# *THE DALAI LAMA'S SPECIAL ENVOY*

# THE DALAI LAMA'S SPECIAL ENVOY

## *Memoirs of a Lifetime in Pursuit of a Reunited Tibet*

LODI GYALTSEN GYARI

*Columbia University Press*
*New York*

Columbia University Press
*Publishers Since 1893*
New York Chichester, West Sussex
cup.columbia.edu


Library of Congress Cataloging-in-Publication Data
Names: Gyari, Lodi G. (Lodi Gyaltsen), author.
Title: The Dalai Lama's special envoy : memoirs of a lifetime in pursuit of a reunited Tibet / Lodi Gyaltsen Gyari.
Other titles: Memoirs of a lifetime in pursuit of a reunited Tibet
Description: New York : Columbia University Press, [2022] | Includes bibliographical references and index.
Identifiers: LCCN 2022000639 (print) | LCCN 2022000640 (ebook) | ISBN 9780231206488 (hardback) | ISBN 9780231556507 (ebook)
Subjects: LCSH: Gyari, Lodi G. (Lodi Gyaltsen) | Exiles—China—Xinlong Xian—Biography. | Exiles—Washington (D.C.)—Biography. | Gyari family. | Bstan-'dzin-rgya-mtsho, Dalai Lama XIV, 1935—Friends and associates. | China—Relations—China—Tibet Autonomous Region. | Tibet Autonomous Region (China)—Relations—China. | Tibetans—Washington (D.C.)—Biography. | Xinlong Xian (China)—Biography.
Classification: LCC DS786.2.G93 A3 2022 (print) | LCC DS786.2.G93 (ebook) | DDC 305.895/410753092 [B]—dc23/eng/20220401
LC record available at https://lccn.loc.gov/2022000639
LC ebook record available at https://lccn.loc.gov/2022000640

Cover design: Milenda Nan Ok Lee
Cover image: Sonam Zoksang

*This book is dedicated to Gyari Nyima Gyaltsen, my late father, and my two wonderful mothers, Milog Nordzin Lhamo and Milog Dorjé Yudrön. These three noble individuals have taught me humility, loyalty, and kindness. I have tried to lead each day of my life based on these qualities as manifested every day of theirs. They taught me and my siblings to have pride in our lineage but, at the same time, they never allowed us to dwell in the past.*

*Contents*

## PART II: TIBET RESTORED: REUNITING THE TIBETAN PEOPLE 105



## PART III. THIRTY YEARS OF ENGAGEMENT WITH THE PRC 231

## *Gratitude*

The Gyari family would never have come into freedom without the dedication, devotion, and sacrifices of the following people:

Uncle Tsultrim
Sonam Tenzing
Kalsang Wangdi
Mimi
Dorji

Following in the footsteps of the Gyari family's loyal retainers such as the Taksen-Drukchu, the Sixty Tigerlike Retainers, these people left their own loved ones behind to help us navigate the arduous journey into exile.

# *Preface*

My original intention was to write a detailed preface, not only explaining what motivated me to write this book but also sharing with readers the essence of all its chapters. But a health issue has arisen that is not allowing me that luxury. To make sure that my personal situation does not become an obstacle for the book's publication, I have settled on these rather brief remarks.

Let me begin by emphasizing that this work is not an autobiography. Nor do I make any claim that it is a contemporary history of Tibet or the Tibetan people's struggle. In one role or another, I have had the privilege of being part of the Tibet movement for the last several decades. As a result, no matter how impartial I may try to be, it is still a narration of events as I saw them.

The first inspiration to write about my experiences and thoughts came from a very close Rinpoche friend. I cannot remember the precise date or even the month of our discussion, but it was sometime in 2008, during one of our visits together. After several hours sharing my experiences over the years, as well as my thoughts on both our past efforts and future undertakings, he strongly urged me to commit them to writing to benefit the Tibetan cause. I declined, giving my usual answer when others, from time to time, have offered the same suggestion. My Rinpoche friend was not to be deterred. He immediately responded: "I am not asking you to write your autobiography. It will be good if you can write it, but that can wait. I am asking you to write the thoughts that you shared about how to bring to fruition the vision of His Holiness the Dalai Lama that will benefit not only the Tibetans but the Chinese and the whole world." He said that so sincerely and with such intensity that it really made me take his advice seriously.

A few months later, when I was visiting my dear friend Ambassador Richard Holbrooke at the Asia Society in New York, he echoed Rinpoche's thoughts. After a lengthy discussion about our then ongoing dialogue with the People's Republic of China (PRC) leadership, he said: "Lodi, you need to get some of these thoughts published because it will complement your efforts and not harm them." I remember, then and there, convincing myself to work on a book.

I am grateful for the inspiration of these two dear friends.

The book has three parts—Land of My Ancestors, Tibet Restored, and Thirty Years of Engagement with the PRC. Part I was actually written as an afterthought upon the advice of friends who thought it important for me to give some context to my life and choice of career as a result of my and my family's background. Parts II and III are the real purpose of this endeavor.

For non-Tibetans, a large section of part II, Tibet Restored, may not be of much interest and, in fact, may be quite confusing and difficult to understand. Some Tibetans may even wonder what is the purpose of my writing about this troubled phase of our life in exile. I consider this period extremely important, however. First, we Tibetans must understand our actual history and not continue to labor under the "make believe" conceptions that, unfortunately, have been created, and under which so many of us in exile have been brought up. Also in part II, I explain the inclusive Tibet for which we are struggling and how that historic Tibet has come to be "restored." Unless we fully understand the tumultuous and complex decades of our early years in exile, we cannot truly appreciate why His Holiness the 14th Dalai Lama took the courageous decision to adopt the Middle Way Approach. Throughout this period, His Holiness faced tremendous internal and external challenges to maintaining the unity of Tibet, the cornerstone upon which the survival of our distinct identity depends. As I have steadfastly maintained, His Holiness's solution to the Tibet situation, embodied in the Middle Way Approach, is not only visionary but also brilliant and, most importantly, has the potential for realization.

In the final part of the book, I provide a fairly extensive narration of how we managed to bring Tibet to the attention of the international community. My hope is that this will remind Tibetans, especially those inside Tibet, of the tremendous efforts His Holiness has made to keep the Tibet issue alive, so that, at a minimum, they realize that he has left no stone unturned on their behalf. This part of the book also acknowledges and expresses my sincere gratitude to all those dedicated friends of Tibet throughout the world who have made it possible for us to take Tibet to the next level. We must learn to always be aware and sincerely appreciative of the support, friendship, and solidarity they have shown us during this, the most difficult period of our history.

Many of these friends pay a high price for standing with us. One example is my dear friend Richard Gere, whose association with Tibet has taken a toll on his professional career. Dozens of other supportive institutions and their members, as well as hundreds of individuals, have been blacklisted, making it impossible for them to even visit the PRC and sometimes even barring them from participating in events held in other international forums. Sulak Sivaraksa of Thailand and Lama Lobzang of Ladakh both come to my mind in this regard. But the wonderful thing is that none of these individuals has the slightest regret for their actions. In fact, they feel honored to support such a just cause and to stand in solidarity with the Dalai Lama, whom they deeply admire and hold in the highest regard.

Sometimes I worry that we Tibetans are losing the honorable qualities for which we as a people have traditionally been known and respected. What is even more disturbing is an arrogance we sometimes display indicating that we are somehow entitled to all this support and sympathy. No entity, be it a nation, organization, or individual, is obligated to support us in our struggle. Any such attitude of entitlement on our part will not be appreciated and, in the long run, will cause tremendous harm to our treasured image as a humble people with noble aspirations.

The majority of part III deals with our relations with the PRC. I had the opportunity to be involved in this process for over thirty years. While my narrative does not relate many previously untold stories, I have tried my best to provide an unbiased account of our relationship, acknowledging both the sincere and serious efforts, as well as the mistakes, both sides have made. Some may wonder what purpose it serves in chronicling this history, but I strongly believe that if both sides reflect on these events, we will understand how much of our difficulties were caused by miscommunication and misunderstanding that in turn aggravated our existing, mutual mistrust, the biggest obstacle that confronted and continues to impede our progress.

What I have written may also not be appreciated by some section of Tibetans and Chinese, but I am not writing this book to please anyone. Rather, I am writing with the hope that, even at this stage, both sides will have the wisdom to look forward and not remain bogged down in the past. The Tibetan leadership must understand that it is only His Holiness, the 14th Dalai Lama, who has both the historic legitimacy and the moral authority to help resolve the issue. No one else can do it. For their part, Chinese leaders must understand that the current Dalai Lama is not the problem, but the only solution. In a nutshell, I would urge them to learn to use their "heart" and the Tibetans, their "head."

Originally, I had planned on addressing two other important issues in the book. The first is the unparalleled role that Buddhism can play in bringing harmony between the Tibetan and Chinese peoples. I decided against including that material because it is too precious to be discussed in the present mix of political issues I have covered. One cannot discuss the essential role of Buddhism, for example, without touching on matters including reincarnation, an institution that is to me not at all political, but an inseparable part of the Tibetan Buddhist tradition.

I also wanted to include a section giving my thoughts on our future relationship with our Chinese brothers and sisters. The working title for this part of the narrative was "Looking Forward." I thought that this was one section I should write in conjunction with a Chinese author knowledgeable on Tibet. I reached out to a well-known scholar through mutual friends, and he was very enthusiastic about the possible collaboration. However, both of us felt that we could not do justice to this crucial subject solely through long-distance communications. Although we wanted to arrange a time for him to come work with me, unfortunately, circumstances did not afford that opportunity. For the Tibetans and the Chinese to live together, we must try to look to our common future with mutual respect for each other's values and aspirations.

I also want to acknowledge with a great sense of gratitude the opportunity I had in serving my people and my teacher, His Holiness the 14th Dalai Lama, in one capacity or another for over four decades. While it was a great honor for those of us who consider His Holiness our root teacher to have the opportunity to serve the Tibetan cause, it was also a daunting task because His Holiness is not just our leader but also, most importantly, our teacher. I take the teacher-disciple relationship seriously because I think it is the very foundation and strength of the Tibetan Buddhist tradition and the unifying factor for our people. Even the deep bond between the Dalai Lama and the Tibetan people arises because he is the Lama, not just the Leader.

The role of the Lama, or the teacher, is the cornerstone of our religious practice, so much so that when we recite the Refuge prayer, Homage to the Guru precedes Homage to the Buddha, the Dharma, and the Sangha. This is not to diminish the central importance of the Three Jewels, but rather to recognize the Lama as the embodiment of all three. Within all the traditions of Tibetan Buddhism, the very first salutation is as follows:

> ༄༅། །བླ་མ་ལ་སྐྱབས་སུ་མཆིའོ།།
> སངས་རྒྱས་ལ་སྐྱབས་སུ་མཆིའོ།།
> ཆོས་ལ་སྐྱབས་སུ་མཆིའོ།།
> དགེ་འདུན་ལ་སྐྱབས་སུ་མཆིའོ།།

> Homage to the Guru;
> Homage to the Buddha;
> Homage to the Dharma;
> Homage to the Sangha.

As a disciple, I have been able to maintain my pure *samaya* with His Holiness. Several years back, I gathered all my courage to inform him that if there were ever a situation in the future when I had to make a choice between him in his capacity as my leader or as my teacher, without any hesitation, I would choose the latter. His Holiness was a little startled and said: "Are you facing some dilemma in this regard?" I said: "No, your Holiness, but I just wanted to let you know my feelings on this important matter." I am glad I had the courage to do that.

I firmly believe that I was destined to serve my people and His Holiness. When I look back over the past decades of my service, it is clear to me that each major change in my life was guided by some unseen force. That said, I want to expressly acknowledge those individuals who complemented destiny in smoothing the path it had in store for me: my father, Gyari Nyima Gyaltsen; Lhamo Tsering; Thupten Nyinje; and my friend Tethong Tenzin Geyche. I only introduce them here, leaving it for the reader to discover their many attributes in the pages that follow.

When I began writing this book, I invoked a set of guiding principles that I want to share. Several years back I came across very poignant words in a Theravadan publication. Basically, it says that if you want to communicate something, either orally or in writing, you should first ask yourself the following questions:

1. Is it the truth?
2. Is it necessary?
3. Is it hurtful?

From that day forward, I have found this guidance both profoundly inspiring and, at the same time, quite challenging. While editing the first draft of the book, I actually deleted several sections for failing to fully meet the first criterion: Is it the truth? I took out additional paragraphs and sentences because they did not satisfy either the second or the third challenges. I do not consider myself a hateful person, and I don't think there is any part of this book that is deliberately written with harmful intentions. There is no doubt, however, that some people may find some passages unpleasant, but in those cases I believe at least the first two questions have been answered in the affirmative: it is the truth, and it is necessary to be told.

While the Tibetans and the leadership in exile were dealing with the historic changes resulting from His Holiness's decision to devolve his political leadership in favor of elected leaders, I myself became a victim of a malicious and well-orchestrated attempt at character assassination instigated by the cowardly authors of an anonymous letter widely circulated within the Tibetan world. Many Tibetans and other friends thought that this must be the work of the Chinese, or maybe the Dolgyal cult group that had been targeting His Holiness and those close to him. They just could not fathom that any Tibetan would be behind such malice, jeopardizing the greater cause of Tibet. But the sad thing is, this was not the work of Chinese agents or the cultists, but very much from within.

Ironically, for the purveyors of this vitriol, their intentional lies and deceit prompted my colleagues to reexamine my contributions and service over the years, generating accolades from numerous sources. This support, once again, made me deeply appreciate the genuine friendship and loyalty not only of my peers but also of all those steadfast supporters of our cause worldwide. The Buddha Dharma is a profound path, and while it humbles me to have been born within its fold, I must say that I have come to deeply respect the sense of justice that informs and manifests itself in the Judeo-Christian tradition.

I am taking the liberty of quoting some parts of the August 4, 2014, letter to me from Richard Gere, Chairman of the Board of the International Campaign for Tibet, sharing a thousand-page public report that looked into all aspects of my work and concluded by expressly acknowledging and appreciating the contributions that I had made during the course of my career:

> The Boards of ICT have always placed their trust in you and have witnessed the enormous devotion to His Holiness and to the Tibetan cause with which you have led the work of the ICT and fulfilled your other functions, in particular that of Special Envoy of His Holiness. We are pleased that this report

> confirms that our trust was not misplaced, and are convinced that the effectiveness of your work was in large measure due to your most genuine devotion.
>
> Given the diverse backgrounds, expertise, and the long association of our Board's members with the Tibetan cause, we are well placed to assess the profound and critical effect of your work. Aside from His Holiness, no Tibetan has contributed as much to the Tibetan cause in the international arena in the past decades. The support you have created, sustained and deepened, especially in the United States, Europe and Asia, is unparalleled. The political credibility of the Tibetan position could not have been achieved without your constant engagement at the highest levels of government throughout the world.
>
> We are deeply mystified and saddened by these false rumors. We trust that this report will clarify any misunderstandings and dispel these untruths that are not only very hurtful, but also potentially damaging to all those concerned, and to the Tibetan movement as a whole.

When people became aware that I was writing this book, many jumped to the conclusion that it might be a rebuttal to the allegations proffered against me. I have no intention of wasting a moment of my time countering these baseless rumors, even though they have caused my family and friends deep pain and, more importantly, greatly harmed the Tibetan movement, especially the ongoing dialogue with the PRC.

I could have shared the above letter publicly together with other important and relevant documents, there and then, completely exonerating me, but I deliberately refrained from doing it, keeping the larger interest of the Tibet issue and the credibility of the Tibetan movement in mind. I wouldn't have even touched the issue now, but for the certainty that some people would question my silence.

I chose Bangkok to work on the book for several reasons. First, I wanted to be nearer my aging mothers, who live in India. I also wanted to distance myself from Washington, D.C., and Delhi, to give space to the new Tibetan leadership, formed after His Holiness devolved his political role, to set its own course. But I also chose Bangkok because in 1972, it was the first country I visited as a member of His Holiness's entourage, the beginning of my many decades of direct service to His Holiness.

In recent days, to complete the "circle" of my service, I revisited Wat Suan Mokkh Ashram in Surat Thani in southern Thailand, where His Holiness spent two days with the renowned and highly respected Buddhist master Ajahn

1972 trip to Thailand
Buddhadasa Indapanno Archives

Buddhadasa during the 1972 visit. Being in the presence of these two extraordinary minds enriched my life in ways too numerous to catalogue. Coming to Bangkok to work on my book was also part of that great "unseen mystery" I previously mentioned, that has been guiding me over the years and has enabled me to further deepen my friendship with Sulak Sivaraksa, a remarkable individual whom we all lovingly call Ajahn. Our stay in Bangkok became even more memorable as we made some very dear Thai friends through Ajahn.

I would not have succeeded in writing this book without the help of my friends Jigmey Passang, Kalsang Tsering, and Jamyang Dorjee. Jigmey Passang and Kalsang Tsering were my colleagues and very much a part of the dialogue process. They even sacrificed their limited personal time and energy to help realize this project. All three of them made multiple trips to Bangkok and within India to work with me. The book is very much my own voice, but it is with the help of my dear friend Suzanne La Pierre that it has become more refined and structured. Besides helping with the book, Suzanne has been acting on my behalf in dealing with my publishers. My youngest, Tenzing Tsering, calls Suzanne "the friend who never says no"—there is definitely a truth there!

I must also not forget to thank Tenzing Tsering herself for all the help she has provided. She put her life on hold for several years to help me by moving to

Bangkok with my wife, Dawa, and me. My second daughter, Tenzing Choyang, also helped me with the "Land of My Ancestors" section that addresses our family and ancestral lineage. Another good friend, Rachel Lostumbo, was also of great help in the initial stages. It is due to the kindness of all these individuals that we have this book. But, of course, the views expressed on the various issues I discuss are mine and mine alone.

In a span of over four decades from Darjeeling to Delhi, from Dharamsala to D.C., I was blessed to have wonderful colleagues, many of whom became lifelong friends. I owe much to them. Some are no longer with us, including Zechutsang Sonam Topgyal, who was a gem of a person, and Melissa Mathison, a fellow ICT Board member. Whatever contributions I have been able to make, it was always through teamwork. The only credit I am sometimes willing to take is being able to identify and enlist people smarter than me to work alongside me.

Of all the responsibilities that I was entrusted with, spearheading our dialogue with the PRC leadership was the most challenging and difficult. I was fortunate to have Kelsang Gyaltsen, a capable and strong-minded person, as my colleague. We pursued the negotiations in the most professional and sophisticated manner, as all high-level diplomatic relations are conducted. To a large extent, our success is attributable to the leadership of Samdhong Rinpoche, who in his capacity as Kalon Tripa made this effort his highest priority, supporting the Envoys with the full weight of his position and authority. In addition, we had a great team assisting us, with Jigmey Passang and Kalsang Tsering running the Task Force Secretariat in Dharamsala and Bhuchung Tsering and Lesley Friedell Rich helping me in Washington, D.C. We also greatly benefited from the active participation of individual members of the Task Force who included concerned senior officials of the Central Tibetan Administration in Dharamsala and the Private Office of His Holiness the Dalai Lama, as well as a number of former Kalons with expertise on the substantive issues and experience in the international community.

I must also acknowledge and compliment the courtesy and hospitality extended to us by our negotiating counterparts during the formal dialogue process, particularly Wang Zhaoguo, Liu Yandong, and Du Qinglin, all of whom were Vice-Chairs of the National Committee of the Chinese People's Political Consultative Conference (CPPCC) and who each headed the United Front Work Department as Minister in charge, during different stages of the negotiations. Most of our talks were conducted with Zhu Weiqun, Executive Vice-Minister of the United Front, assisted by Sithar, a Vice-Minister, as well as other senior officials.

Obviously, the talks were difficult, and we had more disagreements than agreements. Each side had fundamental positions difficult to reconcile, and we had no illusions that these differences could be overcome within a short period of time. Nevertheless, our forthright and frank discussions were extremely constructive. We were able to establish a strong foundation and framework for working together. Responsible government officials have publicly acknowledged that our dialogue process was the most stable and long-lasting of any contact between His Holiness the Dalai Lama and the PRC leadership. Overcoming the profound mistrust that has accumulated between us over the past several decades was a daunting task, but I can say with confidence that both sides have come to have a high degree of respect for each other.

I am proud of both my spiritual and family lineages. It is my good karma that I was born to such wonderful parents and have siblings with strong individual personalities, but who still love and respect their *jhola*, or elder brother. The Gyari family is a large and growing clan, with members living in many places the world over. My life partner, Dawa Chokyi, whom I compare with the biblical Ruth, is my pillar of strength. Dawa and I have been blessed with seven children, one of whom passed away at the tender age of five. It is deeply gratifying to me that all my children are securely rooted in our tradition with great devotion toward the Dharma. Dawa definitely deserves far more credit than me for raising them to become the wonderful individuals they are. We are not only proud grandparents of five grandchildren, but in addition to this blessing, have the bonus of welcoming four "extra" sons into our family, helping our lone "homegrown" one, Minling Penam, not to feel so overwhelmed by his five sisters.

I do not know what the unseen force has in store for me, here or elsewhere. I had a very meaningful life and whatever positive acts I have accumulated, such as of being help to others, I would like to dedicate to the well-being of my fellow Tibetans inside Tibet. They are the custodians of our glorious legacy, and it is they who will sustain our precious heritage.

Lodi Gyaltsen Gyari
Bangkok, Thailand
August 31, 2018

## *Homage*

Even though this is not a spiritual writing, I would nevertheless like to start with paying homage to my lineage masters and teachers. The only time that I, for a moment, regretted devoting my time in service of Tibet was when I heard the devastating news in 1987 of the passing away of His Holiness Dudjom Rinpoche, the Supreme Head of my tradition. I broke down out of deep remorse because I never had the opportunity to devote any time to receiving his nectarlike teachings. However, I was very fortunate to be able to spend many precious hours in Darjeeling, where Kyabjé Dudjom Rinpoche maintained a residence for a number of years in the early 1960s. Quite often, he would send his disciple Amdo Tenzing to call on me when he had free time. It was always on short notice.

Kyabjé Dudjom Rinpoche was very interested in current affairs, both global as well as within the Tibetan community, but, most importantly, he shared with me stories of my predecessor, Khenpo Aten, also known as Jampal Dewé Nyima, and their relationship. He was very kind in promising me that he would transmit back these teachings to me, which he had received from Khenpo Aten. How foolish of me not to take advantage of those treasured hours in requesting some teachings, but then again, I was a teenager of maybe around fifteen or sixteen. But I always console myself that it was Kyabjé Dudjom Rinpoche himself who commanded in our last meeting in New Delhi that my activity in this life was to serve Yidshin Norbu—the Precious Jewel, His Holiness the Dalai Lama.

Sometime in early 1982, I made a special trip from Dharamsala to Dehradun for the sole purpose of asking Mindrolling Trichen Rinpoche to give me some spiritual guidance and formally accept me as his student. When I made this request, Mindrolling Trichen Rinpoche chided me by saying: "Why are you going around looking for a teacher when you are already in the presence of Avalokiteshvara?" He told me that I should accept His Holiness as my teacher. In other words, the Supreme Head of my tradition and the Head of my own lineage both voiced the same command directing me toward His Holiness the 14th Dalai Lama. Because of the profound reverence that I have for these two great masters, serving His Holiness as a devoted disciple has even greater significance.

From my birth until my parents took me to the mountains to join the resistance, I spent all my time at Lumorab Monastery as a young novice. Those formative years greatly influenced me, and I am particularly grateful to Gyalsé Chöying Dorjé (aka Tulku Chodor) for giving me oral transmissions and initiations of the *Treasure Text* of Drupchen Pema Dündul and Tertön Rangrik Dorjé. He was the second son of Tertön Rangrik Dorjé and the younger brother of Tritsab Pema Wangchen of Mindrolling. At the time when he gave these teachings, I was only around six years old. Some other Rinpoches told Tulku Chodor that maybe I was too young to receive them and that it would also distract me from my regular classes. Tulku Chodor insisted that I come for his teachings, saying: "Lodi Gyaltsen may be young, but I am very old." Tulku Chodor passed away the following year. It is due to his kindness that I have at least received the most important teachings of my own lineage.

I also received teachings from Jetsün Kunzang Chödrön, daughter of Tertön Rangrik Dorjé. While I was at Lumorab Monastery, Kyabjé Minling Chung Rinpoche visited us in 1955, on his way back from China as part of the Dalai Lama's entourage. I was fortunate to receive my *getsul* vows from him as well as several other teachings. A few years later, in late 1958, while we were at Mindrolling, Minling Chung Rinpoche gave me additional teachings, but it was Minling Khenchen Rinpoche who made the extra effort to confer many short initiations and several other oral transmissions, almost every day, during our stay there.

My first philosophy teacher was Tulku Sungrab of Lumorab Monastery. It was through him that I had the great opportunity to receive such profound teachings as Ngari Panchen Pema Wangyal's *The Ascertainment of the Three Types of Vows* and especially Shantideva's *Bodhicharyavatara*, as well as commentaries on several other shorter texts. While all the teachings are profound and precious, I found Shantideva's *Bodhicharyavatara* the most inspiring, even when I did not fully understand its essence. I was told that my predecessor, the great scholar Jampal Dewé

Nyima, was a great exponent of this work. Possibly because of his blessings and my position as his reincarnation, this particular teaching deeply resonates with me.

I was fortunate again to receive this great work of Shantideva from His Holiness the 14th Dalai Lama in the early 1980s in the Kullu Valley in Himachal Pradesh. His Holiness gave this teaching at the request of Khenpo Thupten Mewa, who had established a small hermitage in the same valley. In the daytime we received this profound teaching from the Dalai Lama, and in the evenings a few of us would huddle in Khenpo Thupten's small, yet cozy room and receive further instruction on the text.

It was my misfortune not to receive some guidance from Khunu Lama Tenzin Gyaltsen on this text, even though I had the opportunity of meeting him several times as part of His Holiness's entourage. Khunu Lama Tenzin Gyaltsen bestowed the transmission of Shantideva's *Bodhicharyavatara* on His Holiness, and he is the individual the Dalai Lama regards as a real Bodhisattva, an enlightened being. I was fortunate, however, to receive some special guidance on this teaching from the saintly Gyen Rigdzin Tenpa, another great master from the same region as Khunu Lama Tenzin Gyaltsen.

During one of my visits to Bodhgaya with His Holiness, I was fortunate to be right behind Gyen Rigdzin Tenpa when he was in deep prayer in front of the Mahabodhi Stupa. I stood behind him, silently, with full concentration and devotion. I prayed that whatever Gyen Rigdzin Tenpa was aspiring and dedicating his prayers toward, I also might aspire and dedicate my prayers to. I felt that I fully connected with his prayer at that moment. It was an extraordinary experience and most inspiring.

Sometime toward the end of 2005, Kyabjé Trulshik Rinpoche instructed that it was of utmost importance that I undertake a serious spiritual retreat to dispel certain obstacles that I might encounter in my work and for my health. Rinpoche instructed that I do my retreat on the *Chimé Pakmé Nyingtik, The Heart Essence of the Sublime Lady of Immortality*, a long-life practice on Tara and Avalokiteshvara. He wanted me to go to Padmasambhava's cave, Maratika, in Halesi, Nepal, to do the retreat, where he could personally guide me. Rinpoche himself regularly undertook this same retreat at Maratika, where Padmasambhava accomplished immortality. But for a number of reasons, it was not feasible for me. Instead, I decided to go to Pemayangtse Monastery in Sikkim, another holy place blessed by Padmasambhava and with a historical connection to the Mindrolling tradition.

I was able to start my retreat in April 2006. The first few days into it, I was having a tough time and was hardly able to concentrate while trying to do all the elaborate visualizations. On the third day, a member of the staff of the Tibetan Welfare Office drove all the way from Gangtok to Pemayangtse to deliver the cell phone number of His Holiness's Ritual Master, Tashi la, in Dharamsala, with an urgent message to call him immediately. My instant thought was that His Holiness perhaps wanted me to join him on his upcoming trip to the United States, even though no stopovers in Washington, D.C., were planned.

However, when I reached Tashi la, to my pleasant surprise, it was more to do with my retreat than anything else. Tashi la told me that on the day of His Holiness's departure to the United States, just before leaving the Palace, he instructed him: "Lodi Gyaltsen is trying to do some retreat in Pemayangtse. Make sure he gets the message that he spends some time studying the *Bodhicharyavatara* in between sessions." His Holiness definitely knew that I was struggling. This is how a teacher comes to the rescue of his student at his or her time of need. It is also very clear that I have some connection with the *Bodhicharyavatara*. It took two days for me to get hold of the text even with the help of my friend Lopon Tenpa Gyatso of Pemayangtse Monastery. However, even before I had the text in my hand, I became more relaxed and focused. When I was actually able to study the text, it felt as if all my senses were uncloaked, giving me immeasurable and indescribable joy, inspiring me to compose a short prayer dedicated to His Holiness.

> ༄༅། །རྒྱལ་ཀུན་སྙིང་རྗེའི་བདག་ཉིད་སྤྱན་རས་གཟིགས།།
> You are both Avalokiteśvara, the embodiment of all the Buddhas' compassion,
> ཐོགས་མེད་ཕྲིན་ལས་སྟོབས་མཐུ་པདྨ་འབྱུང་།།
> And Padmākara, the one who is unobstructed in powerful enlightened action,
> གཅིག་འདུས་ཇོ་བོ་གངས་ཅན་བསྟན་འགྲོའི་མགོན།།
> Protector of the teachings and beings in the Land of Snows,
> བསྟན་འཛིན་རྒྱ་མཚོའི་ཞབས་ལ་གསོལ་བ་འདེབས།།
> Tenzin Gyatso—to you we pray!

I managed to spend a month in retreat, one of the most meaningful periods of my life. I also built a strong bond with Pemayangtse Monastery. A few years later, I was able to bring to fruition the yearly reading of the *Hundred Thousand*

*Recitations of the Le'u Dünma, Prayer in Seven Chapters to Padmasambhava*, at the urging of Lopon Tenpa Gyatso. In the past, he had been instructed on a few occasions by Kyabjé Dudjom Rinpoche, Kyabjé Dilgo Khyentse Rinpoche, and Kyabjé Chatral Rinpoche on the importance of performing this reading. Due to various circumstances, however, he had been unable to manifest their wishes. I am very happy that this recitation continues to this day, as it has brought great benefit to all, especially to the inhabitants of Sikkim, the sacred land of Beyul Demojong.

I have received many public initiations and teachings, including the Kalachakra and the Sangwa Gyachen, visionary teachings of the Great 5th Dalai Lama, from His Holiness the 14th Dalai Lama. I also received other important public teachings from His Holiness Dilgo Khyentse Rinpoche, His Holiness Ling Rinpoche, His Holiness Penor Rinpoche, and Kyabjé Kalu Rinpoche, and many more teachings from Kyabjé Trulshik Rinpoche and Kyabjé Taklung Tsetrul Rinpoche. I have great reverence for His Holiness Sakya Trichen, and whenever my family had the opportunity to be in his presence, we were fortunate to receive some oral transmissions and blessings from him.

The blessings and guidance of my teachers are priceless, but it is the prayer entitled *Entering the City of Omniscience* by Rigdzin Jigme Lingpa that is my true savior. With the hope that it brings benefit to others, I am attaching the text at the conclusion of this Homage.

I received the first oral transmission of this profound aspirational prayer at Benpa Chakdor Monastery at Lhodrak in early 1959, from Yonru Pon Sonam Gyaltsen, one of the most powerful chieftains of Kham, who had renounced everything to live the life of a wandering yogi. This prayer is so precious to me that whenever I meet masters whom I respect, I request the oral transmission for this prayer. I cannot list all the masters from whom I received it, but they include Kyabjé Chatral Rinpoche, Kyabjé Trulshik Rinpoche, Kyabjé Dodrupchen Rinpoche, Kyabjé Taklung Tsetrul Rinpoche, Kyabjé Yangthang Rinpoche, Nyoshul Khen Rinpoche, Khochhen Rinpoche, Chagdud Tulku Rinpoche, Garje Khamtrul Rinpoche, and Garchen Rinpoche, from whom I also received the very rare *phowa* transmission according to Nyala Pema Dündul's *Treasure Text*. Garchen Rinpoche had received this transmission from the great master Khenpo Munsel while they were both prisoners in Tibet. I also have received the oral transmission of this prayer from several important Rinpoches and Khenpos inside Tibet, whose names I am constrained from mentioning.

While I was at Benpa Chakdor, I also had the opportunity to study Atisha's[1] *The Lamp for the Path to Enlightenment* with the Khenpo of that monastery, who was from Ganden. This text sets forth the entire Buddhist path within the framework of three levels of motivation on the part of the practitioner. I was just beginning to study Je Tsongkhapa's *The Great Treatise on the Stages of the Path to Enlightenment* with the Khenpo when the uprising in Lhasa on March 10, 1959, brought my studies to an abrupt end, forcing me and my family once again to flee, this time to exile in India.

It is usually the disciple who goes out in search of his teacher, but in my case, Nyoshul Khen Rinpoche, with great kindness and affection for me, took it upon himself to seek me out and help me understand the true essence of the Dharma. In particular, he introduced me to the nature of mind, the pinnacle practice of our tradition. Time and again, he encouraged me to visit him and made serious efforts to realize that goal, drilling into my thick head the preciousness of the Dharma. Even though he was already in a declining state of health, my father, who was related to Rinpoche, visited him in Bhutan, returning with a message for me that has remained etched in my memory: "Tell Lodi Gyaltsen, I have not yet achieved the state of immortality." The tone of the message bore both urgency and disappointment.

Sometime later, Nyoshul Khen Rinpoche became critically ill and was flown to Bangkok for treatment at the Samitivej Hospital. This time, I put everything aside and went to Bangkok to be with him. When I entered his hospital room, he lit up and started shedding tears on seeing me, saying: "Why have you not come until now?" Nyoshul Khen Rinpoche was one of those teachers who not only guided you spiritually but also took great concern for the well-being of one's family. Even though he passed away in 1999, years before any of my daughters were married, in a mysterious way, he had a hand in all their alliances—a subject too personal and of little interest to the readers of this book for me to narrate.

Those few days that I was able to be with him were invaluable. Most of the time when I was with him, together with several of his close disciples, he would give us profound teachings, further sharing with us the visions he was experiencing from his hospital bed. It was during one of those sessions that for a fraction of a moment, I had a glimpse into the true nature of my mind. I realized that Nyoshul Khen Rinpoche's persistent efforts in chasing me down had finally paid off in managing to implant a seed of understanding in this ignorant person.

Ever since the parinirvana of His Holiness Mindrolling Trichen Rinpoche in early 2008, at which time he was not only our lineage head but also the Supreme Head of the Nyingma tradition, the Gyari family has relied on the guidance of His Eminence Khochhen Rinpoche, the abbot of Mindrolling Monastery, for all matters big and small. Another Rinpoche from whom we regularly seek guidance is Ringo Tulku Rinpoche, who heads Palyul Choekhorling Monastery. We are ever grateful to them all.

# ༄༅། །བདེན་ཚིག་འགྲུབ་པའི་སྨྲ་ཏི་རྣ་རྣམ་མཁྱེན་གྲོང་འཇུག་ཅེས་བྱ་བ་བཞུགས་སོ། །

## *Entering the City of Omniscience*

## *An Aspiration Prayer for Actualizing Words of Truth*

RIGDZIN JIKME LINGPA

དངོས་གྲུབ་རྒྱ་མཚོའི་འབྱུང་གནས་བླ་མ་དང་མཆོག་གསུམ་བྱང་ཆུབ་སེམས་དཔའ་རྣམས་ལ་ཕྱག་འཚལ་ཞིང་སྐྱབས་སུ་མཆིའོ། །
I offer homage to the source of an ocean of accomplishments: the Lamas and the Three Jewels and the Bodhisattvas. I take refuge in you:

བྱིན་གྱིས་བརླབ་ཏུ་གསོལ།
Grant your blessings, I pray!
མི་ངའི་སྐྱེ་བ་ནས་ཚེ་རབས་ཐམས་ཅད་དུ་དལ་འབྱོར་བཅོ་བརྒྱད་ཚང་བའི་མི་ལུས་རིན་པོ་ཆེ་ཐོབ་སྟེ་རྗེ་བཙུན་བླ་མ་མཚན་ཉིད་དང་ལྡན་པའི་གདུལ་བྱར་འགྱུར་བར་ཤོག་ཅིག
In all my future lives, may I gain a precious human rebirth complete with all the eighteen freedoms and endowments, and may I become the student of an authentic master!
མངོན་མཐོ་དང་ངེས་ལེགས་མཐའ་དག་གི་འབྱུང་ཁུངས་ཐོས་བསམ་སྒོམ་གསུམ་གྱིས་རང་རྒྱུད་བཏུལ་ཏེ་རྒྱལ་བའི་བསྟན་པ་རིན་པོ་ཆེའི་རྗེས་སུ་སློབ་པར་ཤོག་ཅིག
Training my mind through study, reflection, and meditation, which are the source of higher rebirths and of definite goodness, may I follow the Buddha's precious teachings!
ཆོས་ལ་འཇུག་པའི་རྩ་བ་ངེས་འབྱུང་དང་བློ་ལྡོག་རྣམ་པ་བཞི་རྒྱུད་ལ་ངམ་ངམ་ཤུགས་ཀྱིས་སྐྱེས་ནས་འཁོར་བ་མཐའ་མེད་ཀྱི་བྱ་བ་ལ་བཙོན་དོང་དང་མེ་འོབས་ལྟ་བུར་མཐོང་བར་ཤོག་ཅིག
May renunciation, the root of all Dharma practice, and the four thoughts which cause renunciation arise naturally in my mindstream, and may I see *saṃsāra* with all its endless activity as a prison or a fiery pit!

ལས་འབྲས་བསླུ་བ་མེད་པ་ལ་ཡིད་ཆེས་སྐྱེད་ནས་དགེ་སྡིག་གི་ལས་ཕྲ་མོ་ཙམ་ལ་ཡང་འཇུག་ལྡོག་བྱེད་པར་ཤོག་ཅིག

Gaining confidence in the infallibility of karma, may I strive to undertake even the smallest good deeds and abandon even the slightest harmful actions!

གནས་གྲོགས་འདུ་འཛི་རྐྱེན་ངན་ལ་སོགས་པ་བྱང་ཆུབ་བསྒྲུབ་པའི་བར་ཆད་ཀྱི་དབང་དུ་མི་འགྲོ་བར་དཀོན་མཆོག་གསུམ་གྱི་སྐྱབས་འོག་ཏུ་ཚུད་དེ་སྐྱེས་བུ་གསུམ་གྱི་ལམ་ལ་སློབ་པར་ཤོག་ཅིག

Not falling prey to adverse circumstances, busy places, distracting companions, or any other such obstacles on the path to enlightenment, may I take the Three Jewels as my refuge and train in the graduated path for beings of the three levels of spiritual capacity!

བདེ་གཤེགས་ཀུན་འདུས་ཀྱི་ངོ་བོ་བཀའ་དྲིན་ཅན་གྱི་བླ་མ་དམ་པ་ལ་ཐེ་ཚོམ་དང་མཉམ་འགྲོགས་ཀྱི་མི་རུ་བཟུང་བའི་ལོག་ལྟ་སྤངས་ཏེ་སངས་རྒྱས་དངོས་སུ་མཐོང་བར་ཤོག་ཅིག

May I give up all my doubts regarding the master, the embodiment of all the sugatas, and without slipping into the mistaken view of considering him as an equal, may I see him as an actual Buddha!

དེའི་མཐུ་ལས་མཚོན་བྱེད་དཔེའི་དབང་བཞིས་སྒོ་གསུམ་སྨིན་པར་བྱས་ཏེ་རྨད་བྱུང་རྡོ་རྗེ་ཐེག་པའི་གསང་ལམ་ལ་འཇུག་པར་ཤོག་ཅིག

In this way, may my body, speech, and mind be matured through the four empowerments, and so may I embark upon the path of the wondrous vajra vehicle!

གསོལ་འདེབས་དང་མོས་གུས་ཀྱི་མཚམས་སྦྱོར་ལམ་དུ་ཡོངས་ནས་མཚོན་བྱ་དོན་གྱི་དགོངས་བརྒྱུད་བདག་ལ་འཕོས་ཏེ་རྟོགས་པ་ནམ་མཁའ་དང་མཉམ་པར་ཤོག་ཅིག

Through the medium of fervent prayer and devotion, may the wisdom of the lineage be transferred into me, and may my realization become equal to space!

བསྐྱེད་པ་མ་ཧཱ་ཡོ་གའི་ཉམས་ལེན་མཐར་ཕྱིན་ནས་སྣོད་བཅུད་དཀྱིལ་འཁོར་གསུམ་དུ་ཤེས་ཤིང་རིག་འཛིན་རྣམ་པ་བཞིའི་ས་ལ་བགྲོད་པ་རྒྱལ་སྲས་པདྨ་དང་བི་མ་ལ་ལྟ་བུར་འགྱུར་བར་ཤོག་ཅིག

Perfecting the mahāyoga practices of the generation stage, may I come to perceive the whole universe and beings as the three maṇḍalas and traverse the four levels of a vidyādhara, just like the Buddha's heirs Padmasambhava and Vimalamitra!

ལུང་ཨ་ནུ་ཡོ་གའི་ཉམས་ལེན་མཐར་ཕྱིན་ནས་འཁོར་འདས་ཀྱི་འཛིན་རྟོག་བདེ་སྟོང་གཉིས་སུ་མེད་པའི་ངོ་བོར་སངས་རྒྱས་ཏེ་འོག་མིན་སྟུག་པོ་བཀོད་པའི་ཞིང་ཁམས་ལ་དབང་སྒྱུར་བར་ཤོག་ཅིག

Perfecting the practice of anuyoga, may all concepts of saṃsāra and nirvāṇa be purified into the state of indivisible bliss and emptiness, and may I experience the pure realm of Akaniṣṭha!

རྫོགས་ཆེན་ཨ་ཏི་ཡོ་གའི་ཉམས་ལེན་མཐར་ཕྱིན་ནས་ཆོས་ཅན་གྱི་སྣང་བ་ཆོས་ཉིད་ཀྱི་ཀློང་དུ་ཟད་ནས་གཞོན་ནུ་བུམ་སྐུར་གྲོལ་བ་རིག་འཛིན་དགའ་རབ་རྡོ་རྗེ་ལྟ་བུར་འགྱུར་བར་ཤོག་ཅིག

Perfecting the atiyoga practice of Dzogpachenpo, may all experience dissolve into the expanse of intrinsic reality, and may I be liberated into the youthful vase body, just like the vidyādhara Garab Dorje!

མདོར་ན་བདག་གིས་བྱང་ཆུབ་ཀྱི་སྤྱོད་པ་ལ་བསླབ་པ་ནས་བཟུང་སྟེ་སྒོ་གསུམ་གྱིས་བྱ་བ་ཅི་བགྱིས་པ་ཐམས་ཅད་ཕ་མ་སེམས་ཅན་ཐམས་ཅད་ཀྱི་དོན་དུ་འགྱུར་བར་ཤོག་ཅིག

In short, beginning with the training in the conduct of the Bodhisattvas, may whatever I do, with body, speech, or mind, bring nothing but benefit to all sentient beings, my very own parents!

དུས་དང་རྣམ་པ་ཐམས་ཅད་དུ་དམ་པའི་ཆོས་མ་ཡིན་པའི་འཇིག་རྟེན་མཐུན་འཇུག་གི་བསམ་པ་སྐད་ཅིག་མ་ཙམ་ཡང་སེམས་ལ་མི་སྐྱེ་བར་ཤོག་ཅིག

Whatever my situation or circumstance, may I never feel the slightest wish to follow worldly ways, which run contrary to the Dharma!

གལ་ཏེ་ལས་དང་བག་ཆགས་དབང་བཙན་པར་གྱུར་ནས་ཕྱིན་ཅི་ལོག་གི་བློ་སྐྱེས་ནའང་དེ་ཉིད་མི་འགྲུབ་པར་ཤོག་ཅིག

Even if, whilst under the sway of karma and habitual patterns, a mistaken thought occurs to me, may it never be successful!

གཞན་དོན་དུ་འགྱུར་ན་ལུས་སྲོག་འདོར་བ་ལ་ཡང་ཞུམ་ང་མེད་པར་གཞོན་ནུ་དོན་གྲུབ་ལྟ་བུར་འགྱུར་བར་ཤོག་ཅིག

For the sake of others, may I be fearless and ready even to give up my life, just like Prince Siddhārtha!

དོན་གཉིས་ལྷུན་གྲུབ་ཀྱི་ས་ལ་ཕྱིན་ནས་ཁམས་གསུམ་འཁོར་བའི་རྒྱ་མཚོ་དོང་ནས་སྤྲུགས་ནུས་པ་སྟོབས་བཅུ་མི་འཇིགས་རྣམ་བཞིའི་རྩལ་ཅན་དུ་གྱུར་ཅིག

Having reached the state of spontaneously accomplishing the benefit of self and others, may I stir the depths of the ocean of saṃsāra's three worlds by means of the ten strengths and four fearlessnesses!

འདོད་པ་དང་བྲལ་བའི་སྨོན་ལམ་དེ་ལྟ་བུ་ཡོངས་སུ་འགྲུབ་པའི་མཐུན་འགྱུར་མཛད་པར་རྒྱལ་བ་སྲས་བཅས་རྣམས་ཀྱིས་ཞལ་གྱིས་བཞེས་པ་ཡིན་ནོ། །

The Buddhas and Bodhisattvas have vowed to work toward the accomplishment of unselfish aspiration prayers such as these.

དྲང་སྲོང་བདེན་པར་སྨྲ་བ་རྣམས་ལ་ཕྱག་འཚལ་ལོ། །

Homage to the sages who proclaim the truth!

ཨོཾ་དྷ་རེ་དྷ་རེ་བྷནྡྷ་རེ་བྷནྡྷ་རེ་སྭཱ་ཧཱ།

Oṃ dhare dhare bhandare bhandare svāhā.

དགེ་བ་སྟོབས་ཆེ་བར་གྱུར་ཅིག

May the strength of virtue increase!

སྨོན་ལམ་མཐུ་བཙན་པར་གྱུར་ཅིག

May the power of aspiration grow!

སྡིག་པ་འདག་སྐྱེན་པར་གྱུར་ཅིག

May negativity be swiftly purified!

ཛ་ཡ་ཛ་ཡ་སིདྡྷི་སིདྡྷི་ཕ་ལ་ཕ་ལ། འ་ཨ་ཧ་ཤ་ས་མ། མ་མ་ཀོ་ལིང་ས་མནྟ།

jaya jaya siddhi siddhi phala phala | ʻa a ha sha sa ma | mama koling samanta

ཞེས་མདོ་ཁམས་པ་ཆོས་ལྡན་གྱིས་ངོར་རིག་འཛིན་འཇིགས་མེད་གླིང་པས་སོ། །སརྦ་མངྒ་ལཾ།། ||

*Composed by Rigdzin Jikmé Lingpa at the request of Chöden from East Tibet. Sarva maṅgalam.*

Trans. Adam Pearcey, *Lotsawa House* (2018),

https://www.lotsawahouse.org/tibetan-masters/jigme-lingpa/entering-city-omniscience

## *Foreword*

MICHAEL J. GREEN

I first met Lodi Gyaltsen Gyari Rinpoche in 2003 when he was advancing the visit of His Holiness the Dalai Lama for a meeting with President George W. Bush and I was preparing to take over as the senior official responsible for Asia on the National Security Council staff. My own expertise up to that point had been in northeast Asia, and I knew far more about Japan and the Korean peninsula than I did the far-off Himalayan plateau. But I was completely taken by this warm and cerebral man who would teach me so much and soon become a dear friend. I was hardly alone in that, as I saw fifteen years later at a congressional memorial event after his passing, where the most powerful Republicans and Democrats in Congress and senior officials from multiple administrations stood in unified praise for Lodi and renewed commitment to the cause for which he struggled throughout his life.

When Lodi retired from formal service to His Holiness the Dalai Lama in 2012 he came to see me to discuss how he might write his memoir to be of greatest service to scholars, practitioners, and—of course—the Tibetan cause. Like others, I encouraged him to share his experiences negotiating with the Chinese Communist Party (CCP) and to introduce readers to the story of the Tibetan people's struggle for justice. I arranged an affiliation with Georgetown University and promised to organize roundtables to help review drafts. But after a few months Lodi decamped to India and then Thailand, to be with family and to pursue a more contemplative and personal recollection of his life experiences. I only saw the result in 2020 when Suzanne La Pierre reached out to me on behalf of Lodi's amazing wife and daughter, seeking help finding a posthumous publisher for the manuscript. My editor at Columbia University Press, Caelyn Cobb, immediately recognized the value of the manuscript and after peer review produced this exceptional volume.

Perhaps it is well that Lodi left Washington, for he has created an incredible tapestry of personal heroism, Tibetan spiritualism, diplomatic history, and geopolitical analysis. The book is really three tales wrapped in the life story of one Rinpoche.

The first and most eye-opening for me was the story of Lodi's own spiritual lineage; his upbringing in eastern Tibet; and then his harrowing escape from Nyarong to Lhasa, Darjeeling, Dharamsala, and finally Washington, D.C. The story begins even before his birth when Minling Khenchen Rinpoche prophesied that Lodi would be the reincarnation of the Rinpoche's uncle, the venerable Khenpo Aten of Lumorab Monastery in Upper Nyarong. When he was only ten, Lodi's prominent family helped to lead armed separatist resistance against Mao Zedong's campaign to uproot and eliminate Tibetan culture and traditions. When the Communist forces attempted to seize the Gyari family, including young Lodi, the Tibetans routed the invading column and trapped the Communists in their own mountain fortress, killing thousands. Returning in greater numbers, the Communists finally forced Lodi's family and their Sixty Tigerlike Retainers to flee eastern Tibet for Lhasa. Sleeping in caves while his senior mother carried a pair of hand grenades hidden in the folds of her clothing, young Lodi witnessed the massacre of hundreds of his family's retainers and his own childhood friends in bloody Communist ambushes along the escape route. Lodi and his family were then forced to flee again in 1959 after large-scale uprisings in Lhasa incurred Beijing's wrath. By horse and foot, they followed the Dalai Lama over the Himalayan mountains to freedom in India. Lodi would live a landless refugee's life in Darjeeling, seeking alms, until a new settlement was completed at Dharamsala, where he would eventually play a prominent role in Tibet's youth politics and then high diplomacy. He would not return to eastern Tibet or Lumorab Monastery until his Chinese counterparts took him there during negotiations almost five decades later. And then never again.

Many of us who considered Lodi a friend knew that his past contained many tribulations, but few would have been privy to the terrifying and violent experiences and pure heroism conveyed in these pages. Indeed, Lodi confesses that it was not easy for him to relate his family history in such detail, not only because of the trauma involved but also because of the intense internal feuds that had preceded their escape, which his father had once asked his children never to record. Lodi's story of resistance and escape explains the quiet determination we all saw in him and makes all the more profound his generosity of spirit to those who opposed him, including even the CCP. Lodi recounts how his father had always told him that the Chinese as a people were honorable and bore no particular prejudice against Tibet in earlier periods of history. He concludes the volume not by condemning Beijing but by expressing renewed hope for mutual understanding with the people of China.

The second strand in the book explains how the Dalai Lama reestablished the historic unity among Tibetans from three different parts of the Tibetan Plateau: U-Tsang, Kham, and Amdo. Ironically, Chinese repression and the experience of exile reforged cohesion among all Tibetans, expressed in the Great Oath of Unity, which was signed in 1960 by a diverse group of spiritual and secular leaders pledging solidarity behind the Dalai Lama. Lodi focuses throughout these pages, as he did throughout his life, on the effort to rekindle that common identity and purpose. His awe of the Dalai Lama is most apparent when he describes how His Holiness patiently brought his people together despite differences of religious doctrine and the activities of offshoot cults that developed their own alternate narratives to that of the Central Tibetan Administration. In reviewing these developments, Lodi again demonstrates a generosity of spirit—rarely impugning the motives of those whose independent-mindedness vexed His Holiness and the CTA. He has particularly kind words for the brother of the Dalai Lama, Gyalo Thondup, whose towering personality and strong principles impressed Lodi even as the Darjeeling-based operations he ran required careful politicking by Dharamsala to maintain unity of purpose. Though he makes only passing reference to it, Lodi acknowledges that factional infighting undid his own career, but in the end he expresses not grievance or retribution but instead an emphasis on the need for mutual understanding and unity among all Tibetans.

The third story line revealed within these pages and Lodi's own life is that of politics, geopolitics, and diplomatic intrigue. From the account of Tibetans' early contact with the CIA and participation in India's paramilitary Special Frontier Force, one is reminded that Tibetans have long had a warrior culture all their own, as both the Indian Army and the PLA came to appreciate. Lodi himself was never comfortable in that role and instead began his own career working with the Tibetan Youth Congress. A natural leader, he traveled as a young advisor with the Dalai Lama on a trip to Thailand in 1972, beginning a relationship with His Holiness that some thought preordained as Lodi rose to the position of Special Envoy in Washington, D.C., and lead negotiator with the CCP. Political scientists will recognize in these negotiations the classic "two-level game theory," as Lodi sought support among impatient younger pro-independence Tibetans for what His Holiness termed a more realistic "Middle Way Approach" that would achieve Tibet's meaningful autonomy but avoid demands for independence that would cause Beijing to reject talks. Crucial to both internal and external support was the process of democratization within the Tibet movement. This commitment to democratic principles helped His Holiness cement relationships with leaders from Jimmy Carter and George W. Bush to Gordon Brown, but in order to fulfill his commitment, the Dalai Lama eventually sacrificed his own political role in favor of a democratically elected President or *Sikyong*. Lodi describes that day as "one of the saddest" in his life because he recognized that the Tibetan movement would immediately lose diplomatic access and leverage with the devolution of political power from the Dalai Lama. And yet Lodi concludes dispassionately that the democratic election of the Sikyong was the right step. Rather than lamenting the decision, he urges the CTA to move toward NGO-like status in international relations while reminding readers that ultimately the flag bearers for the movement live within Tibet itself, where they bear enormous sacrifices to maintain their way of life—pitting the power of spirituality against a secular dictatorship determined to plow under the search for meaning with roads, bridges, Han immigration, and police surveillance.

Lodi's account of Tibet's relationship with previous Chinese dynasties and his own experience negotiating with the United Front Work Department of the CCP convince him that the spiritual will prevail over the cynical material tools of authoritarianism in the end. It is not that he ignores geopolitics; his analysis of the Great Game around Tibet is Kissingerian in its breadth and realpolitik. Rather, he sees China's success as inextricably linked to success for the Tibetan people. He notes, for example, that Deng Xiaoping saw outreach to the Dalai Lama through Gyalo Thondup in 1979 as part of the same reform and opening process that necessitated China's diplomatic normalization with the United States. This belief that China's reform and opening are inextricably linked with Tibet's own meaningful autonomy animated Lodi's negotiating strategy toward the United Front. In negotiations that began in 2002 he was always careful to avoid the kind of litigious historical claims that marked Beijing's unresolved territorial disputes with her neighbors. Instead, he sought Beijing's understanding of Tibet's unique status and the benefits of treating the Tibetan people as a single administrative entity bonded by cultural and spiritual traditions and guided by the Dalai Lama—building on the now sadly defunct example of the "one country/two systems" treatment of Hong Kong. The high-water mark for Lodi's negotiations came in the eighth and final round of talks in 2008 when he presented the Memorandum on Genuine Autonomy for the Tibetan People—a roadmap that the Chinese themselves had asked for in writing. However, the Chinese side fixated on the geographic implications of a single administrative entity for all Tibetans, claiming it would carve off a quarter of China, despite assurances that "splittism" was not the goal of His Holiness and reminders that the guarantee of autonomy for Tibetans and other ethnic minorities was enshrined in China's own constitution.

Despite some positive signals and optimism on the Tibetan side, the talks foundered and have not resumed since. Lodi blames reactionary elements in the CCP, uncoordinated moves within the Tibetan movement, and the consequences of devolution of political power from the Dalai Lama. Since Lodi's death an even more menacing factor has emerged to cast a shadow over negotiations with Beijing. When it became obvious in 2007 that Xi Jinping was going to be China's next leader, the Tibetan leadership was at first filled with hope. Xi's father, Xi Zhongxun, had led one column of Communist forces into Tibet, where he established a surprisingly warm friendship with the Dalai Lama, wearing a watch given by His Holiness to the end of his days in internal exile. Xi Jinping seemed poised to be a powerful but enlightened leader with his own family connection to Tibet. Yet the Tibetans–and the world–could not have been more wrong about the younger Xi's worldview. A Leninist party man first and last, Xi intended not to open opportunities for ethnic minorities but instead to crush any centers of power or independent thought that might challenge his authority and the legitimacy of the CCP–and spiritual freedom in Tibet became a major target.

Still, Lodi was right about one thing–Beijing will not find a path to success at home or abroad without meaningful autonomy for Tibet. As Beijing passes laws asserting control over selection of the next Dalai Lama and pressures Mongolia and India to deny that right to Tibetan Buddhist spiritual leaders beyond China's borders, it is becoming obvious that the many millions of devout followers of His Holiness across Asia will refuse to accept a pretender. With control of the Himalayan plateau's military vantage points, scarce water resources, and identity politics in the balance, the consequences of mismanaging Tibet's future could be enormous for China and the world.

Lodi Gyari has left a deeply personal, studiously open-minded, and strategically insightful memoir. There will be surprises for Western readers, which Lodi acknowledges may seem unbelievable. At one point he recounts the experience of several Rinpoches under arrest by Chinese authorities who witnessed their teacher calmly announce that he had completed his work on earth and then willingly drop dead before their eyes. He describes seeing a flaming comet streak over Lumorab Monastery the night his family fled Nyarong. He explains how his father's stern expression toward him would suddenly change as he remembered that his son was the reincarnation of the powerful Khenpo Aten. "Tibet," Lodi writes, "is an extraordinary land where extraordinary things do take place."

Lodi Gyari recounts that he began this book after another Rinpoche urged him to "write about how to bring to fruition the vision of His Holiness the Dalai Lama that will benefit not only the Tibetans but the Chinese and the whole world." In this he has succeeded. Despite hardships in Tibet and a harder line in Beijing, the cause of the Tibetan people burns brighter today than it did when Lodi began his journey—in significant measure because of the Special Envoy's own life work.

# PART I

# *Land of My Ancestors*

Although this part of the book is placed first chronologically, it was actually drafted as an afterthought. When I decided to undertake this project, I had no intention of writing anything about my personal life, as the work is not an autobiography. When I sought the advice of a few close friends and colleagues with a rough outline of the book, however, two of them, Michael Green and Gregory Craig, encouraged me to include some details about my life and upbringing to give readers a context in which to understand my perspective. Greg actually asked me: "Lodi, will this be a limited edition that you will send around only to people like me and others who know you well?" I replied that my hope was it would reach a wider audience to help those less familiar with Tibet gain an understanding of the complexity of the issues involved. He then strongly suggested that I include a chapter about my personal background to set the stage for the narrative. Mike was of a similar mind.[1]

My two mothers, Nordzin Lhamo and Dorjé Yudrön, took the opposite view. When I was trying to get some information from them about our family and our ancestral home, my senior mother recited a Khampa allegory: "Those who focus on their past grandeur reveal that they are now nobody. Those who refer to their past great wealth signal that they are destitute now." If my father were still alive, he would also probably not have approved of my writing too much about our family's history. A tragic family feud had left him an orphan. Not wanting to stir up painful memories, he never allowed any of us to revisit the past. When my father learned that my youngest brother, Kunzang Tsewang (aka Gyari Bhutu), was in the process of recording our family's history, he was furious. Even though my brother had already spent months in Nepal working on the project with the late Dogyaltsang (Dogyal) Aten, an elder Nyarongwa and close family friend, my father intervened. He called Aten on the phone expressing his extreme displeasure at Aten's insensitivity in helping Gyari Bhutu rekindle the sad and tragic memories of our family. As inclusion of the material in this section of the book demonstrates, I took the advice of my friends to include some autobiographical information. In deference to my parents' wishes, however, I intentionally limit discussion of the more painful periods in my family's internal affairs.

Even though this part of the book focuses on my childhood in Tibet, my family, and my native land, I have drawn extensively from external sources to tell my story. I rely heavily on the narrations and writings of the previously mentioned Dogyal Aten. Jamyang Norbu's book *Warriors of Tibet: The Story of Aten and the Khampas' Fight for the Freedom of Their Country* provided much of the information about Nyarong. I also consulted contemporary scholar Dr. Yudru Tsomu's book *The Rise of Gönpo Namgyel in Kham: The Blind Warrior of Nyarong.* Finally, I have quoted liberally from the fictional work by Dr. Tsewang Pemba[2] entitled *White Crane, Lend Me Your Wings* that vividly captures the character of the people and the customs of Nyarong, my native land. I have no doubt that the author's personal friendship with my father was a source of inspiration for his story of Nyarong and her people. My father was both Dr. Pemba's patient and a close personal friend when we lived in Darjeeling.

## CHAPTER 1

# History of Nyarong, Kham, My Birthplace

I was born in 1949 in the grasslands of Upper, or Northern, Nyarong in the eastern Tibetan region of Kham, referred to by many as A-zin Nyarong. *A-zin* derives from the Sanskrit word *ajay*, meaning "invincible or great victory." The belief is that during the time of the thirty-eighth Tibetan Emperor, Trisong Detsen (742–796),[1] a contingent of Nyarong cavalry was part of the imperial Tibetan army that staged a successful military expedition over the mighty Himalayas beyond the banks of the river Ganges in India. An iron pillar commemorating the victory of the Tibetan troops is even said to have been erected on the riverbank. Afterward, the Nyarong soldiers proudly added the word *A-zin* to the name of their native place.

Nyarong was traditionally divided into three regions—Upper, Middle, and Lower (Nyatod, Nyakyed, and Nyamed). It is predominately a rural area of relatively isolated towns with farming and animal husbandry as the people's main livelihoods. The nomads constantly move to find suitable pastures for their herds as the seasons change. As early as the seventh century, during the time of the thirty-third Tibetan Emperor, Songtsen Gampo (617–650), Nyarong was an integral part of the Tibetan Empire. With the assassination of the forty-second, and last, Emperor, Udum Tsenpo (815–841), commonly known as Langdarma, the Tibetan nation began to disintegrate. Vast territories of Tibet became self-governing kingdoms and chiefdoms, including Nyarong.

At the turn of the twentieth century, the Qing (Manchu) dynasty annexed some portions of Nyarong into neighboring Lithang County for administrative and taxation purposes. True administrative control by imperial China, however, was ineffective at best and in most areas nonexistent. Large areas of Kham were actually governed independently by Tibetan chieftains (*ponpos*), kings (*gyalpos*),[2] or powerful lamas until Mao's Red Army took control in 1949. Nyarong is now a county within the Kardze Tibetan Autonomous Prefecture of the People's Republic of China's (PRC's) Sichuan Province and today includes only about 8,675 square kilometers.

While Nyarong is not one of the larger kingdoms or regions of Kham, the people of Nyarong have always had a reputation of being great warriors. We are feared even among fellow Khampas, who immortalize our bravery in a curse hurled at enemies—and sometimes at misbehaving children! "May you fall into the hands of the ferocious Nyarongwas." As contemporary scholar Yudru Tsomu notes: "The people of Nyarong were known for their fierce and warlike character, and Nyarong had a reputation as an unruly and troublesome region."[3] During the eighth century, under the reign of Trisong Detsen, when Tibetan military garrisons were stationed in the region, Nyarongwas were part of the Tibetan imperial army, participating in attacks against the Chinese as early as 763, when they helped capture Chang'an, the Chinese Tang-dynasty capital.

Much later, the Qing dynasty had great difficulty imposing its domination over Nyarong even as other areas in Kham coalesced under its rule. As one of the characters in Pemba's *White Crane* narrative explains:

> I hear that the Chinese have hardly any jurisdiction over these Tibetans. They are virtually independent . . . various districts each ruled by a *Ponpo* or chieftain. The people obey no laws except those laid down by their individual *Ponpos*. The Chinese magistrate here at Lithang—the *Gyasago*, as he is called by the Khampas has a very vague tenuous jurisdiction over Nyarong. I hear he is scared of sending his men there, even to collect state taxes.[4]

Nyarongwas are also known for their uncompromising loyalty—be it to the lamas, a chieftain, or even a friend—and many wars were fought precisely to defend this honor. For example, my father's family, the Gyaritsang,[5] ruled Northern Nyarong, wielding complete power over the territories it governed, that also included a large number of subjects known as *gothak*—meaning the "surrendered ones or those who seek protection."[6] While the word "subject" may not sound politically correct today, it accurately depicts the relationship of the time.

Many *gothaks* did not originally live in Nyarong but traveled there seeking the Gyaritsang's protection from harm or injustice, pledging their loyalty in exchange. While having *gothaks* certainly added to a chieftain's prestige and power, it also

Map of Tibet the author maintained in his home office as a reminder of the goal of the Tibetan struggle

Shechen Publications

contributed significantly to his responsibilities in obligating him to protect, defend, and take revenge if any harm were done to them. Given that *gothaks* could include as many as 100 or more households, physically supporting them put tremendous pressure on the chieftain's animal pastures and farmland. At the same time, a chieftain having many *gothaks* was a clear demonstration of his power and influence.

As a direct result of this fierce loyalty, preserving family honor, including the tradition of taking revenge (*drasha len*), is extremely strong in most parts of Kham, particularly in Nyarong. "Whatever you do in our Nyarong, do it cautiously. Keep your eyes on the ground as you tread. Make no enemies whatever you do! We are a very vindictive, revengeful people. Vendettas that last for generations are common amongst us. We have a saying: 'if somebody attacks you, hit back! Take revenge.'"[7] While included in a fictional work, this description of a Nyarongwa's sense of honor is grounded in reality. I personally know several people who sought revenge for the death of a family member when they were but teenagers. One of my family's "retainers"—a polite word for servant—Kalsang Wangdi, was only fourteen when he and his two brothers avenged their father's death by killing three members of the family responsible. He later fled with my family into exile and lived in India for almost forty years. Eventually he returned to Tibet and died peacefully in Nyarong. Had he not avenged the death of his father he would have been considered a coward, undeserving of respect. "A coward—that was the meanest accusation one Nyarong Khampa could make to another. A coward! It was far far better to be dead."[8]

Sadly, revenge killings still occur in Kham. Harsh punishments imposed by the Chinese authorities do not serve as a deterrent. There have been times when my parents, even while living in exile, have been able to settle serious conflicts that could have ended in revenge killings. It is a testament to my parents' evenhanded and compassionate dispensing of justice that, even after so many decades of Chinese rule and their physical absence from Kham, they are still viewed by Nyarongwas with such respect and deep affection.

For the most part, Nyarong is today experiencing genuine peace and reconciliation for the first time in many centuries. To a large extent, this is due to the influence of the esteemed spiritual master Kyabjé Jigmé Phuntsok Rinpoche[9] (1933–2004). Perhaps surprisingly, despite their vaunted ferocity, Nyarongwas are also intensely spiritual people "said to excel at two things—fighting and religion."[10] Kyabjé Rinpoche routinely praised the qualities of the Nyarongwas, noting their trustworthiness and loyalty, as well as their deep religious devotion. Currently, one of his principal disciples, Khenchen Tsultrim Lodrö Rinpoche, visits Nyarong each year to teach and guide the local people, reflecting the special affection that his master had for these ferocious Nyarongwas. I also feel a great sense of personal joy because there are a large number of monks from the various monasteries of Nyarong who are renowned scholars, many of them having studied at Larung Gar Buddhist Academy, the world-famous religious institute established by Kyabjé Rinpoche.[11]

Kyabjé Rinpoche's predecessor, Tertön Lerab Lingpa, commonly known as Tertön Sogyal, not only was from Nyarong but also belonged to the same clan, the Shiwatsang, as my paternal grandfather. Because of this, Kyabjé Rinpoche considered us relatives. Weeks ahead of his visit to India in 1990 he sent personal messages expressing his wish to meet with my father, reflecting his sincere affection. Similarly, when he visited the United States in 1993 as part of his larger world tour, the people in his entourage again inquired about my family and me. I was at that time away in India, but my wife and children had a wonderful audience with him in Maryland, where Kyabjé Rinpoche was staying at a Tibetan Buddhist center.

Kyabjé Jigmé Phuntsok Rinpoche together with the author's family during his 1993 visit to the United States

He gave a beautiful Guru Padmasambhava statue to my son, Tashi Topgyal,[12] that we still honor on our altar. Upon my return from India, I made a special trip to Boston where Kyabjé Rinpoche was visiting and spent several precious hours with this great master. Just a few years before his passing, he sent a precious statue of Buddha as a gift to my father through Khenchen Namdrol Rinpoche, a very senior Nyingmapa Khenpo (abbot) from Namdroling Monastery in South India. Khenchen Namdrol Rinpoche was instrumental in bringing Kyabjé Jigmé Phuntsok Rinpoche to India in 1990.

# CHAPTER 2

# The Gyari Family

*Descendants of Nyarong Gönpo Namgyal*

## NYARONG GÖNPO NAMGYAL

My father, Gyari Nyima Gyaltsen, is a direct descendant of the famed Tibetan warrior Nyarong Gönpo Namgyal (1799–1865), who became one of the region's most powerful chieftains, conquering large parts of Kham in just a few decades. Gönpo Namgyal was a controversial man, considered by some a hero and by others, including both the Central Government in Lhasa (Bod Ü Shung) and the Qing authorities, a "rebellious villain." Many scholars have written about him, including YudruTsomu, who perceptively notes: "The evaluation of individual historical figures . . . has always been influenced by the historian's particular perspective, which is subject to the theoretical, political and ideological concerns of the day."[1] What is undisputed is that Gönpo Namgyal refused to subject himself to Qing authority. When the Qing officials tried to induce him to join their ranks, he not only rejected their overtures but also threw their gifts of enticement into the nearby Nyakchu River, disdainfully remarking:

> I don't need any title from China.
> I don't need a title from Tibet[2] either.
> I will not wear a Chinese hat nor put these feathers on my hat.[3]
> If you are capable there is no restriction in occupying the Gaden Throne.[4]
> I don't need any title or gifts.
> If you want, take them, otherwise throw them away in the river.[5]

Historically, Tibet was composed of three main regions: U-Tsang or Central Tibet, Amdo or the northeast, and Kham, the southeast, with Lhasa as the capital.

At its greatest reach, the Lhasa government's control stretched far into Kham. As Gönpo Namgyal expanded his territory, large numbers of Khampas fleeing his rule, including some influential chieftains, sought refuge in the areas still governed by Lhasa and repeatedly petitioned for its assistance. Citing official documents in his book, Tsepon W.D. Shakabpa, a very senior former Tibetan government official, writes: "Six thousand refugee families poured into Lhasa from Derge, Horkhok, Lithang, Chating and Dzakhok. They submitted petitions to the Tibetan government for help, and in 1863 the government sent troops to Nyarong under the command of Kalon Phulungwa and Dapon Trimon."[6] The presence of six thousand Khampa families seeking refuge in Lhasa in those days must have been overwhelming. Tibetan families are large, but even if you think of an average of only three members per family, the total would have been nearly twenty thousand people. I am a little bit surprised at this staggering figure, but the information appears well documented.

Gönpo Namgyal's domination of Kham also disrupted the historic trade route between China and Central Tibet over which important staples such as black tea from China made their way to Lhasa. Even more than the Lhasa government, the Qing dynasty was deeply concerned with the rise of Gönpo Namgyal. He had taken control of much of Kham on both sides of the Drichu River, disrupting the nominal allegiance accorded to both the Lhasa government and the Qing emperor and, more importantly, the tributes paid to the latter. Some historians believe that it was Qing manipulation of the Lhasa authorities more than the pleas of aggrieved Khampa chieftains that led the Central Government to send troops to suppress Gönpo Namgyal.[7] Although these dissatisfied Khampas eagerly solicited Lhasa's assistance, they only wanted temporary help in ousting Gönpo Namgyal. They were subsequently resentful when the Central Government established a permanent presence in Kham.

The previously mentioned knowledgeable Nyarong elder, Dogyal Aten, astutely expresses how many Nyarongwas feel about the rise and fall of Gönpo Namgyal. He notes that the Central Government's dismantling of Gönpo Namgyal's rule weakened the frontiers of Tibet, making it easier for future Chinese incursions.[8] Aten's position is indirectly confirmed by General Fu Sung-mu in his petition to the Manchu throne seeking to include Nyarong in the newly created Xikang Province when he writes: "The chief of Nyarong, by name Gombu [Gönpo], invaded and ravaged the Five Hor States, Derge and other neighboring Principalities, with the result that the Tibetans possessed themselves of his country."[9] There is also a strong feeling that the subjugation of Nyarong untied one of the "natural knots"[10] of Tibet, thereby weakening its spiritual protection. Traditionally, Tibetans believe that Tibet contains four "knots," and if they are unraveled, Tibet will be thrown into chaos and instability, eventually threatening the Tibetan nation. The four knots are: Nyarong—the iron knot, Golok—the wind knot, Sa-ngen—the earth knot, and Powo—the snow knot. All of these knots have been compromised at one time or another, sadly by the Tibetans themselves.

On the other hand, some Tibetans have, at least publicly, condemned Gönpo Namgyal's activities, although the reasons behind their animosity bear close scrutiny. In his early writings, for example, the late Sherab Özer Rinpoche, a Nyarong scholar, criticized Gönpo Namgyal, seemingly embracing PRC government propaganda in agreeing that he "obstructed the unification of the 'motherland' and harmed harmony among 'nationalities.'"[11] When he visited the United States in 1998, we had lengthy discussions about his research and conclusions. My father was also visiting me at the time, and the two veteran Khampas enjoyed an emotional reunion, as they had been friends since childhood. Sherab Özer Rinpoche confided in us that in some of his earlier writings he had to criticize Gönpo Namgyal solely to appease the Chinese because it was the only way he could get his work published. He also shared with us the draft of his book that was eventually published in 2013, in which he repudiated his earlier views.

In his book on Tibet's history,[12] Thupten Phuntsok gives a very clear narrative of the Central Tibetan Government's involvement in Nyarong. His well-researched narrative explains that these events took place during a break in the Dalai Lama's rule, when the power of the government was in the hands of either Shatra Wangchuk Gyalpo (1862–1864) or Dedrug Khenrab Wangchuk (1864–1872). The 11th Dalai Lama, Khedrup Gyatso, had died suddenly less than a year after being enthroned in 1855.

> In 1863, Nyarong armies invaded Derge, arresting both the queen mother and the daughter of the Derge king. In the same year Kalon Phulungpa Tsewang Dorjee departed Lhasa, leading a contingent of the army that reached Derge in 1864.
>
> In 1865, the armies of the Tibetan government and Derge invaded Nyarong, destroying Nyarong Gönpo Namgyal as well as his followers and the palace.
>
> In 1871, General Phunrabpa invited Kongtrul Yonden Gyatso to Nyarong to conduct a great mercury-purifying process for medicinal use.[13]

Today, among the younger generation of Khampas, Gönpo Namgyal is beginning to be seen as a courageous leader. Young scholars are doing research to better understand him and the sociopolitical situation of that period. However, nearly a century and a half later, some individuals still seem to suffer from the supposed "humiliation" of Gönpo Namgyal's rule, especially members of some of the larger Khampa tribes who don't like being reminded that they were so ruthlessly subjugated by an individual from a much smaller Nyarong family. For example, I have been told that in his contemporary writings, a certain Khampa leader in exile disparagingly refers to Gönpo Namgyal as *Tendra*, which translates as "enemy of the faith." *Tendra* is a derogatory term that most contemporary Tibetan writers will only invoke to describe the Chinese Communists.

The Gyari[14] family had close ties with Gönpo Namgyal's family, the Nyakyedtsang. Gönpo Namgyal's eldest daughter married Gyari Agok (meaning "baldheaded") Sengyé Bhum. Some authors write of Gönpo Namgyal's *sister* being married into our family. Gyari Dorjé Namgyal, my great grandfather, told my senior mother, Nordzin Lhamo, that his great grandmother was the eldest daughter and not the sister of Gönpo Namgyal. This fact was later confirmed by the late king of the Lingtsang clan, Phuntsok Gelek Rabten, who himself was the grandson of Gönpo Namgyal's youngest daughter.

Gyari Lama Tsering, Gönpo Namgyal's grandson from the alliance with the Gyari family, was a close military aide to his grandfather, leading many important campaigns. However, when direct confrontation with Lhasa took place, Gyari Lama Tsering and other senior aides advised Gönpo Namgyal to seek peace with the Central Government in exchange for releasing some of the important lamas and chieftains he was holding hostage. Gönpo Namgyal not only refused to accept this wise counsel but also demoted these true loyalists, labeling them cowards. Consequently, Gyari Lama Tsering and some of the other senior aides did not participate in the last battles fought between the Nyarongwas and the Lhasa government troops, which ended decisively in 1865 in Lhasa's favor.

After Gönpo Namgyal's defeat, the Central Tibetan Government exercised direct control over all the areas that he had conquered, consisting of seventeen districts.[15] This huge area covered most of the Kham region east of the Drichu River, right up to the traditional border with China, as well as several districts that were already under Lhasa's jurisdiction. The famed Drukmo Dzong—Female Dragon Fortress—of Nyarong became the official residence of the Lhasa government's Governor General ruling all of Kham.

Gyari Lama Tsering initially refrained from making direct contact with the newly arrived Lhasa authorities. He felt a deep moral conflict, given his blood relation to the Nyakyedtsang family. He also mistrusted these government officials, having witnessed how Gönpo Namgyal was misled with false promises during the closing hours of the final battle. The Central Government generals, under oath, promised to conclude the conflict through negotiations. Despite his otherwise brutal behavior, as a Buddhist, Gönpo Namgyal never broke an oath. He believed that the Tibetan generals, Buddhist as well, would also honor their word. He thus sent his son Sungdak Gönpo and his senior aides to the Central Government army camp for negotiations. They were immediately ambushed and killed. To this day, the Nyarongwas talk about the treachery of General Trimon with deep anguish.

Gyari Lama Tsering subsequently received urgent instructions from Nyala Pema Dündul (1816–1872), his revered teacher and one of the most renowned Buddhist masters of the period, to proceed immediately to Drukmo Dzong to offer his allegiance to the Central Government generals. Despite his serious misgivings, Gyari Lama Tsering's unwavering faith in his teacher compelled him to make the trip. At that time, many Nyarongwas were still resisting the Lhasa army and had Drukmo Dzong under siege. When they saw Gyari Lama Tsering coming toward the fortress, they aimed their muskets at him, hurling derogatory and demeaning insults and daring him to surrender. Despite the imminent danger he faced, he proudly shouted back that he was proceeding at the command of his spiritual master and henceforth had "decided to pledge my loyalty to the Gaden Phodrang and seek protection and offer my prostration to His Holiness the Dalai Lama."[16] As his fellow Nyarongwas recognized the sincerity of his heartfelt and courageous statement, they gradually lowered their muskets and let him pass. His words subsequently became a popular slogan for many other Nyarongwas who followed his lead in pledging their allegiance to Lhasa.

While some of the governors appointed by the Central Government ruled wisely and were both popular and effective, others ruled with shortsightedness and soon lost the trust and respect of the Khampas. The first Governor General was Phunrabpa Tsering Palden, who came with the military expedition led by Kalon Phulungpa and General Trimon. During his governorship, he reinstated many of the Khampa chieftains to their former positions, patronized local monasteries, and respected many important reincarnated lamas of Kham. He worked closely with local Nyarong chieftains and appointed people including Gyari Lama Tsering to positions of authority.[17] Gyari Lama Tsering's younger son, Gyari

# Gönpo Namgyal's Descendants

## Through his three daughters with focus on the Gyari Family

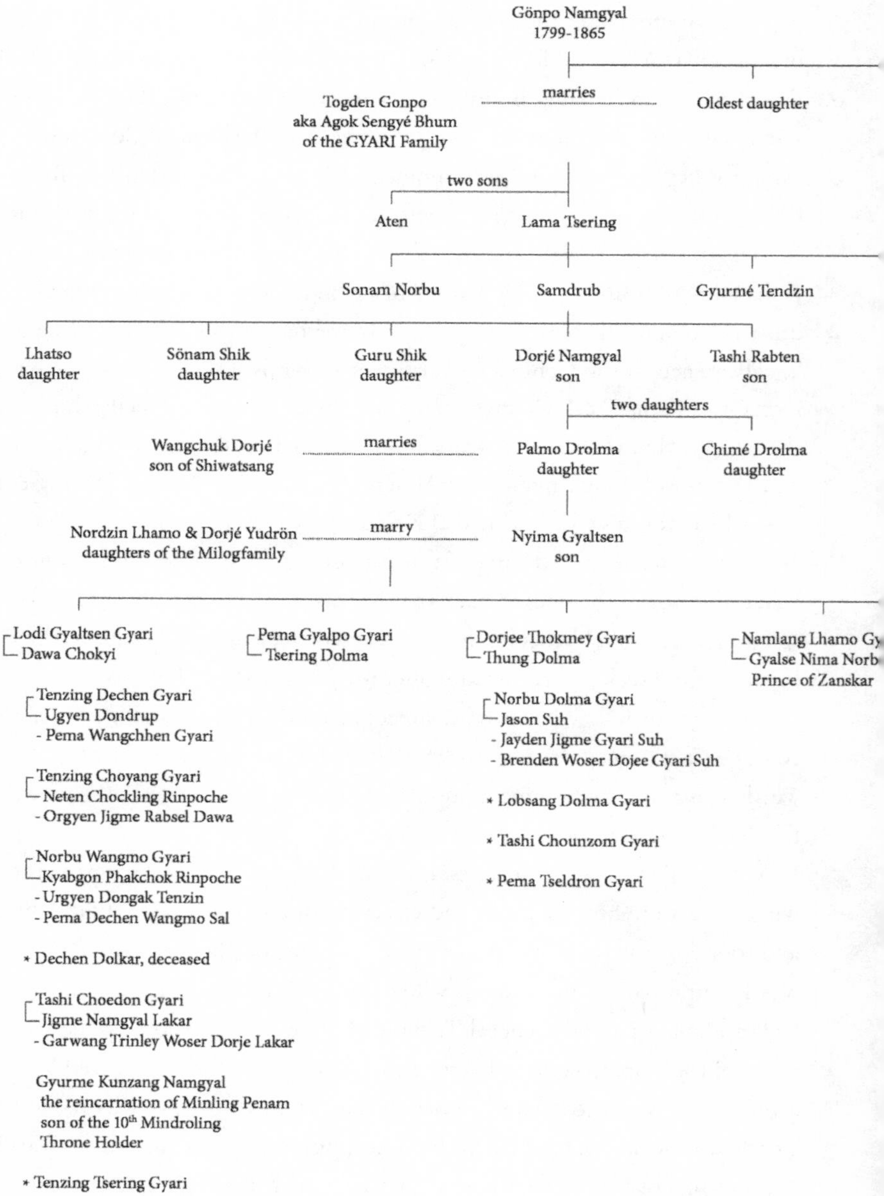

Middle daughter

Vashumewa Family

Youngest daughter

Lingtsang King

Wangchen

Akal

Rinzing Dolma Gyari
Chikaya Noguchi

Thaye Gyari Noguchi

Yulzin Gyari Noguchi

Thinley Kunkyab Gyari
Sherab Tso

* Dorjee Wangchuk Gyari

* Rinzing Lhamo Gyari

Jayang
Dolma Gyari

Kelsang Tsewang
Dorjee Gyari
Samdup Thinley

* Deechen Gyalmo
Gyari

* Tenzing Wangmo
Gyari

* Mipham Dorje
Gyari

Dolma Gyari
formerly married to
Khenrab Thaye Drawu

* Gyari Nima Lhundrub
Dorgee Drawu

Samdrub, was also appointed to be the governor's Special Representative to some areas in Derge.

During one of Gyari Samdrub's return visits to Nyarong to see his family[18] and to report to the governor about his work, Governor Phunrabpa asked: "Have you been personally benefited by your position in Derge?" Gyari Samdrub, thinking that the governor thought he was taking bribes or abusing people, immediately swore in the name of all the deities that he had not misused his office and had not taken anything from the people worth "as little as a needle and a thread." The governor scolded him, saying: "You fool! I appointed you to that position because I thought it would also benefit you and your family." The Gyari family had suffered great personal loss during the many years of instability in Nyarong, and the governor was trying to make amends by appointing Gyari Samdrub to this official position. Governor Phunrabpa felt a genuine fondness and concern for the welfare of the Gyari family, and they in turn conducted themselves in a manner above reproach. After more than a century, one of Governor Phunrabpa's descendants, Phunrab Lobsang Dhargye, and I became close friends. We had the honor of serving together in the Kashag (the Cabinet of the Central Tibetan Administration in Dharamsala), whose members were at the time appointed directly by His Holiness the Dalai Lama.[19]

Unfortunately, many other civil and military officials of the Central Government didn't govern Kham as did Governor Phunrabpa. They behaved like officials of a foreign occupying force despite their common ethnicity as Tibetans. Many of the influential Khampa chieftains who initially pleaded for Lhasa's intervention to subdue Gönpo Namgyal did not favor its strong and permanent presence in Kham. Some of them either directly or indirectly started collaborating with Qing authorities to undermine its influence. Local Sichuan officials took full advantage of this regional discord to reduce the presence and influence of the Central Government in most of Kham east of the Drichu River. At times, Lhasa was able to reassert its authority, only again to be pushed back by the Qing.

A similar pattern emerged during the early period of Chinese Nationalist rule. Khampa rulers, unhappy with the Central Government's presence, established ties with the Kuomintang (KMT). The Nationalists encouraged this regional animosity to weaken Tibetan resistance, setting the stage for China's complete domination of Kham and ultimately all of Tibet. In 1939, the Nationalist government created a province called Xikang that theoretically included all of Kham, even areas to the west of the Drichu River. The Nationalists had no actual control over these areas, as they were directly under Lhasa's rule. Even areas east of the Drichu River were in a fluid administrative situation as the Central Government army periodically reasserted itself. There were a number of additional administrative and territorial changes in the interim, but in 1955 the PRC government eliminated Xikang, merging it into Sichuan Province.

## GÖNPO NAMGYAL'S LINEAGE

In the end, my family, the Gyaritsang, became Gönpo Namgyal's principal inheritor. In addition to the Gyari family, the Lingtsang king and the Washumewa family are his other direct descendants. Besides our family, the Washumewa family also inherited some of the traditional lands owned by Gönpo Namgyal's family—the Nyakyedtsang. In the 1920s, the Washumewa family was compelled to leave Nyarong for Ngapa because of internal conflicts. Before they moved, they donated their inherited lands to Jungkhung Monastery, where they were patrons. After resettling in Ngapa, the Washumewa family became very influential and confidants of the king of Mevo. Tsering Palden, the family head, was able to visit India on a pilgrimage in the late 1980s where he had a wonderful reunion with my father and other relatives. Tsering Palden passed away in 2017 in Barkham, the present capital of the Ngapa Tibetan Autonomous Prefecture, where he was living in retirement. Fortunately, the Washumewa family has many living members to continue its lineage, including some members living in exile. All three of these families have maintained very close ties, even though both Lingtsang and Ngapa are at great distance from Nyarong. Phuntsok Gelek Rabten,[20] the Lingtsang king, escaped into exile and eventually died in Kalimpong, India. When I was a student at Dr. Graham's Homes in Kalimpong in the early 1960s, every Sunday without fail, he would visit me, usually bringing canned pork and a homemade steamed bun or bread. We would sit together on the lawn in front of the school's clock tower. He would not just drop off the food but would make me eat it in front of him. Although Dr. Graham's Homes was an excellent academic institution, food was not plentiful.[21] Besides, I was of weak constitution and used to get bullied a lot by the seniors. The Lingtsang king was worried that the older boys would take the food away from me.

Our two families still maintain very close relations. When I visited Chengdu in 2002 and 2004 as His Holiness the 14th Dalai Lama's Special Envoy for talks with PRC officials, I made it a point to meet the Lingtsang king's elder son, Jigmey Wangdu, where he had permanently settled some years back. I was also able to visit the late king's daughter, Seymo Riyong, just hours before she passed away in Gangtok, Sikkim, in 2013. Fortunately, both the son and daughter of the Lingtsang king have children who will continue the Lingtsang lineage.

While the Lingtsang king and his family, as well as my family, were able to escape into exile in India, only one daughter, Nyendrak Lhamo, from the Washumewa family was able to make the journey out. She was married to the son of a very influential family, the Kirtitsang—the family of the previous Kirti Rinpoche, one of the most revered Rinpoches of the Ngapa region. The present Kirti Rinpoche lives in exile and heads a well-established *sangha*[22] in Dharamsala. He also served as a Kalon in the Kashag.

The Gyaritsang is considered the primary descendant of Gönpo Namgyal not only because of inherited ancestral property but also because it has preserved many of the important traditions and religious practices of the Nyakyedtsang, including the *puja* (ceremony) dedicated to the family's protector deity, Mahakala. This religious tie sprang from an incident during the overthrow of Gönpo Namgyal. When his castle was set on fire many people witnessed a phenomenal sight in broad daylight. Immense balls of clouds burst forth from his Mahakala chapel with a thunderous noise and streamed toward the Gyaritsang manor, dissolving into it. Nyala Pema Dündul, Gyari Lama Tsering's teacher, told him that henceforth the Gyari family must conduct the elaborate recitation of the Mahakala mantra in the same way practiced by the Nyakyedtsang, as this protector deity now resided with the Gyaritsang.

This *puja* is conducted annually from the twenty-fourth to the twenty-ninth day of the ninth month of the Tibetan lunar calendar. As the associated mantra recitations must be done nonstop for six days, there are several shifts of monks involved in the ritual. There is a funny story about Gönpo Namgyal, who apparently became suspicious that the monks on the night shift weren't reciting the mantra properly. Normally, mantras are recited without the accompaniment of any musical instruments. Gönpo Namgyal instructed the monks, however, to use a drum so he could easily check on their diligence and adherence to the text.

Traditionally, small sausage coils were served for lunch to the monks participating in the ritual. Whether this was because Gönpo Namgyal's family was stingy or because of the large number of monks to be served is not certain. My senior mother tells me that the Gyari family preserved this ritual exactly as it had always been done, including serving the same tiny sausages even though my mothers found it quite embarrassing, and also more work to prepare them. My senior mother remembers suggesting a change to this practice by serving regular-sized sausages, but the elders insisted that everything must be done exactly the way it was carried out during the time of Gönpo Namgyal.

## MY PARENTS

By the time my father's grandfather, Gyari Dorjé Namgyal, came of age, the Gyari family exercised supremacy in all parts of Upper and Middle Nyarong. In the absence of any sons[23] to continue the family's power and lineage, a marriage alliance was arranged for his two daughters, Chimé Drolma and Palmo Drolma, to Wangchuk Dorjé, a son of an important family from the neighboring Kardze area, the Shiwatsang. It was a common practice among both Lhasa aristocrats and Khampa chieftain families without male heirs to find a groom who would adopt the name of the bride's family to continue the family line.

My father was born to the younger daughter, Palmo Drolma. She was beautiful with a very strong personality. Her sister, Chimé Drolma, was the opposite: a tomboy who dressed like a man and participated in armed raids and hunting expeditions[24] with the family's loyal retainers, including the Taksen-Drukchu,[25] who truly admired her. After Palmo Drolma's early death, the family fractured and deep divisions formed within the Gyari clan, bringing great tragedy and sorrow.

At the time of my father's birth in 1925, the Qing dynasty had already been overthrown and the Nationalists were in power. Liu Wenhui, a KMT warlord, ruled neighboring Sichuan Province and tried to exert control over parts of Kham, taking full advantage of the internal Gyari family discord. There were numerous fierce battles fought between Liu's troops and Gyari loyalists before Liu Wenhui managed to occupy Nyarong, burning the Gyari manor to the ground and looting the family's famed "speaking Tara"[26] statue. Fortunately, some loyalists recovered the statue and installed it at Shiwa Monastery for safekeeping. My parents wisely decided to keep the statue at the monastery even after they rebuilt the Gyari manor. During the Cultural Revolution, the statue was severely damaged, including the loss of one of its arms, but, once again, people knowing the statue's importance managed to hide it. It survives to this day, residing in its full glory at Shiwa Monastery.

The Gyari family alone lost about fifty-six lives during these fights, including my father's elder mother, Chimé Drolma, who was arrested and executed by firing squad. Her heroic resistance against the Nationalist authorities became legendary, and the Tibetan revolutionary Bapa Phuntsok Wangyal praised her in his 1940s song urging the Tibetans to rise up and take revenge against the Nationalist Chinese:

> Look out, look out, you uncivilized Chinese.
> You were shameless not one time, not two times, not three times.
> First, you killed four Yangchen people,
> Second, you stabbed Sheyngo Kunchog to death.
> Third, you beat Atri to death with a stick,
> Fourth, you used Nyarong Chime Drolma as a target and killed her.
> And you committed serious crimes, stealing the wealth of the people.
> We have never seen such cruel behavior.
> No love and no compassion,
> Treating us Tibetans as animals.
> No love and no compassion,
> You evil and savage Chinese bully the soft and avoid the tough.
> Your usual food is Tibetans' blood and pus.
> Now if we do not take revenge,
> We will no longer tie our belts like real men.[27]

During this period the 9th Panchen Lama, Thupten Choekyi Nyima, was in self-imposed exile in Kham because of his differences with the Central Government. After a visit to Beijing in early 1925, he eventually set up headquarters in Jyekundo to be nearer to Tibetan areas and important monasteries such as Kumbum in Amdo. Seeking local support, he formed an alliance with the Gyaritsang, as well as another powerful Khampa chieftain family, the Khangsartsang. This alliance was mutually beneficial, with the Panchen Labrang[28] gifting the Gyaritsang forty German Mauser rifles. While their provenance is unknown, these weapons were clearly brand new, as they were delivered in their original shipping crates. The Panchen Bureau also gave the family prized Mauser shotguns or pistols. I can remember the monk who looked after me, my Uncle Tsultrim, had one such pistol that fascinated me as a young child. In those days it was rare for one family to have this type and quantity of arms.

Our family ties to the Panchen Lama lineage have endured for decades. When I was in Beijing as part of the Three Member High-Level Delegation of His Holiness the 14th Dalai Lama for exploratory talks with PRC officials in April 1982, I met with His Holiness the 10th Panchen Rinpoche, Choekyi Gyaltsen. At that time, he made inquiries about my father's health and referenced the close relationship that my family had with his predecessor. He even sent my father a personally autographed portrait and a special amulet of Yamantaka, a highly revered Tibetan Buddhist deity, which my family continues to preserve as a precious gift.

After Liu's forces burned our home, the Gyari family began many years of exile, taking refuge in neighboring regions. The family's military power remained strong, however, as it had built a large and experienced contingent of fully armed warriors loyal to Gyari Dorjé Namgyal, my father's grandfather. He was extremely protective of his only grandchild because the very survival of the Gyari clan depended on my father's safety. He sent my father with a group of trusted and loyal retainers to live in the Bureau of the 9th Panchen Rinpoche, also known as Panchen Nangma-Gang. After Thupten Choekyi Nyima's passing in 1937 in Jyekundo, my father moved with the Bureau to China, where he spent his youth studying first at Nanjing and later at Chongqing. Because my father spent so many years in China, he may be the only Khampa chieftain who never had long hair and a ponytail, as is customary of a Khampa man.

Even though he was only in his early teens, my father, with the help of senior officials of the Panchen Lama's Bureau, personally met with Chiang Kai-shek in Chongqing in the late 1930s to protest the atrocities committed by warlord Liu and to seek compensation for the Gyari family's resultant loss of life and property. My father vividly remembered the meeting because General Chiang received them in a reception hall that was partially damaged by daily Japanese aerial bombardments. He later understood the significance of this venue: Chiang Kai-shek was demonstrating the tremendous pressure he was facing as a result of the Sino-Japanese War. While General Chiang expressed sympathy for the plight of the Gyari family, he explained he couldn't take action against Liu Wenhui because it was important for him to retain the unity of the KMT during the conflict with the Japanese. He did, however, offer substantial financial compensation from the Nationalist government and further ensured that my father received an excellent education while in China. Years later, when my father was at the forefront in opposing the Nationalist government's disruptive policies among the Tibetans in exile, he continued to have personal admiration for Chiang Kai-shek. The General's sympathetic hearing of his family's plight made a deep impression on my father's heart.

While in China my father was also fortunate to have the guardianship of Ren Naiqiang (1894–1989), who was considered one of China's top experts on Tibet. He taught at several universities and was the founder of the Tibet-Kangba (Khampa) Research Institute.[29] He was married to a Tibetan woman from Nyarong who was related to my father. She was betrothed to the professor by my father's grandfather.

Nationalist officials encouraged my father in his studies so that he could be nominated to the Nationalist parliament representing Nyarong. My father was surprised to discover that a Chinese person, who had never set foot in Nyarong or any other area of Kham, represented the region. Had my father been able to continue his studies, he was being groomed to join the famous Whampoa Military Academy, the brainchild of Sun Yat-sen that produced some of the finest military leaders of modern China. Chiang Kai-shek subsequently headed this academy, while veteran Communist leader Zhou Enlai served as an instructor at one point. The Sino-Japanese War and the subsequent civil war in China ultimately disrupted these plans.

During his years in Chongqing and Nanjing my father became close friends with several young Tibetans studying or working in China for the Nationalist government, including Bapa Phuntsok Wangyal. Unknown to my father and most others at the time, Phuntsok Wangyal had already joined the underground communist movement and was trying to recruit more Tibetans to its cause. Bapa Phuntsok Wangyal shared with me stories of how he had tried to recruit my father. In those early years Phuntsok Wangyal realized that for the Tibetan Communist Party to get a foothold in Kham, he would need to recruit Tibetans from chieftains' families, as local Khampas are loyal to their *ponpos*. When he met my father, he was thrilled, thinking he was about to land a prize catch. My father was a sophisticated man, educated in China, and a Khampa chieftain. Phuntsok Wangyal took him out on several drinking sessions, but it didn't take long for Phuntsok Wangyal to realize that my father "was too religious minded and I was afraid even to explain [to] him my socialist ideas."[30]

Despite Phuntsok Wangyal's failure to entice my father to join the communists, they remained good friends throughout the years. Even though they were not able to meet in person once my family left Tibet, they had long telephone conversations during the last years of my father's life. Phuntsok Wangyal's youngest brother, Choephel, was also a very close friend of my father. When I met him in 1982 in Beijing, he shared many wonderful stories about their friendship and gave me a lot of information about my father that I was unaware of, as my father was a very private individual not inclined to talk too much about his own life. When I met him, Choephel was the Director of the Bureau of Road Construction in Kardze Tibetan Autonomous Prefecture. He was very proud that he was able to arrange for the building of numerous roads within the prefecture, bringing much benefit to the locals.

Warlord Liu Wenhui's control over Nyarong and other parts of Kham gradually weakened, and the Gyari family was able to reassert its position of power and return to Nyarong. Although the tragic family feud had left my father an orphan, with his coming of age, there was a natural reconciliation between his paternal and maternal relatives, as he was precious to both families. My father subsequently rose to become one of the most powerful and respected chieftains in Nyarong. Even in his later years in exile in India, he remained an imposing figure. Let me quote a dear family friend, Maura Moynihan, of her impressions of my father: "He is, like his wives, an instinctual leader; poised, but not remote, magnanimous, elegant in nothing but a parka and sweatpants. He does not need to draw attention to himself, all attention attaches to him quite naturally."[31]

Kham has always been a volatile region with shifting political alliances between various clans. The region had become even more unstable and unpredictable with increasing interference from neighboring China, combined with its becoming a playground for the struggle of influence and dominance between the Central Tibetan Government and local Chinese authorities. Gyari Dorjé Namgyal realized that the kind of political alliance he had tried to establish by marriage of his daughters was not enough to provide security for the family. Hoping to provide protection for his grandson, he approached the senior Rinpoches of Lumorab Monastery and asked for the hand of their niece, Nordzin Lhamo, the eldest daughter of the Milog family, for my father. He knew that the fame of these Rinpoches and the widespread respect with which they were held would help ensure my father's safety far more than any shifting political alliances.

The Lumorab Rinpoches, especially Gyalsé Chöying Dorjé, the younger son of Tertön Rangrik Dorjé (1847–1903), the founder of Lumorab Monastery, and his cousin Khenpo Aten, were very fond of the Gyari family and were ready to give their blessings to this match. As they didn't have any nephews to carry on their own Milog family lineage, however, they suggested that the two families maintain a distinct identity. To respect this arrangement, my father encouraged our family to adopt both family surnames. Unfortunately, we have not been able to do this, as we felt it too complicated to have two surnames.

In Tibetan, *milog* means "shall not return." It is said that the Milogtsang's ancestors were among the troops of Emperor Trisong Detsen sent from Lhasa to guard the frontiers of Tibet in the eighth century. For generations they performed this duty and were constantly in touch with the Central Government. With the decline of the Tibetan imperial power, many of the soldiers and their families returned to Lhasa. But a section of the garrison refused to return to Central Tibet, saying that unless they received an imperial order directing them otherwise, they would remain at their post, hence the name "Milog." The descendants of these soldiers are the Milog clan of my mothers.

As was often the custom in our region of Tibet, my father ended up marrying both Nordzin Lhamo and her younger sister Dorjé Yudrön. While they have very different personalities, they do share the same fundamental Nyarongwa character, as our dear friend Maura Moynihan notes:

> These sisters have a rare quality, which in the modern world is nearly lost. . . . These women, who were born in Tibet, who fought for their nation and left it against their will, have an innate awareness that they embody much more than their individual selves, but also their clan, their land, the Buddha Dharma, and they know that these are things of great and lasting value. I do not want to call this awareness pride, for pride can veer into hubris. And it is larger than self-respect; it is an innate union of the self with the family, the nation, the cosmos. These Khampa nobles are so utterly and completely sure of who and what they are, because their brand of nobility has not defined itself with tendentious ritual, materialism, or a crippling hierarchy. It was for centuries defined principally by their relation to the natural order, which in Kham is as glorious a creation as anything on this earth. These people have an integral bond with the soil, air, water, trees, birds, animals and people of Kham. They are Khampas and Buddhists, compassionate soldiers, passionate lovers.[32]

The author's parents: (left to right) Nordzin Lhamo, Nyima Gyaltsen, Dorjé Yudrön. Darjeeling, India, circa 1967

My senior mother, Nordzin Lhamo, is more outgoing and approachable—maybe because of her frequent trips with my father beyond Nyarong that gave her wider exposure to the outside world. On the other hand, my younger mother, Dorjé Yudrön, is a bit more reserved but is the epitome of Khampa strength and ferocity. They are both embodiments of an all-encompassing affection and uncompromising loyalty. My siblings and I used to jokingly call our senior mother "the Foreign Minister" and our younger mother "the Home Minister," of course, with our father being the "President"! Let me continue to quote Maura:

> Dorjee Youdon, horsewoman, defender of the citadel, barbarian slayer, protectress, mother . . . this woman is a hero. The moment she enters, I stare, I want to follow her wherever she goes. Clearly, she finds vanity and fashion a waste of time, she wears only a chuba, apron, a sweater, sandals. She needs no jewels, no kajal; she is stunningly beautiful. Two dark braids coil across her shoulders, their tips meet at her heart. Her skin is luminously white, her eyes brilliantly clear. I observe her upright posture, the sure movements of her hands, the keenness of her gaze. She is no doubt highly skilled at many things, able to assume and delegate authority. I suspect her vengeance is something to be feared. But she has that marvelous range of qualities I have seen among Khampas, she is also humorous, thoughtful, affectionate. . . . The first thing she wants to know is if . . . [we] have enough tea. While reaching for the thermos, she takes Surya [her grandson] on her lap and separates two warring children. She takes my hand and asks about her granddaughter. . . . In her presence I feel an amazing comfort, her candour and warmth assure me that I am unconditionally welcome, at once I feel like one of her children. . . .
>
> My parting image of Norzin and Dorjee Youdon is of their bedroom, where they are sitting on pillows with grandchildren in their arms, handsome relatives and admiring friends in their orbit. Painted images of Chenresig and Tara gaze over this scene with calm beneficence. The sisters are living in exile, but not in defeat. As long as this family is whole, Tibet is not lost. Our two queens, they rule the hearts of anyone who loves Tibet, or cares for the welfare of all sentient beings.[33]

I have been truly fortunate for many reasons in my life, but it is my connection with these two exceptional women, who I refer to as my mothers with equal devotion, that has been the cornerstone of all my experiences and achievements. Together they selflessly cared for my siblings and me, guided and instructed us. It was not until I was almost an adult that I finally learned which one of them was my biological mother: Nordzin Lhamo.

CHAPTER 3

# My Spiritual Lineage

*The Mindrolling Tradition and Lumorab Monastery*

Before discussing my birth and recognition as a Rinpoche, I would like to give an overview of my spiritual lineage and the establishment of the associated Lumorab Monastery.

## LUMORAB MONASTERY

My monastery, Thubten Shedrub Yeshen Chog-kye Ling, is located at Lumorab in the Ase region of Upper Nyarong, on the western edge of the Tromthar plateau in eastern Tibet. Because of its location, it is widely known as Lumorab Monastery. It was established in 1896 by Tertön[1] Rangrik Dorjé (aka Rigzin Kusum Lingpa) with the patronage and support of the 13th Dalai Lama, Gyalwa Thubten Gyatso, widely known as the Great Thirteenth.

At the time Lumorab Monastery was established, Nyarong was under the direct rule of the Central Tibetan Government in Lhasa. In fact, most of the Kham region of eastern Tibet was governed out of the Drukmo Dzong, the Female Dragon Fortress of Nyarong, where the Governor General of Lhasa resided. The Great Thirteenth, with whom Tertön Rangrik Dorjé had close spiritual ties, gave him large areas of land, including several villages from the various parts of Nyarong, to support the monastery. He also exempted benefactors of the monastery from any taxation by the Central Government. The name of the monastery, Thubten Shedrub Yeshen Chog-kye Ling, was bestowed by the Great Thirteenth. In fact, the first word, "Thubten," is his first name.

The beauty and size of the temple were believed to be second only to the famous grand temple of Riwoche—the Tragyelma—near Chamdo in Kham. The *labrang*, or the residence of the Rinpoches, was built to reflect the architectural style of the White Chapel of the Dalai Lama's Potala Palace in Lhasa. Lumorab quickly became a famed center of learning in that region of Tibet. Within a short period of time more than thirty monasteries became branches or affiliates.

## THE FOUNDER OF LUMORAB MONASTERY: TERTÖN RANGRIK DORJÉ

Tertön Rangrik Dorjé (1847–1903) is spiritually descended from Terdak Lingpa, the founder of the famed Mindrolling[2] lineage of the Nyingma school of Tibetan Buddhism. Mindrolling Monastery was established in Central Tibet in 1670. Terdak Lingpa was a contemporary of the 5th Dalai Lama, Ngawang Lobsang Gyatso, who was the first Dalai Lama to become the political ruler of Tibet. Terdak Lingpa and the Great Fifth, as he is popularly known, had a very special relationship, as they received teachings from each other. Just before his passing away in 1714, Terdak Lingpa asked his close attendants to help him take seven steps to the east. Seven generations later, in 1847, he took rebirth into the Milog clan in the Nyarong region of eastern Tibet as Tertön Rangrik Dorjé. Studying under the great Nyarong meditation master Nyala Pema Dündul, he reawakened his past aspirations to become a great treasure revealer. Tertön Rangrik Dorjé's collected works consist of forty-two extensive volumes.

Throughout Tertön Rangrik Dorjé's life he made frequent sojourns to Lhasa to give empowerments, oral transmissions, and essential advice on meditation to his many disciples in Central Tibet, including at Namgyal College in the Potala Palace. At the request of the Great Thirteenth and the Lhasa government, he conducted special consecration ceremonies of the Jokhang (the Central Cathedral in Lhasa), important shrine rooms in the Potala Palace, and at Samye Monastery, which had received major restoration work by the Central Tibetan Government at the Tertön's request. As a special honor, he was housed at the Nye Chu Lhakhang situated atop the Jokhang while in Lhasa, where he conducted prayers for the long life of the Dalai Lama and the protection of the Dharma and Tibet. While he was renowned for his extensive learning and his vast treasure revelations, it was his accomplishments as a practitioner that made him widely known and respected across the Tibetan Plateau.

Tertön Rangrik Dorjé demonstrated the highest stage of his spiritual realization by dissolving his body into rainbow light[3] at the time of his passing. His Holiness Kyabjé Dudjom Rinpoche (1904–1987), one of the greatest luminaries of this century, writes:

> It is impossible, too, to enumerate all those who passed into the rainbow body by the paths of the profound treasures of the Great Perfection, as exemplified by the Southern and Northern Treasure tradition. Even during this late age, this may still be illustrated. For example, in 1883/1884 (water sheep year, 15th cycle) the lord among accomplished masters, Rigdzin Pema Duddül, vanished in the body of light. Afterwards, when his personal disciple, Tertön Rangrik Dorjé, passed away at Mindrolling, his remains vanished into light. What was left behind, which was about six inches in size, was taken to Lumorab in Eastern Tibet, where it can still be seen today.[4]

I was among a handful of people who had the opportunity to view Tertön Rangrik Dorjé's actual body when Mindrolling Chung Rinpoche performed the purification ceremony that involved changing the wrappings on the body. Mindrolling Chung Rinpoche had taken the opportunity to stay at Lumorab for an extended time on his way back to Lhasa after visiting various parts of China with His Holiness the 14th Dalai Lama. He, together with His Holiness the 16th Karmapa and Kyabjé Trijang Rinpoche, the Dalai Lama's junior tutor, were asked by the Dalai Lama to visit some of the Nyingma, Kagyu, and Gelug monasteries during their trip back to Lhasa. The body of Tertön Rangrik Dorjé was fresh, and it looked like that of a small child, but as a young child what really caught my attention was the immense size of the head due to the dreadlocks wrapped around it. His body had obviously shrunk, but the hair did not. Some faithful individuals at great risk of their own lives were able to hide his body during the Cultural Revolution, and it is once again enshrined at Lumorab.

Minling Penam Rinpoche, following in his grandfather Tertön Rangrik Dorjé's footsteps, also attained the rainbow body. His mummified miniature is also preserved at Lumorab. Matteo Pistono writes from personal experience of seeing the remains of Minling Penam Rinpoche's body: "Ol' Penam's presence filled the entire valley, though his body was the size of a month-old infant. I noticed the distinct features of an elderly man with large ears and a flat nose; but these features were on a body not sixteen inches long."[5]

## THE MINDROLLING CONNECTION

Near the end of the nineteenth century, there were no male heirs to carry on the Mindrolling lineage, portending a crisis not only for the lineage but also for Tibet. There are prophecies stating that severe negative consequences would befall the Tibetan nation should either the Mindrolling or the Sakya lineages be broken. Fortunately, the Nechung Oracle[6] prophesied that any offspring of Tertön Rangrik Dorjé would be no different from a true son of Terdak Lingpa himself.[7] Heeding the advice of the State Oracle and his own divinations, the Great Thirteenth invited Tertön Rangrik Dorjé's eldest son, Tritsab Pema Wangchen, to Mindrolling to marry the Eighth Mindrolling throne holder Minling Trichen Gyurmé Yishin Wangyal's daughter, Jetsün Chimé Deden Drolma. In this way the great Mindrolling lineage was restored.

With the union of these two important lineages, the Mindrolling and Lumorab Monasteries became inseparable, like the confluence of two great rivers, and became known as the Upper and Lower Monasteries. Mindrolling's ritual traditions, sacred arts, and many annual ceremonies were introduced at Lumorab, while Tertön Rangrik Dorjé's spiritual writings and revealed treasures became its scriptural base. Even ordinary monks of Lumorab who went to Mindrolling were entitled to the same privileges and facilities as a monk from Mindrolling itself. All the principal Rinpoches of Lumorab when residing at Mindrolling enjoyed special status and privileges as part of a family, and similarly, the members of the Mindrolling family were accorded the same when they came down to Nyarong.

The Milogtsang, my maternal family, is the *yabtsang* (paternal home) to the Mindrolling as well as the Lumorab Rinpoches. Quite often, even Tibetans become a little puzzled when we tell them that we are related to the Mindrolling family. This is understandable because the famed Mindrolling Monastery is in Central Tibet while my family was from Nyarong, in the heartland of Kham in eastern Tibet. In fact, Tritsab Pema Wangchen and his son Trichen Gyurmé Döndrub Wangyal[8] both came home to Nyarong and passed away at Lumorab. Maybe they missed their relatives and yearned for the carefree and open space of Nyarong. My mothers shared with me a very poignant scene of Minling Trichen Gyurmé

Kunzang Wangyal (1931–2008) coming to bid farewell to his aunt, who was their mother. He was returning to Mindrolling after spending many years in Nyarong. Even though Sönam Drolma, his aunt, loved her nephew with all her heart, she did not want him to continue in the tradition of his father and grandfather, who had come down to Nyarong and passed away at Lumorab. With a heavy heart she urged him to stay back in Central Tibet to maintain the precious lineage of the Mindrolling. Sadly, Minling Trichen Rinpoche did not return home to Nyarong but went into exile and passed away in India. My grandmother herself had a tragic death that is too sad and personally hurtful for me to narrate, resulting from Communist China's brutal policy in the name of democratic reform.

## KHENPO ATEN

After laying the foundation of Lumorab, Tertön Rangrik Dorjé spent most of his time in Central Tibet at Mindrolling with his son. The task of establishing the monastery in Nyarong and building the associated temples was mainly carried out by Tertön Rangrik Dorjé's younger son, Gyalsé Chöying Dorjé, and his nephew Khenchen Jampal Dewé Nyima, popularly known as Khenpo Aten.[9] The fame and scholarship of Khenpo Aten attracted students from all parts of Tibet to study at Lumorab.

Khenpo Aten was one of the heart disciples[10] of Ju Mipham (1846–1912), who is reverently known as Mipham the Great. Ju Mipham was a master and a scholar, as well as one of the leading figures in the Ri-me (nonsectarian) movement in Tibet. This renowned master bestowed on Khenpo Aten many initiations and transmissions, honoring him by making him the custodian of his Yamantaka lineage.[11] While conferring the lineage, he gifted Khenpo Aten a precious statue of Yamantaka in the Vajrabhairava, or buffalo-headed, form. Khenpo Aten never parted with this precious gift—it was always with him until he gave it to my father with the words: "Hold on to it." Eventually, my father gave it to me as Khenpo Aten's reincarnation. My father truly believed that Khenpo Aten made him the "guardian" of his precious statue until he was reborn. This Yamantaka statue is the central object of my personal shrine.

Khenpo Aten wrote a number of highly acclaimed commentaries and many treatises on various aspects of Buddhist philosophy. Unfortunately, many of them did not survive the destruction of the Cultural Revolution. Today scholars at

# The Spiritual Lineage Tree of Lumorab*

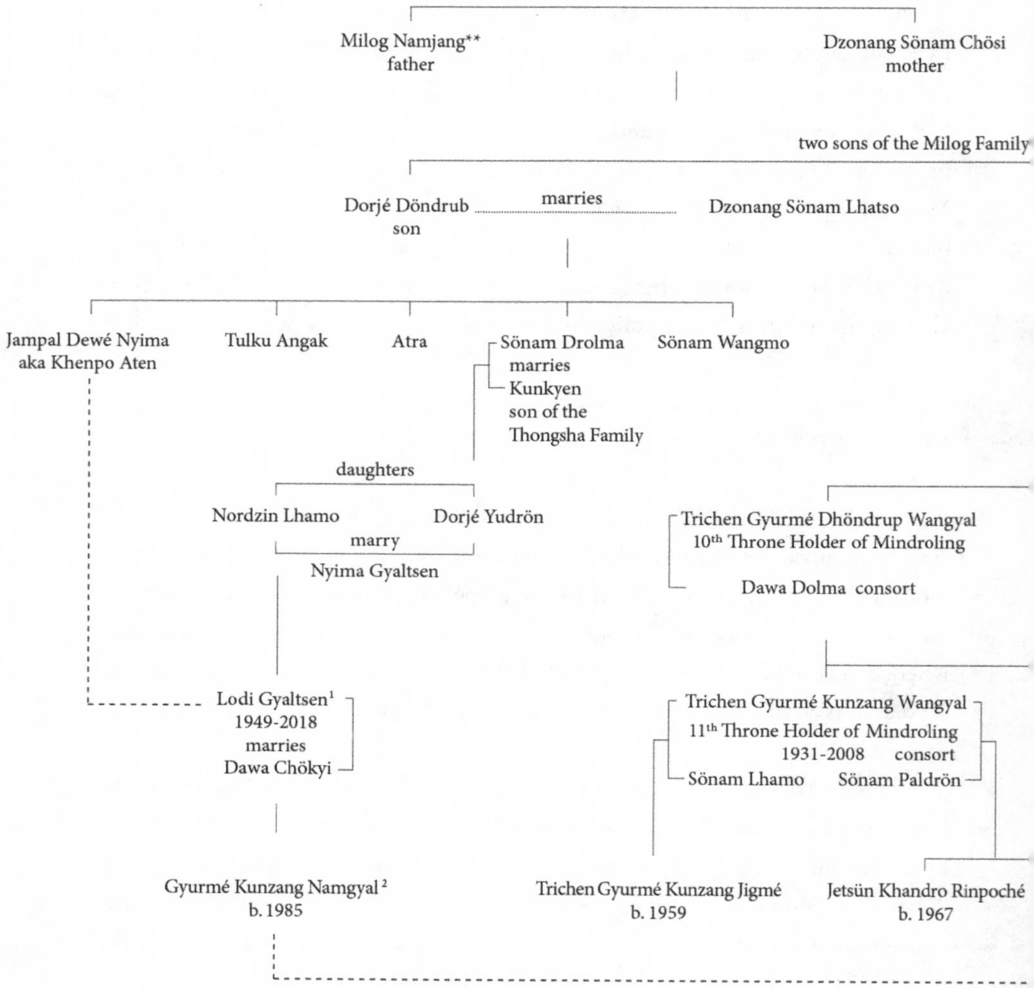


* The spiritual lineage tree of Lumorab is based on the Lumorab lineage prayer. The original prayer was composed by Kunchok at the request of a devotee. Later, each generation of Lumorab masters would compose and add their own lineage prayers to the original prayer. The prayer to Pema Wangchen was composed by Jampal Dewé Nyima. And, the prayers to Kunzang Chödrön, Pema Namgyal, Jamyang Chödrak, and Kunzang Wangyal were composed by Kunzang Wangyal, the 11th Mindroling Throne Holder, at the request of Nordzin Lhamo, the author's mother.

** The Milog family clan dates back to the 8th century during the reign of Tibet's Dharma King Trisong Detsen. The Lumorab lineage sprouted from the Milog family.

[1] The author was the reincarnation of Jampal Dewé Nyima, also known as Khenchen Phendé Özer. In his native land of Nyarong, he is popularly known by the name Khenpo Aten. He was recognized by Minling Khenchen Ngawang Khyentsé Norbu. Jampal Dewé Nyima was one of the heart sons of Ju Mipham Rinpoche (1846-1912), one of the greatest luminaries of Tibetan Buddhism.

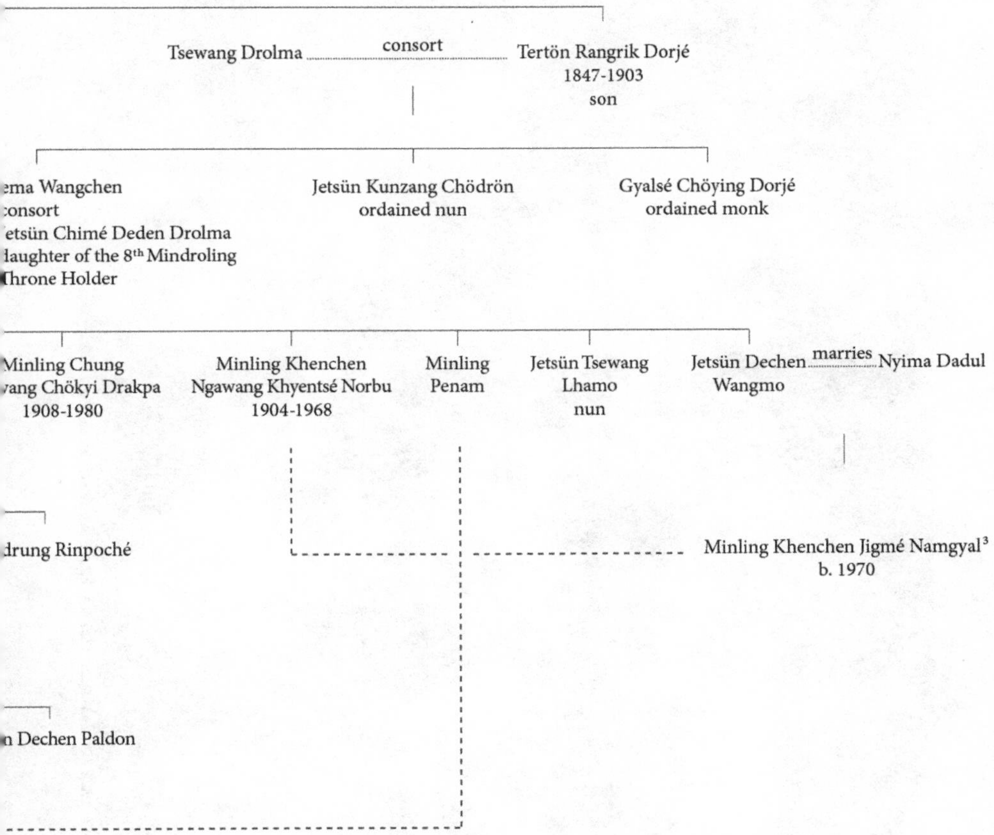


urmé Kunzang Namgyal was given name Tashi Tobgyal while still in his ther's womb by Kunzang Wangyal, the Throne Holder of Mindroling. er his birth, Kunzang Wangyal stated in official recognition letter that Tashi gyal is the reincarnation of my uncle nling Penam and he bestowed officially name Gyurmé Kunzang Namgyal and sonally enthroned him at Mindroling nastery in December 1997.

[3] The reincarnation of Minling Khenchen Ngawang Khyentsé Norbu. He was recognized by the 16th Karmapa and Lhathog Rinpoché. The name Jigmé Namgyal was bestowed by Minling Chung Ngawang Chökyi Drakpa, the brother of the 10th Throne Holder of Mindroling and the uncle of the 11th Mindroling Throne Holder.

Khenchen Jampal Dewé Nyima (aka Khenpo Aten)

Larung Gar Buddhist Academy in Tibet are reverently studying his philosophical commentaries and are planning on publishing his surviving collected works.

The Shedra, or dialectic college, that Khenpo Aten established at Lumorab Monastery was unique because it incorporated some aspects of the Gelug school style of debating while the core curriculum was deeply rooted in Ju Mipham's philosophical writings. Khenpo Aten invited young scholars from Sershi Monastery from the Gelug tradition to be instructors at Lumorab, and they became his devout disciples. When I was six or seven years old, I vividly remember a return visit by two of these monks, who were by then both *geshes*, the highest academic qualification awarded in the Gelug tradition. They came mainly to meet me, as they heard I was the reincarnation of their late teacher.

In his later years, Khenpo Aten also spent a considerable amount of time in Central Tibet, especially at Mindrolling, assisting his cousin with the spiritual and educational needs of the monastery. While there, he became the root teacher to his nephews, the future throne holder of the Mindrolling tradition and his two brothers, Minling Khenchen Rinpoche and Minling Chung Rinpoche. Many members of the noble families of Lhasa, including Samdrup Phodrang, Ragasha, and Ngapo Ngawang Jigme, were also his devout disciples. His Holiness Kyabjé Dudjom Rinpoche considered Khenpo Aten to be one of his principal root gurus. Khenpo Aten acquired the title *khenpo* after his first cousin became the *Tritsab* or Regent of Mindrolling Monastery, where he helped officiate as Khenpo for a while.

## LUMORAB MONASTERY TODAY

Lumorab, like most other Tibetan monasteries, became the target of Communist Chinese destruction. The whole area became totally uninhabited, resembling a ghost town. Precious religious icons of immense value were carted away, while entire libraries and religious images were burned or otherwise destroyed. Almost all the important Rinpoches, including Minling Shabdrung Rinpoche, the younger brother of the Eleventh Mindrolling throne holder, and Ngawang Tenzing (Tulku Angak), who was grand uncle and uncle to both the Mindrolling brothers and my mothers, were arrested and sent to forced labor camps, where the young Minling Shabdrung Rinpoche died of starvation. Tulku Angak survived for many years but died before he could see the reconstruction of his beloved Lumorab Monastery.

Minling Shabdrung Rinpoche, as the younger brother to the future *Trizin* (Throne Holder), was being groomed to become the Khenpo of Mindrolling. In the Mindrolling tradition the elder son becomes the throne holder while the next born becomes the Khenpo. This tradition began with Terdak Lingpa, Mindrolling's founder, and his younger brother, Minling Lochen Dharmashri (1654–1717).

In preparation for him to become the Khenpo, Minling Shabdrung Rinpoche's uncles sent him back to Lumorab so that he could visit important Nyingma monasteries in the nearby region, including Shechen and especially Dzogchen, where the plan was for him to enroll at the famed Dzogchen Shri Singha College. Before his anticipated formal enrollment, he spent many months receiving important initiations and oral transmissions from the great Jamyang Khyentse Chökyi Lodrö (1893–1959) and another great master of that period, the 6th Shechen Rabjam Rinpoche (1910–1959).

Had he not tragically died at the hands of the Communist Chinese, Minling Shabdrung Rinpoche would have first studied at the Dzogchen Shri Singha College and then returned to Mindrolling Monastery. Our senior Rinpoches also wanted Shabdrung Rinpoche and me to establish a personal bond that would continue the close family and spiritual ties between Mindrolling and Lumorab Monasteries in our generation. I was too young to accompany him when he went to receive these teachings, but the plan was for me to go with him on subsequent visits to study with these great masters.

The only senior Rinpoche of the times who managed to stay out of prison was Minling Penam Rinpoche, the youngest of the Mindrolling brothers. The Communists spared him because his eccentric behavior led the Chinese into thinking he was mentally unstable. As a result, they were unable to assign him to any disfavored class to be struggled against. Daringly, during the most tragic period of the Cultural Revolution when no one was allowed to practice any religion, Minling Penam Rinpoche secretly helped conduct prayers and last rites. I was the only Rinpoche of the Lumorab lineage who was able to escape into exile with my family. Most Tibetans refer to me as Gyari Rinpoche because very few people know about my religious background and the Gyari family name is quite well known. This is actually incorrect, but I suppose I must continue to live with that.

With major changes in the PRC's leadership, religious policies became more lenient by 1979–80, and the few remaining monks from Lumorab began the slow process of rebuilding the monastery from scratch. Wangpo Chime[12] and Khenpo

Acho (1918–1998) were the two principal monks who initiated this task. Wangpo Chime was one of the main disciples of Lumorab's senior Rinpoches. He was a great administrator as well as a highly qualified Tibetan physician and Buddhist practitioner, coming from a long line of illustrious scholars. Khenpo Acho, the last abbot before the destruction of Lumorab, was a close disciple of Khenpo Aten and one of the first graduates of the Lumorab School of Dialectics. He later went to Mindrolling Monastery and studied with both Minling brothers and Kyabjé Dudjom Rinpoche for several years, finally joining Sera Monastery[13] at the direction of the Mindrolling Rinpoches.

During Lumorab's reconstruction, Khenpo Acho focused on revitalizing the academic programs while Wangpo Chime took full responsibility for the administrative duties. In addition to the efforts of these two monks, Minling Penam Rinpoche's presence during the initial years was a major factor in encouraging many of the former monks and devotees to return to Lumorab.

Progress on the reconstruction has been slow and difficult, more so than for many other monasteries in the region. The main obstacle is the monastery's connection with the Gyari family, especially my close relationship with His Holiness the 14th Dalai Lama. In spite of these obstacles, the Lumorab monks have managed to complete restoration of the old temple, including its beautiful wall frescoes. Several monks, including some of the most senior individuals, have been able to come quietly into exile to study at Mindrolling Monastery in Dehradun, India.[14] I am very happy that many of them have chosen to return to Lumorab, while some of them have remained at Mindrolling in India, serving in various important capacities.

After forty-six years in exile, I was finally able to visit my monastery in 2004 when I went to the PRC for the Third Round of talks with the PRC government on behalf of His Holiness. Unfortunately, there was no privacy, as I had an entourage of over thirty officials from Beijing, Chengdu, Dartsedo, and, of course, Nyarong County itself accompanying me at all times.

My five-hour visit was memorable and heartwarming, but more than anything, it was heartbreaking. Khenpo Acho had already passed away, but I was able to visit his retreat cabin where he attained the "rainbow body." This extraordinary scholar and practitioner not only demonstrated his personal advancement in practice but also proved to everyone that attaining a rainbow body is possible even in modern times.

Despite the lack of privacy and tremendous tension attending my visit, Wangpo Chime managed to gather together roughly twenty senior monks into

The author with Wangpo Chime at Lumorab Monastery in Nyarong, Tibet, on September 20, 2004, during the Third Round of talks

the protector's chapel and gave me a brief but detailed report on the state of affairs of the monastery. He introduced me to some of the key functionaries who were helping him, particularly singling out Pema Dorjee, upon whom he said I could rely in the future in overseeing Lumorab's affairs. He concluded his remarks by saying in Tibetan, "Iron in the hands of the iron smith, result in the hands of the owner" (མགར་བའི་ལག་ལ་ལྕགས།། བདག་པོའི་ལག་ལ་དོན།།). This is an old Tibetan saying indicating that he had successfully and satisfactorily reported the state of affairs at the monastery and was able to hand over future responsibility to me. It was as if he were just waiting for the opportunity to speak with me, as he did not live long after our meeting.

Today Pema Dorjee and other senior monks faithfully continue the work of restoring Lumorab. I am both proud of and grateful for their successes, even though I cannot make any direct contribution to their efforts. I have not been able to visit the monastery again, nor has any member of my family, but I hope to be able to do so now that I am retired.

## MY BIRTH AND RECOGNITION

Many people ask me how I was recognized as a Rinpoche. Did I have any recollection of my past lives? Was I able to identify some of my personal belongings from a past life? While it is widely known that this was the process of recognizing His Holiness the 14th Dalai Lama, there are no set standards for selection of reincarnates. I was saved from any kind of tests because before my birth I was recognized as a reincarnation, setting into motion a journey that would take me from my birthplace in rural Nyarong, Tibet, to Dharamsala, India, and eventually to Washington, D.C., where I held the position of Special Envoy of His Holiness the 14th Dalai Lama for over twenty-five years. As chronicled in these chapters, my childhood years in Tibet had a profound impact on me, shaping who I became as an adult and laying the foundation for my approach to helping deal with some of the most critical issues facing the Tibetan people.

My birth was prophesied by Minling Khenchen Rinpoche, the nephew and main disciple of my predecessor, Khenpo Aten, whose life I have previously discussed. Before Khenpo Aten passed away in 1945 (twenty-second day of the fourth month of the rooster year), he gave several indications to his close disciples, in particular Minling Khenchen Rinpoche, of his being reborn to my parents. One month before I was conceived, while in Gonjo near Chamdo, Minling Khenchen Rinpoche performed a very elaborate 100,000-*tsok*[15] offering and announced to the monks present that Khenpo Aten would soon be taking rebirth. On learning that my mother was pregnant, he immediately sent a messenger with instructions to perform certain special prayers before my birth. Gyalsé Chöying Dorjé, another of my mothers' uncles and the most senior Rinpoche of Lumorab, further instructed my mother not to deliver the baby at the Gyari manor but rather to go to Lumorab. If the stress of the two days' travel to the monastery was too much, he advised her to go to a pristine and uninhabited place to await my birth. My parents chose the second option, traveling to a beautiful and secluded meadow at Draklhe, not far from my father's ancestral home. My mothers recall that more than thirty monks went with them, together with a large entourage of laypeople, turning this beautiful meadow into a tented community awaiting my birth. After a few days I was born on a full moon day. While there are all kinds of stories of the appearance of auspicious signs, etc., about my birth and the events happening around that time, I don't consider them important for the readers of this book.

My mothers' family, the Milogtsang, maintained a fairly large estate on the outskirts of Lumorab Monastery. After my birth, I was taken straight there, and that is where I grew up. In fact, I never set foot in my father's home, the Gyari manor, until I was about seven years old when I went in my religious capacity as a Rinpoche to participate in the last rites ceremony of my great grandfather, Gyari Dorjé Namgyal,[16] who died under Communist Chinese house arrest in Dartsedo.[17] To commemorate his beloved grandfather's passing, my father organized one of the most elaborate last rites ceremonies ever conducted in our region. Nearly 500 monks participated for several days, in addition to my family's observing the entire forty-nine-day period of ritual prayers at our home.

A number of people were surprised at the extravagance of the funeral, and some of our own older relatives expressed concern that the huge expense would place the family under great financial stress. But my father wanted to honor the kindness of his grandfather, whom he loved deeply and who had always been like a father to him. Candidly, I believe my father's largesse was at least in part motivated by his understanding that the family's wealth and property would not be there forever, so he might as well spend it freely to honor this very special person. Even in his later years, my father spoke of his grandfather with deep emotion, although he also admitted that his grandfather's unrestrained love made him a little spoiled and short-tempered.

CHAPTER 4

# The Gyaritsang's Involvement in the Tibetan Resistance

Friends have encouraged me to write about the Tibetan armed resistance against the Communist Chinese, as many know about my parents' role in the movement. I fully believe that we should have the strength and wisdom to forgive, but we must never forget this troubling past. Remembering the painful events of history encourages us to dedicate our lives to ensuring such events will never be repeated. Despite my inclination, my narration here will be brief, as my mothers lovingly but firmly refused to share any details of their experiences.[1] I know it is painful for them to revisit those memories. Moreover, they wisely believe that nothing can be gained by living in the past. Instead, they have urged me to write about ways to move forward to benefit future generations.

For some additional information about this period of time, there are several good sources. In her book *Arrested Histories: Tibet, the CIA, and Memories of a Forgotten War*, Carole McGranahan writes quite extensively about the role of my parents in the resistance movement. In some ways her book has more information than I will be chronicling here. Jamyang Norbu's *Warriors of Tibet* that I previously mentioned also has detailed accounts of the resistance by the Nyarongwas. His book is primarily based on Aten's writings and recollections, to which my parents contributed in the form of casual conversations during the author's extended stays with my family in Delhi while he was working on his book. Lastly, Holly Elwood interviewed my mothers and wrote extensively about the role they played in the resistance movement in her manuscript "Dorjee Yudon: The Leader of the Rebels" (1989). Unfortunately, I do not think her writings were widely published.

With the Second World War coming to an end, the Nationalist government gained some breathing space that had a ripple effect in Kham. My parents were able to rebuild the Gyari ancestral house that had been destroyed,[2] and my father was able to resume his role as paramount chieftain of Upper Nyarong. My great grandfather's matrimonial arrangement for his grandson, Gyari Nyima Gyaltsen (my father), with the Milogtsang daughters had also helped strengthen the prestige and influence of the Gyari family. Most importantly, as my father was the only heir of the Gyaritsang, his ascendance to rule Upper Nyarong was unopposed. In addition, the Nationalists appointed him head of the entire Nyarong County. In that capacity, he resided at the famous Drukmo Dzong. Later he became Vice Governor of the northern division of the Kardze Tibetan Autonomous Prefecture consisting of seven counties. He also held official rank at the prefecture level in Dartsedo.

During the Gyari family's exile, the head lama of Shiwa Monastery, Lama Jigme Tenzin, asked the well-respected Tertön Anye Tulku for a prophecy regarding the family's future. He composed the following text in reply:

> ཉི་མ་རྒྱལ་མཚན་འབྲུག་ལ་ཞོན་ནས་སླེབས།།
> རྒྱ་བོད་གཉིས་ཀྱི་རལ་པ་གདན་ལ་བཏིང་།།
>
> Nyima Gyaltsen riding the dragon
> Treads the braids of the Chinese and Tibetans.

People interpreted my father's holding office at the Female Dragon Fortress as "riding the dragon." The fact that he had Tibetans, as well as several Chinese, working for him further confirmed the prophecy. Even though the divination came true, it was short-lived, as this period of peace and stability didn't last long. By the early 1950s, Mao's Red Army had infiltrated various parts of Kham that had previously been under the nominal control of the Nationalists, gradually assuming complete control of the region.

In the beginning, the Communists were very respectful of individual religious leaders and institutions, as well as the Tibetan chieftains, giving the impression that they had no intention of disturbing the local system of governance.[3] Some Chinese Communist leaders at the provincial level even encouraged my father to become their ally and hinted that, with his knowledge of Chinese and exposure to contemporary politics, he should consider joining the Communist Party. The Chinese tried this same approach with other senior Tibetan leaders at the time, but few were tempted.

As time passed, it became increasingly clear that Communist China's true intention was the total subjugation of the Tibetan people with the ultimate aim of eradicating Buddhism. My father intuitively grasped this inevitability, given his personal knowledge of China and the Chinese psyche acquired during his years of study there. During this period, my father, like many other important chieftains, spent considerable time in Dartsedo and Chengdu. He found that he was not alone in his deep-seated fear of Beijing's intentions toward Tibet. Many other well-respected leaders shared his view. Secretly, they began to discuss their concerns and developed a shared opposition to the Chinese. My younger mother remembers one such meeting at Dartsedo that was attended by seven very prominent leaders representing some of the most important regions of Kham. She can recall the names of five of the attendees in addition to my father: Gyapon Chemi Dorje and Gya Yonten of the Lingkashi family; Dromo Wangchen, a nomadic chieftain from the Derge area; and Sogri Ahjam and Shendang Ata from the Lithang area. She can't remember the name of the seventh man, a young nomadic chieftain from Derge, who accompanied Dromo Wangchen.

The meeting attendees had all come to believe that the Communist Chinese were the enemy of Buddhism and thus, as devout Buddhists, they must resist by taking up arms. They took an oath of loyalty to each other, binding not only themselves but also their clans. Khampas take such oaths seriously, and one can say that these vows are even more binding than the love between family members.[4] Each leader was tasked with coordinating with the people in his own region. The group also decided to reach out to other prominent leaders who were not present at the meeting. For example, Gyapon Chemi Dorje of the Lingkashi family was responsible for coordinating with the Pondatsang and some of the leaders of Khampa areas west of the Drichu River that were under the direct control of the Central Tibetan Government.

My father and Gyapon Chemi Dorje were deputized to meet with Jagoe Topden, one of the most prominent and influential Khampa leaders of the Derge area, who supported their decision to resist the Communist Chinese but felt that they should think of seeking asylum in Central Tibet if their efforts failed. He confided to them that he didn't think he personally would be able to leave Dartsedo, as he was under heavy surveillance by the Chinese, but that he had advised his family to flee to Lhasa. Heeding Jagoe Topden's advice, my father tried to persuade my mothers to sell the extensive livestock owned by the Gyaritsang and the Milogtsang and take all the children for a pilgrimage to Central Tibet to stay at Mindrolling Monastery. My mothers stubbornly refused to leave without my father. My parents admired and trusted Jagoe Topden, and I remember my father deeply mourning the absence of his leadership when the Khampas in exile became divided.[5]

Toward the end of 1955, during one of my father's short trips back to Nyarong, he took into confidence Lama Jigme Tenzin, a respected lama of Shiwa Monastery,[6] and some of his elder and trusted retainers, including Khenchen Dorjee Samdrup. He instructed them that even if he failed to return to Nyarong, they must never surrender to the Chinese and must prepare for armed resistance against them. By that time, my father had come to the clear realization that there was no choice for the Tibetans other than to take up arms against the Chinese to defend the Tibetan people's freedom and religious beliefs, no matter what the consequences.

When my father was told by the Chinese authorities to return to Dartsedo, an increasingly frequent command, he chose several young men to accompany him up to Kardze, which in those days was the nearest town accessible by road on the way to Dartsedo. En route, they stopped at Zamdo, a beautiful valley, to rest themselves and the horses. My father surreptitiously pulled aside some of the young men accompanying him and had them take an oath of secrecy. He then told them that prior to leaving Nyarong, he had left clear instructions with Lama Jigme Tenzin and his wives, as well as with some of his senior retainers, about certain tasks that needed to be undertaken. He wanted these young men to assist them in coordinating their efforts, primarily by delivering important messages at their instruction.

Nyarong Ating was one of the young men my father took into confidence. He remembers that there were seven of them who took the direct oath from my father. They were further instructed to contact and include eleven others. This group came to be known as the Chogyed Shogkha or the Group of Eighteen.[7] All these young men were personally close to my father. Of the eighteen, six of them ultimately made it into exile: Tsering Sangpo, Atop, Ata, Adom, Atra, and Ating. Ating is the only one who, at the time of this writing, is still alive. Most of the remaining twelve died in battles. The three who survived, Sonam Palden, Jampa Dorji and Gyelu, were each imprisoned for almost twenty-one years. My mothers told me that this group was my father's usual entourage, mostly of the same age, but they thought there were two elderly men who were also part of the group. One of them, Thondup Dorjee, made it into exile, was well cared for by his family, and passed away at an advanced age. His son, Khenpo Ugyen, is a very senior monk at the monastery in Bir where his family settled.

As my father was effectively being held hostage in Dartsedo, in consultation with our family's senior retainers, my mothers decided that the first strike in Nyarong should not be directly tied to the Gyari family but rather led by the respected elder subchieftain Drapa Nyima,[8] who was my father's close relative. At the time, there was a large gathering of respected lamas and chieftains at Shiwa Monastery. More than eighty prominent individuals took yet another oath of secrecy, this time in the presence of the famed "speaking Tara" statue enshrined there. This group came to be known as the Gya-chu Shogkha or the Group of Eighty. While members of the Group of Eighteen were mostly from Ralong, where the Gyari manor is located, or from nearby villages, participants in the Gya-chu Shogkha were from almost all of the areas under the Gyaritsang's rule.

Following this meeting, my younger mother sent messengers or personal communications to many of the chieftains, and even some lamas, in the neighboring areas of Lithang, Drago, Tawu, Derge, and Garje, and, of course, to the other chieftains of Nyarong. As a result, all agreed to take up armed resistance on February 22, 1956. While these Tibetan leaders from Kham were organizing themselves, the Communists began implementing programs aimed at uprooting Tibetan traditions and beliefs under the banner of "democratic reform." This attempted cultural genocide further infuriated the Tibetans, spurring them to openly take up arms against the Chinese.

My younger mother is very insistent that the decision to launch a large-scale armed attack was neither hers alone nor solely a Nyarongwa initiative. Rather, it was a decision taken several months prior at Dartsedo by some of the prominent Khampa leaders, including her husband, my father, Gyari Nyima. What she did do was consult with them and coordinate the specific timing for launching the effort. Moreover, she was not alone in sending messages to organize an attack. Many other leaders were forwarding similar messages and communicating with individuals in areas where they had strong connections. In fact, my younger mother remembers receiving like-minded messages from some other prominent local leaders.

At the same time, the Chinese were not lying idle. Although no vital information was leaked by the resistance organizers, the Chinese authorities at Drukmo Dzong became suspicious that a major rebellion was in the offing. They knew that something was brewing and immediately summoned my senior mother to Drukmo

Dzong for some "important meetings." Once there, they made it very clear that her stay would be for a prolonged period, as many additional "important meetings" would take place over the next several weeks.

This put my junior mother in an impossible position. There was nothing she could do with regard to her husband. She was compelled to carry out his instructions, as he had made it very clear that he might not be able to return to Nyarong and that his absence should not stop the resistance. But her sister's situation was different; she was now being kept at a distance, only a few hours away but at the site of the planned uprising. My younger mother decided that one of the first things she would do when they launched the attack against the Chinese at Drukmo Dzong would be to designate a rescue party for her sister. But that was not to happen.

The Chinese now realized that an assault by the Nyarongwas was imminent. To preempt the attack, they sent about forty soldiers to the Gyari manor to arrest my younger mother and Gyari Ari, a close cousin from an influential subchieftain's family, who was staying there with her. This incident is what finally triggered the Nyarongwas to mount the first ever armed attack against the Chinese Communists. Sometime earlier, an entire Nyarong family, including the wife and children of the Gyarashipa family, had literally been slaughtered by the Chinese. The Gyarashipa family, like the Gyaritsang, was one of the four major chieftain clans of Nyarong. The head of the family, Gyurme, who was away at that time, was the only survivor. It was thus clear that the Chinese intended to start their brutal armed suppression of the Tibetans in Nyarong.

With regard to the Gyari family, the Chinese had a clear game plan: they would attack the Gyari manor, kill my younger mother and some of the family's senior and loyal retainers, and then immediately arrest both my father, who was at Dartsedo, and my senior mother at Drukmo Dzong on charges of "treason" for instigating a sinister plot to revolt against the Chinese authorities. But the Nyarongwas were not about to allow another massacre of a prominent chieftain's family.

The Chinese soldiers advancing on the Gyari manor thus confronted a determined resistance. The Communists met with serious casualties, but they were able to forcefully occupy a few houses near the manor, making it difficult for the Nyarongwas to evict them. Gyari loyalist reinforcements began pouring in from other areas, and it was only a couple of days before all the encircled Chinese soldiers were either killed or arrested. On the third day, however, a contingent of nearly eighty Chinese soldiers marched into Ralong with my senior mother as hostage. She was allowed to mount her horse, but there were Chinese soldiers by her side and her back, with guns pointed at her, and two more soldiers holding the reins of her horse. By then, a large number of Nyarongwa resistance fighters had taken up positions at strategic points, making it impossible for any hostile forces to enter the valley.

Nyarong Ating told me that he was occupying one of these strategic areas along with other Nyarongwas when his group first saw the advancing Chinese troops. They thought it was going to be a great day of victory because they were certain that with their commanding positions, they could literally slaughter the Chinese. But to their shock and dismay, they then saw Nordzin Lhamo being brought along as a hostage, instantly taking away their advantage and instead forcing them to allow these troops to march right into Ralong village and up to the door of the Gyari manor. In a matter of minutes, the tables had turned. The Chinese troops occupied the courtyard and the ground floor, literally trapping Dorjé Yudrön and some of the seniormost leaders of the resistance, who were on the residence's upper floors.

Because the surrounding area was in the hands of an ever-increasing number of Nyarongwas, however, the Chinese could not leave the Gyari manor with their captives for fear of suffering heavy casualties. As the stalemate persisted, and even as the leaders inside were trying to negotiate a truce, the two nearby monasteries of Shiwa and Gyase directly intervened. The monasteries must have worked out a precise plan and thoroughly coordinated their actions, but even so it could have resulted in serious bloodshed, mostly of the monks. At almost the exact same moment, from two different directions and outnumbering the Chinese soldiers, a large number of monks in maroon robes marched right into Ralong village and entered the Gyari manor as well as a few of the nearby houses. They declared that they were unarmed and had come to bring an end to the many senseless deaths. By their hand gestures, they showed that they were indeed unarmed. Then each monk hugged a Chinese soldier and disarmed him. The monks were taking a huge risk. If even one Chinese soldier opened fire, it would have led to a massacre on both sides.

Although the Chinese outnumbered the Tibetans within the Gyari manor, the Gyaritsang retainers were all armed. This was also the case in the few other occupied houses nearby. There were also several hundred armed resistance fighters stationed in the surrounding valley, ready to open fire the moment they saw any

Chinese leaving the houses in an effort to escape. Fortunately, this surprise intervention was a complete success. Within a matter of hours, Ating and his compatriots in the hills guarding the valley saw monks escorting the Chinese out of the occupied houses. The monks were further pleading with the Nyarongwas not to open fire and to give them permission to escort the Chinese soldiers back to Drukmo Dzong, unharmed. The monks even helped carry several of the wounded Chinese soldiers. They would have carried the bodies of those who had died, but the soldiers had already dug makeshift graves in the basements of the houses and buried their comrades.

With the success of the Shiwa and Gyase Monasteries' selfless efforts, the Chinese plan to eliminate my father and my two mothers failed. And the planned uprising went forward as scheduled. At the advice of my mothers, I quote here descriptions of the events of that fateful day and the ensuing battles from Dogyal Aten's comprehensive account. Even though my mothers identified a few factual errors in his narrative, including the statement that my senior mother was at Dartsedo with my father, overall, they consider Aten's account to be accurate. As my father, mostly accompanied by my senior mother, had to make so many trips to Dartsedo, no one can be blamed for being confused about the particulars of one trip.

> The actual revolt began on the fourteenth[9] day of the first moon in 1956, at Upper Nyarong. The Gyari Tsang family were traditionally the chieftains of that area. Gyari Nima, the chieftain and his elder wife were away at Dhartsedo. Nima's younger wife, a beautiful and fearless woman, Dorjee Yudon, was left at home to look after family affairs. As the course of events drew to that one unavoidable conclusion, she made the decision that launched the revolt.
>
> Dorjee Yudon gathered her men and weapons and dispatched missives all over Eastern Tibet, urging the people to rise against the Chinese. Dressed in a man's robe and with a sword and pistol strapped to her side, she rode before her warriors to do battle with the enemy. She ferociously attacked Chinese columns and outposts everywhere in Nyarong. The remaining Chinese soldiers and officials retreated to the Female Dragon.
>
> The castle was stormed, with Dorjee Yudon herself leading the many charges. But the great walls of that old castle were built to withstand such attacks, and without artillery (which the rebels did not have) they were

> virtually impregnable. Casualties soared. Finally, Dorjee Yudon decided to lay siege to the castle.
>
> By now the whole countryside was in ferment and many other villages and tribes rose up to fight. Dorjee Yudon's task at the castle was proving to be difficult. The Chinese garrison was well stocked with food and ammunition, and they also had a spring of clear water within the walls.
>
> After a month, six hundred troops from the 18th Division arrived from Kanze to relieve their beleaguered comrades in the castle. Dorjee Yudon met them at Upper Nyarong and managed to defeat them. About four hundred Chinese soldiers were killed, but two hundred managed to break through the siege lines and enter the castle.
>
> Another column of about fifteen to twenty thousand soldiers poured in from Drango and Tahu in the east. Dorjee Yudon was forced to give way and the siege was lifted. Yet the fighting accelerated and lasted for a month after which the superior numbers and arms of the Chinese began to tell.
>
> The Chinese suffered heavy losses, about two thousand died and many more wounded. Two hundred officers were killed and their bodies were buried with much ceremony outside the old castle.
>
> Finally, the Chinese regained some measure of control in the county, and the rebels had to take to the hills from where they initiated a relentless guerrilla campaign. Day by day their numbers swelled.[10]

The Nyarongwas thus became the first Tibetans to begin open armed resistance against the Chinese. Upper Nyarong was liberated and it, as well as several other areas of Nyarong, remained without any Chinese presence for several more months. In fact, the success of the resistance forced the Chinese authorities in Dartsedo to allow my father, and most of the other local chieftains, to return to their homes and be reconciled with the local people.

Maura Moynihan brought her close friend, the famous Indian filmmaker Shekhar Kapur, to meet my mothers on a few occasions at our house in Delhi as well as in Washington, D.C. She encouraged my mothers to allow Shekhar to make a movie about them. My family highly appreciated Maura's friendship, and they were honored that such a well-known filmmaker was interested in their history, but my parents showed no real enthusiasm for the project. My siblings and I were excited about the possibility, however, and I remember encouraging my parents to consider the offer. Besides, I knew that Maura, with her excellent writing skills and personal affection for our family, would author a compelling and riveting script for the film. However, it was not to be. I remember my father with a stern face admonishing me: "It may glorify our family, but we have a responsibility for many of the people who are still living inside Tibet. One should act responsibly." I not only understood my parents' position but also deeply respected them for their decision not to go forward.

The Chinese did not allow my father to stay in Nyarong for long, instructing him to return to Dartsedo for another "important meeting." They also "suggested" that he bring my younger mother with him this time. They must have thought that if left behind, she would once again go to the mountains and help organize the resistance. Not to be outwitted, this time it was my senior mother who took to the mountains to join the large number of resistance leaders continuing to launch periodic attacks against the Chinese troops.

Resistance against the Chinese became increasingly widespread throughout Kham, causing great anxiety to the Communist rulers. In response, they were compelled to announce major changes to their policies in eastern Tibet and even sent a high-level "Fact Finding and Condolence Mission" to calm Tibetan fears. My father and younger mother as well as many other important Tibetan leaders who had been detained in Dartsedo were sent back to their respective areas to accompany some of these missions. Many promises were made, and amnesty was declared for anyone who had joined the resistance movement. The Chinese officials expressed their condolences to the many Tibetans who had been victims of the recent conflict.

However, my senior mother continued to stay with the resistance groups and did not surrender even after the return of her husband and sister to Nyarong. Secretly, they were in touch and not only encouraged my elder mother to stay back but themselves started making clandestine arrangements to join her and the other resistance fighters. Of course, both my father and younger mother were telling the Chinese authorities that they were encouraging my elder mother and others to surrender. The authorities knew that they would have to adopt some other method to compel my senior mother to return. A contingent of about 300 Chinese soldiers under the command of Colonel ZaHor came to Lumorab Monastery and immediately laid siege, not even permitting the monks to fetch drinking water. Even though Colonel ZaHor himself, together with many senior officers, took up residence in the monastery, the soldiers dug trenches around it and on the second day, fired two warning shots from a cannon that landed in the monastery's main courtyard. The Chinese threatened that if my elder mother did not surrender, the monastery would face consequences of a serious nature. They knew that my family would not allow any harm to be done to the monastery, as it was very precious to them. I think it was on the third day of the siege when my elder mother, accompanied by a few of the elderly resistance fighters, surrendered, bringing with them some obsolete rifles.

My elder mother took me with her when she presented herself to the commanding officer. To the best of my recollection, the colonel was quite courteous and did not treat her in a demeaning manner. A day or two later, they took her to Drukmo Dzong but allowed her to ride her own horse and even to take a maid along with her. When she finally reached the Chinese quarters at the castle, she remembers being coerced into posing for photographs with senior Chinese military officials and civil leaders and having a submachine gun shoved into her hands at the last moment.

This very emotional reunion with my senior mother happened at Lumorab, where I had been living and studying during this entire period. I think this took place somewhere around the end of 1956. I have a vivid memory of it. This was the first time I had seen the Chinese with my own eyes. I remember one young officer[11] giving me lots of cookies and a penknife that I really liked. He also recited the Amitabha Buddha mantra and pointing to himself said, "Ma Ma," indicating that his mother used to recite this chant.[12]

So, while Chinese governmental policies were brutal and suppressive, individual Chinese soldiers were disciplined and in some cases, even friendly. These days you even hear that some United Nations peacekeeping forces misbehave with regard to the civilians they are supposed to protect. Giving credit to the Chinese, you do not hear much about individual soldier misconduct. As a group, however, they were ruthless and destructive because the Chinese Communist Party's (CCP's) policies of the period demanded that. When the Red Army passed through parts of Tibet in the mid-1930s during the Long March, its behavior toward the civilian population was not at all well disciplined, including forced confiscation of food and livestock from the locals. Chairman Mao later lamented the conduct of the Red Army, telling author Edgar Snow: "This is our only foreign debt and some day we must pay the Mantzu and the Tibetans for the provisions we were obliged to take [from] them."[13]

Other senior Chinese officials made similar admissions. In the early 1950s, for example, my father and many other important Tibetan leaders were hosted at a grand reception in Chengdu by Marshal He Long, then Commanding Officer of the Red Army for the Southwest Military and Administrative Bureau, and Deng

Xiaoping, then Political Commissar for the same region. My father used to recount Marshal He Long's speech in Chinese, mimicking the general, even imitating his body postures and mannerisms perfectly, saying:

> I must confess that during the Long March some of our soldiers misbehaved a little bit with your people. I know there have been cases where food, horses, and mules were taken by force, and I must apologize. Even though the strict instruction to follow the Three Cardinal Rules and the Eight Points for Attention was very much there, we were hungry, we had no shoes to wear, and we were being chased by the Kuomintang reactionary forces, and we were also not receiving much help from you. . . . I want to acknowledge that the Tibetan people, especially the people from the areas where the Long March went through, made a huge contribution to the victory of the Communist Party or the Red Army.

In contrast, Deng Xiaoping's remarks were short and blunt, designed solely to command allegiance to the CCP: "I just have one piece of advice: go back to your respective places, work hard, and listen to the Party. And when I say listen to the Party, I mean whoever is the local Communist head—he represents the Communist Party. If you obey his instructions and work together, you will have a good future. If you fail to do that, your future will not be good." Most of the Tibetan leaders did not appreciate Deng Xiaoping's thinly veiled threat. My father, however, thought he was actually giving them valuable advice: if you want to survive, you must be obedient. My father vividly remembered Deng Xiaoping coming to the reception wearing an oversized military uniform. In his position he could easily have had his uniform personally tailored to his measurements. Instead, he wore the uniform issued him by the army, like any other rank-and-file soldier. My father thought that it was a smart move, reflecting Deng Xiaoping's respect for the CCP and his no-nonsense attitude.

Many years later, when Deng Xiaoping began opening up the PRC in the late 1970s and tried reaching out to His Holiness the 14th Dalai Lama, my father felt some sense of optimism because he considered Deng Xiaoping to be a straightforward person. My father told me more than once that the Chinese are not bad people and that many of them are trustworthy. It was only their antireligious policies that my father found unacceptable. He further implied that without that prejudice he would have adjusted to the other reforms and changes proposed by the CCP.

From his comments, I got the feeling that some Chinese officials had in one way or another taken him into confidence about the impending policy changes that would trigger tragic consequences for the Tibetan people. In other words, I believe they were surreptitiously advising him to escape. My mothers lately confided that quite a few senior Chinese officials, at both the county and prefectural levels, took my father into confidence and encouraged him in a number of ways and over a period of time to leave for Central Tibet with his family. My mothers still do not wish to divulge the names of these very empathetic individuals.

My father's view that the Chinese as a people are not inherently prejudiced against the Tibetan race, or any other group for that matter, and can be trusted had a profound influence on my own attitude toward them. In the early 1980s when I was directly dealing with Chinese officials on Tibet's behalf, his words helped me overcome the deep-rooted animosity toward the Chinese that many of us Tibetans unfortunately have cultivated, given the atrocities that they committed in Tibet. This made a huge difference in my outlook toward my Chinese counterparts, contributing to my ability to carry out my official responsibilities with a positive attitude. In later years my family cultivated wonderful friendships with many Chinese in Washington, D.C., Hong Kong, Singapore, and elsewhere. My father's words were vindicated: these individuals were genuine, generous, and reliable. Of course, many of them were Buddhist practitioners, but by no means all of them.

Another person who profoundly changed my attitude toward the Chinese as a people is Julie Tan. Soon after my return from Beijing after our first discussions in 1982, I was invited by Rajmohan Gandhi, grandson of Mahatma Gandhi, to make a presentation at an international meeting that he was organizing at the Moral Re-Armament Center at Panchgani, a beautiful hill station in the Indian state of Maharashtra.

My remarks included a summary of my recently concluded trip to the PRC with a focus on the sufferings of the Tibetan people at the hands of the Chinese Communists. While I was speaking, I noticed that one petite Asian-looking woman was avoiding eye contact with me. I also thought she was deliberately keeping her distance by sitting in the far back of the room. My then prejudiced mind immediately contended that she must be Chinese, resented my remarks, and was deliberately trying to stay as far away from me as possible.

When I finished my presentation, this diminutive figure walked purposely over to me, hugged me, and started crying and apologizing. I really felt very small and guilty in the presence of this tiny woman. She was far taller than me in her moral

The author addressing a conference of the Moral Re-Armament movement (now renamed Initiatives of Change) at Caux, Switzerland, 1984
Tibet Museum, CTA

conduct. I too cried and asked her why she was apologizing. She answered that she was a second- or third-generation Chinese and felt deep responsibility for what the Chinese people had done to the Tibetans. I told her it was not the Chinese people but the wrong policies of the Chinese government that were to blame. After all, the same government had also inflicted tremendous suffering on the Chinese people themselves. I later invited her and another friend to Dharamsala. In those days, very few Chinese visited us.

Early in 1957, my parents sought permission from the Chinese authorities to spend some time at Lumorab. They wanted to consult a Tibetan doctor because my father had a serious ear infection and to spend Losar (Tibetan New Year) with family members. My parents were not hopeful, but to their surprise the Chinese authorities granted them permission to make the trip. They were accompanied by armed guards, however, under the guise of providing security for them. Several days after their arrival at Lumorab all the armed guards were removed under the pretext that there seemed to be no imminent threat. Only later on did it become clear that this was part of a detailed plan to assassinate my father in a staged encounter.

Shortly after his bodyguards were dismissed, my father visited Drakgho Tulku, a great physician and Buddhist practitioner, whose hermitage was a day's horseback ride from Lumorab. While my father's group was in transit, a small group of Chinese soldiers accompanied by a few Tibetan cadres planned to ambush and kill them under the pretense of mistaking them for resistance fighters. Fortunately, one of the Tibetans in the group still felt deep loyalty to my family and managed to derail the plot. He intentionally fired at some people crossing the valley where the ambush was to occur about an hour before my father's group reached the spot, alerting my father's party to their presence. The Chinese officer in charge was enraged, but the Tibetan loyalist insisted that he believed the group he shot at to be resistance fighters, as they were carrying arms. Some days later yet another plot was uncovered. Fortunately, neither of these assassination attempts was successful.

Up until then my father had not been physically involved in the resistance. Chinese intelligence was aware, however, that he was advising Khampa chieftains in their efforts. Nyarong Dogyal Aten recalls my father's words: "Gyari Nyima voiced our convictions: 'I can no longer live under the Chinese,' he declared, 'it is my belief that we should all revolt and overthrow their hated rule. If we are ever to achieve this, then the entire population of Nyarong must unite to form an effective resistance force to fight the Chinese.'"[14]

While all these disturbing events were taking place, ironically, I was quite happy because for the first time in my life all my parents were living together at Lumorab. Every evening I was given permission by my teacher to visit my parents for a few hours. This was really wonderful, even though my younger brother, Pema Gyalpo, bullied me quite a bit. He was being pampered by the Gyari family retainers because he was my father's designated heir, and as a monk, I was considered an outsider. These loyal Khampas deliberately encouraged my brother Pema to be tough and authoritative. They even made him carry a revolver and allowed him to drink alcohol.

I remember one interaction with him very vividly because I really felt humiliated. To get to the upper rooms of our house, you had to go up some steep steps. One day, Pema was standing at the top of the steps when I was climbing up and he started urinating on my head. It deeply hurt my ego, and I threw a knucklebone at him. We played jacks with these colored knucklebones, and while I wasn't a good marksman, the knucklebone hit his forehead and he started bleeding. He was only a young boy of seven or eight, two years younger than me, and the moment he saw the blood he started crying. This infuriated his lieutenants, who were deeply angry with me for "assaulting" their dear little chieftain. Pema still has a small scar on his forehead, a little gift from me! Those days of sibling rivalry are over now, of course, and he genuinely respects me as his elder brother.

## POSTSCRIPT

Much of the narrative in this chapter is based on the recollections and writings of nonfamily members even though my parents were active participants. As I have explained, this is a result of my mothers' unwillingness to talk about this painful and tragic period. In my final editing of this section, however, I found myself a little confused about the details and chronology of some of the events. Fortunately, I was visiting my mothers during this period, spending as much time as possible with them given their advanced years and declining health. One afternoon soon after the 2018 Tibetan New Year celebrations, I sought their permission to read them some of the things I had written, to seek their approval of the narrative and, most importantly, to see if I had accidentally made any major factual errors.

While I don't think they were very enthusiastic about the prospect, they did allow me to read through most of the narrative. When I finished reading, my senior mother said: "Why are you writing so much about the past? It is of no benefit. Write more about what you did outside, serving His Holiness and our people." I assured her that I was including those things in later chapters, but that I could not make an informative presentation without writing something about what happened inside Tibet that led to the present situation. At this point, my younger mother stepped in and said the following, which I am narrating quite faithfully:

> Son, we do not wish to contradict or correct things that have already been written by elders like Aten, which we know has been very articulately written in English by Jamyang Norbu. These things happened a long time ago and I am sure there are some minor mistakes in the narration but on the whole we know Aten's presentation was authentic. So we do not wish to add anything. It is good you are relying on them. We also remember some nice Western girls came to talk to us and they have also kindly written about our suffering.

Since you are writing about those sad events I want to clarify a few important points. When I took up arms against the Chinese, I was carrying out instructions your father left to me, to Lama Jigme Tenzin, and to some of his trusted senior advisors. He was not even sure he would be allowed to return but he was adamant that we carry out the pledge that he had entered into with some of the most prominent Khampa leaders at Dartsedo in the preceding year. If your father and my elder sister were with me then our armed resistance would have been far more successful, and we could have liberated Nyarong for a much longer period of time.

This resistance was not just a unilateral act by the Nyarongwas alone, it was a well-planned and coordinated armed uprising that had been planned for months with other neighboring chieftains and leaders. We were compelled to launch the resistance a few days ahead of the planned date to preempt the Chinese army arresting me and all the important Lamas and the retainers of the Gyari family. That is why the first armed resistance against the Chinese army started from the Gyari house. We are happy that you have acknowledged the critically important role played by the courageous monks of Shiwa Monastery as well as from Gyase Monastery. These two monasteries are very near to the Gyari manor and they have always been loyal to our family. In the thick of our resistance against the Chinese, which was causing heavy casualties on both sides, it was the monks of these two monasteries that in force came to our rescue under the pretense of being there to bring reconciliation. We were under heavy siege by the Chinese and if that situation continued there would have been more casualties on both sides.

Monks in large numbers literally disarmed the Chinese troops but also with compassion they escorted them together with their injured soldiers back to Drukmo Dzong. Most of the dead soldiers the Chinese buried in the basements of the houses that they were occupying and much later when things became more under their control, they dug them up and took them in a military procession to be given heroic burial at Drukmo Dzong. The Chinese cemetery at Drukmo Dzong has hundreds of Chinese soldiers buried there, lost during our armed resistance.

Son, since you are writing it is important you acknowledge and try to write the names of the people who fought for our freedom so that their memory is honored. There seems to be little confusion about the Eighteen Group, Eighteen Bhutsa, Eighty Group and also the Sixty Tigerlike Retainers. They are

> all different and were set up at different time periods, but these people have made so many sacrifices for our family and the dharma. We remain silent about them because we thought that even if most of them are dead, many killed during the armed resistance, they still have family behind and writing about them we thought would cause them harm. That is one reason your father and also my sister and I decided not to speak so much about that period. I think now things are changing a little bit and maybe there is no harm to acknowledge their bravery.

I felt a deep sense of satisfaction after hearing these words from my mothers, not only because they had finally spoken about the events but also because, at least in principle, they approved of what had been narrated. I was not prepared, however, for the enormous task of trying to compile the names of all the faithful and loyal retainers of the Gyari family whom they now wanted me to acknowledge. I candidly told them that it is a task that could not be accomplished in this book, but that I was deeply moved at how much they loved and respected those brave Nyarongwas who made the supreme sacrifice, in many cases, to protect our family.

I must convey how deeply moved I am that my mothers were able to overcome their sorrow and revisit these painful memories to help me provide an accurate chronicle of this tragic but essential period of Tibet's history.

## CHAPTER 5

# Our Flight from Nyarong

One afternoon when I came back from my philosophy lesson, I found Uncle Tsultrim, the monk who looked after me, busily packing some bags. He told me to hurry, as my teacher had apparently given permission for me to stay overnight with my parents. When I went to my maternal grandmother's house, there was lots of activity and I could sense something exciting was happening. That night, people began arriving on horseback. They kept on coming until there were at least fifty people there. I was told that we were leaving that night to go to the nomadic area where we kept our livestock. I was old enough to ride my own horse but not skillful enough to handle it alone. I was literally tied onto my horse, with one of the Gyaritsang retainers leading it by its reins. It was the spring of 1957.

The moment I mounted the horse, there was a huge explosion—not the sound of a detonated bomb, but deeper and more stirring. Instantly, the whole sky lit up like daylight, and I could clearly see the entire valley as an enormous comet flew over us. It was huge, swooping right down over our house, seeming almost to touch the roof. The comet threw off thousands of sparks as it zoomed past our house toward the monastery, then flew upward. With a thunderous sound it then split into three parts. The largest one headed straight toward the west, not diminishing at all in brilliance or size as it went over the mountains. The two smaller ones went east and fizzled out.

It was such an extraordinary sight that people began chanting prayers and shouting war cries. They viewed this unprecedented event as a powerful sign from the protector deities that we were being watched over and that this was the right time to leave and join the resistance.

As we prepared to leave, I had no idea that this would be the last time I would see my grandmother, Sönam Drolma, and my great aunt Atra, not to mention my elder brother, Dorjé Damdul, and my younger brother Tashi Tsegyal. Dorjé Damdul was the most kindhearted person I have ever known. He was an extremely intelligent boy, but he suffered from a speech impediment that made him difficult to understand. He was very protective of me and deeply cared for me. Whenever we shared a meal, he would take pieces of meat from his soup and put them in my bowl. Tashi Tsegyal had a physical disability, and my parents felt it would be safer if the two boys stayed with our grandmother and great aunt because they would have had trouble undertaking the harsh journey before us.

Sadly, none of them survived. My grandmother died as a result of a mass "struggle session," even though the Chinese claimed she had committed suicide, and my great aunt and elder brother Dorjé Damdul died of starvation. My younger brother died of "natural causes," but had he received even rudimentary medical care, we have no doubt he would have survived.

While I don't want to fill this book with seemingly unbelievable stories, I will take a risk in sharing one experience that occurred shortly before we left Lumorab. Watching from an open terrace in the night, I had a vision of large groups of mounted warriors heading west from down below our monastery. Even though they wore beautiful traditional armor and headgear and were well equipped with bow and arrows and spears, everyone looked dejected, their heads hung low. They were all bent over, too exhausted even to pick up their stirrups. They were huge individuals, however, and in spite of their mournful expressions, there was something very majestic about them.

This is not a vision I saw just once but multiple times over the course of several days at the same time after dark. Each time I saw the group, there were different individuals, so it was not like the same footage being played over and over. Later on, I learned that other people, including some lamas, had had similar visions. Senior Rinpoches had identified the warriors as Dharma protectors and mountain deities who had lost their own battles, portending a similar human event. Sadly, as I explain below, this vision became reality all too soon. There is no doubt that Tibet is an extraordinary land where extraordinary things do take place.

We left Lumorab and headed into the mountains. As we departed, our remaining family and friends initially stood silently, not fully comprehending that this would be the last time we would see one another. Silence eventually gave way to the traditional Khampa farewell with volley after volley of rifle shots accompanied by war cries. It was very emotional, but to me, as a young child, it was exhilarating. In fact, the first few weeks of our journey were the most exciting weeks of my life. There was a festive atmosphere, and hundreds of people were visiting my father to convey their respect, loyalty, and genuine love. Every day dozens of families joined our group, and very soon it became a huge village with hundreds of tents. Most afternoons I would see my father holding his war council with other chieftains and senior leaders during which they directed mounted groups to ambush and attack Chinese installations in Nyarong and elsewhere. These armed militias would return with rifles and occasionally submachine guns that they had captured, and often with large quantities of tea, rice, and sometimes even Chinese cabbages. I also remember the days of mourning, however, when these groups returned absent a warrior or two who had been killed in the skirmishes.

Whether the raids were successful or not, everyone relished the freedom we were experiencing without the Chinese breathing down our necks. I remember waking up in my tent some mornings, thinking I was back at Lumorab and panicking because I thought I had overslept and my teachers would be furious with me. But then I would realize I didn't have classes anymore and I was so happy! Of course, I look back now and realize how misplaced my joy was.

Rumors were widespread in those days that outside help was coming soon to fight the Communists. The first batch of Tibetans recruited by the US Central Intelligence Agency were sent in March 1957 from Kalimpong in India to Saipan, a US commonwealth in the western Pacific Ocean, to be trained. On September 13, 1957, Gyato Wangdu from the Gyatotsang, a well-known family from Lithang, was airdropped by the CIA into Lithang with two associates, Tsewang Dorji and Tharlo. This further raised the hopes of many of the resistance fighters, who now expected the Americans to airdrop more fighters into Tibet, along with much-needed supplies.[1]

Some had heard that the American flag had been raised above Ba-choedegon, an important monastery in Bathang. Many people honestly believed the Americans were on their way. As news of my father joining the resistance spread across Kham, emissaries from neighboring chieftains in Lithang, Derge, Drago, and Lingkashi arrived to join forces. Within a short period of a few months at least four thousand resistance fighters gathered at our camp. Among the many chieftains who had joined my father were Thangshatsang Kunkhyen, my mothers' father; his brother, Thangshatsang Thutop Gonpo; and Thangshatsang Nima, my mothers' half-brother.

Had there not been these rumors reinforced by some actual CIA involvement, this large gathering of resistance fighters never would have happened. The Khampa leaders decided to come together in force with the hope of receiving US aid and also to demonstrate their strength and, above all, their determination to fight the Communists. As Tibetan Buddhists, it was our karma to be where we were and to face the attendant suffering. But the Khampa resistance movement never would have congregated in one area if it had believed that no outside help was coming. Individuals and groups would have stayed where they were and continued to carry out their resistance efforts independently. In hindsight, this would have been a much more effective tactic. In a way, CIA involvement brought greater suffering and tragedy to the resistance movement in eastern Tibet than had the agency not participated at all. The Chinese became even more ruthless in uprooting the resistance because of their fear of an outside force entering the theater.[2]

Sometime in the tenth month of the Royal Tibetan year of 2084, corresponding to December 1957 in the Western calendar, we moved to Ba-tsachen Sumdo to join an even larger group of resistance fighters. It became one of the largest gatherings of resistance fighters in Kham. Ba-tsachen Sumdo is now part of Palyul County in the Kardze Tibetan Autonomous Prefecture, not far from present-day Yachen Gar.[3] But with so many of us in one place we could no longer avoid detection by the Chinese, and not long after our arrival a huge contingent of Chinese troops launched a three-pronged attack, causing heavy casualties.

Although I had previously witnessed battles at close quarters where people were killed, nothing could have prepared me for the scene at Ba-tsachen Sumdo. It was horrifying, beyond description. Hundreds of people were gunned down. It was not so much a battle as an ambush. Under the cover of darkness, the Chinese had taken all the positions of strategic importance overlooking the valley where we were camped. The attack began at dawn with shots coming from different directions, terrifying not only the humans but also the animals, especially the horses. There was panic and chaos as people and animals ran in all directions. I was told that the mayhem was intentionally planned to scare away our horses because the Chinese knew that Khampa warriors are dependent on them. In fact, the most prized possessions of a Khampa warrior are his amulet for protection, his gun for battle, and then his horse that serves as both his ride and his companion. A Khampa warrior without his horse is like a fish out of water.

As the individuals in this large gathering of resistance forces came from all over Kham, in the chaos they ran in different directions, some heading toward their home areas while others headed toward the Drichu River. They hoped to cross over to the nearby part of Kham that was under the rule of the Lhasa government and thereby escape the Chinese forces. In those days, the Chinese were still making a show of honoring the Seventeen-Point Agreement[4] that they had signed with the Central Tibetan Government by not being too repressive in areas that fell under Lhasa's jurisdiction.

A majority of the families retreated to areas closer to their ancestral lands with the hope that CIA-supported assistance would soon arrive. My own family chose to head back toward the nomadic areas of Nyarong even though my father had by then decided to leave for Central Tibet. It turned out to be a wise, though treacherous decision. Sadly, those who headed toward the Drichu River were pursued by the main force of Chinese troops, suffering further devastating casualties in the following days. For our part, we had to navigate a turbulent river that was in full swell. I remember it was sometime a little before dusk when we began our crossing. We were halfway across when all of a sudden, from their hidden positions, the Chinese spotted us and started shooting indiscriminately. Right there in front of me, three people, including a young Nyarongwa boy of my age whom I knew quite well, along with their horses, were shot. I saw them literally carried away by the strong river current. I think they were not fully dead. This dawn-to-dusk tragedy was the most horrifying and longest day of my life. The scene I witnessed at Ba-tsachen Sumdo continues to haunt me.

Our family lost almost everything. Most of our livestock was gone. We were able to retrieve only a few horses, mostly the old and weak that could not run away. Until then we were still using the famed Gyari Ba-gyen Ma, the grand yak-hair tent of the Gyari family. When dismantled this portable tent required fourteen yaks to carry all its parts. The tent was large enough to comfortably accommodate a hundred monks during religious ceremonies. Our family was not unusual in having such a large tent. Other prominent nomadic chieftain families, including the Yonru and Tromge, had much grander tents because these structures served as their main residences. I was told that the shrine and family rooms of these tents actually had wooden flooring that could also be dismantled. Being agrarian, our family used such tents only occasionally. I remember my parents, Uncle Tsultrim, and we children had our own separate tents while the Gyari Ba-gyen Ma was a communal tent, serving as a kitchen and space for our retainers.

Some of our retainers sneaked back to Ba-tsachen Sumdo to try to find some utensils, which at the time were far more valuable than jewelry or other traditionally precious items. For several days, we had hardly had anything to eat as we had no pots to boil water in and not even cups to drink from. Someone had a bowl—I think it was my Uncle Tsultrim. It is customary for Khampas to carry their wooden bowl in their *amphag*, the upper fold of their dress, which forms a big pocket where things can be stowed. I remember my mothers making a thin gruel of *tsampa* (roasted barley flour) with cold water and feeding us. There were a few wild plants, including the Himalayan cowslip, that were edible, as well as the ubiquitous nettles, but we lacked pots to cook them in. Fortunately, our capable and devoted retainers came back from Ba-tsachen Sumdo with the much-needed implements. They also managed to bring some *tsampa* and dried cheese that had been abandoned in the wake of the battle.

The stories they brought back from Ba-tsachen Sumdo were heart-wrenching. Many of us, including my mothers, were crying at the accounts being narrated. Human and animal remains were sprawled all over the valley, including women, children, monks, and nuns. There were hundreds of vultures and wild dogs devouring the carcasses. An unbearable stench pervaded the valley. We later met some survivors of the Ba-tsachen Sumdo massacre when we crossed the Drichu River in early 1958. They told us that in the days after the attack, Chinese soldiers accompanied by Tibetan cadres were walking through the valley carrying photographs of Khampa leaders, including my father, Gyapon Chemi Dorje, and others, searching for them among the dead.

The battle at Ba-tsachen Sumdo was in a way the end of the organized resistance in Kham. The majority of the former impressive army of resistance fighters scattered in all directions, while those who remained were completely demoralized. My father felt deeply saddened at the loss of so many lives. Many of his friends and compatriots were either killed or separated from the group. Of his close friends who had only a few years earlier pledged their lives to defend the Buddha Dharma, Gya Yonten of the Lingkashi family was killed and his dear friend Dromo Wangchen was ambushed and assassinated. The fates of Shendang Ata and Sogri Ahjam, who were last heard to be fighting bravely against the Chinese in Lithang, were unknown. My father deeply missed his half-brother, Tashi Wangyal. He later learned that Tashi Wangyal was severely wounded in a skirmish with the Chinese, and his wife was killed. Tashi Wangyal later died from his battle wounds.

Particularly upsetting was the fate of the Lingkashi family, with whom our family had only weeks back formalized a matrimonial alliance. Just before the Chinese attacked, I accompanied some of the senior Gyari family retainers on a visit to the tented encampment of the Lingkashi family, who had also gathered at Ba-tsachen Sumdo. We were there to confirm a marriage between one of their daughters and my brother Pema Gyalpo. Of course, I was too young to understand much of what was going on, but I was the token Gyaritsang representative.

Among the upper classes, it is the Khampa tradition that the head of the family does not personally attend the formal "asking for the hand of the bride" ceremony. On the other hand, it is extremely disrespectful if no one from the immediate family attends. Marriage alliances are very important cultural aspects of Khampa lives. The Lingkashi family, like the Gyari family, was considered very powerful, producing ferocious fighters. This matrimonial relationship would have created a formidable force in this part of Tibet. That is how I ended up going to the Lingkashi encampment that day. The following day, the head of the clan came over to visit my parents with a large entourage bearing lavish gifts, further cementing the alliance.

What I enjoyed most that particular day at the Lingkashi camp was the delicious dried fruit that Gyapon Chemi Dorje gave me. He also had a beautiful, ornate pair of binoculars that he allowed me to play with while the adults were talking. I had never seen anything like them, and I was secretly hoping that because I was the Gyaritsang representative, he might give them to me as a gift. Of course, this didn't happen. That was a childish hope. For a warrior like him, those binoculars must have been extremely precious, as they were both rare and very useful.

Gyapon Chemi Dorje and Gya Yonten fought many more battles with the Communists and eventually both became casualties of our struggle. Gyapon Chemi Dorje was still active with a small band of resistance fighters as late as 1959. The Lingkashi daughter who was to marry my brother was one of the few from her family to survive. She never made it into exile and eventually ended up marrying someone else. In the late 1980s we received a message from her expressing her great joy in knowing that our whole family had made it safely into India. She said her family's fate had been tragic, but she survived and was doing well. Even though the marriage between our families was fated not to happen, her continuing concern and affection for my family reflect her genuine love.

## CHAPTER 6

# The Journey to Lhasa

My father knew that he had to make the journey with his family to Central Tibet for our safety. He thought the Chinese would not breach the agreement they had signed with the Central Tibetan Government that guaranteed it the right of self-rule. Of course, there was the added reason for our family to go there because we had relatives at Mindrolling Monastery. But every time he made this suggestion, his close relatives, senior lieutenants, and followers pleaded with him not to leave Nyarong. Some promised that if he waited a year to see what would happen, they would follow him if the situation hadn't improved. My father was convinced, however, that there would be no real change, and that if any occurred, it would be for the worse.

Finally he made the difficult decision to take his family and anyone who was willing to follow him to the safety of Central Tibet. He was convinced that we weren't safe in Kham. There had also been a divination[1] by Drakgho Tulku, a yogi with the power of clairvoyance, revealing that the Gyari family would have safe passage to Central Tibet, but that we should depart without even a week's delay.

When my senior mother went to receive final blessings from Drakgho Tulku, he gave her a bundle of prayer flags, saying there was one for each of the families that was making the journey. However, after her return to our hideout, we found that there were only four prayer flags, while there were five families in our group. My father immediately distributed the prayer flags, commenting that as my parents were taking care of the Gyaltsoktsang children, he considered them part of our family for purposes of the journey. All five families safely reached Lhasa, but one family did not make the final journey into exile in India: the Ahbehtsang. Only then did we realize the full truth of Drakgho Tulku's prophecy. Fortunately, most of the members of the Ahbehtsang were eventually also able to make it into exile, but with greater hardship.

There are other examples of Drakgho Tulku's prophetic gifts and advanced realizations, but none more remarkable than his actions while in prison in Kardze. He was arrested and given the death sentence for his open defiance of the Communists in encouraging Tibetans to take up armed resistance against them. One of his fellow prisoners[2] later visited us in India while on a pilgrimage in the late 1980s during Deng Xiaoping's policy of limited liberalization. He told my parents that Drakgho Tulku told him and his other cellmates on several occasions that Gyari Nyima had safely reached India. It was only through the power of clairvoyance that he could have known this. Drakgho Tulku further told them that it was the Gyari family's destiny to reach safe haven, and that was why he had counseled us to leave. At the same time, he had encouraged many other families to stay and take active part in the resistance because they did not possess the karma to escape the Communist tyranny.

Our visitor further told us that when the Chinese announced that Drakgho Tulku would be executed the next day, some of his cellmates implored him to take action so he would not die at the hands of the Communists. They had come to deeply revere this great practitioner and were desperate for him to save himself from that fate. He appeared to pay serious attention to their pleas as if just realizing the urgency of the situation, saying: "Yes, that is true, yes, that is true." He then propped himself up, straightened his back, sat in a cross-legged position, and was gone. Just like that. Drakgho Tulku had achieved such a high level of spiritual attainment that he had complete control over his life and his death.

Even after making the firm decision to head toward Lhasa, it still took us several months to prepare. We had no provisions, no horses, and not even suitable warm clothing for the journey. Secretly, Uncle Tsultrim and my younger mother went back to our maternal family house in Lumorab to obtain the supplies and livestock we needed for the upcoming journey. But they had to make it look like all these resources, including a large team of horses, had been forcefully confiscated. Lumorab Monastery had to be in a position to report to the Chinese authorities that the "bandit resistance" had looted the monastery. Otherwise it would have been accused of collaborating with the rebels.

This trip gave my younger mother one last opportunity to see her mother and her aunt Atra, as well as the children we had left behind. By then Nyarong, including the area around Lumorab, was under the complete control of the Chinese Communists. A month or so later, just before we left Nyarong, my senior mother also made a secret trip to see them. During these last two visits, my mothers also managed to secretly meet and receive the blessings of their uncle Rinpoches, Tulku

Angak and Minling Penam, as well as their great aunt Jetsün Kunzang Chödrön and their cousin Minling Shabdrung.[3] Sadly, my mothers never again saw these beloved family members.

Even though we now had the necessary supplies, we had to postpone our departure by several more months because winter had set in. We spent the intervening time mostly hiding in very secluded areas in caves and under rocky cliffs in and around Nyarong. Once we began our arduous journey from Kham to Lhasa, it took about six months. In addition to our family, our group included several Lithang families. Gyato Byughen, the elder brother of Gyato Wangdu, and the family of Ratruk Ngawang, a very well-known Khampa leader who later helped escort His Holiness the 14th Dalai Lama into exile, were among them.

We started from Nyarong in 1958, sometime in the fifth month of the Tibetan calendar (July), reaching Lhasa in the tenth Tibetan month (December). We had to make a huge detour, greatly lengthening our journey, to avoid detection by the Chinese army. Normally, to travel from Kham to Lhasa, one heads due west. In our case, for the first several months, we had to head straight north. We traveled all the way to the border of Xinjiang, bypassing the source of the Machu (Yellow) River, before then turning southwest toward Lhasa. We were also ambushed several times by Chinese troops and went weeks without proper food. We survived only by hunting antelopes and brown bears. Ironically, it turned out that a monk from Lithang was the best marksman amongst us, literally saving our lives through his impressive hunting skills.

This journey would have been even more difficult had we not had the help of three guides from Dzachuka whom my parents hired. While Guru Kyab, the leader, became "oath brother" of my father, it was Nang Lo, an elderly nomad, who was the main guide. He was familiar with the area, having navigated these harsh regions when he went *drong* (wild yak) hunting in his younger days. Thi-Ru was the youngest of the three guides. After accompanying us for more than ten days and reaching the source of the Machu River, they could have returned home under the arrangement my father had struck with them. But by this time, they had become so fond of our family and felt such immense attachment to us children that they accompanied us for another ten days, taking us deep into part of Central Tibet where the Chinese were not supposed to be taking military action.

Years later, in the late 1980s, Guru Kyab's son came on a pilgrimage to India and met with my parents. Through him, we learned that when Guru Kyab and his two companions returned home to their nomadic areas, the Chinese had already attacked and taken their families to different locations. Many of their family members were either killed or imprisoned. Our three guides also soon fell into Chinese hands. Only Thi-Ru survived after twenty-one long years of imprisonment. Even then, he was critically ill and did not live long after his release. My parents always include the names of these dear individuals when we do major religious offerings. We all feel immensely grateful to these three men who sacrificed so much to take us to safety. I still vividly visualize Nang Lo, the eldest one, with his prayer wheel, loudly chanting the name of Guru Padmasambhava and seeking his protection.

During this difficult journey, the duties of family priest fell upon me despite my young age, as my family had no one else to turn to for spiritual guidance. My father and I had a very complicated relationship. He was intimidating because he had such a dominant and forceful presence. But at the same time, he was a disciple of my predecessor and as a result, had deep respect for me, sincerely believing that I was the true reincarnation of Khenpo Aten. Whenever we faced a difficult situation during our journey my father would ask, or rather order, me to do a *mo*. Despite having no training in the practice, which is complex and elaborate, I never dared say no to his "request." While some lamas use dice and others use a rosary, there are specific guidelines as to how to interpret the divination. Ordinarily, one has to receive initiation and oral transmission of the particular deity invoked during the divination before undertaking the practice. As I had not received any of these teachings, I developed my own style. Surprisingly to me, most of my divinations proved sound, and I was able to guide our group through this treacherous journey unscathed.

In my role as family priest, I also became the weatherman. As we were traveling on the northern plateau of Tibet, which is totally uninhabited, the only map we had was the stars. To read them, we needed a clear sky or at least some open patches. I was thus told to do prayers to stop the snow and rain. Apparently the family thought I was successful at this task even though I had neither training nor experience in conducting rituals for affecting the weather. I remember simply visualizing myself as an enormous garuda[4] bird under whose wings our group found shelter from snow or rain. I also imagined myself as a garuda issuing a powerful jet flame through my nose that cleared the skies and made the stars visible. Obviously I was a very imaginative boy! I have no doubt, however, that the reason my divinations and prayers seemed to work was my father's unwavering belief in me as the reincarnation of his former teacher. My father rarely asked me to do divinations after reaching Lhasa or in our later years in India, as there were many other highly qualified Rinpoches from whom he could seek guidance. People from Lithang who had made the journey to Lhasa with us, including our sharpshooter monk, continued to request divinations from me even after I became a layperson living in Dharamsala. I advised them to consult a qualified lama.

Before arriving in Lhasa, we visited Reting and Taklung, two monasteries I feel very close to. My philosophy teacher at Lumorab, Tulku Sungrab, was a disciple of the 5th Reting Rinpoche (1912–1947), Jampal Yeshi, who became Tibet's regent in 1934 after the passing of the Great Thirteenth Dalai Lama. Generally, regents are appointed from a small pool of prominent Gelugpa reincarnates to be caretakers of the government until the new Dalai Lama comes of age. Previous Retings had also been regents of Tibet.

Reting Rinpoche was greatly admired, and a majority of Tibetans felt a deep sense of gratitude to him for successfully identifying and enthroning the 14th Dalai Lama during his regency. In 1941, Reting Rinpoche stepped down to devote a few years to retreat and practice, offering the regency temporarily to his teacher Takdrak Rinpoche, an elderly Gelugpa reincarnate. Reting Rinpoche's intention was to reclaim the regency after the conclusion of his retreat, but sadly, he was never to return. Instead, he was arrested by officials of the Central Tibetan Government in April 1947 and taken to Lhasa as a prisoner, where he died under tragic circumstances on May 8 of the same year. In his autobiography, Gyalo Thondup, the 14th Dalai Lama's elder brother, states that he has no doubts that Reting Rinpoche was murdered. He goes so far as to name certain influential aristocrats as being responsible.[5]

The ill treatment and the manner of Reting Rinpoche's death horrified many Tibetans, including Tulku Sungrab, triggering a serious bout of depression that compelled him to resign as Lumorab's abbot. On our journey to Lhasa, we stayed at Reting Rinpoche's summer residence, and his senior monks shared with us the terrifying story of his arrest. It was difficult for us to believe that the central Tibetan army, themselves Buddhists, could so mistreat a great master like Reting Rinpoche. Near his summer residence there was a big rock Reting Rinpoche used to mount his horse when he was taken to Lhasa as a prisoner. At the time of our journey everyone who visited the area would throw a stone at it simply because it had contributed to Reting Rinpoche being taken prisoner.

The Reting incident caused irreparable and long-standing damage to the prestige and reputation of the Central Tibetan Government. In the mid-1970s, when

I was Additional Cabinet Secretary in the Tibetan Government in Exile (TGiE), I accompanied then senior Kalon Kundeling Woeser Gyaltsen on a visit to several Tibetan monasteries in and around Darjeeling, India. One of the senior lamas we wanted to meet was Kyabjé Chatral Rinpoche, a highly respected Nyingma master. To my dismay, when I visited him to arrange the meeting with Kalon Kundeling, he flatly refused, saying that he had taken an oath "not to maintain any relation with the Tibetan government by even taking a drop of water from them because I consider it as irreligious." He gave me a long lecture, the gist of which was:

> We called the Chinese "the enemy of faith." What is surprising about that? They are atheist and they openly declare us as their enemy. But you know what the Tibetan government did? They killed the great being, the Reting Rinpoche, ransacked and robbed his monastery. They also fired cannons at Sera Monastery. These are the acts of the true "enemy of faith." The Tibetan government is supposed to be a religious government while the Communist Chinese proclaim themselves as antireligious. Ever since this treachery by Tibetan government officials against Reting Rinpoche, I took an oath to never have any relations with it.

Fortunately, Kyabjé Chatral Rinpoche and I are both from Nyarong. He had also taken some teachings from my predecessor, Khenpo Aten, and he felt that we had a special bond. I took advantage of this relationship and explained that I was not asking him to go to the minister, but the minister was coming to visit him. His refusal to meet the Kalon under these circumstances would be personally embarrassing for me. After a lot of discussion, I was able to persuade this grand old Nyingma lama to receive Kalon Kundeling. To my surprise and delight, they had a wonderful meeting, primarily because they were able to trade stories about so many common friends they had in Lhasa. Until his passing, Kyabjé Chatral Rinpoche kept his distance from the Tibetan government in Dharamsala. Nevertheless, he had deep respect for His Holiness the 14th Dalai Lama and always showed his appreciation for my serving His Holiness.

After our visit to Reting, we stopped at Taklung Monastery, the main seat of the Taklung tradition, an important subsect of the Kagyu school.[6] Decades earlier my predecessor, Khenpo Aten, had spent several months at this monastery conferring initiations and giving oral transmissions to the previous Taklung Matrul Rinpoche. He also built a unique *stupa*[7] dedicated to the deity Yamantaka.[8] He had built three similar stupas in his lifetime, the others at Mindrolling

The author with Kyabjé Chatral Rinpoche in Salbari, India, 2005

and Lumorab Monasteries. While we were at Taklung, a peculiar thing happened. I had a *phudkong*, a Dharmapala[9] offering cup, which I used for my daily offerings. One morning I discovered that it was missing. I kept it on the table right next to my bed, so no one could have stolen it. Besides, it was of no great value, as it was only made of brass. It was important to me, however, as it was a gift from the then Taklung Matrul Rinpoche to my predecessor. However, some of the senior monks of Taklung thought that it must have been reclaimed by the Dharmapalas of Taklung Monastery! Who knows?

At both Reting and Taklung Monasteries, the lamas and the monks were very kind to us, especially at Taklung because of their reverence for my predecessor. For the first time in many years we felt free from fear, as we knew that the Chinese would not dare take action against us within the territory governed by the Central Tibetan Government. We took our time in moving toward Lhasa, staying for quite a while at Phenpo, a very fertile and rich valley, not far from Lhasa. Our companions from Lithang had already left us to join a large number of fellow Lithangwas who were part of Andruk Gonpo Tashi's Chushi Gangdrug resistance movement.[10] My father formally joined this movement while we were in Phenpo.

Sometime in December 1958 we finally arrived in Lhasa, the most holy and important city for all Tibetans. We were very excited because we were finally seeing this famed city. How we felt when we had a first glimpse of the majestic Potala Palace is beyond description. The Potala was built by the Emperor Songtsen Gampo in the seventh century and became the home and monastery of the Dalai Lamas beginning in the seventeenth century with the reign of the Great Fifth. The very sight of it, with the immense White Palace rising 100 meters into the air and crowned with the jewel-like Red Palace, both silhouetted against the rich blue Lhasa sky, made us proud to be Tibetan, giving us a sense of the grandeur and richness of our history and culture.

My father and some of his retainers entered Lhasa under cover of darkness in advance of the rest of the party as we waited in Phenpo. My father had received a warning that the Chinese were aware of his pending arrival. They had distributed photos among their informers in Lhasa so that if he were sighted, the authorities could be alerted. While in Lhasa my father moved houses every few nights to avoid detection. He also spent considerable time at the Norbulingka, the Summer Palace of the Dalai Lamas, because one of his relatives was a senior personal attendant of His Holiness. My mothers and the rest of us entered Lhasa openly, although we did take a number of precautions. We rented a dozen donkeys in Phenpo, concealing our arms and ammunitions, including a submachine gun taken during a skirmish with the Chinese, in sacks partially filled with cow dung. It was an excellent ruse, as it was an everyday sight to see donkeys from Phenpo bringing dried dung into the city to be sold for fuel.

My father had made arrangements for us to be accommodated at the Trehor Khamtsen[11] of Sera Monastery in Lhasa. Sera, along with Drepung and Ganden, is one of the three largest Gelug monasteries, each of which has several colleges that in turn operate as hostels or living facilities catering to monks coming from different areas of Tibet. Sera is composed of the Mey and Jey Colleges. Monks coming from Kardze, Dhargye, Drago, or Nyarong are housed in the Trehor Khamtsen hostel of the college they attend.

The monks who were running the guesthouse took excellent care of us, showing us the magnificent sights of Lhasa, including many holy shrines. The Central Cathedral or Jokhang is still vividly etched in my mind. Entering the temple from an expansive central square, the main sanctuary was intimate, yet overwhelming. The walls were adorned with exquisitely detailed *thangkas* depicting the lives of the Buddha and other Tibetan deities. Rich and colorful wall and door hangings framed the chapel and pungent incense perfumed the air. At the far end, the completely gilded and jeweled Buddha statue brought to Tibet by the Tang Princess Wencheng as part of her dowry on her betrothal to the Emperor Songtsen Gampo was beautifully situated on an enclosed altar. As a reincarnate residing in my own monastery, I was familiar with the general beauty and serenity of Tibetan cathedrals, but the grandeur of the Jokhang and the splendor of its decorations left me breathless. We also visited Ramoche Temple, which houses another important Buddha image brought into Tibet by the Nepalese Princess Bhrikuti as part of her dowry when she came as Songtsen Gampo's other bride.

Since my mothers were in a hurry to meet up with their uncles at Mindrolling Monastery, we did not spend too many days in Lhasa, believing we would return during the annual Lhasa Monlam (prayer) festival taking place a few months later. We saved visits to the Potala and other important pilgrimage sites, as well as the monasteries of Sera, Drepung, and Ganden, for a later time. Sadly, that opportunity never arose for my family because of the tragic situation of March 10, 1959, leading to His Holiness's flight into exile. I was finally fortunate enough to visit both the Potala and the Norbulingka in 2002 during our First Round of formal negotiations with the PRC representatives.[12]

One other memory from our days in Lhasa, although of an entirely different nature, remains with me. Having safely reached the city, my senior mother must have felt for the first time in one and a half years of travel, camping in the mountains and dodging Chinese troops, that there was little danger the family would be arrested. She finally put down two hand grenades that she had steadfastly, and almost reverently, carried on her person for the entire journey. Much later, I learned of the plan she and my younger mother had devised and kept entirely to themselves. If we were to fall into Chinese hands, the sisters pledged that they would gather all the children together and detonate the grenades. My senior mother's swift and certain death at her own hands, as well as that of her beloved family, was preferable to the physical and mental torture the Chinese would inevitably have visited upon us.

While I was too young at the time to fully understand how painful it must have been for my mothers even to contemplate such an act of self-sacrifice, their courage and resolve inspire and fortify me to this day when I am confronted with situations where the only available options seem unbearable. My youngest brother, Kunzang Tsewang, who was born in exile, heard this for the first time some years back and remarked: "Thank god our amalas did not panic. Otherwise, you would have all been blown to pieces!" His concern was very apt; there were at least two close encounters with the Chinese during our journey that we feared we might not escape.

In Lhasa, tensions were rising, as the Chinese authorities were putting increasing pressure on the Central Tibetan Government to take action against the Khampa resistance movement that was becoming more active in Central Tibet. The Chinese were also trying to marginalize the role and influence of His Holiness the 14th Dalai Lama and the Central Tibetan Government. They created the Preparatory Committee for the Tibet Autonomous Region in 1956, a parallel Chinese-dominated government whose true purpose was to undermine the Tibetan authorities. Outwardly, this organization seemed to function under His Holiness, who was its Chairman, but in reality His Holiness and the other Tibetan officials participated in name only.

CHAPTER 7

# From Mindrolling to Exile in India

My father did not accompany us to Mindrolling. Instead, he stayed in Lhasa to consolidate his connections and work with the resistance movement. He also felt that his presence at Mindrolling could endanger the monastery and its resident Rinpoches, as the Chinese were keeping a very close watch on his movements.

For my mothers, my siblings, and myself, arriving at Mindrolling was truly like returning home. While Mindrolling was their official monastery, Lumorab was their true home. We were housed in the summer residence of the Mindrolling Rinpoches, where Minling Khenchen Rinpoche, who originally recognized me as the reincarnation of Khenpo Aten, and his two sisters, Jetsün Tsewang Lhamo and Jetsün Dechen Wangmo, also lived. My mothers' uncles, Minling Chung Rinpoche and Minling Khenchen Rinpoche, even had winter clothes ready for all of us. We had a wonderful stay at Mindrolling. We felt very much at home, as many monks from Lumorab were also part of the Rinpoches' households. My mothers and the two Rinpoches conversed in our own Nyarong dialect, sharing stories about the tragic situation in Kham but also making plans for the future.

My mothers, especially my senior mother, spent many hours catching up with Dungse Gyurmé Kunzang Wangyal,[1] the son of the Tenth Mindrolling throne holder. They were very close, as they were of the same age and grew up together at Lumorab. Meanwhile, Minling Khenchen Rinpoche took special care of me. He gave me oral transmissions of important texts and initiations of my lineage. On our arrival, we thought we would stay indefinitely at Mindrolling and that I would resume my formal studies there. But several days into our stay, I learned that the Rinpoches wanted me to enroll for a few years at Sera Monastery back in Lhasa, where the more extensive curriculum would complement the basic training in Buddhist philosophy I had received at Lumorab. They also arranged for my mothers to spend some time in Jhang Dhokya, a nomadic region where Minling Khenchen Rinpoche had considerable livestock that would provide my mothers with a reliable source of income. The Rinpoches further recommended we go on a pilgrimage for a couple of weeks to visit some of the holy places in southern Tibet. After returning to Mindrolling to celebrate Losar with them, we could then go our separate ways. They made all the arrangements for our trip, sending letters of introduction to influential people in the areas we would be visiting.

We first traveled to the Lhodrak district, north of the Bhutanese border, where we visited the Mila Sekhar Gutok, otherwise known as Milarepa's tower, built at the command of his teacher Marpa Lotsawa. I was a bit surprised to learn that the monastery was overseen by the Gelug tradition given that it was the main seat of Marpa and Milarepa, the founders of the Kagyu school. While there, we also visited Lhodrak Kharchu, an important Nyingma monastery that was the seat of Namkhai Nyingpo Rinpoche, whose incarnation could be traced back to the eighth century when Padmasambhava visited Tibet.

Namkhai Nyingpo was one of the main disciples of Padmasambhava. On inquiring about the current incarnation's whereabouts, we were told that he was in retreat somewhere close to the Bhutanese border. Knowing the historical importance of this lineage, I traveled all the way to his hermitage with my Uncle Tsultrim. It was not an easy journey, but well worth it. Not only did we have an audience with Namkhai Nyingpo Rinpoche, but he also invited us to stay overnight, giving us further opportunities to converse with him. After China's occupation of Tibet, Namkhai Nyingpo Rinpoche moved to neighboring Bhutan with many of his monks and followers. He spent the remainder of his life there. His reincarnation, the Seventh Namkhai Nyingpo Rinpoche, was born in Bhutan and has established a thriving sangha at Lhodrak Kharchu Monastery in Bumthang.

When we were about to return to Mindrolling, a special messenger arrived with instructions from the Rinpoches advising us to remain in Lhodrak indefinitely. The situation in Lhasa had become extremely tense and unpredictable. The Rinpoches arranged for us to stay at Benpa Chakdor in monks' quarters belonging to Khenchung Sera, a prominent local family who patronized this Gelug monastery in addition to Mindrolling, of Nyingma heritage. They had enrolled one son at each of these monasteries.

Benpa Chakdor is a historically important monastery built by Drupchen Namkha Gyaltsen, a Nyingma master who was one of the principal teachers of Je Tsongkhapa, who later founded the Gelug school. While the monastery became a Gelug institution in the last century, it maintains special ties to its founder's Nyingma lineage. I was treated very well at Benpa Chakdor. The monks paid me the honor of asking me to wear a prized hat belonging to the revered Nyingma master Namkha Gyaltsen during an important religious ceremony. Some of the senior monks had dreams and had seen other signs indicating that I had some connection to their founder and their monastery. We were also able to celebrate Losar at Benpa Chakdor in a way that we had not been able to for a number of years because of the turbulence in Kham. Of course, my mothers would have preferred to have been with their relatives at Mindrolling for the Tibetan New Year as originally planned, but once again the volatile climate of the times spoiled our plans.

As my father had remained in Lhasa, he began making arrangements for my enrollment at Sera. When the monks from Loseling College at Drepung learned of his intentions, however, they began pressuring him to send me to their monastery instead. Even though both monasteries belong to the Gelug tradition and I follow the Nyingma school, it is not uncommon for monks and lamas from other traditions to study at these renowned Gelug universities. The abbot of my monastery, Khenpo Acho, himself studied at Sera, following the advice of the Mindrolling Rinpoches.

Having these two prestigious and influential institutions vying for my attendance put my father in a very difficult position. These powerful monasteries and their respective colleges were especially keen to have the children of prominent families and reincarnate lamas as their students. Fortunately, the dispute was soon sorted out. During the 13th Dalai Lama's rule, it was decreed that students coming from the Upper Nyarong should join Drepung. Thus, had the tragic uprising of 1959 and the 14th Dalai Lama's flight into exile not occurred, I would have joined Drepung Monastery. Who knows, had this transpired, I might have become a real scholar. I was deeply interested in the study of philosophy and had a good foundation from my studies at Lumorab.

To this day, Drepung Loseling College and its Trehor Khamsten continue to keep in touch with me and have shown me much kindness and affection. I was able to participate in the opening ceremony of the grand Loseling prayer hall of Drepung Monastery in exile in 2008 in Mundgod, India, that was presided over by His Holiness the 14th Dalai Lama. But I must confess I also have strong emotional ties to Sera. The fact that Khenpo Acho had studied there deeply influenced my thinking.

While we waited at Benpa Chakdor Monastery in Lhodrak, Mindrolling Khenchen Rinpoche made arrangements for me to receive philosophy lessons from the monastery's Khenpo. I began studying with this wonderful Khenpo, but, believe it or not, I never knew his full name. Everyone addressed him as Khen Rinpoche.[2] It wasn't until many years later that I first learned his full name from my close friend Geshe Tsultim Gyeltsen, who was his classmate at Ganden Monastery. Unfortunately, I misplaced the piece of paper on which Geshe-la had written Khen Rinpoche's name, but I remember his first name was Lobsang.

It was during my time at Benpa Chakdor that I genuinely began to appreciate my teachers and became deeply interested in my studies. As I think back to my early teachers, I realize how lucky I have been to study with them. I feel great reverence and gratitude, particularly to Tulku Sungrab and Ngawang Choephel, my Tibetan language and grammar instructors at Lumorab. These demanding and dedicated teachers taught me more than I realized, greatly influencing me and preparing me well for the more advanced studies I was to undertake with the Benpa Chakdor's Khenpo.[3]

In addition to igniting my passion for my studies, those few months in Lhodrak opened my eyes to the harsh socioeconomic conditions of Tibetans living in the region. Heavy taxation by the Central Tibetan Government further depleted their already meager resources. An added burden for the population was the presence of a large number of Chushi Gangdrug resistance members, who relied on the locals for support. There were also small bands of Khampas taking advantage of the locals, including stealing their livestock. Even my family encountered some difficulties. Only the timely intervention of some senior resistance leaders stopped the thievery. Amdo Lekshey, who was the senior commander of the resistance fighters in the Lhodrak area, was very helpful in this regard. In exile, he became a senior Central Tibetan Administration (CTA) official, serving for many years until he passed away in Dharamsala. Uncle Tsultrim also met with several senior leaders of Chushi Gangdrug, including Jagoe Namgyal Dorjee, Sadutshang Lo Nyendak, and Jangtsa Choetze, who were visiting the area. Jangtsa Choetze later became the first Khampa to be appointed to the Kashag once the government was established in exile. Given the presence of the entire Gyari family, including children, he confidentially advised Uncle Tsultrim that we should seriously think of leaving Tibet through Bhutan because the situation, in his view, was becoming critical. We highly appreciated his sincere and caring advice.

The system of governance in Tibet at the time was feudal. We should not make any excuses or try to project a different, more politically acceptable image. We should also not be apologetic, as history shows that societies evolve over time. In fact, the feudal systems that then existed in other places, including China, were far more cruel and brutal than that in Tibetan regions. The situation in Kham at the time was considered tribal, not having yet reached the feudal stage. Personally, I prefer the purportedly less developed tribal level. Ordinary people in Kham and Amdo enjoyed a great deal of freedom at the time. The relationship between ruler and ruled was rather relaxed and relatively personal.

One afternoon a middle-aged monk carrying a rather heavy *khur-shing*,[4] a backpack made of bamboo canes, walked into my room unannounced, a not uncommon occurrence among Tibetans. This strange man casually dropped the *khur-shing* and sat down, asking if there were a place for him to spend the night. He had an air of confidence bordering on arrogance. From his dialect, it was clear that he was from a nomadic Khampa tribe. He turned to me and said: "The Tulku is young." Then, turning to Uncle Tsultrim, who was sitting next to me, he quoted a verse from Ngari Panchen Pema Wangyal's *Domsum*:

> རྫོགས་པ་ཆེན་པོ་ཡེ་ཤེས་སྤྱི་ཡི་གཟུགས།།
> ཡོངས་སུ་དག་སྐུ་རྡོ་རྗེ་འཆང་ཆེན་པོ།།
> འབྲས་བུའི་མཐར་ཐུག་སངས་རྒྱས་ཉག་གཅིག་དེ།།

> The general expression of primordial wisdom is the great perfection Atiyoga. The perfectly pure embodiment, *kaya*, of the great Vajradhara is ultimate fruition, the oneness of Buddha.[5]

In a challenging tone, he then asked Uncle Tsultrim to enlighten him as to the meaning of this verse. Uncle Tsultrim was a very pious monk, but he was not a scholar. He could also be short-tempered. He did not like the confrontational attitude of this stranger. But frankly, he did not have an answer to the question. His reply was characteristically curt: "If you want to debate, go upstairs to the Khenpo." At this point, the visitor gave a playful smile, saying: "I think I angered you."

While this exchange was going on, I saw my senior mother darting in and out of the room in a rather excited manner. I later learned that she had had a premonition in her dreams about this visitor and felt this pilgrim monk was someone special. She was thus anxious to make arrangements for his overnight stay with our next-door neighbor, Lagye-la, a very kind, elderly monk. By then it was already dusk. My mother escorted the visitor to Lagye-la's quarters and came back very excited. She was quite certain that he was none other than the famous Yonru Pon Sonam Gyaltsen, otherwise known as Sogyal. He had once been a powerful Yonru chieftain who renounced his family and his chiefdom to pursue the life of a spiritual wanderer under the guidance of Jamyang Khyentse Chökyi Lodrö, the foremost torchbearer of the Ri-me movement of that time.[6] One can say with confidence that there would have been no one in Kham who had not heard of his extraordinary act of renunciation.

That very night, all of us went to Lagye-la's quarters. My mothers immediately prostrated to him, addressing him as Yonru Pon. He did not deny or confirm his identity, but he did confide to us that he was heading to Sikkim to join his teacher, Jamyang Khyentse Chökyi Lodrö. We spent a long time with him talking about the tragic events in Kham. I remember the room was lit by a lone oil lamp placed on the table in front of him, giving me an opportunity to see his face clearly. I thought he became quite emotional and teary-eyed when my senior mother told him about how his son Sonam Wangyal and his nephew Daghoe Sey heroically lost their lives at the hands of the Communists. He made no specific comment about the loss of his son but remarked: "So sad! So sad! My nephew sacrificed his life for my son."

This heroic act by these two young chieftains has become a legend. The Tibetan Institute of Performing Arts in Dharamsala, India, used to stage a play depicting their courageous acts. The two cousins fought together defending Lithang Monastery, causing huge casualties to the Chinese soldiers, but in the end, they both ran out of ammunition. The young Sonam Wangyal announced his willingness to surrender, but only to the seniormost Chinese military official. Bare-chested, both cousins walked toward the officer holding their rifles in their hands. But as they got closer, they threw down their rifles, drew the revolvers they had secreted behind their backs, and opened fire, killing the Chinese commander but also being gunned down on the spot.

We were fortunate to receive some oral transmissions from Yonru Pon, including the profound prayer written by Rigdzin Jigme Lingpa entitled "Entering the City of Omniscience."[7] This became my most treasured prayer, a savior in many regards. This great practitioner showed great affection toward me and my siblings,

Pema Gyalpo, Dorjee Thogmay, Namlhang Lhamo, and Yulzin Dolma (aka Rinzing Dolma).[8] He gave me his wooden tea bowl along with a black-and-white photo of a statue of the Buddha and recited the following verse from the Aspiration Prayer of Maitreya:

> Untainted in ethical conduct,
> In accord with pure precepts,
> Upholding the precepts without arrogance,
> May I perfect the Paramita of Precepts.

The photo must have been very precious to this wandering yogi because it had the thumb impression of his teacher, Jamyang Khyentse Chökyi Lodrö, on the back. He gave a flute to my brother Pema Gyalpo and told my parents that they must add "Zamling Kunkhyab" (meaning "Pervading the World") to his name. To my other brother, Dorjee Thogmay, he gifted a small mirror. I am sure all these gifts had not only profound symbolic but also personal meaning to Yonru Pon.

Even though Yonru Pon was not recognized as a reincarnate, my parents revered him with deep devotion. It is not uncommon in Tibet for ordinary monks or even lay individuals, be they male or female, to achieve positions of great reverence based solely on their spiritual attainments. In fact, many of Tibet's greatest practitioners were solitary, wandering yogis and yoginis. We were naturally hoping to spend more time with Yonru Pon, but early the next morning when my mothers and some of the attendants went to offer him breakfast, he had already departed. According to Lagye-la, his host, Yonru Pon had left before dawn. In the true tradition of a Dzogchen yogi, he wanted to remain inconspicuous and anonymous.

Years later, when my parents were living in Darjeeling and later in Kalimpong, Yonru Pon visited them quite often, sometimes spending hours with them. Whenever he wanted to travel between these two places, he would ask my parents to buy him a ticket on one of the local shuttle taxis that in those days were mostly rickety Land Rovers. Even today these rattletrap shuttle taxis still operate. Back then there were three price categories, the front window seat being the most expensive, followed by the seat between the driver and the passenger next to the window. Those who sat in the back paid the least. The first time, my parents reserved the front window seat for Yonru Pon. He declined, saying: "I am a very ordinary person and I want to sit where I belong." After that, my parents always bought him the back seat.

In 1962, during the China-India border war, Yonru Pon wanted to move from Kalimpong to Rewalsar in Himachal Pradesh. He asked my parents to book him a ticket to Darjeeling to settle some matters before he relocated. As usual, my parents bought him the back seat, but this time he was quite insistent that he sit in the front window seat. Unfortunately, the Bengali gentleman sitting in that seat refused to move even after my father, in a final, desperate effort, offered to reimburse him handsomely. Yonru Pon was not happy with his seating arrangement, and for many years my parents felt that some auspiciousness was not fulfilled. My father actually suggested that Yonru Pon postpone his departure so that my parents could get him the seat that he desired, but he was not willing to do that.

Before departing, he told my parents to go to his hermitage in Kalimpong and collect the *tsam-dho*, the boundary marker for his retreat. There was some delay in my parents making the trip, and when they finally went to his hermitage the *tsam-dho* was gone. In addition to these regrettable failures to comply with his wishes, Uncle Tsultrim had also declined to store three volumes of Buddhist texts and a pair of Tibetan-style shoes that Yonru Pon requested he take for safekeeping. Uncle Tsultrim sincerely felt that the texts would get damaged with the monsoon dampness in the small rental room we had taken in Darjeeling. All these events were seen by my parents as a sign that Yonru Pon had a strong fondness for our family. They honestly felt that if we had fulfilled all the requested tasks, maybe he would have taken rebirth in our family. And perhaps he has!

My sister who was born in 1961 in India was named Jamyang Dolma by this great yogi. Most people do not know that his refuge name was Jamyang Dorjee and refer to him as Yonru Pon or by his lay name, Sogyal. Although I do not know for sure, his root master, Jamyang Khyentse Chökyi Lodrö, most likely gave him his refuge name. Some years later, this great yogi passed away alone under a tree in Manali in Himachal Pradesh without anyone to care for or assist him. On hearing this, my parents were deeply saddened, but they also realized that that was how he chose to die, having renounced everything.[9]

## INTO EXILE

Our happy stay in Lhodrak came to an abrupt end with the March 10, 1959, National Uprising in Lhasa and the subsequent escape of His Holiness the 14th Dalai Lama into exile. So much has been written about this exodus, perhaps most eloquently by His Holiness himself in his autobiography *My Land and My People*, that I have little to add.

In the immediate aftermath of the uprising, we did not get any reliable information about the fate of my father and his retainers in Lhasa, and we were very worried. Fortunately, within a matter of days my father arrived at Benpa Chakdor, where we had a truly relieved and joyful reunion. Our happiness was short-lived, however, as the situation in Lhodrak was becoming increasingly unstable. Seeing the volatile situation in Tibet, the Mindrolling Rinpoches sent us some additional supplies and funds via a special courier. They included several letters of introduction to some disciples of the Rinpoches in Kalimpong, including a successful business family, advising them to make available to my family the money that Mindrolling Chung Rinpoche had left with them to buy gold for the monastery's *ser-yab* or golden roof.

There were also letters of introduction to some members of the Sikkimese royal family and to the Ogyen Choelings, a prominent Bhutanese family residing in Bumthang. Directly descended from the great master Dorji Lingpa and also Pema Lingpa, the Ogyen Choelings family is blessed with powerful religious and secular lineages. Tulku Nuden Dorji of this family studied at Mindrolling Monastery for many years and was a close disciple of both Mindrolling Khenchen Rinpoche and Mindrolling Chung Rinpoche. Because of this connection, as soon as my father joined us, our plan was to travel to Bhutan, as it was much closer to Lhodrak. We also knew that His Holiness the 16th Karmapa with his large entourage had gone to Bhutan just a month earlier. When my father arrived, however, he was keen to be part of the resistance group that was heading toward India through the area then known as NEFA, the North East Frontier Agency, now called Arunachal Pradesh.

Reading the draft of this chapter, some of my children wondered why I didn't focus on the hardships attending our flight from Tibet. After some thought, I realized that the journey from Lhodrak to NEFA did not psychologically traumatize me as much as those horrendous years of hiding in the mountains of Kham, living under constant threat to our lives, and the arduous six-month trip to Lhasa. Of course, the trek from Lhodrak to India was physically very difficult. My siblings were very young, and at a certain point we had to give up most of our mounts and cross the Himalayas on foot. There was also a shortage of food until we reached Tawang on the Indian side. Even there it was very hard to get our staple food, *tsampa*, so my Uncle Tsultrim and I went to villages begging for it. There were other monks in similar pursuit; it is not unusual for people in robes to go for alms.

The author as a young boy with Uncle Tsultrim at the Tibetan Refugee Self Help Centre in Darjeeling
Photo by Diki Gyalo Thondup

Crossing the snowcapped Himalayas into NEFA was quite treacherous. It took an entire day to navigate a single mountain pass. Sometimes the single-file line of men, women, children, and animals through the pass hardly moved. The entire route would be at a halt for hours if a single horse or mule collapsed from exhaustion. I remember one very sad scene when a fatigued mule was literally pushed off the path to make way for the convoy. The journey was clearly physically exhausting, but mentally we did not experience the fear under which we had labored for the last many years. On this final exodus we were accompanied by thousands of resistance fighters armed to the teeth, whose numbers alone provided a great sense of security.

I was deeply saddened, however, to leave behind my beloved pet Lhasa Apso that one of the Rinpoches had given me when we arrived in Lhodrak. This little dog was very protective of me and had an interesting habit. While it is not unusual for a loyal pet to follow his master around, this remarkable Lhasa Apso would jump onto my bed the moment I left the room and stand guard. He would not allow even my family members to touch or remove any of my personal belongings. My senior mother used to joke, saying that he must be the reincarnation of the Lumorab household's old bursar Ahlo, who had a reputation of being very tightfisted.

When my family joined the resistance group for our onward journey into exile, it was strictly forbidden to bring a dog for fear that its barking might alert the Chinese. I was heartbroken to have to abandon him, but I was able to leave him with another Rinpoche who I am sure took very good care of him. Knowing how traumatizing it can be to lose or part with a pet, I never allowed any of my children to have one. Years later, when we were living in Dharamsala, without my knowledge, my eldest daughter, Tenzing Dechen, brought home a Lhasa Apso. I named him Dhondup in memory of my own former pet. But a few years later when we moved to the States, we were once again forced to give up a devoted pet that had become a member of the family. This parting was very difficult for both my daughter and Dhondup, bringing up painful memories for me as well.

A number of senior Tibetan officials, reincarnate lamas, Khampa chieftains, and other leaders were navigating the treacherous mountain passes on their way to freedom at the same time we were. It was then that I had my first glimpse of the legendary Khampa resistance leader, Andruk Gonpo Tashi. I was not initially impressed; as a child, I expected a larger-than-life character and was disappointed by his rather ordinary appearance. Years later, I had the opportunity to get to know him well, and he was anything but ordinary.[10] He was a remarkable man and a born leader.

His Holiness the 14th Dalai Lama and his entourage had also taken the same escape route into exile as we did. By the time we reached the Indian border, His Holiness had already crossed safely into India, and there was great rejoicing amongst the Tibetans. I remember being thrilled when I saw what I then believed to be a regiment of the Indian army. One of the officers gave me a small coin as a welcome present that I convinced myself was gold. I later learned that this group was actually a paramilitary force called the Assam Rifles, and the coin I was given was a mere paisa or Indian penny. Nevertheless, to me this was as good as gold because it was offered with genuine affection.

In the end, as prophesied by Drakgho Tulku, my father was able to bring our family and many others to safety and freedom. He was a great leader and an even better father. He was deeply dedicated to the Tibetan cause but never let those feelings overshadow the needs of our family. He was always home in the evenings, sometimes even helping my mothers around the house, which is quite unusual for a Khampa man, much less a chieftain. He never indulged himself playing mahjong[11] or even joining the seemingly endless card games that, unfortunately, were becoming habits within some sections of the exile community. Despite his achievements, my father never took credit for any of them, truly believing that his successes were entirely due to the blessings of Padmasambhava[12] and Lady Tara, the female Buddha of compassion who is the guardian deity of the Gyari family.

Our family never would have survived and successfully reached India without the love and sacrifice of many other people. Uncle Tsultrim, Sonam Tenzing, Kalsang Wangdi, Dorji, and Mimi immediately come to mind. All of them came with us into exile and continued to serve the family until my father encouraged them to start life afresh. Uncle Tsultrim looked after my younger siblings when my parents had to move to Kalimpong because of my father's appointment as *garthue.*[13] He eventually became a disciple of Kalu Rinpoche (1905–1989) and moved to his master's monastery in Sonada, where he passed away in 1981. Kalu Rinpoche was a highly accomplished Buddhist master and practitioner and one of the first Tibetan Buddhist masters to teach in the West.

Dorji and Mimi later married and moved to the Tibetan settlement in Bylakuppe, South India. Mimi outlived Dorji by decades and only recently passed away after being cared for by Namdroling Monastery because she and her husband were devotees of His Holiness Penor Rinpoche. Sonam Tenzing moved to a Tibetan settlement in Mundgod, South India. He has since passed away, but he has a son who is now settled in Canada. Kalsang Wangdi, together with several other Nyarong families, joined the Tibetan settlement in Himachal Pradesh established by Kathok Ontrul Rinpoche, as he was among the majority of Nyarongwas who followed the Kathok tradition of the Nyingma school. As previously mentioned, in the late 1980s, he returned to Nyarong. Well cared for by his family, after many years he passed away. Ironically, he is the only one from our "family" who managed to go back to our native land. I say "family" because my parents, myself, and my siblings never considered Sonam Tenzing, Kalsang Wangdi, Mimi, and Dorji as mere retainers; they were loved and respected as true family members.

At this point, I must also mention two other individuals who were very important to our family even though they did not make it to freedom in India. Ama Mebo took care of my younger brothers Pema Gyalpo and Dorjee Thogmay. He looked after them for years and was with us for the first year and half that we were hiding in the mountains. His health condition was such that we had to take him back to his family for care. My brother Pema was so fond of him, calling him "Ama," which actually means "mother," even though he was a middle-aged man. The other person is Bhumu, my great grandmother's maid. She was separated from us on our way to Lhasa during a skirmish with the Chinese. Fortunately, years later we learned that she had survived.

After spending a few weeks at Tawang and some time at Bomdila, we were moved to Missamari in Assam, where a huge population of Tibetan refugees had gathered and were being registered. Indian and Tibetan officials were making arrangements to send some refugees to Sikkim and other places in the Indian Himalayas to work as road laborers. These laborers were organized into brigades each led by a Tibetan. It was not compulsory to join a brigade if one felt confident of becoming self-supporting. My father made the latter choice, confident that the introduction letters from the Mindrolling Rinpoches would enable him to make a livelihood. He also had a very close relative in Darjeeling who had moved to India several years before. That is where we headed. I remember arriving in Darjeeling on a very rainy day, barefooted. On our train journey from Tezpur in Assam to Jalpaiguri in the foothills of Darjeeling, I lost one of my brand-new canvas shoes on the crowded train platform. As I thought I would have looked funny wearing only one shoe, I threw the other one away, much to my Ama-las' annoyance. Nevertheless, I felt a tremendous sense of happiness on arriving in Darjeeling. To this day I have very strong feelings about the place.

The majority of Tibetan refugees became road construction workers, building some of the most strategic roads in the Indian Himalayas. Sadly, thousands died from the change in climate, emotional stress, and previously unencountered diseases. Within a few years, vast numbers of Tibetans contracted tuberculosis, an illness unheard of in Tibet. On the other hand, there was freedom. Most importantly, Tibetans were once again able to practice their religion openly without fear of persecution. Out of great generosity, the Indian government slowly began settling Tibetans at more permanent locations, primarily in South India. Much of the land was forest that had to be cleared and prepared for farming. Initially it was a very hard life, but gradually the Tibetans built thriving communities where their religion and culture were rekindled. One of His Holiness's highest priorities was establishing schools exclusively for Tibetan refugee children. Indian Prime Minister Nehru actively supported this effort.

## STARTING OVER IN DARJEELING AND KALIMPONG

While my father must have felt tremendous satisfaction at having brought his family to safety, our arrival in India marked the beginning of a new and difficult life for him and my mothers. My parents were quite extraordinary, refusing to dwell on the past, unlike many other prominent Tibetan families who could not face the trials of being poor refugees. Within a year of our arrival, my parents were running a small restaurant in Darjeeling catering mainly to Indian laborers. Of course, they had no money, so they couldn't buy the restaurant. Instead, they assumed a monthly lease from a Tibetan family who had been settled in the area for a long time. Every morning my mothers would go to the local vegetable market to collect fresh, discarded vegetables to supplement their meager income. Later on, with their hard-earned money they were able to buy a small restaurant that they named Gangjong—Land of Snow—that served a slightly more affluent clientele. As of this writing, the restaurant is still there, now owned by a close family friend.

My parents' effort to run an upscale restaurant, sadly, was a failure. They bought a restaurant called the Blue Star on Gandhi Road, a road frequented by and catering to tourists. Just a few months into their restaurant contract and with the business doing quite well, they had a surprise visit by Kyabjé Chatral Rinpoche at their residence. He expressed deep sadness and disappointment that the chieftain of Nyarong and a great patron of the Dharma was now running a restaurant contributing to the slaughter of many animals. Catering to well-off tourists, not surprisingly, included serving a number of chicken dishes. Even though no chickens were slaughtered in the restaurant, being devoted to Kyabjé Chatral Rinpoche, my parents then and there decided to stop serving any meat dishes, especially chicken. Not surprisingly, this was the end of a promising business. My parents soon sold the restaurant at a considerable loss.

In the early 1960s, providing a positive note amidst the hardship and challenges of their new life in exile, my parents received the uplifting news of the arrival of Minling Dungse Gyurmé Kunzang Wangyal in Bhutan. While they continued to be sad that Minling Chung Rinpoche and Minling Khenchen Rinpoche could not make the journey, the news of Minling Dungse Rinpoche's safe arrival lessened their sorrow.

Soon after, Minling Dungse Rinpoche sent an urgent message to my parents asking them to bring him to Darjeeling. My parents were short on cash and had few other valuables, by then having already sold most of the limited amount of jewelry they had managed to bring out of Tibet. They had owned some beautiful pieces of turquoise and coral that were still on display years later in the glass cabinets of Habeeb Mullick & Son, a curio shop on Chowrasta Mall in Darjeeling. They had only their Dzi beads left to sell, but in those days the beads had little value and fetched almost nothing. With these limited funds Uncle Tsultrim immediately left for Rangia in Assam on the Bhutanese border. He then crossed over to Samdrup Jongkhar in southeast Bhutan. Minling Dungse Rinpoche was accompanied by Khochhen Rinpoche and his attendant Tashi, as well as Jangchup from Lhodrak, who acted as their guide, and three of his faithful dogs, which he had managed to bring all the way from Mindrolling. When Minling Dungse Rinpoche originally contacted my parents, he said there would be seven in the group. To our pleasant surprise it was not seven people, as we were expecting, but four people and three dogs!

Minling Dungse Rinpoche stayed with my parents for over nine months. My siblings were fortunate to be tutored by him in Tibetan reading and writing. With the news of his arrival, officials of the TGiE and many other eminent Rinpoches began visiting him. While this kept my mothers very busy, it was a joyful period for them. Among the most senior Nyingma masters, Kyabjé Dilgo Khyentse Rinpoche was a frequent visitor showing immense respect and fondness for Minling Dungse Rinpoche. In consultation with His Holiness Kyabjé Dudjom Rinpoche, he invited Minling Dungse Rinpoche to Kalimpong, where he was later enthroned in a ceremony presided over by His Holiness Kyabjé Dudjom Rinpoche and attended by many of the most prominent masters of the Nyingma tradition. Minling Dungse Rinpoche thus officially became Minling Trichen Gyurmé Kunzang Wangyal, the Eleventh Trichen (throne holder) of the great Mindrolling lineage. My parents felt a special sense of gratitude to Kyabjé Dilgo Khyentse Rinpoche for the deep affection and respect that he had extended to Minling Trichen Rinpoche.

Our family never made it to either Bhutan or Sikkim. Moreover, despite the letters of introduction we carried from the Mindrolling Rinpoches requesting support, we did not receive much help from the local families devoted to these Rinpoches. Some of them were not in sound financial condition themselves and thus could provide very little. A number of them did become close family friends, however, and their devotion to the Mindrolling Rinpoches was genuine and deep. My father did approach some members of the Sikkimese royal family; their response, however, seems to have been lukewarm.

By contrast, Minling Chung Rinpoche's close friends, His Holiness the 16th Gyalwa Karmapa and Kyabjé Trijang Rinpoche, the junior tutor of His Holiness the 14th Dalai Lama, actively sought us out to offer their help. His Holiness

The author traveling with Minling Trichen Rinpoche by train to Kyoto, Japan, 1983

the Gyalwa Karmapa and Kyabjé Trijang Rinpoche had known my parents since 1955, when they spent many days with them at Dartsedo on their return from Beijing as part of the Dalai Lama's entourage. My senior mother accompanied her uncle Minling Chung Rinpoche to many of the functions and social gatherings to which the two Rinpoches were invited.

During a brief visit to Darjeeling in the early 1960s, His Holiness the 16th Gyalwa Karmapa invited our family to visit him, offering to help in any way he could. He was staying at the Oberoi Everest Hotel, and as a young boy what I remember most clearly is his sitting cross-legged on a huge bed. He affectionately told me to climb up and sit next to him. I remember embarrassingly falling on him as I lost my balance on the spring mattress, a contraption I had never encountered before. His Holiness roared with laughter, amused by my predicament. He had already started gathering young reincarnates and educating them at Rumtek Monastery outside Gangtok in Sikkim. He was quite keen on my coming to join the other young tulkus under his care.[14]

Kyabjé Trijang Rinpoche similarly offered to help. I remember walking from Darjeeling to Samten Choling Monastery at Ghoom, a little over six kilometers, to visit him. I'm not sure why we walked, but most probably we did not have the money to hire a taxi for the trip. He spent a long time with us, mostly talking with my parents about our needs, but also about the situation inside Tibet. He further shared with us details about his visit to Mindrolling Monastery with the Dalai Lama's senior tutor, Kyabjé Ling Rinpoche, on their way into exile, during which they urged Minling Chung Rinpoche to join them.

I think His Holiness wanted all the lineage heads to be with him in exile. By that time the major Sakya lineage holders, as well as the Gyalwa Karmapa, had already reached India. I remember Kyabjé Trijang Rinpoche comforting my parents by saying that even though Minling Chung Rinpoche could not immediately depart, he would leave when there was an opportunity. We independently knew that was Minling Chung Rinpoche's intention, but unfortunately, events turned out differently. As I was still in my robes at the time, Kyabjé Trijang Rinpoche encouraged me to pursue my studies, further offering to look after me provided I also had a tutor guiding me in my own lineage's traditions. He was quite intent on my having a Nyingma tutor, most probably to avoid criticism that he was trying to bring me up in the Gelug tradition. Kyabjé Trijang Rinpoche was so kind as to further tell my parents that even though he himself had limited resources, they should never hesitate to ask him for help.

Years later, in the late 1960s, my father became critically ill while attending meetings in Dharamsala. His symptoms indicated poisoning. Even the divinations were showing grave outcomes. My senior mother, Nordzin Lhamo, and I went to visit Kyabjé Trijang Rinpoche to inform him of my father's critical condition. True to his word, he immediately called his secretary Palden-la, instructing him to bring ten thousand Indian rupees to help with medical expenses. In those days, this was a huge amount. His generosity literally saved my father's life.

Just a few months before he passed away, Kyabjé Trijang Rinpoche asked me to visit him. He gave me several precious relics, all previously belonging to renowned Nyingma masters. They included small scraps of Guru Padmasambhava's clothes, some hair of the great female master Yeshe Tsogyal, clothes belonging to Tertön Guru Chowang and the great Dzogchen master Gyalwa Longchen Rabjam, and many other special relics from Mindrolling. He told me that when the Great Thirteenth Dalai Lama's golden mausoleum was being built, the Tibetan government collected precious relics and substances from the major monasteries of all the Tibetan Buddhist traditions to be enshrined within it. As these items are extremely precious and irreplaceable, they were divided equally among His Holiness the 14th Dalai Lama, His Holiness's senior tutor, Kyabjé Ling Rinpoche, and himself as the junior tutor. When the Dalai Lama fled Tibet, his entourage was unable to carry many personal belongings. Kyabjé Trijang Rinpoche, however, felt that these precious items could not be left behind. He thus carried his share into exile.

A few years after arriving in India, he divided his share into three equal parts, offering one to His Holiness and one to Kyabjé Ling Rinpoche. I remember him mischievously telling me, "Many of your own Nyingma masters may not have some of these precious relics." He was such a thoughtful and caring person. Kyabjé Trijang Rinpoche also took a keen interest in global as well as Tibetan political issues. From his observations and questions, one could see that he kept himself well informed. The senior tutor to His Holiness, Kyabjé Ling Rinpoche, as the following episode demonstrates, was the opposite, totally uninterested in worldly affairs. I had the honor of visiting him from time to time with my close friend Sonam Topgyal, and even received quite a few initiations from him.

Sonam Topgyal and my other good friend, Tethong Tenzin Namgyal, were in those days running Sheja Publications, a Tibetan-language journal. In later days, when I went to visit Kyabjé Ling Rinpoche, he was very kind to make an effort to talk about current events or other worldly matters. He would ask, for example, "How is Sheja Publications?" His secretary would correct him, reminding him that I worked for the CTA and not at Sheja. What I am trying to say is that he took very little interest in mundane affairs; rather, this great teacher and scholar was truly one of those who had the qualities of Khe-Tsun-Zang Sum, "Learned, Virtuous, and Noble," that all great teachers are expected to embody. Sadly, such qualities are becoming increasingly rare, and in the future, I fear there may be even fewer teachers embodying these attributes. Fortunately for me, the late Kyabjé Trulshik Rinpoche was one. He ultimately became the head of the Nyingma tradition and was also one of His Holiness the 14th Dalai Lama's teachers.

Years later, we came into contact with the Bhutanese family to whom Mindrolling Chung Rinpoche had intended to introduce us had we traveled through Bhutan. Tulku Nuden Dorji personally came to Darjeeling to meet with my parents. We have no doubt that his family would have extended all the help my family needed had we chosen to travel through his country. Had we gone through Bhutan, we would have settled down there, and our lives certainly would have been different.

Perhaps the Gyari family has some strong karmic connection or responsibility to serve His Holiness the 14th Dalai Lama and the Tibetan people. Living in India, rather than Bhutan, enabled not only me but also my brothers Pema Gyalpo, Dorjee Thogmay, and Kunzang Tsewang, as well as my sister Dolma Gyari, to serve the Tibetan cause. Pema Gyalpo, who was sent to Japan for his studies, became the first person to set up an office representing His Holiness there. After stepping down from that position, he became a professor at Gifu Women's University and later at Toin University of Yokohama. He is now a professor at Takushoku University, Tokyo, in the Department of Japanese Culture. He continues to be professor emeritus at both Gifu Women's University and Toin. He has authored and translated nearly seventy books, some of them best sellers, all in Japanese.

For many years Dorjee Thogmay worked in Delhi at the Joint Center[15] before moving to the United States as a broadcaster with the Voice of America. Kunzang Tsewang served for twenty years as an elected representative of the Nyingma tradition in the Tibetan Parliament. My youngest sibling, Dolma Gyari, is a born activist and leader. She was active with the Tibetan Youth Congress, the Tibetan Women's Association, and several other NGOs. She was elected to the Tibetan Parliament representing the Kham region for several terms and broke the glass ceiling in 2008 when she became the first woman to be elected Deputy Speaker. As the position of Deputy Speaker outranks that of Kalon in the Tibetan administrative hierarchy, when she held that position she was the highest-ranking female in the Tibetan leadership. In 2013, she was appointed as a Kalon charged with the Home Department portfolio, serving in that position for five years. I think she did a remarkable job bringing many benefits to the Tibetan community.

As I wrote earlier, my parents literally took full responsibility for the children of the Gyaltsoktsang. Their father, Gyaltsok Gonpo, became one of the earliest casualties of the Chinese and left his children virtual orphans. My family formally adopted the youngest, C. Wangdi (aka Sulu), and he thus became a Gyari. He was ultimately sent by the Tibetan authorities to work with Indian Intelligence and served in very difficult and remote areas in northeast India for decades. In the mid-1960s, he was actually the major contributor to the family livelihood. He was definitely receiving far better pay than I was! Every few months he would come home to visit and hand his entire salary over to my parents. His elder brother, Rilu, also worked at the Joint Center until he retired.

After my eldest daughter married a Bhutanese, I met with Ugyen, a Nyarongwa elder then living in Kathmandu. He was very happy that one of my children had moved to Bhutan. He told me of a prophecy by Gyarong Ter-gyen Ma, a Treasure Master of the last century from Gyarong, indicating my family would have a strong connection with that country. I remember telling him that my other daughter, Tenzing Choyang, is also married to a Bhutanese. He was surprised to learn this as he thought her husband, Neten Chokling Rinpoche, was Tibetan. In fact, this was the common belief because Neten Chokling Rinpoche's predecessors were very respected Tibetan Treasure Masters.

Years later, I again went to see Ugyen in Kathmandu, eager to record Gyarong Ter-gyen Ma's exact prophecy. Sadly, by then he was in poor health and his memory was not sufficiently sharp to share the text with me. Not long afterward, he passed away. I do remember that it was a two-verse prophecy, saying something about the female dragon returning to the land of the dragon. Interestingly, as I noted earlier, Nyarong's main castle (*dzong*) is called the Drukmo Dzong, meaning Female Dragon Castle or Fortress. As Bhutan is known as the Land of the Dragon, the prophecy seems to have come true. I am still on the lookout for the original text containing the prophecy, but I am not confident I will ever discover it, as few of Gyarong Ter-gyen Ma's prophecy texts seem to have survived.

As I now have family in Bhutan, I am able to visit often. Every time I land in Paro, I have very strong but mixed emotions, a profound feeling of sadness accompanied by a deep sense of happiness. I'm sad because Bhutan reminds me not only of my home[16] but also of what has been lost in Tibet—our culture, religion, and way of life. At the same time, I feel a great sense of joy because here in this remote Himalayan kingdom our common religion and culture are not only being preserved but actually thriving. The Bhutanese are fortunate to have a monarchy that reveres and cares for its distinct heritage. Even more than I hear Tibetans in Dharamsala, I hear Bhutanese officials and scholars proudly quoting the Ten Moral Principles and Sixteen Rules of Public Conduct proclaimed by the Tibetan Emperor Songtsen Gampo.

The contributions of Her Majesty, the Royal Grandmother, Ashi Kesang Choden Wangchuck, of Bhutan alone have been monumental. When I expressed to her my sincere appreciation of her work, she refused all credit, insisting that it was due to the blessings of the Three Jewels[17] and, most importantly, to the actions of Kyabjé Dilgo Khyentse Rinpoche, her root teacher. Her Majesty also remarked that in her opinion, His Holiness the 14th Dalai Lama's activities blossomed after he became connected to Kyabjé Dilgo Khyentse Rinpoche, to the great benefit of all sentient beings. I shared her comments with His Holiness, which he sincerely appreciated.

My parents taught me and my siblings to have pride and dignity in who we are, but they never allowed our family's privileged heritage to inflate our egos. After learning more details about our family history, one of my sisters, Jamyang Dolma, who was born in exile, exclaimed: "I always thought we were from a poor family!" My parents rarely spoke about the grandeur of the past, instead encouraging us to live our lives in the present.

In exile, my father gave the highest priority to a modern education. While he was convinced that I am the reincarnation of his teacher, he nevertheless also seemed to want me to pursue a nonmonastic life. This may be the reason the very kind offers by His Holiness Gyalwa Karmapa Rinpoche and Kyabjé Trijang Rinpoche were not seriously considered. He also knew that I was too old to go to the regular school my other siblings were attending. With the help of Gyalo Thondup's wife, I went to stay with Gordon Temple, a Scottish tea planter and orchid aficionado, at Marybong Tea Estate in Darjeeling, mainly to study English with his visiting mother from Scotland. Uncle Tsultrim and I looked after his beautiful shrine room and also performed some religious rituals for him. We had a wonderful stay at Marybong, and it was there that I learned my first English, a skill that at the time I had no idea was to become so handy.

During this same time, select groups of young Tibetan men were being given crash courses in English to serve as translators for the CIA operatives. Tenzin Tsering, Tamdin Wangyal, and I were selected for this instruction. We were first sent to Dr. Graham's Homes in Kalimpong and later to Mount Hermon School in Darjeeling. Tenzin and Tamdin were both distant relatives of Yabshi, the Dalai Lama's family. Because of the highly secretive nature of the CIA involvement, only young men whose families were already involved in the program or others who were able to meet strict screening criteria were solicited. We were told to study the language earnestly because at any moment we could be called into service. It was also made clear to us that any chance for a more comprehensive education was not an option, as there was an urgent need for translators.

In early 1963, my friend Tenzin Tsering, who was the oldest among the three of us, stopped coming to classes. Within weeks, he simply vanished. We were not even allowed to ask after his whereabouts. Several months later, I was also informed that I no longer needed to go to school. Rather, I should visit Kalimpong to spend a few days with my parents and prepare to begin my service as a translator. I was just a teenager, and I was very excited. In fact, throughout our time at Mount Hermon, the three of us lived rather different lives from the rest of our schoolmates, who had no clue why we were in the school in the first place. We reveled in the knowledge that we would be serving as translators for the CIA operatives, fantasizing about the actual activities we would undertake and even hoping we would be parachuted into Tibet to join the resistance movement.

When I went to visit my parents in Kalimpong to bid farewell, I remember my mothers were not at all happy. My father, on the other hand, seemed fine with my being sent away. I stayed only two days and then returned to Darjeeling, ready to be shipped off. However, weeks and then months went by, and still there were no instructions for me. One early morning in April 1963, my younger roommate, Tamdin Wangyal, vanished as had Tenzin Tsering before him. This was a clear sign that he was being dispatched while I was not selected. I was very depressed. I felt I wasn't trusted, and this deeply affected me. I was soon told to join *Defend Tibet's Freedom Press*, a Tibetan-language journal that had just been launched by the Chushi Gangdrug and was headed by Barchung Thutop Gonpo, a prominent chieftain from Derge. Four other Chushi Gangdrug leaders were his deputies: Taso Choezey, Bapa Gyen Kelsang, Churu Dhondrup Phuntsok, and Amdo Kato, representing the Amdo region. I later learned that the publication was being funded by the CIA together with another newspaper, *The Tibetan Freedom*, both of which were being published in Darjeeling. It was then that I began contributing to the family's upkeep. I received 75 Indian rupees per month as my salary. This was about the same rate of pay as Tibetan officials serving in Dharamsala and other places.

Years later, in a very casual conversation with Lhamo Tsering, the person principally involved in selecting the individuals to be trained as translators to assist in the CIA operations, I learned that my father had explicitly requested him not to send me for training. My mothers were adamantly opposed to my serving in such a role because of my position as a reincarnate. Unlike my friend Tenzin, who was sent to Colorado for training, Tamdin was sent directly to Nepal to work as a liaison coordinator for the CIA Mustang operation. Unfortunately, the Nepalese authorities became aware of his involvement with the CIA. He was arrested in July 1964 and imprisoned for over a year, enduring much suffering and ill treatment. His CIA collaborator managed to leave Nepal and I am sure was informally warned or even formally advised by the Nepalese to do so. While they did not hesitate to put my friend in prison, the Nepalese authorities certainly did not want to confront the mighty Americans. Tamdin's fate could easily have been mine had my parents not intervened. My friends Tenzin Tsering and Tamdin Wangyal have both emigrated to the United States, where they continue to live with their families. We remain very close but without as many opportunities to meet as we would like.

A number of years later, Cornell University in Ithaca, New York, started a special nondegree program mostly for Tibetans who had worked with the CIA and had not had the opportunity to complete a regular school curriculum. I think three different groups of students participated. I was selected for the last group. Once again, at the last moment, my parents used their "influence" to take me off the list. This time their reason was that I would disrobe if I went to the West. Technically, I had already disrobed in Darjeeling at Gyalo Thondup's house when I went to Kalimpong to study at Dr. Graham's Homes. I literally walked into his second-floor residence at Shiva Bhawan on Gandhi Road with my robes on and came out wearing khaki shorts! Many years later when I was working at the Bureau of His Holiness in New Delhi, I found the identity certificate allowing me to travel to the United States to participate in Cornell's program. Had I gone there or been shipped off like Tamdin and Tenzin for CIA training, my life would have taken an entirely different direction. It was, of course, my parents' immediate actions that guided me toward the professional career I ultimately assumed, but I can't help thinking that some unseen forces were also involved in mapping my future.

## MY FATHER'S LEGACY

Every Tibetan who crossed into exile had one common enemy: Communist China, the enemy of his faith, and one common goal: resisting its rule. Many Khampa leaders hoped to return to Tibet to continue their resistance with increased CIA support. Influential chieftains and lamas from both Kham and Amdo, including my father, were also keen to establish connections with Chiang Kai-shek's Nationalist government in Taiwan. This relationship made sense. Large areas of eastern Tibet were under the nominal rule of the Nationalist government on the eve of the Communist invasion, and powerful chieftains such as my father had been given rank and title by the Nationalists.[18] Being educated in China and fluent in Mandarin gave my father even more incentive to reestablish ties with the KMT. While we were in Darjeeling, one of my father's retainers, Sonam Tenzing, even approached Gyalo Thondup's wife to convey to Chiang Kai-shek that my father had safely arrived in India and was keen to reconnect. There was a rumor that she was Chiang Kai-shek's niece. There is, in fact, some basis for this, as she was the daughter of Zhu Shigui, a general in the KMT military.

However, while we were in Darjeeling my father became close to Andruk Gonpo Tashi, the resistance leader, who impressed upon him the importance of Tibetans of all three regions coming together under the leadership of His Holiness the 14th Dalai Lama to strive for independence for a unified Tibet. Because of his understanding of contemporary politics, my father immediately grasped the importance of a unified nation and became firmly committed to that goal. As I discuss in part II, this shared vision was ultimately formalized on February 3, 1960, in Bodhgaya, when prominent Tibetan religious leaders and laypersons from U-tsang, Kham and Amdo took the Great Oath of Unity in the presence of His Holiness.[19]

My father dedicated the rest of his life to this pursuit, becoming a fierce advocate for a unified Tibet and a staunch supporter of the Dalai Lama. At times, however, he was disappointed with some of the Tibetan leadership's policies. He felt that many dedicated loyalists from all regions of Tibet were being marginalized or disregarded and that certain crucial policies were being manipulated by self-serving individuals, resulting in harm to Tibet's greater interests. During his lifetime, not a single Nyarongwa was involved in any activities against the Central Tibetan Administration; they all remained loyal and devoted to His Holiness. This must have given my father a deep sense of pride and satisfaction.

His dedication and loyalty were graciously acknowledged by His Holiness in a taped message he sent when my father was terminally ill in Delhi. His Holiness applauded my father's commitment and dedication to the Tibetan cause and the loyalty extended to him personally. Most importantly, he gave my father precious instructions on how to face the inevitable. Below is a translation of His Holiness's message:

> You have done your best throughout your life and have been very sincere and loyal to the just cause of Tibet, i.e., to protect the Dharma and secular affairs of Tibet. Sometimes you have been even overenthusiastic. We have known each other closely for the last forty years. You have always been very candid and steadfast in your endeavor to support the position of the Tibetan government. . . .
>
> You have conveyed some points to me that are in a way like your last wishes. I also got emotional. I am very pleased to learn that even in your last wishes you spoke about the Tibetan cause. . . .
>
> Now, the most important thing to do from your side is to take refuge in the Lama, the Three Jewels, and Guru Padmasambhava in particular, as you have been practicing it, by visualizing him upon the crown of your head. Pray to Guru that henceforth whatever happens, whether alive or dead and in circumstances good or bad, you are my only protection—Protect me, Guru Padmasambhava! Pray and invoke Guru with single-pointed devotion so that you are able to unite your mind with Guru. . . .
>
> Similarly, you should generate good motivation, whether it is to think about Bodhicitta or the Tibetan cause. It is important to rejoice and properly dedicate the merits you have accumulated during your lifetime. When you reach the final stage, it will be helpful if you pray and dedicate that by virtue of merits you have accumulated working wholeheartedly for the just cause of Tibet, may you be able to serve the cause of Tibet for many lives to come. And finally, be happy and don't worry. I consider you as my old friend, who is loyal and reliable. Therefore, I will never forget you. I will pray for you.[20]

My father remained lucid until the last moment. On the day of his passing, August 30, 1999, as the first ray of sunlight hit the glass window of his hospital room at Rajiv Gandhi Cancer Institute & Research Center, he became very alert and excitedly tried to sit up. Bringing his right hand to his chest in the gesture of reverence, in a weak but very clear voice he said: "Kundun has come! Kundun has come!"[21] Family members, relatives, and other Nyarongwas were in turn looking after him, and that particular morning my younger mother, my brother Pema Gyalpo, and Lama Tsewang, another relative, were in the room. They all witnessed this extraordinary phenomenon, a manifestation of the power of faith. My father died that afternoon. He was supposed to leave that very night for New York to be treated at Memorial Sloan Kettering Cancer Center. I think he did not wish to make the trip and die in a far-off land. Two of the closest family Rinpoches, Khochhen Rinpoche and Ringo Tulku Rinpoche, had come to Delhi to bless him before his trip. They came immediately to the hospital after my father passed away to conduct the appropriate prayers.

What makes me most proud of my father is that when he was terminally ill, he refused to allow me to prolong my stay with him in Delhi but asked me to return to Washington, D.C., to serve His Holiness and the Tibetan cause. That is precisely what I did, and as a result I was not able to be by his side when he passed away. Despite my grief at his passing, I felt then and still feel a sense of pride and gratitude because I carried out his last wishes. I was able to rush back to India in time for his cremation that took place within the grounds of Mindrolling Monastery in Dehradun.

My father was truly fortunate. Mindrolling Trichen Rinpoche personally came to our house in Dehradun and performed *phowa*, the rite of transferring the consciousness that is important at the time of death in the Tibetan Buddhist tradition. The night before, my mothers, siblings, and many others had accompanied my father's body to Dehradun, making the long journey by road from Delhi. It was quite early when Mindrolling Trichen Rinpoche came unannounced to our house to bless my father. Many of the family were still sleeping, physically exhausted by the trip and mentally distraught by my father's passing. The following day my father was cremated amidst elaborate rituals and prayers. A beautiful stupa has since been erected on the spot where he was cremated. Today, in Mindrolling Monastery's beautiful garden one can still see my father's memorial stupa next to that of Jetsün Tsewang Lhamo, one of the daughters of Mindrolling Tritsab Pema Wangchen,[22] who also passed away in exile.

It must be my father's strong karmic connection with his native land that Rinpoches, Khenpos, and monks from fourteen different monasteries in Nyarong and nearby places came to participate in parts of the last rites prayer ceremonies that we held for forty-nine days at our home in New Delhi. We later learned that many of the monasteries in Nyarong observed the full forty-nine-day prayer rituals for my father as well.

After my father's cremation, besides having several monks conduct the ritual prayers at our Delhi residence, we held the first week passing-away anniversary at Mindrolling Monastery in Dehradun, the second week anniversary at the Palyul Choekhorling Monastery in Bir, and the third week rites at Nechung Monastery in Dharamsala. These three monasteries have very special connections with my family. I wrote extensively about our special relationship with Mindrolling in earlier chapters. Palyul Choekhorling Monastery in Bir is headed by Ringo Tulku Rinpoche, a very close family friend highly respected by my parents. The monastery's founder, Khenpo Pema Rabgey, was also someone my parents highly respected. Nechung, the seat of the State Oracle of Tibet, is another monastery with which my family maintained close connections. The State Oracle has always shown special fondness for me during the trances when it is delivering prophecies. I sometimes deliberately tried to avoid being too visible or establishing eye contact with the Oracle because I did not want to embarrass my colleagues by seeming to receive preferential treatment from it.

His Holiness the 14th Dalai Lama personally graced our family by presiding over my father's last rites ceremony at Nechung Monastery, further offering some extremely kind remarks to our family and friends gathered that day. Such a gesture is extremely rare, virtually unprecedented. "Whether a person has led a meaningful life becomes evident when that person is no more with us. Gyari Nyima led a meaningful life. He had one fault—at times he was too loyal to the Gaden Phodrang and me."

༄༅། །བསྟོད་གངས་རིའི་ར་བས་སྐོར་བའི་ཞིང་ཁམས་འདི།།
ལྷ་ཨོ་རྒྱན་པད་མའི་དམ་ཆོས་སྤེལ་ས་དང་།།
བློན་ཐོན་མིས་ཡི་གེ་སྤེལ་ས་རེད།།
གླིང་གེ་སར་རྒྱལ་པོའི་འཁྲུངས་ས་རེད།།

སྟོད་ཉི་མ་ལྷ་སའི་མན་ཆད་དང་།།
བར་མང་ཡུལ་ཕྱུག་མོའི་རྒྱུན་ཆད་ནས།།
སྨད་མདོ་ཁམས་དར་མདོ་ཡན་ཆད་ཀྱི།།
ཚོལ་གསུམ་སྤུན་ཟླ་ཚོ།།
བསམ་པའི་ཁ་ཕྱོགས་གཅིག་དགོས།།
ཇོག་རྩ་གཅིག་སྒྲིལ་མཉམ་དུ་བསྐྱོད་དགོས།།
མ་འོངས་མདུན་ལམ་མཉམ་དུ་འཚོལ་དགོས།།
ཨ་རོགས། ཨ་རོགས་བོད་པ་ཚོ། མཉམ་དུ་འགྲོ །།

Praise the Land of Snows
Where Padmasambhava transmitted dharma
Where Sambotta composed the script
And the land where King Gesar was born

From the west of Ngari, Lhasa and to the east of Dartsedo
The Tibetans from the three provinces
Must have the same purpose of thought
Must go united hand in hand
And seek future aspirations together
Aro! Tibetans!
Aro! Let's go together![1]

# PART II

# *Tibet Restored*

## Reuniting the Tibetan People

On February 3, 1960, soon after His Holiness came into exile in India, high-ranking officials of the Lhasa government, spiritual masters, chieftains, and resistance leaders from across the Tibetan Plateau assembled at Bodhgaya to affirm the unity of Tibet's three regions—U-Tsang, Kham, and Amdo—under the leadership of His Holiness the 14th Dalai Lama. During the darkest period of our history, leaders of my father's generation from all regions of Tibet came together and took the farsighted decision to once again become one nation, in which no Tibetan would be excluded. On that historic day, at the most holy site of Buddhism, where Lord Buddha was awakened and realized the ultimate truth, the Tibetan people woke up from their historic slumber and realized the necessity to reunite under the common leadership of His Holiness, thus revitalizing the historic bond among them. With single-mindedness of purpose, they put their trust in an individual whose wisdom they believed would guarantee a brighter future for the Tibetan people. They took the Great Oath of Unity[2] and, under the guidance and wise leadership of His Holiness the 14th Dalai Lama, took the first steps toward realizing the vision of a reunited Tibet.

Why did Tibet have to be "restored" or "revitalized"? Why did the Tibetans feel the need to affirm unity? What prompted His Holiness to accept this pledge of allegiance from Tibetans of all three regions and Tibetan Buddhist traditions and to initiate the path of democracy to realize the goal of a reunited Tibet? This section of my narrative explores these fundamental and intriguing questions.

# CHAPTER 8

# A Unified Tibet

## *Centerpiece of the Tibetan Struggle*

The concept of a unified Tibet has become the centerpiece of the Tibetan struggle. The preciousness of this aspiration cannot be appreciated without understanding the complex nature of Tibet's history. This includes consideration of the historic relationship among the different regions of Tibet and of Tibet's interactions with others over the centuries. Added to this must be the Tibetan people's hopes and dreams for the future. The vision of a unified Tibet reflects the Tibetan people's heartfelt desires and motivates our actions. It is the overriding goal of our movement, inspiring many of us to dedicate our lives to achieving that result.

### HISTORICAL BACKGROUND

For too long, Tibet's history has been oversimplified and distorted by the Chinese, and others, who have ignored the historically complicated relationship that existed for centuries amongst Tibetans and between Tibet and its neighbors. The relationship between the various dynasties that ruled China and those institutions administering Tibet was at times adversarial, but for the most part was of a special and rather extraordinary nature. Most importantly, it is a relationship that cannot be interpreted or well understood using the contemporary Eurocentric way of looking at nation-state relations.

The very concept of a "nation-state," based on Western ideas and contemporary usage, is not applicable to Tibet's historical status and its external relations as they existed over time in our part of the world. The Western concept of "suzerainty" is a prime example of this misfit. It is an outdated concept created in medieval Europe to describe relations between the pope and various principalities. In those days it was a useful label for countries seeking the support of the Vatican while having no desire to compromise their sovereignty. That situation bears no resemblance to the complex historical relationship between Tibet and China. Yet the British latched on to the term and somehow planted it in the minds of the Manchu court as defining China's relationship with Tibet. But the incongruous, yet illuminating fact is that there is no Chinese word for this concept. How can one entity assert the existence of this kind of jurisdiction over another without having a word or phrase in its lexicon even remotely describing it?

In 1992, the International People's Tribunal conducted a hearing on Tibet's legal status in Strasbourg, France. We initially engaged Michael van Walt van Praag, an international lawyer with extensive knowledge of Tibet's legal status, to represent our interests. But at the last moment, I decided to defend the case myself to reinforce the message that the status of Tibet and its relations with neighboring countries over the centuries is best explained by a representative of our own people, grounded in our culture and traditions, rather than through Western eyes employing a Eurocentric analysis. I stated:

> It is an honor for me to serve as prosecutor during these proceedings. My name is Lodi Gyaltsen Gyari and I was born in Nyarong, in the Tibetan province of Kham. I am President of the International Campaign for Tibet, a non-governmental organization which promotes and monitors human rights and environmental issues in Tibet and educates policymakers concerning Tibet. I have spent my entire adult life fighting for the Tibetan cause and serving the people of Tibet in the following capacities, among others: editor of *Tibetan Freedom* and founding editor of *Tibetan Review*; one of the founders and President of the Tibetan Youth Congress, member and Chairman of the Tibetan Parliament, member of the Cabinet of the Tibetan Government-in-Exile, member of high-level negotiating teams with the PRC, head of the Tibet UN Initiative, and Cabinet-ranking Special Envoy of His Holiness the Dalai Lama.
>
> I feel particularly qualified to present the story of the suffering of the Tibetan people, as my life and the lives of my family members have been drastically altered as a result of the repressive policies pursued by the Chinese occupiers. In other words, the issue at hand is the issue of the very life and death of my people.[1]

From a Western political perspective, Tibet was not a unified nation for periods of its history. Even the relationship among Tibetans in the three regions of Tibet and that among the different Tibetan Buddhist and non-Buddhist religious sects were very complex. However, deep in their psyche, Tibetans have always thought of themselves as a single people united through shared values and traditions at the deepest level. You ask a Tibetan from any part of Tibet about his or her origin of ancestry, and he or she will tell you without hesitation that we are all children of the monkey Pha Trelgen Changchup Sempa, an emanation of Avalokiteśvara, and the rock ogress Ma Drag Sinmo, a manifestation of the goddess Tara. He or she will also proudly say that we are all descendants of the Choegyal Mewon Namsum, or the Three Supreme Chakravartins,[2] the Emperors of Tibet, specifically: Songtsen Gampo, the thirty-third Emperor; Trisong Deutsen, the thirty-eighth Emperor; and Tri Ralpachen, the forty-first Emperor.

It is only natural that the Tibetan people proudly connect with these three great emperors because it was during their reigns that Tibet as a nation reached the zenith of its glory. The prominence given their reigns, however, reflects a Buddhist-centric approach to Tibet's history, as it was during these periods that Buddhism became firmly established and flourished. But in assessing Tibet's status as a nation, it is essential to include its history in pre-Buddhist times, a period virtually ignored by many scholars until recently. Songtsen Gampo, the most important of these three rulers, was in fact Tibet's thirty-third Emperor, demonstrating that Tibet as a nation existed long before his reign.

Professor Namkhai Norbu was one of the first modern Tibetan scholars to look at Tibet's political status from this historical perspective. But even as recently as the early 1980s, there was quite a bit of opposition from some purportedly "orthodox" elements when the Library of Tibetan Works and Archives in Dharamsala published his work *The Necklace of gZi: A Cultural History of Tibet.* Although the Library is an independent organization, at that time, for publications deemed historically or politically sensitive, it was required to seek approval from the Kashag (the cabinet). While I do not have a clear recollection, I believe my friend Sonam Topgyal, who was then Secretary of the Department of Information and Publicity (DIP), and I played a role in helping Gyatsho Tshering, then Director of the Library, obtain the Kashag's permission. In 1981, the DIP's Sheja Printing Press published a limited English edition that was reprinted in 1984. Sheja's successor ultimately became Narthang Publications under my direction.

Upon my becoming the Kalon of the Department of Information and International Relations (DIIR) in late 1988, we enlarged and modernized Narthang to establish a full-scale publishing house with its own printing press. We also ultimately set up an offset press. Although our primary objective was printing and publishing books in Tibetan, we also wanted to have facilities adequate to undertake printing in English. To meet these goals, the office was relocated to the ground floor of the new three-story Narthang Building that we constructed during my tenure. One of the first projects we undertook as the registered printing entity for DIIR publications was republishing the English version of *The Necklace of gZi*[3] for wider circulation, so that both Tibetans and the international community had access to a full and complete history of Tibet, including its political status.

We Tibetans tend to take a rather casual approach to historical facts, preferring our own rendition and perception of events. While I don't believe our people are alone in adopting such a biased view, it is essential to recognize irrefutable facts in one's background, whether it be that of an individual, an organization, or a nation. Historical research will reveal elements that, upon their very utterance, will make one either raise one's head with pride or lower it and weep with shame. But whatever the case may be, "history" cannot be based on delusion and preconceived notions, as fabricated versions of events cannot withstand scrutiny in the long run. Facts must be acknowledged no matter how difficult or inconvenient.

In the case of the Tibetan people, I have a feeling that many of us do not know, or even care to know, Tibet's history of recent decades, let alone past centuries. The majority of Tibetans who have grown up in exile believe that all three regions of Tibet were under single rule when Mao's Red Army marched into Tibet. This incorrect view is evident in their remarks and writings, including many official documents. Moreover, this misperception is not limited to Tibetans but is also prevalent among many Tibet supporters. This is a mistake that needs correcting. We cannot defend our rights based on alleged "facts," no matter how strongly asserted, that cannot withstand impartial scrutiny. Sadly, however, this erroneous picture has become so strongly ingrained in many people's minds that it is now a deeply emotional issue that prevents many of us from looking objectively at even the most recent events in our history.

Unlike many outside "experts" who write or talk about Tibet's contemporary history, I actually lived it. As discussed in part I, I was born in Kham, an eastern Tibetan region that was not ruled by the Lhasa-based Central Tibetan

The author, then DIIR Kalon, and the Narthang Building's architect, Kazuhiro Nakahara, reviewing the mandala design of the structure (see layout sketch) with His Holiness the 14th Dalai Lama, May 15, 1989. Also present: then Kalon Juchen Thubten, Kalon Alak Jigme, Kalon Shewo Lobsang Dhargye
Tibet Museum, CTA

Government. I belong to a prominent chieftain family that actively engaged in armed resistance against the Communist Chinese beginning in the mid-1950s. In 1959, my parents brought me into exile. From an early age, I became involved with the Tibetan movement, very much inspired by my father, Gyari Nyima Gyaltsen, and others of his generation, who were the architects of the reunification movement. I had the opportunity to serve His Holiness the 14th Dalai Lama until he devolved his political authority in 2011, thereby ending the Gaden Phodrang[4] system of governance. As a result of my personal experiences, I can say unequivocally that I understand the underpinnings and evolution of the Tibetan people's drive toward reunification.

The Great Fifth Dalai Lama, Ngawang Lobsang Gyatso, founded the Gaden Phodrang government in 1642. Centuries later, the Great Thirteenth, Thubten Gyatso, made tremendous efforts to maintain the Tibetan national identity, even as international politics swirled around him, incited by the machinations of imperial Britain, czarist Russia, and the Manchu authorities of China. In my opinion, the Great Thirteenth is the first Tibetan leader who understood the Western concept of a nation-state through his exposure to the outside world, primarily during his exile in India from 1910 to 1912 as a result of Manchu interference in Tibet. There is no question that he made serious efforts to reassert Tibetan political control over the eastern parts of Tibet. His minister Shatra Paljor Dorje reportedly took mule-loads of tax collection records and other documents to the Simla Tripartite Convention of 1914 that was held among representatives of British India, the Republic of China, and Tibet, to justify the legitimacy of the Lhasa government's claim to Tibetan areas east of the Drichu River.

As is the case with almost all Tibetans, the 14th Dalai Lama has deep admiration for his immediate predecessor. During his first visit to the West in 1973, the current Dalai Lama visited England for several days. Many descendants of former British officials who had had relations with Tibet during the reign of the Great Thirteenth called on him, bringing gifts from the previous era. When we were staying at The Abbey near Sutton Coldfield, one visitor brought a portrait of His Holiness's predecessor. I remember walking into His Holiness's living room and seeing him holding the picture, gazing at it with deep emotion. He turned the photo toward me and remarked with heartfelt admiration: "Lar-gan bar-tsag dhie ku-ley she-po chik kyon du-ga," meaning "This pock-faced monk struggled so hard!" His Holiness was referring to the scars from the chicken pox evident on the 13th Dalai Lama's face. Given his intimacy with his immediate predecessor, the 14th Dalai Lama's seemingly disparaging comment must be viewed as being offered with nothing but the sincerest affection.

Despite the accomplishments of the Great Thirteenth, it is Tenzin Gyatso, the 14th Dalai Lama, who gave new hope for Tibet's cohesiveness, creating a watershed moment in Tibet's history that has led to true unification in the Tibetan people's hearts and minds. He is the first among all the Dalai Lamas whose leadership is accepted with deep devotion by *all* Tibetans, no matter which region of Tibet they call home. This achievement alone truly makes His Holiness the 14th Dalai Lama the greatest among all the Dalai Lamas. Ironically, the Tibetan people's tragic suffering under the policies of the Communist Chinese has provided the historic opportunity for us to once again come together as one people and one nation under one leader. I consider realization of this unique opportunity my most sacred mission. I have made every effort to contribute to this goal. Indeed, I feel a deep sense of satisfaction explaining its essence to even one individual.

Obviously, the concept of a unified Tibet has made a deep impression on me. I first began to appreciate its importance in the weeks right after the Great Oath of Unity was taken in Bodhgaya. At the time, we were living in Darjeeling, a small Himalayan town in the state of West Bengal well known for its beautiful and lush tea gardens. Darjeeling was part of the Himalayan kingdom of Sikkim until it was leased to the British Raj, eventually becoming part of the Indian state of West Bengal. The name "Darjeeling" is, in fact, a corrupted version of the Tibetan word *Dorjeling*, which derives from the name of the famous Tibetan Treasure Revealer Dorje Lingpa (1346–1405), who visited Sikkim and Bhutan and established a strong following. I know some of his descendants living in Bhutan and Sikkim today.

Darjeeling and Kalimpong, a smaller town until recently within the same district, were the base for most of the Tibet-focused activities of the British Raj. The 13th Dalai Lama spent considerable time in both places during his exile. Darjeeling also gained prominence as the summer capital of the British Raj until 1911, when the British moved the capital from Calcutta to Delhi.

I remember hearing about the Oath like it was yesterday. The house where we lived, interestingly, was called Lhasa Villa and was situated about two kilometers south of Darjeeling town. It was a chilly morning, and my father was wearing a casual sheepskin *chupa* without a belt. He had convened a meeting of a handful of Nyarongwa members of his own clan who had gathered in Darjeeling. Some of them had fled Tibet with us, while others had arrived months later via different routes. He was holding the meeting on the open terrace of an abandoned construction site near our residence.

I was standing on the upper verandah of our house that overlooked the site. All of a sudden, I heard a commotion and saw one of the senior Nyarongwas, Lama Amba, sobbing and knocking his head repeatedly against my father's chest. As a child I realized it was not normal to see a grown man crying so loudly. I was shocked but also curious about what was going on. I understood later that this was the moment my father explained the details surrounding the Oath. He told his clansmen that Tibetans from Central Tibet, Kham, and Amdo had once again become unified, this time under the leadership of His Holiness the 14th Dalai

Lama. Thus, all Tibetans would be part of a unified Tibet with His Holiness as the collective leader going forward. He further added: "I am no more your *pon* or chieftain."

This last statement is what shocked his clansmen. They could not immediately comprehend its meaning. The assembled Nyarongwas felt that they were being let down by their own chieftain. This is what compelled Lama Amba to make such an outburst. It is our customary way of showing profound sorrow. Many of the people gathered there were loyal to the Gyari family, their forefathers having served our family for generations, some of them even having sacrificed their lives on our family's behalf. Watching my father, such a wise leader who was able to look beyond his personal interests, and a loyalist like Lama Amba, who had no option but to listen, was very inspiring and has remained cemented in my memory ever since.

While some Khampa chieftains formed settlements of their own clans in exile, my father did the opposite. He encouraged his people to integrate into the mainstream community and extend full loyalty to the Central Tibetan Administration (CTA), the exile government established in Dharamsala by His Holiness. This led to a handful of exile Nyarongwas settling in different parts of India and mingling with people from other regions of Tibet. But the bond between the Nyarongwas and my father never weakened. Until his passing away, Nyarongwas respected and were deeply devoted to him. He, in turn, did whatever was within his means to assist and guide them.

Many of the Nyarongwas who were gathered that morning with my father became actively involved with the Tibetan freedom struggle. Lama Amba and his two nephews, together with Rinchen Wangyal and several others, soon left for Nepal to join the CIA-supported guerilla movement based in Mustang. Other Nyarongwas, including Dogyal Aten, Kyowo Abhen, and Kalsang Dorje, were sent to the United States to be trained by the CIA. After completing their training, they served faithfully in various organizations. Dogyal Aten became a senior intelligence officer operating out of Kathmandu, while Kyowo Abhen was deputed to join the Special Frontier Forces (SFF),[5] an Indian paramilitary organization established by the government of India soon after the 1962 India-China war in exclusive cooperation with the Tibetans. Kalsang Dorje was sent to join the Mustang guerilla base, where he became a senior leader serving until the Nepalese government disbanded it.[6]

Most of the Amdowa and Khampa leaders of that time, including my father, had one mission in mind for the first few years in exile—to go back to Tibet and continue the resistance.

## NA-GAN THUMOCHE: THE GREAT OATH OF UNITY

Almost ten months into exile, a large congregation of Tibetans gathered at the holy site of Bodhgaya. His Holiness, the Kashag, and other officials from the Gaden Phodrang government, as well as spiritual masters from all the Tibetan Buddhist schools and important leaders from Kham and Amdo, were all there. For the Tibetan people, this was a defining moment: the collective affirmation that they were all Tibetans united under the leadership of His Holiness the 14th Dalai Lama and that this unity was the only option for fighting their common enemy.

This realization, or awakening, led those present to pledge the Great Oath of Unity on February 3, 1960:

> At such a time, all Tibetans will strongly atone for their past misdeeds, and in future shoulder our responsibility in accordance with the visions of His Holiness the Dalai Lama. Furthermore, we will eschew pursuance of personal name and fame driven by mutual jealousies and narrowmindedness, and remain united like an iron ball.
>
> There is no better way to achieve the short- and long-term collective happiness for all Tibetans other than for each of us to carry out his responsibilities per each person's ability, in accordance with His Holiness the Dalai Lama's deep vision and guidance.
>
> This being the unanimous observation of all of us, we have voluntarily and with our minds filled with happiness resolutely passed this resolution, and pledge never to violate it.[7]

Thus, a "reunited" Tibet emerged, and that Tibet is what the 14th Dalai Lama and Tibetans have been struggling for ever since. The Oath acknowledged past mistakes that had weakened the Tibetan nation and at the same time reaffirmed unity under His Holiness's leadership. It is based on equal respect for the unique characteristics of the three regions of Tibet and Tibet's various religious traditions and sects.

Prominent secular and religious leaders pledged, and then signed, the Oath. It was then carefully wrapped in traditional yellow brocade and offered in a grand ceremony to His Holiness by three specially chosen individuals: the Eighth Khamtrul Rinpoche, Dongyu Nyima, representing all the Tibetan Buddhist schools; Dege Jagoetsang Namgyal Dorjee, representing the Chushi Gangdrug, which at the time represented people from both Amdo and Kham; and Shigatse Leydrung Pelsur Dorjee Norbu, representing the U-Tsang Cholkha. To realize the goals of the Oath, respect for the unique characteristics of each of the three regions of Tibet, as well as for the different religious traditions and sects, on an equal basis was essential. This was the most important condition for restoring unity among our people. Neither coexistence between the Tibetan and Chinese peoples nor unity amongst the Tibetans themselves would be possible in the absence of equality or respect for the different regions and religious traditions of Tibet.

It is not only surprising but also very disappointing that this historic event in Bodhgaya is hardly discussed, let alone commemorated by the Tibetan people. CTA publications rarely speak about it, and books published by senior exile leaders make no mention of it. One of the best-known books on Tibetan history, *Tibet: A Political History* by Tsepon W. D. Shakabpa, glaringly omits any discussion of it as well as the major changes His Holiness introduced that fundamentally transformed the structure of the Gaden Phodrang government once it was reestablished in exile, even though the author was very much a part of the CTA when these historic transformations were taking place. In my view, the pledging of the Oath, combined with the associated political changes, is one of the most important events in our recent history. The Tibetan people cannot, and indeed must not, continue to ignore this iconic event if we genuinely believe in the concept of a unified Tibet. The current amnesiac state of affairs reminds me of an old Tibetan saying: "Ma-thong dhok kyi Un-ku chik par; Thong dhok kyi Yol-la chik kap," meaning "A lamp is lit so that one can see; at the same time a curtain is put up so that nobody can see!"[8]

### *Implementing the Great Oath of Unity Through Democratization*

For over 300 years successive Dalai Lamas ruled Tibet with power vested in a few hundred aristocratic families. It was indeed a feudal system. I am not saying whether it was good or bad. It was a practice that existed in many other parts of the world at some point in history. While it would be foolish to pass judgment on conditions existing hundreds of years ago, that does not mean we shouldn't take lessons from them. Many of the aristocratic officials were indeed very capable leaders, deeply dedicated to their service, whose families for centuries had strong ties to the institution of the Dalai Lama. But the political transformation His Holiness inaugurated following the taking of the Great Oath of Unity was groundbreaking, fundamentally changing the parameters of traditional Tibetan governance. Although the Gaden Phodrang government that came into exile with His Holiness continued after the pledging of the Oath, it was redefined, expanding to become a government inclusive of all Tibetans. This led to a powerful sense of nationalism, after a lapse of several centuries, amongst all Tibetans, who share not only the same ethnicity but also a common religion, culture, language, and set of traditions.

Within a few months after adoption of the Oath, His Holiness began introducing major structural reforms to realize its mandate. He gradually changed the composition of the Kashag; while retaining some of its existing members, he added individuals from nonaristocratic families and from areas outside Central Tibet. Wangdu Dorje and Tsewang Tamding from U-Tsang, Jangtsetsang Tsering Gonpo from Kham, and Tsering Gyaltong from Amdo were some of the earliest to be inducted. Eventually, individuals of nonaristocratic backgrounds and hailing from Kham and Amdo constituted the majority of members. When His Holiness appointed me to the Kashag in 1987, the only person with an aristocratic background was Tethong Tenzin Geyche, who was unquestionably chosen solely on merit.

It is somewhat ironic that only in exile has His Holiness had the opportunity to put into practice his long-standing personal desire to bring major political and social changes to Tibetan society. He did make serious efforts to implement reforms while in Tibet, including establishing the Reforms Committee or Lekchoe Lekhung in 1952, but with little success. Given his past experiences, His Holiness recognized that for the Great Oath of Unity to be fully realized, the people needed a stronger voice in decision making. He thus introduced a democratic system, initially calling for creation of an elected body composed of three representatives from each of Tibet's three regions and one representative from each of the four schools of Tibetan Buddhism. Accordingly, just days after the Oath was taken, delegations representing the different groups met in an open space[9] near the Mahabodhi Temple in Bodhgaya to work out the procedural details, including the manner in which elections were to be conducted. As a result, the first elected representatives took the oath of office on September 2, 1960, and in so doing took a major step toward implementing the Great Oath of Unity. We observe this historic day as Tibetan Democracy Day.

This initial body of elected representatives was called the Commission of Tibetan People's Deputies (CTPD). In 1979, during my tenure as Chairman, the name was changed to the Assembly of Tibetan People's Deputies (ATPD). At that time there were suggestions to call it the "Parliament," but some of us thought it wouldn't be prudent to adopt that seemingly grander name. We also didn't use the title "Speaker," choosing the more neutral term "Chairman" instead. But since October 4, 2006, this body has been called the Tibetan Parliament-in-Exile,[10] and its Chairman and Vice-Chairman are now the Speaker and Deputy Speaker.

The composition of this body, no matter its name, has always been based on giving equal representation to the three regions of Tibet. If it were based on the population in exile, people from U-Tsang, or Central Tibet, would have the largest representation and Amdowas, the least. The total number of members and composition of this representative body have evolved over the years. For example, efforts were made from the very beginning to include women. As a result, starting in 1991, two seats for women from each region have been designated. In 1977, the Bon tradition was given one seat in recognition of its status as a major Tibetan religious tradition, alongside the four Tibetan Buddhist schools. By the time I served as a member of the 7th Parliament (1979–82), each region had four representatives. Between the 8th and 10th Parliaments, regional representation was reduced to two representatives. But in May 1990, to further democratize the Tibetan polity, His Holiness dissolved both the Parliament and the Kashag and established a committee to draft a new charter for governing the exile community,[11] one that better reflected the contemporary situation. With the promulgation of the 1991 Charter, each region was accorded ten representatives, while each of the five religious traditions was given two. Tibetans in Europe and America have subsequently been allotted two seats each, and one seat has been designated for Tibetans residing in Australasia. As of this writing, the Parliament has forty-five members or Deputies.

In its early days, the Parliament's role was much less significant than it is now and was not very well defined. For many years, it did not even have a permanent office or a secretariat. It was during my tenure that we built a complex with

The author (seated, front row center) when he was the Chairman of the Seventh Assembly of the Tibetan People's Deputies Parliament (1979–1982). (Seated, left to right) Tsedhong Ngawang Sangpo, Tsering Gyaltsen, Jharsangling Tsewang Namgyal, the author, Gonshar Dorje Damdul, Samshung Kalsang Yeshi, Yungdrung Wangyal. (Standing, left to right) Chatreng Ngawang, Nangra Rigzin, Nubpa Choedak Gyatso, Lithang Athar Norbu, Cheypa Lobsang Jampel, Dekyi Dolkar, Chabcha Kalden, Ga Tridhupon Chime Namgyal, Tanak Kunsang Paljor, Ngodup Tsering
Tibet Museum, CTA

Chambers, a Secretariat, and offices for the Chairman and Vice-Chairman, thus giving this important institution a much-deserved presence. At that time, the Parliament also asserted final authority over the budget and first adopted formal rules and regulations governing its conduct. We also made the National Working Committee a more regular and authoritative organ. Although it is no longer in existence, at the time, the National Working Committee was the highest policy-making body of the CTA, comprising all the members of the Kashag, the Secretaries of all the major administrative departments, and the elected Parliamentary Deputies. Although the traditional practice was to reach consensus on issues, if differences persisted, the elected Deputies took the final decision.

National Working Committee meetings were chaired and convened by the Chairman and Vice-Chairman, usually in consultation with the Kashag. They had the prerogative to call a meeting, however, even without the concurrence of the Kashag. Conversely, the Kashag could request a meeting of the Committee. Joint meetings of the Kashag and the two Chairmen, referred to as Ka-tsog Lhengye, and of the Kashag and the full Parliament, called Ka-chi Lhentsog, were also sometimes held. The Chairman and the Vice-Chairman quite regularly joined the Kashag in meetings with His Holiness. His Holiness would also summon joint meetings of the Chairman and the Vice-Chairman with the Kashag when important matters needed to be discussed.

It was during the chairmanship of Professor Samdhong Rinpoche[12] from 1991 to 2001 that the Parliament was transformed into a true law-making body that, in my view, enjoys more power today than parliaments in many countries. Samdhong Rinpoche's motto of "rule of law and not [the] individual" was reflected in the numerous rules and regulations enacted under his leadership. Ironically, when he became Kalon Tripa, or head of the Kashag, in 2001, he had a tough time navigating some of the rules he had helped put in place. I used to tease him, saying that he had now become a victim of his own policies. Even His Holiness, who is a very pragmatic person, sometimes became a little impatient with Samdhong Rinpoche's strict observance of the rules. But at the same time, His Holiness took these parliamentary procedures very seriously, recognizing the tremendous importance of adhering to the constitutionally established rules of government in a democratic system.

### *External Interference and Internal Dissension*

After the Great Oath of Unity was pledged, the first major substantive task of the newly formed Tibetan leadership was to formulate clear policy guidelines and a strategy to continue the struggle against Communist China. His Holiness had already publicly rejected the Seventeen-Point Agreement, declaring it invalid because the PRC government had violated every one of its clauses respecting the Tibetan people's rights.[13] The exile leadership decided to focus its efforts on making the world aware of the tragic situation facing the Tibetan people and on taking advantage of every opportunity to seek support for the Tibetan struggle for independence. In support of its agenda, the Tibetan leadership further decided that the Tibetans would neither maintain a relationship with nor seek assistance from any quarter that did not support the Tibetan people's aspiration for independence. Local Tibetan communities also adopted numerous resolutions endorsing this policy and calling for a clear distinction between "friends and foes."

This policy put us at odds with an entity most people would have believed was our most natural ally, Taiwan. While pledging support for the Tibetans in the fight against Chinese Communism, however, the Taiwan-based Nationalist government continued to claim Tibet as part of China. This policy compelled the Tibetan leadership to categorize the Nationalists or Kuomintang Party (KMT) as a "foe." This is the reason that relations with the Nationalist government were discouraged. Moreover, KMT agencies, in particular, the Mongolian and Tibetan Affairs Commission (MTAC), of which I will speak in more detail later, were engaged in activities that created deep divisions within and undermined the Tibet movement. While I am convinced that these KMT operatives justified their activities by telling their leaders they were carrying out anti-Communist activities in collaboration with Tibetan "compatriots," I don't think any serious effort or real resources went into fighting Communism. Rather, these resources were misappropriated by a handful of people and used to create disharmony and divisions amongst Tibetans. Sadly, I am confident that a seasoned leader such as Chiang Kai-shek would have understood the difficulties arising from the MTAC's actions if only the Tibetan leadership had instituted an effort to reach out directly to him and other top leaders in the KMT hierarchy.

The CTA's decision to lump the Chinese Communists and the Nationalist government together as foes was not fully shared by a section of the Tibetan people, especially those from Kham and Amdo. Influential leaders from those regions had had close ties with the Nationalist government in the pre-Communist era. As a matter of fact, quite a few of them had enjoyed high-ranking designations from the KMT and therefore felt a natural connection with the Nationalists. Many Tibetans from Kham and Amdo who had taken up armed resistance on their own home turf against the Red Army long before the CIA-backed Chushi Gangdrug was established felt deep personal outrage against the Chinese Communists for the destruction and suffering inflicted upon them. Many had lost their near and dear ones to the Communist aggression, transforming their animosity into a personal vendetta they felt honor bound to pursue. A section of these devastated individuals was, not surprisingly, lured by the KMT's promise of providing active assistance to continue their fight against the Chinese Communists, adopting the philosophy of "the enemy of my enemy is my friend."

These Tibetans saw a huge difference between the Chinese Communists who had inflicted such pain, humiliation, and destruction on them and their families and the Nationalists, who were at least opposing the Chinese Communist regime. For all Tibetans, no matter which region they call home, the most precious possession, something for which they will lay down their lives, is their religion. Putting atheist Communist China on a par with the Nationalists was thus difficult for some of them to digest. Though publicly, no one initially opposed the CTA's campaign based on recognizing the "enemy, ally, and the leader," differences began to surface within the exile community, especially as the CTA's activities became more focused on anti-KMT measures as opposed to combating the mainland Communists.

When we first arrived as refugees in India in 1959, the view that the Nationalists were our natural ally was actually quite prevalent among the newly displaced Tibetans. I remember seeing leaflets being distributed in Tibetan refugee camps in Missamari, Assam, with pictures of General Chiang Kai-shek saluting in full army uniform, with fighter jets behind him. As a young boy, even I was attracted to this grand-looking photo of the General with so many medals decorating his chest. Moreover, General Chiang publicly announced in his message to his Tibetan "compatriots" that Nationalist policy would be to help the Tibetan diaspora overthrow Communist China's rule in Tibet.

> The Government of the Republic of China has always respected the traditional political and social structures of Tibet, and upheld the religious faith of its people as well as their freedom to have their own way of life. Today I wish to affirm emphatically that regarding Tibet's future political institutions and status as soon as the puppet Communist regime on the mainland is overthrown and the people of Tibet are once again free to express their will, the Government will assist the Tibetan people to realize their own aspirations in accordance with the principle of self-determination.[14]

As previously discussed, my father was among the Khampa chieftains who enjoyed rank and title from the Nationalist government. He was also someone who had actually met Chiang Kai-shek. With this background and his fluent Chinese-language skills, it was natural for him to think of reconnecting with the Nationalists. Interestingly, soon after our arrival in Darjeeling, emissaries of the Nationalist government came to visit him, expressing their happiness at his safe arrival in India and extending an invitation for him to relocate in Taiwan. But having taken the Great Oath of Unity and in accord with the CTA's directive to disassociate from the Nationalists, my father took the difficult but firm decision to sever all his connections with them. I remember some of our retainers expressing their profound unhappiness with his decision, saying that he should think of his family's future and move to Taiwan, where he would be given a suitable position and facilities.

On the other hand, many people deeply admired my father for his resolute decision elevating Tibet's interests over his and his family's personal well-being. In 1999, for example, when my father was critically ill, my younger brother, Pema Gyalpo, came from Tokyo to be with him and the rest of the family. Gyalo Thondup invited us for a meal and told us that he had deep admiration for our father because he chose a difficult life for himself and his family in furtherance of the Tibetan cause. He said: "I know your father could have had a much more comfortable life and facilities if he went to Taiwan in the early 1960s, because the KMT people knew who he was and also because he was fluent in Chinese and knew their ways and customs."[15]

After the initial enthusiasm and excitement of the Great Oath of Unity wore off, cracks began appearing within the Tibetan community, confronting the Tibetan leadership with a divisive crisis beginning in the mid-1960s. If the CTA in Dharamsala had physically governed a territory and had law-and-order responsibilities, I think it would have faced serious consequences. The only factor that kept this fragile unity alive was His Holiness.

When the chieftains and religious leaders from areas that had not been governed by the Lhasa government pledged their loyalty to His Holiness and committed to being part of a unified Tibet, they assumed they would retain their traditional influence and power and, in addition, assume leadership roles in the new, unified CTA. Traditionally, even chieftains who were under the direct rule of the Lhasa government maintained control over their respective areas. When the Manchus and later, warlords from neighboring Chinese provinces periodically imposed nominal rule over areas in eastern Tibet, actual control over the chieftains' territories was also not much disturbed. And when Lhasa extended its rule into areas of Kham, it generally tried not to challenge the powers and functions of local rulers.

But as the days went by under the reconstituted CTA, rather than acquiring new positions of authority, these chieftains saw their power eroding. Some even felt they were being ignored, or at the very least, not treated with sufficient deference. The former aristocrats of the Lhasa government had accepted the new administration with similar expectations, but a few of them were also having a hard time digesting the sweeping changes that were diminishing their traditional roles. Overnight many of these individuals felt they were being not only marginalized but actively pushed out, similar to the situation in Tibet with the invasion of Communist China. The only difference they saw was that in Tibet, the Chinese authorities were doing it violently and ruthlessly.

Some former aristocrats did not find positions in the new administration. I am not certain of the reasons behind these exclusions. It could have been a struggle amongst different factions of the former aristocratic officials. Some even thought that the aristocrats who had lived outside of Tibet, mostly in Kalimpong, had more influence, generating further feelings of resentment in those who had fled Tibet with His Holiness. While there are many stories, I have no personal knowledge of that period. Whatever the cause, the seeming marginalization of some of these former officials led to their troublesome alliance with organs of the KMT government.

In 1963, for example, Surkhang Wangchen Gelek, the seniormost minister in the previous Lhasa government, left India for England and from there went to the United States, where he was offered a position at the University of Washington in Seattle. With funding for that program coming to a halt, he moved to Taiwan in the early 1970s, joining his brother-in-law and former Kashag colleague, Yuthok Tashi Dhondup, in setting up a so-called "Kalon office" that was seen by Dharamsala as a direct challenge to the CTA and its authority. At the same time, the CTA sent two former, very senior officials of the Lhasa administration, Phala Thupten Woeden and Neushar Thupten Tharpa, as Representatives of His Holiness to Geneva and New York, respectively. Some viewed these postings as tantamount to exile from the real leadership emerging in Dharamsala, while others saw them as confirmation that the real power remained in the hands of these former aristocrats who seemed to be filling the most sought-after positions.

Whatever may have caused individuals like Surkhang Wangchen Gelek and Yuthok Tashi Dhondup to leave the Tibetan leadership, their ultimate collaboration with the Nationalists was unfortunate. Surkhang Wangchen Gelek was not only the highest ranking Kalon from the former Lhasa government but also among the handful of people, together with Phala Thupten Woeden and Takla Phuntsok Tashi, His Holiness's brother-in-law, who were privy to the events surrounding His Holiness's historic escape. Chinese Communist statements and publications of the 1950s, in fact, single out Surkhang Wangchen Gelek and His Holiness's junior tutor, Kyabjé Trijang Rinpoche, as among the main instigators of the Tibetan "rebellion" against the Chinese.

The Tibetans deeply resented Surkhang Wangchen Gelek and Yuthok Tashi Dhondup for their open collaboration with the KMT, and there was a widespread campaign denouncing their actions. While it was understandable that some Khampa and Amdo leaders, who had never been under Lhasa's control, continued their prior relationships with the Nationalists, it was an entirely different matter for former Lhasa officials to establish new relations with them. Some leaders from Kham and Amdo, while understanding the importance of having a unified front to fight the Communist Chinese, failed to fully appreciate the process of national reunification. Still others, while very supportive of unification, behaved as though they had become *gothak* to the CTA. As previously discussed, this type of subservient relationship is deeply rooted in the psyche of Tibetans from both Kham and Amdo.[16]

I remember one incident in 1984 when some Tibetan community leaders from Dhondupling Tibetan Settlement near Dehradun came to Dharamsala. I was working as Additional Secretary of the Department of Information and Publicity (DIP), which has now become the Department of Information and International Relations (DIIR). My friend Sonam Topgyal was then the DIP Secretary. The delegation came to our office with *khata* (ceremonial scarfs), as they had done with all the departments they had visited, expressing their deep gratitude for the kindness shown to them by the CTA. They had just met with Tashi Topgyal, Secretary of the Home Department, who had literally given them a truckload of relief supplies, including oil, milk powder, and used clothes. They were acting so subservient, like a typical *gothak*, that I felt compelled to explain:

> It is not a question of being grateful. You are not *gothaks* seeking protection, as Tibetans used to think in the old days. The Home Department has not done you any special favor; they simply discharged their normal duty to give you what is your right. All the settlements under the care of the CTA received the same, and this is not special to you. Earlier, you had remained outside of this administration, which was wrong, but now that you are in, you must not think like a *gothak*. Look, both Sonam Topgyal and I are Khampas, and we are here because this administration belongs to all the three Cholkhas.

I was glad to see their reaction and their body language immediately change from submissiveness to one of equality and pride.

Another stumbling block in the unification process was the challenging relations between former Lhasa officials and Tibetans from other regions. Many people from Kham and Amdo felt that they had submitted their allegiance to the newly formed CTA, while conversely, some of the CTA officials behaved as if they were doing these Tibetans a favor by accepting their loyalty. I was made aware of one incident that occurred immediately after the Great Oath of Unity was

Department of Information and Publicity Staff in 1983. (Seated, left to right) Dekyi Khedup, Zechutsang Sonam Topgyal (Secretary), the author (Add'l Secretary), Tsedrung Drakpa Tendar. (Standing, front row, left to right) Sonam Dolma, Dadrak. (Standing, second row, left to right) Tashi Choegyal, Sonam Tenzing, Gyan Chand, Thubten Samphel, Tenzin Phuntsok (Atisha), Jeshong Tawang, Passang Tsering. (Standing, back row, left to right) Bhutruk, Dawa Dakpa, Sonam Tsering
Tibet Museum, CTA

pledged. Some senior CTA officials visited Buxa Duar refugee camp, where a large number of monks from all schools of Tibetan Buddhism and community leaders were staying. One of the monks later told me that the CTA official had said: "Now that we have accepted you, you all must be careful and behave well." This offensive and insensitive statement reflects the patronizing attitude of some former Lhasa officials whom many Tibetans, especially those from Kham and Amdo, detested, particularly in light of the historic mistrust between the Lhasa rulers and the Khampas.

The foregoing are just a few examples of both the external pressures and the domestic difficulties faced by the new, inclusive Dharamsala administration. While the CTA succeeded in some areas, it failed in others. Nevertheless, it was necessary to promote a sense of inclusiveness and equal participation for everyone who was now a part of this reunified Tibet.

## CHAPTER 9

# Tibetan Exile Organizations

### *Too Often Compromised by Conflicting Agendas and Personality Disputes*

The problems confronting the nascent Tibetan community in exile were not limited to adjusting to the newly minted and still evolving unified political administration. External interferences and internal conflicts within Tibetan-run nongovernmental organizations (NGOs) were also surfacing.

In the following pages, I will briefly introduce some of the important organizations that played major roles in the evolution of the exile community and sometimes, sadly, were involved in conflicts that challenged our cohesiveness. My intention is not to write an "authoritative" history of the first few tumultuous decades of our years in exile. No one who was a participant in or even an observer of the events would be able to write something totally unbiased and objective. In the early 1970s, Tsepon W. D. Shakabpa, author of *Tibet: A Political History*, gave a series of lectures to a select group of people in New Delhi. I was lucky to be among those in attendance. I remember telling him that while I was grateful for his contribution in writing this informative book, I had reservations about his narrative of the periods in which he himself was an active participant. The tragic situation involving the fate of Regent Reting was one prominent example of my concerns.[1]

One may say that my narration suffers from the same flaw. Nevertheless, acutely aware of this potential pitfall, I intend to present the facts as uncolored as possible, giving only a summary of the events of this unfortunate period of Tibet's history with the aim of healing wounds rather than contributing to further misconstruction or misinterpretation. Moreover, as I believe it is unethical to write about individuals who are no longer with us, I have deleted a few names from my original draft, as they passed away during this writing. But I do feel compelled to say that if we can examine this period from a detached and impartial perspective, I am quite sure we will find that many groups and individuals had what they believed to be compelling reasons for acting the way they did. Although the leaders in Dharamsala may have lacked the vision and skills to be fully inclusive, thus contributing to the animosity that led to the conflicting agendas of many of these exile groups, for the most part, I don't believe they were acting with malicious intent. I had the opportunity to know many of the leaders of that generation, both within the CTA and from the different NGO factions, and I have deep respect for many of them and their individual perspectives.

## CHUSHI GANGDRUG (FOUR RIVERS AND SIX RANGES) ORGANIZATION

I begin my discussion of the prominent Tibetan organizations in exile with the Chushi Gangdrug, the Tibetan resistance movement led by Andruk Gonpo Tashi, because it was the most dominant and influential in those initial, formative years in exile. This group not only played a crucial role in providing safety for His Holiness's historic escape to India but also was instrumental in bringing about the Great Oath of Unity. In fact, the largest number of delegates at that historic event was from the Chushi Gangdrug. Its initial, formal name was Tensung Danglang Mag-gar (Volunteer Army to Defend the Faith). Amdo Jinpa Gyatso, a prominent Amdo leader, was Deputy Head. When it was formally established at Drigu-thang in Lhokha, Central Tibet, on June 16, 1958, people from U-Tsang and Central Tibet were also members.

Although most of its members were from Kham, the group did not identify itself with any particular region. On the contrary, it promoted itself as a broader Tibetan national movement. In fact, I don't hesitate in recognizing this organization as the first pan-Tibetan movement with both broad-based support and defined leadership, as well as an organizational structure, meriting its belated designation as an important movement in Tibetan history. Unlike the earlier resistance movements in Kham and Amdo that were mainly led by regional chieftains, Tensung Danglang Mag-gar was the initiative of influential Khampa traders based in Lhasa under Andruk Gonpo Tashi, himself a prominent and very successful businessman. His number two, Amdo Jinpa Gyatso, was also a recognized entrepreneur. Gradually, many other important chieftains and battle-tested resistance leaders from eastern Tibet joined the group after arriving in Central Tibet following years of actively resisting the Chinese in their native areas.

As the Communist Chinese authorities had taken more or less complete control of Central Tibet by this time, the Lhasa government was unable to openly support the movement. Nevertheless, many senior officials, including Phala Thupten Woeden, not only were sympathetic but also secretly kept in close touch. Namseling Paljor Jigme, a senior Tibetan army officer and aristocrat who was initially sent by the Tibetan government under pressure from the Chinese authorities to advise the group to disband, actually ended up joining it, together with the other members of his delegation.

Interestingly, when His Holiness was compelled to leave Lhasa, he initially thought of relocating in southern Tibet in areas under the control of the Tibetan resistance movement and from there making a renewed effort to reach out to the Chinese central leadership for a peaceful resolution of the crisis. He traveled to Lhuntse Dzong, an important administrative center of that region that had a sizeable fortress, arriving on March 26, 1959. One of the first things he did from there was reach out to Andruk Gonpo Tashi, conferring on him the rank of Dzasa[2] and thereby formally making him a senior official of the Tibetan government. A decision was also taken to consolidate the Tibetan army and Tensung Danglang Mag-gar into a single fighting force. But the subsequent March 28 radio broadcast revealing the Chinese government's decision to dissolve the Tibetan government eliminated any hope of reconciliation. So it was also at Lhuntse Dzong that His Holiness repudiated the Seventeen-Point Agreement, announced the establishment of the provisional government, and took the very difficult personal decision to seek asylum in India.

Let me interject one humorous comment concerning the granting of Dzasa rank to Andruk Gonpo Tashi related to me in the early 1960s while I was working at *Defend Tibet's Freedom Press* with several senior Chushi Gangdrug leaders. One of the Khampas made a joke based on the similarity in sound between the two Tibetan words *Dzasa* and *jhatsak*. He said: "When *jindak*[3] was given the *jhatsak*,[4] all the tea had been drunk." Everyone had a hearty laugh. While not intending to convey any disrespect for His Holiness's conferral of the esteemed rank on Andruk Gonpo Tashi, the joke implied that with the loss of Tibet there was not much value to it. This anecdote further reveals that even when referring to the most solemn or tragic circumstances, Tibetans, especially Khampas, can display an engaging sense of humor.

Tensung Danglang Mag-gar gradually came to be called Chushi Gangdrug perhaps because, with the exception of the Mustang guerilla outpost, there was no active resistance base with which the organization was associated. With the passing away of Andruk Gonpo Tashi and soon thereafter of Amdo Jinpa Gyatso, most of the Amdowas drifted away. I think they felt marginalized and underrepresented. KMT agents furthered this separation by recruiting quite a few of the Amdowa members. Some of them, including Amdo Kato, a close associate of Amdo Jinpa Gyatso, did remain with the Chushi Gangdrug. Some people seek to hold the Amdowas alone responsible for this separation, but that is unfair. For whatever reason, a section within the group was keen to make it a purely Khampa organization, as it stands today.

Chushi Gangdrug fighters' hope of returning to southern Tibet, their prior stronghold, to continue their armed resistance became impossible when the Chinese army took complete control of the region. When the US CIA agreed to fund and supply equipment for the Mustang guerilla operation in Nepal, however, there was renewed hope and enthusiasm within the organization. Hundreds volunteered to join the guerilla forces. In the initial recruiting stages, all the important regional leaders and resistance groups were actively involved. My father, Gyari Nyima Gyaltsen, along with a prominent chieftain from Kyegudo, Drawu Pon Rinchen Tsering, and another senior Chushi Gangdrug leader, Chamdo Dortse, were charged with making arrangements for the volunteers, who were mostly from the Gangtok and Darjeeling areas, to be sent secretly to Nepal.

The recruiters set up their clandestine base at Ghoom, a small town near Darjeeling. My father, who had by then picked up some Hindi language skills, volunteered to post himself at Raxaul at the Nepalese border to help the volunteers with the border crossing. He had the added advantage of having quite a few young Nyarongwas he could take with him to assist in his efforts. The task of recruiting and sending volunteers was very daunting because it had to be kept secret from the Indian Intelligence Authority. Similarly, because the Sikkimese government, for whatever reason, put strict restrictions on the movement of Tibetan refugees in and out of Sikkim, the recruiters had to smuggle the volunteers out of the area in small groups of two or three, mostly at night.

Six months at Raxaul took a heavy toll on my father's health. My mothers remember him coming home in very poor physical condition but with great satisfaction at having helped send hundreds of veteran fighters to the Mustang base. He personally took many of them across the border through paddy fields and jungles. Years later, I met several Mustang veterans who expressed their sincere appreciation for my father's help. My mothers also humorously told me that he returned home without the famous Gyari *dzi*, a traditional and very valuable stone as big as a small egg. It wasn't stolen; he was careless and left it at a village well where he went for his usual bath. Not surprisingly, it was gone when he went back to retrieve it.

Members of the CIA-supported Mustang guerilla group were exclusively from the Chushi Gangdrug, and its key leaders were all appointed by Andruk Gonpo Tashi during its early years. Similarly, some of the senior political leaders of the Special Frontier Force were deputed by the Chushi Gangdrug. The organization had significant resources and manpower, but by the early 1960s, differences among the members began to surface. Andruk Gonpo Tashi worked closely with Gyalo Thondup, who ultimately became the undisputed leader of the Darjeeling faction. Andruk Gonpo Tashi remained in Darjeeling, even while the CTA was setting up base in Dharamsala. He encouraged other leaders, including Jagoe Namgyal Dorjee, Sadu Lo Nyedak, and later Drawu Pon Rinchen Tsering,[5] to represent the Kham region in the Parliament in Dharamsala. Some people thought that he intentionally kept these other Khampas at arm's length from the real center of power, which was then in Darjeeling. I don't know whether there is any truth to that, but a division began to form within the Chushi Gangdrug between those based in Darjeeling and those who went to Dharamsala.

Like Andruk Gonpo Tashi, Gyalo Thondup was respected by the dominant Chushi Gangdrug leaders in Darjeeling. Those who were based in Dharamsala, however, became mistrustful and turned against him. Ironically, in later years, those leaders who were initially based in Dharamsala as part of the new CTA distanced themselves from Dharamsala, while those based in Darjeeling became closer to and identified with Dharamsala. It was a very confusing and volatile situation.

Andruk Gonpo Tashi was not a charismatic person, but he was a very strong leader. It was very unfortunate that he died young, leaving a huge vacuum in the Chushi Gangdrug leadership. Even those Khampa leaders based in Dharamsala who felt he was marginalizing them respected this tough fighter. To this day, people including Drawu Pon Rinchen Tsering, a prominent leader of the opposing faction, refer to Andruk Gonpo Tashi with reverence as Jindak. I believe that if he had lived longer, there might have been reconciliation between the two factions that would have eliminated the later divisive politics within the Khampa community that ultimately contributed to undermining the Dharamsala administration.

Andruk Gonpo Tashi was deeply loyal to His Holiness the Dalai Lama. I spent about nine days serving as his translator at the Planter's Hospital in Darjeeling during his last illness. In fact, I was right next to him when he took his last breath. The day he passed away, he revived a bit in the morning, gave me a five-rupee bill out of some small change that he kept under his pillow, and asked me to buy some oranges that he then shared with me. He said he appreciated my help and that upon his recovery he would like to go to Dharamsala to have an audience with His Holiness, and that he would take me with him. I was very excited about the prospect. Unfortunately, that very night he passed away. Gyalo Thondup was not in Darjeeling at the time, and I had to wake up his wife with the sad news. Obviously, I didn't physically make that trip to Dharamsala with Andruk Gonpo Tashi, but eventually I did go to Dharamsala, where I served His Holiness for many decades. So maybe, in a way, he did take me there.

### *Complications Arising from the Chushi Gangdrug's Association with the Dolgyal Cult (Shugden)*

As a Khampa, it has deeply pained me to witness the continued problematic relations between the Chushi Gangdrug and the CTA. In my opinion, one factor that may have caused this disharmony is the Chushi Gangdrug's consultation of the medium of the Dolgyal spirit from the organization's very beginnings. Even after coming into exile, a section of Chushi Gangdrug leaders continued with this practice. In fairness, I must note that His Holiness only publicly started advising against worship of this spirit years after Andruk Gonpo Tashi passed away. Ever since the establishment of the Gaden Phodrang system of government by the Fifth Dalai Lama, however, Palden Lhamo (Sri Devi in Sanskrit) and Nechung Dorje Drakden have been the official protector deities of the Tibetan nation.

Apart from the problematic relations between the CTA and the Chushi Gangdrug, the Dolgyal propitiation may have precipitated unhealthy relations within the Chushi Gangdrug itself. Many members, including very important leaders, were strongly against maintaining any relationship with the Dolgyal spirit and resented the fact that some of their colleagues continued to follow that practice. Seeing the potential to advance Beijing's interests as a result of the problematic relationship between the CTA and the Chushi Gangdrug and the divisiveness within Chushi Gangdrug's ranks, certain agencies of the PRC government even started cultivating relations with some members of the Dolgyal cult group. Their efforts strengthened the Dolgyal adherents in later years and continue to do so today,[6] creating disunity within the Tibetan community both in exile and in Tibet.

While this dispute may sound rather bizarre to many readers, these types of issues play a central role in both the Tibetan psyche and Tibetan society. Even for those of us who consider ourselves independent thinkers and not blind followers of certain religious traditions, the need for pure relations amongst ourselves, and especially with our spiritual leader, is deeply rooted in our genes. His Holiness's efforts to curtail propitiation of the Dolgyal spirit were first and foremost to maintain the purity of the Buddhist doctrine, especially of the Gelug tradition founded by Je Tsongkhapa, of which His Holiness himself is the most important spiritual leader.

His Holiness was extremely disturbed by the harsh sectarian doctrines some of the followers of this cult were promoting against other schools of Tibetan Buddhism, thereby creating deep wounds and widespread animosity. One of the most important Gelug teachers who practiced the worship of the Dolgyal spirit was Kyabjé Trijang Rinpoche, His Holiness's junior tutor. I had the honor of knowing this great scholar intimately, and in my opinion, had he lived longer he never would have allowed any of his students to go against the wishes of His Holiness in continuing to worship that spirit. In fact, the vast majority of his close disciples had no hesitation in heeding the instructions of His Holiness and completely disassociating themselves from the Dolgyal cult. They knew deep in their hearts that their root teacher would have approved of their decisions.

As unfortunately has happened on a number of occasions involving complex issues, individuals supposedly devoted to His Holiness overreacted, causing more harm than good. I know quite a few people who would have immediately distanced themselves from this cult but for the fact that they were incensed over the tremendously disrespectful remarks certain misguided individuals started making against Kyabjé Trijang Rinpoche. These former students were not invested in Dolgyal worship. They maintained the practice because they could not tolerate any perceived insults to their late teacher, whom they profoundly respected.

Chatreng Tenzin Tsultrim is one such person whom I knew well. He was one of the veteran CIA-trained Khampa leaders with unwavering loyalty and devotion to His Holiness and the CTA, but who continued the Dolgyal practice. Throughout the Chushi Gangdrug internal squabbles as well as the Mustang episode, he took a leading role, along with individuals including my father, supporting the CTA. Members of another Khampa faction that was anti-CTA physically assaulted him while he was visiting a Tibetan settlement to galvanize Khampa support for the Dharamsala administration.

I know His Holiness was fond of Tenzin Tsultrim, because he and my father were among the few Khampa leaders who, even with their fierce devotion, did not hesitate to speak their minds, a trait His Holiness greatly values. I believe sometime around 2010, Tenzin Tsultrim reached out seeking my help to gain an audience with His Holiness to share his concerns about certain matters he thought of importance. Prevailing circumstances did not allow me to oblige, however, and I regret my inability to help him. Sadly, I now understand that he has become a prominent figure in the Dolgyal cult movement.

Many other people, including some prominent Gelug lamas and scholars, were fearful of abandoning this spirit worship because they thought it would cause them serious harm. At the same time, they deeply venerated His Holiness and did not wish to go against his directives. A few of them were my friends. I am very happy that I was able to help create space for them to gradually give up the practice during this difficult time and fully restore their spiritual relationship with His Holiness, a bond that is so precious to them.

## CHIGDRIL TSOGPA (UNITED TIBETAN ASSOCIATION)

One of the first NGOs established in exile was the Chigdril Tsogpa or United Tibetan Association. It was launched in Darjeeling on April 23, 1964, to help Tibetans better understand the concept of a unified Tibet. The Tibetan leadership felt the need for an NGO of this nature to work at the grassroots level to popularize the concept of Tibetan unity by facilitating closer relations between the people from Tibet's three regions and the different schools of Tibetan Buddhism. Phenpo Lobsang Yeshi, a senior official of the CTA Security Department, resigned his CTA position to spearhead establishment of the organization. He remained its leader until his passing in 1980.

The establishment of the Chigdril Tsogpa also had the backing of Andruk Gonpo Tashi, though he passed away before its formal launch. In consultation with other senior Khampa leaders, he nominated my father, Gyari Nyima Gyaltsen, and other Khampa leaders, including Tsewang Trinley and Bapa Chagzoe

Kalsang Tashi, to represent Kham in the organization. Tsewang Trinley was later elected to Parliament and became its chairperson. In his capacity as executive member of the Chigdril Tsogpa, Bapa Chagzoe Kalsang Tashi was appointed manager of the *Tibetan Freedom Press* that was launched in early 1965 upon the amalgamation of the two publications *Freedom Press* and *Defend Tibet's Freedom Press.* Theoretically, *Tibetan Freedom Press* was supposed to be an organ of the newly launched Chigdril Tsogpa.

Important leaders from Amdo, including Kirti Lobsang Senge, Chone Phagpa Tsering, and Labrang Sonam Gyal, were also among the organization's founding members. His Holiness Dudjom Rinpoche, then the Supreme Head of the Nyingma tradition of Tibetan Buddhism, and many other leaders and scholars, including Drukpa Thuksey Rinpoche and Sakya Khenchen Sangye Tenzin, as well as many Khenpos from the Gelug tradition, were also actively involved in helping draft the organization's manifesto and constitution. These prominent individuals were also initially elected to assume leadership roles. As they were all very senior religious leaders, each one delegated his authority to a representative of his tradition as follows: Taklung Nyima Sangpo from the Nyingma, Dhondup Gyalpo from the Kagyu, Lopon Tashi Tenzing from the Sakya, and Rigzin Choedar from the Gelug. In addition to Phenpo Lobsang Yeshi, founding members from Central Tibet included Tsen-nyer Nyima Wangyal, Drashi Gyapon Dorjee, and Gyaltse Delang Passang Gyalpo, to name just a few.

I really do not know why the Chigdril Tsogpa was run from Darjeeling and not Dharamsala. It could be that because it was a grassroots organization, or to use today's term, an NGO, senior officials in Dharamsala felt that it should be kept at a distance so as not to be seen as an extension of the government. It could also be because in those days Darjeeling was much more politically vibrant than Dharamsala. However, because the founding president, Phenpo Lobsang Yeshi, was formerly a senior Security Department official, he maintained a very close relationship with that department and especially with Takla Phuntsok Tashi, who was also connected with it. Even though the public perception was that Gyalo Thondup had great influence over the Chigdril Tsogpa, I think it actually sought more guidance from Dharamsala and people such as Takla Phuntsok Tashi. Tibetans are never short on real or imaginary perceptions, and I remember a few people even suspecting that the CTA set up the Chigdril Tsogpa in Darjeeling specifically to keep an eye on Gyalo Thondup and his activities.

Immediately after the formation of the Chigdril Tsogpa, Phenpo Lobsang Yeshi, my father, and Gedun Soepa, a senior leader from Amdo, among others, went to Dharamsala to present its draft constitution to the Tibetan leadership. I remember my father returning home with tremendous enthusiasm and revitalized commitment because they had been received by His Holiness in a private audience in which he gave them guidance and his blessings. My father first participated in the organization representing the Khampas, as directed by Andruk Gonpo Tashi. Once he knew that the Chigdril Tsogpa had the blessing and approval of His Holiness, he became very passionate and played a leading role in establishing branches of the organization in many other parts of India.

As time passed, however, my father became quite disillusioned with some of the Chigdril Tsogpa's activities, as well as with individual members who were pursuing certain matters too aggressively, often in ways that harmed the greater cause of Tibet. He gradually distanced himself from the organization and for the last many years of his life played no official role. However, he had a very strong motto that guided his life: "Tse chik la kye wa nyi len me nyen," roughly meaning "In one lifetime, one should not lead two lives." Thus, even though he was disturbed by some of the Chigdril Tsogpa's activities, he never formally disassociated from it. Sadly, this quality of devotion and loyalty characteristic of many elder Tibetans, both monk and lay, is now an increasing rarity.

The Tibetan community at large initially received the Chigdril Tsogpa very well. It was able to open branches in many places in India and Nepal. It further established a number of enterprises, some supplying traditional Tibetan handicrafts, that provided a livelihood for many Tibetans. I remember two that were very successful, one in Kathmandu and the other in Shimla. I am sure there were quite a few others. Nepal, in fact, became a stronghold of the Chigdril Tsogpa, with veteran CIA-trained individuals including Lithang Athar and Dogyal Aten at the core of the leadership. But soon, a group of Tibetans mainly from Kham and Amdo, but also including some former Lhasa aristocrats, started spreading rumors that the organization's real purpose was to completely do away with religious and regional identities. They distorted its actions, citing them as "proof" of Dharamsala's pursuit of this policy.

There is no doubt that some of the Chigdril Tsogpa's activities, and particularly some remarks by overzealous members, could have created such an impression. Sadly, these divisive allegations caught like wildfire amongst a section of the Tibetan populace, resulting in the organization becoming more of a divisive force than a unifying one as originally intended. While it would be interesting to learn exactly how, when, and who started spreading these rumors, the bottom line is that the campaign was quite effective.

In concert with several other organizations, including the Tibetan Women's Association, Chigdril Tsogpa did spearhead the "Know your enemy, ally, and leader" campaign launched by the CTA that I previously mentioned. The organization's preamble made it very clear that its goal was to confront both Communist and Nationalist China. As a result, the KMT, primarily through the MTAC, devoted significant resources and serious effort to discrediting the Chigdril Tsogpa. Regrettably, to a great extent, it succeeded in creating the impression that the Chigdril Tsogpa was the CTA's instrument not only for doing away with the regional-based system of government but also in promoting the Gelug sect as the dominant religious tradition at the expense of Tibet's other religious schools.

As the MTAC's activities were undermining the very foundation of the unified Tibet movement by creating division and mistrust among the exile Tibetans, it is understandable that the CTA and organizations supportive of it gave the highest priority to confronting and opposing the organization's work. But, sadly, some of the CTA's methods were reminiscent of the "class struggle" sessions conducted by the Communist Chinese. It is even more unfortunate that this element of Communist behavior became prevalent in the conduct of some official proceedings in Dharamsala. While opposing the Communist Chinese, these overzealous individuals adopted some of their ugliest methods. Some of them even convinced the CTA to officially ban the use of family names, a practice that, fortunately, was short-lived. Maybe these few Tibetans suffered from Stockholm syndrome! In any event, there has always been an unfortunate tendency among certain Tibetans to project themselves as "progressive," to counter Communist Chinese propaganda depicting Tibetans as backward, feudal, and reactionary. Adopting our overlord's tactics to defeat this characterization simply makes the situation worse.

Unfortunately, the perception that the CTA was gradually doing away with equal representation of the three regions and seeking to consolidate the four Tibetan Buddhist sects into a single entity was spreading within the Tibetan exile community. In reflecting on the prevailing sentiments of that period, Nyingma scholar Khenpo Tsewang Dongyal writes:

> Though Tibetan culture and religion were nicely taking root in their new environment, a few high Tibetan officials had a different idea about how to maintain and strengthen Tibetan culture and political autonomy. They said, "Due to a lack of unity, we lost our country. Now is the perfect opportunity

> for change. Let us call ourselves Tibetans rather than identify with our local regions. Let's have a single school of Tibetan Buddhism rather than the excess of traditions that exist currently."[7]

I do not know which officials the author is referring to, but such a policy would totally contradict His Holiness's vision for a future Tibet. On the contrary, His Holiness wanted to make the system more inclusive and give more prominence to all of Tibet's religious traditions and the three regions. But the Khenpo is not wrong in his conclusion. There was such a perception among the people, making many of them nervous, particularly devotees of the Nyingma, Kagyu, and Sakya schools. Khenpo Tsewang Dongyal further writes:

> On the street people began saying: "If we make one school, which will it be?" "This is only a plan to destroy the schools of Nyingma, Kagyu and Sakya." "Look how the Tibetan schools are running these days. Morning and evening prayers are from the Gelugpa prayers and the religious teacher in each school is Gelugpa." Rumors spread among the refugees and people began saying: "In Tibet the Communist Party gathered all the children, giving them a Communist education and way of life. In exile, the children are gathered and given Gelugpa teachings."[8]

I myself heard irresponsible remarks of this nature at formal gatherings in Dharamsala during my Chairmanship of the Tibetan Parliament.

His Holiness was mindful of these dynamics and made efforts to introduce a nonsectarian approach to every institution and program, including education. But his policies took time to be implemented and may even have been deliberately delayed by some individuals in some cases. All of this misinformation and the resultant misunderstandings overwhelmed the fledgling exile government, contributing to increasing anti-Dharamsala sentiments among the people.

The unfounded allegations hounded not only the CTA but also individuals supportive of the inclusive policy pursued by the Dalai Lama in compliance with the Great Oath of Unity. One example of the latter is my father, Gyari Nyima. As previously noted, he was one of the Chigdril Tsogpa's founding members. He was not only a devout Buddhist but also a staunch Nyingmapa and a very proud Khampa leader. Nevertheless, there were widespread rumors that he had renounced his faith and become a Gelug practitioner. This vicious lie even reached the ears of prominent religious leaders, including His Holiness the 16th Gyalwa Karmapa. During a visit to Darjeeling, when he was a guest for lunch at the house of a prominent Tibetan family, a certain individual mentioned to the Gyalwa Karmapa, as if he were revealing a big secret, that Gyari Nyima had renounced the Nyingma tradition and become a Gelugpa. Roaring with laughter, His Holiness responded that while Gyari Nyima might be close to Gyalo Thondup, he would never give up his faith.

The late Kalu Rinpoche and his nephew Gyaltsen Lama were present at this luncheon. Kalu Rinpoche was both a great devotee of the 16th Gyalwa Karmapa and a close friend of my family. He was so very happy that His Holiness made such strong remarks in support of my father. I learned from my parents that on more than one public occasion the Gyalwa Karmapa uttered such special words of fondness for my father, trying to send a very clear message that he gave no credence to these baseless rumors. Sadly, however, despite his efforts, a section of the public continued to believe these totally unfounded allegations.

## TSOKHAG CHUSUM (TIBETAN WELFARE ASSOCIATION)

With the passing away of Andruk Gonpo Tashi in 1964 the division within the ranks of the Chushi Gangdrug became even worse. Some of the leaders who had moved away from Darjeeling became prominently involved with the Tibetan Welfare Association, commonly known as the Tsokhag Chusum or the Group of Thirteen because it included thirteen different Tibetan settlements and communities, mainly comprised of people from Kham and Amdo. Many important Nyingma, Kagyu, and Bon religious leaders also became actively associated or sympathized with its mandate. His Holiness the 16th Gyalwa Karmapa became the titular head. Quite a few Sakya followers also participated, although the spiritual head of this tradition, His Holiness Sakya Trizin,[9] did not involve himself with the group or, for that matter, with any potentially controversial issues.

I'd like to digress a moment to share an excerpt from a note regarding the position and role of the Sakya Trizin that I prepared for Shivshankar Menon when he was National Security Advisor to Indian Prime Minister Manmohan Singh. I used to meet with him quite regularly, and during one of our sessions we discussed the role and the importance of Tibetan religious leaders and institutions. While Shivshankar Menon is one of the most well-informed Indian diplomats on matters concerning Tibet, he nevertheless asked me to prepare a note reviewing the matters we had discussed that day with further elaboration. It took me quite a while, but I submitted a rather comprehensive note for him sometime in 2013, several months before he left office in 2014.

> The Sakya Trizin is highly respected by the Tibetans and is venerated by all the four traditions. Although he keeps a low profile, the Sakya Trizin is a highly skilled teacher and scholar. There is a strong personal relationship between the Dalai Lama and the Sakya Trizin. In the 1970s, the Dalai Lama gave a serious thought to creating a position between him and the Kashag (cabinet members) and the person who was foremost to fill (in his mind) this role was Sakya Trizin—though the position was never created. Sakya Trizin's great influence is because of the historical importance of his family as well as because of the outstanding personality and scholarship of the Sakya Trizin himself. The Sakya Trizin has never allowed himself or his family to be seen as being a partisan on any issue that has confronted the Tibetan community in exile.[10]

It seems that Shivshankar Menon shared this note with his peers, because much later some other Indian officials indicated to me that they had found it helpful in their understanding of the Tibetan religious traditions and in trying to reach out to important religious leaders.

I felt that the government of India having a better understanding of the status of our spiritual leaders would not only help it appreciate the vitally important role Buddhism plays in Tibetan society but also benefit our religious institutions and teachers. This could help the Indian government avoid making serious mistakes in the future, as it had done in the early 1960s when it foolishly placed His Holiness Dudjom Rinpoche, the Supreme Head of the Nyingma school of Tibetan Buddhism, under house arrest. This monumental misstep created deep sadness and resentment among a large segment of Buddhists, not only Tibetans but also Buddhist practitioners in the Indian Himalayas stretching from Ladakh to Arunachal Pradesh. The incident further exposed the vulnerability of the Indian intelligence system to manipulation by individuals with biased and vested agendas. The Indian government became aware of their blunder when His Holiness the Dalai Lama and the royal families of Bhutan and Sikkim, along with thousands of other prominent individuals, protested this profoundly disrespectful treatment of one of the towering personalities of Tibetan Buddhism.

A section of both Western and Indian media, as well as some government officials in India and elsewhere, persist in a distorted view of the Tibetan Buddhist hierarchy. For example, the Panchen Lama is often erroneously viewed as holding the "number two" position when in fact, he could only properly be referred to as having this position in the Gelug school. In that tradition, the Dalai Lama and Panchen Lama are identified as "the Sun and Moon," or sometimes "the Father and Son."

Similarly, in the recent past, both the media and certain officials have identified His Holiness the 17th Gyalwa Karmapa, Ogyen Trinley Dorje, as occupying the number two position in Tibetan Buddhism, sometimes even calling him the successor to the Dalai Lama. The Gyalwa Karmapa is actually the head of the Karma Kagyu, a subschool of the Kagyu sect of Tibetan Buddhism. There is no doubt that the current young Karmapa has indeed captured the imagination of Tibetans from all segments of society. Several years back, an influential young Tibetan leader from Amdo, in fact, told me that this Karmapa is highly respected even in areas in Amdo, where there are predominately Gelug followers. His dramatic escape from Tibet, combined with his physical residence close to His Holiness the Dalai Lama and his innate charisma, have contributed to the wide respect and acceptance beyond his own school that he now enjoys.

Tibetan Buddhism simply does not have an official hierarchy similar to that of the Roman Catholic Church, for example. While His Holiness the Dalai Lama is the uncontested supreme leader, even he, except on temporal matters, does not exercise any direct authority over schools of Tibetan Buddhism other than the Gelugpa. Moreover, it is only the present, 14th Dalai Lama who is so deeply venerated by all Tibet's religious traditions.

Returning to the subject of the Tsokhag Chusum, some of its leaders began to feel politically marginalized. They believed the Dharamsala administration was discriminating against certain religious traditions, as well as against Tibetans from Kham and Amdo. It was also an open secret that the Tsokhag Chusum was getting moral encouragement and critical strategic advice from some influential Lhasa aristocrats who were themselves disgruntled with the administrative changes in Dharamsala. Many of these individuals further personally distrusted and disliked Gyalo Thondup, a view commonly shared by leaders of the Group of Thirteen.

The Tsokhag Chusum literally broke away from Dharamsala. There was almost no CTA presence in any of the settlements and communities that were part of the Group of Thirteen, and CTA officials avoided visiting these communities for fear of being harassed. Even I felt some sense of discomfort when I went to do a short retreat with Palyul Dzongnang Rinpoche at Mindrolling Monastery in Dhondupling Tibetan Settlement, which was part of the Tsokhag Chusum at the time. Some of my CTA colleagues were a bit concerned for my safety, while others registered their outright disapproval of my trip. From my side, I always try to separate politics from my personal relations, and it was important for me to do this retreat. To this day I wear a ring that bears the sign of a vajra and bell (symbolizing wisdom and skillful means) that Palyul Dzongnang Rinpoche gave me as part of my initiation during that retreat.

These feelings of uneasiness within the CTA about my association with members of the Group of Thirteen were evident as late as 2000 when my second daughter, Tenzing Choyang, married Neten Chokling Rinpoche, whose monastery in Bir is considered a Tsokhag Chusum stronghold. Some friends and colleagues went so far as to express their disapproval of the marriage. I wouldn't be surprised if Orgyen Topgyal Rinpoche and others in the Chokling family suffered similar criticisms from some of their associates. But in the end, this union actually became a very visible step toward reconciliation between the institutions. I invited all my colleagues and friends from the CTA to the wedding, and to my delight, almost the entire Tibetan leadership attended. For many of my colleagues, including some Kalons, this was their first ever visit to this settlement, even though it is only a few hours away from Dharamsala, the CTA's home base.

Most of the Tibetan communities that were part of the Tsokhag Chusum at one point petitioned the Indian government to grant their residents Indian citizenship, with the intention of making a clean break with the CTA. Had sizeable numbers of Tibetan refugees actually been granted Indian citizenship, it would not only have further divided Tibetan communities but also damaged the CTA's credibility. I remember being in some meetings with senior CTA officials and Indian government officials discussing the issue. While the Indians were appreciative of the CTA's concerns, they also had to follow their government's prescribed rules and regulations regarding immigration matters. While they could deny citizenship to a collective body of people, they could not deny the request of a single individual if that person met the requisite legal qualifications. In the end, the CTA was able to convince the Indian government not to accede to the Tsokhag Chusum's request for blanket citizenship for all its members.

Even though it is difficult to justify many of the actions taken by the Tsokhag Chusum against the Dharamsala administration, it is too simplistic to divide the group into good and bad actors. Rather, it is critical to understand how the grievances dividing them surfaced. The seeds of discontent can be traced back to the founding of the Chushi Gangdrug. The style and the manner in which Andruk Gonpo Tashi and Gyalo Thondup ran the organization, limiting access to resources and leadership roles only to certain Khampa leaders, fueled resentment in a large segment of the Khampa population. Nationalist Chinese operatives and their collaborators then took full advantage of the situation, further widening the divisions within the Chushi Gangdrug as well as between the Tsokhag Chusum and the CTA. It is an undeniable fact that a number of prominent people within the Tsokhag Chusum began receiving financial support from KMT agencies principally through the MTAC.

When His Holiness the 16th Gyalwa Karmapa became the head of the Tsokhag Chusum, he did so with considerable reservations. He only agreed to assume the position after several influential Khampa leaders convinced him that the future of the Dharma was at great risk. One influential aristocrat from Dharamsala baited him, saying: "Gyalo Thondup, the atheist, is the most influential and powerful person running all the affairs. . . . Now we must rely on important leaders like you to safeguard the Buddha Dharma." Another person present that day told me these words were very disheartening to the Gyalwa Karmapa, who took the allegations seriously. It is not unreasonable to assume that this unfounded contention influenced his decision to accept the leadership post.

Years later when the rift between the CTA and the Group of Thirteen had become more manageable, the Gyalwa Karmapa indicated to me that he regretted keeping his distance from Dharamsala, and, in particular, from His Holiness the Dalai Lama. I met him at the residence of the Bhutanese ambassador to India either in late 1980 or early 1981 when he was returning from a trip abroad. Abruptly changing subjects during my audience, he suddenly asked me some logistical questions about traveling to Dharamsala. He then said: "I made fewer trips to Shug-gar (a term referring to where the Dalai Lama resides) than I should have." After some further thought, he added: "You should help me when I visit Shug-gar." It was very odd for the Gyalwa Karmapa to make these remarks, because he had been to Dharamsala a number of times and logistical travel and accommodation matters are always taken care of by staff. But in keeping with traditional decorum, I answered all his questions obligingly. Sadly, he never made the trip, as he passed away shortly after our meeting, in November 1981.

Years later, in January 2000, the present, 17th Karmapa came into exile. He went directly to Dharamsala where he took up residence, the circumstances surrounding his flight making it both possible and necessary for him to be closer to the Dalai Lama. I personally thought that he was fulfilling the wish of his predecessor to go to Dharamsala. I shared this belief when I had my first audience with him a few years after his arrival there.[11]

During my 1981 audience with the 16th Gyalwa Karmapa, there were several lamas and young Tulkus in attendance, including, I believe, Gyaltsab Rinpoche, one of the four most important lineage heads under the Karmapa. The Gyalwa Karmapa's influential General Secretary, Damchoe Yongdu, was also in and out of the room and could have been privy to our conversation about the possibility of the Karmapa visiting Dharamsala. Damchoe Yongdu was seen by some as a problematic personality. A number of people in Dharamsala had a negative impression of him. Whenever there was a problem between the CTA and the 16th Gyalwa Karmapa, they believed Damchoe Yongdu was somehow involved.

I myself had an experience that initially made me question his motives. When I was working at the Bureau of the Dalai Lama in Delhi, His Holiness the 16th Gyalwa Karmapa visited the city. Some of us went for an audience. We were made to wait for over two hours even though there were not too many other people waiting to see him. We all thought it was Damchoe Yongdu who deliberately made us wait because we were from the CTA. Much later, to my surprise, I learned from a reliable person that the General Secretary had, in fact, very strongly advised the 16th Gyalwa Karmapa against accepting any formal role with the Tsokhag Chusum, or for that matter, engaging in any conflict with the CTA. I was told: "I know you (meaning Dharamsala) all think the General Secretary is the one who influences our Yidshin Norbu (Precious Jewel), but it is the opposite. When some of the Khampa leaders around him were advising our Yeshin Norbu to join the Group of Thirteen, the General Secretary strongly opposed it." He added that perhaps because Damchoe Yongdu was from Tsurphu in Central Tibet, he was either fearful of the CTA or loyal to it, in either case, not wanting to cause any difficulties. It was an eye-opener for me. But by the time I learned this, the General Secretary had already passed away.

As I am trying to explain some of the causes that contributed to the serious divisions that plagued the exile community in those days, I think sharing the experience of one prominent Group of Thirteen leader will help communicate the genuine feeling of being marginalized and discriminated against that many individuals from this group had. Palyul Dzongnang Rinpoche was one of the most important and vocal leaders of the Group of Thirteen, but he was also a CTA official. In the early years of the newly formed, inclusive CTA, he was one of those who participated with enthusiasm and dedication. He was also a member of the Tibetan Parliament from 1964 to 1967, undertaking many tasks on behalf of the Tibetan leadership. He was even given some responsibilities directly by His Holiness the Dalai Lama, including building a shrine dedicated to Guru Padmasambhava in Sikkim, which was then a small independent Himalayan kingdom and a protectorate of India.[12]

Dzongnang Rinpoche personally told me of the numerous obstacles and challenges he faced in dealing with the fledgling bureaucracy in Dharamsala. He believed many of these difficulties were due to sectarian and regional prejudices among a certain section of the CTA bureaucracy. He further shared with me his personal anguish in witnessing the disrespectful treatment of Kyabjé Dudjom Rinpoche at a public gathering, an episode intolerable to him and many others. Even though the administrative system had changed when reestablished in exile, the biased protocol and mannerisms of the old system lingered. I myself have seen formal communications addressed to Kyabjé Dudjom Rinpoche, where he is disrespectfully referred to as "Pekod Dudjom" (Dudjom from Pemakod) even though, at the time, he had already been unanimously chosen as the Supreme Head of the Nyingma tradition.

A similar event of apparent sectarian prejudice involved Dharamsala's treatment of His Holiness the 16th Gyalwa Karmapa. Some months after I joined the Kashag, we sent a very senior official from the Secretariat on an inspection tour that included a visit to Rumtek Monastery and a meeting with the 16th. I vividly remember the official's report of his visit. In his capacity representing the Kashag, and in keeping with the institution's Lhasa-based traditions, he entered the Gyalwa Karmapa's chamber and, without making any prostrations, offered him an ordinary *khata*. To show his personal reverence of this eminent spiritual leader, however, he immediately stepped back, prostrated three times, and made a mandala offering with a fine-quality *khata*, and then received His Holiness's blessings.

This senior official, schooled in the protocol decreed by the previous Lhasa-based government, meant no disrespect in initially approaching the Gyalwa Karmapa so informally. He was just faithfully observing an age-old tradition. At the same time, he at least followed up with a proper display of personal reverence, an act some other Dharamsala officials might have failed to undertake. I am sharing this story only to show that in many cases, these seemingly arrogant and prejudicial acts were not deliberate slights reflecting discrimination against religious sects or geographic regions, but rather a failure to understand and appreciate the changed circumstances resulting from the now unified Dharamsala administration.

Dzongnang Rinpoche ultimately left Dharamsala, very disgruntled and vowing never to return. But knowing he still had deep respect for His Holiness the Dalai Lama, I made considerable efforts to heal the breach by helping arrange a personal audience for him. Initially, Rinpoche was extremely reluctant to even consider the idea and skeptical about its realization. He sincerely believed that Dharamsala politics would deny him the opportunity. He was so distrustful of CTA officials that he forbade me even to mention the possibility of an audience to anyone and didn't even want to visit my residence until the audience was over.

Ringo Tulku Rinpoche, a senior Nyingma lama and trusted friend of Dzongnang Rinpoche, accompanied him to the audience. Afterward, Dzongnang Rinpoche immediately came to my residence and spent a long time going over and over the meeting. He kept repeating how well the audience had gone and that His Holiness understood everything. He was genuinely happy, and I saw the sincere respect he felt toward His Holiness. Of course, he still had deep grievances and misgivings about the CTA leadership, but it was obvious that he was able to make a clear distinction between the two.

I can't take full credit for Rinpoche's audience because it was people including my father, Khochhen Rinpoche, and Ringo Tulku Rinpoche who encouraged Dzongnang Rinpoche to seek the audience in the first place. Even when he and my father had big differences on political issues, they maintained a close personal relationship. I was told that both of them were criticized for maintaining their friendship by some individuals of their respective factions. But while my father was firm in his own beliefs, he was also a traditional Khampa leader who deeply cherished personal relationships.

Although Dzongnang Rinpoche was from the Palyul lineage of the Nyingma school, he understood the historic importance of the Mindrolling tradition. He devoted himself to establishing the Mindrolling Monastery in exile in Dehradun, assisted by Khochhen Rinpoche, an eminent scholar and administrator, who had spent most of his adult life at Mindrolling Monastery in Tibet and accompanied His Holiness Mindrolling Trichen Rinpoche into exile. Dzongnang Rinpoche invited Minling Trichen Rinpoche to Dehradun and installed him on the throne of Mindrolling Monastery. Prior to that he was residing in Kalimpong.

Minling Trichen Rinpoche, accompanied by his consort, Sangyum Sonam Paldrön, and their two daughters, Jetsün Tsering Paldrön and Jetsün Dechen Paldrön, arrived in Delhi in the early months of 1976. It was a wonderful reunion for my parents. The family spent three days at our residence in Delhi, resting and getting ready for the historic move to Mindrolling Monastery in Dehradun. My father personally accompanied Minling Trichen Rinpoche with my youngest brother, Kunzang Tsewang.

Minling Trichen Rinpoche's permanent presence in Dehradun contributed to closer relations between his monastery and Dharamsala. As previously discussed, the Mindrolling lineage had an extraordinary relationship with the institution of the Dalai Lamas starting with the Great Fifth, who was both a teacher and a student of Terdak Lingpa, the founder of Mindrolling Monastery in Tibet.

Soon after Dzongnang Rinpoche's audience with His Holiness, the Dhondupling Settlement became a part of the mainstream Tibetan community. However, Rinpoche's personal difficulties did not end, and unfortunately, he passed away at the early age of fifty-six. This was a great loss, especially to Mindrolling Monastery. Today, both Mindrolling Monastery and the settlement are very stable and quite prosperous, ably guided by Khochhen Rinpoche.

In conclusion, these organizations were not solely responsible for the trouble that beset the exile community and relations with the CTA in the early years of our exile. The leaders in Dharamsala may also have lacked the vision and skills to be fully inclusive of the different groups composing the newly unified Tibetan community in exile given their need to demonstrate the strength and leadership to keep the fragile alliance together.

I have no wish to go into more depth about this unfortunate period of Tibet's history. My purpose in writing this book is not to open past wounds but rather to help further heal them. If we were to examine this period in a detached and impartial manner, I am quite certain we would find that many of the groups and individuals had what they considered to be reasonable justifications for acting the way they did. Today, all the settlements and communities that were part of the Group of Thirteen have become fully integrated into mainstream Tibetan society. Some of them are run by officials appointed by the CTA. Others appoint or elect their own leaders, all of whom are officially recognized by the CTA. During my tenure in the Kashag, I strongly suggested bringing these communities closer within the fold of the CTA. I specifically lobbied for two senior leaders from the Group of Thirteen, Drawu Pon Rinchen Tsering and Sey Donyo, to be given Deputy Kalon rank, with one of them given authority within the Department of Home to oversee the communities and settlements formerly belonging to the group. I had the opportunity to know many of the leaders of that generation from all the different factions and I have deep respect for many of them.

## GYALO THONDUP: THE MAN AND THE PERCEPTION

Before I address any of the other organizations established in the early years of our exile, I would like to discuss Gyalo Thondup. Although I have mentioned him several times, I have not explained much about his background, personality, position, and activities undertaken in support of the Tibetan cause. As is evident from the preceding discussion, his role and people's perception of him were crucial factors for over two decades in our recent history. He was an extremely influential, highly controversial, and very much misunderstood individual, but one who dedicated his life's work to advancing Tibet's interests. He was in a way an institution, far larger than any individual.

I had the privilege of working for Gyalo Thondup for some time and got to know him quite intimately. It is true that he could be arrogant and condescending. It is also true that he had very negative feelings toward certain Lhasa aristocrats and felt that the influence of some religious leaders was not helpful in moving Tibetan society forward. But the widely held perception by prominent leaders from all the Tibetan Buddhist traditions that Gyalo Thondup was anti-religion is misplaced. It is unfortunate that this distorted image of him surfaced during the early days of exile, branding him a controversial and divisive figure during this critical period of the Tibetan movement. While he may not have been overtly religious or knowledgeable about the Dharma, he was definitely not an atheist, and his commitment to the Tibetan cause was fierce and unwavering.

It is beyond dispute that Gyalo Thondup dedicated his entire life to advancing Tibet's interests, seeking to work with any person, group, or government that might help, including the KMT, Communists, Americans, Indians, and even the Russians at one point, all because of his profound commitment to the cause. In addition to running our intelligence network, he spearheaded many important initiatives, including the CIA-backed Mustang-based guerilla operation and the Special Frontier Force (SFF). I knew many of the senior Indian officials who worked with Gyalo Thondup, and most of them held him in high regard. It was also very clear that he was not the easiest person to work with and a bit unpredictable. I remember a remark by T. N. Kaul, then Indian Foreign Secretary, at a dinner hosted by his brother-in-law, Anupam Dhar, where both Gyalo Thondup and I were guests. Warmly shaking his hand, T. N. Kaul remarked: "What mischiefs are you up to now?" While his tone was playful, he was actually quite serious. I have also come to know some of the retired CIA officers who worked with Gyalo Thondup and, while they had high respect for his dedication to the Tibet cause, they also found him difficult to deal with.

I wish Gyalo Thondup had exhibited a better understanding of the Tibetan psyche, and I wish he had been more inclusive in his undertakings on our behalf. Even among a section of Western friends of Tibet, he had a controversial image and quite a few people mistrusted him. My friend and colleague John Ackerly, former President of the International Campaign for Tibet (ICT), was one of them. After meeting Gyalo Thondup in person and hearing about all he had done for Tibet, however, I remember John telling me: "Lodi, I must admit that this man, throughout his life, has tried everything and worked with all kinds of people with the purpose of getting something for Tibet." This sentiment sums up Gyalo Thondup perfectly.

It is true, however, that the parallel activities led by Gyalo Thondup, with resources from the CIA, unintentionally undermined Dharamsala's authority. Although I began my career in Darjeeling under him, I became a part of the Dharamsala administration. Beginning in the late 1970s, he gradually started handing over many of his operations to the CTA. By the mid-1980s, hardly any of them were still being carried out from Darjeeling. Some of Gyalo Thondup's critics felt that his devolution of authority was not with the best intentions. They believed he relinquished control solely because the CIA was gradually withdrawing its support and funding of Tibetan operations. I don't subscribe to that view.

Gyalo Thondup never questioned the authority of the CTA, but he did have serious misgivings about its capabilities and a great deal of mistrust of some of its senior officials. Even though the CIA was phasing out its support of Tibetan initiatives, agencies of the Indian government had stepped in to take its place for many of the programs. I accompanied then Senior Kalon W. G. Kundeling and Kalon Wangdu Dorje to most of the meetings with high-level Indian government officials during this initial transition period. I was then an Assistant Cabinet Secretary. Most likely, one of the reasons I was tasked with this responsibility was

The author with Gyalo Thondup in front of the Po Lin Monastery in Hong Kong, 1998

my perceived closeness to Gyalo Thondup, in addition to the fact that I already knew several of the government officials we were meeting.

It was very clear that Gyalo Thondup had already fully briefed these Indian officials about his decision to distance himself from day-to-day responsibilities for the operations previously run out of Darjeeling and that the CTA would henceforth be dealing with the Indian government for these and other matters. These meetings were a very uplifting experience for the two attending Kalons because prior to then, the CTA had had no access to such high-level Indian officials. Dharamsala's contacts had been limited to officials within the Ministry of Rehabilitation and Education and periodic meetings with mid-level officials from the Ministry of External Affairs, the latter of which, sadly, were more reprimanding than supportive in nature. The prominent officials we met through Gyalo Thondup's connections included P. N. Haksar, the powerful Principal Secretary to Prime Minister Indira Gandhi, and R. N. Kao, the founder and Director of the Research and Analysis Wing of India's external intelligence agency.

In my view, one practical reason that prompted Gyalo Thondup's decision to hand over operations to the CTA was the lack of a proper administrative infrastructure supporting him. When his chief lieutenant, Lhamo Tsering, was detained by the Nepalese authorities in 1974 in connection with the Mustang guerilla base, all the activities directed from Darjeeling under Gyalo Thondup's guidance were severely paralyzed. Lhamo Tsering and several other prominent individuals connected with the base were only released by the authorities in December 1980, after having spent almost seven years in prison. While Gyalo Thondup was the leader with his eye on the big picture, it was Lhamo Tsering who ran the day-to-day operations. He was a very humble individual, but meticulous in his handling of any matters entrusted to him. Gyalo Thondup would not have succeeded in many of his efforts had he not had someone like Lhamo Tsering assisting him. As I previously noted, he could be harsh and condescending, hurting the ego and sentiments of the many Tibetans working with him and even those who just came to pay him a courtesy call. On numerous occasions, I personally witnessed how skillfully Lhamo Tsering managed to appease those who were hurt by Gyalo Thondup's dismissive behavior.

Although I appreciated and understood the importance of Gyalo Thondup's work, it was also my firm belief that for the Tibetan movement to become more effective, its activities must be cohesive and unified under the CTA's leadership. Thus, I worked very hard to smooth the transition between Gyalo Thondup's organization and the CTA. I felt strongly that the people who had worked with him should be given ranks and titles within the CTA befitting their positions and previous experience. Certain officials were quite reluctant to fully embrace these individuals, however. Only a very few of them were formally accepted, most being rejected under one pretext or another. A number of dedicated people with good experience and professional training gradually left to pursue private lives and were thus lost to the CTA, which sorely needed them in its ranks.

Having worked with Lhamo Tsering, I knew he had much to offer to the movement and should be given important responsibilities within the CTA upon his release by the Nepalese. Behind the scenes, I worked hard to encourage senior officials in Dharamsala, and Lhamo Tsering himself, to become an integral part of the CTA . I even had the opportunity to bring this matter to His Holiness's notice. I was thus very happy when he joined the CTA and eventually became a member of the Kashag. He proved himself to be a great asset to the Tibetan leadership, and many people who had had misgivings about him became true admirers.

Eventually, one way or another, all of Gyalo Thondup's Darjeeling-based operations came under the CTA's domain. Even responsibility for the SFF was transferred to the CTA's Department of Security, then headed by Minister Wangdu Dorje. Soon thereafter, Gyalo Thondup joined the Kashag. He even served as the Kalon Tripa, or Chairman of the Kashag, for some time. During his tenure, however, he was very frustrated, feeling that all the rules and regulations made it difficult for him to function effectively. During one visit to North America when he was Kalon Tripa, he gave several rather precious thangkas to dedicated Tibetan supporters to show his appreciation for their efforts on Tibet's behalf. He gifted these treasures from his own personal collection, preferring to use his own resources rather than try to get the ponderous bureaucracy in Dharamsala to approve some appropriate gifts.

Gyalo Thondup was an almost mythical person, deeply disliked and feared by many but held in awe by equal numbers. In my view, this reputation served a good purpose, not only for him but also for the Tibetan movement. Some of us used to call him "Toranaga san," after the main character from James Clavell's novel *Shōgun*. His joining and later leading the Kashag in a way detracted from this mythical status. But in assuming that position, he left no room for any speculation about his maintaining a separate center of power. This consolidation of interests clearly projected the CTA as the center and engine of the united Tibetan movement, a clarification needed both to reduce internal tensions and to develop support for the Tibetan cause in the international community.

Gyalo Thondup deserves far greater recognition and appreciation for his contributions than he currently receives. As I previously mentioned, he had a number of drawbacks and made many mistakes, but he was not a vindictive person, despite what others may have thought. For example, I once met him in Delhi during one of his rare visits to the city. At the time, a group of Khampa leaders had launched a brutal character assassination campaign against him. Rather than being angry or upset with these individuals, he asked after their well-being and spent considerable time explaining to me the significant contributions some of them had made in advancing the Tibetan cause. He was actually very unhappy with the Dharamsala establishment for not giving them enough recognition and respect.

There was another time I recall when some Tibetans critical of both Gyalo Thondup and Dharamsala were fearful that the government of India was preparing to curtail their activities and even arrest them, supposedly at his behest. Of course, I knew that he was not involved, even assuming these actions were being contemplated by the Indians, because in those days he spent very little time in India. However, I mentioned the matter to him, and he was very upset to think that the Indian government might take such steps. He immediately telephoned his contacts among senior Indian officials to inquire if there were any truth to the rumor. While I could not hear their responses, it was clear from his expression that no such actions were being planned. He made the further strong plea that these leaders not be harassed in any way, as they were all freedom fighters and "my friends" with whom he had worked very closely over the years.

Gyalo Thondup is also not someone intolerant of criticism. I have personally taken him to task on a number of occasions. I must admit, however, that once he has made up his mind, no amount of persuasion is likely to change his opinion. But he must be remembered as a man who dared to think big and act on his thoughts. Although much of the time he failed to achieve his goals, it was not for lack of effort.

I know there is a widespread belief in the Tibetan world that my family is very loyal to Gyalo Thondup because of some special benefit we supposedly received from him. That is simply false, but perhaps the following account will put an end to the speculation. In 1972, I had the great honor of being selected to accompany His Holiness the Dalai Lama as part of his entourage on a visit to Thailand, which proved to be the beginning of numerous other privileges I received in serving His Holiness. I met Gyalo Thondup at his Delhi residence a week or so before the trip, and he gave me sage advice on how to conduct myself during the visit. He then asked if I had a decent suit to wear as it was very important that I dress properly, because the Thai people are very formal. I told him that although I did not have a suit, I had appropriate clothes. He insisted that I immediately go and get myself a tailored suit, giving me 800 Indian rupees to make the purchase. At the time, that was equivalent to approximately three months of my salary. I was so impressed by his kindness and generosity until about a year and a half later, when one of his senior staff, Tashi Chodar, told me that Gyalo Thondup's notes showed that he had given me 800 rupees and they needed to be reimbursed! It took me several installments to pay back the loan. That is the only occasion on which I, or my family, ever received a "gift" from Gyalo Thondup.

## SPECIAL FRONTIER FORCE

As I have also made several references to the SFF, or the Establishment 22 as it is also known, I want to discuss it in further detail and describe the circumstances in which I was almost assigned to it. As previously mentioned, the SFF is an Indian paramilitary organization led by Indians but having many senior Tibetan officers. It is headed by a senior Indian military officer on deputation as Inspector General (IG) who is assisted by a CTA appointee, a Tibetan officer with the title of Chief Political Leader. There were several other Tibetan officers with the title of Political Leader posted at various SFF bases assisting Indian commanders.

In 1976 I received word from Gyalo Thondup while I was in Dharamsala to come visit him in Delhi to discuss a certain important matter. When I met him, he gave me the most unexpected instruction to join the SFF as a Political Officer, a new position that would be created for me with the main responsibility of providing motivational instruction to the forces. With the veteran fighters aging, a large number of young men and women were being recruited, and Gyalo Thondup was worried that unless strong guidance was provided, they might not have the same commitment as the earlier generation.

I was not at all happy about this prospect and tried to convince Gyalo Thondup that I could serve the cause far better where I was than by becoming part of this paramilitary organization. I also frankly told him that I had no interest in military drills and vigorous physical exercise. There and then, he told me that I need not go through any of the military training because my position would be as a civilian. By then, my parents had already moved from Darjeeling to stay with me, and I told him that if I were to join the SFF I would need to be able to take care of them, including proper housing facilities in Delhi, even though I would spend most of my time at Chakrata, the SFF headquarters. He immediately called a senior Indian government official at the Cabinet Secretariat, briefed him on our discussion, and asked him to comply with my request.

Literally the next day, he was gone. However, he seems to have discussed the decision to send me to the SFF with the Kashag and concerned officials, including J. N. Taring, who was then the Representative of His Holiness in Delhi. J. N. Taring was responsible for finalizing the arrangements, including setting up my meeting with General H. K. Bhardwaj, who was the IG from November 11, 1975, to February 28, 1981. Fortunately, this meeting gave me the opportunity to back out of the assignment. For whatever reason, I had the feeling that the IG was not keen on having me around. I was told that certain senior Tibetan political leaders were also worried that my joining the SFF might undermine the status quo. I never bothered to confirm this speculation because I had no interest in joining.

From the beginning, my conversation with General Bhardwaj did not go very well. Extending his hand, the IG said: "So Mr. Gyari, I understand you want to join us?" To which I replied: "No, General, I do not wish to join, but I am instructed." The General made it clear that I must go through the basic military training before my formal appointment as a Political Officer and that his organization had no accommodations in Delhi. I would be provided with suitable facilities and staff at Chakrata. He did hint that some other branch of the government would most probably look into my accommodation needs in Delhi. In any case, we both agreed that my joining the SFF should be reconsidered after we were able to further discuss the matter with senior people on both sides. Of course, the General had a valid point in insisting that I undergo basic military training, as the SFF is a paramilitary organization, but that was something in which I had absolutely no interest. As Gyalo Thondup vanished from India for more than a year during this period, my appointment as a Political Officer never materialized.

I must be clear that my reluctance to join the SFF was purely personal. I have the highest admiration for this force and for the people who served in it. I had gone on tour to Chakrata and to some of the SFF units in the border areas and witnessed their parachute-jumping and rock-climbing demonstrations, both of which made me very proud. The SFF is definitely one of the best commando forces in India, maybe even in the world, having proven its gallantry and skills in many operations, including in the liberation of Bangladesh.[13] The force holds many world records, including the women's free jump. A relative of mine, Dechen Wangmo, was a senior SFF woman officer. When she did her free jump, she was several months pregnant, a fact she did not disclose because she would have been prohibited from making the jump. Her husband, Ratug Ngawang, was among the first officers, together with Jampa Kalden, appointed by the Tibetan leadership to lead the SFF. Jampa Kalden was the Dapon or the Chief Political Leader. After his retirement, he was appointed Secretary to the Department of the Security of the CTA. Both of these veterans have since passed away. Unlike the Mustang guerrilla force that was manned entirely by Chushi Gangdrug veterans, the SFF had a number of former Tibetan army regulars within its ranks. Among the first batch

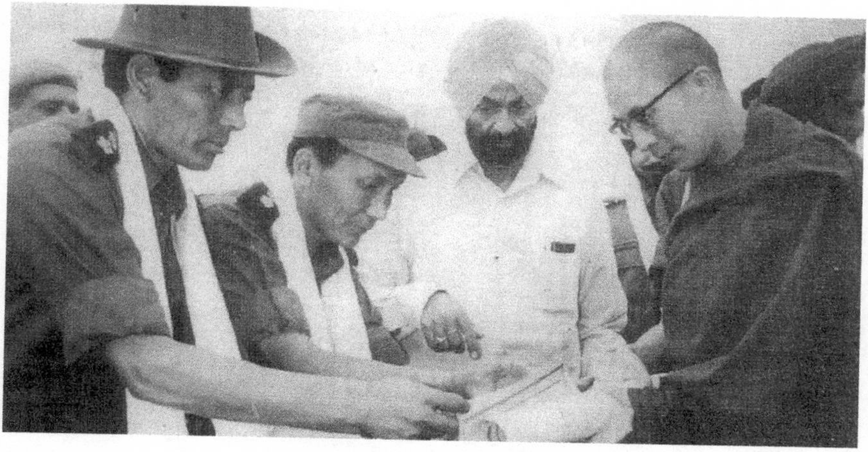

His Holiness the 14th Dalai Lama reviewing maps with members of the SFF, 1972. (Left to right) Ratug Ngawang, Jampa Kalden, General S. S. Uban

of political leaders named to head this organization, Namgyal Wangdu rose to the position of Dapon after Jampa Kalden's retirement.

As I continued to deal with senior Indian government officials even after I moved to Washington, D.C., as His Holiness's Special Envoy, I maintained an interest in the welfare of this organization and its members. I am very pleased that at least they now receive retirement and other benefits quite similar to those given the regular Indian army. I must acknowledge the hard efforts of senior Indian officials in the Cabinet Secretariat with oversight of the SFF in getting these deserved benefits ultimately provided.

We were fortunate to have General S. S. Uban as the founding SFF Inspector General. He provided strong leadership and vigorously maintained the distinctive character of the SFF as a Tibetan force, sometimes even battling his own Indian officials and officers. I knew him very well. After his retirement, we worked together for an extended period, training some of the younger CTA officials and young men of the SFF to become research and intelligence officers. Several of the trainees served in various capacities. One of them, Migyur Dorjee, rose to the highest position in the CTA bureaucracy as Cabinet Secretary. After retirement he ran for elected office and, as of this writing, is a member of the Tibetan Parliament.

## TIBETAN YOUTH CONGRESS

The Tibetan Youth Congress (TYC) was launched on October 7, 1970, by members of the Tibetan youth in exile after years of careful deliberation. Tethong Tenzin Geyche, Zechutsang Sonam Topgyal, Tethong Tenzin Namgyal, and I were the four conveners. In the mid-1960s, Tethong Tenzin Namgyal and I had started discussing the need to create an organization to harness the energy of the younger generation. By that time, I had already left school and was working at *Defend Tibet's Freedom Press*. Tenzin Namgyal was still at the Mount Hermon School. On weekends either I would visit him or he would come to Darjeeling, and we would spend hours discussing our ideas. I vividly remember walking by the Union Church on Gandhi Road on the evening of November 22, 1963, the day John F. Kennedy was assassinated. JFK was someone we both truly admired. We were deeply inspired by his words: "Ask not what your country can do for you—ask what you can do for your country." They became our motto.

During that period, I also translated and read short biographies of several freedom fighters, including that of Subhas Chandra Bose, the Indian nationalist who chose a different path than Gandhi and fought against the British by raising the Indian National Army with Japanese support; David Ben-Gurion, the primary founder and first Prime Minister of Israel; Mustafa Kemal Atatürk, revolutionary reformer and founder of the Republic of Turkey; General Aung San of Myanmar; and Mostefa Ben Boulaïd, Algerian revolutionary and freedom fighter. One can readily see the state of my mind in those days. I chose biographies of revolutionary leaders who did not hesitate to take up arms in pursuit of their hopes for freedom. We published these translated biographies as a series in *Defend Tibet's Freedom Press*, hoping to inspire young Tibetans with revolutionary zeal.

Initially, we thought of establishing youth clubs in various settlements or areas where there were sizeable Tibetan populations. Our hope was that the younger generation could gather on weekends and holidays to participate in various physical activities and listen to recitations of the exploits of King Gesar and other *pathuls* or heroes of Ling.[14] While Tibet had extraordinary, well-known role models in its spiritual tradition, there was a need to popularize the Ling stories to inculcate a sense of pride, loyalty, and courage in our youth that would strengthen their political will. By the end of the 1960s, the first wave of Tibetan graduates from our own schools started entering Indian universities for further studies. We wanted to ensure that the new energy associated with this precious human resource was not wasted but used in the service of our community, particularly in support of our struggle.

Although it was far from the main reason we started the TYC, one thing that worried some of us was that unless we could provide our youth with some meaningful activities, they might devote their energies to frivolous pursuits, including playing mahjong. Though seemingly harmless, the addiction to playing this game for money in my view has not only ruined many lives but also greatly harmed our nation. There is a widespread belief among the Tibetan community that Governor Ngapo Ngawang Jigme's frantic calls for instructions when Mao's Red Army advanced toward Chamdo went unanswered because his governmental colleagues in Lhasa were busy playing mahjong. While we Tibetans have shared so much of our rich spiritual and cultural heritage with our neighbors, we have imported some of their worst vices. It deeply saddens me that today in Nepal, Bhutan, Sikkim, and other Himalayan regions, individuals of the Tibetan elite are wasting their time and money, and in some cases destroying family values and ruining lives, in slavish devotion to this addictive pastime.

For a number of reasons, rather than establishing youth clubs, we decided to launch a more formal organization patterned after some international groups. We initially thought to call it a "league," but taking the wise advice of Tethong Sonam Topjor, the Tethong brothers' father, who in those days was living with me in Delhi, we decided to call it a "congress." Tethong Sonam Topjor thought that the term was much more auspicious because it likened our organization to other prominent groups, such as the Indian National Congress. By contrast, he thought "league" was problematic, potentially associating us with predecessors such as the League of Nations, which was so short-lived.

The suffering, struggle, and success of the Jewish people also profoundly inspired some of us. We even thought of building kibbutz-style communities exclusively for TYC members. Jamyang Norbu and I were the most enthusiastic about learning from the Jewish people's experiences. Jamyang Norbu was the real expert on the subject. One of his primary heroes in those days was the legendary General Moshe Dayan, who was born in a kibbutz. I do not remember very clearly, but I believe we asked Jamyang Norbu to explore this possibility with his uncle, Tethong Tsewang Choegyal, who was then in charge of the Mundgod Tibetan Settlement in South India. Had the Israelis had a diplomatic presence in India, as they do now, I have no doubt we would have made serious efforts to establish some connection with them. In those days, Indian government policy was very pro-Arab; only in recent decades have the Israelis and Indians established direct diplomatic ties. We made some efforts to reach out to the Israelis in this regard, but nothing tangible resulted.

Leon Uris's *Exodus* also greatly inspired me at this point in my life. I spent a considerable part of my meager salary buying copies of this book for my colleagues and friends. It is amazing how one book can have such a powerful and profound impact. His later book *Trinity* was equally inspiring. In recent years, I have wished that someone would write a similar book chronicling Tibet's struggle.

Our hope was that the TYC would not limit itself to being active within the Tibetan community but would expand internationally. At one time we even explored the possibility of creating an affiliation with the Indian Youth Congress, the youth wing of the Indian National Congress. I had discussions with several Youth Congress leaders, including Ambika Soni and Bhim Singh. Ambika Soni is now a senior leader of the Congress Party, while Bhim Singh, whom I see from time to time at the India International Center, heads a regional political party from Jammu and Kashmir State.

We even met with Sanjay Gandhi, the younger son of Indira Gandhi, who really was the paramount leader of the youth wing. I must confess that at one time, I became deeply disappointed with both mother and son because of their authoritarian style, and especially for the way they treated opposition leaders when they imposed the state of Emergency from 1975 to 1977. A number of those targeted were close personal friends. I kept some important documents for George Fernandes, the veteran Socialist leader, and for Pran Nath Lekhi, an eminent lawyer, when they went underground and were eventually arrested and imprisoned. Lekhi's documents included his passport. Ironically, several months after the Emergency was lifted and the opposition Janata Party came into power, I went to return Lekhi's documents, and we had a big laugh because his passport had expired in the meantime!

I must also admit that for ordinary people during the Emergency period, life was easier and definitely safer. Even the trains moved on time, and one did not need to bribe officials to get things done. One truly positive quality shared by mother and son was their decisiveness, a trait lacking in so many political leaders. Thus, from a rather negative first impression, I came to appreciate some of Sanjay Gandhi's good qualities and kept in periodic touch with him. My last meeting with him was in Delhi at his makeshift office on the lawns of 10 Janpath just a day or two before his untimely, tragic death in an airplane accident on June 23, 1980. In January of that year, the Indian electorate had returned the Congress Party and Indira Gandhi to power.

What was uppermost in our minds as TYC founders was instilling and maintaining unity among all Tibetans. One need look no further than the TYC emblem to see our goal: a map of a unified Tibet, announcing our purpose loud and clear. These days there is a perception that the TYC was established for the sole purpose of fighting for Tibet's independence. In fact, in 1970 when the TYC was founded, the entire Tibetan community was engaged in a freedom struggle with the aim of achieving independence. This was years before His Holiness developed the Middle Way Approach.

Tenzin Geyche, one of the co-conveners, was then Secretary to His Holiness, a position that he occupied for decades until his formal retirement in 2007. He continued to serve His Holiness informally for several more years after that. He

His Holiness the 14th Dalai Lama (flanked by His Senior Tutor, Kyabjé Ling Rinpoche, to his right and Junior Tutor, Kyabjé Trijang Rinpoche, to his left) addressing the inaugural meeting of the TYC, Dharamsala, October 7, 1970. (Seated behind, left to right) two of the co-conveners, Tethong Tenzin Namgyal and the author, Kalon W. G. Kundeling. (Note the TYC symbol of a map of unified Tibet as the backdrop.)
Tibet Museum, CTA

also served as a member of the Kashag from 1983 to 1987. Sonam Topgyal, another co-convener, held many important positions in the CTA, including Kalon Tripa, the highest executive position. Sadly, our dear friend is no longer with us. When he passed away in 2012, I happened to be visiting Dharamsala. His family asked me to light the funeral pyre, acknowledging our special relationship. I was deeply touched and honored.

Tenzin Namgyal, also a co-convener, held several important positions in the CTA before being appointed His Holiness's Representative in New York from 1973 to 1986. After that, he served as His Holiness's Special Representative in Washington, D.C., from 1987 until May 1990. He was one of the three members of the interim Kashag directly elected by members of a special assembly called by the Dalai Lama in 1990 when His Holiness was taking major steps toward democratizing Tibetan politics. Subsequently, Tenzin Namgyal also held the post of Kalon Tripa. He was also the founding President of the International Campaign for Tibet (ICT), the Washington, D.C.-based Tibet advocacy group. Tenzin Namgyal and I virtually switched roles when I was appointed Special Envoy of His Holiness and he moved to Dharamsala to join the Kashag. Eventually I became the ICT President. At the time of this writing, Tenzin Namgyal heads the Tibetan unit of the Voice of America in Washington, D.C.

I was fortunate to have these wonderful and talented individuals not only as colleagues but also, more importantly, as personal friends. Over the years, we have never wavered in our friendship and have worked together on many important issues in support of Tibet, a cause dear to us all. Personally, working with this group gave me the opportunity for the first time to interact professionally with individuals my own age. When I joined *Defend Tibet's Freedom Press*, my working colleagues were in most cases twenty to thirty years my senior. While this benefited me immensely in gaining knowledge and experience from seasoned veterans, the vast age difference prompted me to pretend to be much older than I was to fit into the associated social environment. With the TYC, the setting was completely different, and for the first time in a long while I felt like a "youth" again.

Tenzin Geyche was a magnet for bringing people from my generation to Dharamsala to serve His Holiness and the Tibetan cause. I have no doubt that his being Secretary to His Holiness also brought me to His Holiness's attention. Tenzin Geyche was the quintessential civil servant. People such as him and T. C. Tara, who was for a long time His Holiness's Principal Secretary, gave the Private

Office both stability and dignity. For Tenzin Namgyal and myself, Tenzin Geyche's close proximity to His Holiness was, paradoxically, sometimes a handicap. I remember Tenzin Geyche telling us more than once after being briefed about some of our work: "I wish someone else could bring these things to His Holiness's attention. I really don't feel comfortable because of our personal relationship." Tenzin Geyche is such an upright, principled individual, but sometimes, I think, a bit oversensitive. I told him: "You should forget Tenzin being your brother and me your friend. We are talking to you as Secretary to His Holiness, and it is in that position you should also report to His Holiness." While he agreed with my logic, he nevertheless persisted in his discomfort.

While the four of us possibly spent hundreds of hours together, I hardly remember any occasions when we discussed personal issues. Everything was about Tibet. Of course, there were many other people who played important roles in working with us in this formative period as well as after the TYC was launched. Samdhong Rinpoche; Jetsun Pema, younger sister to His Holiness; and Jamyang Norbu were among those elected to the TYC's first Central Executive Committee (Centrex).

The TYC was a purely youth initiative, but we would not have been able to launch it in the manner and scale we wanted without support from the Kashag. We had this great idea, but no funding to realize such an ambitious project. We had serious discussions among ourselves about how to raise the necessary money, but in the end the only feasible option was to approach the Kashag for a grant, at least for convening the first gathering. I cannot remember exactly how much we asked for, but we received 80,000 Indian rupees. Some sharp-tongued critic then nicknamed us the Shon-nu Gye-tri Tsogpa—the 80,000 Youth Organization.

It was not easy obtaining that funding. I have a feeling it took some time for the Kashag to reach a consensus on the matter, as some of the members must have felt a bit uneasy anticipating what trouble this group of youngsters might get them into. During one of our meetings with the Kashag, then seniormost Kalon W. G. Kundeling, in a serious but somewhat humorous manner, asked point blank if we were going to behave like "Red Guards." I think he initially had some serious reservations about the TYC, but later on he became very supportive. He was extremely outgoing and especially good with young people. Many of us visited him on the weekends because he always had a few bottles of beer in his refrigerator, which in those days was a great treat. When he would see us walking in, he would say: "And here they come, just for the beer."

Early in the TYC's existence, we had an opportunity to make our first effort toward furthering unity among the Tibetan community, our principal mission. Shortly after its founding, the TYC hosted a unity dinner for the two factions of the Chushi Gangdrug. Each faction had supporters camped out in different areas of Dharamsala, and the situation was actually quite tense. People were worried that there might even be physical clashes between the two groups. I can't remember the exact month that the dinner occurred, but we had just had the first snowfall of the winter. So we took the opportunity to engage in a traditional Tibetan custom to create a sense of unity amongst all those gathered there.

In Tibet, at the first snowfall, you immediately go outside, gather a fistful of snow, and surprise someone with it. The person to whom you give it is obligated to give you whatever you ask for. Some of us, including Sonam Topgyal, Tenzin Namgyal, Yeshe Gyurme, Jamyang Norbu, Yarphel, Tesur Ngodup, and Kunsang Paljor, quickly went out and delivered fistfuls of snow to the main leaders of the two factions and asked that they join us for the unity dinner. Respecting the age-old tradition, all the Khampa leaders from both sides accepted our invitation, and the dinner was a huge success! It was a joyful and moving event, bringing together veteran leaders who had fought together and shared many personal relations but who had been torn apart by unfortunate misunderstandings and differences. It was like a long overdue family reunion.

The way the elder Chushi Gangdrug leaders conducted themselves was inspirational. In fact, it was almost comical how they all became so busy talking to each other that those of us from the TYC who were hosting the dinner felt totally left out. But I can attest that we were not disappointed; we were so happy seeing the camaraderie among the leaders of these rival groups. In later years, it was painful to see how the whole style and behavior of members of this organization changed. The mature and dignified behavior of the elder leaders was lost in the next generation.

After the success of the dinner, the TYC conducted a special prayer service at the Tsuglagkhang, the main temple near His Holiness's residence, extending invitations not just to the leaders but to all members of both factions. Many CTA officials were worried, as they thought this was dangerous, bordering on the insane. Unlike the dinner, limited to the Chushi Gangdrug leaders, this gathering potentially involved a far larger group of individuals from both factions. But we were confident. Even though the differences ran deep, the senior leaders would never allow any unpleasantness to occur on the doorstep of His Holiness's residence.

Once again, it proved to be a wonderful gathering where battle-tested and highly respected leaders from both sides came together. After the prayer service concluded, people from the two sharply divided factions mingled, talking to one another, cracking jokes, and enjoying themselves. The success of these two events proved the saying that "blood is thicker than water." It also showed that if each side had continued to make an effort to reach out and understand the other's viewpoint, the situation could have turned out quite differently than it did.

Some of us were worried that because of the TYC's dedication to a unified Tibet its public image might fall victim to the rumormongers who created such havoc for the Chigdril Tsogpa. The TYC was very vocal, and as was the case for the Chigdril Tsogpa, our support of a unified Tibet could have been misconstrued as favoring the complete abolishment of regional identities. Having witnessed the mishandling of the issue by some Tibetan activists and officials in the past, we were very cautious and made special efforts to bring people belonging to the Group of Thirteen into leadership positions. For our opening ceremonies, we invited a number of highly respected young leaders from communities associated with the Group, including Dorzong Rinpoche and Drugu Choegyal Rinpoche. Much later, some of us made special efforts to convince Dorzong Rinpoche to accept a position in the Kashag, an idea we knew His Holiness would approve. My friend and colleague Sonam Topgyal had a very close personal relationship with these two Rinpoches. I know he personally discussed these matters with Dorzong Rinpoche, who would have been a great asset to the CTA. Dorzong Rinpoche was deeply committed to his work at Tashi Jong Community, however, and chose to decline. I was deeply saddened to learn of his passing on February 16, 2017, in Taiwan after a prolonged illness.

The TYC's initial events were specifically planned to demonstrate that we had come of age in many respects, including the organization and execution of our activities. Ours were the first ever public events the Tibetan community at large attended. But most importantly, we wanted to give a platform, not only to the Kashag and other important organs of the CTA but also to influential leaders outside the government, to voice their opinions. In fact, our conference was the first public event in Dharamsala at which Gyalo Thondup was invited to speak.

The TYC was seen as an organization loyal to the CTA and dedicated to pursuing the goals His Holiness envisioned, but, at the same time, not a CTA puppet. From the very beginning, we asserted ourselves, sometimes creating rather tense relations with the CTA. But our outspoken positions helped the TYC's image of being truly independent. Within a very short period of time, we established branches in almost all the exile Tibetan settlements and communities. And at one time, almost 80 percent of the CTA staff in Dharamsala were TYC members. The creation of the TYC alone was in my view a needed breath of fresh air in the Tibetan community, providing, at least for a while, a welcome distraction from the internal squabbling.

Although the TYC continues to be an important NGO within the exile community, unfortunately in the recent past it too has had its own internal differences, creating a virtual split among those in favor of independence and those who are proponents of the Middle Way Approach. In my view, the TYC could have handled this explosive issue without triggering a division within its membership. As a founder, I have felt obliged to make an appeal for its unity. As was the case with so many other issues, one of the main reasons for the split was a lack of understanding of the organization's own history, including how and why it came into being.

Even prior to the TYC's founding, I felt that it should eventually become a political party. This was one reason some of us were trying to establish relations with international organizations as well as with political organizations in India, including the Indian Youth Congress. I had serious consultations with several Indian political leaders, including George Fernandes and Rabi Ray, seeking their help in establishing relations with the group Socialist International, which we thought would give Tibet both connections and an international platform. While members of the Indian Socialist Party were staunch friends of Tibet, a number of the prominent socialist leaders in Europe were lukewarm and even hostile to our struggle because they had the misconception of the Communist Chinese as the "real socialists" and the Tibetans as the opposite. Many of the Indian Socialist leaders, including George Fernandes, ultimately became disillusioned with Socialist International and parted company with it.

With or without international connections, I have always felt that we should introduce a political party system within the exile Tibet community if we are truly committed to establishing a democracy. With political parties, elections will be fought on issues and agendas, rather than regional politics, thus fostering greater cohesiveness among Tibetans from all regions. I am not suggesting that this approach supplant or interfere with our regional-based electoral system because maintaining that structure provides the very foundation of our unity. However, if there were political parties, they could field candidates from any and all of the three regions. Whichever party obtained the majority of seats in Parliament could then form the government.

Unfortunately, in my view, there has always been resistance to this idea from virtually every level of Tibetan society. During the days when I was a member of the TYC's Centrex, we called a special meeting of the Working Committee, with many other invitees, to discuss this issue, and in particular, whether or not the TYC should become a party and if so, what kind of ideology or philosophy it should adopt. The discussions at the meeting were lively and informative, but in the end, even the TYC leadership was not prepared to take the plunge. The majority opinion was in favor of defining the TYC as a "movement" rather than a political party. There seems to be an enduring fascination with "partyless democracy" among many Tibetan political leaders that continues to thrive. And while there are a few Tibetan organizations in exile that style themselves as political parties, the current political system has no place for them.

At the time of its founding, the TYC's immediate priority was to build a strong network among the Tibetan community in exile to deepen the understanding of and commitment to the concept of a unified Tibet, consisting of the three regions and the various religious traditions. As I highlighted in my remarks to the Regional TYC of New York and New Jersey in 2014 discussing the TYC's history: "Although there was no one who spoke out against this major historic transformation, it wasn't without some feeling of reservations. These reservations/suspicions were not just limited to regional or religious feelings alone. But some have concerns based on ground reality and historical reasons and it is natural to have reservations for some people. However, these reservations existed mainly during the time of our parents' generation."[15]

As mentioned earlier in this chapter, the exile community was facing serious challenges in fulfilling this vision due to numerous internal and external factors. In almost all his speeches during this period, His Holiness the Dalai Lama strongly urged all Tibetans to remain united, leaving aside regionalism and religious differences, as that was the immediate need. Accordingly, we, the younger generation, felt it necessary to launch the TYC movement to inspire unity so that present and future generations would not carry the baggage of historical differences.

Our primary aim was to promote and protect national unity and integrity by giving up all distinctions based on religion, regionalism, or status. The TYC has continuously and successfully served this mandate since its inception. The other main goal was to reach out to Indian political leaders and parties as well as to other NGOs, not only to help create greater awareness of the Tibet issue but also to broaden our own views and to gain experience, with the ultimate aim of establishing a global platform.

While the TYC was certainly not a militant group, we knew that in those days some young people thought the Tibetans should explore every possibility to achieve their goal of independence. We had conversations with senior people from the Mustang guerilla base as well as with those serving in the SFF, exploring the possibility of the TYC working with these groups either formally or informally. Ultimately, though we hoped TYC members might join them, the TYC as an organization did not engage in any formal recruiting on behalf of either group.

Senior SFF officials were content with our limited involvement, as our work complemented their recruitment activities. Overall, however, our efforts weren't very successful. Many TYC members weren't interested in joining an organization that was firmly under the control of the Indian government and could only act when the government decided to deploy it. In contrast, the Mustang operation was still very much under control of the Tibetans. For any young Tibetan eager to pursue a more active role in the resistance, that was the better choice. Thus, both Jamyang Norbu, a TYC Centrex member, and Lhasang Tsering, another dynamic youth leader, voluntarily joined the Mustang group, gaining valuable experience as a result.

Unfortunately, within a few years the Mustang base was disbanded under very tragic circumstances.[16] Had it remained in operation, more young Tibetans would likely have joined the group. I had several serious discussions with Gyato Wangdu, leader of the Mustang base, and Lhamo Tsering, who was also closely associated with it. Other influential resistance leaders, including Jama Ngagtuk, were very keen for the TYC to help motivate younger, educated Tibetans to join. On the other hand, some leaders were not as enthusiastic because they thought the younger generation would not have the stamina to endure the tough life of a guerilla fighter.

Over the years, the TYC has undertaken numerous initiatives to strengthen democratic principles within the Tibetan community. Ever since its inception, the TYC has functioned as an organization upholding democracy, in both theory and practice. This has contributed to laying a foundation for a democratic culture within the Tibetan community, but we still have a long way to go.

## BHOD RANGWANG DENPAI LEGUL (TIBETAN FREEDOM MOVEMENT)

Another movement or organization that must be mentioned is the Bhod Rangwang Denpai Legul, or Tibetan Freedom Movement, launched by a group of Tibetans mostly hailing from the Central Institute of Higher Tibetan Studies (CIHTS), a university in Sarnath, India, certified by the Indian government. Samdhong Rinpoche, who at the time headed the institute, played a major role in inspiring and supporting the group. Thupten Jungney, a very energetic monk and founder of the Tibetan monastery at Sarnath, lovingly called Gyen Goser or "blonde-headed lama" because of his yellowish hair, was also in the forefront of this movement.

Samdhong Rinpoche was an activist at heart. In early 1968, as the principal of the Central School for Tibetans in Dalhousie, India, one of the earliest Tibetan schools established in exile, he introduced the democratic ethos by setting up the Bal Sabha or Student Council. Even though its mandate was limited to student-related issues, such as food service, hostel accommodations, and disciplinary matters, everything was done according to democratic principles.

Students were allowed to elect members of the Council from two different student groups, the Democratic Party (Mangtso Tsogpa) and the Progressive Party (Yarthon Tsogpa), each having its own principles, platform, and even logo. Potential student leaders competed in debates, promising to deliver on articulated platforms related to student welfare if elected. The party of the candidate who won with a majority of votes assumed the role of ruling party, and the losing group acted as the opposition party. Other student organizations were formed to assume the roles of the judiciary and the press.

A statement by then Indian External Affairs Minister Sardar Swaran Singh, in December 1971 in New York, in which, for the first time, the Indian government unconditionally proclaimed: "Tibet is part of China," is what triggered the creation of the Tibetan Freedom Movement. In general, the Indian people and most of their leaders, with the exception of a few communists who were pro-Beijing, were very sympathetic to the Tibetan cause. Many of them deeply lamented the

Indian government's failure to oppose the PRC's annexation of Tibet. I think even Prime Minister Nehru felt deep anguish about what happened to Tibet and, in my view, also a sense of responsibility for the tragedy that befell us. In a letter to his colleague Gopal Singh on May 24, 1964, just three days before his passing, he wrote: "We are not indifferent to what has happened in Tibet. But we are unable to do anything effective about it." The Prime Minister and his government were, in fact, very generous and genuinely helpful to Tibetan refugees, providing whatever facilities they could. Prime Minister Nehru extended particularly strong support for His Holiness's efforts to educate Tibetan children, whom they agreed were the most important asset for Tibet's future.

With the 1962 armed conflict between India and the PRC at a number of border points, the Indian government took a much stronger interest in the Tibet issue. By the early 1970s, however, there was some shift in its political position. It is too complicated a matter to discuss in detail here. Suffice it to say that many prominent Indian political leaders, as well as both serving and retired senior officials, felt varying degrees of concern about their government's changing Tibet policy. Some viewed it not as a major shift, but simply influenced by the views of Sardar Swaran Singh and some other officials in the Foreign Ministry. During that period, however, the External Affairs Ministry did try to stop His Holiness from issuing his annual March 10th statement.

This yearly statement, issued on the anniversary of the 1959 March 10th uprising, is the most important public announcement that His Holiness makes, similar in importance to the US President's State of the Union address. His Holiness continued to make this statement until 2011, when he devolved his political authority. I remember V. V. Paranjpe, a senior diplomat from the External Affairs Ministry, coming all the way to Dharamsala in 1971 to advise His Holiness against issuing the statement. I was present at this meeting, which took place on a gloomy afternoon. The electricity may also have gone out, because the room was unusually dark when His Holiness received him. There was a "lighter" moment, however, when His Holiness surprised him as he was ushered into the meeting. His Holiness pointed his index finger at the visitor, remarking: "I have seen you before." After another few moments of reflection, His Holiness said: "Ah yes, now I remember, you were with Nehru at a reception in 1954/1955 in Beijing during my visit there." V. V. Paranjpe was speechless. He later mentioned to me that at the meeting His Holiness remembered, he had been a student studying in China who was acting only as a translator during the visit by Prime Minister Nehru.

His Holiness was quite saddened by the Indian government's change in attitude. I have witnessed how decisive and firm he can be under difficult circumstances. After listening to the emissary's message, His Holiness made no effort to respond, telling him only that he would convey his decision to the Indian government in the near future. The very next day I was dispatched to Delhi with His Holiness's message that he had both a historical and a moral responsibility to continue to speak on behalf of his people. Therefore, he would be unable to comply with the Indian government's request. He further said that he understood that it was the prerogative of the government to take whatever actions it wished. One of the drivers for His Holiness's Private Office, Wangdrak, drove me from Dharamsala to Delhi in the record time of nine hours to deliver this message. It was a very scary drive, to say the least.

This injunction by the Indian minister not only was deeply painful to the Tibetan people but also triggered feelings of betrayal. Many Tibetans, especially of the younger generation, felt they must become more active in the struggle and not wait for guidance from the CTA, which they thought was intimidated by the Indian Foreign Ministry. As a result, the students of the CIHTS met for two days on December 23 and 24, 1971, and decided to launch a mass movement, "a struggle for the restoration of Tibet's rightful freedom," they called it. Organizing themselves in small groups, they traveled to various parts of India and Nepal to galvanize public support for their initiative.

The CTA was quite nervous about this movement. This is a natural, inherent reaction of every established government or institution worried about challenges to the status quo. The TYC, which was by then quite well established, was also skeptical and to some extent cooperated with the CTA in trying to absorb the movement into the mainstream. It was yet another momentous event in the insular Tibetan community. With its focus on the Indian government's treatment of the Tibetans, in some respects it was actually a positive development, curtailing the time wasted on internal fights and refocusing attention on the larger agenda this group had adopted. The organizers went to every Tibetan settlement and community, where they were enthusiastically welcomed. They returned from these visits with strong grassroots support. Some of the Tibetan communities belonging to the Group of Thirteen had for some time more or less disassociated themselves from the CTA. Nevertheless, they formally received the Tibetan Freedom Movement delegates, some of them even giving the organization strong endorsements. While this was a healthy trend, there was a concern that unless this movement became much more closely aligned with the CTA, it might become yet another center of power that would do more harm than good for the overall struggle.

Even though the TYC periodically confronted the CTA on larger issues, it remained very supportive. Given that problematic experience, however, in combination with the direct challenge to the CTA leadership by the Group of Thirteen, the Kashag was concerned that another organization under separate leadership with mass support could become difficult to handle. The Tibetan Freedom Movement had a much wider base of support than the TYC, which mainly represented the younger generation. After a rather confrontational and tense beginning, however, the Tibetan Freedom Movement basically became part of the broader CTA infrastructure. It ultimately abandoned its separate leadership, and the Tibetan Parliament became its central coordinating office. All the chapters that it had created evolved into formal committees representing the various Tibetan communities. To this day, whenever there is an important conference, members of this group represent their respective communities and settlements.

Tethong Tsewang Choegyal and I were appointed by the Kashag to represent the CTA at the Tibetan Freedom Movement's first general conference in Dharamsala from July 22 to 31, 1972. We were chosen because members of the Kashag did not wish to personally participate at such a high level. Tsewang Choegyal was then head of all the settlements in South India and had the rank of Deputy Minister. I was then Additional Secretary at the Cabinet Secretariat. Every evening we had to brief the Kashag on the day's deliberations. We also spent a lot of time in informal consultations with key delegates from the Tibetan Freedom Movement and other important participants. After a day or two of tension, the meeting became so productive and the atmosphere so cordial that delegates were able to participate in serious discussions on vital issues confronting the exile community as well as on long-term goals. Then Chairman of the Tibetan Parliament, Venerable Taklung Nyima Sangpo, a very experienced individual who had served in several important positions, presided over the meeting. In the end, it was a highly successful event of significant historical importance. Kalon Wangdu Dorje, Minister for Department of Home of the exile government, hosted a dinner for all the delegates. Senior Kalon W. G. Kundeling came for a special concluding event and presented gifts to Gyen Goser, Samdhong Rinpoche, and all the delegates.

The Tibetan Freedom Movement was also responsible for establishing a very important program, commonly called the Freedom Seed Money, that collects voluntary contributions every Tibetan is encouraged to make. The contribution is recorded in a green booklet that today is viewed as the Tibetan Identity (Tibetan ID) document. I have been told that many people who refused to participate in the program in India but later realized its importance in seeking political asylum in the West managed to obtain the now valuable green book, sometimes through back-door connections.

## TYC AND TIBETAN FREEDOM MOVEMENT INTERACTION AND EVOLUTION

The establishment of both the TYC and the Tibetan Freedom Movement stimulated tremendous political awareness within the broader Tibetan community. Tibetans began to realize that each one of them had the responsibility to make a direct contribution to the Tibetan freedom struggle and that it was their fundamental right to assert themselves. The seed of activism had been planted. The organizations also encouraged allegiance to the CTA and helped defuse regional and sectarian politics. At the same time, the people started demanding more from their leaders. The TYC was also being seen by the public and some of its members as too much a part of the establishment and losing its dynamism. A few key people who launched the Tibetan Freedom Movement confided in me that it was the TYC that had awoken them politically, but it was the TYC's lack of political dynamism that stimulated many of them to start the movement.

There is some truth to this perception. The TYC certainly did become very much a part of the establishment. We felt quite proud of that. As I previously noted, at one time, nearly 80 percent of the CTA staff were members. There were days when the entire Secretariat became paralyzed because they were attending important TYC events. The TYC, in fact, asked the Kashag to declare October 7 TYC Founding Day, a national holiday. Of course, this never happened, but we used to make every TYC member take that day off as casual leave, trying to send the message to the Kashag of our strength and importance. Years later, when I was the Additional Secretary at the Department of Information and Publicity, I remember coming to the office one October 7 morning and finding only two staff members at their desks. I was very irritated. I then realized the inconvenience we must have caused senior officials when we indulged in such actions as TYC members.

As previously noted, the Tibetan Freedom Movement in essence became part of the establishment when the Tibetan Parliament assumed the role of coordinator of all of its subcommittees located throughout India, Nepal, Bhutan, and elsewhere abroad. While this provided administrative efficiency and encouraged the involvement of more Tibetans, many of the movement's architects were dissatisfied. Some of us in the TYC leadership also felt that although we would remain loyal to the CTA, we must assert ourselves politically and project the TYC as an activist organization.

In 1974, the first term of the TYC's executive officers came to an end. As a result of informal consultation among the senior leaders, I was asked to run for the presidency. The outgoing President, Tenzin Geyche, and the two Vice-Presidents, Samdhong Rinpoche and Jetsun Pema, all declined to run for a second term. I was hoping Sonam Topgyal would be willing to accept the position, but he and others were all keen that I step in. This was the heyday of the TYC, and most decisions were taken by consensus; there was no serious politicking. TYC members were respectful of our roles as founders, and most of them thought it was appropriate for me to assume the presidency. Tenzin Namgyal, one of the other conveners, had left for New York the previous year to resume his role as His Holiness's Representative at the Office of Tibet. Jamyang Norbu and I were the only members of the first Executive Committee who stayed on. Others who were elected to the Centrex that year included Yeshe Gyurme, then Secretary of the Home Department, Tashi Wangdi, Tempa Tsering, Lobsang Wangchuk, Tendzin Choegyal, and Kunsang Paljor. Tashi Wangdi and Tempa Tsering both became senior officials and also members of the Kashag in later years.

However, on the morning of the election, Tendzin Choegyal, His Holiness's youngest brother, who had just been elected to the Centrex, told me that he was also thinking of running for the presidency and hoped I did not mind. I welcomed his candidacy and said that if he were seriously interested, I would lend my support. I remember immediately asking for an informal meeting of outgoing and incoming Centrex members to inform them that Tendzin Choegyal was keen to run for the presidency and that I was supportive of him. I also made brief public remarks in his favor just before the vote. Tendzin Choegyal thus became the TYC's second President, while at the urging of the delegates, I agreed to serve as

Vice-President. A year or so later, he left to join the SFF, and I assumed the presidency in 1976 with Lobsang Wangchuk becoming Vice-President.

Some of us began to feel that the CTA was not actively engaged in political issues and even seemed to be trying to curtail the activities of others interested in launching political initiatives. At the same time, I saw ordinary Tibetans becoming more politically conscious, with their focus shifting from regional and sectarian politics to the bigger issues. In those days I used to spend a lot of time with leaders of the Tibetan colony at Majnu-ka-tilla, including Jamyang Tsultrim, Jamyang Sherab, and Ngawang. They were campaigning for some effective political action that would help highlight the Tibetan issue, both in India and abroad. I had come to know Gyen Goser and some of the other prominent students who had started the Tibetan Freedom Movement, and they too urged the TYC to initiate some active political measures. They were clearly not satisfied with the Tibetan Freedom Movement having been completely absorbed into the CTA. They knew that I would be responsive to their views because I was also keen to make the TYC into an activist organization. During this period, on an almost daily basis, some of us were meeting with Indian political leaders sympathetic to our cause. Many of them also urged us to make the Tibetan Freedom Movement more visible and vocal. Some of the regional youth leaders also participated in a number of these meetings.

In fairness, we had very dedicated and hardworking leaders in the Kashag. I understand that they had bigger responsibilities, including maintaining a cordial relationship with the Indian government, which was absolutely critical. The CTA, under the Kashag, was doing excellent work maintaining and running all the Tibetan refugee settlements, looking after the educational needs of thousands of children by running nearly a hundred schools, and above all, trying to obtain financial and other assistance from the Indian government and international institutions. They had their priorities; it's not that they didn't care about the political activism we envisioned.

Indira Gandhi's imposition of the Emergency in India in 1975 caused us a setback, however. While Tibet's support base was not limited to the opposition parties of the Indian government—we had several friends and sympathizers in the Congress Party—the majority of leaders willing to come out openly and forcefully to support us were from the opposition, many of whom were jailed during the Emergency. Indira Gandhi did not spare even highly respected leaders, including J. P. Narayan, whom the Indians lovingly referred to as Lok Nayak, or Acharya

Kripalani, elder statesman and veteran freedom fighter. They were all incarcerated. We had very few people we could consult or seek help from. There were no specific restrictions on Tibetans or our activities, but the atmosphere simply made it difficult to initiate any movement.

## ZUNGDREL TSOGCHUNG (JOINT ACTION COMMITTEE)

One of my most satisfying but also frustrating activities was involvement with the movement that came to be known as Zungdrel Tsogchung or the Joint Action Committee. As previously mentioned, when I was President of the TYC, my colleagues and I wanted the organization to become more activist. We started informally discussing possible options with other like-minded Tibetans. The Majnu-ka-tilla colony leaders continued to urge us to help organize an event around the March 10, 1977, anniversary on a large scale with media participation. The TYC regional unit in Delhi, composed mostly of university students, was also very keen to initiate some political action and started to work very closely with leaders of the Tibetan community. Lobsang Dhargye, a very capable and excellent networker, headed the Regional Youth Congress with an excellent team of youth leaders including Dagpo Sonam Norbu, Tsering Dhondup, Norbu Samphel, and Thubten Samphel, the editor of the TYC journal. The TYC also had a special benefactor, Amdo Phuntsok, a highly accomplished thangka painter whose family ran a very popular vegetarian restaurant at the Ladakh Buddhist Vihara. I remember having many meetings in his room at the Vihara. Some of the conveners of the Tibetan Freedom Movement, including Gyen Goser and Nubpa Choedak Gyatso, a monk activist, were also anxious to join hands in such an effort. Nubpa Choedak Gyatso had become the President of the Regional Chapter of the Tibetan Freedom Movement in Delhi. In later years he would join the Tibetan Parliament and become its Chairman.

Mao Zedong had died a year earlier, and in the United States, Jimmy Carter, a human rights advocate, was elected President. Indira Gandhi ended the state of Emergency and allowed general elections to take place. All these events created an environment of hope and excitement, but the scheduled 1977 March 10th event was forcefully suppressed by the Indian authorities, who attempted to preempt the demonstration by imposing section 144 of India's Criminal Procedure Code, making it illegal for any public gathering or activities to take place near the PRC embassy.

Nevertheless, a few hundred Tibetans managed to break the police cordon and enter the embassy compound on the morning of March 10, which was the eighteenth anniversary of the Lhasa uprising. The Indian police entered the compound to remove the Tibetans and more than forty policemen were injured, some quite seriously. In the end, two hundred Tibetans, including fifty-three women, were arrested. We spent the next twenty-four hours trying to get them released on bail and also visiting senior police officers to extend our apologies for the physical altercations with their men. Most of the officers were actually sympathetic to our cause and expressed remorse for having to resort to violent means to control the situation. Many of them extended small, yet significant gestures to the Tibetan demonstrators that day. This was sincerely appreciated as we saw that in their hearts, the Indian people understood our grievances, but more than that, they recognized and cherished the special cultural and religious bond between our peoples.

The protest not only was noted by the Indian media but also received significant international coverage. Rather than being disheartened, we felt the need to intensify our activities and maintain the spotlight. In the meantime, hundreds of Tibetans started pouring into Delhi from all over India, many saying they were prepared to give their lives for the struggle and would not return home without having done something meaningful. We had very intense, and sometimes heated, meetings lasting hours, and in the end, we decided to focus our attention on the United Nations by staging hunger strikes outside the UN information center in Delhi, urging implementation of the three Tibet Resolutions the UN had previously passed.[17]

The spontaneous support and enthusiasm for this decision were overwhelming. Eighty-seven Tibetans volunteered to go on hunger strikes, until death if need be. Because so many Tibetans had come together from many places, we decided to create a joint committee, the Zungdrel Tsogchung, to spearhead the event, rather than limiting its sponsorship to the TYC or Tibetans from Delhi. There was a lot of work to do. We needed to make sure that the volunteers were serious, taking their decision freely and willingly, and above all, that they would abide by it if they intended to give up their lives. We interviewed almost every individual separately and in some cases, due to their age or health factors, convinced them to withdraw. The remaining individuals we divided into, I believe, three groups. The first group of seven volunteers began their hunger strike on the morning of March 20. This group included one woman, Lhamo Tsering (forty-five years old), and six men: Tamding (thirty), Tsering Wangchuk (twenty-eight), Tenchoe (forty-one), Lobsang Rabten (thirty), Kunchok (forty-eight), and Tenzin Tsultrim (twenty), some of whom were former resistance fighters. We had volunteers lined up to replace them should anyone have to be removed on medical grounds or actually perish.

This was the first instance that the Tibetan people's movement reached out to the international community. We visited embassies handing out petitions. This was my first visit to the US embassy, and at the time I had no idea that one day I would become a US citizen. There is even a photo of me with Gyen Goser and I think Jamyang Norbu, standing right there on the steps, having successfully handed over an appeal addressed to President Carter. Tibet received international media attention the likes of which had not been seen since coverage of His Holiness's 1959 flight into exile. While this hunger strike was going on, scheduled Indian elections took place, giving the opposition parties a massive victory and rejecting Indira Gandhi's authoritarian style of governance.

I must take a moment to compliment the Prime Minister on her decision to go to the electorate for a verdict on her government's policies, and especially on the smooth transfer of power to the opposition party once she lost the election. She could have maintained the state of Emergency and stayed in power for several more years had she so chosen. There was also a fear that she might reject the electoral verdict, but she graciously accepted the people's decision. Her actions proved that the culture of democracy is deeply rooted in India, and in my view, that the reasons leading her to declare the Emergency were not for personal power. Although one might argue that her concerns were misplaced or not agree with the justifications offered in support of her actions, they were political decisions based on what she thought was in the best interests of her country.

For us, the victory of the Janata Party brought tremendous hope and opportunities. I personally knew many of the new party leaders, some of whom were very close friends. One of them was Jayaprakash Narayan, who led the opposition to victory, an event now referred to as the "second revolution" after India's independence. On many occasions, His Holiness sent me either to Patna in the Indian state of Bihar, where Narayan used to reside, or to Delhi, where he would stay at the residence of his friend J. J. Singh at New Friends Colony, to seek advice and help on issues. In his book *In Exile from the Land of Snows*, John Avedon gives a rather vivid description of those days, including a few pithy quotes from Jamyang Norbu.

My personal relationship with Jayaprakash Narayan was such that even when he and other top Janata Party leaders were in the midst of discussions to form the new government, he interrupted the meeting to receive me and my compatriots. I was able to personally congratulate him and offer him a *khata*. The room and the corridors were filled with a "who's who" of the Indian political leadership. I think we became the first outsiders to know the identity of the next Prime Minister. When we were taking our leave, I bent down to pay my respects to him, and he said: "I will mention to Morarji Bai" (*bai* meaning brother). He was indirectly letting me know me that he would tell the next Prime Minister of India to have Tibet on his agenda. A few hours later, he announced to the world the choice of Morarji Desai.

Around this time, the *Tibetan Review*, an informative Tibetan-English publication, published an editorial piece entitled "Enter the People," highlighting the significance of the Tibetan people beginning to actively participate in their struggle rather than leaving all the responsibilities to the CTA. It also gave credence to the Tibetan struggle as one supported by the common people, not only by a handful of "reactionaries," as the PRC propaganda machine was trying to label the Tibetan movement. Although the movement was gaining positive international attention, unfortunately, it was being viewed differently by the Tibetan establishment, or at least by a section of it. We were all staunch loyalists of His Holiness and never for a moment questioned the authority and legitimacy of the CTA, but certain factions saw it differently.

While the hunger strike organizers were immersed in trying to reach out to Indian and global leaders, relations between them and the Kashag, as well as with the Tibetan Parliament, became problematic. I think everyone involved was under tremendous stress, so even small things led to serious misunderstandings and eventually triggered a confrontation. The Tibetan Parliament initially sent some members to Delhi to act as a liaison and help guide the activities surrounding the strike. But as the days went on, relations with the organizers became tense, each side becoming openly critical of the other. Invoking their status as elected Parliamentary Deputies, some of the emissaries from Dharamsala adopted a somewhat condescending attitude, behaving in such a way that people started referring to them as the "new aristocrats." Rather than helping coordinate our efforts, some Deputies were sending reports back to Dharamsala giving the impression that the organizers were challenging the CTA's authority. Some even spoke to the seven hunger strikers directly, urging them to end their fast with the implication that the event organizers were playing with their lives.

These actions sparked a much bigger misunderstanding. It is true that some of the organizers, and even many from the large group of Tibetans who had gathered in Delhi, were sometimes not respectful of the Deputies. They were angry because they thought the elected officials should be joining in their efforts, rather than seeking to control or even stop them. After more than seven days, some of the hunger strikers were showing signs of physical deterioration. His Holiness was also becoming worried and thinking of publicly asking for an end to the strike. We were also concerned about the strikers' health, but we did not want the strike to conclude without some tangible measure of success.

I met with Wangdu Dorje, the most senior member of the Kashag, who happened to be in Delhi. I urged him to help delay any intervention by His Holiness, assuring him that we were working very hard to find ways to conclude the campaign without loss of life. He confirmed His Holiness's intention but promised to try to postpone it. He cautioned, however, that if there were a long delay in finding a solution, he would feel obligated to inform His Holiness. In the meantime, some Deputies who must have been aware of this threatened that if the organizers did not end the hunger strike, they were going to ask His Holiness to publicly urge the strikers to end it. This deeply angered the organizers because they thought His Holiness was being dragged into the situation solely to score political points.

Even though we managed to draw world attention to our plight, the UN was totally unresponsive, failing even to acknowledge our demands. The health of the hunger strikers was becoming worrisome, with some of the participants' conditions becoming critical. Given the global attention we had attracted, in combination with the Janata Party's assumption of power, we believed we had a greater opportunity to pursue our struggle. We thus thought we should start advising the hunger strikers to end their vigil. It was a very difficult decision, and we were not able to come to consensus for some time. Some of the leaders and even some of the hunger strikers were adamant to continue until the UN was compelled either to respond or to bear the responsibility associated with the loss of precious Tibetan lives. Even some of our Indian supporters were urging the strikers to continue and make the UN responsible for the consequences. Several Indian ministers, members of Parliament, and prominent civil service leaders continued to visit the hunger strikers to express their solidarity with our cause. Some Indian friends also joined the strikers in a profound gesture of support. One of them, Captain Virendra Kumar, an Indian war veteran and advocate, joined the strikers for twelve hours and later wrote: "We, the Indians, are responsible for what has happened to Tibet."[18] Diplomats from a number of embassies also started visiting the hunger strikers, some discreetly but many openly, demonstrating that many nations were beginning to take note of the situation.

I began consulting with several Janata Party leaders, including George Fernandes and Raj Narain, who had both become cabinet members; Surendra Mohan, the Party Secretary General; and other veteran leaders including Acharya Kripalani, who was seen as the second most important leader of the Janata Party after Jayaprakash Narayan. I wanted their help in finding a way to bring a conclusion to the strike. These leaders shared my view that the movement had successfully drawn the attention of India and the world and that our energy must now be channeled into more substantively promising activities.

After extensive discussions among the top party leaders, including the Prime Minister, the Janata Party agreed to officially request the UN to immediately implement its existing resolutions on Tibet. The Party also agreed that Surendra Mohan would come in his official capacity as Secretary General to assure the strikers of its support of Tibet and formally request an end to the strike. I am quoting the entire text of the extraordinarily sympathetic message that Surendra Mohan personally read to the strikers on March 30, 1977.

Dear Friends,

On behalf of the Janata Party, I express solidarity with the cause that you have upheld and convey to you our sympathy to all of you who have been fasting in order to press upon the conscience of the world the importance and the urgency of the cause. Leaders of the Janata Party, to whichever political party they have belonged in the past, have consistently supported the cause of Tibet most unequivocally, and I assure you that the Janata Party will continue to do so. We hold the Dalai Lama in the highest esteem and greatly appreciate his sacrifice in the cause of human liberation. In view of your fast, the Janata Party has sent the following telegram to the United Nations: "STRONGLY URGE IMMEDIATE IMPLEMENTATION UNITED NATIONS RESOLUTIONS ON TIBET—SURENDRA MOHAN GENERAL SECRETARY JANATA PARTY."

I also wish to assure you that it will be the endeavor of our Party that whatever disrespect and inconvenience His Holiness and our Tibetan brothers had to face during the past administration in their efforts for their cause will not be allowed to be repeated. I request you that in view of the telegram that we have sent to the United Nations and our assurances as given above, you should kindly accept our request to withdraw your fast. I trust that you will kindly do so and I believe that we can jointly further the cause for which you have so courageously inflicted terrible sufferings on yourselves voluntarily.
Yours sincerely,
SURENDRA MOHAN (sgd.)
General Secretary[19]

The Janata Party also requested Acharya Kripalani to come break the fast by personally offering juice to each of the strikers. I picked up Acharya Kripalani at his residence, having explicitly briefed my colleagues that when he arrived, they must refrain from physically helping him out of the car. Even though he was quite old and very frail, he never liked being made to feel his age. I remember my colleague N. C. Gyatso in his excitement doing precisely the opposite. Acharya Kripalani literally slapped his hand!

George Fernandes joined Acharya Kripalani, fellow Central Minister Raj Narain, and party colleague Surendra Mohan to add his support and show solidarity with the Tibetans. His comments that day were very inspiring: "When the Janata Party is committed to bread and freedom that commitment is not only to the Indian people but it is a commitment to people all over the world that we are on the side of freedom, we are on the side of people fighting for freedom whether it is freedom to go back to one's own country or whether it is freedom to live as free citizens in one's own country. This is our policy today and every day and I would like to assure you that we in this country shall do everything: everything that is necessary and everything that is in our power to help you achieve your objective."[20]

In my view, the Joint Action Committee was a landmark in the freedom struggle by the Tibetans in exile. It excited and motivated the Tibetan people, helping them realize that they were not alone in their struggle, provided they themselves stood up and raised their voices.

With the satisfactory conclusion of the hunger strike, all the participants, especially the seven hunger strikers, were keen to go to Dharamsala to report to the CTA, but most importantly to receive His Holiness the Dalai Lama's blessings.

We were positive that the Kashag would give us a rousing welcome and also encourage us to continue our activities. Sadly, that was not to be the case.

Thirty-seven of us, including the seven hunger strikers, left for Dharamsala, arriving on April 9 to a loud and rousing reception by the people. However, our meetings with the Kashag and the Deputies did not go well. The organizers were all exhausted and stressed out after nearly a month of nonstop, emotionally draining activities. Many of them could not hide their resentment at the attitude members of the leadership had expressed during the strike. The Kashag and the Deputies made it very clear that they would not endorse continuation of the Joint Action Committee. At the same time, the Committee was adamant that it would continue its activities. The meeting ended abruptly with tempers running high. The Kashag and the Deputies hurriedly called a meeting of the National Working Committee, the highest policy-making organ of the CTA in those days.

Although the Kashag certainly did not favor the emergence of a grassroots-based organization that might not always toe the party line, it showed some measure of patience and tried to handle the situation in an accommodating manner. It was the Parliamentary Deputies, especially those who viewed this as a personal battle to suppress the movement, who were the main troublemakers. Of course, there were also some Deputies who were sympathetic and supportive of our activities.

I had some hope that the National Working Committee might come up with a creative solution. Being a civil servant, I had the opportunity to have discussions with some of the senior secretaries. Many had sympathy for the sentiments of the organizers and also saw great value in having strong public participation in political activities. Unfortunately, their voices at the National Working Committee were solely advisory in nature; only the Parliamentary Deputies had the power to vote if there were no consensus among the larger group. We heard rumors that the National Working Committee had decided not to immediately disband the Joint Action Committee but rather to call a special meeting, inviting people from various settlements and organizations to deliberate and come to a decision. I think most of the organizers were not unhappy with this idea, thinking that in a larger gathering they would have a better opportunity to explain their position and the importance of the Joint Action Committee's continued existence. But I felt that whatever the outcome, this large gathering would create more division and disharmony. I was particularly worried that elements not supportive of the CTA would take the opportunity to create further dissension.

I was among those Committee members who argued that we should voluntarily disband the group and not allow the matter to go any further, as it would only defeat the whole purpose of the organization. Many opposed the idea, but we managed to convince most of our colleagues to disband. We then informed the Chairman and the Vice-Chairman of Parliament of our decision. This brought an end to this popular grassroots movement that had such tremendous potential to engage Tibetans from every walk of life in our struggle. Aptly called the Joint Action Committee, it brought together the energy harnessed by the TYC and the Tibetan Freedom Movement with the voices of influential Tibetan leaders from various settlements and communities, including the vibrant group from the Majnu-ka-tilla.

On a personal level, I was deeply saddened by the leadership's failure to take advantage of the energy and commitment that had been aroused in the exile community. If this movement had been allowed to continue, it could have deepened the involvement of our people in our struggle and furthered the culture of democracy within the broader Tibetan community. To this very day, I believe understanding of, and commitment to, democracy is only skin deep within the Tibetan diaspora. Moreover, this unfortunate experience deeply wounded many people, some of whom never relinquished their negative view of the CTA. After our announcement, all kinds of rumors and speculations started surfacing. It was alleged that the CTA had coerced some prominent organizers to disband and that some of us succumbed to Kashag pressure to avoid jeopardizing our careers. I can say with certainty that no one in the Kashag tried to pressure me. Given the climate of the times, for the greater good of the broader Tibetan movement, I felt we had no choice.

Before we began the actual disbanding, I decided to resign from the civil service. I felt it was not right for me to continue to serve, given the major policy differences I had with the administration. I was also trying to set a healthy precedent that when irreconcilable differences arise, resigning rather than continuing in office in an atmosphere lacking mutual trust, at least on major policy issues, was the preferred course. The Kashag made no move to marginalize or "punish" me for my recent activities, but rather reconfirmed my position as the head of the Tibetan Office of Research and Analysis (TORA). Likewise, I felt no animosity toward members of the Kashag. Indeed, I respected and had close friendships with many of them.

The TORA was a unit that was set up at my suggestion to act as an "in-house think tank" for the Kashag. I had two specific areas of interest—international relations and research. I have always felt that we must reach out to the international community through the media, both to create awareness of the Tibet issue and to foster personal relations to gain support. However, I was concerned that we were neither well prepared to argue our case nor well informed on international matters. I was especially alarmed that many CTA officials had almost zero understanding of the PRC, its government, and the current situation. My first efforts were to recruit people with Chinese language skills as part of my staff. That is where the research came in.

I also decided to resign the TYC presidency. While we were proud of having had considerable influence within the CTA, it was crystal clear that the Kashag now had tremendous influence over the TYC. The tables seemed to have turned, at least in Dharamsala. I was beginning to see a move within the TYC questioning its participation with the Joint Action Committee on a permanent basis. Some members wanted the TYC to participate in the March 10th and other individual events but not to join on a long-term basis.

As the lone original convener remaining in the TYC leadership, I did not wish to create a major rift within the organization, one that, unfortunately, became inevitable. The majority of regional youth leaders would have backed the position that Vice-President Lobsang Wangchuk, Jamyang Norbu, and I took, but it was very clear that the Centrex would be divided. With my decision to resign, Lobsang Wangchuk and Jamyang Norbu also decided to leave. After our departure, the TYC continued to have a special relationship with the CTA until Samdhong Rinpoche began implementing the existing civil service rules disallowing CTA staff to have formal affiliation with any outside organizations, including the TYC.

## ACTIVITIES DURING MY PERIOD OF SELF-IMPOSED EXILE

Of course, I did not make the decision to resign from the CTA and the TYC lightheartedly. Recent experiences had convinced me that the Tibetan freedom struggle must make some fundamental changes, giving the people larger roles and more participation. Quite a number of Tibetans, both old and young, shared my view. I thought being away from Dharamsala would give me the opportunity to reflect on a strategy to bring about the needed changes.

*Continuing Efforts in Support of a Democratic Agenda*

With many of my friends now in influential positions in the new Indian government, I was confident of receiving guidance and support from them. I also realized that the Tibetans in exile must become more politically conscious and develop a clear vision as to what kind of society they wanted, not only for a future Tibet but also in exile.

I continued to brainstorm with likeminded friends about launching a political party. I was also keen to establish an institute for democratic studies for Tibetans, because it is an undeniable fact that we do not have a deeply rooted democratic culture among our people. The concept of democracy was a gift from His Holiness. People embraced it more in reverence for him than in understanding its innate value. I viewed it as an important tool for maintaining our unity by institutionalizing proper representation of the three regions of Tibet and all of its religious traditions, not as the goal of our struggle, as some people these days seem to believe. The Tibetan struggle is not about the Tibetan people fighting for democratic rights, but rather about the very survival of our identity as a people.

My good friend George Fernandes designated Kamlesh Shukla, a Socialist colleague of his, to work with me in establishing this institute. My hope was that it would become the breeding ground for future members of the political party we would ultimately launch. As George has acknowledged, my first exposure to his political philosophy arose upon Ram Manohar Lohia's referral of me to him during a meeting I attended with His Holiness:

> My first personal meeting with . . . [His Holiness] was when he came to Delhi in Parliament House. He had come to meet Dr Lohia with a young man (Lodi Gyari) (he has grown older now since; he today deals after the external affairs of His Holiness). His Holiness brought this young man to meet Dr Lohia and after their talks were over, Dr Lohia told Lodi Gyari: "You go to George Fernandes (my house was close by) to learn about our socialist policies." It is how it started, after this first meeting.[21]

Kamlesh and I did start working on the project, even looking around for suitable facilities to house the proposed institute, but it never came to fruition because I found myself back in Dharamsala.

### *Establishment of a Small Family Business*

During this period of self-imposed exile, I also helped my siblings set up a small family business: Middle Path Travels & Tours. Several years before, I had arranged for my brother Thinley, my sister Rinzing, and later my wife's cousin, Tsering Sangpo, to work with my friend Avinash Kohli, a successful Indian tourism entrepreneur, to learn the business. Tourism was our choice not only because we had no resources to invest in any other venture but also because ultimately this could become an important business for Tibet. Under Avinash's tutelage, my siblings gained enough experience to set up their own small agency. I sought Avinash's permission for them to resign from his company and begin building their new enterprise. He was very supportive, even offering to refer to our new company some of his clients who were interested in visiting Buddhist sites. He also wanted my brother Thinley to continue working with him periodically on adventure tours. By that time, Thinley had already made a name for himself in the adventure tourism field, including river-rafting expeditions and trekking. In fact, it was through my brother Thinley that I met Richard Gere, the actor, who eventually became a very close friend and colleague.

Middle Path Travels & Tours was probably the first Tibetan-run travel agency in the world. Not surprisingly, it was initially the official agent for the Bureau of His Holiness the Dalai Lama, remaining so until the CTA set up its own travel agency, Potala Tours. At that point, Lobsang Dhargye, who was then Secretary of the Department of Finance, approached me with an offer for our company to become partners with Potala Tours, a relationship he thought would be beneficial to both sides. Potala Tours needed the experience of Middle Path Travels, and we could benefit from the CTA's resources and connections. I declined for two reasons. First, in principle I am not in favor of government competing with or entering into private enterprise with the intention of trying to monopolize business at the expense of the private sector. Second, I knew that during Lobsang Dhargye's tenure the business relationship would work smoothly because of our personal friendship, but there was no guarantee this would continue in the future with different individuals involved. I was also concerned that people would think my family had received special consideration because of my personal relationship with Lobsang Dhargye, even though it was his suggestion to join forces.

As I am talking about Middle Path Travels & Tours, I thought I should share an interesting story that was churned out by the ever-present Tibetan rumor-mongering factory. A year or so after His Holiness announced his Middle Way Approach at the European Parliament in 1988 in Strasbourg, unkind words traveled through the Tibetan community criticizing the Gyari family for supposedly having the audacity to name our family business after His Holiness's policy. What those ill-informed troublemakers forgot to check was the date that Middle Path Travels & Tours was established: it existed years before His Holiness announced the Middle Way Approach. Interestingly, I recently came across a souvenir program published by the CTA in 1984, four years before His Holiness's policy announcement, commemorating its twenty-five years in exile, which carried a half-page advertisement for Middle Path Travels & Tours.

I also remember at one point my sister Rinzing telling me with great excitement that Gyalo Thondup's wife had offered Middle Path Travels & Tours a very centrally located space in the Khan Market in Delhi, where we could establish a partnership with her son, Khedroop Thondup. For years we had operated out of a tiny cubicle office, so this was a great opportunity, but also an honor in being invited to become partners with His Holiness's brother's family. I disappointed my sister by advising against this promising partnership. I was concerned because sometimes business relations can spoil personal relationships. Given our deep reverence for His Holiness, one that extends to his family, any kind of misunderstanding would be unfortunate.

While I have written quite a bit about Gyalo Thondup, I have said little about his wife, Zhu Dan. Her Tibetan name was Diki Dolkar. She met her future husband while he was studying in China. She was a wonderful person, working with great devotion to help Tibetan refugees. She set up the Tibetan Refugee Self Help Centre in Darjeeling, which has since benefited thousands of Tibetans, continuing its work to this day. The Centre was truly a self-help enterprise. Diki Dolkar not only provided livelihoods for hundreds of people but also helped preserve traditional Tibetan handicrafts and other skills, including carpet weaving, thangka painting, high-quality metal work, and woodcarving. Within a few years of its founding, the Centre became a "must visit" site not only for tourists but also for dignitaries from India and abroad. Diki Dolkar was especially devoted to children. The Centre ran a school and a clinic, both of which were open to all Tibetan refugees, not just those who were members. All of my siblings, in fact, spent their primary school years there.

Even those who deeply disliked her husband had great respect and admiration for Diki Dolkar. I know one old Khampa man who was always so critical of Gyalo Thondup, literally calling him the "devil," while in the same breath recognizing Diki Dolkar as a "true lady Tara." My family all lovingly and respectfully called her Ama Lhacham Kusho.[22] She was especially fond of my brothers Pema Gyalpo and Thinley and my sister Rinzing. To this day, I keep her picture among a small selection of photos of people I personally respect in our home in McLean, Virginia.

His Holiness the 14th Dalai Lama being welcomed at the Tibetan Refugee Self Help Centre in Darjeeling by Mrs. Thondup (Diki Dolkar)
Tibet Museum, CTA

It was my younger brother Pema Gyalpo, however, who had the deepest love and affection for Ama Lhacham Kusho. In the early 1970s, I traveled to Japan with a pair of Tibetan carpets my Ama-las wanted Pema to help sell for them. My mothers had received the carpets in payment of a debt. When I gave Pema the carpets, he made quite a scene, saying he only sold carpets sent to him by Ama Lhacham Kusho's Tibetan Refugee Self Help Centre. Even for his own family, he said he would not break that rule. I was very angry. I remember telling him that while it was admirable to have that degree of loyalty to Yabshi (an honorific Tibetan term for members of the Dalai Lama's family, in this case referring exclusively to the Thondups), there needed to be exceptions. Our own mothers were in dire financial straits, warranting an exception to his sincere and heartfelt practices. In a telling exercise of his innate Khampa headstrong nature, compounded by some unfortunate traits acquired during life in his adopted homeland, he steadfastly refused to accept the carpets for sale at the Tibet Culture Centre. Some Japanese friends kindly took them off my hands.

### *Formation of the All-India Frontier Buddha Mahasabha*

During my time away from Dharamsala, I also helped my friend the Venerable Lama Lobzang from Ladakh, one of the most prominent Buddhist leaders from the Indian Himalayas, organize an important conference of Buddhist leaders that resulted in the formation of the All-India Frontier Buddha Mahasabha. This was the first organization representing Buddhists from the entire Himalayan region, from Ladakh to Himachal Pradesh, Sikkim to Arunachal Pradesh. I have always believed that for the Tibetan Buddhist tradition to survive, we must look beyond the confines of Tibet itself, where our culture and very identity are on the line. I was thus very happy to assist in forming this organization. Moreover, I personally gained a lot of experience and came to know many of the prominent Buddhist and political leaders from the region, including P. K. Thungon, then Chief Minister of Arunachal Pradesh, and Kazi Lhendup Dorjee, Chief Minister of Sikkim.

Initially I was not a fan of Kazi Lhendup Dorjee, who was instrumental in overthrowing the Namgyal Dynasty of Sikkim, leading to annexation of that small Himalayan kingdom by India. Of course, it was not he alone who precipitated this unfortunate event. The Sikkimese royal family, together with some close associates, made many blunders and created deep concerns in New Delhi, all in stark contrast with how the Bhutanese monarchy handled its affairs. Both the Lhasa aristocrats and the Sikkim elitists thought that they were smarter than the Bhutanese. History has proven otherwise. Tibet and Sikkim have both lost their sovereignty, while Bhutan is thriving as an independent nation. The Bhutanese proved to be far more intelligent than their cousins. The catalyst for Bhutan's stability and modernization was the monarchy itself. Like His Holiness introducing a democratic system of governance, the Bhutanese monarchy embraced democracy. Today Bhutan is a constitutional monarchy with legislative power vested in a bicameral parliament, with the majority party running the government.

But while a democratic political system is admirable in theory, it can be abused in practice, sometimes bringing great suffering and unanticipated tragedy. From our own Tibetan experience, I have come to the conclusion that to genuinely practice democracy, the people must have a democratic culture within their society. That is not something that can be implemented or embraced overnight. Many people view democracy only through the lens of the rights they can enjoy without understanding the corresponding duties that citizens of such a system must assume. Quite often, in newly established democracies, individuals and groups with selfish motives take advantage of the system, in some cases even allowing themselves to be pawns of external forces. I have candidly shared some of my concerns based on these thoughts with my Bhutanese friends.

Returning to the situation in Sikkim, meeting and getting to know Kazi Lhendup Dorjee in person and hearing his account of events completely changed my opinion of him. I came to like him very much. He was quite knowledgeable about his own culture and religion and very much committed to maintaining it. He was very helpful to the Tibetans residing in Sikkim, treating them far better and giving them more opportunities than during the Chogyal's[23] time. His successors, Nar Bahadur Bhandari and the current Chief Minister, Pawan Kumar Chamling, have continued his legacy. Both have hosted His Holiness in Sikkim, receiving him with great honor and grand receptions.

The original inhabitants of Sikkim, the Lepcha and Bhutia peoples, unfortunately, have become minorities in their own lands. There has been a strong renaissance of Buddhist culture in recent years, however, enabling them to maintain this important part of their traditional culture that I have personally witnessed as a regular visitor to the region. Younger generations of Sikkimese are taking serious interest in their culture. Buddhist monasteries are thriving, with many young monks undertaking serious Buddhist philosophical studies. Of course, the presence of renowned Tibetan masters and centers of higher Tibetan Buddhist studies in India has made a huge contribution to this revival. Today, in many Tibetan monasteries in various parts of India, there are large number of monks and nuns from all over the Himalayas, including many from Sikkim. After completing their higher studies, some return home, but an equally large number remain at the institutions where they studied, assuming key positions and

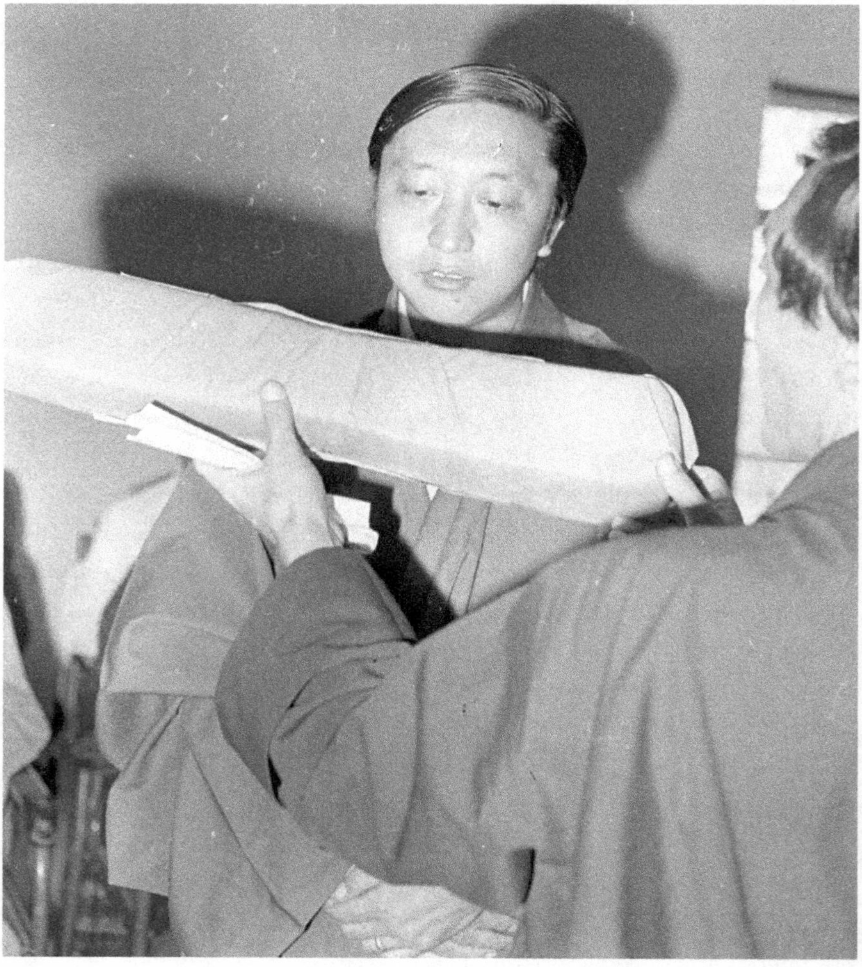

The author taking the oath of office as a Parliament member, Dharamsala, September 2, 1979
Tibet Museum, CTA

responsibilities. Ironically, Tibetans are becoming a minority in many of their own institutions.

## RETURN TO GOVERNMENT SERVICE

My self-imposed exile from Dharamsala and the CTA did not last long. Sometime in the beginning of 1979, Venerable Doboom Tulku, then Secretary to His Holiness, passed on His Holiness's advice that if I were invited by the Kashag, I should rejoin the CTA. Soon thereafter, when I was in Delhi, then Kalon Takla Phuntsok Tashi told me I should anticipate receiving a communication from the Kashag, to which I should respond positively. He seemed unaware of the message I had already received from the Private Office.

In the meantime, preliminary elections for the 7th Tibetan Parliament-in-Exile were being held, and I had scored a large share of the votes from the Dotoe (Kham) constituency. In Delhi sometime soon after that, I had a brief encounter with His Holiness. He said that as I was likely to be elected to the Parliament, judging from the high numbers I had scored in the preliminary election, I should remain in the race and postpone returning to the CTA until after I had served one term.

As expected, I did win a Parliamentary seat with a high percentage of the votes from my region. The Deputies, in turn, elected me Chairman, whereby I became the youngest person to hold that position. As counseled by His Holiness, I served one term and then rejoined the CTA, first as Additional Secretary in the then Department of Information and Publicity and later in the Kashag.

CHAPTER 10

# Repercussions from Divisions Within the Tibetan Community in Exile

The mid-1960s to the 1970s were very tumultuous and challenging years for the Tibetan community in exile. The unity forged in Bodhgaya was being pulled apart by both internal factors and external interferences. This period was especially painful for His Holiness. In addition to the disputes among different exile organizations that I discussed in the preceding chapter, almost every Tibetan leader, including his own brother Gyalo Thondup, and even a number of senior officials were involved in some kind of domestic intrigue. While dealing with these never-ending internal problems, however, His Holiness never lost sight of his priorities: ensuring the well-being of the Tibetans, educating the younger generations, and preserving the Tibetan Buddhist culture and heritage. To help realize these objectives, he began reaching out to the international community, engaging various organizations and individuals in support of the Tibetan cause, in particular to preserve our distinct cultural and religious identities.

His Holiness's deep concern was revealed in both his public remarks and his personal communications. Within a short period of time, he lamented that the Tibetans had lost sight of the real goal. Those ferocious warriors who had fought so valiantly against the Communist Chinese invaders were now obsessed with fighting among themselves and against the Dharamsala leadership. The depth of his despair is evident in a letter written to one of his former ministers, Surkhang Wangchen Gelek, on July 1, 1971:

བོད་ནང་རང་རིགས་རྒྱ་ཆེའི་མི་མང་གིས་མནར་གཅོད་སྡུག་སྦྱོངས་མྱོང་སྟངས་དང་། བོད་རང་དབང་གི་དོན་དུ་འབད་བརྩོན་སེམས་ཤུགས་བྱེད་སྟངས་ལ་བསམ་ན། ཕྱི་རྒྱལ་ས་ཐོག་འགྱོར་བའི་བོད་མི་ཚོས་ནང་ཁུལ་འཐེན་འཁྱེར་འདི་འདྲ་མི་འོས་མི་ཡོད་པ་ལྟ་བུ་ཡང་། རང་རང་སྐྱོང་བྱ་མ་རྟོགས་པ་ཇི་ལྟར་ནང་ཁུལ་བལྟ་ཚུལ་མཐོང་ཚུལ་མི་མཐུན་པའི་ལབ་གླེང་རེ་སྐྱེད་བྱུང་སྐོར། འདི་ནས་སྤྱི་སྒོམས་གཞུང་གནས་ཀྱིས་ཕྱོགས་ཚང་མར་དགེ་སྐྱོན་སྤྱང་བ་ཤོད་ཐབས་ཞིབ་ལོ་བསྟུད་བྱས་ཀྱང་ཕན་ཐོགས་གྲུབ་འབྲས་རེ་བཞིན་མ་ཐོན་ཅིང་། ད་དུང་གོ་ཞིབ་ཕན་ཐོགས་ཡོང་བའི་གོ་སྐབས་ཤར་ཚེ་ཐབས་ལམ་གང་དགེའི་འབད་བརྩོན་མི་བྱ་མཐུ་མེད་དེ་ལྟ་ནའང་། ལས་ཀྱི་འབྲས་བུ་སུས་ཀྱང་བཅོས་སུ་དཀའ་བས་ཅིར་འགྱུར་མ་ངེས།

> If we think about the torture and humiliation our people continue to face inside Tibet and efforts they are making for the cause of freedom, it would be incorrect and even unthinkable for the Tibetans in foreign lands to indulge in such factionalism. However, perhaps due to our destiny, verbal bouts continue to be thrown at each other. For years I have tried my level best, as a third party, to explain to all the sides, but results are hard to come by. I will continue to clear misunderstandings whenever the opportunity presents itself, but the result of bad karma is something nobody can either change or predict.[1]

As mentioned earlier, Surkhang Wangchen Gelek was a former senior cabinet minister who relocated to Taiwan, and in so doing became a target of severe criticism among the Tibetan diaspora. I first met him in 1973 when he called on His Holiness in Switzerland. To be very frank, I thought it was strange for him to receive an audience, given his reputation among the majority of Tibetans as being unpatriotic. His Holiness, however, was very cordial and engaging during the meeting. Surkhang Wangchen Gelek even hosted lunch for His Holiness and his entourage near the Zurich airport because our flight was delayed, and he came to see His Holiness once again in England some days later.

I am sure His Holiness must have been deeply disappointed by Surkhang Wangchen Gelek's decision to go to Taiwan, especially given the machinations of the MTAC designed to undermine the CTA, but it was also evident that on a personal level, he remained in touch with him, as the quoted letter demonstrates. His Holiness's compassionate nature always shines through, as do his respect and support for those who have been in his service for long periods of time. When looking at His Holiness's conduct, it is essential to appreciate how difficult it must have been for him to deal with all the turmoil in Dharamsala generated by the narrow, often conflicting interests of even those closest to him.

Surkhang Wangchen Gelek came to India again, in 1974, I believe. I had the opportunity to spend some quality time with him in Delhi when we were both guests at the official residence of Kushok Bakula Rinpoche, the highly respected leader from Ladakh, who was a minister in the Jammu and Kashmir government and a member of the Indian Parliament for many years. It was quite clear to me that, at the time, he was writing his version of the events precipitating his departure for Taiwan to clear up some of the attendant misunderstandings and misperceptions. It is unfortunate that he never published his narrative. A few years later he passed away, and I do not know if any of his writings survived.

In addition to His Holiness the Dalai Lama, other prominent Tibetan religious leaders were deeply troubled by the bickering within the Tibetan community. Speaking to his followers around this time, His Holiness Dudjom Rinpoche, the Supreme Head of the Nyingma tradition, made the following appeal:

> We are in a foreign country; we should not make an exhibition of our bad behavior! Even if we are unable to have pure vision regarding each other, we should at the very least aim and aspire not to criticize and have wrong views about each other. Sometimes it appears we are completely at loggerheads! As soon as one problem is solved, another one arises. It's quite uncanny! So do your best to avoid such things. Older people should advise the young, and we should all raise our spirits and aspirations. This is so important at the present time. And indeed, this is the best way to pray for the long life of His Holiness and perform a real service for the Dharma.[2]

And, at the same gathering, he further reminded the Tibetan people of the great treasure they had in the person of His Holiness the 14th Dalai Lama:

> And yet, in the midst of this terrible situation, there is at least one good thing: His Holiness the Dalai Lama. Outwardly, he is like an iron fence and inwardly like a precious treasure. He is our refuge in this and future lives, the guide of gods and men. He has been able to come and settle, without any danger to his life, in India, the noble land. To the eye of an impartial observer, it is thanks to this that an amazing development has taken place, both for the Dharma and in the political situation of us Tibetans. You all know this—you don't need me to tell you. It has all happened thanks to His Holiness the Dalai Lama, and to him alone. We should be endlessly grateful to him and pray for his long life. This is vital.[3]

## THE TRAGIC DEMISE OF THE MUSTANG GUERILLA BASE

I know from personal experience the extensive efforts His Holiness undertook, for example, to bring reconciliation between the two factions of the Chushi Gangdrug. In the mid-1970s, on at least two occasions, he personally intervened trying to broker a solution to their differences. One of the major issues dividing the groups was the leadership of the Mustang guerilla base. From the beginning, the US CIA wanted to appoint one of its trainees as the leader, believing that someone with professional training in guerilla warfare would be the most effective. The "old guard" within the Chushi Gangdrug, headed by Andruk Gonpo Tashi, were not in favor of any immediate change.

Indian intelligence became involved in the matter through the Joint Center set up in Delhi to coordinate the efforts of the CIA, Indian intelligence, and the Tibetans.[4] It was given oversight not only of operations based in Mustang but also of the activities of the SFF and several other agencies. The Joint Center recommended that Gyato Wangdu, a CIA-trained veteran who was also Andruk Gonpo Tashi's nephew, be promoted to head the base, replacing Bapa Gyen Yeshe, the first base leader and an appointee of Andruk Gonpo Tashi and Gyalo Thondup.

At the time, the base was facing problems, including financial irregularities and factionalism, that were deeply demoralizing the force. By this time, the Kashag was very much involved because Gyalo Thondup had gradually distanced himself from this kind of responsibility. The Kashag also endorsed Gyato Wangdu's appointment.

Bapa Gyen Yeshe was called to Dharamsala and informed that he would be appointed Deputy Minister of the Security Department and that Gyato Wangdu would succeed him. While saying he appreciated his appointment to this important position within the CTA, Bapa Gyen Yeshe nevertheless insisted upon returning to Mustang to oversee a proper handover to Gyato Wangdu and to take care of some personal matters. For a variety of reasons, the Kashag and the Joint Center were not in favor of his plan and advised him accordingly. However, he made secret arrangements to return and once there, immediately created his own faction within the guerilla group, signaling that he was not going to relinquish his position voluntarily.

Before he left for Nepal, he spent several days in Delhi at a safe house run by the Joint Center where I visited him several times. His nephews Lochung, Lobsang Palden, and Kalsang Tashi were very close friends of mine from the Darjeeling days. Perhaps for this reason, Bapa Gyen Yeshe also showed considerable fondness toward me. He made it very clear that he had to go back to Mustang regardless of the advice of others as he did not wish to depart without clearing up his accounts and taking care of some other matters that might damage his reputation if left unattended.

The appointment of Gyato Wangdu and the return of Bapa Gyen Yeshe to Mustang against the advice of the Tibetan leadership created a major rift at the base. A small but vocal faction, mostly from his own native area, supported Bapa Gyen Yeshe. This unfortunate leadership struggle soon became a major source of division within the broader Chushi Gangdrug organization, leading to not only the dismantlement of the Mustang base but also the appalling death of Gyato Wangdu at the hands of the Nepalese army.

Meanwhile, Beijing took full advantage of the discord to pressure the Nepalese government to take military action to disband the base. The highly trained and well-equipped Tibetan guerillas, however, were unwilling to surrender. Fearing great loss of life and creation of deep animosity between the Tibetan and the Nepalese peoples, who had for centuries enjoyed close relations, His Holiness personally intervened, sending a recorded voice message urging the Tibetans to surrender. Although this timely and farsighted intervention prevented a large-scale tragedy, some of the guerilla fighters were so torn between their personal commitment to continuing their struggle versus their moral responsibility to respect their leader's command that some of them, including Gyen Pachen, felt compelled to take their own lives.

It is indeed heartbreaking that factionalism and individual power struggles precipitated such a disastrous end to the guerilla movement. With the CIA withdrawing its support and Beijing becoming more influential in Nepal, the Tibetan leadership and the Joint Center had already come to the conclusion that it would not be possible to sustain the base. Alternative sites were already under serious consideration, and during W. G. Kundeling's meeting with P. N. Haksar and R. N. Kao, this was one of the primary issues discussed. But with the situation in Mustang getting out of control, such deliberations became irrelevant and even the gradual transition of the elder guerilla fighters into civilian life was disrupted.

The termination of the Mustang program, ending with the death of Gyato Wangdu and many others, was a profoundly sad and devastating event. I knew Gyato Wangdu very intimately. His elder brother, Gyato Bhugyen, joined my family on our six-month flight from Kham to Lhasa. This trying and dangerous experience had bonded our two families, and the deep relationship remained alive in exile. Gyato Wangdu was a very capable and charismatic person, someone who had the potential to become an important leader of the Chushi Gangdrug, maybe even capable of filling his illustrious uncle Andruk Gonpo Tashi's shoes.[5]

Bapa Gyen Yeshe himself kept a low profile after this disaster, living in Kathmandu under Nepalese protection. I understand that he was shunned by the Tibetan community but devoted his remaining years to his spiritual practice, foregoing any active partisan activities. He too must have felt deeply saddened at the tragic demise of the Mustang operation, given that he was one of the main architects of the guerilla movement.

In the aftermath, some Khampa leaders, mostly in the Group of Thirteen, took advantage of the situation by siding with Bapa Gyen Yeshe. This effectively ended the domination of the Darjeeling-based faction of the Chushi Gangdrug under Andruk Gonpo Tashi that included individuals primarily hailing from Lithang, Bathang, and Chatreng. Once again, agents of the MTAC meddled in our internal affairs further muddying the waters and eventually splitting the Chushi Gangdrug movement into two factions, one of which eventually signed a Memorandum of Understanding (MOU) with the MTAC.

Although I was not directly involved with the Mustang program, I felt deep remorse over what had transpired and always wanted to do something to help mitigate the suffering of the valiant fighters who had so staunchly defended Tibet's interests. As I was based in Washington, D.C., as His Holiness's Special Envoy, I made efforts to bring some of them to the United States under a special program. Some members of Congress and their senior staffers were very sympathetic to the plight of these patriots. In consultation with Lithang Wangyal and others charged with looking after the welfare of these individuals, we prepared a comprehensive list of veterans and their dependents. There was precedent for bringing individuals to the United States who had worked in concert with the government. Even though my efforts in Washington, D.C., were bearing fruit, internal politics at the Chushi Gangdrug and the CTA bureaucracy derailed the initiative.

In March 2015, upon my retirement from the ICT, the organization and some members of Congress held a memorable farewell ceremony for me at the Senate Russell building in Washington, D.C. Despite the warm and sincere compliments delivered by these dear friends and supporters, my parting words voiced my heartfelt despair at being unable to help these deserving Tibetan heroes:

> One area where we were not successful was in helping the families of Tibetan freedom fighters who were at one time assisted by the CIA. Even though His

> Holiness the Dalai Lama and the Tibetan leadership are deeply committed to the non-violent approach, these Tibetans made many sacrifices and I firmly believe that it is our responsibility to take care of them. Due to a number of obstacles, however, we were unable to provide for them. This was particularly distressing when the U.S. State Department was ready to be creative in facilitating their exit from Nepal and receiving them in the United States. I continue to believe that it is our duty to not forget their contributions.[6]

The split within the Chushi Gangdrug even created rifts between relatives and close friends. In many cases, people were dragged into the dispute through emotional manipulation or adverse personal circumstances, including financial hardship. As so frequently happens in politics, there was quite a bit of switching of loyalty between the factions, not so much based on policy differences but driven by personal animosities and interests. We may have adopted this unfortunate practice from the Indian political parties of the period. At one time, there was so much floor crossing or changing of parties within the Indian political system that the phenomenon was reflected in this commonplace saying: "Aaya ram, gaya ram," meaning "Ram has come, Ram has gone."

One of the most prominent individuals who switched allegiances was Athar Norbu, also known as Lithang Athar. In 1957, he was one of the first Tibetans to be selected for training by the CIA. After a few months of intensive training in guerilla warfare and radio communications, he and his colleague Lotse, also from Lithang, were parachuted back into Tibet in September. Athar was known as "Tom" to the CIA instructors, while Lotse was called "Lou." They were the first Tibetans ever to parachute. In my opinion, their behind-the-scenes role was critical to the establishment of the Chushi Gangdrug.

Unlike the second CIA-trained team that was airdropped sometime later into Lithang, Athar and Lotse were able to persuasively communicate with their CIA counterparts, resulting in the needed airdropping of arms and ammunition. But even more than the valued weapons, their participation brought great hope to the fighters, enabling them to sustain their efforts with the knowledge that their movement was being supported by the United States. Lithang Athar and Lotse also played major roles in facilitating His Holiness's safe passage into exile. In his book, Gyalo Thondup writes in detail about how he received a message from these two men notifying him of the Dalai Lama's decision to seek asylum in India. This advance notice enabled Gyalo Thondup to rush to Delhi to meet with India's Prime Minister Nehru and present him with His Holiness's request.[7]

Early in his career, Lithang Athar was a staunch supporter of Gyalo Thondup and the CTA. He was among the most outspoken whenever key issues erupted within the Tibetan community, always supporting the CTA. Together with Dogyal Aten, another US-trained veteran, Athar was also instrumental in establishing the Chigdril Tsogpa in Nepal, one of the most organized and efficient among all the organization's branches. Athar and I served together in the 7th Tibetan Parliament-in-Exile, both representing the Kham region. The Tibetan leadership considered him a trustworthy and capable ally, and he has always proven to be one. On a personal level, he was a very generous and well-liked individual.

But later in life, Lithang Athar became one of the most vocal critics of the CTA. He went so far as to be involved in the Chushi Gangdrug's open collaboration with the KMT. This deeply saddened my family and me because, unlike others involved in this unfortunate alliance, here was a man who had made so many contributions and played such a crucial role in Tibet's struggle. But I think I actually witnessed the moment when he first "snapped" and lost his confidence in the CTA.

Toward the end of our term as members of the 7th Parliament, he came back one day after visiting the Department of Education, where he had gone to seek financial support for one of his daughters' university tuition fees. The CTA was providing various scholarships for higher studies, and Athar took it for granted that because of his unwavering loyalty and commitment to the cause, he would receive the requested aid. This was the first time in his life that he asked for something in return for his lifelong service. Moreover, he genuinely needed the funds, unlike many others who had the necessary resources but nevertheless took advantage of the program.

Not only was his request denied, I don't think he even received the basic courtesy that he deserved. His lodgings were next to mine, an arrangement we deliberately chose because of our almost familial relationship. Athar was a relative of my mothers. My siblings and I were very fond of him because he was one of the few relatives we had from their side. I had never seen him so visibly upset and hurt. He kept on saying: "Now I have seen the true nature of these people." In the days following, I offered to speak to the Secretary of the Department seeking reconsideration of its decision, but Athar absolutely forbade me from doing so. He vowed he would never seek anything from the CTA again. Athar was also facing certain personal difficulties and as a result, was unable to participate in Parliamentary proceedings for some time. This situation was deliberately made into a public issue, primarily by members of the Tibetan community hostile to the CTA. What saddened Athar the most, however, was the participation of some senior CTA officials in this spiteful smear campaign.

This kind of insensitive handling and, more important, total disregard and lack of acknowledgment of the contributions made by such individuals, by officials within the CTA, has broken the hearts of many Tibetans, driving them away from Dharamsala and the greater interests of the Tibetan movement. This callous treatment may well have been the event leading Athar to become a vocal critic of the CTA. I am not trying to justify his later actions; he knew he was causing serious damage to our cause. The Chushi Gangdrug's open collaboration with the KMT under Lithang Athar's leadership, including signing of the MOU with the MTAC, was one of the most divisive acts taken by any of the Tibetan organizations in exile. It was in direct defiance of His Holiness's advice and CTA policy. It was also done without the knowledge of the majority of Khampa members of the organization. However, through very clever manipulation, the whole matter was made to look like a conflict within the Chushi Gangdrug, resulting in the formation of rival factions.

An official publication of the Department of Security entitled *Den-dhon Dorje Drak-ri* (Truth Revealed Like a Vajra Rock) meticulously recounts the activities of the Chushi Gangdrug as led by Lithang Athar and others. Such publications are important. The CTA has always been reluctant to defend its positions even when baseless and ill-intended accusations were leveled against it. The usual explanation for its silence is that it is beneath the dignity of the leadership to even comment on such patently false and outrageous allegations. While this sounds very noble, and I am sure may be the case most of the time, future generations will, unfortunately, read what has been published and preserved in libraries believing it to be accurate. The truth must be revealed and chronicled. While I was in the Kashag, a number of times His Holiness himself advised us on the importance of having the truth stated and being transparent with our people. I remember he once explicitly said that whether we succeeded or not in our struggle, future generations of Tibetans must at least know that we have done the best we can, in spite of both external and internal challenges and obstacles.

Because of my personal affection for him, I asked to see Athar during one of my visits to India. We spent some precious time together, uncle and nephew, at the Bureau of His Holiness the Dalai Lama. I urged him to reconcile with the CTA because his actions were even disturbing His Holiness. He emotionally explained the sacrifices he had made, the services he had rendered to the cause, and the disappointments and rejections he had suffered. As he is no longer with us, it is not proper for me to share our in-depth conversation. However, his parting words were: "I have served well, and I have no regrets. But you be careful now, I am worried about you."

This was the last time we were together. He passed away in New York in 2004. I flew in specifically to participate in his memorial service. When I walked into the room where people were gathered, many were clearly shocked, and some were even a bit hostile toward me. In the end, however, some of the organizers asked if I could say a few words, an offer I declined. Given my official position as the Special Envoy of His Holiness the Dalai Lama, my remarks could have been interpreted as representing the CTA. Some pro-CTA individuals were also not happy that I had attended the service, but I have never allowed my official position to interfere with my personal relations, a principle I learned from my father.

Soon after Athar's passing, I made a special request to His Holiness's office for a letter to be prepared and sent to his children recognizing the contributions their father had made to the Tibetan cause. I am really very happy that I was able to facilitate this gesture of official appreciation for his efforts and personally deliver it to his daughter Dolma Tsering. I hope it was of some value to the family. There are so many tragic stories similar to this that have needlessly divided our people.

## THWARTED EFFORTS TO COUNTER THE MTAC'S DESTRUCTIVE MACHINATIONS

It should now be apparent that one of the main causes of disunity among the Tibetan community was the destructive activities of the KMT government's MTAC. Its operatives managed to infiltrate many Tibetan organizations and interfere in almost every major issue with the sole intent of discrediting the CTA's work. Its interference became increasingly bold and aggressive over the years, with these troublemakers and their Tibetan collaborators openly challenging not only the CTA leadership but also His Holiness personally. Some of the Tibetan stooges went so far as to say they had never been ruled by the Lhasa-based Tibetan government and their allegiance had always been to the Nationalist government. This was a not so thinly veiled attempt to repudiate the Great Oath of Unity. The

MTAC also started funding projects in some Tibetan settlements and communities to win the loyalty of the residents and simultaneously turn them against the CTA and its unification policy. They also openly paraded handpicked Tibetans to "celebrate" the double tenth anniversary in Taiwan, commemorating the founding of the Republic of China.

The unity of the Tibetan people was under serious threat. His Holiness felt compelled to speak out publicly, explaining the great harm being inflicted by these external forces. He openly challenged the Tibetan people, especially those from Kham, saying that if the majority of them really felt they did not wish to be part of the inclusive Tibet that had been reestablished in accordance with the Oath, he would not stand in the way and would immediately stop talking about a unified Tibet composed of the three regions. His Holiness's public challenge was intended to identify, expose, and isolate this small faction of malcontents. He knew that the vast majority of Tibetans from all regions, both inside Tibet and in exile, were committed to a reunified Tibet and that it was only a handful of individuals, for a variety of primarily selfish reasons, who were seeking to undermine Tibetan unity and the all-inclusive leadership of the CTA.

At the same time, His Holiness realized that a direct confrontation with the MTAC and its collaborators would not cure the fundamental problem. He needed to make efforts to build a relationship with the Nationalist government in Taiwan. Thus, in 1982, the CTA Department of Security secretly established direct relations with the Taiwanese National Security Bureau. The principal people involved were Minister of the Department of Security Tashi Wangdi; Department of Security Secretary Jampa Kalden; and Tempa Tsering, Secretary at the Office of His Holiness the Dalai Lama; with my brother Pema Gyalpo, who was then His Holiness's representative for the Asia Pacific region, as the main interlocutor. The contact was kept highly confidential and in the initial stages even the Kashag seemed not to be involved. I only became fully aware of the initiative toward the end of 1987 when the relationship was exposed and became hugely controversial in Dharamsala. By that time, I was in the Kashag.

I do recall, however, when I was Chairman of the Tibetan Parliament in the early 1980s, during some of my brother's visits, Jampa Kalden and Tempa Tsering used to pick him up at my house to take him to meetings. Sometimes they had hurried consultations on the small veranda of my residence. Only later did I realize they had been discussing their work with the Taiwanese Security Department. Even though this burgeoning relationship came to an end with its public exposure, its initial efforts did deal a severe blow to the MTAC's operations.

This whole disastrous episode could have been avoided if the Kashag had acted according to His Holiness's advice. Soon after the public exposure of this relationship the entire Kashag briefed His Holiness on the delicate situation confronting the CTA. His Holiness responded directly and unequivocally, advising that in the future we be open and transparent about the relationship. He said we had done nothing wrong in establishing relations with the Taiwanese National Security Bureau and that these types of relations are normal between countries. He further recognized that we had established the relationship to safeguard and promote Tibet's interests, and thus there was nothing to be embarrassed about. He did specifically acknowledge, however, that if there were any financial or administrative irregularities, they should be thoroughly investigated.

After extensive discussions in the Kashag, unfortunately, we decided to handle the matter differently, including continuing to keep the involvement of His Holiness's office confidential. In the end, everything backfired. I am consciously refraining from writing in detail how this relationship was blown out of proportion by vested interests because my brother Pema Gyalpo was a key participant in the events and my views could be seen as biased in his favor. For a very thorough and objective presentation of the events, I recommend the *Memoir of Jampa Kalden*, published by the Library of Tibetan Works and Archives in 2015 as part of its oral history collection. Jampa Kalden devotes nearly forty pages to this event, including an explicit revelation of the parties responsible for bringing the promising relationship between the Department of Security and the Taiwanese National Security Bureau to an unfortunate end.

When this relationship became public, Alak Jigme Rinpoche had taken over as Minister for the Department of Security from Tashi Wangdi, and Lobsang Tsultrim had succeeded Jampa Kalden as Department Secretary. It became very clear during the internal investigations that there was a lack of transparency among the three principal people involved, Kalon Alak Jigme Rinpoche, Secretary Lobsang Tsultrim, and Pema Gyalpo, which was also very unfortunate.

Years later, after I had moved to the United States from India, I learned much more about how this whole relationship was painstakingly planned and carried out from T. T. Chen, who was a close friend of my brother. He was from a very prominent KMT family and played a key role in building the relationship between the two security departments. He had relocated to the United States and was running a family business in Nashville, Tennessee, when we spoke. To say the least, he was disgusted with how the Tibetan leadership had handled the matter and did not mince his words in criticizing me, because during that period I was a member of the Kashag. By then he was also not happy with the CTA for having established close relations with Taiwan's Democratic Progressive Party because he remained a staunch Nationalist in spite of being very critical of the MTAC's harmful activities among the Tibetans.

The MTAC and its agents and collaborators took this opportunity to retaliate against my family by implying that because of my brother's involvement, the Gyari family was also a beneficiary of KMT funding. Overnight, unsigned leaflets and posters started appearing accusing us of having relations with the KMT. This whole controversy was traumatizing for our entire family, especially the children. One of our distant relatives overheard a well-known MTAC collaborator boastfully telling a group of Tibetans at a restaurant at the Tibetan refugee camp in Delhi that "We gave it back to Gyari Nyima," meaning they had managed to drag the Gyari family name into this mess in retaliation for my father having been at the forefront in opposing the KMT's activities.

What was most upsetting for my parents was that these totally unfounded allegations caused a direct confrontation with Kunsang Lama, a senior attendant of His Holiness Penor Rinpoche. Kunsang Lama was the main individual openly challenging the CTA's restriction on Tibetans receiving funding from the KMT, pointing to the alleged hypocrisy of the CTA's position given its supposed receipt of KMT funds.

My parents have always been deeply religious. They have never allowed themselves to be placed in a situation that confronted our religious leaders or institutions. Fortunately, in anticipation of a visit to India in 1990 by His Holiness Khenchen Jigmé Phuntsok Rinpoche, there was full reconciliation between my family and Penor Rinpoche's monastery. Realizing how much Khenchen Jigmé Phuntsok Rinpoche cared for my family, Kunsang Lama later wrote a very detailed letter to us in which he explained the circumstances under which he had been misled and expressed regret for causing pain for our family. Some of our close relatives wanted this letter made public, not only to clear the family name but primarily to expose the individual who had instigated the whole issue that not only harmed our family but more importantly, destroyed the fragile relationship that had been forged between the Taiwanese and Tibetan security departments.

My father not only refused to make the letter public but actually tore it to pieces so that no one could misuse it in the future. He was concerned that it might be used not only to betray Kunsang Lama's confidences but also to show disrespect for Khenchen Jigmé Phuntsok Rinpoche and Penor Rinpoche. He was satisfied that our family relationship with this important monastic institution was restored.[8]

This unfortunate confrontation actually bonded my family very closely with Penor Rinpoche and his monastery. My youngest brother, Kunzang Tsewang, was subsequently elected to represent the Nyingma tradition in the Tibetan Parliament for four consecutive terms—a total of twenty years—mainly with their backing and support. As I write elsewhere, it is admirable to see this quality of loyalty and unwavering friendship in some of the elder Tibetan Rinpoches and leaders. Even after Penor Rinpoche's passing, other prominent Rinpoches and Khenpos of his monastic institution continued to support my brother as a mark of respect for their late teacher. He declined to continue this representation, however, with gratitude for their continuing confidence in him, knowing there were many other deserving and capable individuals representing the Nyingma tradition in Parliament.

His Holiness did not give up his effort to reach out to the Nationalist leadership in Taiwan to uproot the cause for the continued obstacles and problems instigated by some of its operatives. During the presidency of Lee Teng-hui, His Holiness's efforts bore fruit, ultimately leading to His Holiness personally visiting Taiwan and meeting with President Lee. I write more on this later in the book.[9] I am happy I was able to play some role in facilitating that.

## COMPLICATIONS ARISING FROM HIS HOLINESS THE 14TH DALAI LAMA'S DEVOLUTION OF POLITICAL AUTHORITY

Despite the history of obstacles and internal discord within our community, Tibetans today enjoy an unprecedented level of unity that is even stronger inside Tibet. The seed of this restored cohesion was sown in the Great Oath of Unity under the guidance of His Holiness and earlier generations of both lay and religious Tibetan leaders. The Oath bound together the Gaden Phodrang government in the person of His Holiness the 14th Dalai Lama and the Tibetan people, serving as a pledge by the people to their temporal and spiritual ruler. Its goal was to ensure the continuation of the historical and traditional legacy of the Tibetan government of Gaden Phodrang while fulfilling the hopes and aspirations of the entire Tibetan people in their changing circumstances. Establishing a unified entity did not take away any authority from the Gaden Phodrang. On the contrary, it broadened its sphere of administration to include all three Tibetan regions.

Mindful of the long-term aspirations of the Tibetan people, His Holiness gradually moved the Tibetan polity toward democratization. He has always firmly believed that the true masters of Tibet's destiny must be the Tibetan people, not Tibetan institutions, nor even the institution of the Dalai Lama. However, the fact remains that there is a spiritual as well as a moral authority of the Dalai Lama that is not bestowed by rule of law. No political act can terminate this inherent power or destroy the extraordinary relationship His Holiness has with the inhabitants of the Land of Snows.

Given this profound and unshakeable bond, His Holiness's 2011 decision to devolve all his political authority and to separate the Gaden Phodrang from the Tibetan administration saddened and disturbed many of us very deeply, not because of any blind faith in him but because of the impact on the immediate and long-term interests of the Tibetan people. It is my firm belief that we could have worked toward the goal of democratization without making such a drastic change. While technically the CTA and its various organs are led by people elected by a majority of the Tibetans in exile, as I previously noted, the CTA is a continuation of the government that came into exile with His Holiness. In my opinion, the very legitimacy of the CTA as representing all Tibetans becomes questionable in the absence of a direct relationship between it and His Holiness.

I have raised this issue time and time again. Some may think I have taken my concerns too far. However, I remember the day His Holiness relinquished his political role as one of the saddest days of my life. I am not alone in my feelings; many others felt the anguish of this unprecedented change. Tulku Orgyen Topgyal, then a sitting member of the Tibetan Parliament representing the Dotoe (Kham) region, resigned his seat, saying he had no desire to be a party to the dismantling of the Gaden Phodrang government that was established by the Great Fifth Dalai Lama, Ngawang Lobsang Gyatso. His action surprised many because he was often critical of the CTA.

From my years of experience, however, I have learned that many Tibetans make a clear distinction between the CTA and His Holiness. Even though individuals critical of the CTA are routinely viewed as disrespectful of His Holiness, this is neither true nor fair. Even in my own writing, I make a clear distinction: when I talk about the Tibetan leadership, I am referring to the Kashag, Parliament, and other institutions, not His Holiness personally.

I want to share with my readers another story that has relevance here. Several years back, a Japanese television crew interviewed a Tibetan woman still living in Tibet who was identified as a former "serf" of the Phala family. During the interview, which took place at the Phala estate in Gyangtse, she denounces the old system in Tibet with so much anguish and angry emotions that at times she breaks down crying. She goes on to say how happy she now is, sharing how her children have all received good educations and hold positions of responsibility. She is now the happiest person due to the kindness of the Chinese Communist Party.

Anyone listening to her story would think that this was propaganda designed by the Chinese Communists to denounce the old system and glorify current Chinese rule. However, I heard from an individual who was present during the interview about the following exchange. When asked a final question about her last wish for this life, without a blink of the eye, she responded: "The only wish I have now is to gaze upon the face of Gyalwa Tenzin Gyatso (the 14th Dalai Lama) before I die." With that answer it becomes clear that all her prior remarks were genuine and heartfelt.[10]

What I am trying to say is that even Tibetans who have a deep dislike of or even animosity toward the prior Lhasa government or the CTA in exile have a deep reverence for the institution of the Dalai Lamas, and particularly for His Holiness the 14th Dalai Lama. Some Tibetan government officials, however, make the gross mistake of seeing this profound reverence as somehow applying to them. They then take full advantage of this position, lording their presumed "status" over others, including people from other Himalayan regions and other non-Tibetans. I think some Tibetan functionaries feel that every individual who wears a red robe is one of their "subjects," an unacceptable, ego-driven perception that must be eliminated.

During one of my visits with Kushok Bakula Rinpoche in Delhi, a group of Ladakhi leaders called on him to respectfully express their concerns about how he always remains submissive when dealing with Tibetan officials, tolerating their improper treatment without objection. I am sure that they were indirectly conveying a message to me, criticizing my role as a government official. I remember one of the younger leaders saying that His Holiness the Dalai Lama is our supreme religious leader and most precious to us, but Tibetan government officials should not think that they have jurisdiction over us. I do not disagree with this sentiment. I have heard such comments from many others in the Himalayan region.

The most important historical and moral responsibility that faces us today is to find a solution to the tragic situation that we as a people continue to endure. Emotional and sentimental issues aside, the only way to find a reasonably beneficial solution is through dialogue with the PRC government. No Tibetan institution or leader other than His Holiness the 14th Dalai Lama can help us in this regard. Likewise, even in the international arena, the Tibet issue has become inseparable from the person of the 14th Dalai Lama. In fact, many of our international efforts and activities were carried out under his direction and in his name. Even within the Tibetan community itself, it is difficult to imagine being part of a government that has no formal or direct connection with His Holiness. I have mentioned these concerns repeatedly over the years, including in memoranda I submitted when those sweeping changes were under consideration in Dharamsala.

Nor do I understand why there was such a rush to complete the devolution process. In a very hurried manner, even the CTA emblem was changed to reflect the new motto: Denpa Nyid Nampar Gyal Gyurchig (May the Truth Always Prevail). The old motto was *Bod gzhung dga' ldan pho brang phyogs las rnam rgyal* (Tibetan Government, Ganden Palace, Victorious in All Directions). Similarly, the Gaden Phodrang, which has now simply become the household or the Secretariat of the Dalai Lama, quickly adopted a new logo. Most disturbingly, the Tibetan name for the CTA was hurriedly changed from Bodshung (Tibetan Government) to Bod-mie Drig-zug (Tibetan Administration). While it is true the use of the word "government" was awkward for our host country and we need to be sensitive to its concerns, the change was puzzling and obviously made many people unhappy.

But now, looking back and thinking rationally, the new name for the administration, in fact, accurately reflects today's changed reality. The CTA is well run, with an impressive track record representing the exiled Tibetan community. The recent change of the designation of the head of CTA to President (Sikyong) seems to convey the intent of the organization to style itself more as an NGO. As I discuss in part III, I believe this is a welcome shift in emphasis.

## CHAPTER 11

# Tibetans Inside Tibet

### *Flag Bearers of a Unified Tibet*

When Deng Xiaoping proceeded with his open-door policy in 1979, it became possible for Tibetans in exile to visit Tibet and those inside to visit their relatives outside. This allowed the message of a reunified Tibet to spread far and wide. Tibetans inside Tibet understood its significance and deeply appreciated the exile leadership's actions. Decades of suffering and marginalization under Communist Chinese rule made the Tibetans inside Tibet acutely aware of the importance of self-identity, much more than those of us living in freedom in exile.

Today, Tibetans inside Tibet, whether in the Tibet Autonomous Region (TAR) or other Tibetan areas, maintain their strong desire for solidarity and unity. They comfortably use the term Do-U-Kham sum, referring to a collective entity comprising the three regions of Tibet, as well as the more common term Cholkhasum (Three regions). Folk songs, paintings, stories, and poems from inside Tibet, as well as the tragic political message conveyed through self-immolations, demonstrate an uncompromising and genuine commitment to the concept of a unified Tibet. It is ironic that one of the most beneficial effects of Deng Xiaoping's open-door policy was the opportunity for reunification of the Tibetan people. After visiting their homelands, exile Tibetans from Kham and Amdo, including those who were earlier keeping their distance from the CTA, returned to India much more supportive and appreciative of the concept of unity.

With Tibet opening up and reports generated by our three Fact-Finding Delegations, as well as my official 1982 visit to the PRC,[1] I was convinced that the idea had now caught the imagination of the Tibetans inside Tibet. At the same time, however, I realized that we must give even greater respect to preserving the individual identities of the three regions. Maintaining their distinctive character and uniqueness was, in fact, the unifying factor and not the other way around.

Delegates of the First Exploratory Talks mission visiting Mount Wutai, along with some of their Chinese hosts, 1982

During my 1982 visit, my delegation was taken to Mount Wutai, known as Riwo Tse-nga in Tibetan. It is the most important pilgrimage destination for Tibetans in all of China. While there, we met some Tibetan nomads from the Kirti region of Amdo. We were all wearing casual Western attire, so they did not recognize us as Tibetans. As they were wearing their traditional clothes and speaking Tibetan, I immediately recognized them and rushed over, saying in a rather loud voice: "We have come from India! We are His Holiness the Dalai Lama's representatives!"

For a while they froze, speechless, neither uttering a word nor moving a limb. Then slowly, a very tall and elegant-looking Amdowa recovered and tentatively asked me: "So you have all come from India?" Again, I responded by telling them that, yes, we had come from India at His Holiness the Dalai Lama's instruction to meet with Chinese leaders.

This small group of about six to seven individuals then rushed over to us. Many of them started crying. At that point, I thought it important to introduce ourselves and identify where in Tibet we were originally from, so that they would be encouraged to see that representatives from the different regions were working together as one. I first introduced Takla Phuntsok Tashi, emphasizing his background and connections: "He is from Amdo. He is the brother-in-law of His Holiness the Dalai Lama." Then I introduced my other colleague, Juchen Thubten Namgyal, noting that he was a Khampa from Derge. Lastly, I introduced myself also as a Khampa, but from Nyarong.

I could see our hosts becoming uncomfortable. They started whispering to Phuntsok Tashi, who spoke Chinese, that we needed to move on as it was getting late. I knew I had to communicate one more important fact to the nomads before we parted. I said: "They are both Kalons, members of the Kashag. I am the Chairman of the Parliament." I somehow knew the Chinese word for the PRC's National People's Congress and for "chairman." I uttered these Chinese words to the nomads and with my own eyes saw the electrifying effect. They started talking among themselves in the Amdo dialect, which I understood, saying: "Yes, it seems true. Yes, it seems true." It was very clear that they had already heard that the Tibetans in exile had formed a common government under His Holiness, and here they were seeing two Khampas and one Amdowa in the flesh, representing the Dalai Lama and the Tibetan leadership in exile, confirming the information. This was a precious moment for me as well because I realized how deeply the concept of a unified Tibet was appreciated by the Tibetans inside.

While in Beijing on this trip I met with many other Tibetan leaders and scholars, all of whom confirmed this enthusiasm, even though many of them are not able to freely express their desires. But I also realized that no matter what difficulties we might face, we must not make any changes to the existing electoral system. To maintain the eagerness and support of the Tibetans inside, the distinct identities of the three regions had to be respected. It was worth tolerating the views of a few irresponsible members overly concerned with narrow, regional interests to avoid sending the wrong message to the vast majority inside Tibet who ultimately would be the decision makers. Understandably, some Tibetans in exile, including the then leaders of the TYC, criticized me, while others went so far as to denounce me as a regionalist.

Unfortunately, there were also others who mistakenly viewed the TAR as something "special" that people from other regions were envious to join and who were only invoking the "unity" slogan to realize their selfish goals. But this is absolute nonsense. The PRC government had already designated almost all Tibetan regions in Kham and Amdo as "autonomous." For example, my birthplace,

Nyarong, is today a part of the Kardze Tibetan Autonomous Prefecture in Sichuan Province. Moreover, some of the Tibetan autonomous areas outside of the TAR actually enjoy more freedom than does the TAR. The decision to unify had nothing to do with any one region trying to join another or one attempting to assert dominance over another; it was an effort to reestablish a unified Tibet in which every Tibetan would be an equal participant and stakeholder.

While Tibetans, especially those inside Tibet, are deeply committed to a unified Tibet, this does not mean that they have forsaken their devotion to their own religious traditions, traditional rulers, and lamas. Disregard of these traditional values and concepts could weaken our collective strength and unity. We should all be proud of our birthplaces, as well as our local social and religious traditions. As I have even told His Holiness, I would personally be reluctant to trust anyone who totally disavowed his or her regional roots or spiritual lineage. In the early 1980s, for example, when I was Chairman of Parliament, the Tibetan community in exile once again faced some critical fissures along regional lines. During one meeting convened in Dharamsala to discuss some of these explosive issues, one of the delegates, who was a great orator, spoke quite eloquently, saying he was neither U-Tsangpa, Khampa, nor Amdowa, nor Nyingmapa, Kagyupa, Sakyapa, or Gelugpa, but just a Tibetan and a Buddhist. His Holiness heard his speech, and a few days later during one of my audiences, he commented that he thought it was a refreshing statement in light of the pervasive factionalism and divisiveness afflicting our community.

His Holiness has always been very observant of body language, and he immediately sensed that I had some reservations about his views. He kindly asked me to speak my mind. I told him that as far as I was concerned, one should be cautious in making such remarks. I am sure the speaker meant what he said, but while I consider myself a Tibetan nationalist, when I think of Tibet, the first thing that comes to my mind is not Tibet, nor Kham, nor even Nyarong, but Lumorab, the small monastery where I grew up. From there, step by step I extend my affection and attachment to Nyarong, then to Kham, and then eventually I feel a sense of pride in being a Tibetan. I submitted to His Holiness that my nationalistic loyalty is firmly rooted in a strong local foundation. Similarly, while I consider myself a very devout Tibetan Buddhist, that devotion comes from my deeply rooted pride in my own Nyingma school, and within that, specifically the Mindrolling tradition. This understanding and devotion make me a true nonsectarian, because they stem from a strong feeling of identity with my tradition, yet with a respect for all others. A tree without firm roots won't bear fruit. After listening to my view, His Holiness said he sincerely appreciated my perspective.

For Tibetans inside Tibet, this sense of pride extends to the highest levels of society. During my 1982 trip to the PRC as part of the delegation sent by His Holiness for exploratory talks, I had an additional personal goal of understanding the thinking of prominent Tibetan leaders on the issue of a unified Tibet. We carried three letters from His Holiness (referred to as *kayig*) to three of them: Panchen Rinpoche, Ngapo Ngawang Jigme, and Bapa Phuntsok Wangyal. When we delivered them and I explained our achievements in creating unity in the exile community, I learned that these individuals not only supported our efforts but already had committed themselves to realizing the same objective.

We first met with Panchen Rinpoche at his residence. After the usual courtesies and official briefings, we presented the letter to him. Panchen Rinpoche immediately took it with both hands, touched it to his forehead, and prayed for some time. He then read the letter quietly, put it back into its envelope, touched it to his forehead once again, and placed it on a high table on his right side, while all of us watched in total silence and with deep emotion. After exchanges of views on a number of issues, I took the opportunity to ask Panchen Rinpoche his view on unification. With a rather strained look, Panchen Rinpoche composed himself and without annoyance, but in a thick, stammering voice with a mixed accent of Tsang and Amdo unique to him, said, "Lodi Gyaltsen, Dhon ney ga-shig gi thog-la, rangwang chen gyi chigyal yuldru la neypai punda tsoi sam ma nyongwa nga tsoe je nyong ta" ("On some issues, we have done what our brethren in free countries may not even have thought of"). Even today I remember very vividly the emotions I immediately felt after posing what I realized had been an unintentionally insensitive question. I felt so uncomfortable, a kind of regret, asking such a direct question to one of our bravest leaders, a hero who had suffered so much physical as well as mental pain in his life, all in furtherance of our cause.

Panchen Rinpoche then told us that recently nine Tibetan Communist Party members from Kanlho Tibetan Autonomous Prefecture of Gansu Province had submitted a very strong memorandum to the central Chinese government on this very issue. The memorandum was entitled: *Opinions on Reorganizing the Tibet Autonomous Region Administrative Division and Ensuring Its Right of Self-Determination*, dated November 17, 1980.[2] It argued for the inclusion of all the Tibetan regions that are today in Qinghai, Sichuan, Gansu, and Yunnan Provinces within a single Tibetan autonomous region along with the TAR. If this were not possible,

Bapa Phuntsok Wangyal, Panchen Rinpoche, Juchen Thubten Namgyal, and the author at Panchen Rinpoche's residence in Beijing during the First High-Level Exploratory Talks meeting, 1982
Tibet Museum, CTA

then all the Tibetan areas outside the TAR should be consolidated and given separate regional autonomy in one entity designated as the "East Tibet Autonomous Region."

Panchen Rinpoche made it very obvious that this petition had his blessing. He was such a courageous person who never failed to speak up on behalf of his people. He once again asserted his support for a unified Tibet, saying: "The wish of Kundun (the Dalai Lama) that you just explained to me is one and the same." I was completely overwhelmed by his response, and even today each precious word and the sound of his voice resonate in my mind.

Encouraged by his words, I ventured to once again speak freely. He was kind enough to indulge me, saying: "Sung-dhang sung-dhang" ("Say it, say it"). I gathered up all my courage and requested that in the future when talking about unifying all three Tibetan regions in one autonomous zone, one should not include an alternative based on the proviso "if that is not possible." Offering this option would weaken our demand. Tibetans both inside and outside Tibet must ask with one voice for all the Tibetan areas to be unified. Rinpoche thought for a while, seemed very pleased, and said: "Gyu tsen denpa re, gyu tsen denpa re, nge par du sem la shak chok" ("Very valid, very valid reason. Surely will keep this in mind"). Panchen Rinpoche was no ordinary person.

We next met Ngapo Ngawang Jigme at his residence, where we were invited for a private dinner. His style of receiving His Holiness's letter was the exact opposite of Panchen Rinpoche's and puzzles me to this day. He took it from us and placed it on the table without even opening it. One possible reason for his failure to read it could be that the day before, he had met privately with Takla Phuntsok Tashi, one of the other members of our delegation. As they were quite close friends, it is possible that Takla Phuntsok Tashi had already informally shared the letter with him; he had custody of the letters because of his position as team leader. But this is only a guess, and common courtesy should have prompted Ngapo Ngawang Jigme to at least open the letter and scan its contents.

I did not have the opportunity to ask Takla Phuntsok Tashi about the matter before he passed away, but I know Ngapo Ngawang Jigme did highly respect His Holiness. This is evident from his formal remarks, including a public speech delivered to the Fifth People's Congress of the TAR on July 31, 1989, in which he said: "I am a Tibetan and served the Dalai Lama as Minister prior to 1959 for eight to nine years and played a major role on behalf of the Tibetan Government. Therefore, I have respect for the Dalai Lama and always wished good relations between the Dalai Lama and the Central Government and hope that he will return to Tibet as soon as possible."[3]

We explained to Ngapo Ngawang Jigme the purpose of our visit and solicited his guidance and advice. After some formal discussion, I asked him the same question on Tibetan unity that I had posed to Panchen Rinpoche. He looked at Takla Phuntsok Tashi and addressed him with his former title, Dapon (Chief Security Officer of His Holiness), saying: "Do you remember this was one of our very strong points we raised during the discussion of the Seventeen-Point Agreement in Beijing?" Phuntsok Tashi had been the interpreter for Ngapo Ngawang Jigme's delegation that signed the 1951 agreement. Phuntsok Tashi had never mentioned this to us because, as it turned out, he did not clearly remember the discussion. At that moment I realized the different experiences of individuals who are present at events in secondary roles versus those with primary responsibilities. As the leader of the negotiating team representing the government of Tibet, Ngapo

Ngawang Jigme remembered every word spoken. Now having his memory jogged, Phuntsok Tashi remembered and replied, saying: "Yes, yes, yes it was like that."

This conversation convinced me that the unity issue was raised very strongly and had reached the desk of Premier Zhou Enlai as early as 1951, although I don't know whether the delegation discussed it directly with the Premier or it was conveyed through the Chairman of the United Front office. Ngapo Ngawang Jigme told us that Zhou Enlai responded: "The desire for unification of Tibetan nationality is appropriate, but the time is not yet ripe . . . because the present discussion concerns the Tibetan areas yet to be liberated." At that time most of the Tibetan areas that were not under the political rule of the Lhasa government had already been overrun by the Chinese Communist army. By sharing his recollections, it was clear to us that Ngapo Ngawang Jigme was conveying his current support for a unified Tibet.

Finally, we met with Bapa Phuntsok Wangyal (Phünwang) and offered him His Holiness's letter. He received it with both hands and was visibly moved. We could see the emotions on his face for what must have been a historic moment—His Holiness the Dalai Lama had personally written to the founder of the Tibetan Communist Party! He read the letter carefully, put it back in its envelope, and placed it on the table. I did not need to ask him the unification question, as his views were well known. Phünwang was a revolutionary and a committed nationalist. When he and his comrades established the Tibetan Communist Party, it was with the intention of establishing an independent and united Tibet, fundamentally transforming the prior feudal structure.

During the nineteenth century, the strongest proponents of Tibetan nationalism came from the Kham region of eastern Tibet bordering China. I am not saying this because I was born there. The reason is simple. In 1911, Sun Yat-sen, recognized as the father of modern China, overthrew the Manchu Dynasty with his vision of a new China based on "Three Principles of the People"—nationalism, democracy, and people's livelihood (interpreted to be "welfare and socialism"). The Tibetan areas adjacent to China, especially the Bathang region, were the first exposed to this ideology. As previously mentioned, repeated brutal incursions by the Manchus, especially General Zhao Er Feng's butchery, not only made the Khampas wary of Chinese rule but also revealed the need for unity among the Tibetan people. At the time, prominent Khampa chieftains launched several initiatives to create a closer alliance among them and establish a structure to consolidate their efforts. Other factors also contributed to their nationalist feelings.

A number of young Khampas had traveled to China and been exposed to the concept, while Christian missionaries active in the region provided a window to the outside world in which this doctrine was evident. The extension of the concept of Tibetan nationalism to encompass Tibetan unification is thus logical and based on historic events.

As can be seen from his voluminous writings, Phünwang was an expert on the rights of nationalities. Many Chinese experts tell me that he is regarded as one of the top scholars on Marxist and Leninist thought regarding nationalities. Why did he devote himself to this field of study? Precisely because as a Tibetan, he felt very strongly about the rights of his own people. As a communist, he had to work to have these rights respected within a system dominated by Marxist-Leninist ideology. So he studied and eventually became an expert on the subject. It is important for Tibetans to take note of Phünwang's writings.

I have tried to learn from Phuntsok Wangyal himself, a direct transmission of sorts! He has visited Europe and America quite a few times, giving me extensive opportunities to meet with him. I also arranged for Samdhong Rinpoche to meet with him in the United States, and we had several meetings all together. It was very exciting to see these two Tibetan scholars interact, each trained in a totally different belief system. As a scholar, Samdhong Rinpoche was able to understand some of the subtleties of what Phuntsok Wangyal was trying to convey on issues such as the Marxist approach to nationalities.

I deeply regret that Phünwang never had the opportunity to meet His Holiness in exile. In my view, such a personal and intimate meeting would have greatly benefited our cause. Although I worked hard to make this a reality, in the end, Phünwang believed that he might be able to do more for the cause if he did not make the Chinese suspicious of him. President Jiang Zemin's invitation to a special meeting in 1998 to discuss the Tibet issue gave Phünwang some hope of being able to influence the matter from within, but in the end, he was unable to do anything substantive. He also began to have periodic health problems. If he had had another opportunity to leave the PRC, there is no doubt that he would have met His Holiness.

Not surprisingly, for a long time many Tibetans considered Phünwang a virtual traitor, even believing he played an active role in bringing the Chinese Communists to Tibet. In recent years, fortunately, that perception has greatly changed. Now a majority are able to see him as a true Tibetan nationalist. Many Tibetans at one time also believed Amdo Gendun Chophel to be a communist sympathizer and antinationalist. In the early 1970s, at a TYC Centrex meeting, I proposed that we create a literary award in his name to encourage young Tibetans to give more importance to their native language. At the time, some Centrex members were strongly opposed, effectively killing the idea. Ironically, these days, everyone seems to be a Gendun Chophel admirer.

## THE FUTURE OF TIBET MUST BE GUIDED BY THE TIBETANS INSIDE

As the Special Envoy of His Holiness the Dalai Lama for dialogue with the PRC leadership, I gave the highest priority to trying to ascertain the sentiments of the Tibetans from inside. They understand the situation far better than we in exile do, and most importantly, it was their future that I was tasked with addressing in my negotiations with Beijing. Toward this end, I have had the opportunity to meet with quite a number of Tibetans from inside who were visiting India, Nepal, or the United States. I even made some special trips to Europe to meet with visiting Tibetan scholars. In all these meetings, I raised the issue of a unified Tibet and requested their thoughts. To the best of my recollection, all the Tibetans to whom I spoke not only expressed their appreciation for the initiative but also gave their personal commitment to realizing this goal. Of course, most of them understood the reality on the ground and how difficult it will be to bring our concept of unity to fruition. They also understood that a unified Tibet does not depend on geographic unification alone, but most importantly on the mindset of the Tibetan people and the activities undertaken to preserve the distinct Tibetan identity in every aspect of life. It is truly inspiring how Tibetans inside Tibet pursue these goals.

The Plateauwide spontaneous demonstrations in 2008 and the repressive measures Beijing took to suppress them caused deep anguish to His Holiness and all of us Tibetans. We were helpless bystanders as the PRC government remained totally unresponsive to our appeals. Yet in a strange way, I was proud to see that the Tibetan people's struggle for their legitimate rights is now being led by Tibetans from inside. As a result, Tibetans outside, including the leadership in Dharamsala, started to pursue activities reacting to events in Tibet. In my opinion, this is a needed and welcome aspect of our struggle, one that imbues it with an immediacy and legitimacy that cannot easily be ignored or dismissed by the international community.

Those of us in exile must applaud the courageous efforts of our countrymen and women and let the movement inside Tibet progress. We must do nothing to hamper that trajectory. Some of us on the outside, including NGOs and even some CTA leaders, try to take credit for things that are happening inside Tibet. We must not do that. First of all, such pretension plays right into the hands of the PRC authorities: they use such claims as proof that the dissatisfaction and unrest are being instigated from the outside. Even more importantly, I don't think the Tibetans inside Tibet appreciate those of us outside taking credit for their efforts and sacrifices. It is neither fair nor just.

Achieving the long-term dream of geographic and emotional unity of the Tibetan people rests primarily with our brothers and sisters in Tibet. Even though the generation has turned over and conditions inside Tibet have changed, Tibetans retain their commitment to unity. Their power is growing stronger year by year. Tibetans often express themselves through literary avenues. The songs and poems composed in Tibet today show this shared vision of unity. Here is one example:

> མཐུན་སྒྲིལ་གྱི་བརྩེ་སེམས་ཡོད་ན།།
> གཞིས་བྱེས་ཀྱི་བོད་རིགས་སྤུན་ཟླ།།
> ལྷན་འཛོམས་ཀྱི་ཉི་མ་བསྒུགས་ནས།།
> ཆོལ་གསུམ་གྱི་ཕ་ས་ཟིན་ཡོང་།།

> If Tibetans have love for unity
> Brethren in and outside of Tibet
> Should wait for the day of reunion
> To own our fatherland; the three Cholkas.[4]

## UNITY AND THE MIDDLE WAY APPROACH

In this part of the book, I have focused on the many challenges faced by the Tibetan leadership and the Tibetan people in the first few decades of exile following the adoption of a policy of reunification. Much of this information may be new to non-Tibetan readers, and even the younger generation of Tibetans may not fully appreciate its importance. There may be people who disagree with the way I see the situation or think that I should not write about the internal discord that beset our community. I believe it is essential, however, to discuss this sensitive and unfortunate period in our history to fully appreciate the significance and brilliance of His Holiness's Middle Way Approach, which I discuss in part III.

Just as Tibetan leaders in exile from all regions of Tibet became morally bound by the Great Oath of Unity, His Holiness too is bound by this Oath. Any solution that he seeks for the future of his people must benefit all Tibetans, not only those over which the Gaden Phodrang had political jurisdiction pre-1951. I have heard His Holiness say on numerous occasions that even if it is just a single piece of bread, he must make sure that it is equally shared with the Tibetans of all three regions. His Holiness's unwavering ethical commitment deserves our deep respect. While some Tibetans have wavered and even disregarded the Great Oath of Unity that they took at Bodhgaya, His Holiness is ever mindful of the trust and faith that was then bestowed, or more accurately imposed, on him by the Tibetan people through that vehicle.

His Holiness did not haphazardly adopt the Middle Way Approach. He developed it in light of history and the contemporary needs and aspirations of the Tibetan people. There is no doubt in my mind that it wasn't an easy decision for him and that he fully understood the historical, legal, and practical implications. But ultimately, he knew that whatever proposal he offered must be inclusive and benefit all Tibetans, and at the same time have some possibility of acceptance by the PRC leadership. The sad but inescapable reality is that Tibet is now fully governed by the Chinese. Any idea of an independent Tibet, even if it is limited to the present TAR, will never be accepted by Beijing. Deng Xiaoping was very clear and explicit on this point in his first message reaching out to His Holiness in 1979. Successive Chinese leaders to this day have consistently maintained this position.

Looking at both the Tibetan people's historical experiences and the challenges they were destined to face in the future, His Holiness came to the firm conclusion that maintaining the distinct identity of the Tibetan people is of paramount importance. He further concluded that this highly advanced and vibrant civilization would be weakened and might even disappear if the Tibetan people failed to remain unified. Recognizing that politically created regions, labels, and slogans come and go, His Holiness devoted his energies to the ambitious and visionary task of creating a strong foundation for protecting the unique Tibetan identity. The cornerstone is the unity of the Tibetan people.

As early as 1974, His Holiness had internal discussions with the Kashag, as well as with the Chairman and Vice-Chairman of the Tibetan Parliament, about the need to formulate a solution for Tibet that did not envision independence but safeguarded Tibet's unique identity. On June 15, 1988, His Holiness formally offered his proposal in a public announcement to the European Parliament in Strasbourg. This policy came to be known as the Middle Way Approach.

I believe the Middle Way Approach is a truly visionary solution to a complex problem. It accommodates Beijing's uncompromising position of maintaining the PRC's sovereignty while simultaneously providing the opportunity for all Tibetans to be united and able to preserve their distinct identity as a people without being constrained by historical or legalistic complications. I completely agree with His Holiness's conclusions. As long as Tibetans are able to maintain their distinct cultural and religious identity, Tibet will never vanish. On the other hand, if we remain bogged down and consumed with high-sounding political rhetoric, our condition remains perilous, our struggle becomes marginalized, and our chances of achieving any positive results continue to diminish. If realities on the ground in Tibet were stable with regard to cultural, linguistic, environmental, and especially demographic freedoms, perhaps we could justify taking an uncompromising position. But the truth that confronts us is just the opposite. We do not have the luxury of time.

His Holiness's Middle Way Approach has been intensely debated over the years. I sincerely believe that most Tibetans engaged with the struggle, whether they support the Middle Way Approach or continue to hope for independence, are doing it out of their passionate love for Tibet. It is a healthy sign of democracy when everyone can express their views, however conflicting. In fact, I believe we should have more open debate on the subject.

His Holiness personally respects people holding differing views; he actively encourages it. Immediately after delivering the historic speech at the European Parliament, which has come to be known as the Strasbourg Proposal, for example, he asked me to call his brother, Taktser Rinpoche (aka Thupten Jigme Norbu), at his home in Indiana. He wanted me to personally tell Taktser Rinpoche that although His Holiness had made the formal announcement of his Middle Way Approach, his brother must continue advocating for independence, as His Holiness knew he was sincerely committed to that goal. Similarly, a day or two later, in Bern, Switzerland, His Holiness made his first public speech to the Tibetan people sharing his vision of the Middle Way philosophy. While we were escorting him backstage, he saw Lhasang Tsering, who was then the TYC President. His Holiness went right over to him and said: "I am very sincere about my Middle Way Approach, but you all can continue to pursue your own beliefs." I share these conversations to show that while His Holiness is fully committed to the Middle Way Approach without any hidden agenda, he has always tolerated and even solicited different opinions.

Almost a decade after His Holiness's formal announcement of the Middle Way Approach, he and the CTA not only continued to allow but also actively encouraged serious discussion of different approaches. In 1997, for example, the CTA organized a conference in Dharamsala where nearly 400 delegates met to discuss different possibilities. The options presented included the Middle Way Approach, independence, self-determination, and satyagraha. Together with my colleague Kelsang Gyaltsen, I was tasked with giving a presentation on the Middle Way Approach. After making what I believe was a passionate statement on its significance and importance, I ended with a strong plea that my fellow Tibetans should not hastily make a decision in choosing one approach over another. I said that even I, an ardent supporter of the Middle Way Approach, would not urge the Tibetan people to adopt that option at that stage. I believed that a premature decision would only weaken His Holiness's efforts.

Samdhong Rinpoche, who was the next speaker, then introduced his proposal based on the principles of satyagraha as exemplified by Mahatma Gandhi's campaign against the British. He started with a humorous remark: "The previous presenter, while making a passionate presentation of the merits of the Middle Way Approach, concluded by urging everyone not to support the issue he is advocating. My stand is to make my presentation with the hope that you all give it a strong endorsement!"

As I write this book, it is now mid-2018, and I am profoundly disappointed to see the Tibetan exile community deeply polarized between those who support the Middle Way Approach and those who only want to pursue independence. The CTA's manner and style of promoting the Middle Way Approach over the last several years has further contributed to this polarization. This divisiveness does not help us at all.

In today's electronic age, we must be aware that any campaign launched by Tibetans is noticed and analyzed by a much wider, indeed global audience, and certainly by Beijing. We must therefore avoid creating the impression that the Middle Way Approach, the bedrock of His Holiness's philosophy, is being challenged or facing huge opposition, as this is decidedly not true. I can say with confidence that the silent Tibetan majority is supportive of His Holiness's vision and not the other way around.

I support His Holiness's initiative not out of blind faith but because I know this approach will benefit the Tibetan people. Moreover, I have learned from my own experience how the international community perceives the Tibet issue, and what it will and will not support. It is thus through logical reasoning that I have come to my conviction. In addition to ensuring the unity of the Tibetan people, the Middle Way Approach seeks to preserve and promote their unique identity. I am constantly impressed by the wisdom behind His Holiness's proposal and wholeheartedly respect it. And while I firmly believe that we must fully debate all options, I also believe that some of the opposition to his policy has been misleading and biased, generating unwarranted criticism of His Holiness. These misstatements must be revealed for what they are, and corrected, although not in an adversarial manner or with personal animosity.

Some of those who advocate independence allege that the Middle Way Approach is at best a compromise and at worst a complete selling out of Tibet's interests. Some even point fingers directly at His Holiness. How can they? His Holiness assumed both temporal and spiritual leadership of the Tibetan people from Sikyong Tagdrak Rinpoche at the tender age of sixteen.[5] The unvarnished truth is that the political situation in Tibet had by that time already reached a very critical stage. It was becoming unmanageable, and there was no option but to request His Holiness to take over. In those days, as there were no formal media, people expressed their observations and feelings through street songs. In the streets of Lhasa they started singing:

> རྒྱལ་ཁབ་རྩབ་ཧྲུལ་དགུ་ཧྲུལ།།
> རྒྱལ་བའི་ཕྱག་ལ་ཕུལ་སོང་།།
>
> The country, which is tattered from all sides,
> Is handed over to His Holiness.[6]

This sentiment aptly describes the state of the country at the time. My questions to those who today accuse His Holiness are: "What has been cut? What has been sold? What has been compromised?"

My criticism is not aimed at those who sincerely advocate independence. I believe that most of them are dedicated to and working hard for the common cause and are equally devoted to His Holiness. But at the same time, I must assume that their efforts are on behalf of the Tibetans belonging to all three Cholkhas. They certainly project that view, but without clearly articulating it. If some believe that it would be more acceptable, both legally and historically, to strive for independence solely for the area previously directly ruled by the Gaden Phodrang government, the present-day TAR, then they should state their position openly and unequivocally. I personally know and respect individuals sincerely advocating that view. What I do not appreciate is people of that belief who mask their true opinions with high-sounding, populist slogans like *Rangzen* (Independence) or, worse yet, goad others into undertaking activities that further divide our community. People who sincerely and strongly hold their opinions should very candidly speak their minds. As I previously noted, free expression is the bedrock of a true democracy.

I sometimes hear independence advocates referring to the resolutions passed by the United Nations regarding Tibet in 1959, 1961, and 1965 in support of their position. Examining them with care, however, reveals that they only refer to the Tibet that was previously governed by Lhasa and not the Tibet of our objective. This is because the UN resolutions were passed as a result of efforts by officials of the old Tibetan government. The memorandum submitted to the UN General Assembly on November 7, 1950, from Shakabpa House in Kalimpong by the Tibetan government clearly says: "Chinese troops, without warning or provocation, crossed the Di Chu river, which has for long been the boundary of Tibetan territory."[7]

I am not criticizing the Lhasa-based government, because its appeal to the UN reflected the political reality of the time. I am also certainly not trying to minimize the significance and the importance of these resolutions. What I am saying is that when people cite these resolutions in favor of their demand for independence, what are they suggesting? Are they seeking independence only for the areas of Tibet that were previously governed by Lhasa, or are they unaware of the substance of the resolutions they are supporting?

In my view, some of them have full knowledge of the substance and breadth of these resolutions and the potential factors limiting their reach. The language of the 1961 resolution, however, does provide some latitude for a more expansive reading by referring to one of the earlier resolutions that specifically calls for respect of the Tibetan people's fundamental human rights, including "their right of self-determination." This provision lends very strong support for His Holiness's position: our struggle is a justified and internationally recognized campaign for protection of the fundamental rights of all Tibetans.

Those Tibetan leaders who, through their tireless efforts, succeeded in having the UN General Assembly discuss the Tibet issue and pass these resolutions must be applauded because they faced tremendous difficulties and challenges. Even though the PRC had no representation at the UN at that time, many countries, surprisingly including both India and Great Britain, served Beijing's interests in opposing the 1961 resolution. Similarly, the KMT government, in those days not only a member of the UN but also a permanent member of the Security Council, did not support any resolutions containing language that indicated in any way that Tibet was a separate nation that had been invaded.

The operative part of the 1961 resolution does not even mention the PRC by name. It is limited in expression to the need for respecting the Tibetan people's fundamental human rights. It was passed thanks to forceful statements by Irish and Malaysian delegates, among others, who: (1) spoke in favor of the resolutions; (2) did not hesitate to condemn Chinese aggression; and (3) unequivocally stated that the Tibetan government, headed by the Dalai Lama, represented an independent nation.

The last UN Resolution on Tibet, passed in 1965, actually received strong support from the Indian government through its delegate Rafiq Zakaria. His remarks were some of the most supportive of our cause. Unfortunately, the term "self-determination" was deleted from the final text because of India's fear that the concept would be applied to its own Kashmir issue.

In the late 1960s there was a renewed effort to raise the Tibet issue at the UN once again. I remember typing a personal letter from His Holiness to Dinesh Singh, who was then India's Minister for External Affairs. I can recall the event vividly because of one terrifying moment. I was at the Ashok Hotel in Delhi, typing the draft I had received from His Holiness's Secretary Tenzin Geyche. I was pecking away at the keys of Tenzin Geyche's portable Brother typewriter with my two fingers when all of a sudden I heard His Holiness's voice behind me. I was paralyzed: my half-smoked cigarette lay accusingly in the ashtray beside me!

When Tibetans in exile who never were subjects of the Gaden Phodrang government criticize His Holiness in saying that he has abandoned independence, it actually amuses me. If it weren't for his strong commitment to an inclusive Tibet, these critics wouldn't even be in the class of potential beneficiaries of his efforts. It is not only hypocritical but also a total abnegation of reality. Sometimes I suspect the intent of their statements is the opposite of their superficial meaning. I am not making any sweeping criticism, but certain individuals among those voicing these allegations are the same ones who, some decades back, took great pains to contend that they were subjects not of the Gaden Phodrang but rather of Nationalist China, and by implication China.

In examining the wisdom of any policy, we must give serious thought to whether it has international support and whether we can rationally present our position to the PRC government. In sum, we have to seriously ask ourselves the question: Would the initiative give us an opportunity? Tibetans in exile are well aware of how much backing the Middle Way Approach enjoys in the international community. I have been intimately involved in shouldering the responsibility for generating support for this position for decades. Internationally, many governments, parliaments, and politically influential people have not only favored this effort, recognizing the pragmatic nature of the approach, but also become personally invested in its success. As I discuss in detail in part III, the United States' long-standing tacit support is of great significance. But even more important was the US government's first public expression of support for the Middle Way Approach on February 18, 2010, after a meeting between His Holiness and President Barack Obama.

As far as the PRC's view of the Middle Way Approach, none of us believed that the issue would be resolved through dialogue in the short time span of a few years. The Tibetan-Chinese issue is centuries old and historically complex. It is thus way too early to say that the policy has failed just because the PRC government has not yet accepted it. In delicate and serious negotiations, parties will make critical remarks of the opposing side's stance, but this does not mean the discussions have failed.

Because Beijing cannot rationally challenge the Middle Way Approach, it has attempted to misrepresent the policy, making numerous false accusations. But no credible organizations or governments subscribe to Beijing's rhetoric in criticizing it as independence in disguise. Moreover, an increasing number of Chinese, particularly intellectuals and those from the younger generations who are knowledgeable about the Tibet situation, are beginning to express their support and understanding of this approach. Even Beijing confirms the existence of the "Tibetan Nationality" (*Zang zu* in Chinese) as distinct and separate. Perhaps surprisingly, the map published by the PRC government showing the location of different nationalities is quite similar to the maps published by the CTA depicting the three regions of Tibet as a unified entity. Even under the PRC's constitution and other laws governing nationalities, the Tibetan people are a single nationality with the right to live together and maintain their distinct cultural identity.[8]

The Middle Way Approach is both brilliant and achievable. If the Tibetan people carefully study their recent history and remain strongly committed to the concept of a unified Tibet, they will come to the conclusion that it is the most viable proposal for attaining our goals, rather than seeing it as a "sell out" or even a compromise. The core is the preservation of the Tibetan people's distinct identity in every aspect—culture, language, religion, history, and way of life. If these attributes are maintained, Tibet and the Tibetan people will never cease to exist. Genuine autonomy within the PRC with clear constitutional and legal safeguards guaranteeing the legitimate rights of the Tibetan people will benefit both the Tibetans and the Chinese. The Beijing leadership must realize that it cannot maintain unity and stability through the use of power or by economic and other incentives.

Present-day Chinese leaders seem to pay a great deal of attention to Confucian philosophy. Mencius, one of China's great Confucius scholars, said the following, a sentiment I hope Beijing will embrace: "When one by force subdues men, they do not submit to him in heart; when one subdues men by virtue, in their hearts' core they are pleased and sincerely submit." As I constantly reminded my counterparts throughout the formal dialogue process, the Dalai Lama is not the problem but rather the solution. Tibetans, especially the exile leadership, must also understand that it is only His Holiness the 14th Dalai Lama who has the historical legitimacy and moral authority to help find a solution to save Tibet. As I discuss in part III, in addressing our outreach to and dialogue with Beijing, both sides must accept this reality. Time is not anyone's friend, especially in this regard, a fact I hope both Chinese and Tibetans alike will quickly come to understand.

# PART III

# *Thirty Years of Engagement with the PRC*

*Tibetans Betrayed by Suspicion, Chinese Betrayed by Unrealistic Hope*
བོད་དོགས་པས་འཕུང་། རྒྱ་རེ་བས་འཕུང་།

## THE TIBETAN APPROACH TO NEGOTIATIONS

When one talks about the need for dialogue or negotiations between parties, the underlying premise is the existence of conflict, misunderstanding, disagreement, or other problem requiring resolution. History is replete with examples of conflicts among nations and peoples, even leading to war between them on many occasions. Engaging in dialogue is a centuries-old method of peacefully addressing adversaries' differences. While over time it has become a refined and sophisticated art, there is no one uniform pattern or method applicable to all issues or to every conflict between competing parties.

As a number of my close friends who have dealt with the People's Republic of China (PRC) can attest, the Chinese are universally acknowledged as being some of the most difficult people with whom to negotiate. I think there are more books addressing the "how to" of negotiating with the PRC than for any other country. Some of the world's foremost think tanks, including the Rand Corporation, have many well-respected scholars studying the art of negotiating with Chinese officials.

In the United States, major governmental organizations, including the Department of Defense, Department of State, and of course, the Central Intelligence Agency (CIA) and the National Security Administration (NSA) have large staffs exclusively focused on this issue. I am thus proud to say that, given our limited experience in international relations and our scarce resources, during the formal dialogue process from 2002 to 2012, we conducted our negotiations with the PRC in a sophisticated and professional manner. Employing techniques tailored to our situation and taking into account both the unequal bargaining power and the disparate natures of the parties, we developed and implemented a negotiating strategy recognized by veteran diplomats as unprecedented in the field of diplomacy.

President Carter, for example, acknowledged the unique nature of our strategy when I consulted with him on the draft of His Holiness's proposed remarks to the European Parliament announcing his Middle Way Approach. When informed that the steps outlined in the proposal were not inflated negotiating positions but rather the actual outcome His Holiness was committed to achieving, the President responded: "If this succeeds, it will be a new chapter in the art of diplomacy." I know our stripped-down, morally based approach has already attracted the attention of many experts and scholars in the field. I continue to hope that one day it will fulfill President Carter's sentiments.

The strategy that we adopted is indeed unique. The heart of the approach is deeply grounded in the Buddhist philosophy of His Holiness. It has a characteristically open and transparent quality whose straightforward nature is unfamiliar in diplomatic circles, creating doubts in the minds of veteran negotiators. I must admit that in the early years, because all of us were amateurs without any formal experience, our actions were a bit ad hoc, suffering from a lack of coordination among all the individuals addressing the issue. His Holiness, however, was able to articulate a clear and unambiguous position that we adopted and advocated both in our direct dealings with Beijing and indirectly in our efforts to persuade the international community to embrace our cause. Credit for imposing discipline on our internal deliberations must go to Samdhong Rinpoche, who, throughout the formal dialogue process, paid attention to the smallest details of our work. Together with my near obsession with institutionalization, the collective experience, drive, and commitment of the team gave our Nine Rounds of negotiations a strong and uncompromising character.

## UNEQUAL BARGAINING POWER

Complicating our unorthodox approach were obstacles that others negotiating with Beijing have not faced. The typical Chinese negotiator dealing with foreign affairs is an official either in the Ministry of Foreign Affairs or one of the ministries dealing with trade and commerce that are familiar with international norms and standards of diplomacy. These officials also interact with their counterparts as representatives of equal, sovereign nations. By contrast, we were dealing with the United Front Work Department (United Front or UFWD), an institution that has very little exposure to or experience in dealing with the international community. Moreover, the United Front has a historically entrenched disdain for Tibet and all things Tibetan, a bias not encountered by other groups or nations in dialogue with the PRC. In other words, our negotiating partners assumed a condescending attitude, constantly reminding us that we were not equals.

And indeed, we were not. We had to earn the respect of our counterparts. With patience and self-confidence, stemming from our firm belief in the justness of our cause, we not only began but also sustained a formal, substantive dialogue with the PRC representatives. Through several years of engagement and, most importantly, by developing close personal relationships, we were able to elevate our stature in the eyes of our counterparts and conduct our discussions as peers.

When formal dialogue began in 2002, meetings were conducted very informally or, alternatively, in a highly ceremonial atmosphere. The pomp and circumstance of these rituals did little to mask the lack of substance. After the first two of these fundamentally meaningless "get-togethers," we prevailed in our determination to conduct substantive meetings with the delegations formally seated at a table facing each other. Our counterparts also agreed to rotate the opportunity to make the opening remarks, a privilege they initially kept to themselves.

We also alternated between formal and informal meetings. When tempers became heated during formal talks, we would adjourn and retire to a different room for "off the record" discussions, giving us the opportunity to sort out issues that would have been impossible to handle in a formal setting. We also had principals-only meetings, with just the seniormost members of the negotiating teams participating. All these steps may sound familiar to seasoned diplomats, but to us naïve delegates, they were hard-fought victories.

I would also like to emphasize that had we not succeeded in both bringing the plight of Tibet to the attention of the international community and maintaining its presence on the international agenda, Beijing would never have come to the bargaining table. I am intentionally avoiding the use of the word "pressure." No one pressured the Chinese into sitting down with us. It would have been a self-defeating tactic; Chinese negotiators' initial reaction is to rebel when they feel they are under attack or being strong-armed.

Rather, once we adopted a strategy of international engagement, we first set about convincing members of the international community that resolving the issue of Tibet would improve their own bilateral relations with the PRC. Then, working together, we were able to convince Beijing that it is in both the PRC's short- and long-term interests to engage with His Holiness. When some say that we walked into a trap, I think they are really giving a measure of credit to the Chinese rather than criticizing us. But to say we brought the Chinese to the negotiating table only by pressure also is not correct. The Chinese came to the table recognizing that it is in the PRC's interests to do so. This is a lesson for the future: Tibetans and Tibetan friends should not be under any illusion that we can bring the Chinese back to the negotiating table through sheer pressure.

As I chronicle the events of our thirty-year engagement with the Chinese, I will sometimes be critical, even harsh, in referring to the practices and behavior of the PRC government. I am not writing anything, however, that I have not, at one time or another, conveyed to PRC officials during our various meetings. As a Tibetan, I do harbor deep grievances for the pain and suffering Beijing has inflicted on the Tibetan people. I also strongly oppose many of its policies. But I must acknowledge that our negotiating counterparts conducted themselves respectfully in our face-to-face meetings. I have also come to the conclusion, albeit after harboring many doubts, that they paid serious attention to our presentations and in many areas have come to a better understanding not only of our position but also of the nature of the issue itself. Did they have a hidden agenda? Most probably they did. It would be naïve to think otherwise. In negotiations between adversaries, the opposing parties always have their own agendas. Some people even believe that the whole purpose of the PRC government engaging us in dialogue was simply a grand deception. I wholeheartedly disagree. The dialogue was a result of tremendous efforts by His Holiness combined with our direct approach to Beijing, bolstered by the goodwill of many individuals and governments.

I also want to make one other thing very clear. It is not my intention to be critical of any individual or the overall policy that we Tibetans adopted in dealing with the PRC leadership. In one role or another, I have been involved in this issue from the beginning. When I identify specific areas where we made mistakes or should have adopted a different strategy, I accept full responsibility for my part in our missteps.

## SCOPE OF THE NARRATIVE

In the nearly five decades of my active involvement in serving Tibet and His Holiness, I have spent over thirty years dealing with PRC-related matters, sometimes directly and sometimes indirectly. I am narrating what happened during this period not only to provide an accurate record of events but also to share my personal observations and reflections, hoping that my analysis of both our successes and our failures will be of some benefit to those continuing to engage the PRC on Tibet's behalf.

Quite a few people have already written accounts of Dharamsala-Beijing relations. I have purposely not read any of these, with the exception of Gyalo Thondup's memoir, *The Noodle Maker of Kalimpong*. Although I may not agree with all his observations and differ with him on a few of the facts, there is no doubt he played a crucial and pioneering role, particularly in the early years of our engagement with the Chinese, and his narrative is of great value. I have great respect for him and have always tried to learn as much as I could from him.

Many of my friends and colleagues have urged me to read and comment on some of these other publications. I know their exhortations are based on concern about the accuracy of these renditions. I also know it is important that future generations have access to true and unbiased accounts of our history. However, I have decided to refrain from attempting to correct any inaccuracies or exaggerations included in these other works; ultimately the facts will become known.

The Chinese, in fact, maintain precise and detailed accounts of Dharamsala-Beijing relations. They keep a record of everything, not only minutes of meetings but also of verbal messages and other communications. It is only a matter of time before those documents become declassified and available to all. Inaccuracies or misstatements will then be revealed for what they are and the consequences of those errors, intentional or otherwise, will manifest. The Tibetan leadership has already been caught in this awkward situation a number of times, as I discuss in detail herein, and suffered the consequences of our lack of clear coordination.

It is also not my intention to dwell on the long and complex history of Tibetan-Chinese relations. I am not trying to minimize the importance of history; it can't be ignored. But what happened, happened. While differing perceptions and interpretations of events are to be expected, no one should be foolish enough to try to rewrite history. Many an attempt to revise or massage past events to suit political ends has failed miserably. A mutually beneficial solution to the Tibet issue will not be found by peering backward, but only by embracing the present and looking forward with unjaundiced eyes.

On numerous occasions I have urged my negotiating counterparts to adopt this perspective. I remember one time vividly challenging one of them when he sought to raise a historical event to justify his position. I advised him that looking back, even only to the past few decades of our relationship, would only serve to bring deep wounds, anger, and resentment to the surface, impeding any progress on resolving our differences. I even shared my personal sorrow about the tragic suffering of my family and the destruction of monasteries with which I have a personal connection. Focusing on the past, I told him, would bring nothing but discord, disagreement, and divisiveness, creating more obstacles to be overcome. His Holiness has always maintained that the solution to the Tibet issue cannot be based on history, as it does not lend itself to a simple black-and-white interpretation. His forward-looking Middle Way Approach is a brilliant, mutually beneficial solution to a problem that will only continue to fester if the parties persist in sparring over their respective versions of the past.

## CHAPTER 12

# The Early Years

*1979–1984*

### INITIAL CONTACTS

To begin, I want to share an episode that epitomizes one of the major obstacles that plagued the early years of our engagement with the PRC: lack of coordination. In February 1979, a group of young Tibetans announced their decision to go to Tibet as volunteer teachers. I was then residing in Delhi as a private citizen, having resigned from the Central Tibetan Administration (CTA)[1] as well as from the presidency of the Tibetan Youth Congress (TYC). Together with a few like-minded friends, we had just announced the formation of the National Democratic Movement of Tibet. We established this organization believing that the formation of political parties would further our struggle by bringing genuine democratization to Tibetan politics.

We were seriously opposed to the idea of these volunteers heading to the PRC, feeling it was premature and would only be exploited by the Chinese. We held a press conference to oppose the trip. My colleagues, Lobsang Wangchuk and Jamyang Norbu, and I sought a meeting in Delhi with Gyalo Thondup to share our concerns. He listened to us very patiently and expressed his sympathy with our view. However, he delivered a lengthy monologue praising Deng Xiaoping and the unprecedented changes that were taking place in the PRC under his leadership. "This little man really is very courageous," said Gyalo Thondup. "Under his leadership, China is going to change."

It wasn't until much later that I learned the teachers' proposed visit was the direct outcome of a suggestion by Deng Xiaoping taken to His Holiness through Gyalo Thondup. The visit was not what we thought, an idea dreamed up by some individual Tibetans, but rather a first step in engagement with the PRC, mutually agreed upon by the parties and having His Holiness's blessing.[2]

At the time we met with Gyalo Thondup, we had no clue that there were any communications between Dharamsala and Beijing, much less that he was acting as intermediary. I felt rather embarrassed to have approached him, being totally ignorant of his key role in this initiative. No wonder he was speaking so highly of Deng Xiaoping. He didn't want to confide in us, and at that juncture, he had no reason to, as none of us held any official position. But, as later events would show, the lack of coordinated efforts among entities and individuals in Dharamsala addressing the Tibet issue seriously complicated our relations with the PRC over the years.[3]

## HIS HOLINESS'S RATIONALE FOR ENGAGEMENT

In 1979, Deng Xiaoping reached out to His Holiness through Gyalo Thondup, saying that aside from independence, all matters concerning Tibet could be discussed. When the message came, His Holiness was ready. But the Tibetan population at large, including myself, was not so prepared. Although I was a member of the younger generation of Tibetans, with a slightly better understanding of global politics than our older compatriots, nevertheless, we were all very much the product of our experiences both in Tibet after the Chinese invasion and in exile in India. Because of the wide-scale physical destruction and personal suffering inflicted on our culture and our people by the Chinese, combined with their record of broken promises, the exile Tibetan community harbored deep animosity and mistrust. There was very little hope in any of our minds that an amicable solution to the Tibet issue could be reached by dealing with the Chinese. The Chinese were our enemy. For the twenty years we had been in exile, every Tibetan, with one notable exception, was committed to regaining Tibet's independence, waiting only for some appropriate opportunity.

As previously discussed, as early as the mid-1970s, His Holiness believed that the Tibet issue could only be resolved through dialogue with the Chinese leadership. He further recognized that in all likelihood, Tibetan independence would not be an option. Even though His Holiness had taken the Kashag into confidence at the time, by 1979, the incumbent Kalons were not yet prepared to digest this possibility. I remember vividly the cynicism and skepticism expressed by individual Kalons as news of Gyalo Thondup's message circulated.

As I was not a member of the Kashag when His Holiness first mentioned the possibility of a negotiated settlement with Beijing in which Tibet would remain part of the PRC, I have no knowledge of its reaction. However, I do recall years later, when I was Chair of the Assembly (Parliament) and included in some briefings with the Kashag, His Holiness reminding the Kalons of his earlier remarks and some of them nodding their heads and saying, "Oh! Yes, yes!" as his comments refreshed their memories. I don't think there had been any real discussion, much less deliberation, on the matter years earlier. There was likely nothing more than His Holiness sharing with them his farsighted thoughts. My guess is that the Kalons didn't pay much attention, as the likelihood of such an event, given the circumstances in the PRC at the time, was extremely remote.

That His Holiness held on to his view of the need for dialogue even as Mao's Red Guards went on a rampage, destroying everything in their path under the guise of the Cultural Revolution, is testimony to both his brilliance and his belief in man's fundamental good nature and the value of human relationships. A number of other factors also contributed to this difficult and courageous decision.

First, because of his unwavering commitment to nonviolence as a Buddhist monk, he could never endorse any policy that included violence, even if undertaken in pursuit of a legitimate right. Thus, armed conflict with the Chinese was not an option for the Dalai Lama.

Second, even though at the time he had not had much exposure to world politics, His Holiness kept himself fully informed of the international situation through conversations with eminent scholars and political leaders from both India and the West. As a result, he recognized the limits of what the international community could do and was willing to do in support of Tibet.

Third, and most importantly, even though His Holiness was in exile without a country, he was the first Dalai Lama to command the loyalty and allegiance of the entire Tibetan populace. Even though the PRC physically governed Tibet, His Holiness ruled the hearts and minds of all Tibetans from his home in exile in the small Himalayan town of Dharamsala. This unprecedented and unqualified support, reaffirmed in the Great Oath of Unity,[4] obligated His Holiness to seek a solution benefiting *all* Tibetans, regardless of where they resided in the PRC. Because many of them live in areas now included in four Chinese provinces, together constituting 25 percent of the PRC's landmass, the possibility of gaining independence for Tibet was unrealistic.

His Holiness also felt that citing history, including statements about the prior geographic extent of Tibet, would hinder rather than promote a resolution.

Whatever might be the historical truth, any solution would have to be based on current realities. Although the term "Middle Way Approach" was coined much later, the concept of seeking genuine autonomy within the PRC was born years before Deng Xiaoping made his initial overtures to His Holiness in 1979.

## DENG XIAOPING'S MOTIVATION IN REACHING OUT TO HIS HOLINESS

In 1979, Deng Xiaoping's message to His Holiness was unequivocal: the PRC government was ready to discuss all matters concerning Tibet, with the exception of independence. On the latter point, Deng Xiaoping was firm.

It was very clear that Deng Xiaoping and the other leaders of that period had thoroughly thought out their strategy for handling the Tibet issue, including their bottom line, before reaching out to His Holiness. Despite its provocative rhetoric, Beijing remained very consistent in its position. Deng Xiaoping, who took the lead, spent considerable time with Gyalo Thondup, sharing his thoughts in a candid and almost accommodating way. But the essence of all his communications was explicit and unyielding. If what the Dalai Lama and the Tibetans had in mind was either "separation or independence," there was no point in holding any meetings, as there was no room for debate on this subject. On the other hand, if they were looking for a solution whereby Tibet remained within the PRC, then everything could be discussed.

During that period, Deng Xiaoping and other senior leaders publicly acknowledged that they had made grave mistakes in handling Tibet-related policies that had triggered deep resentment, and even anger, in the hearts of Tibetans across the Plateau. When Deng Xiaoping told Gyalo Thondup that "everything could be discussed," he was signaling that the PRC government was prepared to make major changes in its policies to satisfy Tibetans both inside and outside of Tibet.

Deng Xiaoping's goal was not just to convince His Holiness to return to Tibet but also to start looking for a way to solve the broader Tibet issue. But from day one, the PRC leaders were clear that they would deal only with His Holiness and not with any representatives of the Tibetan Government-in-Exile (TGiE). The Chinese have a very firm position on this. For them, the only Tibetan government is the one they set up in Lhasa under the direct control of the Chinese Communist Party (CCP).

The Tibetan exile leadership reconciled itself to these conditions. And as a practical matter, it really didn't make any difference. In those days, the Dalai Lama was the head of the TGiE; any decisions or activities he outwardly undertook in his "personal capacity" were in fact actions of the TGiE. Both sides took advantage of this semantic cover to creatively conduct their relations without triggering any controversial issues that could potentially derail a dialogue.

At the same time, Deng Xiaoping's outreach to His Holiness was not motivated solely or even in large part by a desire to improve conditions for the Tibetan people. While I agree with Gyalo Thondup's observation that Deng Xiaoping was sincere in reaching out to His Holiness,[5] the motives behind his efforts arose from other problems his government was then confronting. Deng Xiaoping was a strong-minded and pragmatic leader. An early resolution of the Tibet problem would help him in these other areas. Even though his primary focus was on domestic issues, he was also keen to create a new image of the PRC on the global stage, entirely different from that of Mao's era. He knew that the Tibet issue had both domestic and international ramifications.

Specifically, in 1979, Deng Xiaoping had both Taiwan and Hong Kong reunification to address. He was committed to having Hong Kong returned to Beijing's rule during his leadership. Even though the PRC leaders viewed these situations as far more complex than the Tibet issue, they hoped that a breakthrough on Tibet, resulting in some form of autonomy within the PRC, would demonstrate their commitment to a peaceful resolution of the other two matters. In fact, in early January 1979, Wang Ping-nan, who represented the PRC in ambassadorial talks with the United States in the late 1950s, suggested that Tibet could be the role model for Taiwan's future status.

From our conversations with PRC leaders at various levels, it was clear that they were giving highest priority to Hong Kong and were worried that Prime Minister Margaret Thatcher, the "Iron Lady," would give them a tough time. Her stern image was also an unpleasant reminder of Britain's lingering imperial power. I remember some casual remarks by Chinese officials worrying that although Britain would have to hand over the New Territories in 1997 on expiration of its ninety-nine-year lease, it would likely prolong discussions on Hong Kong Island and Kowloon, as these areas had a different legal status. Beijing thought that if some understanding could be reached with His Holiness, it would give it better leverage in negotiations with the British. But ultimately, as discussed hereafter, this potential enticement disappeared.

## BEGINNING OF MY INVOLVEMENT IN TIBETAN–CHINESE RELATIONS

In September 1979, I was elected to the Assembly of Tibetan People's Deputies, now known as the Tibetan Parliament-in-Exile, and I became its Chair. In those days the role of the body was much less influential than it is now. During my tenure as Chair, we did try to increase its responsibilities, arguing, for example, that it should be the final authority regarding financial matters, including the budget. Despite its limited powers, however, the Parliament was an important institution. Not only was its establishment a first step in the democratic process initiated by His Holiness once he reached exile in India, even more importantly, it was the first expression of unity among all the regions of Tibet as well as all the religious traditions following affirmation of the Great Oath of Unity.[6] Moreover, both the Chair and Vice-Chair of the Parliament were included in important discussions with the Kashag on certain matters.

During my tenure in the Parliament, I continued to have strong reservations about the wisdom of pursuing any relationship with the PRC. Yet in 1982, while I was still Chair, His Holiness chose me as part of a three-member High-Level Delegation for Exploratory Talks to Beijing. Given my vocal skepticism about engaging with the PRC, I was somewhat surprised. I can only think that His Holiness selected me precisely because of my many reservations, thinking I would adopt a very cautious approach.

The appointment was not totally unanticipated. Several months earlier, after attending an important religious ceremony at the Tsuglagkhang,[7] the then seniormost Kalon, Wangdu Dorje, had pulled me aside to say that the Kashag was keen on my involvement in the discussions concerning our relations with the PRC. He concluded by noting the importance of members of the younger generation becoming more actively involved and hinted that it was also His Holiness's wish that I become one of the individuals assuming this role. This appointment proved to be the beginning of my thirty-year involvement in Tibetan–Chinese relations.

## DIRECT INVOLVEMENT OF THE CTA FROM THE BEGINNING

While Beijing officially refuses to deal with any members of the Dharamsala government, agreeing only to communications with His Holiness or his personal representatives, it has, in fact, from the very beginning worked with CTA officials. All the Fact-Finding Delegations His Holiness sent to observe conditions in Tibetan areas had senior CTA members. The PRC government made no issue of their participation. While Beijing could tacitly ignore the team members' political connections by labeling them personal representatives of His Holiness, it knew the political offices these people held and the significance of their participating in the various delegations.

More importantly, when His Holiness sent the First High-Level Exploratory Talks Delegation to Beijing in 1982 to begin discussions, all three of us on the team held prominent positions in the CTA. I was Chair of the Parliament, while my two colleagues, Takla Phuntsok Tashi and Juchen Thubten Namgyal, were both members of the Kashag. During our second trip in 1984, although Takla Phuntsok Tashi was retired from the Kashag, Juchen Thubten Namgyal was the senior Kalon and I was Additional Secretary of the Department of Information and Publicity (DIP), which later became the Department of Information and International Relations (DIIR).

Similarly, during the Nine Rounds of formal talks that I led starting in 2002, our negotiating team included other prominent CTA officials including Envoy Kelsang Gyaltsen and Dagpo Sonam Norbu. Additional CTA members participated in later meetings. Beijing was well aware of my team's political connections. In fact, during the Fourth Round of Talks, our negotiating counterparts explicitly congratulated Dagpo Sonam Norbu, as he had been promoted to Secretary of the DIIR in the time since our third meeting. I remember jokingly saying: "Yes, this may be the result of our last visit. The Kashag must have felt we did a good job, so he got promoted."

Beginning in 1979, when Dharamsala–Beijing relations were first established, the PRC government's public stance was that dialogue with the Dalai Lama was limited to discussions about his status, including his return to Tibet. But both parties knew that the real subject was Tibet and the Tibetans. Starting with the Deng–Thondup conversation, up to and including our formal dialogue, this was our focus.

Indeed, His Holiness has always been adamant that the Tibet issue and his personal position must not be linked, and we were explicitly instructed in this regard. Accordingly, during our negotiations, we always highlighted the role of the Kashag. During our meetings, I deliberately instructed my colleagues to bring me files containing our talking points that were emblazoned with the Kashag's official logo. I would then go through the points, making certain that my negotiating counterparts were aware that I was conducting myself as instructed by the Kashag. Sometimes in the middle of my remarks, I would intentionally turn to my colleague Kelsang Gyaltsen and ask him whether I had conveyed all the instructions given us by Kalon Tripa Samdhong Rinpoche, thereby highlighting the central role that the Kashag was playing in the deliberations. After several rounds, our negotiating partners themselves began to ask us to convey messages to both His Holiness and Samdhong Rinpoche as head of the Kashag. They referred to him as Samdhong *Huofo* (*Trulku* or Living Buddha).

Thus, through skillful means, we were able to sidestep one of the major issues that threatened to derail our discussions. With the total devolution of political power by His Holiness to the elected leadership in Dharamsala in 2011, however, the opportunities for such creative maneuvering have been significantly reduced.

## THE CLIMATE OF OPPORTUNITY

In my view, confusion, misunderstandings, and miscommunications combined to spoil some real opportunities for progress in the first few years of the Dharamsala-Beijing relationship. This is not to say that what was in the minds of Deng Xiaoping and other PRC leaders was anywhere near what His Holiness and the Tibetan leaders were contemplating. But Deng Xiaoping was definitely giving high priority to Tibet, and he was a very determined person. His grip over the CCP and the government was firm and unchallenged. What he wanted to accomplish had a high probability of success.

There were other factors that contributed to a relatively conciliatory mood within the leadership of the Deng era. Many of the officials, for example, were empathetic toward the situation in Tibet, as they too had suffered horrible atrocities during the Cultural Revolution and its aftermath. In 1982, during our First Exploratory Talks meeting, when we shared with our counterparts the destruction in Tibet and suffering of the Tibetan people chronicled in the Fact-Finding Delegations' reports, many of them, including Ulanhu, Xi Zhongxun, and Yang Jingren, did not protest, deny the findings, or try to defend the PRC's actions. Rather, they related stories of their own suffering and the cruel treatment they had received under the same policies. Ulanhu, the grand old Mongolian Communist leader, even shared with us some of the tragic events visited on the Mongolian people during that era of unbridled madness. These individuals' own personal sufferings, combined with their having witnessed the unprecedented upheaval in the PRC at the time, made them quite sensitive to the Tibetans' plight. To be very frank, our counterparts had many more examples of personal suffering to share with us than we did with them. We had been fortunate to be living in freedom in exile while Mao created havoc in the PRC, not sparing even his closest comrades-in-arms.

In addition, many of these leaders, including Deng Xiaoping, Li Xiannian, and Xi Zhongxun, had previously met His Holiness, and he had made a very positive impression upon them. I personally experienced the fondness that many of them felt for His Holiness during our 1982 meetings. Xi Zhongxun, for example, not once but several times wistfully recounted his memories of His Holiness's 1954–55 visit, which he had overseen as then Secretary General of the State Council.

It is unfortunate that His Holiness did not have a chance to establish a close personal rapport with any of these "second generation" officials in the PRC leadership, even though he had met many of them during that visit. Understandably, he relied on the personal relationship he thought he had built with Chairman Mao. Other members of the Tibetan leadership of that period were also unable to cultivate relationships with these "up and coming" officials.

One exception was Panchen Rinpoche, who developed a close relationship with Xi Zhongxun that benefited not only him personally but the broader Tibet issue as well. What happened during the madness of the Cultural Revolution is a different matter, as even Xi Zhongxun himself fell victim to its barbaric practices. He was the first senior CCP leader to establish contact with Panchen Rinpoche. They met in 1951 and from then on, Xi Zhongxun was concerned about Panchen Rinpoche's well-being. I know at one point there was even a perception in both Beijing and Lhasa that Xi Zhongxun was partial to Panchen Rinpoche. Although later events clearly demonstrated otherwise, he was one of those visionary leaders who understood that for the PRC to be strong and unified, the leadership needed to understand and respect the aspirations of all the nationalities residing within it. I myself had the opportunity to see this aspect of Xi Zhongxun during our formal negotiations, including the sincere affection he had for His Holiness the 14th Dalai Lama.

### *Beijing's Recognition of Tibet's Unique Status*

Many PRC leaders in the early 1980s publicly acknowledged Tibet's special status among the PRC's other "nationalities." Party General Secretary Hu Yaobang, for example, stated: "In the case of Tibet, as everyone knows, it is special amongst the specials. Nationality task can never be successful if we generalize all without talking about these specialties." In spite of increasingly strained relations, even as late as 1989, the PRC leadership still seemed to be acknowledging Tibet's special status. In a formal address delivered to the Second Session of the 5th National People's Congress of the Tibet Autonomous Region (TAR) on July 31, 1989, Ngapo Ngawang Jigme, Vice Chair of the National People's Congress, commented:

> If we perceive Tibet similar to other minority nationalities then it will not be in line with the historical ground realities. In the past there were many incidences where we failed in recognizing the special weather, scarcity of oxygen, more than 90% of its population being religious, its unique language, art, culture, custom and tradition. Moreover, the special characteristics of Tibet are evident in its history. . . . In 1949 after the liberation of China, excluding Taiwan, there was no other nationality except Tibet whose local government sent a delegation to Beijing and signed the 17-Point Agreement. Therefore, from this point also it is clear that Tibet enjoys special character in the field of history and politics. . . . From my perspective, if we want to carry the task of Tibet successfully and accelerate the speed of development in Tibet, then I feel it is utmost importance to accept and recognize the special characteristics of Tibet and these should never be ignored. Dividing line of whether our policy and implementations are successful or not and whether it addresses the ground reality or not will be decided by our (CCP) ability to accept and recognize the special characteristics of Tibet or not.[8]

Although Ngapo Ngawang Jigme is a Tibetan, and one might think his remarks were not government policy, that is not the case. In the Chinese Communist system, formal remarks by national leaders are not only approved but actually drafted by the CCP leadership.

### *The Tibet Work Forums and the Tibet Working Group*

Other second-generation leaders, including Hu Yaobang, Zhao Ziyang, Hu Qili, and Yan Mingfu, were more open to addressing the Tibet issue as part of a broader plan to liberalize Chinese society, both economically and politically. As a result of the Tibetan Fact-Finding Delegations, they learned not only of the Tibetans' deep loyalty to the Dalai Lama but also of the animosity the Tibetans harbored toward Chinese rule. This deeply worried them. They realized that while the PRC as a whole was economically still very backward, the situation in Tibet was far worse than in any other region.

Both to respond to His Holiness's concerns and to increase leverage in their negotiating positions, the PRC government decided to give top priority not only to providing economic incentives but also to trying to give more meaning to autonomous regions' special status in areas including culture, religion, and education. On March 14–15, 1980, it convened the First Tibet Work Forum to revise its policies. A high-level committee called the Tibet Working Group was created to oversee implementation of the policies adopted during the Forum. Party Secretary General of the Central Committee and member of the Standing Committee of the Politburo Hu Yaobang was appointed Chair. The other Committee members were Wan Li, member of the Central Committee and Vice Premier of the State Council; Ngapo Ngawang Jigme; Yang Jingren, member of the Central Committee and Minister of the Nationalities Affairs Commission (NAC); and Zhao Zhengqing, Deputy Head of the CCP Organization Department. Ngapo Ngawang Jigme was the lone Tibetan in the group.

In the beginning, the State Council also played a direct role through its NAC. This is the department that officially hosted the visits of the two Exploratory Talks Delegations of His Holiness even though the United Front controlled the agenda. Even at the beginning of the formal dialogue process in 2002, the head of the NAC acted as our formal host while the substantive talks were handled by the United Front.[9]

Close examination of the deliberations of the successive Tibet Work Forums gives an idea of the shift in Beijing's policies on Tibet over the years, and especially its attitude toward His Holiness. The substantive deliberations and decisions of the first two Forums focused on economic development. In addition, they decided to give priority to preserving the Tibetan language and culture as well as promoting freedom of religion. Although the PRC government was making unilateral decisions, not discussing them with either His Holiness's representatives or local Tibetans, it was very clear that Beijing was actively trying to redress the atrocious conditions in Tibet. It hoped to convince the Tibetans, especially His Holiness, that it was making real efforts to improve the situation inside Tibet.

## *Hu Yaobang's Efforts*

Hu Yaobang's politics, with the underlying question of whether he was liberal or conservative, have been the subject of much scholarly debate. While I do not wish to comment on that broader discussion, I do know we must be careful when using terms like that in describing Chinese leaders. These words have far different meanings in the Chinese context than they do in the West. Rather than using these labels, I'm offering my observations and comments on Hu Yaobang's approach solely regarding Tibet.

As I said earlier, the PRC leadership of the early 1980s was giving high priority to resolving the Tibet issue. Hu Yaobang had just come into prominence as the Secretary General of the CPC Central Secretariat. After the meeting of the First Tibet Work Forum, in his capacity as Chair of the Tibet Working Group, he personally visited Tibet. Unlike some of his peers, whose visits were purely ceremonial, Hu Yaobang made a serious effort to examine the true situation. His reaction to the conditions he observed during his visit to Lhasa in May 1980 is well documented. He was utterly shocked by the pathetic conditions under which the Tibetans labored.

I have a lot of admiration for Hu Yaobang. While Deng Xiaoping was a strategic, risk-taking politician, Hu Yaobang had an emotional reaction to the hardships suffered by the Tibetans that motivated his policies. Deng Xiaoping was far-sighted and courageous, but at bottom, his decision to reach out to His Holiness was only taken in the broader context of realizing his overall political agenda. Conversely, Hu Yaobang was genuinely affected by the appalling conditions he encountered and had a sincere desire to remedy them. He was also known to be quite impulsive. His emotional outburst when he saw the poverty in Tibet, combined with the lack of representation by Tibetans in the TAR leadership, deeply troubled him. These factors led him to convene a meeting of more than 4,500 cadres, both Chinese and Tibetans, in Lhasa. He did not hide his revulsion at the situation.

He scolded CCP officials in Tibet for their callous and despicable behavior, causing them and the Party itself embarrassment and great loss of face. He compared the situation in Tibet with colonialism, saying that in some regards it seemed to be worse than it had been before "liberation." He demanded to know where all the money had gone that Beijing had poured into Tibet over the years. Was it "thrown into the Yarlung Tsangpo River"? He further expressed regret for the

CCP's actions, saying: "We feel that our Party has let the Tibetan people down. We feel bad! The sole purpose of our Communist Party is to work for the happiness of the people, to do good things for them. We have worked nearly thirty years, but the life of the Tibetan people hasn't improved. Are we, the Party, not to blame?"[10] Tibetans who were present when Hu Yaobang made these statements agree that they were really quite remarkable.

In addition to publicly rebuking the responsible CCP leaders, Hu Yaobang immediately took action, including removing General Ren Rong, the Party Secretary, and replacing him with Yin Fatang, a Tibetan-speaking Chinese. He further issued clear instructions to CCP officials to include more Tibetan cadres in leadership roles. He proposed that within the next few years, two-thirds of all government functionaries should be Tibetans. He ordered the gradual withdrawal of thousands of Chinese cadres from Tibet. Those under the age of fifty remaining in Tibet would be required to learn Tibetan with sufficient fluency to be able to read papers and documents written in the language.

### The Six-Point Reform Program

With the approval of the more pragmatic Deng Xiaoping, Hu Yaobang spearheaded further policy changes, although opposition from the hard-line faction of the CCP continued to create obstacles. Soon after his public chastising of Party leaders for their gross mishandling of the situation in Tibet, Hu Yaobang announced the Six-Point Reform Program at a large Party meeting on May 29, 1980, in Lhasa. Bapa Phuntsok Wangyal (Phünwang) accurately summarizes the essential points of the Program in the book *A Tibetan Revolutionary*:

> (1) Full play must be given to the right of regional autonomy of minority nationalities under the unified leadership of the party Central Committee.... The right to decide for oneself under unified leadership should not be abolished. It is necessary to exercise this right fully and independently. Anything that is not suited to Tibet's conditions should be rejected or modified, along with anything that is not beneficial to national unity or the development of production. The autonomous region should fully exercise its right to decide for itself under the unified leadership of the party Central Committee, and it should lay down law, rules and regulations according to its special characteristics to protect the right of national autonomy and its special national interests.

(2) . . . Compared with other provinces and autonomous regions of the country, it is conspicuous that in Tibet the people's living standards lag far behind. This situation means that the burden of the masses must be considerably lightened. The people in Tibet should be exempt from paying taxes and meeting purchase quotas for the next few years. . . . All kinds of exactions must be abolished. The people should not be assigned any additional work without pay. Peasants' and herdsmens' produce may be purchased at negotiated prices or bartered to supply mutual needs, and they should be exempt from meeting state purchase quotas. . . .

(3) Specific and flexible policies suited to conditions in Tibet must be carried out on the whole economic front of the region, including the agricultural, animal husbandry, financial and trade, commercial, handicraft and communication fronts, with a view of promoting Tibet's economic development more rapidly. . . .

(5) So long as the socialist orientation is upheld, vigorous efforts must be made to revive and develop Tibetan culture, education and science. The Tibetan people have a long history and a rich culture. The world-renowned ancient Tibetan culture included fine Buddhism, graceful music and dance as well as medicine and opera, all of which are worthy of serious study and development. All ideas that ignore and weaken Tibetan culture are wrong. It is necessary to do a good job in inheriting and developing Tibetan culture.

Education has not progressed well in Tibet. Taking Tibet's special characteristics into consideration, efforts should be made to set up universities and middle and primary schools in the region. Some cultural relics and Buddhist scriptures in temples have been damaged, and conscientious effort should be made to protect, sort and study them. Cadres of Han nationality working in Tibet should learn the spoken and written Tibetan language. It should be required subject; otherwise they will be divorced from the masses. Cherishing the people of minority nationalities is not empty talk. The Tibetan people's habits, customs, history and culture must be respected.

(6) The party's policy on minority cadres must be correctly implemented and unity between Han and Tibetan cadres must be even more closely enhanced. . . .

Full time cadres of Tibetan nationality should account for more than 2/3rds of all government functionaries in Xizang, within the next 2–3 years.[11]

Hu Yaobang's Program forms the essence of Document No. 31, issued on April 7, 1980, by the central leadership based on the deliberations of the First Tibet Work Forum. This document puts forth policies that give Tibet a substantial degree of self-governance. Later that year, the PRC leadership published Document No. 46, which, while mainly focusing on the Xinjiang Autonomous Region, also included Tibet. Again quoting the policy as cited in *A Tibetan Revolutionary*: "Document Number 46, concerning Xinjiang . . . went further. It said that in the future, in special nationality areas like Xinjiang and Tibet, the central government would retain authority over only three areas: foreign relations, national defense, and veto power. All other rights belonged to the minority areas."[12]

Even though *A Tibetan Revolutionary* refers to *six* points, one of them, number 4, is missing. It seems that the authors combined points 3 and 4, as they both dealt with development. Wang Yao's report entitled "Hu Yaobang's Visit to Tibet, May 22–31, 1980, An Important Development in the Chinese Government's Tibet Policy" lists all six:

1. To exercise nationality autonomy in the region fully—that is to say, to let Tibetans really be the masters of their own lives.
2. A commitment by the Central Government to relieve and reduce burdens of the people, exempting them from agriculture and animal husbandry tax over the next three to five years in order to allow the Tibetan people a chance to recover.
3. To adopt a special policy to revive the Tibetan economy, including the adoption or a system of private economy in line with Tibetan circumstances. Nationwide this initiative was developed into the economic (household) responsibility system.
4. To make great efforts to develop agriculture and animal husbandry as well as the manufacture of consumer goods, in order to promote economic prosperity and enrich people's lives.
5. To make efforts to develop Tibetan science, culture and education, and to prepare for the establishing of the University of Tibet.
6. To implement the policy on minority nationality cadres correctly, to strengthen the unity between the Han and Tibetan cadres, and to transfer a large quantity of Chinese cadres who had worked in Tibet for many years back to the interior.[13]

Wang Yao was a Tibetan specialist who accompanied Hu Yaobang on his historic trip. He wrote this detailed account of Hu Yaobang's Tibet visit as a tribute after Hu Yaobang passed away on April 15, 1989. I first met him in 1982 and I really thought he was a Tibetan from Lhasa because his Tibetan was so perfect. He was one of those Chinese scholars who really understood Tibet and made sincere contributions in trying to bring reconciliation between the parties. I kept in touch with him periodically, directly and indirectly. More than once, he sent me very moving messages of encouragement, always urging me not to give up when he saw relations between the parties facing obstacles and under stress. I was saddened to learn of his passing in 2015.

If the provisions of the Six-Point Reform Program, Document 31, and Document 46 are read without the Communist rhetoric, the essence of the proposals is surprisingly close to the genuine autonomy that His Holiness is seeking through the Middle Way Approach. These policies have never been formally repudiated.

### Lessening of Bureaucratic Control Over Tibetans' Daily Lives

Two of His Holiness's and the TGiE's major concerns about conditions in Tibet were the marginalization of Tibetans in every aspect of daily life and the demographic changes caused by the influx of Chinese that could ultimately reduce the Tibetans to a minority in their traditional homelands. In response, the PRC leadership made some concrete efforts to remedy these problems in the early 1980s, especially after Hu Yaobang's visit to Tibet and his clear directives calling for improvements. While many of the rather forward-looking reforms did not materialize, two very important benefits that had a profound positive impact were realized: Tibetans were freed from the shackles of collectivism in both agriculture and animal husbandry and exempted from taxation. Bureaucratic control of day-to-day life lessened, providing an opportunity for Tibetans to pursue their livelihoods with considerable freedom.

For a long period of time prior to these reforms, Tibetans were not even able to consume their staple food, tsampa (roasted barley flour), but rather were compelled to eat rice as did the Chinese. Hu Yaobang even commented on the negative consequences of this specific practice: "Are we not currently proposing that production teams should have the right to decide for themselves? In fact, as individuals, we all have the right to decide for ourselves, we all have our own individual enthusiasms. You Tibetan comrades like to eat butter and tsampa, as a southerner, I like to eat rice. If you abolish his right to decide to eat tsampa, and if you abolish my right to decide to eat rice, then we couldn't be united."[14]

**Hu Yaobang Offers the Governorship to Bapa Phuntsok Wangyal**

In addition to these decisions proposing broad devolutions of authority to local Tibetan officials, Hu Yaobang approached Phuntsok Wangyal, offering him the position of TAR governor. Hu Yaobang made this offer in person not only with Deng Xiaoping's blessing but also knowing that His Holiness personally admired Phuntsok Wangyal. This was a clear signal to Dharamsala that the PRC leadership was sincere in its attempts to make amends for past practices and to undertake concrete initiatives both to improve conditions on the ground and to give Tibetans some control over their lives. Hu Yaobang's remarks to Phuntsok Wangyal encouraging him to move to Tibet clearly show that at that time, Deng Xiaoping and Hu Yaobang were looking for an individual who would have the courage to speak the truth and bring the Tibetan people's views to the central leadership. "Many of them (Tibetan cadres) simply do what the Chinese cadres tell them. They don't speak up on behalf of their nationality, and so they can't really be called Tibetan cadres, since they don't express or advocate the thoughts and concerns of Tibetans."[15] Hu Yaobang further mentioned that in a few years' time, a *Tibetan* cadre could become the Party Secretary of the TAR. He went so far as to hint that if Phuntsok Wangyal accepted the position as governor, he could be that person, thus becoming the first Tibetan to hold the most powerful position in the TAR.

## MISUNDERSTANDINGS, MISCOMMUNICATIONS, MISSTEPS, AND POOR TIMING

His Holiness the Dalai Lama welcomed Hu Yaobang's proposals, emphasizing his heartfelt pleasure with these gestures. In a letter to Deng Xiaoping dated March 23, 1981, he applauded Hu Yaobang's sincere and far-ranging efforts to correct the wrongs inflicted by CCP officials as well as his honest and frank admission of the Party's past mistakes. He placed great faith in the PRC leadership of that period, sincerely hoping that with Deng Xiaoping's pragmatic and bold leadership, assisted by Hu Yaobang as head of the CCP and Zhao Ziyang as Premier, a resolution of the conflict could be reached. In September 1982 when Hu Yaobang was reelected Party Secretary, His Holiness sent him a congratulatory message, further expressing his hope that they would have an opportunity for an in-person meeting in the future.

All these conditions seemed promising for improving the situation in Tibet and moving the parties toward a mutually acceptable resolution of their differences. However, this was not to be. A number of factors, including the machinations of the hard-liners in Beijing undermining the efforts toward reconciliation and Dharamsala's missteps and unfocused activities, combined with other events in the PRC and on the world stage to shut down this promising window of opportunity.

### *Unanticipated Consequences of the Fact-Finding Delegations*

In response to Deng Xiaoping's original overtures, His Holiness initially requested the ability to send several "fact-finding" delegations to Tibet to accurately assess the situation on the ground before putting forward any concrete proposals. From the beginning, he conveyed to the PRC leadership that these delegations needed to visit *all* the regions of Tibet. His Holiness was sending a clear message to both the Chinese and the Tibetan people at large that he was concerned with the plight of all Tibetans, not just those residing in the TAR.

Deng Xiaoping complied with His Holiness's request and over the next six years, four delegations made the trip. Even though in those days the PRC was quite poor, Beijing made elaborate arrangements to accommodate the visitors. And while Deng Xiaoping and other senior leaders knew there had been immense destruction and suffering inflicted on the Tibetans, they allowed relatively unrestricted visits by the delegates.

The visits of the first three Fact-Finding Delegations took place one after another. The First Delegation had five members: two members of the Kashag, Takla Phuntsok Tashi and Juchen Thubten Namgyal; His Holiness's elder brother, Taklha Lobsang Samten; Deputy Chair of the Commission of Tibetan People's Deputies Phunrab Lobsang Dhargye; and Secretary of the Home Department Tashi Topgyal. Juchen Thubten Namgyal headed the delegation at the suggestion of his senior colleague Takla Phuntsok Tashi. The group left Dharamsala in early August 1979 and spent over six months visiting Tibetan areas in all three regions of Tibet.

The Second Delegation departed in early May 1980 and spent about three months in Tibet. It also had five members, including His Holiness's representatives to the United States, Switzerland, and East Asia, respectively Tethong Tenzin Namgyal, Sangling Tsering Dorjee, and my brother Pema Gyalpo. The remaining members of the team were Lobsang Jinpa, President of the TYC, and Phuntsog Wangyal, Chair of the Tibetan Community in Britain. All these individuals were younger generation Tibetans brought up and educated in exile. Tethong Tenzin Namgyal led the delegation.

The members of the Third Fact-Finding Delegation were all educators sent specifically to assess the educational status and needs of Tibetan children. Jetsun Pema, His Holiness's younger sister and Director of the Tibetan Children's Village (TCV) in Dharamsala, was the team leader. She was accompanied by Chazotsang Sonam Rapten, Principal of the Central School for Tibetans in Mussoorie. Other members of the delegation were Rev. Tenzin, Lhagon Trulku, Wangdu, and Yangmo Tso, all of whom were teachers in Tibetan schools in India. The delegation left in early June 1980, returning in early October after about four months touring various Tibetan areas.

As discussed hereafter, following the return of the Third Fact-Finding Delegation, our relations with Beijing suffered a major setback. As a result, Beijing was unwilling to entertain the idea of allowing any more delegations to visit. With some renewed efforts on our part, it finally allowed the Fourth Fact-Finding Delegation to visit in June 1985, after a gap of several years. It included current and former members of the CTA, and its main task was to assess the state of religious practices in Tibet. Kundeling Woeser Gyaltsen, a former senior Kalon, headed the delegation. His personal assistant was Atisha Tenzin Phuntsok, a junior staff member of the DIIR. Two former Assembly members, Chabcha Kalden and Drawu Pon Rinchen Tsering, were also part of the team, as were Jigme Lhundup (Alak Jigme Rinpoche), Auditor General of the CTA, and Thubten Samphel, Deputy Secretary of the DIIR. The delegation's visit lasted about four months and was limited to Tibetan areas in present-day Qinghai Province.

The reports of the Fact-Finding Delegations on conditions in Tibet were indeed heartbreaking. They revealed tragic stories of the sufferings of their fellow countrymen far beyond their imagination. Dharamsala shared the reports with the public, which made the Tibetans even more resentful and angry with the Chinese. But the findings also energized the exile movement in showing the deep devotion of the Tibetans inside Tibet to His Holiness as well as their unshakable courage and determination to pursue the struggle. In this emotionally driven environment, what should have been an unequivocal decision to begin talks with

Beijing was compromised. Rather than reinforcing the need for immediate dialogue, the release of information had the opposite effect. To be frank, we did not handle the dissemination of the findings of the delegations with a clear strategy. Delegation members wrote and shared their views with the public without any clear guidance from Dharamsala on the best way to present the information.

From its side, Beijing was infuriated by our uncontrolled release of the findings and our failure to offer any proposals to address the conditions the delegations had witnessed. The PRC authorities knew that what the delegates would see would not be pleasant. Nevertheless, Deng Xiaoping had allowed them unrestricted access to many parts of Tibet. What deeply disappointed Deng Xiaoping and other senior leaders was our lack of any acknowledgment of their transparency in letting us see the true situation. All that the PRC government saw was international publication of the report, which it believed to be a deliberate attempt by us to humiliate and embarrass Beijing. Both sides lost their appetite for discussions, each for different but equally tragic reasons.

Although His Holiness's purpose in sending the delegations was sincere and based on a desire to assess ground realities before offering any solutions, the negative publicity in the international community simply fueled the hard-liners in Beijing, who had always mistrusted His Holiness's motives. You could almost hear them gloating in their conviction that His Holiness did have a hidden agenda, that his intention was to portray the PRC in the worst possible light and take advantage of international outrage to attain his goal, which, despite his statements to the contrary, was independence for Tibet. What else were they to think? Nothing positive or constructive had come from the Tibetans in response to Beijing's courageous gesture—only scorn and loathing from both Tibetans and the international community.

The PRC leaders were also shocked to see the deep animosity and resentment that the Tibetans throughout the Tibetan Plateau had toward Chinese rule. While they must have known that there was some unhappiness, they never imagined how unpopular their policies in Tibet were. They assumed that many of the problems were the result of the misguided polices of Mao and the Gang of Four under which they had all suffered. They actually thought they might have to control outbursts by the Tibetan people who might resent the delegations, seeing them as representatives of the former feudal regime.

Deng Xiaoping and the other leaders knew that the Tibetans held His Holiness the Dalai Lama in high regard. They also knew that because of the historic role of the institution of the Dalai Lamas, they had to reach out to him to resolve the Tibet issue. But they were totally unprepared for the escalating reverence, devotion, and loyalty in the hearts and minds of the Tibetans throughout Tibet for Tenzin Gyatso, the 14th Dalai Lama of Tibet. It was simply mind-boggling to them. So, just as the findings of the delegations hardened Tibetans' resolve against dealing with the Chinese persecutors, they simultaneously turned suspicion into fear in the minds of many senior PRC leaders.

### *Bapa Phuntsok Wangyal Declines the Governorship to Support the Efforts of Other Influential Tibetans in Beijing*

Bapa Phuntsok Wangyal then declined the proffered post as Governor of Tibet. I discussed this decision with him several times in later years. While I felt he should have accepted the offer, he had many valid reasons for rejecting it. With Deng Xiaoping and other leaders, including Hu Yaobang and Xi Zhongxun, taking serious and positive interest in Tibet, he believed he could make more substantive contributions to the cause by remaining in Beijing. Given the relatively small but disruptive group of hard-liners continuing to cause problems for him, he felt it would be detrimental if he went to Tibet, from where he could not effectively monitor and stymie their efforts. Remaining in Beijing, he believed, was also necessary to continue supporting the 10th Panchen Rinpoche, who relied very heavily on Phuntsok Wangyal's views, and to a lesser extent, Ngapo Ngawang Jigme.

To fully appreciate the roles of these three influential individuals during the early years of our efforts at reconciliation, further discussion of their backgrounds and the influence of those factors on their motives and actions is essential.[16] Strong criticisms expressed by the 10th Panchen Rinpoche no doubt finally registered with government policymakers and brought about some significant improvements in the lives of everyday Tibetans. At about the same time Phünwang, who had just been "rehabilitated," was making his own efforts from within the Party as a Marxist theoretician. He was urging amendments to the PRC Constitution to reflect a genuine Marxist approach in dealing with the different nationalities within the PRC. Although Ngapo Ngawang Jigme was cautious and unwilling to take the lead in risking his own well-being, his efforts must also be recognized.

### **Bapa Phuntsok Wangyal**

Bapa Phuntsok Wangyal was a committed Marxist but at the same time a staunch nationalist. When I say "nationalist," I mean Tibetan nationalist, yet his position was rooted in Marxist theory. I sometimes felt he knew more about communist ideology than many of his Chinese peers. As was the case with Panchen Rinpoche, when you asked him a question, you got a very clear answer, but it could sometimes be overly dialectical in nature because of his profound understanding of Marxism. He would also quite often answer a question replete with historic references and analytical interpretation, all of which I found very stimulating. Also, like Panchen Rinpoche, Phünwang never compromised his views or abandoned his beliefs. He endured eighteen years of solitary confinement, emerging from prison both a stronger and more refined individual.

As previously mentioned, some Tibetans persist in calling him a "traitor," a totally unjustified characterization. The views of these critics are most likely based on Phünwang's prominent position with the Chinese authorities in Lhasa in the early 1950s as well as his opposition to the aristocratically controlled Tibetan government that preceded the Chinese invasion. As a committed Marxist, he certainly did not appreciate Lhasa's feudal system of government that exploited the vast majority of Tibetans. That said, when he was in Lhasa from the end of 1947 until 1949, he actively tried to encourage the "up and coming" generation of aristocrats to institute social reforms to alleviate the unequal treatment of the lower classes.

Quite a few progressive young aristocrats, including Sonam Tomjor (Trendong Sey), shared his view of the need for social and political reform. Phünwang writes about his good friend: "He had democratic and reformist instincts and told us right away that there were lots of things he deplored about the old Tibetan system." Phünwang further writes: "We used to talk late into the night about Tibetan society and the country's future, and we talked frankly, holding nothing back. Trendong and I thought alike in many ways."[17] Phünwang was eventually expelled from Tibet, while forward-thinking individuals, including Trendong Sey, became suspect in the eyes of the orthodox Chinese leadership and were marginalized.

Phuntsok Wangyal's dream in the wake of the Chinese invasion was for the Tibetan people to reassert themselves and enter the modern era as a progressive and unified nation. To achieve this goal, he felt that the outdated and inefficient Lhasa government must be removed and replaced. It was with that passion that he cofounded the Tibetan Communist Party in 1942. Unfortunately, realities on the ground resulted in the co-opting of the Tibetan movement by the CCP. I encourage people, especially Tibetans of the younger generation who still harbor doubts about Phuntsok Wangyal's lifelong dedication and fierce loyalty to bettering conditions for the Tibetan people, to read his biography.[18]

### The 10th Panchen Rinpoche

Panchen Rinpoche was one of the most courageous leaders Tibet has ever had. His greatest accomplishment was pioneering the effort to revive Tibet's distinct national, cultural, and religious identity. He personally visited many Tibetan areas to launch this initiative, lending crucial support to other spiritual and community leaders. His effort to revive the Buddha Dharma was not limited to Tibet. During the 1982 and 1984 Exploratory Talks, our team had the opportunity to visit several historically important Buddhist sites and monasteries in China. In a number of these places, his portrait was prominently displayed in recognition of the important role he played in helping reopen them.

While Panchen Rinpoche firmly believed that the Tibetans must find their future within the PRC, sharing their destiny with the Chinese people, he was equally adamant that the unique identity of the Tibetan people be preserved. In 1962, at the age of twenty-four, he submitted his 70,000-Character Petition to the government, which reads in part as follows:

> Before democratic reform, there were more than 2500 large, medium and small monasteries in Tibet (TAR). After democratic reform, only 70 or so monasteries were kept in existence by the Chinese government. This was a reduction of more than 97 percent. . . . The number of monks and nuns living in the monasteries was about 7000 people, which is a reduction of 93 percent. . . . The number of monasteries and monks in the Tibetan brother provinces has been reduced by between 98 percent and 99 percent.
>
> We have no way of knowing in detail the number of Tibetans who were arrested after the rebellion, but from the appearance of things it may be inferred that the number of people who were locked up reached about ten thousand and or more than ten thousand in every area. Therefore, if we say that all these people were the enemy, we can affirm that hardly anyone is left among us Tibetans, apart from women, old people, children and a very small number of young men.[19]

This forthright and provocative document is testimony to both his courage and his commitment in fighting for the rights of the Tibetan people. In the petition, he further urged Beijing to improve the social, economic, and cultural lives of the Tibetans. He also raised other major issues, including the right to religious freedom and maintenance of the distinct Tibetan identity, and further expounded on the numerous other inequalities Tibetans faced. As a result of his commitment to the truth and defense of the Tibetan people, he was tortured, humiliated, and imprisoned in solitary confinement for more than twelve years.

Panchen Rinpoche was released from prison in 1977 but was kept under house arrest in Beijing until he was "rehabilitated" and inducted into the central leadership as Vice Chair of the National People's Congress. He did not hesitate to speak out and act forcefully on behalf of his fellow Tibetans, taking full advantage of his new position and platform. While he knew his penchant for telling these unpopular truths could deprive him of his position within a matter of hours, he stood firm and fought for the rights of his people.

His very presence made you proud to be Tibetan. During our 1982 Exploratory Talks visit to Beijing we were invited to a cultural extravaganza attended by the "who's who" of Beijing, missing only Deng Xiaoping and a few elders. When Panchen Rinpoche walked into the hall just about ten minutes before the curtain went up, the entire audience erupted, whispering: "Panchen, Panchen, Panchen." Many of the seniormost CCP officials, some of them very advanced in age, rose to greet him. The sight was overwhelming. I had goose bumps.

His passing away in 1989 at the age of fifty-one (according to the Tibetan system for calculating age) was an irreparable loss to the Tibetan people. With His Holiness spearheading the movement from outside Tibet and Panchen Rinpoche battling from within, unprecedented changes could have been made. I had the great fortune of being in his presence several times. No matter what the politics of his recognition,[20] there can be no doubt that he was an extraordinary human being. When you asked Panchen Rinpoche a question, you got a straightforward, no-nonsense answer. Everything he said is what he truly believed. He proved his uncompromising loyalty to his people, the Dharma, and His Holiness through the multitude of sufferings he endured on their behalf.

### Ngapo Ngawang Jigme

Ngapo Ngawang Jigme was a former Lhasa aristocrat who was part of the Central Tibetan Government prior to the Chinese invasion. He spent most of his later years in Beijing. He was very much integrated into the PRC leadership system. I believe he joined the CCP but was advised not to make it public because Beijing felt he would be more effective in influencing the Tibetan people if they didn't see him as a Communist. If true, that was a smart decision.

In spite of his absence from Lhasa for many years and his daily routine being very much part of the Beijing scene, Ngapo Ngawang Jigme remained very aristocratic in his behavior. Of course, he did not dress in the rich brocade outfits he wore as a member of the Kashag in Lhasa, rather adopting the standard Mao jacket of his contemporaries in the PRC leadership, but his style remained aloof and disparaging. He was rumored to have become an atheist. Although this is quite difficult to imagine given his cultural roots, during my meetings with him he did try very hard to convey that he was a nonbeliever. He was from one of the few influential aristocratic families from Lhasa that follow the Nyingma Buddhist tradition. He also had a close relationship with the Mindrolling Monastery, especially with Mindrolling Chung Rinpoche. He knew that I am a close relative of Chung Rinpoche, and we talked quite a bit about the tragic situations that Chung Rinpoche endured before and particularly during the Cultural Revolution. While he spoke of Mindrolling Chung Rinpoche with great fondness, he described his spiritual relationship in the past tense. However, he went out of his way to get special permission for Chung Rinpoche's two sisters, Minling Trichen Rinpoche's son, and the young Khenchen Rinpoche to leave Tibet to join Minling Trichen Rinpoche in India.

Unlike the behavior of Panchen Rinpoche and Bapa Phuntsok Wangyal, one has to do a lot of "between the lines" reading of Ngapo Ngawang Jigme's comments and actions to assess his true feelings. He was a guarded speaker with every word meticulously vetted before delivery, so his true intentions were hard to discern. While he did not oppose Panchen Rinpoche's efforts on behalf of the Tibetan people, he certainly kept his distance from him and even from Phuntsok Wangyal. Although Phünwang told me that both he and Panchen Rinpoche were sometimes disappointed with Ngapo Ngawang Jigme, on a few core issues he took the right position, admittedly with caution.

For example, as previously discussed,[21] he was quite supportive of the Tibetan people's right to become unified. Similarly, on another important issue in the history of Tibetan-Chinese relations, he stalwartly defended the Tibetan position, publicly criticizing the Kuomintang (KMT) government for its distorted and exaggerated role purportedly "overseeing" the February 22, 1940, enthronement of the 14th Dalai Lama in Lhasa. On July 31, 1989, at the TAR People's Congress in his capacity as its Chair, he stated that the role of the KMT representative Wu Zhongxin was no different from that of the representatives of any of the other neighboring countries, including British India, Nepal, Bhutan, and Sikkim, who were all participating in the ceremony. He explicitly stated: "To 'oversee' and to 'participate' have entirely different meanings, which one should never mistake."[22] He further recounted in detail the search for and recognition of the Dalai Lama's reincarnation by the Tibetans. While technically referring to that event, he was actually using it to mask a direct challenge to the Chinese historic claim over Tibet.

Despite his views of the historic relationship between the countries, however, he was firm and unambiguous in his position that Tibet became part of the PRC with the controversial signing of the Seventeen-Point Agreement in 1951. I don't think he took that position simply because he was the signatory on Tibet's behalf. In his mind, whatever may have precipitated the signing, the agreement was a valid document that he signed with full authority and the knowledge of the Central Tibetan Government. He further noted that the Lhasa regime was well aware of the contents. Indeed, upon his return from Beijing after signing the agreement, in briefing a gathering of government officials as well as representatives from the monastic institutions, he gave a detailed account of how the negotiations, including the signing of the final agreement, were conducted with the approval of the Tibetan leadership.

I don't wish to get into any serious debate over the validity of the Seventeen-Point Agreement other than to say that it was signed under duress, precipitated by the Chinese military invasion of Tibet, the defeat of the Tibetan army, and the threat of further military incursions if Tibetans refused to sign. Putting aside the question of the validity of the agreement under international law, it is the document routinely cited as establishing the date Tibet became part of the PRC. It provides crucial background for assessing the merits of the parties' respective positions as expressed today. Under its provisions, Tibet did not become a province of the PRC but was incorporated into the PRC as an autonomous region, specifically the Tibet Autonomous Region (TAR), while Tibetan areas lying outside the TAR were also given autonomous status. Designation of these areas as autonomous was a clear and unambiguous acknowledgment by Beijing of the Tibetan people's distinct identity. Indeed, Zhou Enlai went so far as to inform foreign dignitaries, including Pandit Jawaharlal Nehru, India's first Prime Minister, that Beijing didn't consider Tibet to be a PRC province and further, that it had no intention of turning it into one because the Tibetans are a separate people.[23]

Ngapo Ngawang Jigme strongly believed that a final settlement of the Tibet issue requires His Holiness's full participation. I believe this is the same position he consistently conveyed to the PRC leadership. He also said it more than once to those of us participating in the Exploratory Talks Delegations at both our 1982 and 1984 meetings. Ultimately, he said, the principals must meet to come to a resolution. He used a Tibetan term, དོན་གྱི་བདག་པོ།, which has a much deeper meaning. The closest translation may be the "real owners."

When the Second Fact-Finding Delegation met Ngapo Ngawang Jigme in 1980 in Beijing, he seemed to be citing a much-quoted Tibetan proverb when he said: "Tibetans are betrayed by suspicion, Chinese are betrayed by hope." Some of the delegation members thought he had simply misquoted the well-known proverb that actually reverses the phrases: "The Chinese are betrayed by suspicion and the Tibetans by hope." He wasn't misquoting; he was deliberately trying to deliver a message that he felt was very pertinent at that time.

Ngapo Ngawang Jigme's view of the need for the principals to sit down together was evident in the active role he later played in persuading Deng Xiaoping to invite His Holiness for the 10th Panchen Rinpoche's funeral service, which he knew would provide the opportunity for His Holiness and Deng Xiaoping to meet personally. While we had heard of his involvement from several others, I had it confirmed by none other than Bapa Phuntsok Wangyal. Despite his position as a senior member of the PRC government, Ngapo Ngawang Jigme was adamant that a real breakthrough in relations can only happen if and when His Holiness personally engages with the top leadership officials.

In my view, Ngapo Ngawang Jigme was a victim of circumstances resulting from political infighting amongst the aristocratic rulers of Tibet. He did not volunteer to go to Chamdo as its governor in 1950 but was sent there by a faction of the Lhasa central government that was worried about his quick rise in power. Heading an ill-equipped and outnumbered army led to a humiliating defeat and his capture by the Chinese toward the end of that same year. I need not go into detail about what followed. Did he demonstrate the kind of courage that Panchen Rinpoche and Phuntsok Wangyal showed during their years of incarceration? He certainly did not. But I don't think it is fair to call him a "traitor." Having said that, I was a little surprised by the glorifying tribute the Kashag paid him when he passed away in 2009. However, I came to the conclusion that this elaborate remembrance ceremony must reflect His Holiness's view of Ngapo Ngawang Jigme, whom he apparently held in high regard as a true Tibetan patriot.

### *Britain's Gifted Return of Hong Kong to Beijing's Control*

In 1982, when I was in Beijing for our First Exploratory Talks mission, PRC leaders were considering options for Hong Kong's status upon its return to Chinese rule from the British. In the process, they were drafting the text establishing the so-called Special Administrative Regions (SAR) for approval by the National People's Congress. An official of the United Front gave each of our team members a copy for our comments. A day or two later, when we were away on tour in Shanghai, this official reminded us not to forget to share our thoughts, making the cryptic comment: "This can have relevance to Tibet." The provision for creating the SAR entity was incorporated into the PRC Constitution as Article 31, which reads as follows: "The state may establish special administrative regions when necessary. The systems to be instituted in special administrative regions shall be prescribed by law enacted by the National People's Congress in the light of the specific conditions."

**One Country, Two Systems**

As previously noted, the Seventeen-Point Agreement is historic evidence of Tibet's special status in the eyes of the PRC government. Indeed, it was the first example of a "One Country, Two Systems" formula similar to that ultimately promised to both Taiwan and Hong Kong. However, as CCP rule had been established in Tibet, unlike in Hong Kong (at the time) and Taiwan, the Chinese Communist leadership would never relinquish its control over Tibet as part of the solution to our differences. But in sharing the draft text of the SAR proposal with us, inviting our comments on it, and explicitly informing us that the provisions could have relevance to Tibet, the gesture was a subtle but unambiguous indication that Beijing continued to recognize Tibet's special status. It was clearly considering including Tibet as an SAR, based on that historic, unique status, at least while Beijing was negotiating with the British on the future status of Hong Kong.

But that need disappeared in 1984, eliminating one of Deng Xiaoping's primary reasons for considering an early resolution of the Tibet issue. Despite Beijing's worries, Prime Minister Thatcher handed Hong Kong back without demanding or receiving any significant concessions in return. Her rapid conclusion of the matter adversely affected our nascent relations with the PRC by removing a major incentive for Beijing to engage us. By the time we returned for the Second Exploratory Talks meeting in October 1984, there was a noticeable hardening of attitude and even a sense of arrogance on the part of the PRC representatives. Although the Sino-British Joint Declaration on Hong Kong was not formally announced until December 19, 1984, the British and Chinese had settled all the critical issues before our fall visit. One of the main reasons motivating Beijing to talk with us had simply evaporated through no fault of our own.

*Unintended Negative Effects of Hu Yaobang's Reforms*

As previously noted, during his visit to Tibet, Hu Yaobang called for repatriation of more than 80 percent of the Chinese cadres then residing there. Throughout his remarks there was a clear message that the Tibetans must be in charge of their lives. He went so far as to cite the positions of earlier leaders, including Mao Zedong and Zhou Enlai, who intended the Han cadres to return to China once the Tibetan cadres had been well trained to carry out their responsibilities.

Ironically, a number of subsequent programs initiated as a result of Hu Yaobang's policies actually worsened the situation in Tibet. The launching of major infrastructure projects brought more Chinese to the Plateau, as many of the associated contracts were awarded to Chinese companies. By May 1984, more than 60,000 Chinese had arrived from various provinces to work on forty-three projects approved by the Second Tibet Work Forum, adding to the more than 50,000 Chinese workers who had migrated to the Plateau the year before.[24] Many of the funds allocated for these projects thus ended up enriching large Chinese companies and Chinese workers. A large portion never even reached Tibet, while some of the projects were neither wanted nor needed by the local Tibetans. During the First Round of our formal talks in 2002, I visited some of these projects, including a "state of the art" stadium in Shigatse. This beautiful facility, built as one of the forty-three projects, was already in shambles; it was simply not of any practical use to the locals.

Beijing was very unhappy that His Holiness and the exile Tibetan leadership never acknowledged or appreciated any of their efforts to improve conditions in Tibet, particularly in the early years when they were serious in their desire to respond to the dire conditions highlighted by His Holiness's Fact-Finding Delegations and Panchen Rinpoche. From our side, we were from the beginning skeptical about Beijing's sincerity and then disillusioned by the programs that brought more Chinese to the Plateau and seemed to benefit them disproportionately.

Sometimes those of us in exile have different perspectives than our people inside. One example of our lack of understanding of local needs was the railway line built from Xining to Lhasa. Tibetans in exile vigorously opposed it for several legitimate reasons. The ease of access would enable more Chinese to reach the Plateau, threatening to reduce Tibetans to a minority in their own land. The environmental consequences were also negative: the railway threatened sensitive ecological regions and enhanced Beijing's ability to drain Tibet of its natural resources for the benefit of the Chinese. But these considerations did not take into account the resulting benefits to the Tibetans inside Tibet. I remember reading the petitions written by Derong Tsering Dhondup from 1986 to 1993 that were submitted to Jiang Zemin, Li Peng, Deng Xiaoping, and various administrative departments, in which he lists how many ways the Chinese discriminated against the Tibetans.[25] One example he cited was the lack of railway systems in Tibetan areas.

We in exile have clearly been remiss in not always accounting for the different perceptions and needs of Tibetans inside Tibet when evaluating the pros and cons of Beijing's projects, a failure that created unnecessary animosity in the PRC leadership's minds and contributed to the deterioration of our relations in the early 1980s. Sometimes we cannot fully appreciate the changes that have taken place inside Tibet. Even dismissing the PRC authorities' disdain for our insensitivity to these positive events, some of our own people inside lament the exile community's lack of understanding and appreciation of these changes that have materially improved their lives.

### *Reactionary Elements Within the Chinese Communist Party*

While Deng Xiaoping, Hu Yaobang, Xi Zhongxun, and other senior leaders were making serious efforts to redress past mistakes in Tibet through fundamental policy changes, as well as on-the-ground improvements to ease tensions and promote harmony, reactionary elements within the CCP in Beijing and Lhasa were busy trying to undermine their efforts. With the backing of influential senior CCP leaders, these hard-line cadres launched vicious campaigns warning about the danger posed by the Dalai Lama from outside, the Panchen Lama from within the country, and Phuntsok Wangyal from within the Party. A conspiratorial plot instituted against Phünwang is clear evidence of the sinister and deeply rooted animosity this small, yet influential group of CCP officials felt toward Tibet and the Tibetan people.

One of the group's ringleaders was Yang Jingren, Minister of the NAC and later a United Front Minister. He went so far as to delete Phuntsok Wangyal's name as a Sichuan Province member of the 6th National People's Congress even though Phünwang was both a member of the Standing Committee of the NPC and Deputy Party Secretary of the Nationalities Committee. In his memoirs, Phünwang gives a detailed account of how he had to seek out Xi Zhongxun to help reinstate him as a delegate. Xi Zhongxun not only instructed that Phuntsok Wangyal's position be maintained but also expressly scolded Yang Jingren, saying: "You made a big mistake. Phünwang's position should not be changed. I am going to report this to Hu Yaobang! You must reinstate Phünwang immediately. Do you understand?"[26]

The machinations of this group would prove to be more than inconvenient and disruptive. Even though Yang Jingren had to reinstate Phuntsok Wangyal as a member of the NPC, these hard-liners never gave up attempting to disrupt the process of reconciliation between His Holiness and the leadership in Beijing. They became brazen enough to launch an open campaign against the Dalai Lama, Panchen Rinpoche, and Phuntsok Wangyal under the banner "Three Enemies of the Party." The TAR Party Secretary, Yin Fatang, actively collaborated with Yang Jingren and others in Beijing. Although technically their campaign targeted only these three individuals, the real goal was to oppose the central leadership's policy on Tibet. This group had deep animosity toward Hu Yaobang, Zhao Ziyang, and the other more reform-minded officials. It is quite mind-boggling how they managed to carry out their conspiratorial activities right under the nose of Deng Xiaoping and Hu Yaobang.

Unfortunately, some Tibetan cadres joined hands with these reactionary elements, convinced that any reconciliation between the Dalai Lama and Beijing would result in their loss of power and position. This fear was very prevalent even in the early 2000s. When my delegation had the opportunity to meet Tibetan cadres during our visits to Tibetan areas in conjunction with the formal dialogue process, we made it very clear that resolving the Tibet issue would in no way diminish their power and prestige but rather enhance it. I assured them that no one was going to come from outside to take over. Fortunately, there were other Tibetan cadres, such as Yangling Dorje, who played crucial roles in exposing the sinister plots hatched by this handful of senior Tibetan Party members. Because of Yangling Dorje's personal relationship with Premier Zhao Ziyang, he was able to directly warn the Prime Minister of these attempts to undermine the central leadership's forward-looking policies.

After the direct intervention of senior, more progressive leaders, this reactionary group became less vocal and less effective. TAR Party Secretary Yin Fatang even went to Phuntsok Wangyal to apologize. But the seeds of these negative thoughts had been planted and from time to time resurfaced. The hard-liners within the CCP were able to get closer to Deng Xiaoping and take advantage of internal and external situations, eventually leading to the marginalization of the more progressive leaders, including Xi Zhongxun, and the purging of Hu Yaobang and Zhao Ziyang from the leadership. Our actions, or more accurately inactions, also played into the hands of these reactionary groups.

### *Dharamsala's Failure to Formulate and Implement a Coordinated Strategy Exacerbated by Gyalo Thondup's Independent Style*

As is evident from the previous discussion, we handled our relations with Beijing in an ad hoc and sometimes chaotic manner in the early 1980s, generating misunderstandings and resulting in the loss of opportunities for dialogue. Obviously, the relationship with Beijing was given high priority by the Tibetan leadership, but a lack of internal coordination and institutionalization unintentionally sabotaged it. There was no designated individual or office charged with responsibility for these important issues on a day-to-day basis, and there was no overall strategy informing our actions. While Gyalo Thondup continued as the principal interlocutor and Beijing interacted with the Tibetan leadership occasionally through its embassy in New Delhi, these communications were sporadic and uncoordinated at best.

Moreover, His Holiness's Secretariat and the Kashag only addressed matters if and when Beijing relayed information through Gyalo Thondup, or His Holiness, on his own, thought of a new initiative. Gyalo Thondup's efforts were handicapped not only by a lack of clear direction from Dharamsala but also by the absence of any staff assistance. Periodically, his two sons and senior officials from Dharamsala lent some support, but most of the time he was on his own dealing with the Tibetan people's most important and delicate issue.

In my view, some real progress could have been made in the early 1980s if matters had been handled in a more coordinated, professional, and institutionalized manner. Gyalo Thondup's role was indispensable, and while the Chinese did not fully trust him, they acknowledged him as credible and reliable. The problem lies at our feet. While the Tibetan leadership should have formally empowered him and given him an official role, he should have made more of an effort to coordinate and work as a team with Dharamsala. This internal failure to communicate and work together was instrumental in the breakdown of our relations with Beijing at the time.

Gyalo Thondup's style and personality, in combination with the lack of a coordinated and streamlined decision-making process in Dharamsala, unfortunately did contribute to miscommunications and misunderstandings with Beijing that caused us to lose an important opportunity for engagement with the PRC. None of us is perfect; we are all profoundly influenced by the society and the political system in which we grow up. As clearly revealed in his biography, Gyalo Thondup deeply mistrusted the Lhasa government of old, faulting the leadership as shortsighted and riddled with corruption and nepotism.

Even though the old aristocratic form of governance changed upon our exile from Tibet, gradually being replaced by a new generation of leaders, including many commoners as well as people from Kham and Amdo, Gyalo Thondup still viewed the Dharamsala establishment with a degree of mistrust. The feeling was mutual. Dharamsala continued to treat him with suspicion, not making a serious effort to create a formal role for him or integrate him into the leadership. His decades-long secretive and unilateral handling of relations with the PRC did not help matters. The lack of a concerted, transparent, and open relationship between the Kashag and Gyalo Thondup torpedoed one of the early promising opportunities we had to advance our interests with the PRC and further hindered His Holiness's ability to pursue this critically important issue in the most effective way. I am specifically referring to our handling, or more accurately mishandling, of the events surrounding the PRC government's Five-Point Policy Toward the Dalai Lama.

### *Beijing's Proposed Five-Point Policy Toward the Dalai Lama Falls Through the Cracks*

On July 27, 1981, Party General Secretary Hu Yaobang conveyed to Gyalo Thondup Beijing's proposal for His Holiness the 14th Dalai Lama's return. The major substantive components of the proposal specified that: His Holiness and his followers could return to the PRC; His Holiness would enjoy the same political status and living conditions as in the past; he would be reinstated in his position as Vice Chair of the NPC Standing Committee and could also hold the position of Vice Chair of the Chinese People's Political Consultative Conference; and he should reside in Beijing but could visit Tibet periodically. It further delineated the logistical details concerning his physical return. At Gyalo Thondup's request, this Five-Point Policy Toward the Dalai Lama was given to him in writing under seal of the United Front as a record of his meeting with Hu Yaobang.

This document was destined to trigger a misunderstanding between Beijing and Dharamsala, prompting the first major obstacle to dialogue between the parties. While there are different versions of the actual events, lack of communication between Gyalo Thondup and the Kashag, as well as lapses in communication between His Holiness's office and the Kashag, are the true culprits. In fairness, no one was trying to keep anyone in the dark. The debilitating result was just the most blatant and tragic example of Dharamsala's lack of a clearly defined strategy for engaging with the PRC combined with the failure to appoint one individual or department as responsible for overseeing this, the most fundamental of Tibet's concerns.

In late April 1982, when we went to Beijing for the first of our Exploratory Talks, none of my team was aware of this document, even though Gyalo Thondup had received it about ten months earlier. I was not then a member of the Kashag, but my two colleagues, Takla Phuntsok Tashi and Juchen Thubten Namgyal, were—yet neither of them had ever heard of it. I had no reason to doubt their denials, as our pretrip briefing by the Kashag also made no mention of it. Accordingly, we had not received any explicit instructions on how to respond.

As the PRC leadership had forwarded this proposal to His Holiness via Gyalo Thondup almost a year earlier, they were under the impression that the sole purpose of our visit was to follow up on their initiative and iron out the related details. Under the circumstances, one cannot blame them for making that assumption. Even Panchen Rinpoche, Ngapo Ngawang Jigme, and Phuntsok Wangyal thought that our visit was solely to discuss the proposal. That these individuals were under the impression that the talks would be limited to Beijing's Five-Point Policy subsequently explained some remarks that Panchen Rinpoche and Ngapo Ngawang Jigme made to us before our meetings. Panchen Rinpoche cautioned us several times that His Holiness should not be in a rush to return. Ngapo Ngawang Jigme, the veteran Tibetan politician, further remarked: "Since decision on the important matter has already been made, don't make issue on less important matters." I remember that when we were driving back to our guesthouse, we were asking one another what Ngapo Ngawang Jigme was hinting at.

Taken aback by our reaction, our counterparts must have thought we were deliberately feigning ignorance. They then presented each of us with a photocopy of the signed and dated letter while forcefully reiterating Beijing's position.

Needless to say, we were shocked by both the existence of the document and its contents. We couldn't hide our surprise. Although we were very embarrassed, we couldn't pretend we had been aware of the proposal. Being totally unprepared to respond, we initially thought that one or all of us should immediately return to Dharamsala to seek guidance from His Holiness. In the end, we decided to stay, but we reacted very negatively to the substance of the proposal, as it was limited to a discussion of the status of His Holiness and the conditions attending his return. This misunderstanding, resulting from miscommunication within the Tibetan leadership, made the first round of the Exploratory Talks confrontational and unproductive.

### *Missed Opportunities at the 1982 Exploratory Talks Meeting from Lack of Communication*

When one examines the Five-Point Policy calmly and objectively in the context of the times, almost all its points are neither new nor surprising. Deng Xiaoping had orally conveyed the essence of them to Gyalo Thondup in 1979, and Li Xiannian had made similar remarks to the First Fact-Finding Delegation, in which both Takla Phuntsok Tashi and Juchen Thubten Namgyal had participated. But it creates much more of an impact to see these ideas expressed formally in writing, set out as individual requirements. The only new condition was the explicit mention that His Holiness need not stay in Tibet but should live in Beijing, making periodic visits to Tibet. Only later on did we learn that a number of other PRC leaders had previously publicly advanced this idea.[27]

Not only did the miscommunication surrounding Beijing's Five-Point Policy jeopardize our relationship with Beijing, but it also became a matter of controversy in Dharamsala upon our return. Some aspects of the internal distribution of the document are still not very clear. In fairness to Gyalo Thondup, it seems that he did transmit the contents of Beijing's proposal to His Holiness, at least the gist of it. When our team, together with other members of the Kashag, briefed His Holiness on the details of our meetings in Beijing, sharing with him our surprise and consternation at the existence of the Five-Point Policy, I remember His Holiness looking at his Principal Secretary, Reverend T. C. Tara, and rather matter-of-factly acknowledging that the information had previously been brought to his attention.

I believe His Holiness's casual reaction to our revelation stemmed from his having attached little importance to the contents of the proposal when it was initially brought to his attention by Gyalo Thondup. As I wrote earlier, many of the things included in the Five-Point Policy were familiar to him, as they had previously been conveyed through various channels at different times. Most importantly, because His Holiness never considered his personal status or future role as the priority, he was always dismissive when the subject arose in conversation. And his explicit instructions had always been not to allow matters concerning his position to detract from discussions on the real issue, the needs of the Tibetan people. On the other hand, from the perspective of the Tibetan people, including those of us in the leadership, his role is inseparable from the larger issue of Tibet. It is difficult for any of us to fathom a solution to the Tibet issue without His Holiness playing a central role.

Not surprisingly, there were heated discussions both within the leadership and with the Tibetan public about this unfortunate series of events. It became a seriously divisive issue for quite some time, and there was considerable finger pointing, with Gyalo Thondup being the main scapegoat. But that is neither fair nor accurate. His Holiness is always eager to embrace new ideas and encourage individuals to carry them out. Gyalo Thondup was anxious to facilitate a meeting between His Holiness and Deng Xiaoping, believing, as many of us do, that a face-to-face meeting of the principals holds the most promise for resolving the conflict. Knowing Gyalo Thondup, I am certain he did everything in his power to bring this about, including praising each individual to the other party and portraying the negative consequences to their respective constituencies of failing to come to a resolution. All of this was done with the best of intentions. But, as I mentioned earlier, in the absence of an institutionalized approach, with a clear strategy and defined responsibilities for involved individuals, it was simply a matter of time before something like this happened.

I have always felt that if our team had had prior knowledge of the Five-Point Policy and time to strategize, we not only could have avoided the embarrassing situation in Beijing but also could have turned the proposal to our benefit. Obviously, the PRC government is most comfortable operating under the fiction that there is no Tibet issue, only the matter of the Dalai Lama's return. Steadfastly adhering to this position, advocates of dialogue then appear to their countrymen, and more importantly, to the hard-liners in Beijing, as maintaining the upper hand and not acceding to any of Dharamsala's demands. Armed with this knowledge and with time to develop a counterproposal, rather than impulsively reacting and rejecting out of hand Beijing's conditions for His Holiness's return, we could have traveled to Beijing equipped with our own list of requirements for the PRC government to meet in order to create the right environment for his return.

In other words, we could have drafted our proposal within the context put forward by Beijing. We would have reminded our counterparts that His Holiness had left Tibet because of the tragic situation facing the Tibetan people, not for any personal reasons. For him to return, the circumstances compelling him to leave and remain in exile obviously must be rectified. Under this "cover," we could have advanced our own proposals for resolving the Tibet issue without rejecting theirs. Most importantly, unlike Beijing's more recent conditions, this proposal did not include a requirement that His Holiness accept Tibet as having always been part of China, something he can never do, as it is historically incorrect. The proposal was actually forward-looking and indicated that we should not focus on past events. But we never had the chance.

The miscommunications within Dharamsala led to the breakdown of our relationship with Beijing for several years. While there were some setbacks here and there prior to this time, we had worked hard to develop professional as well as personal relationships with several of the senior PRC leaders. Our communications had been both respectful and promising. Hu Yaobang and other influential leaders had consistently referred to the future of Tibet positively in their remarks. But the fallout from our ignorance of the Five-Point Policy destroyed this hard-earned connection. It was apparent to our team that any further talks would not yield any substantive results. It was thus time for His Holiness and Dharamsala to develop a new strategy to try to reengage Beijing.

## CHAPTER 13

# Tibet's Rise to Prominence on the International Stage

### *Adoption of the Middle Way Approach*

Over and over again the PRC government has criticized His Holiness the 14th Dalai Lama and the Tibetan movement for "internationalizing" the Tibet issue, mischaracterizing our efforts to mobilize the international community to embrace our cause as a deliberate attempt to tarnish the PRC's image and harm its standing in that forum. While I completely disagree with the motives the Chinese assign to us for pursuing this path, they are correct in their conclusion: His Holiness and the Tibetan movement have successfully elevated Tibet's plight to a prominent place on the world stage.

In the face of Beijing's decision to curtail discussions with us by the mid-1980s, we had no choice but to develop and implement a strategy designed to reengage Beijing. Any sensible party finding itself frozen out of dialogue with its adversary but still desiring a resolution to the underlying dispute would have followed the same course. Accordingly, His Holiness adopted the Middle Way Approach, and one of the methods employed in its service was a concerted effort to bring Tibet's plight to the attention of the international community. This chapter details the circumstances that compelled us to embrace this new strategy, the efforts we made to further it, and the successes we achieved in its pursuit.

As I have said on many occasions, renewed dialogue with the PRC never would have occurred absent our success in placing and maintaining the issue of Tibet on the world's agenda. The Tibetan people must further recognize, however, that active involvement of the international community on the Tibet issue only became possible because of His Holiness's adoption of the Middle Way Approach. I understand that the sentiment for independence runs very deep among the majority of Tibetans. I myself held that strong belief for many years. People have legitimate reasons for that position and the absolute right to aspire to that goal. Moreover, this view should not be interpreted as being disrespectful to His Holiness. Everyone is entitled to his or her own opinion, a position His Holiness wholeheartedly endorses.

Not once but several times during my talks with my PRC counterparts, I bluntly told them that the vast majority of Tibetans deep in their hearts wish for total freedom, including independence. I used to urge them that, precisely because such strong sentiments prevail among Tibetans both inside and outside Tibet, they should view His Holiness's Middle Way Approach as a mutually beneficial way to preserve the stability of the PRC. While many Tibetans long for independence, they will embrace a solution formulated and supported by His Holiness the 14th Dalai Lama. No other Dalai Lama in the history of Tibet has commanded the love and respect that His Holiness Tenzin Gyatso enjoys. Any future Dalai Lama developing the allegiance of all Tibetans, regardless of religious belief or geographic origin, is extremely unlikely.

In all his proposals to Beijing, His Holiness has remained, and remains, very firm on two principles. First, while he is fully and sincerely committed to finding a way to achieve the well-being of the Tibetan people without seeking independence, he is unwilling to rewrite the history of Tibet. Second, he is explicit and firm in speaking on behalf of Tibetans from *all* regions of Tibet, not only those who were once governed by his Lhasa-based government. He deeply feels this moral obligation to all Tibetans because of their confidence in him as their guide and leader. Most importantly, he sincerely believes that the distinct identity of the Tibetan people can be preserved only if the Tibetan people have the opportunity to be united.

## OPTIONS IN THE ABSENCE OF CONTINUING DIRECT DISCUSSIONS

As previously mentioned, at the close of the Second Exploratory Talks meeting in October 1984, it was clear Beijing was no longer interested in pursuing any serious discussions with us. Despite its continuing denial of any such change in its position, the facts speak otherwise. While Gyalo Thondup was periodically in touch with some PRC officials, they were no longer willing to engage with us, effectively slamming the door in our face. It was clear that the hard-liners within the upper echelons of the CCP hierarchy had gained increased access to Deng Xiaoping, even managing to create a deep wedge between him and Hu Yaobang and the other more "liberal"-minded leaders. The struggle within the leadership was not just about Tibet but about the overall direction the PRC was headed. Inaccurate intelligence about our motives was also used by the hard-liners to support their views. And sadly, our own unprofessional and uncoordinated approach provided additional support for this mistaken perception. At the same time, some individuals and institutions in both Lhasa and Beijing deliberately distorted and sometimes even manufactured events to advance their own agendas.

When the Second Exploratory Talks team returned to Dharamsala, we submitted a report to His Holiness sharing our views. In addition, I sought a separate audience to elaborate on the report's conclusions and provide suggestions for alternative action. I remember that my audience was on a weekend, as I was received at His Holiness's residence rather than his office. I conveyed my personal observations, explaining that I did not see any desire on the part of the PRC government to make a serious effort to engage in any further dialogue. "They are just playing for time," I told His Holiness, "so therefore, we ourselves must seriously think about alternatives." I offered two specific recommendations: to strengthen our connection with Tibetans inside Tibet and to take the Tibet issue to the global arena.

### *Strengthening Ties with Tibetans Inside Tibet*

I am a firm believer that the most valuable asset in our struggle is the Tibetan people themselves, particularly those residing inside Tibet. As long as all of us, both inside Tibet and in exile, maintain a strong commitment to realizing our fundamental rights and the concept of a unified Tibet, I know there is reason to be optimistic that a solution will be found. Therefore, in the wake of our 1984 trip to Beijing, I recommended not only to His Holiness but also to other officials of the exile administration that we strengthen our connections inside Tibet. I did not mean we should encourage violent activity or any kind of sabotage. Instead, I spoke of the importance of mobilizing the Tibetan people behind the vision and plan of His Holiness, whom all Tibetans undisputedly regard as our leader.

I specifically remember speaking about the need to increase our outreach inside Tibet to then Secretary of the Department of Security Jampa Kalden. I remarked that in some ways Beijing had simplified our task because all Tibetan areas, not just the TAR, were governed under an easily defined administrative structure. To start with, I recommended creating a file for each county containing information about prominent individuals both currently residing inside Tibet and in exile, including lamas, recognized scholars, former chieftains, and other influential individuals. I said to Jampa Kalden: "You are from the Chamdo area and I myself from Nyarong. Who are the prominent people from our own counties who are in exile? Just collect the names and their connections inside Tibet."

In this way, we gradually began to collect data about the situation in Tibet and to build a strong network there. During my audience with His Holiness, I further recommended that we create a separate department to manage this effort. I remember saying: "Your Holiness, the name that I propose for that department may not be appropriate, but I suggest it be རྒྱལ་ནང་ལས་དོན་ཁང་།." The English translation would be something like the "Department for Inside Tibet Affairs." I also suggested that His Holiness recruit the best minds to work in the department and that its mandate be restricted solely to matters inside Tibet. "Everything done in the office should be about 'inside Tibet,'" I said, "so that even in their dreams, the staff thinks only about Tibet." I believed that even though Beijing had stonewalled us, this was an opportune time for us to build connections, understand the real feelings of the people inside Tibet, and galvanize their support behind His Holiness's efforts.

I also took the opportunity of my audience with His Holiness to request that I be excused from taking any further part in our effort to reach out to Beijing. I confessed that with no Chinese-language skills or understanding of the Chinese mind, combined with the lack of progress we had made during the two Exploratory Talks missions, there was very little more that I could contribute in that area. Instead, I told His Holiness that I believed I would be more useful to the Tibetan cause working with officials in India or other foreign countries. Thus began my over thirty-year-career bolstering Tibet's visibility in the international community.

## *Going Global*

For many years, His Holiness and dear friends of Tibet from all over the world had been working to gain recognition and support from the international community for the cause of Tibet. But it wasn't until the mid-1980s that the Tibetan leadership in Dharamsala developed a formal strategy that, among other things, included a decision to concentrate its efforts on engaging the international community. Our revised plan was not a result of expanded resources or a desire to poison the PRC's international relations. Indeed, the opposite was true. As discussed in the previous chapter, for a number of reasons, Beijing was no longer interested in carrying out any serious, direct discussions with us. In the face of these altered circumstances, we needed to adopt new methods to try to reestablish communication. We had to be realistic. We had scant resources, precious little experience in foreign relations, and no political power vis-à-vis our well-equipped adversary. Moreover, only a very few Tibetans were working on the issue, and we were all learning how to advocate as we went along, seeking advice whenever and wherever we had the opportunity.

## EVOLUTION OF THE DEPARTMENT OF INFORMATION AND INTERNATIONAL RELATIONS

Ever since I joined the service of His Holiness the Dalai Lama in the late 1960s as a staff member of the CTA, my main interest has been trying to create global awareness of the Tibetan cause. His Holiness has also always been aware of my long-standing passion for this aspect of our work. After serving one term (1979–1982) as an elected member and Chair of the Tibetan Parliament, I rejoined the CTA in 1982 as Additional Secretary in the Department of Information and Publicity (DIP). I was very happy with this appointment because being part of the DIP gave me the opportunity to carry out some of the things that I had been envisioning for a long time.

In those days, all the major governmental departments were headed by Secretaries, not by Kalons. My close friend and cofounder of the Tibetan Youth Congress (TYC), Sonam Topgyal, was then Secretary of the DIP. This was an additional benefit for me, as he and I held very similar views, predisposing him toward supporting the activities I wanted to pursue. At that time the DIP was the least important among the existing departments. This was clearly reflected in all matters down to and including the office space provided to it. But it had a dedicated staff, many of whom were keen to take on new initiatives and think "outside the box."

Secretary Topgyal and I agreed that to make the department an effective vehicle for creating greater global awareness of Tibet, we needed to broaden its mandate. At the time I joined, the responsibility of this office was precisely what its name indicated: providing information about Tibet and preparing publications. By contrast, we wanted the DIP's focus to be on international relations, in essence reviving the previous, short-lived Chi-sid Khang or Foreign Office.

When His Holiness first reorganized the administrative system after reaching India, he designated an office for foreign relations headed by Neushar Thupten Tharpa, a monk official who had held a senior administrative position in Tibet, assisted by Gyalo Thondup and a few others. One of the main initiatives of the original Foreign Office, it seems, was lobbying at the United Nations. That is the reason the Office of Tibet was originally set up in New York rather than Washington, D.C. Neushar Thupten Tharpa, with his full ministerial position, moved to New York to head the newly established office.

But the Foreign Office soon met with its demise, although the precise reason for its closure is difficult to ascertain. It appears that both Gyalo Thondup personally and the Office itself were purged from the administrative structure of the Dharamsala government. The Foreign Office's work was divided among different offices including the Private Office of His Holiness, the Bureau of His Holiness the Dalai Lama in Delhi, and the newly designated DIP. In my view, internal politics played a pivotal role in shutting down the Foreign Office. It would have been difficult to maintain the office without giving Gyalo Thondup a prominent formal role, which the Dharamsala establishment was reluctant to do.

Gyalo Thondup was one of the very few Tibetans with the necessary experience and connections in that universe. Maintaining the office yet failing to give him an official role would have been insulting. Closing the office avoided that potential embarrassment. Many of the official Tibetan documents of the time went further in not even listing Gyalo Thondup as having been a Minister or Kalon during that period. In others, however, he is referenced as co-Kalon or Minister with Neushar Thupten Tharpa, or as Assistant Kalon. At the same time, people supportive of Gyalo Thondup to this day refer to him as "Sa-wang Chenpo," a title given to full-fledged Ministers in the old Tibetan system.

Because of sensitivities of the Indian government and other practical concerns, we could not establish a formal Foreign Office in India. Precisely for that reason, the "Foreign Office" that was set up in Dharamsala was just called Chi-sid Khang. Its old signboard remained in place for many years after the office itself was shut down. We decided to rename the DIP the Department of Information and International Relations (DIIR), with the clear mandate of not only providing information about Tibet to interested parties but also actively taking the Tibet issue to the international arena.

Accomplishing this refocus was not an easy task. For some reason, the nature of which I am still unclear about, there was strong pushback from the Kashag. Not until I was appointed to the Kashag by His Holiness in 1986 was I able to get the necessary approval. Even then, it took considerable time and effort. Finally, on April 4, 1988, we were rewarded with a department that had the clear mandate of raising Tibet's profile in the eyes of the global community. We also gradually brought administration of all of the worldwide Offices of Tibet under our control, a restructuring that was absolutely essential for working effectively at the international level.

When I was first inducted into the Kashag in 1986 as a Deputy Kalon, I was given independent charge of the Departments of Religion and Culture, Health, and, briefly, Education because Tethong Tenzin Geyche, who was then holding those portfolios, had rejoined the Private Office as a Secretary to His Holiness, while maintaining his position as a Kalon. I didn't hesitate to tell my colleagues very bluntly that my interests, and I believed my talents, lay in the field of international relations, and that I didn't think I could be of much value overseeing the portfolios I had been assigned. It took a while for me to get the portfolio that I wanted and to upgrade the DIP to the DIIR. To achieve that result, I had to invoke His Holiness's name. I recall frankly telling my colleagues that each one of us was appointed by His Holiness for a specific reason based on our interests and our skills. I knew for sure that he didn't appoint me to look after the departments of Culture, Religion, Health, or Education.

I inherited a small but very enthusiastic staff from the DIP that had now become a full department. My friend and colleague Sonam Topgyal continued as Secretary. We didn't have as many officers as the department does now, but those few were capable and dedicated individuals, including Dekyi Khedrup and Thubten Samphel, as well as Kelsang Gyaltsen. Other early staffers included Lhasang Tsering, who has since left government service but continues to remain active with the Tibet issue and who headed the TYC for many years with great passion. Bhuchung Tsering, Atisha Tenzin Phuntsok, and Dagpo Sonam Norbu, all committed Tibetan advocates, were products of the DIIR. A good team was in place.

I also tried to get the best equipment for the office, including computers, which in those days were not only expensive but also a very rare commodity. The DIIR was the first office to have them. I installed a telephone at my residence, again the first person within the CTA hierarchy to acquire such a modern convenience. While I knew some people thought I was simply showing off, the telephone was essential to my work. Given the time differences between Dharamsala and the various Offices of Tibet abroad, most of my conversations took place in either the late evening or early morning. Not surprisingly, soon thereafter, all my colleagues in the Kashag followed my lead in installing telephones at their residences. I am very happy to have been a convenient excuse for them to modernize their offices.

I also realized that those of us charged with representing Tibet's interests in the international community must be well versed in diplomacy. Not only did we need to forge relationships on a personal level, but we also had to master even such small things as how to conduct ourselves at meetings and formal events. I started sending my colleagues on as many trips abroad as possible so they could become comfortable in their roles as Tibet's ambassadors. We also realized we needed larger and more formal facilities to welcome foreign dignitaries and other government guests to Dharamsala. While I was able to convince my fellow Kashag members of our needs, budgetary constraints precluded building the complex I had in mind. In consultation with Secretary Topgyal and other senior colleagues, we decided to raise the funds ourselves if the Kashag would allocate a site for us on the grounds of the CTA Secretariat. Although it was not easy, we succeeded not only in raising the funds necessary to build a basic facility but also in giving the building a distinctive Tibetan look. As it is the first building you see when you enter the Secretariat, we thought it was important that the face of the CTA reflect the beauty of traditional Tibetan architecture.

Once again, even though I suffered criticism from some of my colleagues who believed I was giving special treatment to my office and my staff, our efforts were richly rewarded. We were ready not only to welcome the world to Dharamsala but also to venture out seeking friendship, support, and guidance. I think we did remarkably well, given the constraints under which we had to function. Of course, our greatest fortune was and is having His Holiness as our leader, supported by the large number of dedicated friends without whose wisdom, experience, and compassion we could not have elevated the issue of Tibet to the level of prominence on the international stage that it has reached today.

## INITIAL OUTREACH TO THE INTERNATIONAL COMMUNITY

In the 1980s, the highest priority of the PRC leadership, particularly of Deng Xiaoping, was to bolster the PRC's standing in the world so that it would be accepted as a legitimate, respected member of the international community. Beijing understood the tremendous advantage to be gained by building relations with Western countries, particularly the United States. In light of this, we realized it would be to our advantage to reach out to Western leaders with the goal of encouraging them to use their leverage to convince Beijing to restart meaningful discussions with us. Thus, our clear and unambiguous purpose in taking the Tibet issue to the international stage was to reestablish a direct connection with the PRC leadership through this new route.

Although I have explained our motivation to PRC officials on numerous occasions, they remain intent on accusing us of undertaking this initiative primarily to harm the PRC's interests. As a Tibetan Buddhist, I believe it is essential for the world to understand the true reasons underlying our international efforts. In our religious tradition, motive is more important than the act itself. I try to remember and apply this principle in all aspects of my life—that I shouldn't judge an event by simply looking at the act. Instead, I need to examine the motivation behind the conduct. Under this standard, the true nature of all our acts on behalf of Tibet must be viewed as the concrete expression of our honest and sincere motivation to reengage Beijing in meaningful discussions. Sadly, this is the exact opposite of what the Chinese allege and for which they persist in vilifying us.

I am sure that scholars one day will write a much more detailed analysis than I have about how the Tibetan people succeeded in making Tibet an international issue, because succeed we did. This was, of course, a joint effort undertaken by many Tibetans, but we would not have had the success we did without the dedicated and continuing help of our friends in the international community. One of my main goals of this chapter is thus to pay respect and express sincere gratitude on behalf of the entire Tibetan community to the many friends who helped us so selflessly and steadfastly in this endeavor.

### *Focus on the United States*

Because of our limited resources for bringing Tibet's concerns to the international stage, we had to pick the one area of the world most likely to influence Beijing.

We eliminated the developing world from consideration, as the PRC government's only interest in the region was the potential reward of massive resource exploitation. It didn't care about the PRC's political standing in the eyes of these "marginal" states. We also recognized that because the PRC was beginning to engage economically in these regions, particularly in Asia, we would have less success in obtaining support from those leaders anxious to capitalize on Beijing's overtures. Because the United States was the PRC's main diplomatic focus, and we simply didn't have the resources to reach out to all the European nations at the same time, it became our priority.

By the late 1980s, the PRC was positioning itself to become increasingly important to both US government and business interests. It hired some of the most prominent public relations firms to polish its image and was aggressively exploring how to exploit its increasing leverage with multinational corporations eager to invest in the PRC. Their greed for business opportunities had already led many corporations to become Beijing's most influential lobbyists. These firms contributed to Beijing's public relations campaign both by hiring prestigious lobbyists to carry their message and in commissioning purported "experts" to write articles for influential newspapers and to publish "scholarly" books. We faced a formidable challenge from this diplomatically savvy and well-funded machine. But despite our minimal resources, we managed to hold our own and often fare better than the PRC in the court of public opinion.

For some time, we had known how important it was to establish a physical presence in the United States, particularly in Washington, D.C. In the 1980s, with the assistance of longtime Tibet supporter Michael van Walt van Praag, the Washington, D.C., law firm of Wilmer, Cutler & Pickering began providing pro bono representation to His Holiness and the CTA, even registering as a Foreign Agent on our behalf. While we have been blessed with many wise and steadfast friends over the years, Michael is the one who has maintained the longest uninterrupted association with us. He has worked closely with His Holiness and the Tibetan leadership since the early 1970s. He was the main organizer of His Holiness's first visit to the West, the 1973 trip to Europe.

In addition to our many dear and committed friends, what we had that Beijing didn't was a group of extremely dedicated people working with us, including our staff at the International Campaign for Tibet (ICT), where I was based for more than twenty-five years, until my retirement at the end of 2014. The guidance and support we received from many members of the US Congress and their staff were unprecedented. They took an interest because of a heart connection to the Tibetan people and our rich culture. I used to boast that while Beijing had these prominent, expensive public relations firms working for it from 9:00 a.m. to 6:00 p.m., that was the limit of their efforts. But for those individuals helping the Tibetans, the cause became a part of their lives. Not only did they work from 9 to 6, but Tibet followed them home and everywhere else they went. It was because of the steadfast dedication of these individuals, many of whom volunteered their time, that we enjoyed the successes we did.

Was it easy? No, it was very difficult, particularly in the beginning. It was one thing to get expressions of support for human rights and religious freedom in Tibet because most Western politicians feel comfortable with these issues, which are ingrained in their respective cultures. But when we started talking about substantive political matters, it became much more difficult. We couldn't convince governments to support our efforts to begin negotiations, as they all assumed we were seeking Tibet's independence, something, unfortunately, they weren't willing to support. It wasn't until His Holiness announced his Middle Way Approach, first articulated in his speech to the European Parliament in 1988 in Strasbourg, France, that governments became more comfortable with our political aspirations.

## ADDRESSING CONCERNS OF LACK OF CLARITY

His Holiness has always been committed to resolving the Tibet issue through direct communication with the PRC leadership. He has personally written Chinese leaders seeking opportunities for dialogue as well as contacted them through the PRC Ambassador in Delhi and through other intermediaries, including foreign government representatives and private individuals, about whom I will speak in later chapters. But a looming impediment to expanding our outreach was the lack of a clear and defined proposal to present to Beijing.

Beginning with his response to Deng Xiaoping's 1979 overtures, His Holiness has never included a demand for Tibet's independence. In fairness, however, early on, we did not provide Beijing with a clear and specific proposal outlining the parameters of the relationship we envisioned. At the time, we were in the midst of serious discussions in Dharamsala, and our position was constantly evolving based on past communications with Beijing and contemporary events. For example, when Deng Xiaoping first reached out to His Holiness, he also articulated his famous "one country, two systems" approach. While we knew that this option was formulated primarily with Taiwan and Hong Kong in mind, we had reason to believe that Tibet might also be addressed within this or a similar framework. We were waiting to see what Beijing might propose before offering any details from our side, but we knew any solution would require Tibet to remain part of the PRC.

During our Exploratory Talks meetings in 1982 and 1984, we were also very clear with our counterparts that we were not seeking independence. Rather, we communicated our hope that any solution would take into consideration Tibet's special status as specifically acknowledged under PRC law. We expressly complimented Beijing on its Nine-Point Reunification proposal for Taiwan, noting that Marshal Ye Jianying's September 30, 1981, statement on the issue was very promising. While Taiwan would remain within the PRC, the proposed solution gave it tremendous opportunities, including the right to pursue its own political and economic systems, maintain its own armed forces, and so forth. Because the conflict between Beijing and Taipei was ideologically based, there were no differences between them with regard to the integrity of China. Moreover, both parties were predominantly Chinese with a common cultural heritage. By contrast, Tibet and the Tibetan people have their own distinct and separate identity, with a unique culture, language, and religion, important factors we contended should be taken into consideration in devising a solution.

Not surprisingly, our counterparts immediately rejected our proposal and underlying analysis. I don't know whether one should read their response as arrogant or simply matter-of-fact, but it was both brief and to the point: "No, you cannot expect to get what we are willing to give to Taiwan, because Taiwan is yet to be 'liberated.' Tibet has already been 'liberated' and is now very much a part of the PRC. We are offering these things to Taiwan because it is not under our jurisdiction, while you people are physically under our control. So don't even think about it." Thus they made it clear that no special circumstances would be considered; any resolution would be based on politics alone.

I recap these considerations here to highlight the context in which we were formulating our proposal. We were evaluating various options, including the idea of a federation that, at the time, was the recommendation of a number of international experts, including scholars from the PRC. Given that the PRC was a multiethnic state composed of many peoples, including the Tibetans, Mongols, Uyghurs, Hui, and others, the thought was that the best way to preserve unity was a federation model offering substantial autonomy to each of these groups in return for their acceptance of PRC sovereignty. We sincerely believed that the best way to maintain the PRC's unity, to which Beijing was uncompromisingly committed, was not by suppressing but rather by recognizing the unique and distinct identities of these different peoples.

Beijing, however, felt that we were not being sincere and were deliberately playing for time. Even some international observers sympathetic to our cause felt we had not been sufficiently explicit. Sadly, this further fueled the PRC propaganda machine. As the PRC was very aggressively trying to win global recognition and access to the international arena at the time, when questioned by foreign governments on the status of Tibet, they answered that we were the ones holding up progress. Beijing argued that it had reached out to us, but we had not communicated what we wanted. Beijing then went even further, alleging that our failure to provide a concrete proposal revealed our insincerity and our true agenda to obtain independence.

## DEVELOPMENT OF THE MIDDLE WAY APPROACH: A MAJOR BREAKTHROUGH

In the late 1980s His Holiness responded to this call for clarification by propounding what has come to be known as the Middle Way Approach. This proposal is not at all complex. It is exactly what it says it is—a middle way, or an accommodation between parties with two widely divergent viewpoints. On the one hand, the vast majority of Tibetans desire to be totally free of external rule and operate as a sovereign nation. At the other extreme lies the PRC government, with its uncompromising position on the issue of sovereignty and integrity of the PRC. The Middle Way Approach basically acknowledges the PRC's entrenched position that the country not be divided while recognizing that the Tibetans are a distinct people with a rich civilization who will not accept total absorption into the PRC. Through the vehicle of the Middle Way Approach, the Tibetan people would be given the opportunity to preserve their identity while the PRC would achieve the desired recognition of its sovereignty.

A discussion of the background leading to the development of this strategy and the attendant obstacles that had to be overcome reveals its true genius. As I wrote in the preceding chapter, by the mid-1980s formal relations between Dharamsala and Beijing had come to a standstill, partially due to miscommunication and misreading of each other's positions. The PRC leadership had also become much more arrogant and assertive, realizing it no longer needed to resolve the Tibet issue to further some of its immediate objectives.

While His Holiness has always believed that a solution to the Tibet issue can only be achieved through direct dialogue with the PRC leadership, in the late 1980s, the Tibetan people were inspired by the unprecedented global movements for democracy and freedom then occurring around the world. In the Soviet Union and Eastern European countries, earth-shattering changes were taking place that not even the most experienced political pundits had foreseen. It was but natural that the exile Tibetan movement sought to take advantage of this global trend, warmly accepting the generous and sincere support of these emerging democracies. But Beijing viewed Tibet's new opportunities and enthusiastic support from these nations as indicative of our "true colors," i.e., a desire for Tibet's independence.

In some ways Beijing's hostile reaction to our global activities is understandable. However, during this period, through various channels, His Holiness continued to reach out to Beijing, never wavering from his commitment to resolve the issue without seeking separation. Some of the more farsighted and broadminded PRC leaders, including Yan Mingfu, then Minister of the United Front, also tried to maintain some connection with us. But it was also very clear that by this time hard-line CCP members had gained more influence over Deng Xiaoping, greatly undermining any effort by the more liberally minded individuals to move the issue forward.

One question kept on surfacing in the minds of the senior leaders who remained committed to resuming talks: the need for His Holiness to be very specific and make a public announcement rejecting independence as an option. Many of our friends in the international community expressed similar thoughts. His Holiness and some of us assisting him also came to the same conclusion: he needed to issue a formal statement not only to publicly reaffirm his message to the PRC leadership but also to clarify his position in the eyes of the international community.

### *The Five-Point Peace Plan*

Accordingly, on September 21, 1987, at a special meeting of the Human Rights Caucus of the US Congress, expressly convened to afford the Dalai Lama the opportunity to announce his policy, he presented the Five-Point Peace Plan.[1] While the proposal neither explicitly rejects independence nor specifies autonomy as the goal, its substance makes clear that independence was not being suggested.

His Holiness the Dalai Lama addressing the US Congressional Human Rights Caucus and announcing his Five-Point Peace Plan for Tibet, Washington, D.C., September 21, 1987. (Left to right) Congressman Charlie Rose, Tethong Tenzin Geyche (Secretary to His Holiness), the author, His Holiness, Congressman Tom Lantos
International Campaign for Tibet

Rather, His Holiness had two primary objectives: creation of a Zone of Ahimsa and stopping the relocation of Chinese into Tibet. Both of these proposals were premised on Tibet remaining within the PRC. The wider international audience welcomed this statement as both forward-looking and containing concrete goals. It also treated the Plan as a clear signal that His Holiness was not talking about independence.

His Holiness deliberately used the Sanskrit word *ahimsa*, rather than "peace," as the latter has a much more limited meaning. *Ahimsa* means much more than nonviolence or even peace. In selecting this term, there is no doubt His Holiness was inspired by Mahatma Gandhi's philosophy. But one must be careful not to confuse or equate His Holiness's proposal with King Birendra's declaration of Nepal as a "zone of peace," first proposed in 1975 during his coronation. Although the idea was not embraced at the time, in the mid-1980s there was a renewed effort by a section of the Nepalese people to resurrect it. And while Beijing did not formally endorse the plan, it was widely viewed, especially by Indian officials, as a Chinese-inspired attempt to remove Nepal from India's sphere of influence.

While historically a sovereign nation, because of similarities in culture, ethnicity, and geographical location, Nepal is viewed by many, if not uniformly by the Nepalese people, as a satellite state of India. So when the King of Nepal declared: "I want to make my kingdom into a zone of peace," he seemed to be indicating a desire to distance Nepal from India thereby becoming a "genuine" buffer state. This Nepalese dream has remained unfulfilled. Nepal continues to sway back and forth in allegiance between its two formidable neighbors as realities on the ground change and as politicians more interested in their personal power than in the well-being of their country pursue their selfish interests.

Beijing, however, and even a few Western observers thought His Holiness's proposal was in fact retaliation by India in light of King Birendra's declaration. They thought that India was trying to expand its influence farther north to cover the entire Tibetan Plateau, in an effort to counteract the perceived extension of the PRC's influence over Nepal. As evinced by contemporary media accounts, some members of the Indian government also believed that His Holiness's proposal was somehow connected with King Birendra's declaration, lending further credence to Beijing's suspicions.

I can assure you that this contention is baseless. I was very involved in assisting His Holiness with formalizing his proposal and am aware of the factors that went into his decision. The Five-Point Peace Plan was the result of serious contemplation, inspired by His Holiness's commitment to nonviolence, his Tibetan heritage, and the hope that Tibet could become a positive factor easing tensions in the region. While he did consult with senior leaders of the exile Tibetan leadership, the proposal was very much the personal vision of His Holiness from his perspective as a Buddhist monk and a man of peace. If one examines the Five-Point Peace Plan, it is clear that he is thinking about stability and peace in the whole region, not just in Tibet. His inspiration was very much rooted in his philosophy of Universal Responsibility.[2]

Unfortunately, while the international community responded favorably to the plan, Beijing reacted very negatively. On October 17, 1987, in the PRC's own "Five point" memorandum, pointedly written in Chinese, Yan Mingfu, then Minister of the United Front, conveyed Beijing's rejection and criticism of the Plan to His Holiness as follows:

> This year, the Dalai Lama visited the United States and openly raised an outcry about "Tibet's independence" on 21 September by propounding a "Five

> Point Peace Plan" at the Congressional Human Rights Caucus. A few splittists in Lhasa supported the Dalai Lama's splittist activities and created disturbances on 27 September and 1 October. The Dalai group has made "Tibet's independence" a major issue in foreign countries. Bolstered by foreign support, they harbored an empty hope of sponsoring splittist activities in Tibet. Taking advantage of our policy of allowing our overseas Tibetan brethren to visit Tibet, they sent people into Tibet and instigated the formation of underground organizations.

The memorandum continued:

> It is the mistake of the US Congress to offer the Dalai Lama a forum to talk about splitting the Motherland. This is in violation of the Shanghai Communiqué as well as the Communiqué on the Establishment of Sino-US diplomatic relations. Some members of the US Congress are among the foreigners indulging in such practices. These people are stretching out long arms to interfere openly in our domestic matters. Their actions have come under strong criticism from our people. Their intrigue will never bear fruits.[3]

### *The Strasbourg Proposal*

After discussion in Dharamsala and consultations with friends, His Holiness decided to elaborate on the Five-Point Peace Plan, to focus on Tibet and address Beijing's concerns. This led to the Strasbourg Proposal,[4] so labeled because it was announced on June 15, 1988, before the European Parliament then in session at Strasbourg, France. Like the Five-Point Peace Plan, this proposal was very well received internationally. There was consensus among our supporters and more neutral observers that this was an unambiguous statement that should alleviate Beijing's concerns. The bold and innovative Strasbourg Proposal was applauded by the global community, resulting in His Holiness's receipt of the Nobel Peace Prize in 1989.

The Strasbourg Proposal expressly conveyed His Holiness's commitment to a solution with Tibet remaining within the PRC. It further explicitly ceded control over defense and foreign policy to the PRC government. Under its terms, Tibetans were only looking to assume responsibility for culture, religion, language, traditional way of life, and other related areas. The only "foreign relations"

His Holiness the Dalai Lama addressing the European Parliament and elaborating on the Five-Point Peace Plan in a speech now known as the Strasbourg Proposal, Strasbourg, France, June 15, 1988
International Campaign for Tibet

Tibetans sought to undertake were with neighboring countries solely on matters of religion, culture, and regional or local trade.

The courageous decision of His Holiness to adopt and promote the Middle Way Approach created tremendous opportunity for Tibet at the global level. The explicit commitment to forego independence in favor of protecting the fundamental rights of the Tibetan people within the political framework of the PRC made it possible for governments to support His Holiness's efforts. Presidents, prime ministers, and many other government officials who had been reluctant to receive him in the past or to support Tibet's cause now openly welcomed him to their offices.

Unfortunately, Beijing not only criticized these meetings but also adopted all kinds of tactics to sabotage these burgeoning relationships, including downgrading governmental relations and canceling business and commercial engagements. But global leaders felt justified in their willingness to receive His Holiness because the proposal nowhere contradicted nor violated the "one China" policy that the PRC had successfully imposed on most of the nations of the world.

## *Misrepresentation of the One China Policy*

I would like to digress for a moment to clear up an issue that has hampered some governments from feeling they could support our cause. Despite the PRC's contentions, its current "one China" policy has nothing to do with the Tibet issue. Reference to my remarks to the Council on Foreign Relations on April 23, 2012, in Washington, D.C., should make this abundantly clear.

> The history of relations between Tibet and China—and between Tibetans and Chinese—is complex and cannot be understood simply in the context of the relatively young People's Republic of China. This may seem like an obvious assertion were it not for the fact that many of us do not study history sufficiently, and our friends in Beijing seem intent on convincing today's policy-makers not only that 'Tibet is an inalienable part of China' but also that relations with the PRC must be predicated on a notion—incorrectly applied to Tibet—that support for the Tibetan struggle violates the 'one China' principle . . .
>
> As I mentioned already, I wish to address a phantom cause for paralysis affecting the ability of some governments to put in place a credible and flexible policy on Tibet and the worsening situation there. This is the well-known—but apparently ill understood—'one-China' policy invoked by the Chinese government to prevent legitimate inquiry or engagement by members of the international community with respect to Tibet.
>
> The 'one-China' policy, as you must know, was created in the early 1970s as the instrument that enabled the United States to establish relations with the People's Republic of China and maintain relations with the Republic of China or Taiwan.
>
> Then U.S. President Richard Nixon and his national security assistant Henry Kissinger were responding to the Communist Chinese leaders' need for assurances on U.S. policy with respect to Taiwan when they told Chinese Premier Zhou Enlai and Communist Party Chairman Mao Zedong that the United States was not pursuing a 'two-Chinas' policy. In the 1972 Shanghai Communiqué, the United States artfully acknowledge that "all Chinese on either side of the Taiwan Strait claim that there is but one China and that Taiwan is part of China . . . and the United States does not challenge that position."

This 'one-China' policy paved the way for the joint communiqué establishing diplomatic relations between the United States and the People's Republic of China on January 1, 1979, and the adoption by the United States Congress of the Taiwan Relations Act that same year. Under the 1979 agreement, the United States recognizes the PRC government as the sole legal government of China, while the Taiwan Relations Act set out the nature of relations the United States would maintain with Taiwan in terms that were not inconsistent with the 'one-China' policy but protected the status quo and therefore the status of Taiwan, whatever that might be.

Adherence to the 'one-China' policy has been reiterated by successive American Administrations, sometimes making explicit reference to the communiqués mentioned above or to Taiwan's unchanging status. Although the 'one-China' policy was articulated in the context of U.S.-China and U.S.-Taiwan relations, Beijing increasingly demands that other governments with whom it establishes or maintains relations also endorse this 'one-China' policy.

What is the relevance of this discussion to Tibet? If one has to look for any reference point for China-Tibet relations, it is not the 1972 Shanghai communiqué, but the '17-Point Agreement.' In fact, the lack of relevance of the 'one-China' policy is precisely what I would like to address. No Tibetan government has ever claimed to be the government of China, so the application of the 'one-China' policy to Tibet—or for that matter, the PRC government's 'one-China' principle that stresses the inalienability of both Taiwan and mainland China as parts of a single 'China'—simply does not arise.

We have our differences with China's leaders when it comes to the history of Tibet and our historical independence from China but, as you well know, His Holiness the Dalai Lama's proposals and statements concerning ways to resolve the Tibetan question all envisage solutions that respect the sovereignty and territorial integrity of the People's Republic of China as the state is constituted today. These proposed solutions call for the exercise by Tibetans of genuine autonomy within the People's Republic of China and within the framework of its constitution—not for independence.

Yet, the PRC government vigorously pursues efforts to extend the applicability of 'one-China' to Tibet and, in recent years, it has misled a number of governments into believing not only that the 'one-China' policy applies to Tibet, but that it restricts the extent to which their government officials can

> interact with Tibetan leaders in exile, including His Holiness the Dalai Lama. We believe that the intended effect of China's initiative is to limit outside governments from playing a constructive role in promoting a mutually acceptable negotiated solution for Tibet. Indeed, by accepting the applicability of 'one-China' to Tibet, governments are subtly aligning themselves with the Chinese position that the Dalai Lama is trying to 'split' China.
>
> While the PRC government is trying to intimidate some governments into believing that meeting with Tibetan exile leaders would violate the 'one-China' policy, in reality, this assertion is counter-intuitive to the policy. If there were a connection, the adherence by any government to the 'one-China' policy would have the opposite effect. Since the policy was developed precisely to make it possible for the United States to continue to conduct relations with Taiwan while recognizing the PRC government as the sole government of China, if the policy were at all relevant to Tibet, it then should enable governments to conduct relations with the Tibetan exile leadership and His Holiness the Dalai Lama without incurring Beijing's displeasure.[5]

Beijing's resort to this argument in an attempt to thwart nations from embracing the Tibet cause is telling. Our efforts to elevate the Tibet issue to a prominent place on the global stage have been extremely successful. The PRC, in its concern over this united support, is forced to resort to this contrived and irrelevant contention.

### *Chinese Reaction to the Strasbourg Proposal*

Beijing's reaction to the Strasbourg Proposal was the same as its response to the Five-Point Peace Plan: total rejection. Beijing also stepped up its campaign to label His Holiness a "splittist," alleging that our activities were aimed at achieving independence. Our close relationship with some of the prominent leaders of emerging democracies in Eastern Europe and their sympathy for the Tibet movement gave the PRC leaders grounds for their suspicions. But we were not working with these individuals and groups in an effort to "split" the PRC. Particularly with regard to our support of the emerging democracies that were appearing around the globe, I never tried to hide or deny our actions. As people longing for freedom, it was natural for us to be inspired by these global insurgencies.

Some of us visited many of the emerging democracies in Eastern Europe, primarily in the Baltic states, more than once in those days. I even went to

Mongolia and some of the Central Asian republics. My visits were very inspiring, and we were able to forge strong relations with a number of these movements, ultimately leading to formation of the Unrepresented Nations and Peoples Organization (UNPO) in 1991.[6] In some ways, His Holiness's philosophy of nonviolence and seeking a solution through dialogue inspired many of the individuals involved in the democracy movements of that era. Yet, even at the peak of the global movement for democracy, when totalitarian and communist governments were crumbling, His Holiness remained true to his word, reaffirming his commitment to seeking only genuine autonomy for the Tibetan people within the PRC and explicitly rejecting independence.

During some of our formal dialogue sessions with Beijing between 2002 and 2010, I had the opportunity to explain our activities of the mid-to-late 1980s to our counterparts. Several times they criticized us for our relations with the Uyghurs of East Turkistan, or Xinjiang Uyghur Autonomous Region, as the Chinese call it. At the time, few Uyghurs lived outside the PRC, and their issue was not high on the agenda of the international community. But there was a very cohesive and committed group of people speaking on their behalf, including my good friend Erkin Alptekin, son of the highly respected Uyghur leader Isa Alptekin. I remember telling my counterparts that rather than criticizing us for having relations with the Uyghurs, they should praise us for keeping the Uyghur movement fully committed to nonviolence and dialogue and away from relationships with militant Islamic groups.

When Rebiya Kadeer assumed leadership of the Uyghur movement, she met with me more than once seeking our help and support. I was very explicit that their efforts must remain nonviolent and that she should not give up hope of engaging Beijing in dialogue to find a solution. Sometime later she had the opportunity to meet His Holiness. He explicitly told her: "As far as I am concerned, I am committed to find a solution for Tibet without seeking independence." What more proof and reassurance of His Holiness's sincerity is needed?

## THE MIDDLE WAY APPROACH: HIS HOLINESS'S DEEPLY HELD VIEW

Some of us in Dharamsala had the great honor of assisting His Holiness in developing the Strasbourg Proposal, but very few outsiders were consulted. Nevertheless, for quite some time, the perception persisted that the Strasbourg Proposal was the work of non-Tibetans. There were even rumors that no Tibetan text of the proposal even existed or that it was originally written in English and then translated into Tibetan. This is totally false.

His Holiness is a very strong-minded personality and not someone who does things at the urging of others. Be it the Five-Point Peace Plan, the Strasbourg Proposal, or any other important pronouncement, each one is the result of his thoughts and vision. Of course, he does discuss his ideas with senior aides, Tibetan leaders, and close friends, but the basic ideas are always his own. I know from personal experience that he takes considerable time in developing his ideas before sharing them with others. The few non-Tibetans who were consulted either deeply cared about Tibet or were experts in international law. It would have been foolish for us not to consult professionals on matters where we lacked experience or knowledge, particularly as we were presenting the proposal to, and trying to convince, the PRC leadership as well as a sophisticated international audience.

Moreover, as many of these proposals needed to be translated into English, we tried to be sure that the translation accurately reflected His Holiness's intent, so much so that at times, we unintentionally invoked his displeasure. Occasionally we rejected a literal translation of His Holiness's words in favor of an English expression that captured his intent and avoided what we viewed to be the perils of an exact translation. For example, in the Strasbourg Proposal, while it was very clear he was not talking about independence, we did not use the word "autonomy." Instead, we defined the proposed relationship between Tibet's existing autonomous regions and the PRC central government as "in association." Many of us working on the English version were uncomfortable using "autonomy" because the Chinese historic interpretation of that term had proved meaningless. All the Tibetan areas within the PRC were already officially designated as "autonomous," yet the Tibetans had no practical control over any aspect of their affairs.

His Holiness was very unhappy with our suggestion. "I am talking about autonomy, why are you not using that word?" Even with our explanation, he remained skeptical. "What is the word that you people were using?" We said, "in association." He thought for a while and said, "I may not even be able to repeat that word. What I am asking is genuine autonomy. So, I am going to talk about autonomy."

In retrospect, I must admit that we were not as careful as we should have been with some of the terms we used in translating these important documents. We could have been far more creative and consciously chosen words more familiar to the Chinese, who were our most important audience, a fact I think we failed to fully appreciate. As those of us assisting His Holiness had all grown up in India, our understanding of terms such as "autonomy," "self-rule," and "self-governance" were Eurocentric or Western in perspective. So I think we unintentionally did some disservice in this regard.

Learning from our past mistakes, during our formal negotiations beginning in 2002, we were very careful with our diction. Samdhong Rinpoche, then head of the Kashag and an eminent scholar, played a leading role in preparing all the associated documents. We tried to use terms that could be better understood by the Chinese and were less confrontational. Of course, our positions had not changed; we were just presenting them in what we hoped was a less provocative manner. The best example of this is the Memorandum on Genuine Autonomy for the Tibetan People,[7] presented to Beijing in 2008 during the Eighth Round of talks. Not only were we extremely sensitive with our verbiage, but also we made an extra effort to consult with and include suggestions from Tibetans inside Tibet. Quite a few of them, in fact, pointed out that we had been a bit careless and inconsistent in our language in the past.

The Chinese, especially the Communist Chinese, assess the meaning of every word very carefully. If different terms are used in different documents to describe the same situation, they become suspicious, believing we are not sincere or have a hidden agenda. In addition, I have learned that some Tibetan words when translated into Chinese can have several meanings conveying very different messages. We therefore learned to have a document translated into Chinese before we shared it with Beijing. That way, it was not left to the discretion of some Chinese bureaucrat who might have his own agenda or personal bias that might give our words an unintended meaning. Having the document already translated into Chinese further assured us that the leadership at the highest levels could read it immediately, precluding the ability of any lower-level bureaucrats to delay, alter, or suppress our intended meaning.

## THE INTERNATIONAL COMMUNITY EMBRACES THE MIDDLE WAY APPROACH

In conjunction with His Holiness's delivery of the Five-Point Peace Plan and the Strasbourg Proposal, we devoted our efforts to educating and gaining the support of the international community. To draw Beijing back to the negotiating table, we needed help. We did not restrict our efforts to governments and international forums but also lobbied individuals who had close, friendly relationships with Beijing. Our goals remained unchanged; we were still knocking at the PRC's door, but this time accompanied by mutual friends. His Holiness personally led this effort, and it was his personality, commitment, and unwavering allegiance to the truth that opened all the doors and created all the opportunities.

His Holiness's dedication to seeking a solution benefiting all Tibetans through his Middle Way Approach was indeed visionary, enabling us to take the Tibet issue to the next level on the international stage. Influential world leaders started paying serious attention. They began meeting with His Holiness and his envoys, including myself, and including Tibet as part of their discussions with the PRC leadership, urging them to resolve the issue through dialogue. Some even made special trips to Beijing carrying personal communications from His Holiness to Deng Xiaoping and later to Jiang Zemin. PRC leaders at the highest level received these dignitaries with great courtesy, engaging them in substantive discussions on Tibet. We fully recognized that Beijing was not motivated to undertake these discussions with global leaders out of a newfound desire to appease us. It did so out of self-interest. Beijing did not wish to alienate influential Western leaders or jeopardize its own developing friendships in the international community. In those days, Beijing was giving the highest priority to improving relationships with the West, particularly the United States. It thus evinced a willingness to engage with the Dalai Lama to demonstrate its seriousness and sincerity.

This turnaround in the international community's position on Tibet did not happen solely as a result of the efforts of the Tibetan leadership. The nonstop hard work and dedication of thousands upon thousands of Tibet friends throughout Europe and America were instrumental to our success. Tibet's support base was unique and extraordinary. It included prominent politicians, Hollywood celebrities, scholars, students, environmentalists, human rights activists, and of course, Dharma students of various Buddhist teachers. It touched every level of society and included people of differing political and social views.

But our efforts to fully engage the support of the international community were not without significant obstacles. Even though the Middle Way Approach was farsighted, there was considerable opposition and numerous objections to the proposal when the specifics were delineated, proving the age-old adage that "the devil is in the details." Beijing, for example, started telling some visiting Western dignitaries that the Dalai Lama's proposals were "unreasonable," "unobtainable," and "totally unacceptable." One of their main arguments was our purportedly exaggerated view of the geographic extent of Tibet. Beijing contended that His Holiness was unjustifiably trying to expand Tibet's traditional borders by including vast areas within the Chinese provinces of Qinghai, Sichuan, Gansu, and Yunnan, to encompass an area covering one-fourth of the PRC's total landmass. Unfortunately, their contentions had an adverse impact on some of our most committed supporters.

### *President Carter's Efforts and Concerns*

Former US President Jimmy Carter is one of those influential world leaders we consulted when formulating the Strasbourg Proposal. His Holiness reached out to President Carter early on, knowing that the former president is a very spiritual person with a strong commitment to human rights and other global humanitarian issues, and at the same time, a close friend of Deng Xiaoping. Even though President Nixon was the first US President to go to the PRC (1972), it was President Carter who formally recognized the PRC in 1979. We were first introduced to President Carter by Richard Blum, the husband of Senator Dianne Feinstein, who even accompanied us on some of our visits to the Carter Center. Another friend who was helpful in our relationship with President Carter and his staff is Joel McCleary, a Buddhist and ardent friend of Tibet who had worked in the Carter White House.

When we internally finalized the Strasbourg Proposal, I was sent from Dharamsala to the United States to consult with President Carter on the text. I remember that long flight from New Delhi to New York, where I met Tethong Tenzin Namgyal, who was then head of the US-based Office of Tibet. We then flew together to Minneapolis, Minnesota, where President Carter was attending a conference.

Our meeting is vividly etched in my mind. President Carter was an extremely meticulous person. He read the text of the Proposal very carefully. Then he read it through a second time, but more quickly. In total, this must have taken him about a half hour, and you could have heard a pin drop in the silence. Finally he put the document down and asked what the Dalai Lama's "bottom line" was. I responded: "Mr. President, this is His Holiness's bottom line." President Carter then replied that if that were true, we should begin by asking for something more. I explained to him that many of us felt the same way, but His Holiness remained adamant, declaring that he wasn't a politician but a Buddhist monk, and bargaining is not in his nature. His Holiness wanted to be straightforward and clear about what he was asking for. After listening carefully to my explanation, President Carter admiringly observed that if His Holiness's approach succeeded, it could revolutionize the field of negotiations.

He made some comments on the text, but nothing substantial. I am sure he probably had other ideas, but I now understand that he wanted to be respectful of His Holiness, particularly after I explained to him that this was a sincere, straightforward proposal from a Buddhist monk, not from a politician.

When we began making efforts to reach out to Beijing again in the mid-1990s, after another period of isolation, I went back to President Carter for his guidance and support. In all, I must have gone to the Carter Center to meet with him dozens of times. He was always very gracious and kind. He was also extremely thorough, and I had to be well prepared for each of our meetings. The only other person I remember being as conscientious as President Carter was India's former Foreign and Education Minister M. C. Chagla, who chaired the All-Party Indian Parliamentary Forum for Tibet (APIPFT). At one point I worked full-time as a consultant to this group. I learned so much from President Carter, Minister Chagla, and a number of other seasoned diplomats. They provided essential guidance and support for those of us just entering the minefield of diplomatic relations and political intrigue.

President Carter was also very helpful in facilitating communications with the PRC leadership at the highest levels. In 1987, he went to the PRC mainly to discuss Tibet with Deng Xiaoping, trying to jump-start a dialogue between us. He was visiting Asia for other purposes, but his trip to Beijing was the primary focus of the tour. Before he left, I went to Atlanta twice to brief him, and we agreed to meet in London after his visit.

After his trip, I called President Carter's staff as planned to arrange an opportunity for him to brief me. I never got through and my calls weren't returned. After a few days I knew something was wrong. In the past, if the President were busy, his staff would tell me, and they might suggest I come to Atlanta. But nothing like that happened this time. Weeks went by without any response from the President or his Atlanta office. Very concerned, I finally asked for help from Joel McCleary, who had helped facilitate our initial meetings.

After my call, Joel contacted several of President Carter's senior staff. They reported that the President was unhappy, feeling that we had not properly briefed him, and as a result, he had been put in an uncomfortable situation with Deng Xiaoping. After weeks of Joel's efforts, President Carter agreed to receive me at the Carter Center. To my surprise, he was as pleasant as ever, but he was clearly very unhappy with me. He said: "I never knew the Dalai Lama was demanding 'Greater Tibet,' which includes large areas of neighboring provinces," including Qinghai, Sichuan, Yunnan, and Gansu. He said he couldn't understand why we were making such "unreasonable" demands on Beijing.

He told me he had strongly urged Chairman Deng to resolve the Tibet issue through dialogue and to allow the Dalai Lama to visit Tibet, as he and I had discussed prior to his trip. While Deng Xiaoping was receptive to our overtures, he told the President that the Dalai Lama was making an "unobtainable" and "unreasonable" demand. Deng Xiaoping had showed President Carter a map and said that we were not just talking about Tibet but asking for huge areas of China, in fact one-quarter of China's land mass. I am also extremely confident that Deng Xiaoping further mischaracterized the proposal as one seeking independence, even though His Holiness was explicit that he was looking for a solution that would keep Tibet within the PRC.

It was only then that I realized our mistake. I had not explained to President Carter the parameters of a unified Tibet. I apologized, acknowledging that we should have been more specific about our proposal. I then explained that His Holiness's prime objective is, and has always been, safeguarding the Tibetan people's distinct identity. Any negotiated political resolution is but the handmaiden to this paramount goal. Accordingly, His Holiness advocates on behalf of *all* Tibetans, not just those residing in the TAR. He feels morally bound to speak on behalf of us all because, as demonstrated by our undertaking the Great Oath of Unity, we have designated him as our common leader and spokesperson. Moreover, he is fully convinced that for the Tibetan people's unique cultural, linguistic, and religious identity to survive, all Tibetans inside the PRC must find some way of being together. His proposals for the future thus include all Tibetan-inhabited areas, including those currently subsumed in the existing Tibetan autonomous regions lying within the Chinese provinces of Qinghai, Sichuan, Yunnan, and Gansu.[8]

For me, this episode was a painful but important lesson about the need to be explicit. It was clear that President Carter had been put in a very awkward situation, particularly for someone who is so careful and thorough. He must have been very embarrassed. By the time of our follow-up meeting, I had already had the opportunity to brief his senior staff on our position, and it seemed that President Carter had been thoroughly briefed by them. I think he understood the rationale behind His Holiness's view, but he made it very clear that Beijing would never accept our proposal. At least I was happy to convince him that we had not deliberately misled him, and I was able to leave the Carter Center with the assurance of his continued interest and support.

His Holiness was planning a trip to the United States later in the year. President Carter not only agreed to meet him but even invited him to his home in Plains, Georgia. It was a wonderful gesture. I had the opportunity of accompanying His Holiness to many important and historic meetings, but this visit to Plains is among the most memorable. His Holiness took the opportunity to personally explain to President Carter why he was asking for a unified Tibet, discussing his moral obligation to obtain a solution addressing the needs of all Tibetans regardless of where they reside inside the PRC. His Holiness asked for a map so that he could support his view of the true geographic reach of Tibet. We managed to get one from a book in the President's personal library. His Holiness humorously remarked that if we used the Chinese definition of Tibet, then he wasn't actually a Tibetan. I could clearly see the President beginning to grasp the legitimacy of His Holiness's arguments. However, from his knowledge of politics and having seen the reaction of Deng Xiaoping, he remained skeptical of the viability of our position.

We were all deeply impressed with the President's and Rosalynn Carter's down-to-earth sincerity and lack of ostentation. They returned to the house he had built in Plains after his term ended. The Carters also had a small cabin in Ellijay, Georgia, called Blue Ridge Pine. I remember visiting him there in July 1991 with Rinchen Dharlo, who was then head of the Office of Tibet.[9] Walking into this cabin was like walking into a hermitage. I was very moved that someone who had been the most powerful person in the world, the President of the United States, was living so simply. When I was in President Carter's presence, I felt as if I were with a truly spiritual person. His honesty, faith, and integrity infuse his entire being. He has been such a good friend of Tibet, and I am grateful for his support, advice, and goodwill.

### *Senator Dianne Feinstein's and Richard Blum's Support*

Richard Blum had long been interested in the Himalayas and its culture when in 1978 he took his future bride, Dianne Feinstein, on a visit to Dharamsala. Since then, their support of His Holiness and the Tibetan people has grown stronger and stronger. In 1979, they were the first to invite him to visit the United States. Their very personal friendship spans decades and their affection for His Holiness is intense. Senator Feinstein's excellent political and diplomacy skills are much complimented by her husband's straightforward, and to be honest, sometimes blunt, approach. Richard's respect and love for His Holiness run very deep. He will not tolerate any remarks disrespectful of His Holiness. Surprisingly, his wife often has to "kick him under the table" to restrain him from making "undiplomatic comments" to PRC leaders and officials in defense of his dear friend, the Dalai Lama.

In 1985, when Jiang Zemin became mayor of Shanghai and Dianne Feinstein was San Francisco's mayor, the existing sister city relationship became even stronger. Unlike some of these matches where the relationship is primarily symbolic, these two mayors took the alliance far deeper than just a public relations exercise, broadening US-PRC relations in general. Because of their long-standing

The author and Richard Blum in Washington, D.C.

friendship with His Holiness and the relationship they had forged with Jiang Zemin, Dianne and Richard became very important players in our relationship with senior PRC leaders.

Over the years, the two of them visited the PRC many times. Three of their trips, in 1991, 1993, and 1997, were undertaken solely to carry important messages from His Holiness to Jiang Zemin. In his book *An Accident of Geography*, Richard writes in detail about the Senator's and his efforts, a brief excerpt from which is reproduced here:

> For more than twenty-five years, working with Lodi Gyari, the Dalai Lama's chief envoy in Washington until a few years ago, Dianne and I tried to establish a sensible dialogue between the Chinese leadership and the Tibetans—the same kind of dialogue we've been able to have with those same leaders on many topics. Dianne very much shares my strong views on Tibet. A Chinese official in Beijing once accused me of brainwashing her. "Guilty," I responded, quickly and proudly.[10]

However, just as Deng Xiaoping was able to convey a very strong message rejecting the notion of a "greater Tibet" to President Carter in their meeting, Jiang Zemin forcefully argued to Senator Feinstein that our demands were "unrealistic," "unreasonable," and "unobtainable." As I have a close personal relationship with the Senator, I have been able to discuss this with her in a very frank manner. I told her that even if she felt our definition of Tibet was "unrealistic" and therefore "unobtainable," I hoped that as a friend, she would not see it as "unreasonable." I asked: "What is unfair or unreasonable about a people yearning to be unified in this day and age? The Tibetan people's desire for unification has undeniably strong historic, religious, cultural, and linguistic bases."

I further explained in detail the evolution of the unified Tibet concept that had been embraced by the Tibetan people, as evinced by the Great Oath of Unity and put into place in the exile government, specifically through geographic representation in the Tibetan Administration, the Tibetan Parliament, and the Kashag. I told her that His Holiness was morally committed to a unified Tibet, that the Tibetan people had put their faith in him, and if he departed from that position, the institutions in Dharamsala would become irrelevant. I also reminded her that almost all the areas for which His Holiness is advocating are already designated by the Chinese as Tibetan autonomous areas.

I asked the Senator if she would try to convey to President Jiang Zemin His Holiness's thinking as articulated in his Middle Way Approach. She candidly shared her concerns with me that Beijing would never agree to His Holiness's proposal. I responded that with wise guidance from friends such as her, we would find a way. In any event, our fundamental position should be respected, just as the world respects the PRC's existing dominion over Tibet. I further reminded her that prominent Chinese leaders, including Zhou Enlai, were on record stating that the desire of the Tibetans to be collectively governed in one administrative unit was a legitimate request. Marshal Chen Yi had, in fact, specifically advocated our approach in suggesting merging the Tibetan areas of Qinghai, Sichuan, Gansu, and Yunnan provinces with the TAR to form one unified Tibetan autonomous region.

Whenever His Holiness visits Washington, D.C., the Senator and her husband host him either in the Senate Dining Room or at their residence. They invite senior administration officials, diplomats, congressional colleagues, and other people of influence to meet His Holiness. Over the years they have developed a sophisticated understanding of the Tibet issue, and Senator Feinstein has given serious thought to finding a way to bring the Tibetans and Chinese closer to an understanding. It would be premature for me to write about these ideas because the issue remains unresolved and any hypothetical ideas could be misunderstood. Nevertheless, both the Senator and Richard continue to be engaged on the Tibet issue and to help in all ways possible.

## RENEWED OUTREACH TO BEIJING

Despite Beijing's negative reaction to the Strasbourg Proposal, His Holiness continued to want to reach out to restart discussions. Sometime in mid-July 1988, at the conclusion of one of the rather lengthy sessions of a routine meeting with the Kashag, together with his senior Secretaries the Reverend T. C. Tara and Tethong Tenzin Geyche, His Holiness rather casually said: "Oh, since I have already publicly announced that we are ready to have a dialogue with the Chinese government and I have already selected my team, we need to do something about appointing our representatives." Everyone present responded in agreement. His Holiness paused for a little while and then said: "Maybe Lodi Gyaltsen should lead this." I was quite surprised because after my return from the PRC as part of the Second

Exploratory Talks delegation in 1984, I strongly conveyed to His Holiness that this was one task I felt inadequate to undertake.

There was silence in the room. I immediately responded that while I could not say "no" to His Holiness, the team should be led by someone else. I would be honored to participate, even acting in the number two position, but I should not be the leader. I had joined the Kashag not too long before and was still only a Deputy Kalon. The Chinese people, like many others, are very status conscious. I was concerned that they might erroneously interpret a team led by a Deputy Kalon as indicating that the initiative was not of the highest priority. One of my colleagues, Phunrab Lobsang Dhargye, then mentioned some other names. But at that point, His Holiness abruptly ended the meeting, saying: "Anyway, let's see about it." I could clearly see he was not happy with my reaction.

A few days later, I sought an audience with His Holiness because I was about to leave on a trip to Europe, including several Eastern European countries. I apologized for my impulsive reaction, saying that if His Holiness felt I would be of some service, then I would certainly undertake the responsibility. I did ask, however, for His Holiness's approval to appoint his Secretary, Tethong Tenzin Geyche, who at the time was also a member of the Kashag, to be the team's leader. I assured him that I would devote my full time and energy and do most of the legwork required for this important task, but that Tenzin Geyche was the best choice as head of the delegation.

His Holiness was quite surprised by my suggestion, expressing some reservations because of Tenzin Geyche's rather strong views and forthright manner. I agreed with His Holiness's assessment wholeheartedly but said that the designated leader should be someone with the public image of being critical, and Tenzin Geyche fit the bill. In addition, while it was entirely up to His Holiness to decide on the members of the team, its success would depend a lot on the personal relationships between them. I have a close personal friendship with Tenzin Geyche and tremendous respect for him as a person. Even though we might differ on some issues, we trust each other. These were some of the reasons I thought he would be a good choice.

I further said that while Beijing might also not feel comfortable with someone like Tenzin Geyche because of his rather tough views, his being the Secretary to the Dalai Lama would add a great deal of credibility to the team. This would make the Chinese more comfortable and maybe make them take us more seriously. I emphasized this point because I knew that Beijing has always been suspicious about whether people acting as His Holiness's emissaries were truly speaking on his behalf, were being faithful messengers, or enjoyed his complete trust.

His Holiness agreed with my reasoning and approved my proposition. I had, of course, taken Tenzin Geyche into confidence before I spoke with His Holiness. Initially, he was absolutely against the idea for the exact same reasons as his Holiness. He said: "I am very frank and blunt, and somehow I may even damage the relationship rather than help." But I gave him my reasons, and in the end, he did not forbid me from bringing the matter up with His Holiness.

The next day I left for Europe. It was a rather long trip. During those days we were making serious efforts and enjoying considerable success in reaching out to international communities. We were building stronger ties with the newly emerging democracies in Eastern Europe, particularly with the three Baltic nations, who were struggling to come out of the Soviet Union's political control. I returned to Dharamsala after several weeks. Either the very next day or the day after, I went to brief His Holiness on my trip. Before I walked into the meeting, Tenzin Geyche pulled me aside and said: "You will be very unhappy with me, but after giving it much thought I went to His Holiness and told him to remove my name from consideration." He really felt like he was the wrong candidate for this important position. I was personally disappointed, but I had to respect his decision.

During this period, we were again able to reconnect with Beijing, principally through Gyalo Thondup. My colleague Tashi Wangdi, who was then a member of the Kashag and concurrently His Holiness's Representative in Delhi, was also in close touch via the local PRC embassy. Another Kashag colleague, Alak Jigme Rinpoche, who was personally keen to be involved in the dialogue efforts, was also periodically in touch with the PRC embassy in Delhi.

In addition to our direct efforts, several international personalities approached the PRC government, encouraging dialogue with His Holiness. These efforts were no doubt an important factor contributing to Beijing's willingness to restart discussions, although His Holiness's historic speech at Strasbourg was the key factor. Even though Beijing publicly criticized the Strasbourg Proposal, it gradually indicated that some of the proposal's provisions could be considered.

Upon my return from abroad, my colleagues in the Kashag informed me of the possibility of resuming direct dialogue with Beijing and that they had chosen the negotiating team members, and His Holiness had approved their choices. They had waited for my return before making the formal announcement. My colleague Tashi Wangdi and I were appointed as coleaders. I accepted the position because

I was very happy that Tashi Wangdi was the other team leader. He had been in the Kashag several years ahead of me and was rich in experience, as well as being calm and patient in nature.

On July 27, 1988, the Kashag issued a press statement saying that the negotiating team would be headed by Tashi Wangdi, Kalon for Information and Security, and Lodi Gyaltsen Gyari, Deputy Kalon for Culture, Religion and Health. Other members included Jigme Lhundup (Alak Jigme Rinpoche), Deputy Kalon for Security; Wangdu Dorjee, Former Kalon; Sonam Topgyal, Secretary of the Office of Information and International Relations; and Lhamo Tsering, Former Additional Secretary of the Security Office.[11] The team would be assisted by Pema Gyalpo, His Holiness the Dalai Lama's Representative in Tokyo; Kelsang Gyaltsen, His Holiness the Dalai Lama's Representative in Geneva; and Michael van Walt van Praag as legal adviser.

I was also very comfortable with the composition of the team. All of the proposed members had been discussed several times in the past. My only suggestion was adding Tethong Tenzin Namgyal. He had earlier been removed from consideration at the suggestion of his brother, Tenzin Geyche, who at the time was slated to lead the team. Tenzin Geyche thought that two brothers being part of the same delegation would not be appropriate. He was adamant. At the time, I opposed his position because Tethong Tenzin Namgyal had a great deal of experience. I further pointed out that my younger brother Pema Gyalpo was also under consideration and that did not make me uncomfortable; nor should he be with regard to his own brother's participation. Each of them had the requisite skills and expertise and would be a valuable addition to the team. In any event, as Tenzin Geyche was no longer part of the delegation, I thought Tenzin Namgyal should be reinstated. Despite my urgings, the team's composition was finalized for the time being. My colleagues noted, however, that should the dialogue actually take place, team membership could always be changed.

I understand Beijing expressed some unhappiness with the proposed composition of the delegation primarily because of the youth of most of the members. They suggested we should include some more senior leaders. I was not at all involved in any direct discussions with the PRC leadership in those days, as most of the time I was away from India in Europe and the United States, trying to build up our international support base. The first half of 1988, I was focused on laying the groundwork for His Holiness's speech at Strasbourg, holding strategy meetings with various Offices of Tibet and influential friends of Tibet. My colleague Tashi Wangdi was also very much involved in these efforts.

Communication with Beijing was primarily through Gyalo Thondup. I remember some conversations with him during which he gave me the impression that the Chinese were not so concerned with the supposed youth of the delegation but rather had objections to particular individuals. At the same time, in the formal briefings he gave us, he reverted to the youth argument, with the implication that Tashi Wangdi's and my membership in the TYC was the source of the problem. In any case, I do not wish to write too much about this particular period, as I was not directly dealing with the PRC authorities and thus not privy to their real concerns. In the end, Beijing seems to have agreed to the team's composition, but was adamant in not accepting any non-Tibetans. Their opposition to Michael van Walt van Praag's participation was not subject to negotiation.

The PRC representatives further indicated their willingness to receive us in Beijing, Hong Kong, or, if we thought it more convenient, at any of the PRC's embassies or consulates abroad. However, due to a variety of factors, the opportunity for this dialogue never materialized.

In his book, Gyalo Thondup has a chapter entitled "Our Negotiations Fail" in which he holds Dharamsala responsible for the breakdown in relations during this period. He further singles out Kalon Tashi Wangdi for criticism in this regard, a conclusion I think is completely unfair. He also implies that the Indian government had a hand in derailing the process, in part by supposedly encouraging us to choose Geneva as a venue for the talks without considering all the factors.[12]

Geneva was, in fact, selected after detailed discussions and consultations within the Tibetan leadership. The choice was certainly not made under the influence of any other person or institution. In those days, we felt that if the talks were held outside the PRC, it would give us a better opportunity for discussion among team members and potentially for consultation with His Holiness. In addition, because of past experience, we felt we would be psychologically handicapped if the talks were held in the PRC. I remember many foreign diplomats I met during that time who were quite pleased that the Chinese were willing to meet us outside the PRC. They saw this flexibility as a positive signal demonstrating serious effort on Beijing's part to build confidence.

Almost everyone thought that we should take the opportunity to have the first round of talks outside the PRC. We would have preferred Delhi or Washington,

D.C., where we had better facilities, but we thought we should be sensitive to Beijing's concerns. A section of the PRC leadership, especially the intelligence branch, always harbored suspicions that the American and Indian governments were using us to stir up anti-China sentiment. Given these factors, we thought Geneva was a neutral choice and therefore more acceptable.

It is true that we could have handled the situation more skillfully. Gyalo Thondup should certainly have been taken into confidence before these important announcements, including composition of the negotiating team and suggested venue, were made. Beginning around mid-1983, he withdrew from any involvement on Dharmasala's behalf in dealing with Beijing. I do not know why that happened. Dharamsala certainly needed his help, and with his departure, the whole process slowly broke down. By the time I joined the Kashag in 1986, I strongly urged my peers to once again seek his help in reaching out to Beijing. Even though we were building strong international support, in the end we had to have a way to contact Beijing directly to take advantage of our diplomatic successes.

I remember visiting Gyalo Thondup by myself several times, and with my colleagues from the Kashag on other occasions, asking for his help. Both in my private audiences with His Holiness and during formal Kashag meetings with him, I urged him to encourage his brother to reengage. From the beginning I have known that Gyalo Thondup is not a team player, and there is always a danger of his taking unilateral decisions without proper consultations with Dharamsala. That is not a correct practice, and it should not happen. Because of my personal relationship with him, however, I thought I could help work things out. I think to some extent my efforts were helpful, but in the end, I also realized that he is strong-minded and unlikely to change his ways. In my view, the Tibetan leadership's failure to engage his service, combined with his refusal to become a team player, was most unfortunate.

## PROPOSED VISIT BY HIS HOLINESS FOR THE 10TH PANCHEN RINPOCHE'S MEMORIAL SERVICE

As our relations with Beijing were at a standstill, the tragic passing away of the 10th Panchen Rinpoche on January 28, 1989, actually presented us with another opportunity for reengagement. Gyalo Thondup called Dharamsala from Hong Kong, saying that he had just come back from Beijing and was carrying an invitation from the PRC government for His Holiness to participate in Panchen Rinpoche's memorial service.

The initial reaction among us in Dharamsala was quite positive, even though there were obvious concerns over such a visit. After a quick consultation, the Kashag decided to ask Gyalo Thondup to come to Dharamsala immediately to personally brief His Holiness and the Kashag and bring the official invitation. In fact, I was asked to call him, as was often the case because of my perceived close relationship with him. When I spoke with him, he was very excited and kept on saying: "This is great opportunity, this is great change. Deng Xiaoping himself took the decision, etc. . . ." Gyalo Thondup promised to take the earliest flight to Delhi and head to Dharamsala. I knew His Holiness was also keen to meet with him, as he had instructed one of his secretaries to urge him to come to Dharamsala. I remember Tenzin Geyche sharing with me the gist of his conversations with him. We were both impressed by his excitement and optimism.

A few days later, Gyalo Thondup arrived. He first briefed His Holiness and then came to meet the Kashag. He was very animated, speaking at length and offering many good reasons we should take advantage of the opportunity. Throughout his presentation, however, he kept referring to the proposal as an "official invitation." We all believed that he meant it was issued by the PRC government. However, at one point late in the meeting, it became clear that this "official invitation" was actually from Zhao Puchu, then Chair of the Chinese Buddhist Association.

It was like pouring water over fire. Silence descended over the room, and the whole mood of the Kashag abruptly changed. Individual Kalons were visibly upset and offended, offering dismissive comments such as: "This is not an official invitation, it is only from a Buddhist organization." Gyalo Thondup tried to explain, saying that the invitation was extended at the explicit instruction of Deng Xiaoping. Yan Mingfu, then Minister of the United Front, had personally approached Zhao Puchu to issue the special handwritten invitation on Deng Xiaoping's behalf. The proposal was therefore very much official.

One important point that Gyalo Thondup repeatedly raised during the briefing was that such a visit by His Holiness would give him the opportunity to reconnect with Deng Xiaoping and a few other senior leaders he had personally met during his 1954–55 visit to Beijing. Everyone agreed on the importance of such a face-to-face meeting, but Gyalo Thondup was asked again and again whether he had concrete assurances from Yan Mingfu that it would actually occur. While acknowledging that he had not explicitly discussed this with Yan Mingfu, he asked why Deng Xiaoping would make such an effort to invite His Holiness if he didn't intend to meet with him.

I fully agreed with Gyalo Thondup's arguments and firmly believed His Holiness should make the trip. In fact, I thought the invitation coming from the Chinese Buddhist Association, rather than directly from the government, made it even more convenient for His Holiness to accept. But the damage was done. The interest and guarded enthusiasm initially expressed by the Kashag was lost. Had Gyalo Thondup been explicit from the very beginning that he was carrying an invitation from Zhao Puchu, who was asked to extend the invitation on behalf of Deng Xiaoping, the reception would have been quite different.

After lengthy and heated discussions, there was no consensus in the Kashag. Both the Kashag and Gyalo Thondup sought an opportunity to discuss the matter in the presence of His Holiness. Secretary Reverend T. C. Tara also participated.[13] The arguments for and against the visit were extensively reviewed, although in a more formal and respectful manner. The major concern, of course, was His Holiness's safety, but the other two issues were the likelihood of a meeting with Deng Xiaoping and whether His Holiness would be given the opportunity to visit Tibet. Reverend Tara was particularly concerned that if His Holiness went to Beijing but not to Tibet, it would deeply sadden the Tibetans inside Tibet. We ultimately agreed that asking for a visit to Lhasa would not be feasible. Even if Beijing dared to allow His Holiness to go, which was extremely unlikely, such an important visit would need to be planned far ahead of time.

His Holiness patiently listened to everyone's views. He understood the importance of the opportunity, but he also appreciated the concerns that people expressed. In the end it was decided that Gyalo Thondup should go to Delhi and, through the Chinese Ambassador, ask if the meeting with Deng Xiaoping and other leaders could be confirmed and whether His Holiness could make a short visit to Kumbum, a monastery in a Tibetan area of Qinghai Province. We thought that a visit to Kumbum might be seen by Beijing as more appropriate and less risky than one to Lhasa, as Qinghai Province is the birthplace of both His Holiness and Panchen Rinpoche. A final decision would be made depending on Beijing's response.

Gyalo Thondup enthusiastically assumed the task. Unlike his rather forceful and assertive attitude during the meeting with the Kashag, in the presence of His Holiness he remained respectful of the views expressed by those strongly opposed to the visit. One of the things that I admire and appreciate in Gyalo Thondup is the genuine respect that he shows His Holiness, his biological younger brother. His whole personality softens, as does that of many strong-willed individuals, in the presence of His Holiness. The ability to bring forth calm, reflection, and warmth in those he meets is indeed one of His Holiness's most precious attributes.

After the audience, Gyalo Thondup and I happened to queue up together for use of the lavatory. He leaned over to me and asked: "Rinpoche, what did you think?" I candidly told him: "It didn't go well. You know very well that you will get no positive response from the Chinese Ambassador for both the matters that you have agreed to raise. I do not know why, knowing the situation well, you so readily agreed to take this matter to the Chinese Ambassador for consideration." He reflected for a while and nodded his head. "I know, I know."

Everyone who had taken a position either for or against the trip was sincere. The concern for His Holiness's safety was the main negative factor, but past experiences of betrayal and broken promises by Beijing were also very much on people's minds. Some of us were quite certain that if the visit took place, His Holiness would definitely meet Deng Xiaoping and other senior leaders. It was simply not in the nature of the Chinese Communist regime to confirm such a meeting ahead of time. I reminded our colleagues that when US President Nixon journeyed all the way to Beijing, he was not assured of meeting Chairman Mao. And when the meeting finally happened, it was with very short notice and at a very unusual hour. That's just how the Chinese behave.

Not surprisingly, Gyalo Thondup was not able to acquire the requested assurances. Consequently, His Holiness did not make the trip. Much later I confirmed through Phuntsok Wangyal and a few others that the decision to invite His Holiness was the result of very heated and complex deliberations at the highest level of the PRC leadership. Many of the conservative and leftist elements vehemently opposed the idea, but in the end, Deng Xiaoping prevailed and gave the go-ahead to Yan Mingfu to invite His Holiness. As I wrote in the preceding chapter, Ngapo Ngawang Jigme strongly argued in favor of issuing the invitation, as he too felt that only a direct face-to-face meeting between His Holiness and Deng Xiaoping could move the Tibet issue forward.

Gyalo Thondup devotes a full chapter in his book to this event, entitled "Another Opportunity Lost." Sadly, I wholeheartedly agree with his opinion that we missed a major opportunity when we failed to approve the proposed visit.[14]

However, he too must bear some responsibility. I believe this happened for two reasons: lack of clear communication internally and lack of formal institutional procedures for addressing the matter. I was told that the hard-liners in Beijing took full advantage of our refusal to let His Holiness visit. They started spreading the word that our failure to agree to the trip vindicated their position that the Dalai Lama was actually not at all interested in returning.

## LOSS OF CONTACT IN 1989

In addition to this missed opportunity to reengage with Beijing, we suffered another setback later that year. With renewed efforts, through both direct contacts and various other connections, we obtained Beijing's commitment to a meeting in Hong Kong later in 1989. But, once again, events conspired to eliminate this opportunity. The domestic situation in the PRC dramatically changed in the wake of the June 4 Tiananmen Square tragedy, while the subsequent disintegration of the Soviet Union had a profoundly negative impact. These events combined to preclude any opportunity for serious dialogue between us and Beijing, then and for several years to come.[15]

## CHAPTER 14

# Developing United States Support for Tibet

Our communications with Beijing once again suspended, in the early 1990s we focused on strengthening our internal institutions and streamlining communications in Dharamsala while continuing our outreach to the international community. We remained focused on the United States, as by the late 1980s we had begun to develop close relations with members of Congress and the executive branch, yielding tangible results.

### EFFECTS OF HIS HOLINESS'S CONTINUING EFFORTS TOWARD DEMOCRATIZATION

His Holiness the 14th Dalai Lama's efforts toward democratization have been a lifelong endeavor. Even as a young man in Tibet he wanted to bring major reforms to the political system. After coming into exile, slowly but steadily he instituted changes to afford the people a more direct role in governance. He has always wanted Tibetans, either directly or through institutions such as the Tibetan Parliament, to play a greater role in the selection of cabinet members. In the late 1980s, he instructed the Kashag to accelerate this process. In August 1989, it responded by convening a brainstorming session with members of the Parliament, government officials, and NGOs, as well as representatives of new arrivals from Tibet, numbering about 230 participants. Soon afterward, the Kashag prepared a five-point discussion paper for wider circulation within the Tibetan community at large to get further feedback. The five issues included the following:

1. The desirability of having a Prime Minister in the existing government.
2. Whether the Kalons (Ministers) should be elected or continue to be appointed by His Holiness.
3. Possible introduction of a political party system.
4. Whether the number and/or responsibilities of members of the Tibetan Parliament should be changed.
5. What other democratic changes should be made.[1]

Based on the feedback to these questions, and after serious discussion among the leadership, a consensus was reached to call for a conference of Tibetan leaders to take a formal decision on these important matters.

As I recall, the Tibetan community strongly favored a continued role for His Holiness in appointing members of the Kashag. Those of us in the Cabinet, however, realized that His Holiness was keen to make a major change. To pave the way for him to guide the Tibetan people toward his own farsighted vision, we all submitted our resignations on May 9, 1990, just days ahead of the conference called for May 11. With our resignations, the institution of the Kashag as originally constituted during the reign of the 7th Dalai Lama (1708–1757) came to an end. To this day, I feel a great sense of honor in being one of those who served in the Dalai Lama's Kashag as a direct appointee. We were the last such officials.

His Holiness personally addressed the May 11 gathering. He announced that to build a strong and viable community, the existing democratic institutions of the CTA needed to be strengthened. He then announced his decision to dissolve not only the Kashag but also the Parliament. He further suggested that those attending the conference should elect an interim cabinet lasting for one year. During that period, a new charter should be drafted that would establish the rules and regulations for future governance, including how the Kashag and members of Parliament should be elected.

Most of the conference participants found it very difficult to comprehend and accept such drastic changes, but His Holiness left no room for compromise or reversal of his position. He concluded his remarks: "The Dalai Lama's strength can be used only at critical situations where only the Dalai Lama can handle, at which time, I will put all my strength." The depth of his affection for the Tibetan people was further reflected in his promise "to serve the Tibetan people until my death." Many of us at that gathering, both old and young, could not hold back our tears. We all felt an overwhelming sense of gratitude and reverence toward him. His Holiness is so very precious. I hope my fellow Tibetans remember and appreciate his dedication to our collective well-being. We will face a situation where we need him to act upon his promise. In fact, I think we are facing it right now.[2]

While many of my colleagues in the outgoing Kashag decided to retire, I was among the few who decided to stay on, if elected, for the simple reason that I wanted to complete the restructuring I had started at the DIIR. Specifically, I wanted to set up a special Foreign Service cadre that would staff the DIIR, the Offices of Tibet, and the Kashag Secretariat, as well as His Holiness's Private Office. At the time, I was facing considerable resistance not only from the Kashag but also from a broader segment of the senior staff who thought I was trying to create an "elite" group that would have the best resources and facilities, as well as opportunities to fly around the world in supposed luxury. Perhaps I am to blame for this criticism in not showing them how tough it was to be perpetually on the move, begging for support and assistance from anyone who would listen.

Of the remaining Kalons who ran for election, only Kalsang Yeshi, who was then a Deputy Kalon and a recent inductee, managed to secure the minimum requirement set by His Holiness of over 70 percent of the vote. There was definitely incumbent fatigue. Under this strict standard, the delegates were able to elect only three individuals, the two others being Jetsun Pema, His Holiness's sister, and Tethong Tenzin Namgyal, who was then President of the International Campaign for Tibet (ICT) and His Holiness's Special Representative in Washington, D.C. The very afternoon of the election, His Holiness summoned all the outgoing and incoming Kashag members to the Palace for consultations. Of the newly elected Kalons, only Kalsang Yeshi and Tethong Tenzin Namgyal were present, as Jetsun Pema had not participated in the special conference. When all of us who had run for office walked in, His Holiness was roaring with laughter, saying that his advice of requiring more than 70 percent of the vote to be elected seemed to be too stiff a hurdle for some of us to jump over!

He immediately got down to serious matters, saying that even though it was to be an interim Kashag lasting only a year, it would be difficult for just three people to run it. Addressing the two newly elected Kalons, His Holiness complimented my international work, singling out my then recent visits to Russia, Mongolia, and some of the Baltic nations. He then advised them to ask me to continue taking responsibility for international relations. He said that of course, I could not be called a Kalon, but they should find a suitable designation for me.

What was important was that they should ask me to help with international relations as I was currently doing. Further commenting that neither of the two Kalons who were present, nor Jetsun Pema, had any experience in finance, he also counseled them to ask Phunrab Lobsang Dhargye, the outgoing Finance Minister, to continue being responsible for financial matters. These were quite explicit "suggestions."

He then turned to one of my colleagues, Alak Jigme Lhundup, who was the outgoing Minister for Security, complimenting him for establishing and maintaining close relationships with Tibetans inside Tibet. His Holiness said that of all the members of the different Fact-Finding Delegations he had sent to Tibet, Alak Jigme was the one who had kept in closest touch with the people inside by doing excellent follow-up work. I thought he was suggesting that Alak Jigme should also be retained, but he didn't continue with the same type of "suggestion" that he had offered with respect to myself and Lobsang Dhargye. It may be that His Holiness felt he should not give too many instructions to the now "elected" Kalons but just express his views.

There was immediate discussion of His Holiness's ideas. I remember Tenzin Namgyal suggesting that a good title for me would be "Advisor for International Relations for the Kashag," with the mandate of continuing my work. Kalsang Yeshi also expressed strong support for my continuing with international relations. He further suggested that since Tenzin Namgyal had been elected to the Kashag, I should take up residence in Washington, D.C., which had by then become a critically important venue, and from there conduct my responsibilities and oversee our broader international relations.

His Holiness's immediate reaction was not favorable. I remember him telling the gathering that I could travel to Washington from time to time as I had been doing, but that they needed me there in Dharamsala. Interestingly, Kalsang Yeshi made a rather forceful presentation of the importance of my being in Washington, and at that point His Holiness turned toward me and asked: "What do you think?" I replied that as it was only to be for one year, it didn't really matter. I wasn't intending to spend much of my time in that part of the world in any case.

After a few moments' thought, His Holiness approved the idea. That's how, within just a few hours of this historic political change in Dharamsala, my future also dramatically changed. Who could have foreseen this? In fact, when I returned home after the meeting, my wife thought that I was joking when I told her we were moving to the United States.

In keeping with His Holiness's instructions, the Kashag appointed me as Special Envoy of the Dalai Lama with broad responsibilities for international relations and a primary focus on the United States and Europe. Elevating the true needs of the Tibetan people over the early steps of a fledgling democracy was a very skillful exercise of Tibetan governmental authority. I was thus able to continue carrying out my former responsibilities, albeit with a much more Washington-oriented focus, despite my failure to meet His Holiness's well-intentioned but perhaps somewhat unrealistic election standard.

I was, however, very keen to offer myself as a candidate once the new charter establishing the permanent election criteria was introduced and adopted. I wanted to come back to Dharamsala, at least for a few years, to complete the projects I had set in motion at the DIIR. Halfway through my scheduled stay in Washington, however, I realized that I could be of more value by remaining there. I saw tremendous possibilities for advancing the cause of Tibet, especially in working with the US Congress. As in Dharamsala, I was again lucky to inherit a small but dedicated and professional team this time at the ICT. I gave up the idea of returning to Dharamsala and made arrangements for some of my children to join my wife and me, recognizing that the United States was to become our home, at least for the foreseeable future. At the time, I did not know that it would ultimately span twenty-five years.

Not surprisingly, my perspective on our efforts to elevate the Tibet issue in the international arena centered on our activities in the United States. I know that during this period there were many important events happening in other parts of the world, especially in Europe, that I may fail to mention but that undoubtedly contributed to the rise of the Tibetan cause on the international agenda. My colleagues, including Kasur Tashi Wangdi and Kelsang Gyaltsen, who were stationed in Europe, can contribute much more to this discussion than I can. Kasur Tashi Wangdi, for example, who studied in the United Kingdom and later served in Europe as His Holiness's Representative, was intimately involved with our efforts there and is thus an extremely knowledgeable source of information.

Just days after my appointment as His Holiness's Special Envoy, I left for Washington to formally take over the responsibilities from my friend and colleague Tenzin Namgyal, arriving around May 19, 1990. Because my family did not immediately join me and I was also shuttling back and forth between Dharamsala, Europe, and the States, I initially stayed with my friend Keith Pitts, who was then senior staff to Congressman Charlie Rose. I made the formal move with my wife, Dawa, and our two youngest children, Tashi Topgyal and Tenzing Tsering, in late February 1991. Our son was only around five and our youngest daughter was just three. We arrived on a bright and sunny but freezingly cold day. Fortunately, we already had accommodations in Takoma Park, arranged by John Ackerly from the ICT. He had even stocked the refrigerator with food. While we made many friends during our stay in Washington, Keith and John have a special spot in my wife's heart. A good personal friend, Tenzing Chodak, who was in those days working at the Office of Tibet in New York, also came to D.C., specifically to help us settle in.

This sudden move was very difficult for my wife, who had not traveled outside India except for a short trip to Switzerland and Germany a few years before. It was also heartbreaking for her to leave behind the rest of our children, who were in boarding school, and her father, with whom she was very close after the death of her mother when my wife was very young. But it is amazing how Dawa adapted to and adopted this new land as her home. Within a few years, she learned to drive and became our family's ever cheerful chauffeur. Almost every weekend, and sometimes even on weekdays, she would also host my colleagues and other friends of Tibet for her famous *momos*—Tibetan dumplings.

Her open house and open heart have been of immense help in my work. I am grateful to have a life partner who has always been selfless and understanding, but also strong-willed. Dawa is like the biblical Ruth. You may find my quoting a biblical figure rather strange, but I actually so excelled in my Bible studies at Mount Hermon School in Darjeeling that some of my Methodist teachers thought I was ready to convert. Ironically, their praise of my endeavors made me stop my Bible studies!

In addition to my responsibility as Special Envoy, the ICT Board appointed me as its President. I continued with this dual position until 1999, when I stepped down as the President with John Ackerly succeeding me. I continued on the ICT Board as Executive Chair until December 2014, retiring about two and a half years after my retirement as Special Envoy in June 2012.

A few years after the new charter was adopted on June 14, 1991, in accordance with its dictates, those of us who had been members of the earlier appointed Kashag were told we were permitted to maintain our title and the attendant protocol as a *Kasur* (former Minister). If we were interested in serving in the CTA, however, we would be appointed to suitable positions but lose our Kasur status.

I decided not to seek a further position with the CTA because maintaining the Kasur status was more precious to me, reflecting my position as one of the last direct appointees of His Holiness to the Kashag and having had the honor of taking the oath of office directly from him. Technically, with this decision I ceased to be a part of the CTA bureaucracy. Because His Holiness continued to head the government, as Special Envoy I remained very much a part of the Tibetan leadership, continuing to work with guidance from the Kashag.

## ALLIES IN THE US CONGRESS

Over the past thirty years we have been able to build tremendous support for Tibet in the US Congress. But this did not happen overnight.

### *Elected Officials*

Congressman Charlie Rose, a Democrat from North Carolina, was one of the first members of Congress to take an interest in the Tibet issue. In 1979, he became the first member of the House of Representatives to invite His Holiness to Capitol Hill. He remained at the forefront of all Tibet-related legislation until he retired in 1997. In 1987, the US Congress welcomed His Holiness to Washington, D.C., via resolutions introduced by Senator Claiborne Pell and Congressman Rose. The visit was officially hosted by the Chairmen of the Congressional Human Rights Caucus, Congressmen Tom Lantos, a Democrat, and John Porter, a Republican. As previously discussed, His Holiness took the opportunity of this invitation to deliver his Five-Point Peace Plan.

Encouraged by the overwhelming response of Congress to His Holiness's presentation, in consultation with some of our close friends, we took the decision to establish a permanent presence in Washington, D.C. His Holiness and the CTA already had a formal presence in New York (the Office of Tibet). We were advised to set up an NGO in Washington that could both lobby the US Congress and the administration and work very closely with the CTA and the Office of Tibet, to strengthen the CTA's global strategy.

Rinchen Dharlo had recently been appointed as His Holiness's Representative at the Office of Tibet in New York, replacing Tethong Tenzin Namgyal, who was planning to return to Dharamsala to fill a key position. In my capacity as the

Kalon for International Relations and in consultation with Rinchen, I sought His Holiness's approval to ask Tenzin Namgyal to stay in the States for some time to help establish our presence in Washington. Rinchen was also very keen to have Tenzin Namgyal remain for a while because of his many years of experience and his immensely valuable personal connections. Accordingly, a few months later we opened the ICT, and from then on legislative activity on Tibet rapidly escalated. Since then, the US Congress has passed more than fifty resolutions expressing support for His Holiness, condemning the PRC's human rights and environmental policies in Tibet, and providing direct assistance to the Tibetan people, both inside and outside Tibet.

Former Speaker of the House[3] Nancy Pelosi is one of those friends who always felt that our "ask" was too modest. She has tremendous respect for His Holiness and has always supported our initiatives. She has been such a loyal supporter of Tibet that I always felt comfortable approaching her even in the early morning hours or late at night if we had a pressing issue needing attention. She has also always been very candid with us, doubting the PRC's sincerity in fulfilling their promises to us, even if we supported awarding Most Favored Nation Status or the Olympics to the PRC. She is also among a handful of leaders in Congress, including Congressmen Frank Wolf and Chris Smith, who felt that it is a legitimate right of the Tibetan people to seek independence.

When Congresswoman Pelosi visited His Holiness in India in March 2008, in the wake of massive demonstrations throughout Tibet that were being brutally suppressed by the PRC government, she sent a very strong message of support for the Tibetan cause that was not lost on Beijing. She became the highest US dignitary to visit Dharamsala. I could see that even His Holiness was visibly moved by her visit. For the Tibetans, especially those inside Tibet, it was a huge morale booster, providing great encouragement for our struggle.

Visits by other members of Congress to Dharamsala and Tibet have also provided needed support for the Tibetan people. Congressman Frank Wolf visited Tibet "incognito" to investigate conditions on the ground. Congressman Chris Smith adopted Gedun Choekyi Nyima, the 10th Panchen Rinpoche's reincarnation, as a prisoner of conscience, ensuring that his plight would not be forgotten. Congressman Benjamin Gilman, a Republican from New York, was another great friend of Tibet, taking the lead on several legislative proposals. He was a very warm and wonderful supporter. When Congressman Gilman was Chair of

Former Speaker of the House Nancy Pelosi (center) holding a statue of Tara presented to her by the author and his wife, Dawa Chokyi Gyari, at her office soon after the 2016 US Presidential election

the House International Relations Committee, he led a congressional delegation on a visit to Dharamsala.

In 1995, Congressman Rose told me that he wanted to visit India to meet His Holiness and to learn firsthand about the resident Tibetan settlements. We arranged a trip for him at a time when His Holiness was giving teachings in Mundgod, in the southern Indian state of Karnataka, which is home to one of the largest Tibetan settlements in India. Together he and I flew to Goa and then made the long road trip in a small, rusty Maruti van to Hubli, the Indian town nearest the Tibetan settlement. It was an exhausting journey, and the road was quite rough, but Congressman Rose did not complain about the discomforts. When we arrived, His Holiness was very happy to receive him and introduced him to a congregation of over 50,000 people. Many important religious leaders were there, as was the entire Tibetan political leadership.

Friendships like these must be duly recognized. We must remember to acknowledge these individuals' contributions with sincere gratitude. These ardent supporters of our cause did not advocate on our behalf to receive medals, but out of human compassion. Over the years, many people have acknowledged and appreciated the loyal nature of Tibetans. We have always been known for our outward displays of gratitude. Our struggle is a moral one, and I hope we are not losing these values. While we have not had the resources to hire prestigious law firms or contribute to election campaigns, many people have recognized the effectiveness of our "Tibet lobby" in changing US policy, making Tibet a core issue in its bilateral relations with the PRC.

When they see the results that we have achieved, some people, however, think that we have a huge number of people working for us, as well as unlimited financial resources. But this is not the case. We have been successful because with careful planning, we built a strong and very influential group of bipartisan friends upon whom we could fully rely for help. We had brilliant minds such as Senator Patrick Moynihan to guide us. The Senator, who had previously served as US Ambassador to India and to the United Nations, was very knowledgeable about international issues. Some of us were fortunate to spend hours with him planning and strategizing how to advance our issue in the US Congress and present it to the international community. The Senator's then son-in-law, John Avedon, and his daughter Maura[4] have also been very active in the Tibet world. John's book *In Exile from the Land of Snows* is one of the most informative books covering the first few decades of our life in exile.

Finally, I must mention Senator John Kerry. I worked more closely and on more issues with Senator Kerry than with almost any other member of Congress. He was instrumental in developing support for all the major Tibet legislation that was enacted during his tenure in the Senate. Beginning in the 1980s, he supported legislation including S. Res. 82 (1989) and S. Res. 271 (1992), each of which highlighted human rights violations in Tibet. He helped incorporate policy and programmatic measures broadening and institutionalizing US support for Tibet in the annually enacted US Foreign Relations Authorization Acts. He was also a strong advocate of the Fourteenth Dalai Lama Congressional Gold Medal Act of 2006, which sent a strong message to the international community of US support of His Holiness's policies. These and other initiatives that he championed not only provided critical assistance to Tibetans struggling to preserve their culture and identity but also promoted dialogue between the parties toward negotiating a solution to the Tibetan-Chinese conflict. His work on behalf of Tibet did not end with passage of legislation but continued in his subsequent efforts to encourage full implementation of the Acts, in particular the dictates of the Tibetan Policy Act of 2002.

In addition to his professional efforts on behalf of Tibet, Senator Kerry was personally engaged, reflecting his deep reverence for His Holiness. With a welcoming "open door" policy, he was always available when I sought his counsel. I was deeply touched when upon my retirement in 2012, he introduced a resolution (S. Res. 557) honoring my contribution "as Special Envoy of His Holiness the Dalai Lama and in promoting the legitimate rights and aspirations of the Tibetan people."

### *Congressional Staff*

Members of the US Congress are certainly key, but in many cases, equally important are their staff. In fact, some of our most important initiatives were based on ideas generated by concerned congressional staff. The Voice of America–Tibet program is one example. We had had many discussions in Dharamsala about the need for access to broadcasting facilities, at one stage even exploring the possibility of launching our own broadcast from a ship located in international waters. We had to abandon this idea, however, as it was prohibitively expensive. We also lobbied the BBC to create a Tibetan-language program, but at the time it was downsizing because of financial constraints and was not in a position to undertake any new programming.

During one of my visits to Washington as Kalon for the DIIR, along with Tenzin Namgyal, then the Representative of the Office of Tibet in New York, we mentioned our disappointment with the BBC's decision to some congressional staff. Keith Pitts surprised us by suggesting that we explore the possibility of having a Tibetan-language program with Voice of America. Soon he and others, including Paul Berkowitz, staff to Congressman Benjamin Gilman, were actively investigating this possibility. When Tenzin and I returned to D.C. after visiting some other parts of the United States, a bill establishing a Tibetan-language Voice of America program had been drafted and was ready to be introduced! This is but one example of how much can be accomplished with the support of committed staff.

When I came to Washington in 1990 to live full-time, we already had a solid circle of friends in the US Congress. Tenzin Namgyal and others had done excellent work in building support, bolstered by periodic visits from some of us from Dharamsala. Nevertheless, Tibet was still seen primarily as an issue concerning human rights and religious freedom.

## GROUNDBREAKING US CONGRESSIONAL POLICY ACTS

### *1991 Senate Concurrent Resolution 41: A Unified Tibet*

Of all the US Congressional legislation addressing Tibet, the most important to me was Senate Concurrent Resolution 41, acknowledging our vision of a unified Tibet under occupation by the Chinese. Although the legislation compelled no action, it was the first time that the United States, or any government, formally acknowledged that Tibet was more than just the Tibet Autonomous Region, that it encompassed the entire area that His Holiness and the Tibetan people know to be Tibet. The passage of this resolution gave an enormous boost to the morale of Tibetans everywhere who were yearning for a unified Tibet. While I worked hard on all of our congressional efforts, I may have worked the hardest on this one. This was the first, and remains today the only, official declaration by any government recognizing a unified Tibet, reflecting the historic decision by the Tibetan people to reassert ourselves as one nation: "To express the sense of the Congress that Tibet, including those areas incorporated into the Chinese provinces of Sichuan, Yunnan, Gansu and Qinghai that have historically been a part of Tibet, is an occupied country under established principles of international law whose true representatives are the Dalai Lama and the Tibetan Government in exile as recognized by the Tibetan people."

Procuring this resolution was not an easy task. The State Department strongly opposed it, actively lobbying against it. In State's view, it undermined the US "one China" policy that viewed Tibet as part of the PRC. Senior officials told members of Congress that rather than helping, this resolution would work against the possibility of the PRC taking a lenient position on Tibet. But we prevailed and the resolution was passed, giving needed legitimacy to the concept of a unified Tibet.

By this time, His Holiness had already publicly announced that he was not seeking independence for Tibet but rather striving to find genuine autonomy for the Tibetans, to preserve their distinct identity while remaining within the PRC. Some critics thought that the resolution, particularly the reference to Tibet as an occupied country, contradicted His Holiness's position. We had serious discussions among ourselves and with the bill's congressional sponsors on this point and concluded that the wording in no way precluded negotiating a future solution to the Tibet issue that would be mutually beneficial and acceptable to both parties. The language of the resolution merely stated a historical fact, albeit one that supported the legitimate aspiration of the Tibetans to remain united as a people.

### *The Tibetan Policy Act of 2002*

Objectively speaking, the most important US Congressional legislation addressing Tibet is the Tibetan Policy Act of 2002 (TPA), which established firm and explicit US policies regarding Tibet. This is not simply a resolution expressing the sense of Congress but rather a binding law requiring action on behalf of the US government. Over the years, Congress had passed a number of laws, as well as resolutions, concerning Tibet. In consultation with our supporters in the Senate and the House, we decided it was time to bring all our foreseeable legislation into one bill, with the goal of codifying US support and assistance that would be honored by successive administrations.

While we looked to the Taiwan Relations Act as a model, we recognized the differences between the two situations and were careful not to overstep boundaries and needlessly alienate Beijing. For example, we consciously didn't use the term "Tibet" or "relations," but rather "Tibetan" and "policy," so as not to imply Tibetan sovereignty. The Act specifically details actions the administration must undertake, including: (1) creation of the Office of Special Coordinator for Tibetan Issues; (2) encouraging dialogue between the government of the PRC and representatives of His Holiness and subsequent monitoring of any negotiated agreement; (3) consultation with Congress and the submission of annual reports on the situation in Tibet; (4) support for economic development, cultural preservation, health care, education, and environmental sustainability for Tibetans inside Tibet; and (5) release of individuals imprisoned because of their political or religious views, including release of the 11th Panchen Lama.

The State Department complained that these activities interfered with its role, alleging that Congress was improperly micromanaging the Tibet issue. The

Department's Bureau of Legislative Affairs aggressively lobbied individual members and their staff against passing the bill. Despite this opposition, the legislation passed and has been faithfully implemented by successive US administrations, notwithstanding a delay in appointing the Special Coordinator under the Trump presidency at the time of this writing.

Although I discuss several of the most important provisions of this landmark legislation below, I have included the full text of the bill as an appendix because of the law's importance and the fact that many of its provisions are too often misunderstood or overlooked.[5]

### Highlights of the Provisions

**1. ENCOURAGE NEGOTIATIONS AND MONITOR COMPLIANCE WITH ANY NEGOTIATED AGREEMENT** The law contemplates US involvement in a negotiated settlement to resolve the Tibet issue by encouraging dialogue between the parties and monitoring the agreement once it is negotiated. We have always accepted the fact that the substantive talks must take place between His Holiness, through his representatives, and Beijing, with no third-party involvement. That said, in my work, I have always lobbied the international community to encourage the PRC to start talks with us. International interest and support for our efforts is critical because, despite the PRC's rhetoric, its leaders are pragmatic, understanding that they cannot totally ignore international sentiments.

**2. CREATION OF US SPECIAL COORDINATOR FOR TIBETAN ISSUES** In the beginning of our lobbying efforts in the United States we spent our time seeking support from Congress rather than the executive branch. At the State Department, even senior officials who were dealing with the Tibet issue often tilted toward the PRC's view. They were not deliberately being unsympathetic to Tibet, but that is how they were trained. We were trying to show that Tibet was a geopolitical issue, not just a human rights concern. While acknowledging that the abuses in Tibet were egregious, I argued that they were the symptoms of the PRC's repressive policies. I stressed that we had to look for the cause—the Buddhist approach is to always seek out cause and effect. But it was a struggle to present Tibet as a political issue.

Even before I started working in the United States, representatives of the Tibetan Government-in-Exile (TGiE) didn't have physical access to the State

Department. We were not allowed in the building, and officials would only meet us offsite. There was one notable exception in the early 1980s when Elliott Abrams was Assistant Secretary for Human Rights in the Reagan administration. He received Tenzin Namgyal and me in his State Department office. This was a short-lived practice, however. When we went to see him for our follow-up meeting, he met us in the lobby and took us to the cafeteria in the basement. Apparently his counterparts from the Bureau of East Asian and Pacific Affairs (EAPA) were displeased with his formally receiving us in his office.

Even when we met with officials from State, they had very little information on Tibet. It was difficult and disheartening to encounter such a Sinocentric attitude. Eventually I got to know many of these officials and came to respect them. Quite a few of them later admitted to me that because of our work together they were able to gain a better understanding of the issue and see it from a broader perspective.

Today there is a new generation of experts and diplomats who have a different, less accommodating attitude toward the PRC. I would, in fact, discourage them from becoming hostile toward the PRC because I sincerely believe that a strong US–PRC relationship is not only in the United States' interest but selfishly in Tibet's interest as well. I think those Tibetans who would prefer to see a rift between the US and the PRC are misguided. I understand this position because we feel vindicated when the PRC is condemned and criticized. But it is very clear that when relations between Washington and Beijing are cordial and they are working on a number of global issues together, the United States is far more effective in encouraging the Chinese to engage with us. When relations are frosty, the United States has decidedly less influence, and the Chinese sometimes vent their displeasure by hardening their attitude toward us.

Because of the work we did shoring up support for Tibet in Congress and our efforts to cultivate contacts in the executive branch, eventually we were able to effect a change in State Department policy. By the time I retired from the ICT Board in 2014, not only were we welcomed in the State Department building, but also a new office had been created on the prestigious seventh floor for the Special Coordinator for Tibetan Issues, established in compliance with the TPA. Even though I did not enjoy formal diplomatic status, as the Dalai Lama's Special Envoy, I was always received at State with the same courtesy extended toward ambassadors and other dignitaries.

**Evolution of the Legislation**

We achieved these milestones by harnessing the tremendous support we enjoyed in the US Congress, resulting in passage of the TPA. The evolution of this pivotal legislation bears discussion. In 1993, bipartisan bills were introduced in the House and Senate to create a "United States Special Envoy for Tibet." Under this initial formulation, the Special Envoy was to be appointed by the President, have the rank of Ambassador, and be housed in the State Department. This effort was spearheaded by Senator Dianne Feinstein, a Democrat, and Senator Jesse Helms, a Republican. As previously discussed, Senator Feinstein is one of His Holiness's oldest friends in the United States. Senator Helms was very conservative and a committed Christian, but he was also a great friend of Tibet who had tremendous admiration for His Holiness. I was deeply touched when during one of His Holiness's visits to Washington, D.C., Senator Helms had several of his grandsons come all the way from North Carolina just to meet him. Senator Helms was well respected by many, but he was also feared and disliked by many others. To me personally, and on the Tibet issue, he was always helpful and gracious.

For four years we worked to garner support for the creation of the Special Envoy position. Madeleine Albright was Secretary of State at the time, and she understood the level of support we enjoyed in Congress. Some of her senior colleagues reached out to me and suggested that I work with the State Department's Bureau of Legislative Affairs to help negotiate with Congress, particularly the Senate Foreign Relations Committee, which was then chaired by Senator Helms, to establish the Special Envoy position in a way that would be workable for State.

As we negotiated, State voluntarily offered to create an executive branch position covering Tibet. State did not want the position to be that of an "envoy," as it would be difficult for the department to handle diplomatically. I felt we should be understanding of these concerns and not create a situation where our efforts were counterproductive. As a result, the original bill was amended to replace the proposed "Special Envoy for Tibet" with "Special Coordinator for Tibetan Issues." With the State Department's official announcement of the creation of the office of Special Coordinator in 1997, the pending legislation was preempted. During this sensitive negotiating process, we managed to maintain excellent relations with both Congress and the State Department.

Even after State's announcement, we didn't give up on the legislation. We knew that Secretary Albright would appoint a Special Coordinator, but there was no guarantee that the next Secretary of State or President would fill the position.

Therefore, we continued to work for language in the bill establishing the position to match the State Department's nomenclature, thereby ensuring that the position would be permanent. It was subsequently codified by Congress in the TPA.

**The Special Coordinator's Office: Appointees and Initiatives**

Our next hurdle was determining where, within the State Department, the Special Coordinator's Office should be located. Stanley Owen Roth, who was then Assistant Secretary of State for the EAPA region, insisted that it be placed within his bureau. He felt that no matter the name, Tibet was part of the larger PRC issue, so the office must be housed within that bureau. I vigorously opposed his stance, but he was equally committed to his position. Our good personal relationship allowed us to have a frank and open discussion on this and other matters. I said that if I were him, I would not want the Special Coordinator to be in my bureau, as it would be a hindrance. If it were outside, he would have some deniability for its activities but could still have influence over it.

My effort to keep the Special Coordinator Office out of the EAPA Bureau was not in any way an attempt to challenge its jurisdiction. I knew that if the Office were within that Bureau, every matter would be viewed through a Beijing-centric lens that would not help the Tibet issue. Therefore, I also strongly lobbied Secretary Albright on this point. In the end, the decision was made to keep the Special Coordinator Office out of the EAPA Bureau. But the question remained—where to place it.

We successfully worked with the State Department to have the Special Coordinator be closely associated with the Secretary of State to give the office a certain amount of political cachet. In 1997, Secretary Albright appointed her Director of Policy Planning, Gregory Craig, to be the first Special Coordinator. Directly associated with and physically adjacent to the Secretary of State's office, the office of the Director of Policy Planning served as a sort of "think tank" for the department. This appointment was of enormous importance to us, not only because of the close professional relationship Greg had with Secretary Albright but also because of his office's physical proximity to hers.

Unfortunately, shortly after his appointment, Greg was asked by President Clinton to be his primary legal advisor. Secretary Albright then appointed her Counselor, Wendy Sherman, a very senior State Department official and her close personal friend, to fill the position. She invited me to the State Department to tell me personally of the Secretary's decision, but, as luck would have it, she never assumed the office. Instead, she was tapped to be the key interlocutor for the US government on the Korean peninsula. That position made it very inconvenient for her to assume the Special Coordinator role. Beijing strongly criticized the creation of the Special Coordinator Office and refused to have any dealings with individuals who were heading it. On issues related to the Korean peninsula, maintaining close relations with the Chinese government is critical; thus her appointment was no longer acceptable.

Julia Taft was selected next, and she actually assumed the position. She was the Assistant Secretary of the Bureau of Population, Refugees and Migration, issues that are sometimes seen as "soft" and less political. In the end, I built a very close relationship with her. She consulted me on matters of importance and always took me into confidence regarding decisions, even when she was not obligated to do so. She was very active in the position, and in 2000 she became the first Special Coordinator to visit Dharamsala.

As a result of our efforts and with congressional support, the administration began to open its doors to His Holiness at the White House and the State Department. At the same time, the administration maintained a clear distinction between His Holiness and his direct representatives versus other Tibetan officials, in other words, the exile government. State would not receive any officials of the CTA at Foggy Bottom, and there was reluctance to hold any meetings even offsite.

With the close personal relationships we built, I was ultimately able to convince senior State Department officials, including the Special Coordinator, to have direct contact with CTA representatives. Julia Taft was very helpful in this effort. In consultation with her and other friends in the administration, we initiated informal brainstorming sessions that came to be known as "Tibet Summits," in which senior CTA officials were able to participate. In fact, the first meeting was held at her farm in Maryland. Then Head of the Kashag Kalon Sonam Topgyal participated in this maiden event. Ever the diplomat, she did insist that the main agenda focus on humanitarian matters, steering clear of any issues that might seem too political.

Eventually the Tibet Summit became an institutionalized vehicle for senior US officials, congressional staff, CTA representatives, and ICT Board members to discuss Tibet-related issues. I have hosted the meeting both in my capacity as Special Envoy and as Executive Chair of the ICT. Organizations including the National Endowment for Democracy (NED) have also acted as host. The success of these gatherings demonstrates that if one thinks creatively, but at the same time honestly and transparently, there is often a way to achieve seemingly impossible results. In this case, CTA officials were afforded the opportunity to deal directly with senior members of the US administration despite problematic diplomatic protocols. The professional manner in which the CTA officials conducted themselves during these meetings also contributed to the event's success, helping ensure continuation of these unique and valuable discussions. Our goal, which I am proud to say we achieved, was for substantive and tangible results, not just public relations kudos or photo opportunities.

In 2001, George W. Bush succeeded Bill Clinton as US President, leading to a change in many of the executive appointments. Again I fought very hard to upgrade the Special Coordinator position. Eventually Ambassador Paula Dobriansky was appointed. She was an Under Secretary of State, which at the time was one of the three most senior official positions at State.[6] She occupied this position during the entire Bush presidency, significantly raising the political profile of the office during her tenure, primarily in actively engaging US-based diplomats of nations receptive to our endeavors. She was also a firm advocate in favor of exerting a strong US influence on the dialogue process and a very active participant in the informal Tibet Summits, being quite flexible regarding the agenda and elevating the subject of dialogue between His Holiness and Beijing as a major topic of discussion. Samdhong Rinpoche, then Kalon Tripa (Head of the CTA), personally participated in quite a few of these meetings under Ambassador Dobriansky's leadership.

Under President Obama there were two Special Coordinators. The first, Under Secretary Maria Otero, was named after some delay, but she proved to be a strong advocate for Tibet. In September 2009, her first act upon receiving the Tibet portfolio (even before it was formally announced) was to travel to Dharamsala with presidential advisor Valerie Jarrett to meet His Holiness. In 2011, she visited the Tibetan settlement in Bylakuppe in the southern Indian state of Karnataka. Her visit to this settlement, the largest in India, was the first by a US Special Coordinator for Tibetan Issues.

One of the main reasons we were keen for her visit to Bylakuppe was to jumpstart an effort that Kalon Tripa Samdhong Rinpoche had initiated, called "Revitalization of Settlements." This idea was first discussed during Under Secretary Dobriansky's time as Special Coordinator and was viewed favorably by Washington, even earning the support of First Lady Laura Bush, with whom Ambassador

Dobriansky and I each met several times to discuss the initiative. With the change of administration, the project was delayed, but Maria Otero enthusiastically embraced it.

Visits to Tibetan communities by senior US officials such as Under Secretary Otero not only sent a very strong message to the international community of US support for the Tibet issue but also were of incalculable value in raising the morale of the Tibetan people, both inside Tibet and in exile. Because she was a senior member of the State Department, the first difficulty in realizing the visit was persuading other State Department bureaus and offices to agree to the trip. They were all concerned about the major political significance of her visit. We also had to clear the trip with the government of India for the same reasons. Not surprisingly, visits of this prominence take weeks, if not months, of planning, requiring close consultation among Dharamsala, the State Department, and the host country. I was still sorting out the details with senior officials of the Indian Foreign Ministry as Under Secretary Otero's flight was about to touch down at Bangalore Airport, where I was waiting to greet her.

Under Secretary of State Sarah Sewall succeeded Maria Otero as Special Coordinator in early 2014. By then, there had been historic changes in Dharamsala, with His Holiness's devolution of political authority and my own transition. I am pleased to know that after my departure, she visited Nepal and India to draw further attention to Tibet. She was very kind in 2015 to invite me as a special guest for the first ever Tibetan New Year celebration held at the State Department. Seemingly minor actions such as this send extremely important messages to Beijing and the international community of the US administration's commitment to protecting the distinct Tibetan identity, a stance I praised in my remarks at the event.[7]

As of this writing, we are already midway through Donald Trump's presidency, and no one has been appointed Special Coordinator. Although US law mandates this position, there is no guarantee that it will continue to be staffed by a high-level State Department official or housed within an influential bureau. I hope that the office will not fade into the background, as happens too frequently in Washington when advocates fail to vigorously pursue their interests. Each Special Coordinator has been very helpful to our cause, and Beijing pays very close attention to the office's activities. If the position remains unfilled or is given to a low-ranking official, Beijing will most certainly interpret it as a downgrading of the Tibet issue in the administration's eyes, even if that is not the State

Department's intent. It is thus essential for those continuing to work on Tibet's behalf, as I did when I was Special Envoy, to build a strong case to keep the position at as high a rank and as political as possible each time a new appointment is under consideration.

At one time there was a suggestion to move the office into the State Department Bureau of Human Rights by appointing Gare Smith, one of the Deputy Assistant Secretaries, as Special Coordinator. Gare is a longtime friend of Tibet with whom I first worked closely when he was senior staff to Senator Ted Kennedy, another committed Tibet supporter. Gare was also among the earliest congressional staff for whom the ICT arranged visits to both Dharamsala and Tibetan settlements in India. He was thoroughly informed and extremely knowledgeable about Tibet. On substantive grounds, no other individual could have been a better choice for this post than him. When I learned of the possibility, however, I approached him and then Secretary Albright's office. I explained that if the Tibet issue were placed in the Human Rights Bureau, it would be seen solely as a human rights issue, not a political one, a perception we were trying to move away from. Gare completely understood, as did the Secretary. Gare today remains one of the pillars of the Tibet movement, serving on the ICT's board for the last many years and giving so much of his precious time and energy.

The passage of the TPA in 2002 and the appointment of the Special Coordinator for Tibetan Issues were defining moments for Tibet. For the first time in our history, a US government official was mandated to become an expert on and coordinate US policy toward Tibet. For the first time, Congress was able to influence State Department policy on Tibet through the mission of the Special Coordinator. Congress could keep tabs on the administration's efforts through the annual reports that the Act further requires the State Department to submit to the legislature. Truly, Tibet's coming of age.

In 2014, the ICT published "My Personal Words of Gratitude," in which I commented that many Tibet-related programs are now on "autopilot" as a result of the TPA. I cautioned the ICT to remain vigilant, however, for its leadership might be needed in the future if an indifferent administration or an increasingly powerful PRC threatens to disturb the status quo. With the exception of what is hopefully just a delay in appointing the Special Coordinator under the Trump presidency, successive administrations have complied with the law and not sought to amend it. Should we fail to keep the issue of Tibet at the forefront of US concerns, however, this could change to our serious detriment.

As is evident from the foregoing discussion of the TPA and other Tibet-related bills, the bulk of US assistance to Tibet comes through legislation. This is much more reliable than resources provided through executive branch agencies. However, we must be vigilant in maintaining relationships with both branches of government, lest another cause supplant ours. The ICT has done a remarkable job in this respect. Here again we have relied heavily on friends, including Senator Patrick Leahy on the Senate side and Congresswomen Nancy Pelosi and Ileana Ros-Lehtinen on the House side. In recent years Congressman James P. McGovern has also been the watchdog for Tibet-related issues in the House.

## RICHARD HOLBROOKE

No single individual did more to elevate the issue of Tibet as an important geopolitical concern in the United States than Richard Holbrooke. He was personally very kind to me, and while he credited me for bringing him to the Tibet issue, it was actually Richard Blum and Melvyn Goldstein who introduced him to Tibet. And it was the Tibetans inside Tibet who truly inspired him, particularly some of the nomads with whom he spent significant periods of time.[8] His interest took everyone in Washington, D.C., by surprise. But as a result of his concern, others began to take Tibet seriously: if Richard Holbrooke saw it as important, it must be. He brought the issue to the attention not only of his close circle of associates but also of a much wider audience as he began to speak out publicly on Tibet's behalf.

Richard was of the realpolitik school of international affairs, in the mold of Henry Kissinger.[9] He took a no-nonsense approach to diplomacy, looking at the substance of each situation. Once he became interested in Tibet, he skillfully maneuvered to give the issue a political dimension. At one point, he even publicly proclaimed that the issue of Tibet could potentially determine the future bilateral relationship between the United States and the PRC.

Richard had a brilliant mind and was constantly strategizing. When I went to see him, he would bombard me with questions, and by the time I left, I would have numerous scraps of paper covered with scribbled notes, diagrams, and names. He referred to these as his "roadmaps" on how to move the Tibet issue to the next level. He would even host lunches for His Holiness in New York to which he invited dozens of influential people. Sometimes we didn't even know who these people were, as they were completely outside our own circle of friends and professional contacts. But when I now review the lists of invitees, I see that they were luminaries from the world of business, politics, and even the media, including the likes of Tom Brokaw. Richard was always seeking to maximize contacts and opportunities for us to introduce individuals to the cause of Tibet and make our case. He would even personally work on the seating arrangements at these lunches to make sure that the most could be gained from each event. And when Richard Holbrooke invited people to lunch, they came, even if his domineering personality put some people off. The respect in which his colleagues, acquaintances, and even his adversaries held him assured that no one would miss an opportunity to interact with him personally.

For a number of years, Richard served on the board of the National Endowment for Democracy. Carl Gershman, the NED President, who is also a very dear friend, once invited me to make a presentation to his board. This was a very important opportunity for me, as the list of NED Board members reads like a "who's who" of Washington. Even though he had served on the board for quite some time, I believe this was the first time Richard participated in an event. After the Chair and President of NED made their remarks, Richard gave me a glowing introduction. After I finished my presentation, he continued to discuss Tibet, turning the entire board meeting into a Tibet-focused discussion. Carl Gershman was pleased, but understandably a bit frustrated, as the board ran out of time to discuss the other issues on its agenda, and a few members felt sidelined. But that was classic Richard Holbrooke.

It is a true tragedy that Richard passed away so young. Had he lived, he certainly would have risen to even greater heights than he did. It was his ambition to become Secretary of State. In fact, he thought he should have been given that position many years ago. I am so grateful I had the opportunity to learn from him. He devoted considerable time to helping us strategize, as he was a master negotiator. He also created every opportunity to advance our issue. For example, Richard was well aware that the United Nations wouldn't allow access to His Holiness or any of his representatives. So when he was the US Permanent Representative, he would invite me to walk with him to the UN, which is just opposite the US mission in New York. He would defiantly introduce me as the "Dalai Lama's Envoy" to the other ambassadors, envoys, and diplomats and see if anyone would dare to protest. He deliberately pushed the envelope to raise awareness about the issues he cared about.

Richard Holbrooke visiting the author at his office in Washington, D.C., in the early 1990s

Richard Holbrooke's most important contribution to our cause was his role in restarting our dialogue with the PRC. He was instrumental in connecting me with his Norwegian friends, particularly with Jan Egeland, who was at one time State Secretary at the Norwegian Foreign Ministry. I remember the three of us meeting at a ski resort above Oslo City, with Richard, as usual, preparing his "roadmaps," jotting down diagrams and lists of things for all of us to do.

If I remember correctly, Jan was one of the earliest senior foreign diplomats to visit Lhasa, if not the first. Wegger Strommen, who succeeded Jan at the Foreign Ministry, also became part of our discussions. The relationships that Richard facilitated with the Norwegians made it possible in early 2002 for my colleague Kelsang Gyaltsen and I to use this channel to send a letter to President Jiang Zemin detailing how we thought our process of engagement should be undertaken.[10]

Richard was also very keen that we reach out to Henry Kissinger, President Richard Nixon's National Security Advisor and later Secretary of State. Richard accompanied him on at least two important trips to the PRC after he left the government to help promote the business interests of several megacorporations. On each trip, when they met with the PRC President, Richard would raise the

Tibet issue, much to his partner's displeasure. I am told that on one of their later trips, Henry Kissinger chided that he was sure his friend Richard Holbrooke would not leave the meeting without discussing his "favorite topic"!

There is no doubt that Henry Kissinger was a brilliant political operative and strategist, but he is not generally admired for his commitment to principle. As many friends of Tibet pride themselves on their strong ethical values, he was not well loved within the Tibet movement. But everyone knew he was very influential when it came to the PRC, being one of the few non-Chinese to whom Beijing would listen. Time and time again there would be a discussion about whether we should try to reach out to him. The idea was almost always rejected because His Holiness and Henry Kissinger represent such different sets of values. There was also some concern that he was not entirely trustworthy because of his close relationships with both Beijing and the corporate world, the latter sometimes being the main ally of the PRC in helping influence US policies favorable to Beijing.

Despite these concerns, Richard advised me that we should at a minimum try to neutralize him, if not gain his support. Richard was thus extremely keen on arranging a meeting between Kissinger and His Holiness. Eventually His Holiness agreed, and a meeting was organized in 1998 in New York.

It was funny how meticulous Kissinger's secretaries were in managing the details of the meeting. They were concerned not only with the usual issues, e.g., how many people would be there and who they were, but also with which "back door" we were to use and repeated requests for assurances that no press would be present. The list of conditions was as stringent as if he were still the National Security Advisor or Secretary of State, even though at the time of the meeting he was a private citizen. Then, two days before the meeting, Ambassador Paul Bremer, then Director of Kissinger & Associates, who later became US Special Envoy for Iraq, called to ensure that the meeting be kept confidential.[11] "Ambassador," I replied, "I am so happy that you have rescued me from a very embarrassing situation. I was just thinking of calling you to say the same thing." I also wanted this meeting to remain confidential, but for entirely different reasons. Many of our human rights activist friends, as well as leaders of the Tibet movement and other friends of His Holiness, had strong reservations regarding Henry Kissinger.

The meeting itself went quite well, and he was cordial in his behavior. His Holiness's gentle demeanor often disarms people. His Holiness was, as usual, very casual in his conversation, but I was concerned that he was speaking more to Richard Holbrooke than to Henry Kissinger. I actually took the liberty of whispering to His Holiness to look toward him, something I would not normally presume to do, because I didn't want him to feel neglected.

It was very clear that Henry Kissinger had been thoroughly briefed before the meeting. He even asked a few questions on some sensitive issues that were clearly designed to provoke His Holiness. At one point, he also seemed to be trying to put words into His Holiness's mouth, some of which could later be misconstrued. I was supposed to accompany His Holiness to the West Coast the next day, but I sought his permission to stay back for a few days to write a detailed memo memorializing the meeting to share with Kissinger's office so that there would be no opportunity for misinterpretation of the matters they had discussed.

I do believe that Henry Kissinger came to understand the Tibet issue a little better because of his meeting with His Holiness, although he never became actively involved. Several months later I saw him at the National Correspondents' Dinner, where I was invited as a guest by *Newsweek*'s Melinda Liu. To my surprise, he remembered me and came over to chat for a few minutes, in the end asking me to "keep him posted." A seemingly promising encounter, although nothing ever came of our overtures.

## US STATE DEPARTMENT LEADERSHIP IN BRINGING LIKE-MINDED COUNTRIES TOGETHER

While US support for Tibet is the most critical, we recognized that total dependence on the United States has its disadvantages, as the US-PRC relationship is unpredictable and volatile. This relationship is undoubtedly the world's most important on issues including trade, defense, and international affairs. Given the breadth of the two countries' interaction, the relationship might at any given time be moving in the right direction in one respect while moving in the totally opposite direction in another. Whenever relations deteriorate, secondary issues including Tibet become the first casualties. PRC leaders are very careful, especially regarding domestic politics, to avoid giving the impression of being too accommodating to the United States.

Understanding this, we began serious efforts to broaden the Tibet support base by reaching out to sympathetic European countries. His Holiness personally attached great importance to this initiative, and I remember him specifically mentioning it to senior US administration officials. This was not an easy task, however. Americans and Europeans have a "love/hate" relationship that often creates difficulties when they try to work together. Again, with our limited resources, we had to choose the objects of our attention very carefully. We settled on Germany, France, Norway, and the Netherlands and, I am pleased to say, with considerable success.

With the appointment of the US Special Coordinator for Tibet, we had an unprecedented opportunity to pursue our efforts. Our friends in Congress had included specific language in the TPA directing the Special Coordinator to make "efforts to establish contacts in the foreign ministries of other countries to pursue a negotiated solution for Tibet." This led to the creation of a working group of officials from governments around the world who had shown a serious interest in the Tibet issue. Paula Dobriansky took the lead and was able to bring the effort to fruition.

As previously mentioned, Under Secretary Dobriansky gave the highest priority to reestablishing dialogue between the parties. She encouraged us to reach out to concerned countries to assist in this effort, both in Europe and elsewhere, offering US support whenever she could. She hosted formal working lunch meetings at the State Department, inviting ambassadors to strategize with us to make their countries' support for Tibet more effective and meaningful. Her senior position within the administration, combined with her personal relationships with many of these ambassadors, made a big difference.

I had also built strong personal ties with several senior European diplomats that complemented our other efforts. French Ambassador Jean-David Levitte and Norwegian Ambassador Wegger Strommen, for example, were very active supporters. Wegger Strommen was involved in developing our strategy for resuming dialogue with the PRC from the very beginning. Over the years my colleague Kelsang Gyaltsen and I also worked very closely with Ambassador Levitte, who was Jacques Chirac's senior diplomatic advisor. We knew him from his days in the French Foreign Ministry. He was later appointed as France's Permanent Representative to the United Nations, serving from 2000 to 2002, and from there he came to Washington, D.C., as the French Ambassador, remaining in his post until 2007.

With Under Secretary Dobriansky's leadership, these ad hoc meetings developed into more formal gatherings, often held at one of the ambassadors' private residences. I believe the first formal meeting occurred when Knut Vollebaek was Norwegian Ambassador to the United States. He was very supportive of our cause and knowledgeable about the issue, having served in India as a young diplomat. His diplomatic expertise eventually led him to become Norway's Foreign Minister. When French Ambassador Levitte returned to Paris to become diplomatic advisor to President Nicolas Sarkozy, Pierre Vimont became the next ambassador. He took the same level of interest in our cause as his predecessor, hosting two of our group's meetings, the first in his capacity as the chair of the European Group of Ambassadors and the second in his role as the French Ambassador.

Other senior State Department officials, including James Kelly, Assistant Secretary of the EAPA Bureau, as well as senior White House officials began attending the meetings. With the French and Norwegians taking the lead, and in coordination with Under Secretary Dobriansky, ambassadors and senior diplomats from other countries gradually became part of the group. At the December 2011 meeting at the Norwegian Embassy, for example, participants included: the Czech Ambassador; the Mongolian Ambassador; the Australian Embassy's Deputy Chief of Mission; the British Embassy's Deputy Head of Mission; the Swiss Embassy's Deputy Head of Mission; the Dutch Embassy's Deputy Chief of Mission; the Head of the Political Department of the German Embassy; the Chief of Staff for the Political Affairs Department of the French Embassy; the Counsel of the Political Section of the Japanese Embassy; and the Minister-Counselor of Canada. The Ambassadors of Sweden and New Zealand ultimately joined the group, and even the relatively small country of Slovenia wanted to be involved.

These meetings gave us a tremendous opportunity to broaden our ties with both the US administration and the international community and develop a coordinated approach for encouraging Beijing to have substantive, not just cursory, dialogue with us. We were able to brief the group on our activities, while the ambassadors shared the efforts their countries were making on our behalf. At the same time, the participants shared their views and experiences with regard to the broader PRC issue, a valuable exercise for us all.

From the start, I kept the Indian Ambassador fully briefed on these discussions, but I didn't request his formal participation to avoid any unnecessary complications with the PRC. My American friends, however, were very keen to have India's participation. They encouraged me to take the matter up with the Indian leadership in Delhi, hoping that the ambassador would be formally instructed to participate. I explained to them that India is the most important country for us, as it is home to His Holiness and the Tibetan leadership. We needed to remain appreciative of its kindness and generosity at all times, and avoid jeopardizing its relationship with the PRC to the maximum extent possible. Because of similar sensitivities, while I kept the Mongolian Ambassador in the loop, I didn't initially press for his participation. After careful consideration, somewhat surprisingly, the Mongolian government decided to become involved, and from then on the Mongolian Ambassador was always present at our meetings.

All of the ambassadors attending these meetings accepted the United States taking the lead role. There was no sensitivity about this, which was of great benefit to us. As the main focus was on methods for encouraging substantive dialogue with the PRC, I always invited my colleague based in Europe, Envoy Kelsang Gyaltsen, to participate in the discussions. He was able to brief the group on his efforts. I also invited His Holiness's Representative from the Office of Tibet in New York as part of my continuing effort to bring the CTA into an active role. Unlike my position as the Special Envoy, the Office of Tibet is part of the CTA, directly responsible to the Kashag. The respective Heads of the Offices of Tibet worldwide, however, are also the personal Representatives of His Holiness, a designation making it easier for me politically to include them in the meetings. Had they just been representing the CTA, the US administration would not have agreed to their formal participation.

I believe Kasur Tashi Wangdi was the first Office of Tibet participant in these meetings. Starting in 2009, his successor, Kasur Lobsang Nyendak, attended most of the meetings. I also began inviting Lobsang Nyendak to some of the meetings at the State Department with either the Special Coordinator or other senior officials, including the Assistant Secretary for the EAPA Bureau. I remember he and I attending many of these meetings with Kurt Campbell, the Assistant Secretary of State for EAPA, one of the most thought-provoking and engaging officials with whom we were privileged to work.

Every task has to be done with patience, skillfulness, and respect, always mindful of the other side's interests and sensitivities. These periodic high-level consultations created a uniform and unified approach on the issue of Tibet among the major Western nations and other interested parties. Quite often, different roles were assigned to or agreed upon by participating nations to accelerate our efforts to reestablish substantive dialogue. I have always been careful not to betray the trust of any individuals, be they senior US administration officials, ambassadors, or other senior diplomats with whom I worked. They all know that my efforts were directed toward substantive and constructive advances and not for any superficial political points or transient media exposure. I have also always respected the importance of the bilateral relations each of these countries maintains with the PRC. Our sincere efforts convinced them that we would never do anything to hinder or harm their respective relationships with the PRC. Of course, Beijing knew very well of this high-level diplomatic engagement, and I am sure it was not pleased. However, as these meetings were conducted in a very low-profile manner, Beijing never made any protests—either to the group as a whole or to the individual nation participants.

## CONGRESSIONAL GOLD MEDAL

In 1991, at the invitation of several members of Congress from both houses, including Senators Mitchell, Akaka, and Kerry as well as Congressmen Rose and Gilman, members assembled in the US Capitol Rotunda to welcome His Holiness the Dalai Lama. This historic event helped pave the way for another equally transformative moment when, in 2007, the US Congress awarded His Holiness the Congressional Gold Medal. For some years I had lobbied hard for His Holiness to address a joint session of Congress. Not only did I believe he deserved this honor, I thought of it as a personal mandala offering to him. Close friends and advisors, however, prevailed in proposing the more prestigious Congressional Gold Medal as an alternative.

His Holiness's receipt of the medal represented hundreds of hours of ICT advocacy, from coordinating grassroots campaigns in support of the legislation to discussions by me and other senior Tibetan officials with members of Congress and the administration. We had thousands of volunteers engaged on every level. At the ICT, we had a massive "countdown" calendar posted on the office wall, listing goals and benchmarks. As was the case with the Nobel Peace Prize, the success of our effort demonstrated the deep respect His Holiness engenders in people in the United States and worldwide.

When the Senate and the House decided to confer this prestigious award on His Holiness, the United States Mint was instructed to design and make the actual medal. Each gold medal is unique because it commemorates the person and the achievement for which the medal is awarded. Authorities at the US Mint were very kind in consulting me when designing His Holiness's Medal, and the final design was shared with the Office of His Holiness. The mint did a beautiful job. The medal has an image of His Holiness with three mountain peaks in the background, symbolically depicting Tibet—the Land of Snows. On the back of the medal is the following quote rising up from a lotus flower: "World peace must develop from inner peace. Peace is not the absence of violence; peace is the manifestation of human compassion." The text was taken from a public address His Holiness gave in 1995 in Boston.

We wanted to include three sacred mountains on the medal, one from each of the three regions of Tibet. Our choice for Amdo was not difficult because Amnye Machen Pomra is not only the most prominent in the region but also the abode of the Tibetan mountain god Machen Pomra. Similar to the Native American concept of a spirit animal that guides and protects a person on his or her journey in life, the Tibetans believe that a person is protected and bound to the local deity of his birthplace. Hence, this mountain in Amdo where His Holiness was born is also his *bla-ri* or "spirit mountain." For Central Tibet, our first choice was Nyenchen Thanglha because it is the home of the supreme mountain deity for all of Tibet.

The US Mint designers wanted us to submit images of several mountains so they could make the most aesthetically pleasing picture. As the medal was being presented to His Holiness, we definitely wanted to include Amyne Machen Pomra. The two other mountain images thus had to complement its shape and contours. This is how Chomolungma (Mount Everest) and Khawalungri, a sacred mountain in the Kham region, were chosen. Our other submissions included Kailash, Khawakarpo, Minyak Gangkar, and several others.

Although it is not mandatory that the US President participate in the gold medal presentation because it is a legislative branch ceremony, we were honored to have President George W. Bush in attendance. This event marked the first time that an American President publicly honored His Holiness the 14th Dalai Lama for his leadership. President Bush spoke sincerely of his support and admiration for His Holiness. The congressional leadership flanked the President as he spoke, while thousands of supporters gathered in D.C. for the ceremony and attendant festivities. All of the speakers' remarks at the ceremony came from the heart, and for a moment, there was a true sense of unity among all those present in the Rotunda. This is His Holiness's major strength: bringing people of various backgrounds and views together.

The leadership of the US Congress most appropriately invited Elie Wiesel, a fellow Nobel Laureate and a Holocaust survivor, but most importantly for this ceremony, a previous recipient of the Congressional Gold Medal, to introduce His Holiness. I want to share with you his words as well as those of President

President George W. Bush and Congresswoman Nancy Pelosi with His Holiness the 14th Dalai Lama at the ceremony conferring the Congressional Gold Medal in 2007. The author is to the left of His Holiness.
International Campaign for Tibet

George W. Bush and the leadership of Congress on this occasion. Their remarks reveal the true depth of their admiration and respect for His Holiness and their genuine support for his effort not only to bring solace to his people but also to encourage harmony between the Tibetan and Chinese peoples. Through sharing their poignant sentiments, I also want to express my own heartfelt gratitude to these true leaders, many of whom I am honored to call my friends.

Congresswoman Ileana Ros-Lehtinen, Ranking Republican Member of the House Foreign Affairs Committee

Through this award, we are recognizing his lifelong advocacy on behalf of peace, tolerance, human rights, non-violence, and religious understanding, as well as his heroic efforts on behalf of 6 million Tibetan people who continue to suffer under the iron grip of Beijing's communist rule. They continue to brave systematic attacks aimed at destroying their national and cultural identity. But they do not waver, they do not falter, they know, that truth and justice will prevail over evil and repression. Their guide and inspiration, is His Holiness.

Congressman Tom Lantos, Democratic Chair of the House Committee on International Relations

What accounts for the rise of this humble Buddhist monk from near-obscurity to the global phenomenon that he has become? It is not lobbies. It is not economic power. It is not political influence. It is moral authority.

At a moment in world history when nothing is in as short a supply as moral authority, this humble Buddhist monk has an inexhaustible supply. And this accounts for the respect, the admiration, the love that people have for him across the globe. . . .

I want our friends in Beijing to know that while occasionally we look like a divided country, we are all united, the President and Mrs. Bush and the Speaker and all of us across the aisle in making this plea: Let this man of peace visit Beijing.

Senator Dianne Feinstein, Democratic Chair of the Senate Rules Committee

The simple truth is this: I can think of no one who more embodies the spirit of the Congressional Gold Medal than His Holiness, the Dalai Lama. People flock by the thousands to his lectures all over the world. They yearn to hear his voice, to be enveloped by his spirit of compassion.

His teachings resonate across religions, cultures, and ethnic lines. And his message of peace, non-violence and understanding has never been more relevant.

Elie Wiesel, Nobel Peace Prize Laureate and Congressional Gold Medal Recipient

Today, in honoring a great man of faith and courage, you—members of Congress and you, Mr. President—are giving power to truth. Admired by millions all over the world, true to his tradition and open to all others, forever ready to listen, and willing to learn, H.H. the Dalai Lama is a man of profound spiritual conviction, who believes that like all people, his own in Tibet have the right to live a sovereign religious and cultural life.

Congressman John Boehner, Republican House of Representatives Minority Leader

The Dalai Lama, who we honor today, has taken on the burden of his people. And he has become a symbol of dignity, of tolerance, and religious freedom. Tonight, when this work is done, this ceremony is over, all of you will go home. Members of Congress will finish their work tomorrow, and they will go home. We will go to our districts and we will see our families. But the Dalai Lama will not go home. He has not been home in 50 years. So today we honor his sacrifice, and his struggle, and with a firm commitment, that we will never forget, the people of Tibet.

Senator Mitch McConnell, Republican Senate Minority Leader

Truth is persistent, and in the case of the Dalai Lama, so is the messenger. He's carried the plight of his people to the world for nearly 50 years, never growing tired or frustrated. It's this constancy and hope in the face of violence and intimidation that inspires Tibetan teenagers and grandfathers to risk arrest, or worse, by keeping pictures of him in their homes or by scrawling his name on a schoolhouse wall. In recent weeks he has inspired the suffering people of Burma to similar acts of heroism. And he has inspired Congress to give him the greatest honor in our power to bestow.

Senator Harry Reid, Democratic Senate Majority Leader

Today we gather in this great chamber, a President, and a Poet, members of Congress and members of the Clergy, to award the 146th Gold Medal.

I can think of no one living on this Earth today more deserving of this honor, than His Holiness, the 14th Dalai Lama of Tibet. For the people of his nation, he is a spiritual leader, and emissary to the world, the voice of their suffering, and the steady hand that guides their path. For those who are oppressed throughout the world, and beyond the borders of Tibet, he is a voice of reason in crisis, and wisdom in chaos. For all of us, he represents the very best of humanity. A child of humble farmers from a town of just a few hundred, who rose to inspire millions, and move the world closer to peace.

Congresswoman Nancy Pelosi, Democratic Speaker of the House

Members of Congress are afforded many special opportunities. The opportunity to join the President of the United States and Congressional leaders to award His Holiness the Dalai Lama with the Congressional Gold Medal is an unsurpassed honor. . . .

To meet with the Dalai Lama, Tibetans flee the repression in their own country, under the threat of torture and imprisonment for even having a picture of His Holiness. They walk for weeks, without adequate food or clothing, across the freezing Himalayan mountain passes. It is the most perilous escape route on earth.

After their audience, they make the trip once again, returning to Tibet to rejoin their families. . . .

Today, with this Congressional Gold Medal, we honor the Tibetan people and His Holiness the Dalai Lama for his many enduring and outstanding contributions to peace, nonviolence, human rights and religious understanding.

President George W. Bush, Republican

Nearly two decades have passed since the Dalai Lama was welcomed to the White House for the very first time. Members of both of our political parties and world leaders have seen His Holiness as a man of faith and sincerity and peace. He's won the respect and affection of the American people—and America has earned his respect and affection, as well. . . .

Throughout our history, we have stood proudly with those who offer a message of hope and freedom to the world's downtrodden and oppressed. This is why all of us are drawn to a noble and spiritual leader who lives a world away. Today we honor him as a universal symbol of peace and tolerance, a shepherd for the faithful, and the keeper of the flame for his people.[12]

The *Roll Call*, a newspaper covering the activities of the US Congress, once wrote that it was only the Dalai Lama who could bring together in the same room the most liberal voices of the Senate, such as Senator Ted Kennedy, with the most conservative, Senator Jesse Helms, and create a palpable feeling of solidarity. It is so true. I was just reviewing the official publication entitled *Congressional Ceremony to Welcome His Holiness the Dalai Lama of Tibet* and reading the list of Senators and members of the House who attended. One can clearly see that politicians from the most liberal left to the most conservative right were working together in great harmony on the issue of Tibet and extending their warm friendship to the Dalai Lama.

I would also like to mention the sponsor and cosponsors of Senate Concurrent Resolution 41 of 1991 welcoming the Dalai Lama to give an idea of the mosaic of political leaders supporting Tibet. Senators Pell, Moynihan, Helms, Akaka, Kennedy, Jeffords, D'Amato, Sarbanes, Wallop, Dixon, Robb, Cranston, Bradley, and Hatfield joined together to sponsor the resolution. Those familiar with the US political scene will know that these are some of the most influential politicians of that time from both parties. These leaders did not just lend their names to the Act, they felt and spoke passionately on the issue of Tibet, further demonstrating our success in reaching out and providing them and their staff with the information regarding the true situation in Tibet.

## FINANCIAL AND OTHER SUPPORT FROM THE US CONGRESS

Over the years the US Congress has also passed legislation directly benefiting Tibetans inside Tibet as well as Tibetan refugees. One early program provided for a one-time allocation of a thousand special immigration visas for Tibetans. This eventually led to several thousand additional Tibetans coming to the United States through the family reunification program. Whether keeping Tibetan people informed about current events around the world through the Tibetan-language programs of Voice of America and Radio Free Asia or providing much-needed educational support through humanitarian assistance, programs like these have brought untold benefits to Tibetans both inside and outside Tibet.

When I stepped down from the ICT Board in 2014, I asked then ICT Director of Governmental Relations Todd Stein to give me a rough idea of how much money the US government had provided to the Tibetan cause in response to the ICT's efforts over the years so that I could make a proper expression of gratitude. I was astounded to learn that from 1988 to 2013, the United States had provided over $225 million, including direct aid to Tibetan refugees and Tibetans in Tibet, educational grants such as Fulbright scholarships, and Voice of America and Radio Free Asia programming. Before I left Washington, D.C., in 2014, Senator Feinstein, her husband, and Richard Gere, Chair of the ICT, hosted an intimate farewell dinner for me attended by senior officials from the State Department as well as several ambassadors. I asked the Senator and Congresswoman Pelosi, who was also there, if they knew how much money the US Congress had provided for Tibet. I remember both of them instantly asking: "Did we give you enough?" I sincerely thanked them for their generosity and said that it was only recently that we had compiled the total amount.

Financial assistance from the United States has helped us sustain our lives and maintain our unique culture and identity, particularly when Dharamsala was inundated with refugees. Without this American help, the CTA would have been overwhelmed.

Our generous friends in Congress never mentioned or bragged about the funding they helped authorize for Tibetans. We also never advertised our success in procuring these funds. Of course, the Tibetan community knew of the substantial assistance being provided by the United States. Some of them thought, however, that all of the funds were received by the ICT. While it is true that all were received as a result of the ICT's hard work and lobbying, not a single penny was ever allocated to or used by the ICT itself. US law forbids any organization or institution lobbying for specific funding to be the beneficiary of that endeavor.

Initially, I was able to ask our friends in Congress to earmark money for Tibetan assistance through the Tibet Fund, a New York-based NGO specifically established to help the Tibetan people. I had been on the board of Tibet Fund for many years before my move to the United States. When Tibet Fund started receiving US funding, however, I resigned my position to comply with the law. Through this organization, we knew that the bulk of the money would be spent on actual projects rather than on administrative, consulting, and other expenses, as is too often the case with NGOs.

We also successfully lobbied Congress to earmark money for the Bridge Fund, an NGO I helped establish that was fully engaged in facilitating cultural, educational, and economic programs for Tibetans inside Tibet. Gradually, some other NGOs started competing for these limited funds. While I have nothing against other organizations seeking financial aid for Tibet-related projects, I only hope that these entities have the best interests of Tibetans in mind and that the bulk of any allocated funds reaches the targeted population.

While speaking of financial aid from our friends in the international community, I must take a moment to acknowledge India's unsurpassed largesse. India has provided the greatest amount of aid, both financial and programmatic, of any nation. I remember expressing my gratitude to one of its Foreign Secretaries at one point. He told me that he considered it India's moral obligation to help the Tibetan people, so it wasn't a burden. How lucky we have been that even when struggling with its own challenging economic situation, India has been so generous.

## RISE IN IMPORTANCE OF THE TIBET ISSUE OVER THE COURSE OF SUCCESSIVE US ADMINISTRATIONS

During our early years of outreach to the international community, the US Congress took the lead in embracing our cause. Over successive US administrations, the executive branch slowly followed its lead, ultimately publicly endorsing His Holiness's Middle Way Approach.

In the early years of our advocacy in the United States, receptions by senior administration officials as well as the President were entirely unofficial. As previously noted, neither His Holiness nor any of his representatives were even allowed on State Department premises. Meetings at the White House were termed "drop-by" and not included on the President's official schedule. The White House was not prepared to make any public announcement of meetings with His Holiness. Even when some members of the White House press corps specifically asked during briefings whether the President had met His Holiness, the press secretary would often avoid giving a clear answer.

The situation gradually changed when President Clinton started receiving His Holiness for one-on-one meetings, departing from his earlier practice of "drop-bys" at Vice President Gore's office. The White House also started issuing press releases about the meetings. In recent years, the deference accorded His Holiness by the US administration has escalated to a point almost equaling that given to senior foreign dignitaries.

President Obama met with His Holiness twice during my tenure as Special Envoy. Each time, the President articulated his support for the Middle Way Approach, complimenting His Holiness on his continued efforts to find a solution to the Tibet issue through dialogue with Beijing and urging the PRC leadership to come to the table. Gaining this official and public support for His Holiness's position was not an easy undertaking. It reflects years of work cultivating and maintaining political connections while simultaneously clearly articulating His Holiness's proposal to diverse audiences and understanding how to most effectively position the Tibet issue within the broader context of US–PRC and indeed global relations.

This rise in importance accorded to the Tibet issue is in large measure due to the efforts of our longtime supporters in Congress but also to those of sympathetic officials of successive administrations as well as the tireless efforts of the countless individuals, both professional and volunteer, who have made the cause of Tibet their lifelong calling.

### *George H.W. Bush Administration*

I have been privileged to be responsible for arranging all the meetings His Holiness had with US Presidents, beginning in 1991 until I stepped down from my position as Special Envoy of His Holiness the 14th Dalai Lama in 2012. When His Holiness met President George H.W. Bush on April 16, 1991, it was the first meeting between His Holiness and a sitting American President. It set the precedent for all subsequent meetings between His Holiness and other world leaders.

Arranging this meeting took a tremendous amount of hard work, and I was fortunate to receive guidance and support from many friends both inside and outside the government. Elsie Walker, the President's cousin, was of great help in this regard. At the advice of some friends, I hesitantly wrote an op-ed for the *Boston Globe*, "The US Obligation to Tibet," on April 14, 1991, urging the President to receive His Holiness at the White House. I say hesitantly because normally I don't think it is proper to pressure a person to do something that he or she is uncomfortable with or unwilling to do. My fears were soothed, however, by very wise friends, including some members of Congress with close personal ties to the President, who counseled that it would not be seen negatively by the White House and might even strengthen the hands of people advising the President to meet His Holiness.

In those days, His Holiness was not accorded diplomatic security or any of the other prerequisites provided foreign dignitaries that he now receives. We were fortunate to have friends in Congress who arranged for Capitol Hill police to escort His Holiness. The Washington city police were also very helpful. After we had left the hotel for the meeting with the President, we learned that the meeting would be delayed. Rather than returning to the hotel, the police decided to take His Holiness to visit the Washington Monument. Although I had lived in the city for some time, this was to be both my first and only visit inside the memorial. From the top of the monument, our park ranger guide was very kind to point out the White House to His Holiness, showing him where he would soon be meeting the President.

When we finally arrived at the White House, President Bush was still caught up in a press conference. Sichan Siv,[13] Deputy Assistant to the President, received us and escorted us to the family quarters, where First Lady Barbara Bush greeted His Holiness. She was apologetic that the President was not there, pointing to the television showing him still answering questions in the press briefing room. Millie the dog's immediate liking of His Holiness delighted the First Lady, adding an unexpected note of intimacy to our meeting.

When the President arrived, his National Security Advisor, Brent Scowcroft, accompanied him. One could see that the President was very well informed about the PRC and the situation in Tibet. This was not surprising, as he had previously served as CIA Director and Chief of the US Liaison Office to the PRC, as well as Vice President in the Reagan administration. It was a very relaxed and friendly meeting. President Bush was a good listener, but while sympathetic, he made no specific commitments. We were not expecting anything substantive because of his focus on the "larger" PRC issue, but the mere fact that he met His Holiness greatly enhanced the profile of both Tibet and His Holiness. But it was with his son, President George W. Bush, that His Holiness developed a deep personal friendship.

### *The Clinton Administration*

Through the tremendous efforts of many people, by the late 1990s Tibet had become a mainstream issue in the United States, as well as an important factor in US-PRC relations. It became routine practice that during any formal or informal discussions between US and PRC officials above a certain level, the issue of Tibet would be on the agenda.

The importance of Tibet in Sino-American relations was highlighted in the globally publicized joint press statement issued by Presidents Clinton and Jiang on June 27, 1998, in Beijing.[14] Jeff Bader, who would go on to become US Ambassador to Namibia, was then a senior staff member at the White House dealing with Asian affairs. He was of tremendous assistance in making sure that the Tibet issue was not only included as an important topic of discussion but also mentioned during the joint press conference following the meeting. He worked with all the parties—the Americans, the Chinese, and me, as representative of the Tibetans, to accommodate each party's concerns. As a result of this and other collaborations, we became close personal friends.

We worked so closely with the US administration in preparing for this meeting that I knew in what context President Clinton would take up the issue of

Tibet, including the formulation he would use. We even had some knowledge of how Beijing would react. The following excerpts from the transcript of the conference illustrate the high level of the parties' engagement on the issue:

**PRESIDENT CLINTON:** I reaffirmed our longstanding "one China" policy to President Jiang and urged the pursuit of cross-strait discussions recently resumed as the best path to a peaceful resolution. In a similar vein, I urged President Jiang to assume a dialogue with the Dalai Lama in return for the recognition that Tibet is a part of China and in recognition of the unique cultural and religious heritage of that region.

**PRESIDENT JIANG:** I'm sorry, I have to take up an additional 5 minutes. [*Laughter*] So I'd like to say a few words on Dalai Lama. President Clinton is also interested in this question, in Dalai Lama. Actually, since the Dalai Lama left in 1959, earth-shaking changes have taken place in Tibet.

First, the system of theocracy has forever become bygones, though it is unfortunate that the disappearance of this theocracy was much later than the demise of theocracy in Europe, that's before the Renaissance. And the more than 1 million serfs under the rule of the Dalai Lama were liberated. In 1990 when I was in Tibet, I went to visit the liberated serfs. And now the system of national autonomy is in practice in Tibet, and the people there, they have their Tibetan autonomous region government.

Since I came to work in the central government, I have urged the rest 29 Provinces, Municipalities, and Autonomous Regions to assist Tibet in its development, even including those provinces that are not very developed, such as Qinghai Province. So all together, nearly 8 billion RMB-yuan financial resources were raised, and already 62 projects have been completed in Tibet.

As for the freedom of religious belief, there is clear stipulations in our constitution for the protection of religious belief, and this also includes in Tibet. And we have also spent a lot of money in renovating the lamaseries and temples in Tibet. And we have spent 100 million RMB-yuan and one ton of gold in renovating the Potala Palace.

Just now President Clinton also mentioned the Tibetan issue and the dialogue with the Dalai Lama. Actually, as long as the Dalai Lama can publicly make a statement and a commitment that Tibet is an inalienable part of China and he must also recognize Taiwan as a province of China, then the door to dialogue and negotiation is open. Actually, we are having several channels of communications with the Dalai Lama. So I hope the Dalai Lama will make positive response in this regard.

Finally, I want to emphasize that according to China's constitution, the freedom of religious belief in Tibet and also throughout China is protected. But as the President of the People's Republic of China and as a Communist member, a member of the Communist Party, I myself am an atheist. But this will by no means affect my respect for the religious freedom in Tibet.

But still, I have a question. That is, during my visit to the United States last year and also during my previous visits to other European countries, I found that although the education in science and technology have developed to a very high level and people are now enjoying modern civilization, but still quite a number of them have a belief in Lamaism. So this is a question that I'm still studying and still looking into. I want to find out the reason why.

I think President Clinton is a strong defender of the American interests, and I am a strong defender of the Chinese interests. But despite that, we still can have very friendly exchanges of views and discussions. And I think that is democracy. And I want to stress that, actually, there are a lot of areas in which we can learn from each other.

If you agree, we will finish this. [*Laughter*]

**PRESIDENT CLINTON:** I agree, but I have—you have to let me say one thing about the Dalai Lama, since you brought it up. [*Laughter*]

First, I agree that Tibet is a part of China, an autonomous region of China. And I can understand why the acknowledgement of that would be a precondition of dialogue with the Dalai Lama. But I also believe that there are many, many Tibetans who still revere the Dalai Lama and view him as their spiritual leader. President Jiang pointed out that he has a few followers of Tibetan Buddhism even in the United States and Europe. But most of his followers have not given up their own religious faith. He has followers who are Christians—supporters, excuse me, not followers, supporters—who are Christians, who are Jews, who are Muslims, who believe in the unity of God, and who believe he is a holy man.

But for us, the question is not fundamentally religious; it is political. That is, we believe that other people should have the right to fully practice their religious beliefs and that if he, in good faith, presents himself on those terms, it is a legitimate thing for China to engage him in dialogue.

> And let me say something that will perhaps be unpopular with everyone. I have spent time with the Dalai Lama. I believe him to be an honest man, and I believe if he had a conversation with President Jiang, they would like each other very much. [*Laughter*]

Sadly, while the prominence of this press conference was very beneficial for us on some levels, it also created tremendous obstacles, as I discuss in a later chapter.[15] I must credit President Clinton and his team, particularly Jeff Bader, however, for helping us build the foundation upon which direct dialogue with Beijing ultimately resumed during President George W. Bush's administration.

**Hillary Clinton: First Lady, Senator, and Secretary of State**

During the Clinton presidency, First Lady Hillary Clinton took considerable interest in Tibet. While President Clinton was sympathetic, our issue was just one among many on his busy agenda. But his wife took a special interest in Tibet, with a visit to Mongolia in 1995 sparking in her a deeper understanding and appreciation of Tibetan culture and the institution of the Dalai Lama.

When the First Lady decided to lead the US delegation to the Global Women's Conference in Beijing in the fall of 1995, many human rights organizations strongly opposed her participation. They believed it gave unwarranted legitimacy to the PRC. But others, including many women's organizations, lobbied for her participation to elevate the substantive issues being addressed. I felt that her participation was important, but even more crucial than her attending was what she would say and do while she was there.

In the end it was decided that the First Lady would attend, but that the conference would be just one stop as part of a regional visit, not solely a visit to the PRC. At the time Mongolia was lobbying for a high-level US visit. The Mongolian Ambassador to the United States, Jalbuugin Choinhor, approached the State Department and the White House to see if the First Lady would include Mongolia on her trip. Many other countries in the region were also requesting visits and had very strong advocates. To support Ambassador Choinhor's efforts, I also lobbied the White House on Mongolia's behalf. The First Lady ultimately visited Mongolia in September 1995, following the Global Women's Conference.

When the First Lady returned from her trip, senior White House officials told me that she was very impressed with Mongolia, particularly with the popularity of His Holiness. Encouraged by this, I approached her office, with the result that when His Holiness came to Washington, D.C., soon thereafter, the First Lady hosted an intimate dinner for him at the residence of her very close friend Vernon Jordan. At her table, it was only His Holiness, His Holiness's Secretary Tenzin Geyche, and me.

As the dinner was held soon after the First Lady's return, the visit was very fresh in her mind. She told His Holiness that he was so popular in Mongolia that if he ran for office there, no local politician would have any chance of beating him. She also shared the details of her trip, including visits to nomadic areas and private citizens' homes. Wherever she went, she found that a person's most prized possession was a photograph of His Holiness. This made her realize that the influence of His Holiness and the Tibetan culture extended far beyond Tibet.

His Holiness very much enjoyed getting to know the First Lady, appreciating her candor and warmth. They discussed a number of issues of mutual interest in a very relaxed manner. His Holiness even felt comfortable enough to share his concerns about the Christian missionaries then aggressively trying to convert Buddhists in Mongolia. His Holiness raised this concern not for sectarian reasons but from a larger perspective based on maintaining stability in the region. He pointed out that the Mongolians had suffered half a century under Soviet Communist rule and even though they had technical "sovereignty," for all practical purposes Mongolia was a satellite of the Soviet Union. As a result, Mongolian culture, particularly Mongolian Buddhist culture, had been severely undermined by the Communists. While attempting to recover from this onslaught, they were being challenged yet again by another alien culture, this time Christianity. He further told her that for Mongolia to be a strong and sovereign nation, Mongolians must be encouraged to retain their identity, their self-respect, and their confidence.

I could see that the First Lady was a bit taken aback by His Holiness's candor, but I think this kind of frank discussion is one of his strengths. While his direct and forthright manner sometimes makes those of us in his entourage a little nervous, surprisingly, it actually brings people closer to him.

This dinner was held the day before His Holiness's third meeting with President Clinton. The prior two meetings had been "drop-bys" at the Vice President's office, but this was a formal meeting scheduled on the President's official calendar. After their initial discussion, the First Lady joined the President and His Holiness for tea. She then told her husband that His Holiness had been quite blunt with her about some issues at dinner the night before. She recounted for the

President their discussion on Christian missionary activities in Mongolia, and His Holiness further elaborated on his views.

Later, when she became a Senator, Hillary Clinton became actively involved in Tibet issues, supporting every Tibet-related bill that was introduced during her tenure in Congress. An added advantage for us was Senator Dianne Feinstein's personal friendship with her. The two Senators hosted His Holiness together on a number of occasions. As Secretary of State in the Obama administration, Senator Clinton continued to show her support for Tibet, including receiving His Holiness in 2010.

I must acknowledge here that Vice President Al Gore was of great help in the initial years of the Clinton administration. I had built a close personal friendship with him when he was the Senator from Tennessee and very active on environmental issues. I was among those who were deeply disappointed when he lost the presidential election, personally visiting him to convey my sincere regret. But I

Vice President Al Gore greeting His Holiness, accompanied by the author, at the White House, 1993
International Campaign for Tibet

must confess that, despite my support for him, a few years later I voted to reelect George W. Bush because of his deep understanding of and sympathy for Tibet and his genuine friendship with His Holiness.

*George W. Bush Administration*

I can say with a great degree of confidence that a special chemistry existed between His Holiness and President George W. Bush. "W," as he is widely known, is deeply religious, and I think he regarded His Holiness with special reverence as a spiritual leader. He was always extremely polite in the presence of His Holiness, tempering his behavior so as not to give even the slightest offense. One example I recall is his determination not to sit cross-legged, as was his usual seated posture. Someone must have told him that this could be perceived as disrespectful. I noticed that during many of their meetings, the President would consciously try to sit properly, further addressing His Holiness as "Sir, Sir." As the conversation became more animated, he would forget himself and cross his legs again before immediately coming to attention and trying to sit respectfully. It was very touching.

Over the years the President and His Holiness met a number of times. During their last meeting while he was President, First Lady Laura Bush joined them as they were walking out of the meeting. His Holiness was actually between the two of them, warmly holding their hands. At their parting, the President looked directly into His Holiness's eyes and said: "We love this man." The President again said: "You tell me what I can do for you. Just tell me." He said this in such a sincere manner that it was clear he really meant it. Those were powerful words of commitment coming from the President of the United States.

**Dialogue with the PRC**

When we first started the dialogue process with Beijing in the 1980s, I was tasked with creating an opportunity for His Holiness to make a private pilgrimage to the PRC that would give him the opportunity to meet personally with some senior leaders. Both the Clinton and Bush administrations felt that this was achievable and the best way to help bring some understanding between the Chinese and the Tibetans. We were very committed to this approach. George W. Bush really hoped he could help make this happen. Unfortunately, Beijing was lukewarm to the proposal. Moreover, even when we finally started directly negotiating with them, the PRC leadership continued to regale the international community with their favorite propaganda: "There is no Tibet issue. The only issue is the relation of Dalai Lama with Central Government."

This persistent attitude compelled His Holiness to deprioritize the idea of a visit to the PRC out of concern that Beijing would use it as evidence of its position that the dialogue was all about him. I was instructed to convey this to the Bush administration. Kelsang Gyaltsen and I, the primary negotiators, were also instructed no longer to raise it in our discussions with our counterparts.

The Bush administration understood our position but was deeply disappointed by it. Senior officials sincerely felt that we should continue making a visit a priority. Some of the President's national security staff asked me whether President Bush directly raising the matter with His Holiness would be appropriate. It was very clear that the administration felt it could help arrange a face-to-face meeting between His Holiness and PRC leaders and that it would be a meaningful event. I reiterated His Holiness's concern about the PRC's potential propaganda use of such a meeting and that we saw no sincere effort on Beijing's part to agree to a visit. In his meetings with His Holiness, President Bush never urged him to reconsider his decision even though the President still believed that a personal meeting with the PRC leaders would be the catalyst for resolving the Tibet issue. Knowing how respectful President Bush is of His Holiness, I believe he may have decided not to pursue the matter because his advisors had already briefed him on His Holiness's resolute position.

**Senior Staff of the George W. Bush Administration**

We were also very fortunate during George W. Bush's presidency to have a very sympathetic team of senior officials. Condoleezza Rice, his National Security Advisor and well-regarded academician from Stanford University, was extraordinarily helpful. I met her within a few months of her appointment. I took Bhuchung Tsering, who later became the ICT's Vice President, with me for this visit. Whenever I went for meetings at the White House or State Department, I went in my capacity as the Special Envoy of His Holiness the Dalai Lama. Most of the time I took Bhuchung Tsering with me to emphasize my ties with the Tibetan community. Sometimes for visits to State I also took senior ICT staff, although I was always careful to emphasize our different roles. As an American NGO, the ICT could lobby for US policies that would have been improper for me, as the Dalai Lama's Special Envoy, to advocate.

Let me first share an interesting anecdote of my initial meeting with Condoleezza Rice. I went to meet her armed with a few books about Tibet and a *khata*, a ceremonial scarf that we Tibetans always offer when visiting respected individuals. She has a far better memory than I do. The moment I walked into her office, she said: "We met before, remember? I was among a small group of faculty members at Stanford that had a lovely discussion with His Holiness the Dalai Lama, which you organized." After looking through the book titles, she kept only one book, saying: "Lodi, you need not educate me. I have always been interested in your issue. Give the remaining books to people who need to be educated more."

A few weeks after our meeting, I received a package from the White House that created quite a bit of excitement at my office. When we opened it, there was the *khata* I had given National Security Advisor Rice together with a short but polite note saying that due to restrictions on the value of gifts administration officials were allowed to receive, the scarf was being returned. Of course, it was a rather long and elegant silk scarf, but the offering is an entirely symbolic gesture of respect with scant monetary value. I explained this aspect of Tibetan protocol and custom by writing a rather lengthy response to her office, but of course, I didn't return the scarf. Some years later, when she became Secretary of State, I walked in again with my ceremonial scarf. With a big smile, Secretary Rice said: "Lodi, I will keep your scarf. I know what it is and the importance of it in your tradition."

Normally it is not my habit to seek appointments with such high-profile dignitaries as Secretaries of State or National Security Advisors. Working with their senior staff or with people at the level of Assistant Secretaries, who head bureaus and do the substantive work, tends to yield the most concrete results. But sometimes these officials encourage me to meet with their senior colleagues and even facilitate such meetings.[16] This was the case for my initial meeting with Condoleezza Rice. Mike Green, the Senior Director for Asian Affairs, not only encouraged but also arranged the meeting. During the Bush administration, Mike was the key person I relied on at the White House. Previously, work on Asia had been split between two White House departments as it was at State. The Bush administration wanted to adopt a policy that looked at Asia holistically. As Mike was already working with East Asia as well as South and Southeast Asia, consolidation of all Asian affairs under his direction was natural. I really appreciated that approach, but it didn't last long. President Obama reversed it soon after assuming office.

Relations with the PRC are often managed directly by the President, frequently leading to senior staff at the National Security Council having more influence over policy than their counterparts at State. Of course, this also depends on the personal relationship between the President and the Secretary of State. Depending on the personalities involved, there are times when relations between State and the White House can be tense. Fortunately for us, there was full cooperation on Tibet, with Special Coordinator Dobriansky working well with both James Kelly, Assistant Secretary of State for the EAPA Bureau, and Mike Green at the White House.

On too many occasions, the Assistant Secretary for the EAPA Bureau has raised objections to policies suggested by the Special Coordinator for Tibetan Issues. We never had this happen when James Kelly held the position. He often joined former Special Coordinator Dobriansky at the Tibet Summit meetings that she organized. Moreover, the Special Coordinator enjoyed the full confidence of Secretary of State Colin Powell during his tenure from 2001 to 2005. We also had a strong ally in Richard Armitage, who was Colin Powell's number two at State.

I remember Richard Armitage very fondly. He had a wonderful sense of humor. One time, during a meeting with Secretary Powell and His Holiness, he asked His Holiness to spend some additional time with him in his office. At one point, he told His Holiness about a recent conversation he had had with President Chen Shui-bian of Taiwan. His Holiness thought that Richard must have met with the Taiwan President America a few weeks earlier. "Oh, you met him?" His Holiness asked. Pointing to several of the senior State Department officials in the room taking notes, Richard replied: "Oh no, these people never allow me to do that. I wish I could do that. But I spoke to him on the phone, which they couldn't stop." They both had a big laugh. His Holiness very much liked Richard. Every time they met, His Holiness assumed a boxing posture, as he saw Richard as having the strong body and mind of a boxer.

A few months before the end of his presidency in 2009, President George W. Bush and First Lady Laura Bush kindly included me among a small group of people they invited to Governors Island in New York for an intimate luncheon. They told the group that after leaving the White House, they would like to remain engaged with some issues that they felt a special connection to, and Tibet was one of them. They invited each of us present at the lunch, in our individual capacities, to be part of the effort. The First Lady would take the lead until the President completed his term. She further invited me to the White House to introduce me to her personal assistant, who would help arrange the meetings.

Governors Island lunch meeting, fall 2009
International Campaign for Tibet

At my subsequent meeting with the First Lady, I expressed my deep gratitude for the interest she and the President had shown in Tibet and for inviting me to be part of this esteemed group of individuals. Because of my heavy responsibilities in Washington, coupled with our ongoing dialogue with PRC officials, I didn't think I would do justice to the group's efforts, at least in the initial stages. I proposed that my colleague Thubten Samphel, a senior staff member of the CTA, take my place. Unfortunately, primarily because of lack of funding as well as a change of personalities at the Bush Center, the project was never realized.

*The Obama Administration*

As previously mentioned, Jeff Bader was the Senior Director for Asian Affairs when the joint Jiang-Clinton press conference took place. The close working and personal relationship I developed with him during that period was of immense value in the beginning of the Obama presidency. While the President had supported most of the Tibet initiatives when he was a Senator, he was not among our active supporters, so we didn't have a personal relationship with him. He appointed Ambassador Bader as his Senior Director for East Asian Affairs on the National Security Council, however, thus giving me immediate access to a senior member of his staff.

In addition to Jeff Bader, Greg Craig, the first appointed Special Coordinator for Tibetan Issues during the Clinton administration, was another important conduit to the new administration. President Obama appointed him White House legal counsel. A close personal friend from Chicago also introduced me to Valerie Jarrett, who became Senior Advisor to the President. She was probably the President's closest confidante and one of the most influential persons in the Obama administration. All of these individuals were of immense help.

Senator Feinstein and her husband, Richard Blum, continued to be extremely helpful. The Senator, who chaired the ceremonies for President Obama's inauguration, attended the customary postinauguration breakfast hosted by the outgoing President, along with her husband. As recorded in *An Accident of Geography*, Richard took the opportunity to present the President-elect with a *khata*, saying that it carried the blessings of His Holiness the Dalai Lama:

> The morning of January 20, 2009, Dianne and I were at the White House to join other members of the official inaugural party for Senator Barack Obama at a breakfast hosted by George W. and Laura Bush, one of their last official acts as President and First Lady.
>
> It is a Tibetan tradition to present a silk scarf, or khata, as a sign of greeting when meeting someone. His Holiness had blessed and given me a beautiful white khata on his previous visit to the United States. I said to the President-elect during breakfast that His Holiness had wanted me to convey his congratulations, adding that I thought the khata would be a fitting gift and wanted to give it to him. I figured he would add the khata to the pile of inaugural gifts streaming in. "Who do I give it to?" I asked.
>
> "Let me have it," he said, reaching out. "I'm going to put it in my back pocket and keep it there while I've got my hand on the Bible." And he did.
>
> Not long after, Dianne, who was leading the inaugural ceremonies, announced, "It is my great personal honor to present the forty-fourth President of these United States, Barack Obama." Word spread on pro-Tibetan websites and elsewhere that the new American President had carried a scarf blessed by the Dalai Lama while taking the oath of office. The White House wanted to avoid antagonizing China in the President's first days in office and declined comment about the khata. I did mention the khata story privately

but never confirmed it publicly—until now. My belief is that in reaching out for the khata by his own hand that morning, the incoming President was expressing his respect for the Tibetan people's continuing struggle.[17]

### 2010 Meeting of President Obama and His Holiness

A few months into the Obama presidency, His Holiness's Private Office advised me that as part of his US tour, His Holiness would be visiting Washington, D.C., in October 2009. I was asked to start working with the White House for a meeting with President Obama. As official meetings with the President had become well established during the preceding administrations, I was not at all worried that the White House might not receive him. I was also quite sure the President had a personal interest in meeting His Holiness. In recent years, however, the US-PRC relationship had become one of the most important of the US bilateral relationships, and it was only natural that the administration would want to be extremely careful in planning the meeting. I also knew from past experience that a request for a meeting this early in a presidency was a significant "ask," as new administrations appreciate some time to settle into the job, first focusing on acute or high-priority issues.

Nevertheless, I immediately approached Jeff Bader, as well as other friends both in and outside the administration. In fact, even before I received instructions from Dharamsala, Jeff and I discussed a visit by His Holiness and how to maximize the benefits of the meeting. Jeff felt a visit as early as the suggested October date, however, could be problematic because of the President's planned visit to the PRC in November. He asked me to communicate with Dharamsala to find some other possible dates toward the end of the year.

I have always felt that good results require mutual respect and an appreciation of our counterpart's situation and priorities. Jeff knew from his experience working with us during the Clinton administration that our request for an October White House meeting was built around His Holiness's existing itinerary. As a friend, he once chided me, saying: "Lodi, do you know that you are the only person who walks into the White House and tells us the month and date that *we* need to arrange a meeting with the President?" The White House's receptivity to our unorthodox behavior reflects nothing more than the high regard in which it held His Holiness.

What might be viewed as arrogance on our part was not born of any disrespect for the Office of the President but rather was a result of the CTA's inexperience with Washington protocol. To remedy this naïveté, I even explored the possibility of His Holiness's senior staff visiting Washington, D.C., to gain some understanding of the complexity of the process. They would then know how best to navigate it in the future. This proposed meeting, for example, was the subject of lengthy discussions at the highest level of the US administration, requiring clearance at many different levels. A complicating factor was the Defense Department's contemporaneous effort to conclude a large arms sale to Taiwan, a transaction that also required the President's approval. If I recall correctly, the proposed arms sale was a several-billion-dollar deal and thus a high priority for the Defense Department. In the midst of planning a summit meeting between President Obama and Hu Jintao, needless to say, the recently inaugurated Obama administration wanted to avoid offending the PRC by signing off on a big arms sale to Taiwan and at the same time receiving the Dalai Lama at the White House.

The potential complications arising from the arms sale were first discussed by the Deputies Committee, which was then chaired by Deputy National Security Advisor Tom Donilon. After that, it was considered by the Principals Committee, at the time chaired by NSA General Jim Jones. The Principals Committee included Secretary of State Clinton, Secretary of Defense Robert Gates, Chairman of the Joint Chiefs of Staff Admiral Michael Mullen, Director of National Intelligence Dennis Blair, and Director of Central Intelligence Leon Panetta,[18] with other senior officials, including Tom Donilon and James Steinberg, Deputy Secretary of State, also participating.

By contrast, the decision to meet His Holiness was taken unilaterally by the President. In his book, Jeff Bader quotes the President telling both him and Tom Donilon: "Let me cut this argument short. I am going to meet him." And thus, the certainty of a meeting was confirmed. The timing of that meeting still needed to be determined, however.

As I mentioned, we were hoping His Holiness could meet the President in October because of his previously scheduled US trip, during which he was committed to giving teachings to large numbers of Buddhist practitioners in multiple cities. Many of the venues had already been booked, programs publicly announced, and substantial funds collected and expended by the event organizers. Changes to that itinerary to accommodate a meeting with the President were simply not possible. My colleagues in Dharamsala were responsive to the White House's concerns, however, and suggested that His Holiness make a separate trip in August to meet with the President, giving the administration several months before President Obama's November visit to the PRC. To my surprise, Jeff thought the timing might work, even though he felt that the ideal situation would be for His Holiness to come after the PRC trip.

Unfortunately, this option died quickly. Not only were Jeff's colleagues at the White House and State Department unsupportive, some of them expressed their deep disappointment at our lack of appreciation of the President's situation. James Steinberg was among those who vigorously opposed any meeting before the November PRC visit.

I had known James for several years, beginning when he was the Deputy National Security Advisor in the Clinton White House. He had always been very approachable and helpful. I went to see him to argue our case, but he was quite firm in his position, urging us to be more understanding of the importance and delicacy of US–PRC relations and not to cause any inconvenience to the President, who had genuine respect for His Holiness. I appreciated his candor and completely understood his position. I too have always fully subscribed to the view that good relations between the United States and the PRC do more for the Tibetan cause than a hostile situation, in which case the United States has no influence over the PRC whatsoever.

Sometimes our passionate friends in the Tibetan world tend to see things in black and white, categorizing people into friends and enemies. I remember there were a lot of harsh words uttered against the Obama administration for its refusal to schedule a presidential meeting with His Holiness before the PRC trip. There were also some critical media reports. All of this negativity was expressed without any understanding of the behind-the-scenes discussions that led to our *mutual* decision to delay the visit. This negative publicity not only unfairly criticized the administration but also diminished the statesmanship that His Holiness demonstrated in being mindful of the administration's concerns.

Our candid conversations with administration officials regarding the proposed October visit ultimately triggered some unexpected benefits. The President sent Valerie Jarrett to Dharamsala to personally explain the situation to His Holiness and ask for his understanding. This in itself was a major accomplishment, as it reflected the President's respect for His Holiness and his concern for Tibet. I was naturally very pleased with the decision, but there was a complicating factor. As is customary under these circumstances, the administration wanted clear assurances in advance that His Holiness would agree to a meeting after the November trip to the PRC.

Although it wasn't an unreasonable request, I suggested that the purpose of the visit be slightly recharacterized. Valerie Jarrett, as the President's personal emissary, would convey to His Holiness the President's sympathy and support for the Tibetan cause and his sincere commitment to helping resolve the situation through dialogue with the PRC. As the President was planning to visit the PRC in the near future, with the Tibet issue high on his list of priorities, she also wanted to seek His Holiness's advice. In addition, she would convey an invitation from the President for His Holiness to visit him at the White House.

The administration accepted my proposal but still wanted a definitive answer to the question whether His Holiness would agree to a post-November meeting. I explained that I could not speak for His Holiness, but after working for him for so many years and knowing his understanding nature, I was confident that he would see the benefits of the proposed timing. At the same time, I was in close contact with Samdhong Rinpoche, Head of the Kashag, who shared my view that His Holiness would respond positively to the administration's suggestion. The meeting was ultimately set for February 2010.

This initial hiccup in timing greatly benefited us in the long run. Valerie Jarrett's visit, much like that of Nancy Pelosi the prior year, was noted by everyone concerned, especially Beijing and the government of our host country, India. It was quite uplifting to see the importance attached to a visit by a presidential emissary. The protocol and associated security arrangements also kept the local Indian operatives, as well as my colleagues in Dharamsala, on their toes.

Valerie Jarrett became a committed friend of Tibet. More than once, I went to her seeking some special assistance where a word from the White House was necessary. Because of her September 2009 visit, she became a key player in the Obama administration on issues relating to Tibet. She joined President Obama during his meetings with His Holiness in 2010 and 2011, and I am quite certain that she participated in subsequent meetings between them held after my retirement.

I was hoping that Jeff Bader would accompany her on her trip to Dharmasala, but we lost him to an urgent matter in East Asia. His colleague Evan Medeiros took his place. This actually worked out quite well, as it gave Jeff's colleague an opportunity to better understand the issue and for us to begin building a personal friendship. Evan Medeiros remained at the White House for several years, becoming the Senior Director for Asian Affairs when Jeff departed for the Brookings Institution.

**A Milestone: The 2010 Press Release Endorsing the Middle Way Approach**

As is standard practice before a meeting of His Holiness with prominent governmental officials, I started working on the content of the associated press release weeks ahead of the scheduled visit, this time with Jeff Bader and his colleagues Daniel Russel[19] and Evan Medeiros. I knew that the White House would issue a very supportive statement on both the importance of preserving the distinct Tibetan identity and the necessity of continuing dialogue with Beijing, but I was keen on having the statement include specific mention of the Middle Way Approach.

Over the years, successive Presidents of the United States have come to understand the essence of our position, giving full support to His Holiness's efforts to resolve the issue through dialogue. However, while they would urge Beijing to engage in dialogue with us and compliment His Holiness on his efforts to reach out to the PRC leadership, they would never specifically endorse the Middle Way Approach. It was President Obama's administration that first explicitly supported it. The official press release issued after His Holiness's first meeting with the President on February 18, 2010, states:

> The President met this morning at the White House with His Holiness the XIV Dalai Lama.
>
> The President stated his strong support for the preservation of Tibet's unique religious, cultural and linguistic identity and the protection of human rights for Tibetans in the People's Republic of China. The President commended the Dalai Lama's "Middle Way" approach, his commitment to nonviolence and his pursuit of dialogue with the Chinese government. The President stressed and was pleased to hear about the recent resumption of talks. The President and the Dalai Lama agreed on the importance of a positive and cooperative relationship between the United States and China.

This was a momentous event.

His Holiness developed the approach as a true compromise between the parties' opposing views. President Obama was the first head of state to publicly endorse it. This was of great significance. Once a government takes a position, it becomes part of the official narrative that can take considerable effort to reverse. The US's official "seal of approval" of the Middle Way Approach at long last elevated His Holiness's proposal to a prominent place on the US's and the international community's foreign policy agendas, confirming its substance as the core of the solution to the issue. This never could have happened without the concerted efforts of all the individuals, both in Congress and in the executive branch, who championed our cause.

## Discussions Leading to the 2011 Meeting of President Obama with His Holiness

With the historic changes taking place in Dharamsala following His Holiness's decision in 2011 to devolve political leadership to a democratically elected body, I had decided to resign my position as Special Envoy. As I knew His Holiness's second meeting with President Obama would be the last one I arranged, I took special care in organizing it. I was particularly concerned that the Obama administration reiterate its support for the Middle Way Approach, a public commitment that had taken so long to realize. Per the usual routine, I started working with the Senior Director for East Asian Affairs at the White House, who by this time was Daniel Russel, and Evan Medeiros. We developed the agenda for the meeting and drafted the press release that the White House would issue afterward. The following excerpt is taken from the memorandum summarizing the discussion I was having with the White House that I prepared for His Holiness, his staff, and other senior Tibetan leaders just a day before the White House visit.

> I have spent considerable time discussing with them the content of the statement. They have agreed to reaffirm the President's support for the Middle Way Approach. I have also strongly insisted that when they talk about the distinctive Tibetan identity the language does not limit it to culture and highlights linguistic identity because of the current Chinese policy to limit the Tibetan language. They are playing with the formulation with regards to saying "that His Holiness the Dalai Lama is not seeking Tibet's independence" and changing the word "Tibet" to "Tibetan" in that sentence. I emphasized that they should use the formulation "People's Republic of China" and not "China" when talking about Tibet being a part of the PRC.
>
> The most important issue that I tried to get them to include is complimenting His Holiness on the devolution of his political power. There was very strong pushback on that because it is very clear they do not want in any manner to give the impression that they are acknowledging the political setup. They convey to me strongly that the area where the President can be helpful

> is in supporting the Tibetan people's distinctive identity and getting strongly behind a negotiated settlement of the Tibet issue between His Holiness and the PRC leadership.[20]

As you can see, besides asking for reaffirmation of President Obama's support for the Middle Way Approach, I urged the White House to expressly compliment His Holiness on his devolution of political power. While I wasn't personally pleased with this sweeping change, I knew His Holiness was taking a long-term view and fulfilling his personal commitment to confer political leadership on the Tibetan people.

A number of Tibetan political leaders, as well as many members of the public, were also very excited about "democratization," a noble pursuit in the abstract. In the particular context of our struggle, however, I sometimes felt that our immediate mission was being supplanted by this long-term objective. No one can deny that among all the political systems, democracy is the best, despite its faults. But we did not leave Tibet to pursue democratization as an alternative to the communist system of the PRC. Our goal is clear and simple: preservation and continuation of the unique identity of our great civilization and avoidance of becoming a mere relic of our past, fit only for display in a museum, as has happened to so many other nations and peoples dominated by a more powerful regime.

As my memorandum further noted, the administration was reluctant to make any reference to this historic change. Several hours before His Holiness's scheduled meeting with President Obama, I was asked to meet with Daniel Russel and Evan Medeiros. I was initially concerned that the meeting with the President was going to be postponed, but my fears were alleviated. Not only did they reconfirm the meeting, but further advised me that in addition to the scheduled forty-five minutes, they had kept some additional time should the President and His Holiness wish to continue their discussions. I was elated. Many visiting heads of state aren't accorded that amount of time with the President of the United States.

They further assured me that there would be specific reference in the ensuing press release to the Middle Way Approach and some of the other concerns I had raised, including consistent reference to China as the PRC. But they also made it very clear that the statement would not refer to the devolution of leadership. Although the President deeply admired His Holiness's decision and might personally compliment him for it, the White House could not publicly endorse the transition. Doing so could be viewed as US acknowledgment or even official recognition of the institution to which His Holiness had transferred power. While the US government's long-standing policy acknowledges His Holiness's leadership of the Tibetan people, it does not recognize the CTA or the TGiE in any capacity.

Some people may be surprised at this news and wonder why I am publicly acknowledging it. I believe Tibetans and our supporters must clearly understand the complexity of the political situation in which we must maneuver. If we accept this reality, it will help us design and adopt strategies and policies that can help us move forward despite existing limitations and obstacles.

I previously mentioned my request that the White House refer to China as the PRC. This seemingly inconsequential distinction is actually of vital importance. His Holiness's commitment in the Middle Way Approach and seeking room for the Tibetan people within the *PRC* as opposed to *China* is based on history. The PRC is a political entity that only came into being on October 1, 1949. Saying that Tibet is or will remain a part of *China* can be read to imply that a political relationship predates the formation of the PRC, a contention categorically denied by the Tibetan people.

My request was also made to help diffuse criticism of Dharamsala by some Tibetan leaders receiving funding from the Nationalist Chinese in Taiwan. These individuals accused the CTA of invoking a double standard: while it was acceptable for the CTA to negotiate with Beijing, it was inappropriate for them to deal with the Kuomintang, even though both groups claim Tibet to be part of "China."

During one of my visits to Taiwan, some senior Kuomintang leaders pointed out this seeming contradiction. As I have previously discussed, while there is controversy about the legality of the Seventeen-Point Agreement signed in 1951, it is the *only* document that can be used to support the position that Tibet is now part of the PRC. If we were to accept the Kuomintang's position that Tibet is part of "China," we would not only contradict the legal status of Tibet but also undermine our negotiations with the PRC.

## The 2011 Meeting: Misperceptions Arising from Even the Best-Laid Plans

My primary purpose in writing this book is not only to accurately chronicle the history of our relations with the PRC over the last thirty years but also to provide a guide and resource for future discussions between the principals. While inclusion of so many details makes the narrative lengthy, and perhaps tedious to some, a factually correct portrayal of the individuals involved, the tenor of the discussions, and lessons to be learned cannot be communicated in their absence. The circumstances surrounding the issuance of President Obama's press release after the 2011 meeting with His Holiness are illustrative.

The importance of negotiating in advance both the particulars attendant on high-level meetings and the official statements issued in their wake, down to the seemingly most inconsequential details or language, cannot be overstated. Even with the most meticulous planning, unforeseen events can and do engender significant unintended consequences. The incident I am about to relate serves as a constant reminder to me of both the necessity of excruciatingly detailed planning and the vagaries of life over which we have no control.

Arranging a visit to the White House is a monumental undertaking. His Holiness's visits to Washington, D.C., and especially his meetings with an incumbent president, are planned months in advance. One could easily write a quite impressive book on each trip, from the planning stage to the elaborate and complicated discussions with the White House, the State Department, and members of Congress. In addition to these conversations, there are literally volumes of internal memos sent to His Holiness's Private Office and the Kashag, as well as a division of responsibilities at the ICT. Equal numbers of communications are circulated among the White House, the State Department, and congressional staff. In addition, we prepare a visit book not only cataloging His Holiness's minute-by-minute itinerary but also including extensive background information on every person His Holiness will meet.

As Washington visits are almost exclusively for political purposes, we plan each one to serve a specific and well-defined objective. On the advice of veteran diplomats and experienced congressional staff, we arrange these visits in accordance with the formal protocol accorded heads of state. The details of His Holiness's meetings are planned in close coordination with his Private Office and the head of the Kashag, the Kalon Tripa, in Dharamsala. When I was Special Envoy, I also met numerous times with senior White House staff so that both sides knew most of the major issues that would be discussed.

One of the most important substantive issues that we have historically succeeded in having on the agenda is US affirmation of its core policy on Tibet, specifically its commitment to the protection and preservation of Tibet's distinct cultural, religious, and national identity. This is no minor commitment, and it is something that has been achieved only as a result of years of effort. The culmination of these efforts was President Obama's specific endorsement of the Middle

Way Approach in the press statements following his meetings with His Holiness in 2010 and 2011. While I am not in any way seeking credit for the success of our work, I will acknowledge that I took the lead in making the effort. The real credit for institutionalizing this landmark commitment must go not only to our friends in Congress, both members and staff, but also to senior administration officials at the White House and at the State Department headed by the Special Coordinator for Tibetan Issues.

Below is an excerpt from the White House statement issued by President Obama's press secretary immediately following the President's 2011 meeting with His Holiness. Given the detailed planning I have outlined regarding the preparation and content of these statements, I am sure readers will now examine every word, as we have, to determine its true meaning. One may also wonder why I am emphasizing the White House's reaffirmation of its support for the Middle Way Approach given that it had already been stated in the wake of their 2010 meeting. Even important policy commitments can fall between the cracks unless they are periodically reaffirmed. As this was to be my last time arranging a presidential meeting, I wanted to make sure this important endorsement of the Middle Way Approach became a standard component of the US government narrative.

> The President met this morning at the White House with His Holiness the XIV Dalai Lama.
>
> The President reiterated his strong support for the preservation of the unique religious, cultural, and linguistic traditions of Tibet and the Tibetan people throughout the world. He underscored the importance of the protection of human rights of Tibetans in China. The President commended the Dalai Lama's commitment to nonviolence and dialogue with China and his pursuit of the "Middle Way" approach. Reiterating the US policy that Tibet is a part of the People's Republic of China and the United States does not support independence for Tibet, the President stressed that he encourages direct dialogue to resolve long-standing differences and that a dialogue that produces results would be positive for China and Tibetans.
>
> The President stressed the importance he attaches to building a US-China cooperative partnership. The Dalai Lama stated that he is not seeking independence for Tibet and hopes that dialogue between his representatives and the Chinese government can soon resume.[21]

Our elation over the substance of this press statement reaffirming the US administration's explicit support for the Middle Way Approach was short-lived, however, as subsequent events of the day curtailed our enthusiasm.

In addition to planning the agenda for the substantive issues to be discussed at a Presidential meeting and working on the wording of official White House statements, we even micromanage logistics, including, for example, His Holiness's points of entry and exit from the White House. After a great deal of resistance, I arranged for His Holiness to speak to the White House press corps after the 2011 meeting. The opportunity conveyed a very powerful message of support of the Tibetan cause by the US government.

Despite all our careful planning, and goodwill on behalf of the administration, an unfortunate incident sabotaged the event. My good friend Jeff Bader best captures this in his book:

> Providing evidence of the maxim that no good deed goes unpunished, the Dalai Lama walked out the front door of the White House to speak to cameras in front of the West Wing at a prearranged photo op. Because of yet another record snowstorm a couple of days earlier, the cleaning crew had failed to clear out some trash bags in front of the White House, and cameras perched at the West Wing site captured him walking past them. The likes of Rush Limbaugh quickly offered outraged commentaries at this supposed calculated insult, charging that the Dalai Lama was banished to the back door of the White House to appease the Chinese. In fact, he had gone out the front door."[22]

I felt very badly, not only that the amazing opportunity for His Holiness to garner the attention of the world had been tarnished but also that the President and many of his senior staff, who had extended the highest courtesy to His Holiness, were being so unfairly criticized. But such is life. Even to this day, I see periodic reference to this incident as supposed "proof" of US insincerity with respect to Tibet, offered by some journalists and academicians who pride themselves as being the "experts" on this issue.

# CHAPTER 15

# India, Our Home Away from Home

## HOMAGE

Let me start this chapter by paying homage to our adopted home of India, as is done in traditional Tibetan style when writing about something precious that deserves reverence. The quote is from "My Personal Words of Gratitude" that I shared with friends and associates on the eve of my retirement from the ICT in 2014.

> I spent my formative years in India. Growing up in that great country and being mentored by some of the extraordinary leaders of India has given me the opportunity to broaden my understanding of global issues, while also sharpening my own sense of dedication to the Tibetan cause. My gratitude and love for the people of India is profound.[1]

When we talk about bringing the issue of Tibet to the international stage, we often forget to discuss India. As India is home to many of us Tibetans, we tend not to think of it as a foreign nation. But India is not our country, and our relationship with it is the most important of all our international relations.

## INITIAL ENCOUNTERS WITH INDIAN LEADERS AND OFFICIALS

In the mid-1960s, as a young man, I had not yet awoken to the fact that the issue of Tibet had relevance to others outside our community. My first inkling of its importance arose when I began interacting with Indian leaders. I was then editor of the Darjeeling-based magazine *Tibetan Freedom*, where I also started the first

Tibetan-published English-language journal, the *Voice of Tibet* (now the *Tibetan Review*). I had my first eye-opening experience when I had the opportunity to go to Delhi, where I met some of the giants of the Indian freedom struggle. I met all of those luminaries with the exception of those who had already passed away, i.e., Mahatma Gandhi, Sardar Patel, and Maulana Azad.

When Pandit Nehru visited Darjeeling in the early 1960s, Lhawang Paljor, a prominent local citizen who was then principal of the Central School for Tibetans, and I were among the few Tibetans chosen to greet him. As Pandit Nehru was such an enormous public figure, I thought he would be physically taller and more imposing in real life than he actually was. But what he lacked in physical stature he more than made up for in personality. You were humbled in his presence.

But the one leader who really opened my eyes to Tibet's relevance in the broader international community was Ram Manohar Lohia, whom I was privileged to get to know quite well. I met him in 1967 and in typical Tibetan style, I thanked him

At the *Tibetan Freedom Press*, the author greets Dharma Vira, Governor of West Bengal, Darjeeling, India

for being such a great supporter of Tibet. I vividly remember his reply because he told me he was not supporting us just for Tibet's sake, but for India's greater good. He further told me that if any Indian leader said he was supporting Tibet on our behalf, either he didn't understand what he was talking about or he was just trying to please us. He then gave me a long explanation of his reasoning. He was very critical of Pandit Nehru and the then Congress government's successive failures to protect Tibet as a buffer state, in his view thereby compromising India's security. This was the first time I realized Tibet's political status was of major interest and relevance to India, and also of importance for regional stability.

Even though at that age I was deeply committed to Tibet's welfare, I was very naïve. I remember him inviting me to visit the Indian Parliament. This was during the days when access to Parliament House, and even the Prime Minister's office, was relatively easy. I was overwhelmed by the majesty and grandeur of Parliament House. It was thrilling for a young man like me to be in the visitor's gallery looking down at all those people whose names and photographs I'd only seen in newspapers.

On the day of my visit, July 14, 1967, member of Parliament Shri Chand Goel offered a private member resolution stating: "The Dalai Lama should be recognized as the Head of the Émigré Government of Tibet and all facilities and help should be extended to him by the Government of India to liberate Tibet from the colonial rule of Communist China." Ram Manohar Lohia rose to speak in support of the resolution, starting his remarks by passionately recounting my recent visit with him:

> A few days before a young Tibetan named Lodi Gyaltsen, who is the editor of a Tibetan newspaper, came to see me. He was on his way to meet the Dalai Lama. He asked me one question with anxiety, "Will Tibet ever become independent?" My anxious heart started aching. Today, while listening to Shri Randhir Singh, I realize that I could have answered him with conviction if I had strength in my heart. I was also young one time and I also used to speak anxiously about the independence of my country. But I was stronger because, after all, we were a population of around thirty-five crore (350 million). The question whether India will become independent or not, never came to my mind. But when Lodi Gyaltsen asked would Tibet ever become independent, I felt very sad. With saddened heart I could only say that if the world is to be progressive and follow the path of independence, then I think she will become independent.[2]

He then went on to criticize the government of India for all of its missteps, using extremely strong language. I was both excited and intimidated by the august nature of the Parliament and the fact that I had triggered a discussion on Tibet, including very critical comments about the government.

His socialist colleague Jayaprakash Narayan, another iconic Indian leader, characterized Dr. Lohia's unabashedly straightforward demeanor as rather unpleasant at times. I experienced that very sentiment myself on occasion. During one of our meetings, he spoke bluntly about his opposition to the sociopolitical system that had existed in Tibet. "Lodi, I am very much against the theocratic system that prevailed in Tibet. I am glad it is gone! But I like the young man." By "young man," he was referring to the Dalai Lama.

I became deeply drawn to this outspoken Indian socialist leader. I went to see him several times during my month-long stay in Delhi. He also took a special interest in, and I believe had a fondness for, me in introducing me to two of his closest young prodigies, Rabi Ray and George Fernandes. These two individuals became lifelong friends, but more importantly, pillars of the Tibet support movement in India. They never wavered in their commitment to the Tibetan cause even when they became prominent Cabinet Ministers in the Indian government. Looking back, I sometimes feel as if Ram Manohar Lohia entrusted me to their care, knowing that he did not have much time to live. He died on October 12, 1967, a few months after our meeting. I consider him one of my early mentors and, had I been Indian, I definitely would have joined the socialist movement under his tutelage. On hearing of his passing, I wrote his obituary in the November 1967 issue of *Voice of Tibet*:

> A Great Loss—The death of Dr. Ram Manohar Lohia has been a great loss to the Tibetans. His courage, sincerity and devotion to the cause of the downtrodden has earned him everlasting gratitude and his name will always be ranked among the greatest sons of India. At the beginning of August, I had the opportunity of exchanging views with him in his residence at Delhi. Little did I know then what fate had in store for him. Now he is no more and with his passing away, we have lost a great defender of our cause.

Besides holding many important ministerial positions, Rabi Ray was also the Speaker of the Lok Sabha, the lower house of the Indian Parliament. At my request, he also served on the ICT's International Council of Advisors. When the

The author being congratulated as editor of the *Tibetan Freedom Press*, Darjeeling, India

ICT presented its Light of Truth award to the people of India, it was Rabi Ray who accepted it on their behalf at a very moving ceremony in Delhi on December 18, 2002. The Light of Truth award is the Tibetan community's highest honor, conferred on individuals and institutions that have helped bring the Tibet issue to international attention. ICT Board Chair Richard Gere and several other board and staff members traveled all the way to Delhi for the ceremony. His Holiness the Dalai Lama personally conferred the award. As President, and later Executive Chair of the ICT, I participated in the presentation of the award on many occasions, but this ceremony was the most fulfilling for me personally, not only because of the sincere gratitude I feel for the people of India but also because my dear friend Rabi Ray accepted it on their behalf.

Rabi Ray passed away on March 6, 2017. Because I do not live in India, I only learned of his passing several months after the fact. Had I known, I definitely would have gone to pay my final respects to him.

My other dear friend, George Fernandes, has been critically ill with Alzheimer's and Parkinson's disease for many years now. I still try to visit him on my periodic trips to Delhi, but it is very painful for me to see this brilliant mind and influential politician in a declining state. During my visits, his wife, Leila, bends near his ear and says: "George, your friend Lodi is here." He will sometimes open his eyes, but it is very difficult to know if he really recognizes me. However, one time when I was visiting him with my son, Minling Penam Rinpoche, I am certain he had at least a moment of recognition. As my son was in his monk's robes, I think it sparked a memory for him because quite often I used to take my children, especially my son, to visit him at his ministerial residence in Delhi. He was very fond of my son as well as my youngest daughter, Tenzing Tsering. When they were young and he came to stay with us in Washington, D.C., he would often hold them on his lap and read to them.

Returning to July 1967, the day following Ram Manohar Lohia's fiery speech in the Indian Parliament condemning the inaction of the Indian government on Tibet's behalf, I was summoned by Gyalo Thondup, His Holiness's elder brother, to his residence at Golf Links. As I previously mentioned, I was working under his leadership, although not directly because he was very busy during those days. He sent Namsey, one of his assistants, to fetch me. When I met him, he was very upset, severely scolding me and giving me no opportunity to sit down or explain what had happened. He bombarded me with questions: "What do you think you are doing? Why are you going around meeting with Indian opposition leaders? You made the government of India very angry." And then he asked Kungo Thupten Nyinje, head of His Holiness's Bureau in Delhi, whose nickname is Palchoe, to set up meetings for me with some very senior Indian officials to explain my actions and apologize.

The next day, Lobsang Tsultrim, one of the Deputy Secretaries of His Holiness's Bureau, brought me to South Block, which houses the offices of the Indian Prime Minister and the Ministry of External Affairs. It was my first visit to these prestigious offices, and I was intimidated upon entering the enormous red stone gates guarding the entrance. The Secretariat building with its colonnaded balconies and extensive roofs dominated by huge domes was overwhelming to someone as young and naïve as I was. Designed by Herbert Baker, one of Britain's most distinguished architects of the early twentieth century, the building was designed to convey the power and prestige of imperial Britain. It was indeed grand, imposing, and majestic, intimidating me as I sheepishly stood in front of its magnificent facade feeling insignificant, insecure, and anxious, as I knew I was not going to be welcomed inside.

Lobsang Tsultrim left me at the office of an official of the Northern Division in the Ministry of External Affairs that handled Tibet-related matters.[3] After waiting for some time, I was escorted to the office of M. K. Rasgotra, who was then heading the Northern Division. He had a very impressive office with a massive desk. He held a small pipe in his hand, and there were six or seven more stored on a pipe rack on his desk. He was reading a file and did not even acknowledge that I had entered the room. I stood there for what felt like ages. Finally, without looking at me and while still seeming to read the file, he pointed to a chair. I slowly walked over and timidly sat down. Again, he made me sit there for some time before finally putting the file down, looking me in the eye, and saying: "So you are the editor of *Freedom Press*." I said, "Yes, sir." "What is the policy and purpose of *Freedom Press*?" I told him that it had no policy, but rather followed the directions of His Holiness the Dalai Lama and the Tibetan government.

My answer clearly did not please him. He became extremely annoyed, delivering a scathing monologue criticizing my remarks and my conduct at the Parliament. "What do you mean by the 'Tibetan government'? There is no Tibetan government," he said. He then proceeded with a long lecture about how His Holiness was welcomed to India solely on humanitarian grounds, not in support of any political agenda, vehemently reciting what has come to be India's oft-repeated, canned speech on the Tibet situation.

His harsh words and aggressive body language were quite intimidating. I was very upset hearing these statements from a senior official of the Indian government. While I knew the government was cautious in its public statements about Tibet and His Holiness to avoid unnecessary conflict with Beijing, the intensity and severity of his denunciation shattered me. As I was young and inexperienced, I reacted without thinking, saying: "Sir, the way you are treating me today clearly demonstrates to me that you yourself had no role in your country's freedom struggle since you don't seem to understand such values." This infuriated him, prompting him to literally say: "Get out of my office."

Needless to say, this first visit to South Block was far from auspicious. Fortunately, during my years of service to His Holiness I have had the opportunity to go back to that imposing building hundreds of times. And on those later occasions, I was well received. In fact, as a result of those visits, I became close personal friends with some of the most brilliant Foreign Service officers ever to serve India.

Many years later, in 1973, I had the opportunity to accompany His Holiness on his first visit to the West. By then I had left Darjeeling and joined the CTA.

During the trip we visited London, where M. K. Rasgotra was then serving as Indian Deputy High Commissioner. Because of the long history of relations with Britain, the Indian government always posts very senior officials in London, and even the Deputy High Commissioners are given full ambassadorial rank. Ambassador Rasgotra was at Heathrow Airport to receive His Holiness when we landed.

I felt very uncomfortable. The Ambassador had aged a little since I first met him, and I had also become a little more mature, though I was still very young. When he received His Holiness, I managed to keep myself to the side, but when His Holiness went to address the media in another room, I was left alone with him in the VIP room. I gathered all my courage, approached him, and asked: "Sir, do you remember me?" He looked at me and responded: "Yes, when I saw you, your face looked very familiar. Have we met before?" I said: "Yes, sir, several years back in your office." Immediately remembering our former, unpleasant interaction, he was unexpectedly kind in trying to smooth over the animosity of that encounter, saying: "Well, I was doing my job." Then he added: "I must tell you that I thought even at that time that this young man would go places. I am really happy that you are serving His Holiness directly." To my great surprise, he was genuinely pleased with my advancement.

Since then, I have had many opportunities to meet him, particularly since he became Foreign Secretary. He was in that position in the early 1980s when I went to the PRC for the first time as a member of the Exploratory Talks Delegation. Even after his retirement from the Foreign Service, I met him from time to time. Romesh Bhandari, who succeeded M. K. Rasgotra, was another Foreign Secretary with whom I worked in the early 1980s.

## RETURN TO DELHI

A chance encounter with the eminent Indian journalist Frank Moraes brought me back to Delhi less than a year after my meeting with Ram Manohar Lohia. When I was the editor of the *Freedom Press*, I tried not only to increase my knowledge of Tibet and how its situation fit into the international picture but also to connect the magazine with the mainstream Indian media, including becoming a member of the All-India Small Newspaper Editors' Conference. It was in Calcutta at one of this group's meetings that I met Frank Moraes, who was then Editor-in-Chief of the *Indian Express*, an English daily paper that had the largest combined circulation in India at that time. He was well informed about Tibet's situation, having even authored a book on the subject entitled *The Revolt in Tibet*. He was obviously pleased to see a young Tibetan refugee boy attending the conference, but he must have also seen how raw and inexperienced I was. He suggested that I come to Delhi to join the *Indian Express* staff for some time, where I could gain needed experience. I decided to take advantage of his kind offer, recognizing not only my lack of experience but also the importance of gaining media attention for advancing Tibet's cause. In those days, it was quite rare to find any newspaper or other media stories about Tibet.

In Gyalo Thondup's absence, in those days Lhamo Tsering, in addition to undertaking many other activities, supervised work at the *Freedom Press*. He was very supportive of my joining the *Indian Express* and further suggested that I ask Frank Moraes to allow a colleague of mine, Tenzing Choegyal, to join me. We both ended up spending several months working in various departments, including advertising and editing, and eventually became subeditors on the night shift. I never returned to the *Freedom Press* after my stint at the *Indian Express* because while working there, Thupten Nyinje, who was then His Holiness's Personal Representative in Delhi, asked me to volunteer at the Bureau of His Holiness the Dalai Lama (the Bureau).

Looking back, my encounters with these prominent Indian political leaders, including the rather confrontational meeting with M. K. Rasgotra at the Foreign Ministry, must have made a rather positive impression on Thupten Nyinje. At a minimum, he must have believed that I had some skills and certainly a lot of enthusiasm. He had discussed his proposal with Gyalo Thondup and with the latter's concurrence, I was appointed a full-time staff member at the Bureau with the main responsibility of editing the *Tibetan Bulletin*, the official publication of the Tibetan Government-in-Exile that in those days was published by the Bureau in Delhi. Becoming a part of the Tibetan civil service through this appointment was a major turning point in my life.

Even after joining the Bureau, I kept in touch with Frank Moraes. I was a frequent visitor to his house in Maharani Bagh in Delhi, where he lived with his companion Marilyn Silverstone, a well-known photojournalist who also had deep passion for Tibet. She was among those journalists who covered His Holiness's historic press conference at Tezpur, soon after his arrival in India in 1959. I had the opportunity to meet this wonderful couple again in 1973 in London, where they had moved, when I was part of His Holiness's entourage. I took time from His Holiness's heavy schedule to visit their home for a lovely evening. Frank Moraes died the following year.

## THE ALL-PARTY INDIAN PARLIAMENTARY FORUM FOR TIBET (APIPFT)

India also has the distinction of establishing the first Parliamentarian group for Tibet, long before any other similar group was formed, a fact too often overlooked in conversations about these influential bodies. In working with the APIPFT, we learned the importance of building a strong network among Parliamentarians. This became one of the best vehicles for raising the profile of the Tibet issue around the world and for providing prominent platforms for His Holiness to speak publicly.

The Indian group's leaders came from all corners of the Indian political spectrum and included such luminaries as M. C. Chagla, Acharya Kripalani, Sucheta Kripalani, Minoo Masani, Madhu Limaye, S. M. Joshi, Atal Bihari Vajpayee, Nanaji Deshmukh, Acharya N.G. Ranga, L. K. Advani, Madhu Dandavate, P. Venkatasubbaiah, Chandra Shekhar, Nanasaheb Goray, Raj Narain, George Fernandes, M. L. Sondhi, and of course, Kushok Bakula, the highly respected Buddhist leader from Ladakh.

Among the Indians from the Himalayan region, Ladakhis have been, in my view, the most helpful to the Tibetans. Kushok Bakula was one of them. He was someone whom Tibetans from many walks of life would rush to consult and seek help from whenever they faced difficulties or problems. Members of His Holiness's office, Kalons, the heads of different Buddhist lineages, and ordinary Tibetans sought and relied on his sage advice over the years. I myself personally received much guidance and support from him. As a senior member of the Indian Parliament, with a spacious official residence centrally located in Delhi, he hosted many Tibetans at his home, including my family and me.

Another supportive Ladakhi who comes to mind is Lama Lobzang. Besides being helpful in many other regards, he literally saved the lives of hundreds of Tibetans. In the early years of exile, tuberculosis (TB) was a chronic disease rampantly killing hundreds of newly arrived Tibetans who had no immunity, as the disease was not present on the world's highest plateau. Lama Lobzang made arrangements with a number of TB sanatoriums to accommodate scores of Tibetans. He went so far as to provide financial assistance and chaperones to personally transport many of the victims to the facilities.

People like Kushok Bakula and Lama Lobzang thought helping the Tibetans was both a privilege and a duty. It was a privilege because His Holiness the

14th Dalai Lama was their spiritual teacher, and it was a duty because the Tibetan people are fellow followers of their revered mentor. Many of the Indian leaders of that generation possessed a unique quality. While many of them were very much on the left politically, they were all deeply rooted in India's spiritual tradition. I sometimes feel deeply saddened when my fellow Tibetans fail to appreciate their extraordinary acts of kindness on our behalf.

We were so fortunate to have the support of all the APIPFT members. Kushok Bakula and George Fernandes helped me recruit many of them. They would personally take me to Parliament House and assist in enrolling their colleagues in the group. M. C. Chagla was a brilliant, eminent lawyer and a former Foreign Minister. He was the first chairman of the APIPFT. M. L. Sondhi, who was elected to the Indian Parliament in 1967, was helpful beyond his activities as part of the group. He left an exemplary Foreign Service career dissatisfied with the direction of India's foreign policy, including India's failure to intervene in the Soviet Union's actions in Czechoslovakia. He and his wife, Madhuri, kept their door open for us at all times. Their cozy little living room in their house near Lodi Gardens was a regular haunt for us to meet and strategize. The Sondhis were an inseparable husband-and-wife team, very similar to my dear American friends, Congressman Tom Lantos and his wife, Annette.

Thupten Nyinje was His Holiness's Representative in Delhi, a very senior posting. He was also the person responsible for recruiting me into the CTA. He later became the Kalon for the Education Department. In addition to helping establish the APIPFT, I served as its lone staff member for over a year. Thupten Nyinje selflessly gave up his weekends to chauffeur me, then just a Deputy Secretary at the Bureau, around Delhi, waiting patiently in the car while I went to persuade individual Parliamentarians to join the group. True dedication! Indeed, I had the honor of working with a number of Tibetan leaders of his generation who were totally committed when it came to advancing our cause.

In advance of my visits to prospective APIPFT members, most of the time M. C. Chagla, Atal Bihari Vajpayee, George Fernandes, Rabi Ray, P. Venkatasubbaiah, or one of the other members of the group's Executive Committee would have spoken to their colleagues, advising them of my hope to recruit them and collect their signatures affirming their commitment on a form we had prepared. I had a very interesting experience during one of these visits. M. C. Chagla had directed me to collect the signature of a Parliamentary group leader of an important regional party from South India. When I arrived and told him who had sent me, he immediately signed the form. Saying that he would be supportive, he told me, however, that I must ask my own member of Parliament to take the lead. It was very clear that he believed we Tibetans had our own Member of Parliament. Most probably he thought that this was an issue concerning Ladakh or Arunachal. When I told him that we didn't have a Member of Parliament and this was a support group for Tibet, he immediately took the form and expunged his name. He argued that he needed to check with his party hierarchy and meet with Foreign Ministry officials, as this was a *foreign policy* matter. He never did understand the nature of the group, although much later, some of his party colleagues did, becoming active participants in the organization.

The APIPFT was also the first group of its kind to visit Dharamsala to call on His Holiness and meet with the Tibetan leadership, including the Kashag. M. C. Chagla was unable to come because of health issues, but the delegation included members from all of India's political parties, except the Communist Party, which never participated in the group.

When it comes to the question of Tibet, Indian Communist Parties have always faced a dilemma. I had an interesting encounter with Jyoti Basu, who was the longest serving Chief Minister of West Bengal, when I was attending the All-India Small Newspaper Editors' Conference previously mentioned. Jyoti Basu was then the editor of *People's Democracy*, the Indian Communist Party's official newspaper, which is still in publication as of this writing. Raj Bahadur, the Union Minister for Information and Broadcasting, was presiding over the conference. After his remarks, people began to ask questions. I remember sitting next to some Urdu newspaper editors from Lucknow, and for the first time I saw people wearing typical Muslim hats who didn't speak English. They were repeatedly raising their hands along with everyone else, but few of them were actually called on. I thought I should also participate, so I raised my hand, assuming I, like them, wouldn't be acknowledged.

Unfortunately, I had become an object of interest, as I was the first Tibetan to participate in the conference. When the Minister saw me raise my hand, he said: "Yes, young man, what do you have to say, my friend?" We had met one-on-one the day before, and he remembered me. Now I was stuck and thoroughly embarrassed. Once again, my nineteen-year-old naïveté surpassed my judgment.[4] Jyoti Basu had spoken just before, offering remarks very critical of the government. This was a few years after the 1962 Sino-Indian War, which was still very fresh in everyone's mind. Showing my inexperience, I challenged Jyoti Basu, stating that it was embarrassing to see Indians criticizing their own government and at the same time supporting the PRC. I am sure the other delegates were aghast at my lack of diplomacy, but I was passionate and spoke from the heart.

The conference was held at Spence's Hotel, one of the upscale establishments in Calcutta. At the end of the proceedings, I was standing outside the hotel entrance trying to get a taxi. It was raining quite heavily, and most of the other delegates must have already made transportation arrangements. Jyoti Basu was one of the few still there. To my surprise, he came over and said: "Where are you heading? Can I give you a lift?" This offer was both a surprise and a challenge to me. Sadly, because of ill treatment by the Chinese Communists, most of us Tibetans felt that every communist was an enemy.

My arrogant, youthful mind told me that I should accept his offer to demonstrate that he did not intimidate me. He then invited me to come to his office for a cup of tea, after which his driver would take me to my accommodation. This further invitation was yet another challenge, one I also felt I had to accept. He led me through a large office with lots of papers and books lying around and imposing portraits of Marx, Lenin, and Stalin. I thought I was in real enemy territory. But Jyoti Basu had a very warm, disarming personality. I cannot remember very clearly all the details of our conversation, but one thing I do remember is his saying he understood that we Tibetans had legitimate grievances, that many of our people had suffered terribly. He offered to put me on the mailing list of his publication. *People's Democracy* was thus sent to Darjeeling in my name for many years even after I left the *Freedom Press*.

That was my first, quite unanticipated encounter with an Indian Communist leader. Since then, I have met quite a few. Although some of them have shown personal sympathy for our cause, none of them openly associated with the Tibet issue in any meaningful way.

## CONSULTATIONS WITH OFFICIALS IN DELHI

We have always kept the government of India fully informed about our communications with Beijing. I have had the opportunity to work very closely with many eminent Indian diplomats and policy makers and greatly benefited as a result. In a professional career spanning over four decades, I have dealt with many officials and diplomats from all over the world. Some of the Indian government officials with whom I worked stand out among this group as being of the highest caliber.

In addition to the Foreign Secretaries already mentioned, I had the opportunity to work closely with Lalit Mansingh, Shyam Saran, Shivshankar Menon, and Nirupama Rao. Lalit Mansingh and Nirupama Rao also served as Indian Ambassadors to the United States, postings that gave me further opportunity to get to know them well. Each of them took a special interest in Tibet because of their personal understanding and knowledge of the situation.

In 2002, when we restarted formal dialogue with the PRC leadership, we briefed senior Indian government officials thoroughly both before and after every visit of my delegation. By then the Office of the National Security Adviser (NSA) had been created. It did not exist in the 1980s. The NSAs with whom I worked included Brajesh Mishra, J. N. Dixit, M. K. Narayanan, and Shivshankar Menon, the former Foreign Secretary, who had been appointed by Prime Minister Manmohan Singh. I greatly benefited from the wise input of all these experienced policy makers. I also met with Ajit Doval, NSA to Indian Prime Minister Narendra Modi, a few times. I did not have any opportunity to work closely with him because by the time the Modi government came into power, I had already resigned as the Dalai Lama's Special Envoy. In our few meetings, however, I got the impression that he is very decisive and a "no nonsense" individual.

With His Holiness's devolution of his political role and an elected leadership taking the helm of the CTA in 2011, I realized that maintaining any relations with government officials in either Delhi or Washington, D.C., might be inappropriate. While these officials knew that my relations with them were now personal in nature, I entered a self-imposed exile to give space to the new leadership in Dharamsala, even though in some cases it might have been beneficial for our cause for me to keep up these meetings. In any event, I not only stopped visiting my former colleagues at Foggy Bottom, the White House, and South Block but even physically kept my distance. I did and continue to maintain relationships with my old friends, who are themselves also retired. And I truly cherish these friendships.

Some of the first NSAs with whom we worked were interested in learning about both the PRC's and our view of the Indo-Tibetan border issue. Brajesh Mishra, who became the Special Representative for border talks, and M. K. Narayanan, who led the majority of those talks, were particularly keen to hear our thoughts. Aside from Shivshankar Menon, I had more opportunities to meet with Brajesh Mishra than with any other NSA. I had the feeling that he and Prime Minister Atal Bihari Vajpayee, whom he served, wanted to pave the way for a better relationship with the PRC by trying to settle their territorial dispute. Sometimes the leader of a party that is perceived as being hawkish and nationalist has a certain advantage and can take some radical steps. President Nixon's policy tilt toward the PRC is one good example. I am not criticizing this approach because, as I discuss hereafter, I believe a conflict-free relationship between the two Asian giants would only benefit Tibet. Whether or not a mutually acceptable solution can be found by both parties is a different question, however.

Soon after Prime Minister Vajpayee's visit to the PRC in June 2003, I had to write to Brajesh Mishra expressing my concerns regarding the references to Tibet in both the joint declaration issued following the meeting and Prime Minister Vajpayee's remarks to the Indian Parliament. While I applauded him for correctly referring to Tibet being a part of the "People's Republic of China" and not "China," I expressed my deep disappointment at the definition of Tibet being limited to the Tibet Autonomous Region (TAR).

In those days we were seriously trying to convince the White House and the State Department to broaden their definition of Tibet to include all Tibetan areas, or at least leave it ambiguous or indeterminate.[5] Beijing was very much aware of our efforts, and I think it deliberately boxed India into a position of declaring that Tibet is only the TAR. While trying to defend this as being consistent with India's "decades-old policy," on July 23, 2003, the Prime Minister told India's Lower House: "We have never doubted that the Tibet Autonomous Region is a part of the territory of the People's Republic of China." I took issue with the expression "never doubted," as it is in fact not consistent with the actual "decades-old policy" of the Indian government.

I hand delivered my letter to the Indian Ambassador in Washington, Lalit Mansingh. My frank expression of concern seemed to have hurt Brajesh Mishra's feelings. In a later telephone conversation I had with Samdhong Rinpoche, he mentioned: "Your friend the NSA is unhappy with your letter." I met with Brajesh Mishra at least once after that, before the change of government in 2004, and he was as cordial as ever, showing no signs of being upset with me. Perhaps Samdhong Rinpoche was pulling my leg.

I must also say that there were some Indian leaders and officials, including members of the Foreign Service, who were intimidated by Beijing. They were, and in some cases remain, overly cautious in their remarks, going out of their way in hopes of appeasing the Chinese. On occasion, for example, an Indian politician will remark that the Tibet issue is an internal matter of the PRC and India should not interfere. Others have also conveyed to Beijing that the Dalai Lama was welcomed into India on humanitarian grounds and as a respected religious leader but is not allowed to indulge in any political activities. While these individuals may think they are mollifying Beijing, the reality is just the opposite. Statements like these have always made the Chinese suspicious. Any person with even an elementary knowledge of the geopolitical situation of India, Tibet, and the PRC knows that Tibet is vitally important to and inseparable from India's future.[6]

Taking advantage of my long association and personal friendship with many senior Indian government officials, I have shared my views on this subject with them many times over the years. I have suggested that rather than shying away from discussing Tibet, the government of India should take a clear position and share it openly with Beijing. Whether it was the mistake of Pandit Nehru and some of his close associates or the failure of the Tibetan government to galvanize support for independence, the fact is that India recognizes the status quo, that the TAR is an autonomous region within the PRC. This position, however, does not contradict His Holiness's Middle Way Approach, which eschews independence for the TAR and the other historic regions of Tibet in exchange for *genuine* autonomy for the Tibetan people regardless of where they reside.

A number of senior Indian leaders have publicly embraced His Holiness's position, including George Fernandes, who was on Beijing's blacklist for decades because of his harsh criticism of Chinese rule in Tibet. But when he became India's Defense Minister, he was invited to the PRC and was able to build close personal relations with quite a few important PRC leaders, in particular Premier Wen Jiabao. George was an ardent supporter of Tibet's independence and very skeptical about our efforts to negotiate a settlement. But after visiting the PRC and getting to know some of its leaders, he felt a sense of hope. George spoke passionately about Tibet to these officials and even mentioned his friendship with me. This transparent and sincere sharing of genuine concern was actually welcomed by PRC officials. They had become accustomed to Indian diplomats trying to avoid mentioning Tibet or becoming very defensive if the topic were raised and distancing themselves from the issue. George's experience validated my belief that if Indian officials were proactive on Tibet without challenging Beijing's core insistence on sovereignty, it would be enormously helpful in building a relationship of trust between them that would also benefit us.

As I previously mentioned, since coming into exile in India, we have regularly consulted with Delhi, diligently briefing the government on our efforts at dialogue with Beijing. For example, in 1982 and again in 1984 before I went to

The author with George Fernandes

the PRC as a member of the Exploratory Talks Delegations, we consulted many senior Indian government officials. We met frequently with M. K. Rasgotra, the Foreign Secretary, as well as his successor, Romesh Bhandari, who also took a keen interest in Tibet. Even after Romesh Bhandari left the Foreign Office I kept in touch with him, especially in Delhi, where he resided during his tenure as Lieutenant Governor.

In 1982, when we were in Beijing during the First Exploratory Talks, I suggested to my two colleagues that we pay a courtesy call on A. P. Venkateswaran, the Indian Ambassador, who I personally knew. My colleagues were quite hesitant, and for good reason. They thought that it might unnecessarily create suspicion in the minds of the PRC authorities. I remember telling them: "I am sure they are suspicious. We live in India, and most probably Beijing thinks not only that we consult the Indian government but also that Delhi actually tells us what to do and what not to do. But calling on the Indian Ambassador here is not going to make them either more or less suspicious. After all, India is where we live; it is quite natural for us to call on him."

In the end we all agreed on the visit. To be very frank, I don't think our hosts minded very much, as they made all the necessary arrangements. It turned out to be a really wonderful visit. The Ambassador made us feel very much at home and also showed keen interest in our effort, giving us much-needed encouragement.

I went to visit the Ambassador again by myself before we left Beijing. He was a very knowledgeable and principled individual, never afraid to speak his mind. In my opinion, it was a great loss to India when he was unceremoniously made to resign from his position as Foreign Secretary by Rajiv Gandhi. We stayed in touch over the years. He was a wonderful person and a good friend. I sincerely miss him.

At this point, I think it's important for me to make it clear that while we regularly consulted with Indian government officials and took them into confidence, at no time did they pressure us or try to induce us to adopt a particular position. I have dealt with officials at various levels over many years, particularly on matters relating to our dealings with the PRC. We have certainly benefited from the advice we received from many of these very experienced individuals, but there was never a single time during my service when New Delhi tried to dictate our actions. This I can say with absolute certainty. I cannot speak of today's relations between New Delhi and the CTA, however, or how Indian government officials are conducting themselves. But periodically, I read newspaper accounts quoting remarks from both sides that do worry me a great deal.

If I have any criticism of India, it is not about interference but rather about its reluctance to act. It would be naïve for us to think that other nations would give priority to the Tibet issue at the expense of their own interests, but India's approach toward the PRC has been at times overly cautious and unrealistically optimistic. Of course, there are many Indians from every walk of life, including political leaders, who are ardent supporters of Tibetan independence. Many of them feel a moral responsibility to help us because one of the factors that contributed to our loss of independence was the policy of Prime Minister Nehru's government that these critics bluntly decry as a "betrayal of Tibet." The humiliating outcome of the 1962 border war between India and the PRC no doubt also influences their opinions. Quite a few of them were even disappointed when His Holiness formulated the Middle Way Approach not because of the effect on Tibet, but out of concern for the ramifications for India. Much like Ram Manohar Lohia, many Indian leaders are not being "pro-Tibetan" when they speak up on our behalf; they are acting either in India's national interest or in some cases because of their ideological beliefs.

Pandit Nehru was a true visionary, but he was also overly idealistic. He genuinely believed that the PRC and India, the two foremost emerging Asian nations, could become formidable allies, adopting a common policy of anti-imperialism and anticolonialism. All these dreams were shattered by the 1962 war between them. It is unfair, however, to hold Pandit Nehru fully responsible for the fate of Tibet. Even though he made mistakes, being misled by his own advisors and having his sincerity and good will manipulated by Beijing, it is we Tibetans, particularly the Lhasa government, who must shoulder more of the blame for not taking advantage of India's support. Both before and after Indian independence, Pandit Nehru and other Indian leaders made serious efforts to reach out to the Tibetan government, but all their efforts were ignored by Lhasa. As Gyalo Thondup, who has more intimate knowledge of that period than I, recounts in his book:

> Nehru wanted me to serve as an intermediary between him and the government of Tibet. I was still the only Tibetan he had ever met. Nehru was suspicious of the Communists. They had yet to give any overt sign of attacking Tibet, but he urged the Tibetan government to prepare for the possibility nonetheless. He thought the Tibetans would be foolish not to begin mobilizing their military, even if in the end no attack occurred. And he wanted the Tibetan government to know that India was willing to help with arms and military aid.[7]

He further notes that he forwarded two messages to the Lhasa government from Pandit Nehru but never received any reply. He then asks some thought-provoking and troubling questions: "What was the Tibetan government doing? Sleeping? Dreaming? Why weren't they answering?"[8]

Apa Pant, who was closely associated with Pandit Nehru on matters relating to Tibet, Bhutan, and Sikkim, also told me of some of the serious efforts Pandit Nehru made to help Tibet, further corroborating Gyalo Thondup's narrative. On two occasions, His Holiness sent me to consult with Apa Pant on some important issues at Pune, where he lived in retirement. While I was there, he told me of these events, but unfortunately I did not take any notes of our conversations. In his book, B. N. Mullik, Pandit Nehru's spymaster, further indicates that Pandit Nehru even voluntarily terminated India's special privileges in Tibet, inherited from the British, to encourage Beijing to respect Tibet's autonomy.[9] We have only ourselves to blame for failure to follow through on any of these initiatives.

I think some Tibetan aristocrats actually looked down on Indian Congress leaders, somehow feeling more kinship with the British. Even though Tibetans hold India in high esteem as being the Land of the Buddha Dharma, reverentially referring to it as Phagpai-Yul, the Land of the Holy Beings, many influential religious leaders and powerful monastic institutions maintained closer relations with the Chinese. By this time, Buddhism had almost vanished in India, represented only by physical ruins in a few holy places such as Nalanda in Bihar.

## THE SIMLA CONVENTION AND CURRENT BORDER DISCUSSIONS

Over the years His Holiness has made statements supporting India's position with regard to the long-standing border dispute between India and the PRC. This has led to some resentment from Tibetans both inside and outside Tibet. The 10th Panchen Rinpoche and other Tibetan leaders, for example, were not pleased. I can fully understand and appreciate their views and know that they were not acting at the instigation of Beijing. Even some Tibetan leaders in exile thought His Holiness was ill advised on this matter by Samdhong Rinpoche and those of us counseling him. What they failed to understand is that His Holiness did not take this position to appease New Delhi or to provoke Beijing, but rather to validate the 1914 Simla Convention. Nevertheless, Beijing was infuriated.

During some of our formal dialogue meetings, our counterparts brought up His Holiness's position, accusing him of acting against Tibetan interests. I remember Zhu Weiqun, Executive Vice Minister, telling us that if the Chinese people became aware of his views, there would be a nationwide backlash against him. They branded Samdhong Rinpoche as "unpatriotic" for adhering to the same view. I responded that we weren't taking any sides on the current matter, but when His Holiness or other Tibetan leaders are asked to comment, they cannot deny the historical facts even if they are, in some respects, detrimental to our position. Any future agreements that are worked out between the PRC and Indian governments are an entirely different matter, however.

Some years back I was invited to speak at the Observer Research Foundation (ORF), a prominent think tank in New Delhi. One of the participants, Jyoti Malhotra, a well-known journalist, asked about my position on the border issue, particularly regarding Arunachal Pradesh. I do not have the precise wording of my reply, but it was along the following lines:

> What kind of settlement India and the PRC reach on the border issue, including the eastern sector, is unfortunately none of our business. Tibet is now totally under the control of the PRC. Even the government of India acknowledges that situation and is currently negotiating with Beijing to determine what is actually the Indo-Tibetan boundary. When His Holiness and other Tibetan officials say, for example, that Tawang is a part of India, they are stating a historical fact that cannot be denied. They are not making a political statement or trying to influence the outcome of current negotiations. No matter what the circumstances may have been or whether or not it was an "unequal treaty," the Tibetan government is a signatory to the Simla Convention of 1914 that established the McMahon Line as the international boundary between British India and Tibet.

I did go on to note the irony that while the McMahon Line is respected, the legitimacy of one of the signatories to the treaty establishing it is disregarded.

While it is the prerogative of the Indian government to take whatever decision it feels is in India's long-term interests, if resolution of the border dispute is a serious consideration from the perspective of regional stability, India must at the same time be supportive of finding a solution to the Tibet issue. Indian leaders seem to forget that in the past Beijing has explicitly sought India's involvement in the Tibet situation. I am referring to Prime Minister Zhou Enlai's visits to Delhi in 1956, seeking Pandit Nehru's help in encouraging His Holiness to return to Tibet while making promises of Beijing's respect for Tibetan autonomy. At the time, His Holiness was visiting India on a pilgrimage and giving serious thought to prolonging his stay, as many of his advisors and family members were advocating. He decided to return to Tibet mainly on Pandit Nehru's advice. There is thus unambiguous precedent for New Delhi taking an active role in the dispute between the Dalai Lama and the PRC leadership.

I firmly believe that a hostile or even stressful relationship between Beijing and New Delhi is of no benefit to the Tibetans but actually the opposite. Even though we may not be in a position to make any meaningful and positive contribution to the relationship, we must certainly not do anything to further escalate tensions between the parties. I also believe that the Tibet issue is one of the critical elements in the Indo-Chinese relationship, even if neither side, for different reasons, chooses to acknowledge the fact.

His Holiness the 14th Dalai Lama's unwavering commitment to finding an amicable solution to the Tibet issue through the Middle Way Approach must be genuinely appreciated by the Indian government because its success will benefit not only Tibet but also India. The Dalai Lama has proven himself to be a staunch and loyal friend of India, a lifelong commitment that he will honor no matter the consequences. The loyalty and friendship of the Dalai Lama are of inestimable value. At the same time, no one should expect him to become a "cheerleader," a position he simply will not embrace. Indian friends must also understand that His Holiness's first and foremost moral obligation is the welfare and future of the Tibetan people. His efforts in pursuit of that goal must be respected. Indeed, he has spent the vast majority of his time in exile devoted to alleviating the suffering of his people.

## THE IMPORTANCE OF CLOSE RELATIONS WITH THE INDIAN GOVERNMENT

His Holiness has enjoyed very special and rather extraordinary relations with the government of India. I am certainly not privy to all the details, but it is abundantly clear that the people and government of India have come to deeply respect him and to view him as a dependable friend. His Holiness frequently shares with world leaders not only his personal gratitude to India but also his heartfelt admiration for its democratic system and tolerant attitude toward different religions and peoples. India is our second home, and the government as well as the people have shown us great kindness during a very critical and sad period in our history.

Throughout my service to His Holiness, I have assigned the highest importance to maintaining a very close and transparent relationship with the government of India. We have nothing to hide from them. In any event, even if we did want to keep certain matters confidential, the Indian intelligence services could easily learn the facts. Quite a few Indian government agencies post officers in Dharamsala who are constantly on the lookout for any news. Many Tibetan officials do not feel comfortable sharing information with them. I don't blame my colleagues because the attitude of some of these officers is disturbing, to the point of making you feel you are doing something improper by briefing them. This has sometimes led to us sending important communications to the Indian leadership in New Delhi without sharing the details with local officials. I used to encourage my colleagues to be more open with the locals because information transmitted by them as political or intelligence briefings has a better chance of actually being read by senior leaders than our formal communications, which have a tendency to get bogged down within the bureaucracy.

Even while I was away from India for over twenty-five years in Washington, D.C., I continued to encourage my Tibetan colleagues who were there to maintain a close relationship with the Indian government. In my formal memos, I highlighted the importance of this relationship. I also personally maintained close relations with senior Indian diplomats posted in the United States. Every time I returned to India to report to His Holiness or for consultations in Dharamsala, I took the opportunity to visit my Indian friends, not only those in office but also those who had retired. Somewhat ironically, many of India's senior civil servants have been more helpful to our cause since their retirement, when they were no longer bound by official constraints.

I have many wonderful memories of the extraordinary and very generous help that we have received from so many Indian officials. Rameshwar Nath Kao immediately comes to mind. He occupied a very influential position in the Indian government as the founding Director of the Research and Analysis Wing (RAW), India's external intelligence service, an organization similar to the US CIA. Even after his retirement, I visited him from time to time. During one such visit, I had my youngest brother, Kunzang Gyari (aka Kalsang Gyari), drive me. As I had nothing confidential to discuss, I took the liberty of including him in the meeting. By then Rameshwar Nath Kao was mostly wheelchair bound, but he remained very sharp. I was so touched when he said: "Lodi, in my profession we are supposed to be pragmatic, no sentiments and emotions. We are supposed to carry out our responsibilities with detachment to any emotions. But I must confess, I became very emotionally involved with your cause and with your people." My brother, who is not usually emotional, was so moved by his sentiments that he thanked me for including him in "this great experience." That was actually my last meeting with Rameshwar Nath Kao. The following year he passed away.

I share this anecdote to illustrate the reason so many people have helped us: they are genuinely motivated by the justness of our cause. I have many more stories like this to tell, but this is not an autobiography and there simply isn't space! It is a sad thing that extraordinary people such as these wonderful, sincere, and selfless individuals are becoming increasingly rare. Maybe it is just the passage of time. Or maybe people today are driven more by professional advancement than by moral responsibility.

It is my fervent hope that our close relationship with India continues at every level. It is critical, especially for the leadership in Dharamsala, not to lose the confidence of the people and government of India. His Holiness has earned the genuine respect and trust of many Indians and their leaders, but Tibetan leaders should not become complacent. With the elder generation of Indian leaders and civil servants the bond was strong because there was genuine sympathy for the tragedy that had befallen Tibet and the circumstances that led to it. We must accept the fact that such sentiments are fading away along with our elder generation and make renewed efforts to establish strong ties with the new leadership. Similarly, Indian leaders must understand that they cannot take the trust and confidence of the Tibetans for granted. A new generation of Tibetans is emerging that has a broader understanding of politics and expanded opportunities to pursue Tibet's and their own personal interests. I hope that Indian political leaders will neither take advantage of Tibet inappropriately, using it as leverage to further their periodic political goals and interests, nor, conversely, view it as a liability.

I sometimes have concerns in this regard. An article written by R. K. Sinha, a Parliamentary member of the ruling BJP Party, published on July 24, 2017, in the very prestigious mainstream English daily *The Statesman*, is illustrative. Entitled "Why Is The Dalai Lama Silent?,"[10] the article criticizes His Holiness for not publicly supporting India in its border dispute with Beijing. What saddened me more than the article's insensitive and disrespectful tone was the lack of any published rebuttal to or correction of the piece. It was hard for me to accept the fact that no responsible individual in India felt compelled to respond. Sometime after its publication I spoke with several well-connected Indians about the article's outrageous sentiments. They all deeply regretted the irresponsible nature of the remarks, trying to assure me that the article need not be taken seriously. While I am sure they felt justified in ignoring it, remarks such as these can have a widespread negative impact, particularly among the new generation of Indians with very little knowledge about Tibet and at a time when nationalist sentiments are on the rise.

For that reason, I want to share a note I wrote on this issue while living in Bangkok in 2017. I sent it to a number of senior government officials, both active and retired, all of whom are well informed on these matters, because it is vitally important that a wider section of people become aware of these concerns.

### Some personal concerns to share with close Indian friends—August 9, 2017

Last week a friend forwarded to me an article titled "Why is the Dalai Lama Silent?" I just skimmed through and dismissed it as a remark by some uninformed individual. This Sunday I reread it and I could no more be dismissive because the author of the article, Mr. R. K. Sinha, seems to be a member of parliament and that too from the ruling party, the BJP. When I did a quick Google search, he is not just a ruling party parliamentarian, but a prominent journalist, entrepreneur, and also described as a security professional. I also realized that his article was also published in a very prestigious and mainstream English daily, The Statesman.

I next tried to see if anyone had responded to Mr. Sinha's article, and so far I found nothing written either by the Tibetans or by Indian friends.

I do not know what is Mr. Sinha's motive; it certainly cannot be ignorance because he seems to be very well informed and a well-connected person. This article made me concerned because such a view publicly expressed at a time with national sentiments running high can give a very negative view of His Holiness and the Tibetans as being unappreciative of India's kindness, and unwilling to come to India's aid in its ongoing border conflict with China.

India has been very generous and we could not have found a better place to seek refuge, but you all know His Holiness has been an unwavering friend of India and one of its strongest advocates. From my personal experience of serving as His Special Envoy for decades, there were times he would speak more of India, its importance and its virtues than his own issues during important meetings. These efforts by His Holiness do help. It is not only His Holiness but also most of us Tibetans who in our own way try to do what we can to support India. Some of you know of my own humble contributions during my 25 years' stay in Washington, D.C. But much more than that, thousands of young Tibetans stand guarding India's borders, facing tremendous danger and hardships in the Himalayas as part of SFF and other agencies. Scores of Tibetans have even made the highest sacrifice of their lives fighting for and with the Indian soldiers in important battles like the liberation of Bangladesh. Such a statement from a well-placed and well-informed person is not only unfortunate but also unfair.

I have very little access to information, the only source being Bangkok Post and the NHK English broadcast . . . and periodic information sent by friends. However, I get the feeling that the Indian government is trying to handle the current border situation and doing everything possible not to escalate it further. Will a statement by His Holiness be helpful under such circumstances? If Mr. Sinha cared to check with PMO or South Block, I think he would have been advised differently. In any case, that is my assumption. Furthermore, unlike Tawang, where the Tibetans can take a clear stand because of our treaty obligations, I do not know how well Tibet-Bhutan borders were defined. I am not an expert, but one may find an unfavorable situation by bringing the Tibetans into the mix in this regard. However, if there were very clear border demarcations between Tibet and Bhutan, His Holiness will not hesitate to speak because he always believes in stating the truth, as he did with regard to Arunachal Pradesh, even though his statement caused further complications in our own fragile relation with PRC.

I have no responsibility to take any public stand on this issue; however, I felt that I should share my concerns with some of my close Indian friends such as you. We are deeply indebted to the people of India, but new leaders like Mr. Sinha should also understand that India is not totally innocent of the tragedy that had befallen Tibet. Anyway, all that is history now.

As someone who had the honor of working closely with the various branches of the Indian government for decades, I am highly appreciative of the genuine respect and support that India extended to His Holiness, never thinking of him or the Tibetans as either leverage or liability. I am sure this continues to be the attitude in Delhi.

I hope I am not taking too much liberty of our friendship, and I do hope that these expressions of mine will be seen as a contribution to our mutual interest.

Some people may wonder why I persist in saying that India is the most important country for us. Many Tibetans, and of course, a large number of Indian friends as well as international support groups, feel deeply disappointed with India's lack of visible political support. As I have written elsewhere in this book, sometimes the Foreign Ministry even tried to stop His Holiness from making his annual March 10th Statement.

But to understand and appreciate India's generosity, we must first ask ourselves what the core of our struggle is. For me, it is the survival and maintenance of the distinct cultural and religious identity of Tibet. As long as we maintain that identity, Tibet will never be lost. Had it not been for the kindness and support of the Indian government and her people, we would not have been able to maintain this great civilization that was terrorized and displaced within our own country, especially during the Cultural Revolution. Today every aspect of Tibetan culture, religion, and daily way of life not only survives but actively thrives in India, our adopted homeland. In addition, the Indian government has provided modern educational opportunities for our children. It set up a special department within the Ministry of Education to run both residential and day-student educational institutions, annually funded by millions of rupees. These institutions were created exclusively to give the highest priority to the transmission and protection of the Tibetan language, culture, and even customs. This stands in stark contrast to what happened in our native homeland, where an entire generation of Tibetans was denied the opportunity to study their own language and culture for a long period of time.

Pandit Nehru must be acknowledged for launching this educational endeavor, which I can only describe as precious. I hope Tibetan leaders continue to give high priority to this sector. I know there have been some ongoing efforts to try to run these educational institutions by the CTA directly. I have always been nervous about that. I am sure there are certain drawbacks and even disadvantages resulting from their being run by the large official Indian bureaucracy, but in my view, the continued direct role of the Indian government carries a very powerful message.

Tibetan refugees are also not parasites. From day one in exile, they started working hard on some of the most hazardous projects in the Indian Himalayas, including road building, that were difficult for Indian laborers to handle because of the high altitude and extreme weather conditions. Tibetans have paved some of India's most strategic roads in the Himalayas. Once the government of India started providing land for resettlement, Tibetans started reclamation of forest lands, sometimes literally with their bare hands. Today there are thriving Tibetan communities contributing to local development. Most importantly, Tibetans did not arrive empty-handed. They brought with them priceless knowledge of India's ancient wisdom, having been its custodians for hundreds of years while vast components of that knowledge had been lost in India itself. Many Indian and Tibetan institutions today are translating back into the original Sanskrit works of great value not only about Buddhism but also about other important subjects.

What I write in this chapter does not do justice to the ongoing activities of numerous Indian organizations on behalf of Tibet and India. There must be hundreds of Tibet support groups in various parts of India, voluntarily run by devoted Indian friends. There is also a new generation of Tibetans who are engaged with their Indian brothers and sisters in a much more effective and intimate partnership than my generation was able to forge. The Tibetan leadership has also realized the importance of giving the highest priority to building a strong grassroots support base, even creating a special cell at the Bureau of His Holiness the Dalai Lama in Delhi in the late 1990s with Jamyang Dorjee as its head.

Jamyang Dorjee was one of the first of his generation whom I came to know and whose work I appreciated. Even though of Tibetan origin, he was a senior civil servant in the Sikkimese government who sought permission from it to serve the CTA. Among the present Tibetan leadership there are now several who on a daily basis are actively working with Indian friends to broaden the support for the Tibet cause and to deepen the friendship between our two peoples. My sister Gyari Dolma and Acharya Yeshi Phuntsok, at the time of this writing Deputy Speaker, are among these leaders. Some years back at a function at the India International Center in New Delhi, a prominent Indian political leader came over to greet me and said: "So you are Gyari Dolma's brother." I really felt happy that members of the new generation of Tibetan leaders have firmly established themselves and cemented their friendship with India. It also made me aware that today my younger sister knows many more people than I do. And the ones I know are obviously my own age or several years my senior—a fading generation, whether we like it or not.

Some of these new generation Tibetan leaders have taken Indian citizenship and are fluent Hindi speakers. Indian law explicitly allows this status, and in my view, this gives them a better opportunity to pursue their efforts on behalf of

Tibet. There is a significant difference of opinion on whether Tibetans should take Indian citizenship. But the fact is that for decades, we have had Tibetans with American or European passports occupying top positions in the Tibetan leadership. As far as I am concerned, even questioning the right of an individual to take Indian citizenship is hypocritical. The question implies that citizenship of one country has greater value than that of another, a proposition that should not be countenanced.

CHAPTER 16

# Assistance from Other Asian Nations, Europe, Nongovernmental Organizations, and Dharma Centers

## ASIAN NATIONS

I have been asked many times why we have not made a greater effort to reach out to countries in our immediate neighborhood, especially some of the Buddhist nations in Asia. As I explain in the first part of this chapter, our relations with some of these important players were complicated by both historical realities and contemporary geopolitics.

### *Support in Southeast Asia*

When His Holiness left Tibet in 1959, he walked into the polarized world of the Cold War. Many Asian nations were very much a part of the Western camp and were anti-Beijing. In those days, there were also some strong leaders, in Indonesia and Malaysia, for example, who had themselves fought against Western colonization and therefore had deep sympathy for and understanding of Tibet's plight. The United States even suggested that His Holiness move to Thailand, a Buddhist country and in those days a close US ally, rather than seeking asylum in India. And as previously discussed, earlier in 1956, when His Holiness was giving serious thought to not returning to Tibet from India, Sri Lanka was also under consideration, I think not so much because it is predominantly a Buddhist country, but more to do with politics. I am sure there must have been a strong temptation among some of His Holiness's advisors to counsel him to follow one of these suggestions and capitalize on the offers of immediate support, both economic and political. But His Holiness made what in the long run has proven to be the wise decision to stay in India.

This is not to discount the efforts taken on our behalf by several Asian countries. Malaysia, Thailand, and the Philippines, for example, raised the issue of Tibet at the United Nations by sponsoring resolutions. In addition, in 1959, His Holiness became one of the earliest Ramon Magsaysay Award recipients. This is Asia's premier prize and highest honor, celebrating greatness of spirit and transformative leadership in Asia and quite often referred to as the alternative Nobel Peace Prize. In 1972, on one of his early visits to Thailand, His Holiness was received almost like a head of state. Both the King and the Prime Minister hosted him with deep reverence. I have a wonderful memory of that visit; it was my first-ever opportunity to accompany His Holiness on a trip abroad. I was overwhelmed by the hospitality extended to His Holiness, but above all by the genuine friendship of the Thai people.

After New Delhi, Tokyo was the first Asian city to open an Office of Tibet. Of course, there were representative offices in Kathmandu, Thimphu, and even Gangtok, as Sikkim was then only a protectorate, not a province, of India. But these offices were mostly engaged in looking after the needs of the sizeable local Tibetan populations and settlements being established in those countries, working under the direction of the CTA's Department of Home. The Tokyo office, by contrast, was very much a part of the Tibetan leadership's international relations and outreach, being responsible for the entire Asia Pacific region. My brother Pema Gyalpo was the founding head of that office. In 1982 he arranged His Holiness's visits to Malaysia, Singapore, and Indonesia, where His Holiness was received by some of the respective countries' most senior leaders, including Adam Malik in Indonesia and Tunku Abdul Rahman in Malaysia.

Everything changed when the United States did a complete about-face during the Nixon administration regarding its policy on the PRC. Nixon's "opening" to the PRC was the first of a series of political acts that resulted in President Carter abandoning Taiwan. As a result, all of these formerly sympathetic countries started moving closer to the PRC, distancing themselves from problematic issues such as Tibet. It thus became very difficult for us to reach out to these countries for any meaningful assistance. While I don't blame them for their change in position, I think they could have been more creative, at least by continuing to receive His Holiness as a paramount religious leader and later as a Nobel laureate. From our side, we also could have made more serious efforts to reach out to our neighbors, but our lack of resources compelled us to concentrate on the West.

With our renewed effort to establish direct dialogue with Beijing, however, I saw the need for us once again to reach out to some of the more influential leaders in the region. PRC leaders always view Western interest in the Tibet issue as politically motivated and not genuine. Too much pressure by the United States and other Western nations on Beijing often triggers a negative reaction. I thought encouragement by prominent Asian leaders might be seen as more acceptable and "genuine."

When I learned that then PRC Vice President and designated future leader Hu Jintao was visiting Thailand in July 2000 to take part in the Silver Jubilee celebration of the two countries' diplomatic relations, I reached out to the prominent Thai intellectual and social activist Ajahn[1] Sulak Sivaraksa. He has kept the issue of Tibet and the message of His Holiness alive for decades in his country. He has translated into Thai and published many of His Holiness's books. If you walk into any Thai bookstore, including at the airports, you will find several of these translations. They are widely read by the Thai public.

I sought Ajahn Sulak's help in contacting Khun Anand Panyarachun, who was cochairing the Silver Jubilee celebration from the Thai side. Khun Anand has served as Thailand's Prime Minister on two occasions. Ajahn Sulak personally arranged my meeting with him, and Khun Anand very kindly agreed to take up the Tibet issue with Hu Jintao. When he raised the issue, however, the Vice President gave the usual official response, saying that Beijing's door for dialogue was always open, but the Dalai Lama must stop his "splittist" activities. Hu Jintao further told Khun Anand that Beijing was actually in contact with the Dalai Lama through his brother Gyalo Thondup, who had recently been in Beijing.

When I met with Khun Anand some days after his meeting with the Vice President, he was quite disappointed because he thought that I had not taken him into full confidence. He said: "Lodi, you people *are* in touch with Beijing. Hu Jintao said that the Dalai Lama's brother was in Beijing, and you didn't tell me that." In response, I confessed that I had no knowledge of Gyalo Thondup's visit. I told him: "While Mr. Thondup may have gone there, and he may even have met with Chinese friends or officials, we are not looking for this type of informal communication. We are seeking the formal resumption of dialogue that came to an end in the mid-1980s." As I have previously lamented, this kind of lack of internal coordination and sharing of information within Dharamsala and among those representing His Holiness in other capacities has constantly hampered our efforts.

On this trip, Hu Jintao's next stop was Jakarta, where he was meeting with then Indonesian President Abdurrahman Wahid. Through the efforts of Ajahn Sulak and Jeffery Sng, a Singaporean friend living in Bangkok, we approached President Wahid seeking his support in encouraging Vice President Hu to engage in dialogue with His Holiness. I remember meeting the President in Jakarta hours before Hu Jintao came to see him. Both Ajahn Sulak and Jeffery had known the President for a long time and were kind enough to accompany me. We spent almost two hours in the President's office. I repeatedly tried to signal to Ajahn Sulak and Jeffery that we should leave because when we walked in, his staff was making last-minute arrangements for the formal meeting with the Chinese Vice President. But President Wahid remained very relaxed and engaged in our conversation, clearly in no hurry for us to leave. Tibet wasn't the only matter we discussed; Ajahn Sulak and Jeffery had many other interests in common with the President.

I remember President Wahid had a beautiful image of Mahatma Gandhi in his office and very soft Beethoven music playing in the background. He was a respected Islamic cleric and an eminent scholar. He was one of those rare and enlightened leaders fully committed to peace, nonviolence, and interfaith dialogue. I wish we had more leaders like him, especially with the world becoming as polarized as it has in recent years.

A few days later when I was back in Bangkok staying as usual with Ajahn Sulak, President Wahid called to brief him about his meeting with Hu Jintao. Ajahn Sulak gave me the opportunity to speak directly with the Indonesian President. It is interesting to note how differently Hu Jintao addressed President Wahid as opposed to Khun Anand. Vice President Hu had been very formal and on guard while speaking with Khun Anand, a very sophisticated and well-informed political leader, spouting the standard Chinese rhetoric. By contrast, Hu Jintao uncharacteristically opened up to President Wahid, even sharing some personal thoughts with him.

President Wahid reported: "Hu Jintao told me he was the governor of Tibet." He was actually not the governor but CCP Secretary, a higher rank than governor in the Chinese Communist system. Acting as if he were divulging a secret, the President further said: "Did you know he is going to be the President of China in two years' time?" Of course, we all knew that, but I simply said: "Yes, Mr. President, I know he is going to be President of the PRC." Then he said: "The bad news is he said that nothing will happen before that. He can't do anything before that.

But the good news is, after he becomes President, since he has been the governor in Tibet and since he knows the issue, he said he will try to solve the Tibet problem with the Dalai Lama." Here Hu Jintao really did open up to President Wahid, I think because he was talking with someone of genuine warmth and sincerity whose disarming personality encourages the same traits in others. It was a very interesting glimpse into Hu Jintao as a person, but I share this story mainly to show that a number of Asian leaders did take steps to help us.

The highly respected Singaporean diplomat Ambassador Tommy Koh is another person who has been very kind and provided much-needed guidance. My brother Pema Gyalpo introduced me to this veteran statesman. I remember meeting him in Rome, Washington, D.C., and of course, several times in Singapore. He is widely respected in the international community, with many people thinking he would make an excellent UN Secretary-General.

I also became friends with George Yeo, who held many cabinet positions in the Singaporean government, including Foreign Minister. He first came to my attention when he visited Lhasa in 2009 and subsequently wrote an article highlighting the importance of Tibet in the Sino-Indian bilateral relationship. Ironically, I first contacted him to raise my concerns over a few points in his article. But it was the kind introduction of our mutual friend Jon Huntsman, former US Ambassador to the PRC and US Ambassador to Russia as of this writing, that moved our relationship to the personal level. George's essay, "Tibet in the 21st Century," is worth reading for its regional, if not global perspective on Tibet.[2] He ultimately became another wise counselor whose opinions I greatly value.

These respected Asian leaders were not providing me guidance in a partisan, pro-Tibet or anti-PRC manner, but rather from a broader, regional perspective. They felt comfortable trying to help bridge the gap between Beijing and Dharamsala precisely because His Holiness had decided to seek space for the Tibetan people within the PRC. They felt that resolving the Tibet issue in this way would not only enhance the PRC's international standing but also provide the Tibetan people the opportunity to maintain their distinct identity.

While trying not to sound presumptuous, I am sure they further believe in the widely held perception that the next century will be the "Asian century." In accordance with that sentiment, it is not surprising that they would like to see countries such as the PRC and India behave in a manner that brings harmony to the region and projects them as principled and tolerant nations on the world stage. As confirmed in his essay, individuals such as George Yeo also believe that better

Sino-Indian relations are important in this regard: "How China and India relate to each other in the coming decades will affect everyone. If peaceful, this will be a golden age for Asia."[3]

Besides influential leaders and diplomats, I also sought the advice of many scholars in Hong Kong, Tokyo, Singapore, Taiwan, and Australia who had a thorough understanding of the PRC and its history. Wang Gungwu at the National University of Singapore is one such person who has been very generous with his time.

### *Taiwan*

As I have previously written, in our initial years of exile, one of the major obstacles we faced was interference by the Nationalist government of Taiwan. The Tibetan leadership tried very hard to build a mutually beneficial relationship with Taipei, urging it to stop interfering in our affairs. None of our efforts succeeded. With the election of President Lee Teng-hui in 1996, we hoped there could be some change in our relations, and His Holiness asked me if I could suggest someone from the United States who could meet with President Lee to talk about Tibet, without involving the Kuomintang (KMT) bureaucracy. As our direct efforts always met with difficulties, and because of the good relationship between Washington and Taipei, His Holiness felt an American effort might be helpful. Without any hesitation, I suggested US Congressman Charlie Rose, not because he was an expert in that area or had a personal relationship with Lee Teng-hui but because he was a senior Congressman who would certainly be received by President Lee and was someone we could unreservedly trust.

His Holiness immediately instructed me to talk to Congressman Rose about a possible trip to Taiwan. During one of his visits to Washington, His Holiness personally briefed him at length about our problems with the KMT government. He specifically requested the Congressman to ask President Lee if he would be willing to reconsider his government's policy and, should he show any willingness to do so, to further ask the President to designate someone to start serious discussions with me on His Holiness's behalf. Knowing how important the matter was to His Holiness and the Tibetan people, the Congressman traveled to Taiwan in 1996 to meet President Lee.

The two engaged in very detailed and intimate discussions. The President gave Congressman Rose firm assurances that he would reexamine relations with

Dharamsala. In addition, he gave him the name of one of his senior aides with ambassador rank as the point of contact for me, with whom to lay the foundation for a new relationship with Dharamsala. Congressman Rose came back very much encouraged by his meeting with Lee Teng-hui. He told me to convey to His Holiness that he thought the Taiwanese President was an honorable person whom His Holiness could trust. He then gave me the name and telephone number of President Lee's designated interlocutor and encouraged me to reach out to him without delay.

Within days, I called President Lee's representative, but I found his demeanor lukewarm and unresponsive. I called him a couple more times before giving up, thinking that the KMT old guard had once again managed to forestall our efforts. But soon thereafter, a senior KMT official, Jason Hu, was appointed to head the Taipei Economic and Cultural Representative Office (TECRO), the KMT's office in Washington. Within days of his arrival, his office called me to set up a meeting. I learned that President Lee had personally appointed him to be the interlocutor and that Taiwan was developing a new approach to Tibet. He had even been entrusted to discuss a possible trip to Taiwan by His Holiness to meet President Lee in person. For the first time in decades, relations between us were headed in a mutually beneficial direction.

I reported the welcome news to Dharamsala and suggested that Kelsang Gyaltsen, one of the Secretaries in His Holiness's Private Office, join me in future meetings because discussions would also involve logistics of a possible visit by His Holiness to Taiwan. Ultimately, we had several rounds of fruitful discussions that laid the foundation for a major shift in KMT policy toward Dharamsala. We also agreed on a visit to Taiwan by His Holiness. I was unable to attend the meeting that worked out the final details of His Holiness's 1997 visit because of ill health, so I had my office colleague Bhuchung Tsering participate with Kelsang Gyaltsen. This meeting ushered in a new chapter in Taipei–Dharamsala relations. Since then, His Holiness has made quite a few visits to Taipei, even establishing a permanent presence there through the office of the Tibet Religious Foundation of His Holiness the Dalai Lama.

Years later when I went to Taiwan and met my now good friend Jason Hu, we kiddingly complimented each other for successfully keeping the initial contact with President Lee confidential until the 1997 trip was cemented. I say "kiddingly" because we had both been involved in situations in the past when we miserably failed to keep matters private as a result of vested interests on both sides deliberately leaking information.

I have also made several visits to Taiwan, meeting with successive Presidents and senior leaders. My main interest has been to learn more about the PRC. Not surprisingly, Taiwan is home to a number of experts in the field, many of whom were born on the Mainland and thus have personal knowledge. But one has to be careful to distinguish KMT propaganda from the facts, especially when talking to old-school Taiwanese officials trained by the KMT whose knowledge might be accurate, but whose perspective is ideological. By contrast, the younger generation of Taiwanese scholars and leaders, including Tsai Ing-wen, Taiwan's President as of this writing, offers a much more realistic assessment. I met with her several times when she was Minister for Mainland Affairs under President Chen Shui-bian, and I found her to be quite knowledgeable.

The positive turn in our relations with Taiwan understandably caused new problems with Beijing. In outlining the conditions for the resumption of direct talks, Beijing continued to insist not only that we must accept Tibet as an "inalienable part of China" but also that we must further acknowledge Taiwan as a province of China. As I have previously discussed, this precondition posed, and continues to pose, a major obstacle in our relations, spawning intense discussion within the Tibetan leadership and with Tibetan friends in the West, especially in the United States.

After resumption of our formal dialogue with Beijing in 2002, I decided not to make any further trips to Taiwan. I was concerned it would be counterproductive and might even jeopardize the fragile relationship we were starting to rebuild with Beijing. Many well-wishers, including senior US officials and European diplomats, also advised that we not allow our relations with Taiwan to upset our fledging efforts with Beijing. Many of them further strongly urged His Holiness not to make any personal visits for a while.

### *Activities in Other Asian and Australasian States*

While the PRC's ever increasing global influence, especially in Asia, deterred some governments from continuing their support of Tibet, many individuals and organizations remained steadfast in their commitment to our cause. Reverence for His Holiness and support for his moderate political stance had generated unprecedented support. Tibet-focused organizations and institutions sprang up in many of these countries, and every year thousands of people were coming to India to receive teachings from His Holiness or just to pay their respects.

Aside from my brief remarks about the establishment of an Office of Tibet in Tokyo, you will find a conspicuous absence of any comments about our activities in Japan. I have tended to stay away from the region to avoid any appearance of nepotism because my brother Pema Gyalpo was His Holiness's Representative there in the early days. There has always been a small but very committed group of friends of Tibet in Japan, however, and I have on occasion attended a few brainstorming sessions with them, together with my Kashag colleagues, heads of other Offices of Tibet, and some special Tibet friends. After moving to Washington, while I concentrated my time and energy on our work in the United States, I did maintain close relations with senior Japanese diplomats who took the initiative to remain in touch. They were very keen on developing a deeper understanding of the Tibet issue. Because of the special Tokyo–Washington relationship, I was also able to effectively integrate the Japanese delegation into our core group of supportive diplomats who met regularly at the State Department or in the privacy of some of the embassies.[4]

At the same time, I was cautious not to foster much of a visible relationship with Japanese officials because the Chinese have a lingering mistrust, or shall we say hangover from history, when it comes to Japan. Some of my American friends, however, including senior NSC officials such as Mike Green, encouraged me to maintain my relations with the Japanese. I followed their advice, making stopovers in Tokyo to meet with senior officials in the Prime Minister's office from time to time. Governor of Tokyo Yuriko Koike was one of those individuals with whom I dealt when she was in Junichirō Koizumi's government. All of these meetings were directly arranged by my American friends without the participation of either the Tokyo Office of Tibet or my brother. Moreover, our discussions were limited to the dialogue between Dharamsala and Beijing, an area for which I had full responsibility.

I have also not made any reference to Australia or New Zealand because I had very limited dealings in this part of the world. With the advice and assistance of Richard Holbrooke and some senior National Security staff at the White House, however, we did make efforts to engage Australian Prime Minister Kevin Rudd. Richard, in fact, arranged a meeting for us with the Prime Minister in New York during a visit to the United States, but bad weather intervened, and the Prime Minister had to forego his stopover in the city.

I made my first-ever visit to the region in 2011. I was very impressed with the solid grassroots support developed by the Office of Tibet and various Tibet support groups, including the Australia Tibet Council (ATC). I saw tremendous potential for further growth. I had been working closely with Paul Bourke at the ATC and knew the organization had been extremely successful in its lobbying efforts in Australia. I was also very impressed with the professionalism and commitment of Dhongdue Kyinzom, a young Tibetan woman also on ATC's staff. It was very clear that she had been working closely with many members of the Australian Parliament, as she was on a first-name basis with most of the people we met. In 2016 she was elected to the Tibetan Parliament, representing Tibetans in Australasia. She is very deserving and a good choice.

The Office of Tibet in Australia and the ATC work together in the same way that the ICT and the Office of Tibet function in the United States, complementing each other's efforts rather than competing with one another. Before I left the ICT, I laid the foundation for a much stronger institutional relationship between it and the ATC, and I believe the two organizations have in the intervening years taken steps to realize that goal.

I was also very much impressed with the perspective of several Australian scholars I met. They had a very balanced and pragmatic approach toward the PRC. Australians look at the PRC from a different angle than their counterparts in America and Europe because Australia is geopolitically more connected to Asia than other Western nations. The Australian All-Party Parliamentary Group for Tibet was also one of the most active Parliamentary Groups working on our behalf that I have had the privilege of getting to know.

### *Nepal*

We have always understood Nepal's inability to take a public stand on Tibet for fear of displeasing Beijing. Sadly, however, over the last few decades, successive Nepalese governments have become increasingly less generous to the Tibetan people, causing tremendous hardship even for those Tibetans who either were born there or lived in the country for decades. Nepal, which is the natural exit point for Tibetans fleeing Tibet, has not only denied entry to many of these refugees but often forcibly repatriated some of them. While one can understand the political difficulties for a small country like Nepal in dealing with its temperamental and more powerful neighbors, its callous treatment of its Tibetan population is deeply disappointing. Our two peoples have a historic, long-standing relationship and share many important cultural and religious traditions. Immediately in the aftermath of the Chinese invasion of Tibet in 1959, Nepal was very welcoming, and second to India, hosted the largest number of Tibetan refugees. King Mahendra even allowed the CIA-backed Tibetan guerilla base to be established in the Mustang region.

Kathmandu has become home to many Tibetan enterprises and institutions, including the carpet industry, which for a long time was Nepal's second-highest foreign exchange earner after tourism. The refugee population has thus not been a burden to the host government but rather a boost to Nepal's economy. Many senior Tibetan lamas established their centers in Nepal, providing the unprecedented opportunity for thousands of young Nepalese to undertake advanced studies in Buddhist philosophy and culture, as well as other fields. While Mount Everest is no doubt a huge tourist attraction, more foreigners actually come to Kathmandu in search of Tibetan Buddhist teachers and scholars. Many of these highly revered and knowledgeable individuals have become long-term residents making stable and substantial economic contributions to the country.

The opportunities and benefits for many Nepalese are not limited to those residing in Nepal. Thousands of young Nepalese men and women study at Tibetan Buddhist monasteries and institutions in India. While traditionally large numbers of Nepalese young men were recruited by the British to serve in its armed forces, today it is Tibetan institutions, primarily monasteries, that host many more of these young people.

No matter how some Nepalese politicians treat Tibetans, I have always felt that we must assist them whenever possible because of our historic ties, and even more so because at a social level, Tibetans and ordinary Nepalese have always lived amicably like members of the same family. Richard Blum, who served as Nepal's Honorary Consul in San Francisco for years, introduced me to several Nepalese Ambassadors to the United States and other senior officials. At one point, some members of the US Congress were trying to deny Nepal its export textile quota to the United States to show displeasure about its treatment of the Tibetans. Rather than encouraging the denial, I effectively lobbied for its restoration. Imposition of this penalty would have not only harmed the hardworking Nepalese people but also created unnecessary animosity between the Tibetans and their Nepalese brothers and sisters. I knew the Nepalese authorities would cover their own failures by blaming the Tibetans and their friends for depriving Nepal of its textile quota.

In 2008 the Maoist Party came out of the jungle and joined the mainstream political system in contested elections. With the overwhelming support of the people, the party won a majority of seats and was able to form a government. Regardless, the US State Department continued to list the Maoist Party and its leaders as terrorists and blacklisted them from visiting the United States. At one point Barsaman Pun, who was very senior in the Maoist Party and viewed as head of its militant wing, was scheduled to come to the United States for some UN-related work and wanted to spend some additional days in the country. A mutual friend must have told him that I might be able to help get a special waiver for his visit, as he soon contacted me. As I knew it would not be an easy task, I approached James Steinberg, then Deputy Secretary of State, with whom I had worked on a number of issues.

I explained to him how the situation in Nepal was changing. There had been an honestly contested election in April 2008, and Barsaman Pun's party had won the majority. They were now the legitimate Nepalese leaders. I told him that the United States should support the Maoists' efforts to abandon their guerilla bases in the jungle and integrate into the mainstream. As Barsaman Pun was a young and influential leader, it would be in the US's interests to begin building a relationship with him. Although the visit was approved, I can't clearly remember whether Barsaman Pun actually made the trip.

Another time, the Nepalese Finance Minister, Baburam Bhattarai, came to D.C. for a World Bank meeting. He wanted to meet with Senator John Kerry, who was then Chairman of the Senate Foreign Relations Committee. I was contacted through a mutual friend to help arrange this. I was confidant that the Senator would meet with the Nepalese Minister, as we had developed a strong professional and personal relationship from our continuing work on Tibet legislation.[5] The Nepalese, however, were extremely concerned that their Minister would be put in an embarrassing situation should the meeting be canceled at the last minute. They thus called the Senator's office for confirmation of the appointment. After receiving the standard, noncommittal response of the Senator's scheduler that the Minister's name was on the Senator's schedule, but things could always change depending on the Senator's commitments, the Nepalese feared cancellation of the meeting and left town. At the appointed meeting time, Senator Kerry's office started calling me, asking where the Nepalese Minister was, as the Senator was waiting. A few minutes later, Senator Kerry himself called me, saying: "Lodi, where is your friend?" I apologized profusely, telling him frankly that I couldn't reach them. Sometime later, Minister Bhattarai did write a very nice note to our mutual friend in Nepal thanking us for our help and apologizing for not keeping the appointment.

Because I grew up in Darjeeling and speak Nepalese fluently, I have always had a very special feeling toward the Nepalese. I have many close Nepalese friends and know that many of them are also deeply saddened about how a handful of politicians have so callously treated the Tibetans to placate Beijing. I have told them that, based on the way Beijing dictates Nepal's politics and the behavior of some Nepalese politicians, it's almost as if Nepal has become a "prefecture" of the Tibet Autonomous Region. Nevertheless, the bond between the Nepalese and Tibetan peoples remains strong, and I have no doubt that it will grow stronger as a new generation of Nepalese comes to power with a much greater sense of self-respect and pride in their cultural roots.

I also feel that Tibetans are to some extent victims of deteriorating relations between New Delhi and Kathmandu. If the Indians were able to pursue a far-sighted and pragmatic relationship with Nepal, the latter's dependence on the PRC would be far less, and the Nepalese would also pay some attention to New Delhi's views. I have candidly told some of the most senior Indian officials I know that Delhi's marginalization of Nepal is a matter of "shame." Not only does India provide generous economic and other assistance to Nepal, but the countries also have much in common both culturally and politically, in stark contrast with Nepal's relationship with the PRC. Despite those commonalities, today Beijing seems to have more influence in Kathmandu than does New Delhi. It's really not fair of me to sweepingly criticize India, because I know many Indian politicians, senior diplomats, and intelligence officials who have made concerted efforts to do the right thing. Indian leaders and officials, however, must understand that people would be willing to go hungry rather than have their dignity and self-respect disregarded. I sometimes fear that India may make the same mistake in Bhutan that it has in Nepal.

When Prime Minister Narendra Modi came into office, one of the things that impressed me was his attitude toward immediately neighboring countries. He chose Bhutan as the first country to visit and soon thereafter went to Nepal. I happened to be in the region at the time and saw the live coverage of his address to the Nepalese Parliament on August 3, 2014. At the conclusion of his speech, all these Nepalese politicians—from far right to the left—gave him a standing ovation, totally in contrast to their indifferent and even dismissive body language when he first walked into the chamber.

Disappointingly, the Indian government's subsequent policies and actions do not reflect what I believe Prime Minister Modi was trying to convey in his speech. I am not suggesting or advocating a "turf fight" between New Delhi and Beijing over Nepal, but realization of Prime Minister Modi's expressed vision would be beneficial not only to India and Nepal but also to the whole region. The political situation in Nepal has changed, and everyone should adjust to the new realities. Adversarial relations between the two Asian giants will certainly not benefit the Tibetans. We are always on the receiving end when turf fights such as this escalate.

The communist coalition that governs Nepal at the time of this writing may prove to be more sympathetic, at least to the plight of the Tibetans born and raised there, than its recent predecessors, if their attitude toward their own indigenous people is any indication. In addition, I am sure they understand that the deplorable shortsighted policies of prior Kathmandu governments, which changed on an almost yearly basis, significantly damaged Nepal's standing in the international community.

## EUROPE

In the late 1980s as the Minister responsible for international relations, I was deeply involved in formulating our strategy for engaging governments in Europe. Much later when I was serving as His Holiness's Special Envoy, I made frequent trips to Europe to assist in our efforts there. Fortunately, we had very capable people at the Offices of Tibet in Europe pursuing our agenda.

In Geneva, for example, we had Gyaltsen Gyaltag, who ran the office expertly with his calm and sophisticated manner. He was completely at ease in his diplomatic role, particularly in lobbying at the United Nations. His passing away in 2002, at the young age of fifty-three, was a tremendous loss to the Tibetan movement.

As previously mentioned, Kelsang Gyaltsen, who headed the Geneva office for several terms, and I worked together in numerous capacities. I am very fortunate to have always had capable, intelligent, and dependable colleagues, but Kelsang Gyaltsen tops the list. He was highly regarded by senior officials around the world.

Envoy Kelsang Gyaltsen (left), the author, and DIIR Additional Secretary Dagpo Sonam Norbu (far right) receiving final instructions from Kalon Tripa Prof. Samdhong Rinpoche before departing to Beijing for the Second Round of talks, Delhi, 2003

He was a formidable member of our negotiating team, as he is definitely not a "yes" man. We are both Khampas, but I think he demonstrates more Khampa character than I with his forthright attitude. Over the years I came to appreciate his no-nonsense style, as did Samdhong Rinpoche, our immediate superior during the formal dialogue with Beijing. He would just laugh at Kelsang Gyaltsen's bluntness.

As a general matter, I must note that individual European governments have been very cautious in embracing the Tibetan cause. Fortunately, this reticence has been counterbalanced, by the European Parliament, where we have a powerful support base, as well as by a select number of national parliaments. All of this hard-won support is due to the tireless efforts of European friends, NGOs, and our representatives in the various Offices of Tibet. I hope our future leaders will put even greater emphasis on our efforts in the region.

*Norway's Efforts Through Its Peace and Reconciliation Bureau*

In its support of Tibet, Norway has played a very different role from that of any other country. The Norwegian government has not made strong public statements, nor has it made Tibet a major issue in its bilateral relations with the PRC. When it does voice public support for Tibet, its statements tend to be limited to inclusion in its yearly dialogue on human rights. Instead, Norway has acted in a subtle supportive role, complementing the more public efforts of the United States and others. Indeed, Norway has a history of working closely with the United States on global issues, sometimes stepping in where the United States faces political constraints.

As there has been some misunderstanding over the years with respect to Norway's role, I want to take this opportunity to dispel any notion that Norway supported Tibetan independence or that the government was in any way "anti-Chinese." This was absolutely not the case. When Norway became involved, it did so with a clear understanding that it would not take a confrontational or partisan position. Its interest was in supporting the genuine effort of His Holiness to reach out to the PRC leadership to find a solution to our differences. It wanted to help preserve and protect the distinct Tibetan identity and improve the lives of Tibetans, at the same time contributing to the stability and unity of the PRC. Norway's conduct has always been transparent and very much in keeping with its tradition of supporting peace and reconciliation efforts. The assistance extended to our negotiating team was thus provided by Norway's Peace and Reconciliation Bureau. Because of its mission and experience, the Bureau had a clear understanding of the complexities of our issue and the difficulties in reconciling the needs of the conflicting parties.

Beginning in 2002, Norway played a crucial role during our formal negotiations with the PRC. It helped my team on several occasions by conveying important communications to Beijing. In addition to professional advice and expert guidance, at my request, the Norwegians also provided much-needed material assistance for my team's work. This is very much in keeping with Norway's tradition of helping jump-start sensitive dialogues. Norway also has very strict funding guidelines for the international assistance it provides. The cause and recipient must be clearly identified, the procedure transparent, and the funds dispersed through proper channels. Jan Egeland, the former State Secretary at the Norwegian Foreign Ministry, who had previously helped us from that position, had assumed leadership of the Norwegian Red Cross, making the funding arrangement possible through that organization. Jan was the senior Norwegian official who initiated Norway's involvement in helping start the negotiations. Because the recipient of Norway's financial assistance had to be an NGO whose financial records are regularly audited by competent authorities, I suggested the International Campaign for Tibet (ICT) as the vehicle. As I was then affiliated with the organization and was receiving its full support for my efforts, it was the logical choice.

I would also like to comment on the criticism expressed by some members of the Tibetan community when His Holiness did not meet with any representatives of the Norwegian government during his 2014 visit to Norway. The lack of a meeting had nothing to do with Norway's policy regarding Tibet. The government simply had no advance notice of his trip. A senior Norwegian official told me that they only learned about His Holiness's plan to visit Norway through the media. Dharamsala did not reach out to the government before arranging the trip. Had there been prior consultation, I am certain a meeting of some nature could have been put together. After all, His Holiness is a Nobel laureate, and there is profound and genuine respect for him in Norway.

The Norwegian government was disappointed by Dharamsala's behavior, particularly its seeming lack of appreciation of the delicate relationship Norway had with the PRC following its awarding of the Nobel Peace Prize to Liu Xiaobo in 2010. In response to this perceived insult, Beijing chose to punish the Norwegian government and intimidate its officials. For years their diplomatic relations were downgraded. Norway was hesitant even to send a new ambassador to the PRC, concerned that the Chinese might keep their appointee for a long period of time without accepting his credentials. As a result, Ambassador Svein Ole Saether, a dear friend of mine, was compelled to remain in his station far beyond his expected tour of duty. To this day Beijing does not seem to have forgiven Norway. We should have been more sensitive to Norway's delicate situation.

### *French Support for Dialogue*

Along with the United States and Norway, France ranks top among the nations that have engaged with us and supported our cause. While it is easy to judge governments and individuals by their public stance on Tibet, those of us actively engaged in the struggle know that support can often take place quietly and in less obvious forums. One example is the disappointment some Tibetans felt with the seeming change in behavior of former Mayor of Paris Jacques Chirac once he became the French President. Having received His Holiness in a grand celebration when he was mayor and been a vocal critic of the French government for its failure to meet with him at the time, he subsequently met with His Holiness only once during his decades-long tenure as President.

The truth of the matter is that as President, Jacques Chirac was very active on the Tibetan issue, albeit in quiet but instrumental ways. His efforts on our behalf were done in close consultation with us and have been of immense value. He decided not to take a public position on Tibet, believing it would create obstacles to implementing his ambitious initiative for France to play a more active and prominent role in Asia, especially regarding the PRC. In his book *My Life in Politics*, he shares many details of the discussions he had with President Jiang Zemin, including his efforts to encourage him to start a dialogue with His Holiness.[6] His undertakings were not tailored for public acclaim but rather toward obtaining substantive results.

In the mid-1990s, President Chirac was seriously committed to helping us reconnect with Beijing. Even though no breakthrough immediately materialized, the efforts of the French government contributed to Jiang Zemin's decision to restart engagement. By 2000, the US administration had begun to take a leadership role in encouraging resumption of the dialogue. Through the efforts of Ambassador to the United States Levitte, the French became an important partner in these efforts, which eventually led to the Nine Rounds of formal dialogue we began with Beijing in 2002.

When Nicolas Sarkozy was elected President in 2007, Ambassador Levitte returned to Paris and once again served as a diplomatic advisor. He continued his efforts to make sure that Tibet remained high on the new President's agenda. In the beginning of his tenure, President Sarkozy took a very strong public position on Tibet and even threatened to boycott the formal ceremonies of the Beijing Olympics. To be very frank, I was a little surprised and concerned with the tenor of his public remarks. I can't imagine he did this on the advice of Ambassador Levitte, whose style was much more behind the scenes. Not surprisingly, Tibet supporters, in concert with the broader human rights world, welcomed his position. Quite a few even praised his bold public stance, disparagingly contrasting it to the "weak" position taken by President Chirac. Despite the superficial appeal of his rhetoric, as some of us feared, political realities pressured President Sarkozy to pull back from his public posture, rendering him ineffective on our issue for quite some time. Still, throughout his term in office, President Sarkozy continued to make efforts on our behalf.

My extensive working relationship with Ambassador Levitte over the years led to a close personal friendship. We have deep respect for each other. Issues discussed in private remain absolutely confidential. He was a major supporter of our cause and the individual within the French government most responsible for spearheading initiatives on our behalf. Once, right in the middle of one of our meetings, someone interrupted us, beckoning the Ambassador. A few minutes later he came back and asked if I wanted a quick meeting with President Sarkozy. Without any hesitation I said I didn't need to meet with the President, as I had discussed all matters of importance in our meeting. I suggested that the President should meet with His Holiness and that there was no need to waste his time with me. The Ambassador offered this opportunity to me out of friendship, but I didn't need this type of formal support. His substantive actions on our behalf were the ones of true benefit.

I would also like to acknowledge the genuine support and interest that Bernard Kouchner has consistently shown on the Tibet issue. He received His Holiness in 2008 when he was Minister of Foreign and European Affairs for the French government, publicly expressing his concern for the plight of the Tibetans without hesitation. He has a track record of boldly championing humanitarian issues, sometimes causing displeasure within his own government. His whole life reflects his principled stance on human rights issues, as evinced by his founding of Médecins sans Frontieres (Doctors Without Borders), a Nobel Prize-winning NGO.

One also cannot overstate the passionate support that Danielle Mitterrand, the former First Lady of France, extended to His Holiness and the Tibetan people. She officially met with His Holiness when her husband was still in office, and her door was always open to those of us seeking her support and advice. She was a powerful voice for human rights and for the cause of Tibet. She became one of the earliest recipients of the ICT's Light of Truth award, receiving it from the hands of His Holiness himself in Los Angeles in 1999, together with Hugh Richardson[7] and Richard Blum.

In addition to the genuine and long-standing support we received from French government officials, I would also like to acknowledge the efforts of the French people. France has an extremely active grassroots movement and is home to the largest number of Tibet support groups in the world.

### *Efforts of Senior German Leaders*

Tibet has always enjoyed support from German leaders and private citizens. Angela Merkel officially received His Holiness on two occasions: first in 2005 in her capacity as leader of the Christian Democratic Union/Christian Social Union (CDU/CSU) parties, and again in 2007 as Germany's Chancellor. I also must give special mention to the late Green Party leader, Petra Kelly. She was key in bringing the issue of Tibet to the attention of the German people. Her death in 1992 at the young age of forty-four was a huge loss not only to the environmental lobby but also to the Tibetan movement, and indeed the world. She was a powerful voice for nuclear disarmament, for environmental protection, and on issues of human rights. If she were still alive, she would be in the forefront of the global movement supporting total abolition of nuclear weapons.

Otto Count Lambsdorff, a prominent German politician, was also instrumental in providing meaningful assistance to Tibet through the Friedrich Naumann Foundation. The foundation maintained a very active office in India and devoted considerable resources to various Tibet programs, among other activities sponsoring several of the International Tibet Support Group meetings. Its bold association with the Tibet issue greatly jeopardized the organization's relations with the PRC, ultimately leading to the forced closure of its office there.

Christian Schwarz-Schilling, a senior member of the CDU, was another extremely helpful individual. Like US President Jimmy Carter, he had personal ties with Beijing. In the early 1980s, as Minister for Postal Services and Telecommunications, he was instrumental in jump-starting the PRC's telecommunications program. Ever since he was a young man, he had been interested in China and Tibet. I remember going to see him in the 1980s before moving to the United States. Equipped with a doctorate in East Asian studies, over the years he developed a deep understanding of historic China and its contemporary manifestation as the PRC. As a friend of the PRC, and concerned about Tibet, he was able to engage Beijing, including the United Front, on our behalf.

He also played a key role during the years of our formal dialogue in annually organizing a special "roundtable" meeting on the Tibet issue, giving Kelsang Gyaltsen and me the opportunity to brainstorm with him and other experts. In later years a representative of the German Foreign Ministry participated in these sessions, giving us the opportunity both to brief the Ministry on our efforts and to listen to their thoughts and proposals. It was through this medium that the Ministry become actively involved in the dialogue process. As these meetings were "off the record," the Foreign Ministry participants spoke very candidly, providing us with insights and options we otherwise would not have heard. Christian Schwarz-Schilling held most of these meetings at his home, and his wife,

Marie-Luise, joined in some of the discussions. Being with the Schwarz-Schillings reminded me of two other husband-wife teams that have been so helpful to our cause.[8]

These roundtable meetings, held sometimes before and at other times after a formal negotiating session with our PRC counterparts, also gave us the opportunity to analyze the state of our dialogue and come up with suggestions for moving the discussions forward. Christian Schwarz-Schilling prepared a report after each session, offering specific recommendations that he shared with us, Beijing, and the German government. These were very useful, as they took into consideration the sensitivities and limitations expressed by both parties. They were practical suggestions that were not difficult for either party to accept. For example, one proposal was to reduce time spent on the more problematic "big-picture" issues and focus on less contentious issues such as education and environment, matters viewed as less political by Beijing. In this way, each party could maintain its fundamental negotiating position while at the same time taking some steps forward to build confidence between us.

I participated in seven of these discussions prior to my retirement. I know they are ongoing, and I am certain they continue to be of great benefit to the Tibetan leadership.[9]

### *Ireland*

One European country I wish to specially mention is Ireland. Tibetan leaders in the late 1950s and early 1960s must have had hopes that their old friends the British would speak up on our behalf because of the historic relation between our countries and their knowledge of the Tibet issue. But it was Ireland, a small nation, that ultimately became Tibet's champion. Then Irish Foreign Minister Frank Aiken took almost personal charge in raising the Tibet issue at the United Nations. His role was paramount in all three UN resolutions addressing Tibet, those in 1959, 1961, and 1965.[10] When His Holiness made his maiden visit to Ireland in 1973, he was received officially like a head of government. The most memorable moment was when Frank Aiken came out of retirement to personally meet His Holiness at a government reception. His Holiness and all of us in his entourage were so deeply touched to be able to meet and shake hands with this stalwart supporter who had so tirelessly championed our cause for so many years, never giving up.

Because of the suffering the Irish endured under British rule, Irish people everywhere have a special understanding of and sympathy for our plight. Even in America, people of Irish origin have shown strong solidarity with the Tibetan people. There was a very energetic Tibet support group in Ireland spearheaded by Neil Steedman and Anthony O'Brien. Mary Robinson, who later became the President of Ireland, was also actively involved with this group. I remember having strategy meetings with Tibet friends at her home when I visited Ireland. She later became the UN High Commissioner for Human Rights, and many of us worked with her in that capacity. Although her hands were tied as a UN official, in her personal capacity she has always remained supportive. Mairead Maguire, another Nobel laureate, has also been a strong supporter of Tibet and was someone I could always approach for guidance. She continues to serve on the ICT's International Council of Advisors. Betty Williams, corecipient of the Nobel Prize with Mairead Maguire, has also been an active participant with His Holiness on a number of global issues. She further chaired the board of the Institute for Asian Democracy (IAD), led by Michele Bohana after Michele left the ICT as its founding director. I was very supportive of the IAD's efforts because we agreed that building a strong network of democratic movements in Asia would benefit our cause. Michele's work addressing the struggle of the peoples in Burma from her position at the IAD provided one such avenue.

### *Other European Initiatives*

As my colleague Kelsang Gyaltsen was posted in Switzerland, he maintained far closer relations with the Swiss, and indeed other European governments, than I did. When in 2005 Beijing agreed to hold one of our formal dialogue meetings outside the PRC, Switzerland's historically neutral stance, combined with its generosity in providing a home to many Tibetan refugees and its close relations with Beijing, made it an obvious choice. With the concurrence of our negotiating counterparts, Kelsang Gyaltsen worked very closely with the Swiss Foreign Ministry to arrange the logistics. The Swiss authorities were not only supportive but very pleased that their country would be the venue for this important meeting. The ETH Zurich University further provided valuable training in the art of negotiation to my team on more than one occasion.

In addition to the Office of Tibet in Geneva, we had offices in London, Paris, Budapest, and Brussels, each headed by a senior CTA official. All of these offices were very successful in bringing a broader understanding of the Tibet issue to the people in their respective regions, while some of them further developed close relations with senior government officials. As in the United States, our goal was to build strong parliamentary support groups in these countries, recognizing that legislative support tends to be more reliable and long-lasting than that provided by the executive branch.

*United Kingdom: Disappointing Inaction*

Because of the British colonization of India, the United Kingdom is the European country with which Tibet has had the longest relationship. Consequently, it has been a great disappointment to the Tibetan people that we have never been able to gain the full support of the British government in our struggle. In the early 1950s, the US State Department sought British guidance on how to handle the Tibet issue because of the UK's historic relations with India and Tibet. I am quite sure that when the United States first started consulting the British, it thought the UK would be a willing partner in advancing Tibet's interests because of its past involvement in the region. However, the UK's position was just the opposite. As early as the late 1950s, when the Tibetan government was trying to refer the Tibet issue to the United Nations, our main obstacle was the United Kingdom. It advised other countries, including the United States, to be very cautious, actually complicating matters by needlessly raising issues of "suzerainty and sovereignty"[11] and "China's special position in Tibet."

We have been deeply disappointed by the British government's lack of support. Veteran UK diplomats, including Hugh Richardson and other British scholars, have also voiced concerns about their government's lukewarm measures. We never asked the UK to support Tibetan independence, but it has even failed to support His Holiness's Middle Way Approach. On some occasions, select British Prime Ministers and the Foreign Office may have raised the Tibet issue with their counterparts behind closed doors because of strong public sympathy for Tibet and at the urging of British members of Parliament and other noted public figures, but that has been the limit of the UK's involvement.

The only time the British Foreign Ministry publicly issued a rather detailed statement on the issue was David Miliband's 2008 comments when my team was on the eve of our departure for our Eighth Round of dialogue. Then Foreign

Secretary, he talked about the importance of dialogue, touched on human rights issues, and even had a complimentary word for His Holiness's decision not to seek independence. But the underlying purpose of his statement seemed to be more a formal rejection of Britain's historical position on Tibet based on its now acknowledged misguided suzerainty notion than support of our cause.

> But our position is unusual for one reason of history that has been imported into the present: the anachronism of our formal position on whether Tibet is part of China, and whether in fact we harbor continued designs to see the break-up of China. We do not.
>
> Our recognition of China's "special position" in Tibet developed from the outdated concept of suzerainty. Some have used this to cast doubt on the aims we are pursuing and to claim that we are denying Chinese sovereignty over a large part of its own territory. We have made clear to the Chinese Government, and publicly, that we do not support Tibetan independence.[12]

I have also wondered about the timing of this statement. Was it truly to help with the dialogue, or did Beijing encourage the British to make the statement at that particular time? I believe someone in the British government made a commitment to Beijing to make this "clarification" in an effort to bolster Beijing's negotiating position. To be very candid, the statement was not particularly detrimental to us at that stage of the dialogue process. Rather, it reflects poorly on a nation that is so proud of its imperial legacy that it joins the club of disingenuous nations seeking to rewrite history for the political conveniences of the day.

By contrast, we have had a very strong support base among the British people. They have been in the forefront in providing humanitarian and other assistance to Tibetan refugees. The Tibet Society of the United Kingdom, established soon after the Tibetan exodus in 1959, is the oldest Tibet support organization. When His Holiness made his first visit to the West, the UK was one of his most important stops. He was received with great warmth and friendship by the British people. I was part of his entourage and can attest that he thoroughly enjoyed his visit, even reconnecting with some friends he had first met when he was still living in Tibet.

Our disappointment with the position of successive British governments has been tempered, however, by the personal support of Prince Charles, who has acted

His Holiness the 14th Dalai Lama arriving in Zurich from Italy in 1973 for his first visit to the West. (Left to right) the author, Ven. Paljor (His Holiness's longest serving personal assistant), Michael van Walt van Praag (Liaison Officer), Lhundup Negi, Tenzin Gyeche (behind flower bouquet), Ven T. C. Tara (behind His Holiness), His Holiness, Kunga, Phala Thubten Woeden

Tibet Museum, CTA

admirably on our behalf on many occasions. He has often taken a principled stand on Tibet, at times refusing to attend formal events honoring visiting Chinese leaders in protest over Beijing's policies on Tibet. In 2012, he went out of his way to receive His Holiness, no doubt over the strong objection of the British Foreign Ministry. I think His Royal Highness has done a great service for his country, uplifting the dignity and prestige of the UK particularly in the eyes of the Tibetan people, who feel a personal connection to the British. Tibetans, in fact, refer to all Westerners as *Enji*, meaning "English," because our first direct contact with the Western world was with the British.

Among the small but very active group of British friends of Tibet, Lord David Ennals comes immediately to mind. This dedicated human rights campaigner even went on a parliamentary fact-finding mission to Tibet in 1988. He was a tireless

Tibet supporter, involved in all the major Tibet-related conferences and activities worldwide. A number of us in the Tibetan leadership, particularly Kasur Tashi Wangdi and myself, have worked with him for many years. His support echoed that of President Carter and Senator Feinstein in eschewing a claim for Tibetan independence in favor of His Holiness's Middle Way Approach, a position that led some people within the Tibetan movement to be critical of him.

Lord Ennals always sought to help us by trying to be a bridge with Beijing. When the PRC first started its charm offensive to the West, it had some of its most skillful diplomats posted in London. Lord Ennals worked very hard to reach out to them on our behalf. They responded negatively to his overtures, as they did to others during this time, claiming that His Holiness was in fact seeking independence. Lord Ennals knew that not to be the case and suggested that a clear statement from His Holiness could help dispel Beijing's rhetoric. His Holiness considered his arguments and agreed to make the statement, as it accurately reflected his position.

Unfortunately, when the statement was actually issued, Lord Ennals was disappointed. The language that we had worked on with him was there, but other paragraphs had been inserted, significantly altering the intended message. I must admit that I too was disappointed with the final statement. Once again, in a pattern all too familiar, our internal lack of communication and coordination impeded an opportunity for reconnecting with Beijing.

British friends, including parliamentarians such as Lord Ennals and the Tibet Society of the UK, have worked tremendously hard on our behalf, making it less painful to remember that the Foreign Office has been so unhelpful. While I understand that each country must put its own interests first, the British could have adopted a more supportive position without jeopardizing their relations with the PRC. Indeed, I don't believe the PRC has reciprocated in any positive way for the UK's accommodating posture on Tibet.

I understand when Tibetans and Tibet supporters are critical of the lack of support from the British government. And as I mention elsewhere, many Tibetans and our friends feel emotional satisfaction when people talk about independence or condemn Chinese leaders in the harshest manner. But I am deeply disappointed when they speak out against individuals such as Lord Ennals. He, together with other parliamentarians including Sir Bernard Braine, Lord Eric Avebury, and Fabian Hamilton, were some of the leading members of the All-Party Parliamentary Group for Tibet (APPGT) actively working for our benefit. Given that many of the actions they took on our behalf occurred behind the scenes, the public is unaware of their contributions. But we must be outspoken in their defense when such unjustified criticisms arise, doing our best to explain the crucial roles these steadfast individuals played out of public view.

With Lord Ennals's passing in 1995, we lost a great campaigner for our cause and a valued personal friend. I was thus deeply honored when I was asked to give the Third Annual Lord Ennals Memorial Lecture, hosted by the Tibet Society of the United Kingdom in 1998 in London. My introductory remarks sum up the deep respect and appreciation I have for all his efforts on Tibet's behalf:

> Lord Ennals was both a personal friend to me and a tireless advocate for the issue of Tibet. He made countless contributions to the issue of Tibet and with wisdom and compassion he always offered invaluable advice when sought out. Lord Ennals also had a rare quality amongst Tibet's friends—not only did he respect the views of the Tibetans and His Holiness the Dalai Lama, he understood it was for the Tibetans to make the ultimate decisions about their own cause. It was this quality that endeared him to me and earned him the respect and friendship of His Holiness.[13]

### *Eastern European Countries and Soviet Republics*

From the late 1980s to the early 1990s I made frequent trips to Europe, including Eastern European countries, as well as to Mongolia and other Soviet Republics, including Buryatia. Our initial efforts in Eastern Europe and in the Baltics were during the Soviet era. Many of my visits to the Baltic nations were without proper visas. In those days, the Russian visa specified the areas that one could visit. As the Soviets did not approve of my Baltic trips, I used to stay in St. Petersburg, at the time called Leningrad, and travel back and forth by train or bus on a daily basis to the Baltic countries. One was not really restricted from visiting these areas, but without a visa, hotel accommodations were unavailable.

Alex Berzin was one of the key people who helped open doors for us in Eastern Europe, and he accompanied me on quite a few of my trips. In Hungary, many people knew about Tibet not only because of the recent tragedy but more because of the famous Hungarian Tibetologist, Alexander Csoma de Koros. I visited the room in Zangla in Zanskar where he lived and studied for a long time and his memorial at Darjeeling, where he died in 1842. In addition, quite a few Hungarians thought that their ancestors came from Central Asia and were thus distantly related to the Tibetan people.

The late Linnart Mall from Estonia played an important role in helping us build connections there, as well as in Latvia and Lithuania. Andrey Terentyev from Leningrad also supported our efforts, hosting me several times. Because of my visits and activities in Eastern Europe, I had the great honor of meeting Vaclav Havel, Vytautas Landsbergis, Lech Walesa, and other leaders who were in the forefront of their respective countries' democratic movements. Both Vaclav and Vytautas kindly agreed to be on the ICT's International Council of Advisors. In 2004, the ICT had the great honor of presenting the Light of Truth award to the Honorable Vaclav Havel.

## ISRAEL

I have already mentioned the special bond that we feel with the Jewish people. His Holiness also has great admiration for them. In one of his earliest dialogues with Jewish religious leaders, he asked several prominent rabbis to share with him the secret of their survival. His Holiness always advised us to hope for an early end to our suffering, but to be ready for the long haul. I am sure he had this perspective in mind when he posed this question.

I had the pleasure of arranging many of His Holiness's visits and meetings, many of which were of historic importance, but nothing gave me as much satisfaction as arranging His Holiness's visit to Israel. This was different from all other visits; this was truly a pilgrimage, not a meeting with politicians or to lobby parliamentarians on Tibet's behalf. Arranging the trip was not an easy task. It took over a year, and at one point I thought it was not going to work out. Had I not had the help and support of a prominent American friend who had strong connections in Israel, it likely would have remained unrealized.[14]

In those days India had yet to establish diplomatic relations with Israel. In both its domestic and international relations, India pursued a pro-Arab policy and was quite often unfriendly to Israel. Because His Holiness not only resides in India but also travels on an Indian travel document, it took time for the government of India to approve his visit. I worked very closely with senior Israeli diplomats in Washington, D.C., who were very helpful, but it also took time before the Israelis gave the green light.

My American friend and I, accompanied by a rabbi friend of his, made a special trip to Israel to work out the details of the visit. When we arrived, I was overwhelmed. It was unbelievable visiting these prominent biblical sites and those places described in Exodus. My most memorable experience was a visit to Masada, where nearly a thousand Jewish patriots took their own lives rather than be subjugated by the Romans. I took as much time to learn about and enjoy these memorable sites on this scouting trip as possible because I knew during His Holiness's visit it would be very hectic and there would be no time for sightseeing.

His Holiness finally visited in November 1999. As I mentioned, for him, this was a pilgrimage to the most holy sites of the three great Abrahamic religious traditions and the opportunity to meet all their current, most prominent leaders. There was one meeting where I think three chief rabbis together received His Holiness. I was told this was a very rare event, as these rabbis do not usually meet together. For His Holiness's visit to the Wailing Wall, our Jewish friends even produced a maroon-colored yarmulke to match his robes!

Our intention was for His Holiness to go overland to Jordan, but that portion of the trip had to be canceled because tension between the Palestinians and the Israelis forced closure of the border. I was able to organize a visit for His Holiness to Jordan some years later, however, although I could not join him on the trip. My special assistant and Director of the ICT's Special Programs, Lesley Friedell Rich, accompanied him in my stead. As we do not maintain an Office of Tibet in that part of the world, it made sense for me to handle the logistics of these visits from Washington, D.C., where these countries have strong diplomatic presences. In that regard, I thoroughly enjoyed working with the Jordanian Ambassador in D.C., who was very supportive of the visit.

## THE NOBEL PEACE PRIZE

Because of his unwavering moral compass, His Holiness the 14th Dalai Lama has become one of the most respected figures in the international community. But this esteemed position did not materialize instantaneously. Had he not developed the brilliant Middle Way Approach, I don't think he would have been awarded the Nobel Peace Prize in 1989. Moreover, had he not been awarded the prize, I don't believe the Tibet issue ever would have reached the prominence it has. The receipt of the Nobel Peace Prize was like a rocket booster, elevating the Tibet issue to a higher level on the global stage virtually overnight.

The idea of pursuing the Peace Prize for His Holiness was first brought to my attention by Riki Hyde-Chambers, a very dear friend of Tibet, during one of my trips to London. Years later, with his customary modesty, Riki told me that it was actually John Billington, then Chairman of the UK Tibet Society, who originally came up with the idea. Notwithstanding that fact, Riki played a key role, together with Lord Ennals and Edward Carpenter, then Dean of Westminster, in bringing the proposal to fruition. In support of their efforts, long-standing friends of Tibet, including Robert Thurman and Michele Bohana in the United States, Michael van Walt van Praag and Jan Andersson in Europe, and Kushok Bakula and M. L. Sondhi in India, among many others from several countries, became active campaigners for this effort.

When Riki first mentioned the idea, to be very frank, many of us were unaware of the strict protocol attending the nominating procedure. The committee does not independently decide on the awardees; only a select few individuals, as detailed in the Statutes of the Nobel Foundation, can nominate candidates. After His Holiness received the award, Riki wrote an article in the *Tibetan Review* saying how pleased he was, further mentioning the names of those of us, including himself, who had been involved with the effort. Some Tibetans were upset, criticizing us as taking credit for His Holiness receiving the award. But they simply didn't understand the nominating process and the tremendous organizing effort a successful campaign entails. Everyone who has been a recipient of the Peace Prize has gone through this arduous process. Indeed, it was only in the third year of our efforts that they bore fruit.

When I asked Riki how he felt when he learned that His Holiness had been nominated, he responded: "It had a major impact on me emotionally, as I knew it would for Tibetans inside Tibet, because it was something tangible, a recognition of the justness of the cause and the nobility of the approach, and it would help His Holiness in his advocacy. It was a privilege to attend the presentation of the prize in Oslo, but those first moments of hearing he had been awarded the prize was a unique experience and feeling of great joy." The prize is awarded to the candidate who has "done the most or the best work for fraternity between nations, for the abolition or reduction of standing armies and for the holding and promotion of peace congresses." His Holiness unquestionably meets these criteria.

Even those of us in the Tibetan leadership didn't immediately realize how enormous the impact of the award would be. Traditionally, the Norwegian Ambassador personally delivers the news to the winning candidate. When His Holiness learned of his award we were in California, where he was giving a major Buddhist teaching to a large audience. We received a message that the Norwegian Ambassador was coming to see him. Tenzin Geyche and I were so excited. We could barely contain our glee, as we suspected the reason for his visit. But His Holiness was almost indifferent and lightly chided us, asking what the commotion was all about.

As the Ambassador had to catch a flight back to Washington immediately, he wanted to visit His Holiness very early in the morning. We were staying at a private residence, and when the Ambassador arrived, Tenzin Geyche and I received him. Tenzin Geyche went upstairs to inform His Holiness. His Holiness came down wearing his rubber bathroom slippers, and there was the Norwegian Ambassador in formal dress—it was quite the sight. While gracious and welcoming, His Holiness showed no excitement when he was informed of the reason for the Ambassador's visit. A few years later, however, His Holiness did mention to me that his receiving the Peace Prize had given tremendous credence to the cause of Tibet. It not only catapulted the Tibet issue to international prominence but also greatly enhanced His Holiness's acceptance by global leaders. Those who wanted to meet him but previously worried about the PRC's reaction could now say they had a nonpolitical reason for the meeting. Conversely, it became difficult for those who might not have wanted to meet him to say no to a Nobel laureate!

His Holiness has become one of the most active laureates in joining hands to work on critical global issues. Archbishop Desmond Tutu was one of those with whom His Holiness worked most closely. Seeing the two of them together is a great treat, one that is certain to leave you with unforgettable memories. They can both be very funny, but most importantly, very inspiring. His Holiness could make a much more profound contribution as a Nobel laureate in the absence of the PRC's objections. Because of political pressure by Beijing, His Holiness is sometimes precluded from joining his fellow laureates at their gatherings.

For the Tibetans and Tibet friends, I remember no other event that was as joyous as the occasion when hundreds of us journeyed to Oslo to be there for this

His Holiness the 14th Dalai Lama receiving the Nobel Peace Prize from Egil Aarvik, Chair of the Norwegian Nobel Committee, December 10, 1989
Tibet Museum, CTA

momentous day. We really celebrated, loudly singing: "We shall overcome, we shall overcome," with candles in our hands, parading through the evening streets of Oslo. His Holiness, coming out onto the balcony of his hotel room, was so deeply moved to see so many of his friends gathered together that he came outside and joined us in the candlelight vigil. I simply do not have the English vocabulary to communicate the joy we felt that day. I asked a few of the participants, Joel McCleary from the United States, Jan Andersson from Europe, and Rajiv Mehrotra from India, to express their feelings that night and the significance of the award. Their remarks[15] beautifully capture the experience in all its joy, intensity, and camaraderie.

> Over the decades of the global movement to protect the Tibetan people, religion, and culture, there have been and will be many high and low points. The 1989 Nobel Peace Prize for His Holiness is one high point. The electric feelings of support running through the people of Norway and those international Tibet supporters, who had come from afar to witness and celebrate, will never be forgotten. Standing with torches and on frozen feet at night before His Holiness' hotel with my dear friends and Tibet allies; Congressman Charlie Rose (NC), Lodi Gyari, Tenzin Tethong, Richard Gere, Bob Thurman, Michael and Lavinia Currier, John Avedon, Michele Bohana, and of course a large contingent of friends from Europe, Japan, India and I am sure many other countries, was a moment to be cherished forever. I left Norway with the realization the spirit and will of the Tibetan people will never be broken. Nothing has occurred since Norway to make me doubt that Norway-inspired realization.
>
> Joel McCleary

> In October, when the news came, I was in my chemical laboratory but was too stunned to react—after several years of working for this occasion, and two years of other laureates being selected, it took several minutes for me to realize that it was true and to react, and then tears came out of an overwhelming happiness. In Oslo, in the dark, bitterly cold December night, marching through the streets with all those other people supporting justice for Tibet, a feeling of immense optimism rose, of strength, that the Tibetan cause is not at all lost. When the large torch-bearing crowd arrived at His Holiness' hotel and he entered his balcony to greet us, it felt like the heart would burst of joy. And he then came down on the street in his simple monk's robe and mingled with us, sharing our exaltation, it was an emotional earthquake. A jubilation, a confirmation that the noble forces in the world cannot be defeated.
>
> I have never had such an intense emotional moment in my life, neither before nor later. You may remember those moments yourself, Lodi la, and how

exalted we all were. To this day I am happy to have experienced that once, and especially that it was such a worthy occasion.

Jan Andersson

It was an unexpected and undeserved blessing, a great privilege to be invited by His Holiness the Dalai Lama to accompany him to the Nobel Peace Prize Ceremony in Oslo.

For this most unworthy chela December 10th 1989 remains an indelible memory—of joy, of tears and inspiration that I will cherish for lifetimes to come.

It was a decisive moment that accelerated The Dalai Lama's emergence on the global stage, not merely as an embodiment of the legitimate aspirations of the Tibetan people or an apostle of non-violence—for many it also represented a gesture of atonement for the Nobel that was due but never awarded to Mahatma Gandhi.

Rajiv Mehrotra

His Holiness's primary message delivered upon receiving the Peace Prize was the sharing of his deeply felt philosophy based on the principle of universal responsibility. Not only does this philosophy underpin His Holiness's Middle Way Approach for resolving the Tibet issue, but it also informs all of His Holiness's activities, on behalf of the Tibetan people and for the benefit of us all. The following excerpts from his "Acceptance Speech" and his "Nobel Lecture" eloquently express his views.

### December 10, 1989, "Nobel Peace Prize Acceptance Speech"

As a Buddhist monk, my concern extends to all members of the human family and, indeed, to all sentient beings who suffer. I believe all suffering is caused by ignorance. People inflict pain on others in the selfish pursuit of their happiness or satisfaction. Yet true happiness comes from a sense of brotherhood and sisterhood. We need to cultivate a universal responsibility for one another and the planet we share. Although I have found my own Buddhist religion helpful in generating love and compassion, even for those we consider our enemies, I am convinced that everyone can develop a good heart and a sense of universal responsibility with or without religion.[16]

### December 11, 1989, "Nobel Lecture"

Today, we are truly a global family. What happens in one part of the world may affect us all . . . War or peace; the destruction or the protection of nature; the violation or promotion of human rights and democratic freedoms; poverty or material well-being; the lack of moral and spiritual values or their existence and development; and the breakdown or development of human understanding, [these] are not isolated phenomena that can be analysed and tackled independently of one another. . . .

Clearly, it is of great importance, therefore, to understand the interrelationship among these and other phenomena, and to approach and attempt to solve problems in a balanced way that takes these different aspects into consideration. Of course, it is not easy. But it is of little benefit to try to solve one problem if doing so creates an equally serious new one. So really we have no alternative: we must develop a sense of universal responsibility not only in the geographic sense, but also in respect to the different issues that confront our planet.

Responsibility does not only lie with the leaders of our countries or with those who have been appointed or elected to do a particular job. It lies with each one of us individually. Peace, for example, starts with each one of us. When we have inner peace, we can be at peace with those around us. When our community is in a state of peace, it can share that peace with neighbouring communities, and so on. When we feel love and kindness toward others, it not only makes others feel loved and cared for, but it helps us also to develop inner happiness and peace. . . .

The awarding of the Nobel Prize to me, a simple monk from faraway Tibet, here in Norway, also fills us Tibetans with hope. It means, despite the fact that we have not drawn attention to our plight by means of violence, we have not been forgotten. It also means that the values we cherish, in particular our respect for all forms of life and the belief in the power of truth, are today recognised and encouraged. It is also a tribute to my mentor, Mahatma Gandhi, whose example is an inspiration to so many of us.

This year's award is an indication that this sense of universal responsibility is developing.[17]

Of course, we could not include all of those who journeyed to Oslo to celebrate His Holiness's prize to the formal dinner hosted by the Norwegian Nobel Committee. In my capacity as Kalon for International Relations, I hosted a separate earlier dinner for our friends at the same venue because His Holiness was keen to personally greet his friends before the official dinner. The DIIR of the CTA issued a special commemorative medal for all those who participated in the event. The medal has a drawing of a lotus on one side, with "Chagna Padmo" (meaning "Holder of Lotus," another name for Chenrezig) written above it and "Shidhey Depon" (Peace Captain) written underneath, all symbolizing His Holiness the 14th Dalai Lama. The CTA seal is featured on the other side, with the English inscription "His Holiness the Dalai Lama XIV" above the seal and "1989 Nobel Peace Laureate" underneath it.

His Holiness gave away all of the prize money associated with receipt of the Peace Prize, donating it to various international charities and using a portion of it to create the Foundation for Universal Responsibility of His Holiness the Dalai Lama in November 1990, a not-for-profit, nonsectarian, nondenominational organization devoted to His Holiness's call for Universal Responsibility and led by Rajiv Mehrotra with great devotion. While the Tibetan movement as a whole has, for some reason, never embraced this profound way of thinking, I am happy that a separate NGO is there to promote this truly selfless, wise, and compassionate philosophy.

## FORMATION OF THE UNREPRESENTED NATIONS AND PEOPLES ORGANIZATION

When we first fled Tibet and were establishing ourselves in exile, we had little energy to devote to any cause other than our own. But the suffering of other peoples around the world could not go unacknowledged forever. This first led us to examine the situation of two of the other peoples suffering under PRC rule, the Uyghurs and the Mongolians.

Takla Phuntsok Tashi, who was at one time in the Kashag, was one of the individuals initiating these efforts. He was fluent in Chinese and was married to His

Holiness's older sister Tsering Dolma. The two of them had been part of His Holiness's delegation to Beijing in 1954–55. Takla Phuntsok Tashi knew quite a few Mongolians as well as other individuals in Taiwan. Another key person who was instrumental in this effort was Erkin Alptekin. As I previously mentioned, he is the son of Isa Alptekin, a prominent East Turkistan leader who came into exile in India in the late 1940s/early 1950s and stayed in Kashmir for a long time, becoming personal friends with Pandit Nehru. Eventually he immigrated to Turkey, but he visited His Holiness soon after the Dalai Lama's arrival in India and they maintained a close relationship over the years. His Holiness went to Turkey in 1983 to visit Isa, and as far as I know, it is the only time that His Holiness made a specific trip to a country just to meet with one individual.

Talka Phuntsok Tashi, Erkin Alptekin, and others realized the importance of creating an alliance among the Tibetans, Uyghurs, and Mongolians to learn from one another's experiences. My cabinet colleague Tashi Wangdi and I also were involved from the beginning, launching a support organization called the Allied Committee. Later, at the explicit suggestion of His Holiness, some Manchurians were also invited to participate, although there was a great deal of resistance from our Uyghur friends to their inclusion. The Uyghurs deeply resent the Manchurians, as the latter's policy toward the Uyghurs when they ruled the region was ruthless, possibly even rising to the level of genocide. It was also not easy to find an ethnic Manchurian. One individual we located in Taiwan was more Chinese than Manchurian. He eventually felt his participation in the group was actually a liability, so he left.

In the early 1990s we decided to create a wider alliance so that our combined voices would have more resonance in the international community. With the changes that were unfolding in the former Soviet Union, there were a number of groups bringing their historical suffering to the public's attention. While I took the lead on behalf of the Tibetans in expanding our alliance, Michael van Walt van Praag, Linnart Mall, and Erkin Alptekin were key in pulling all the other groups together. As I wrote earlier, Michael is a longtime friend of Tibet, but also an international lawyer deeply concerned about the plight of suffering peoples the world over. He is a staunch advocate of a people's right to self-determination. His book, *Status of Tibet*, is an important work that those interested in the issue of Tibet, particularly its historical and legal status, should definitely read.

As a result of our collective efforts, on February 11, 1991, we founded the Unrepresented Nations and Peoples Organization (UNPO) in The Hague,

Netherlands, merging the Allied Committee into it. The founding members were Armenia, Australian Aboriginals, Cordillera, Crimean Tatars, East Turkestan, Estonia, Georgia, the Greek Minority in Albania, Iraqi Kurdistan, Latvia, Palau, Taiwan, Tatarstan, Tibet, and West Papua. East Timor, Kosovo, Abkhazia, Somaliland, Chittagong Hill Tracts, Nagaland, Bougainville, Acheh, Ogoni, Zanzibar, Mapuche, and the Burmese exile government, among others, soon joined. As of this writing, UNPO has about forty-three members. It held its XIII General Assembly meeting at Edinburg, Scotland, in June 2017. The organization is led by a General Secretary elected by the General Assembly. Michael van Walt van Praag served as the first General Secretary.

The Burmese exile government was treated as a Nation. Armenia, Georgia, and other Baltic states also joined as Nations. Many of the UNPO members later became sovereign nations, and we instituted a provision that any member who became a full-fledged independent nation could remain in UNPO as an associate member. Ultimately this included East Timor, Armenia, Estonia, Latvia, Georgia, and Palau. Jose Ramos-Horta, who later became President of East Timor, was not only very active but also a UNPO office holder and a Nobel Peace Prize recipient, awarded the honor in 1996.

Some of these now sovereign nations forgot about UNPO as time went on, although UNPO must share some of the responsibility for not cultivating a continuing relationship with them. But others remained close to the group and were quite helpful to the membership. The Democratic Progressive Party of Taiwan (DPP) is one example. When the party formed the government in Taiwan, it remained very supportive of UNPO, including hosting UNPO gatherings. Similarly, some of the Baltic nations continue to maintain relations, even hosting quite a few UNPO-related workshops and conferences.

Tibet was not only one of the founders of this organization but also able to provide substantial logistical support because we had the advantage of having several Offices of Tibet in Europe. For many years, the driving force behind this organization was Tsering Jampa, who served as Deputy General Secretary for the first six years and Acting General Secretary for an additional year following Michael van Walt van Praag's resignation. While Michael was a great leader with a global vision, UNPO would not have succeeded without the dedicated and hard work of Tsering Jampa. Another Tibetan who played a very important role with UNPO is Ngawang Choephel, who served as UNPO President from 2010 to 2017, the longest term of anyone occupying that position to date. In this way we

Tibetans have been able to lend support to other peoples in circumstances similar to our own. We are often seen as a role model, thanks to the towering leadership of His Holiness the 14th Dalai Lama. Using our Office in Geneva, the Tibetan team has been able to provide crucial assistance to others who are trying to be heard at the United Nations, many of whom are making their first approach to the organization. We had the benefit of experienced diplomats who understood the UN helping them, even though our efforts on behalf of Tibet have been blocked at every level.

In the course of our work, we have influenced organizations including UNPO to accept His Holiness's philosophy of nonviolence. The UNPO constitution makes it clear that anyone who wants to be a member must commit to nonviolence. If an organization has engaged in an armed struggle in the past, it must renounce the practice. UNPO has in fact rejected a few applications because there was clear evidence that the applicants were actually armed resistance movements.

## NONGOVERNMENTAL ORGANIZATION SUPPORT

While we have been fortunate to receive support at the highest levels from a number of governments, in many cases, it was active grassroots organizations that initially triggered this official interest. It is indeed wonderful that in a democracy, politicians respond to public views.

Many Tibet support groups throughout the world have made significant contributions in garnering support for the cause by educating policy makers and the public on the issue of Tibet. In some countries, there are multiple groups; in France and several other countries, as many as fifty, each of them performing valuable work. While I wish to acknowledge the hard work of all these groups, I focus my discussion on US-based groups because Washington, D.C., was the base of my activities for over a quarter of a century and I am most familiar with their work.

### *International Campaign for Tibet*

A large part of our success in creating awareness of the Tibet issue and having an influence on US policy regarding Tibet is due to the efforts of the ICT. Even though we had excellent access to the political leadership in global institutions, governments, and parliaments, we still faced practical and legal limitations, and the ICT's role in overcoming them has been enormous. It would not be an exaggeration to say that this organization played the most important role in our efforts at global outreach, second only to the CTA itself.

Tethong Tenzin Namgyal was the ICT's first President when it opened its doors in 1988, but when he was elected to the Kashag in 1990, I succeeded him. I was closely associated with the ICT from its founding years until my retirement in 2014. Accordingly, many of my activities were conducted either in my capacity as ICT President or later as Executive Chair. Establishing this NGO in Washington, D.C., was a brilliant and farsighted idea by friends of Tibet. With the blessing of His Holiness, the ICT continues to be in the forefront of the Tibet movement, keeping the issue alive internationally.

Since its inception the ICT has functioned as an independent NGO. It is not, and never has been, an extension of the CTA, although it works in close coordination with Dharamsala. The ICT and its founders adopted a clear policy, enunciated in its bylaws, that its mandate is to support His Holiness on whatever path he and the Tibetan people choose to pursue. Thus, whenever His Holiness or the CTA puts forth an initiative, the ICT extends its full support. This has included dialogue with Beijing, an area in which the ICT played a key role.

As I was the Special Envoy for the formal dialogue, all the logistics and secretarial assistance for this endeavor were handled by the ICT. Of course, those of us involved were very fortunate to have a capable group of people in Dharamsala under Samdhong Rinpoche's direct guidance, further assisting us. The CTA's Task Force on Sino-Tibetan Negotiations dealt with the most sensitive and important policy-related matters, including preparation of major documents.[18]

From its beginning, the ICT had highly dedicated, capable, and experienced people on its staff and Board of Directors. Richard Gere has been Chair of the Board since 2003. Many NGO boards meet only infrequently and have a ceremonial chair. By contrast, Richard takes tremendous interest in our cause, routinely visiting the office and motivating the staff. Whenever he comes, he spends quality time with individual staff members, listening to their ideas and concerns and making them feel that the work they are doing is both understood and appreciated by the Board.

Because he is a globally recognized artist, Richard's involvement also helps create wider awareness of Tibet. I have been very fortunate to work closely with him. With his deep knowledge of the issue and profound appreciation of the Tibetan Buddhist cultural heritage, Richard is one of the most visible and

ICT Board Chair Richard Gere and the author, Washington, D.C., 2016

effective spokespersons for the Tibet issue on the international stage. He has met with political leaders and government officials all over the world and has testified on our behalf numerous times before the US Congress, the European Parliament, and other legislative bodies. He is also one of the most generous donors to the ICT. Finally, as a devout Buddhist practitioner, Richard understands the true essence of the struggle as articulated by His Holiness: the preservation of the unique Tibetan culture and Tibetan Buddhist doctrines.

I could devote this entire book to the efforts of each member of the ICT's Board and staff but I will refrain. I would be remiss, however, in failing to acknowledge the ICT's first Director, Michele Bohana, and two of the ICT's former Presidents, John Ackerly and Mary Beth Markey. Michele's deep commitment to and passion for the Tibetan cause were essential in building support with policy makers in the early years. I vividly remember traveling to California with Tenzin Namgyal to recruit Michele to move to Washington and join our ICT team. Although I felt some guilt in taking Michelle away from sunny California when the weather in Washington, D.C., became gloomy and overcast, her selfless contributions to our cause erased my unease.

John Ackerly, who succeeded me as the ICT President, expanded the organization into the largest and most effective Tibet-focused NGO in the world. He integrated a strong grassroots advocacy approach into the ICT's mission, understanding the strength of a membership-based organization. John's vision became the model for other ICT offices in Europe and is the reason for much of their success thus far. John came to the Tibetan movement because of his encounter with Tibetans inside Tibet. He is one of the few foreigners who was present in Lhasa, and detained by the Chinese, when major demonstrations broke out in the streets in 1987. The iconic photograph of Jampa Tenzin demonstrating with one burned hand was taken by John. He returned to the United States deeply saddened by the situation but inspired by the determination of the Tibetans, compelling him to act. I have always identified John as a direct recruit for our cause by the Tibetans inside Tibet, similar to my view of Richard Holbrooke.

Mary Beth Markey joined the ICT in 1996 as Director of Government Relations, succeeding John Ackerly as President in 2010. Mary Beth came to us with many years of experience working for the late Senator Claiborne Pell in the Senate Foreign Relations Committee, where she worked on significant early Tibet legislation. Mary Beth was a skilled advocate instrumental in developing a comprehensive global advocacy strategy for the ICT during her presidency. We have been extremely fortunate to have several individuals in that position with rich Capitol Hill experience, including Rachel Lostumbo, Kelley Currie, Charlotte Oldham-Moore, and Todd Stein.

The ICT has been an extraordinary vehicle for the Tibet movement. When I retired in 2014, my parting advice to the staff was to be sure not to neglect relations with Congress, as it has been the backbone of our success in the United States. While we may enjoy excellent access to Congress now, this could easily change. I know the ICT's current President, Matteo Mecacci, will give the highest priority to maintaining and furthering relations with Congress because of his own background as a member of the Italian Parliament. In that capacity, he played a leading role in the International Network of Parliamentarians on Tibet, which he cochaired with Thomas Mann, a member of the European Parliament from Germany.

The current elected leaders in Dharamsala are keen to have direct relations with the US administration, preferring not to use vehicles such as the ICT. The ICT should respect this decision, as the organization's mandate is to support the Tibetan people in their cause. That said, the ICT is an American-based NGO, entirely separate from the CTA, that has always maintained its own relations with members of Congress. This separation is good for both groups and, most importantly, for the benefit of the Tibetan people. In the past, the ICT had one clear guiding principle—to do whatever was needed to support the policies and guidelines of His Holiness the 14th Dalai Lama. With His Holiness devolving his political position and the subsequent political changes in Dharamsala, the situation has changed. Therefore, if tomorrow the ICT, as the foremost Tibet support group, feels that the NGO needs to go to Congress with some ideas, I think it has every right to do so, particularly knowing that the organization would never pursue any policies contradictory to His Holiness's views.

### *The Tibet Fund*

For many years, the Tibet Fund has been an important vehicle assisting the Tibetans in humanitarian endeavors, as well as with initiatives to preserve Tibet's distinct cultural identity. It was established long before I came to the United States, initially to manage the funds from the sale of property left to His Holiness by Geshe Wangyal, the legendary Kalmyk monk who lived and taught Buddhism in the United States from 1955 until his passing in 1983. The Fund is registered as an NGO, but it originally shared space with the Office of Tibet in New York.

Over the years the Tibet Fund has grown under the leadership of people including Tenzin Namgyal and Rinchen Dharlo. It has provided a tremendous amount of assistance to the Tibetan people. Under Rinchen Dharlo's leadership, the Fund's growth was phenomenal. At one time Rinchen was a strong candidate to be inducted into the Kashag, an extremely prestigious position. As a close personal friend, I encouraged him to forego the honor. He and I both understood that he could benefit the Tibetans more by continuing in his position at the Tibet Fund. At that time, we were also lobbying for more funding from the US Congress. The

ICT's excellent relations with both staff and members of Congress enabled us to obtain substantial funding for the Tibetans and earmark funds for the Tibet Fund in *Congressional Report* language.

While maintaining their independent identities, both the ICT and the Tibet Fund worked very closely with the CTA to fund programs that the CTA deemed important. At times leaders in Dharamsala have not understood and appreciated the importance of respecting the independent status of NGOs, including the ICT and the Tibet Fund. While it is understandable that the older generation wants to incorporate these organizations into the CTA, I am disappointed that the younger generation is so aggressively trying to control them, especially given the historic and continuing benefits these institutions provide. Some cynics go so far as to allege that the ICT's success in lobbying for substantial funding must have inured to its own financial advantage. As I previously noted, not one penny of US funds benefited the ICT.

## *Students for a Free Tibet*

When Students for a Free Tibet (SFT) was launched in 1994, the ICT extended valuable support and encouragement to its efforts but never attempted to interfere in its mandate or activities. Originally SFT worked solely on university campuses, at one time having chapters at virtually every prominent center of higher education in the United States. It harnessed tremendous energy, enthusiasm, and commitment for Tibet, and in the 1990s and 2000s, SFT and the ICT created a formidable alliance.

I could be wrong, but in recent years SFT seems to be less focused on university campuses and more on internal Tibetan politics like the Tibetan Youth Congress and other Tibetan NGOs. Historically, the strength and uniqueness of SFT has been its success in reaching out to the broader world, and especially to the younger generation who are its future leaders. I hope that it once again sets itself apart from other Tibetan NGOs, returning to its original mandate. Today I often come across Americans in prominent positions in various fields who were once members of SFT. Their prior involvement continues to positively influence them on our behalf so many years later. Encouraging this engagement early in an individual's life is critical to keeping the Tibet movement alive and moving it forward.

## DHARMA CENTERS

One may wonder why I am addressing religious centers in a book concerning Tibet's political status. I am not talking about the Buddhist traditions of these organizations; rather, I am identifying them to acknowledge the tremendous help that the Tibetan leadership received from them and their associated spiritual communities (*sangha*). In particular, I wish to mention Sogyal Rinpoche, the founder of Rigpa; Geshe Tsultim Gyeltsen, founder of the Los Angeles-based Thubten Dhargye Ling; Lama Zopa Rinpoche, founder of the Foundation for the Preservation of the Mahayana Tradition (FPMT); Geshe Sopa of the Deer Park Institute in Wisconsin; and Gelek Rinpoche of Jewel Heart, as well as Lama Kata in Belgium, who for years headed the Kalu Rinpoche centers there. Sogyal Rinpoche, Geshe Tsultim Gyeltsen, and Geshe Sopa served on the ICT's Board for several years. Geshe Tsultim Gyeltsen actively participated in ICT Board meetings and was lovingly referred to as "Rangzen Geshe" because he was passionate about Tibetan independence (*rangzen*).

I must say that at times in the past I have been disappointed as a Tibetan when some of the Tibetan Buddhist centers and teachers were hesitant about identifying themselves with the "political issue of Tibet." The core of the Dalai Lama's effort is the preservation of Tibet's unique and distinct identity, which is nothing less than Tibetan Buddhism. I am very happy to see that Tibetan Buddhist teachers and centers now uniformly seek to be associated with His Holiness and to project themselves as having special relations or connections with him. That is wonderful, but it is important not to forget those who supported His Holiness's efforts from day one.

In the 1980s when we began our efforts to bring Tibet to the attention of the international community, we had scarce resources and traveled on a shoestring budget. We didn't even have the funds to stay in hotels. Sometimes we would stay with local Tibetan families, but most often it was Dharma centers that hosted us. I remember an early trip that Rinchen Dharlo and I took to Latin America in 1990 to organize a visit for His Holiness. We traveled to Argentina, Costa Rica, Mexico, Brazil, and Chile, among other countries. Except for Costa Rica, where we stayed in a hotel paid for by a Costa Rican friend, in every country we visited we stayed at Dharma centers or in the houses of local Buddhist practitioners. In Latin America, Namkhai Norbu Rinpoche's centers were the most generous. Not only did they house us, but their members also chauffeured us, translated for us, and helped us in every other possible way. Even in countries where we had our own Office of Tibet, from the very beginning we relied heavily on the support of Dharma centers, especially Rigpa, which has centers in most European countries as well as the United States.

I could go on and on extolling the kindness and generosity of these and the many other Dharma centers that have so selflessly and steadfastly given us their support. I mention a few only to give a taste of the widespread, global support our movement has received from the Dharma community. Many Tibetans have not fully appreciated the contribution these Dharma teachers and centers have extended to our efforts, a perspective I hope to help change. Not only did they provide their own important leadership, they were also the inspiration motivating some of our core supporters.

Kalmyk Buddhist teacher Geshe Wangyal was one of the first Buddhist teachers from the Tibetan tradition to establish a center in the United States. He was an extraordinary person with diverse interests and seemingly unlimited talents. He was a resource person for the CIA for many years and was involved when the CIA was training Tibetan resistance fighters. A great devotee of His Holiness, when he passed away, he left his house to His Holiness. Proceeds from its sale became the seed money for the Tibet Fund, as I previously mentioned. In my view the most important gift that Geshe Wangyal left His Holiness and the Tibetan people, however, was his students, especially Professors Robert Thurman and Jeffrey Hopkins, and Joel McCleary.

Bob Thurman and Jeffrey Hopkins chose academic careers, each specializing in aspects of Tibetan Buddhism. They are both highly respected and, through their scholarship, have made significant contributions to the field. They have both served as translators for His Holiness on multiple occasions, with Jeffrey serving as His Holiness's main translator when he was giving teachings on important and complex Buddhist texts.

Joel's contribution has been different because he chose a different path. As previously discussed,[19] when he won the election, President Carter brought Joel to the White House as a member of his staff. Joel chose to use his experience gained from his time there to assist us in formulating long-term strategies. He became a part of the team that spearheaded our international efforts. He played an enormous role in obtaining State Department approval for His Holiness's first visit to the United States in 1979.

Chögyam Trungpa is one of those pioneers who brought Tibetan Buddhism to the West, and even though Rinpoche himself didn't speak publicly on the Tibet issue, he laid a deep and lasting foundation in the minds of thousands of people, greatly benefiting Tibet. Many of his students are involved with the Tibet issue in one way or another.

Tibetans also tend to look at the issue of Tibet from a very narrow political view. The issue is far bigger and more precious than politics. We should pay more attention to Western scholars who have not only helped deepen understanding of Tibetan culture but also, more importantly, helped preserve it. The work of one scholar alone, Gene Smith, is priceless. But most Tibetans, I am sorry to say, pay very little attention to these vital contributions. Tibet will live on not because of its politics but because of its rich Buddhist-inspired culture.

Furthermore, the support that we receive from those people who are passionate about Tibetan Buddhism and culture often lasts much longer than that we enjoy from others who act out of political ideology or with other motivations. Take the example of human rights. There are many people who care deeply about human rights who have come aboard the Tibetan movement at one time or another to help us. Their main commitment, however, is to the broader issue, which is a very noble fight. But whereas today the popular human rights issue might be Tibet, tomorrow it might be another cause. I sometimes see old friends I have known from the Tibet movement and now find them busy with a different issue. This is understandable, as their devotion to the greater human rights agenda is their primary motivation. Similarly, we have had friends involved with Tibet out of concern for the environment, but they too moved on.

Capturing the enduring attention and compassion of individuals who are truly captivated by Tibetan culture, including its religious component, is a task we must continue to undertake for Tibet to remain in the public eye and on the world's agenda. Dharma centers around the world have played, and continue to play, an unparalleled role in that endeavor. For that alone we must continue to offer them our utmost gratitude and heartfelt thanks.

CHAPTER 17

# The 1990s

## *Renewal of Efforts to Engage Beijing*

Sometime in the mid-1990s, I think during His Holiness's July–August 1996 visit to the United States, His Holiness instructed me to try to reconnect with the PRC government. Although there were no visible signs of interest on Beijing's side, he was convinced that it was the right time to make an effort. During my many years of service, I experienced a number of times when His Holiness gave guidance seemingly based on intuition. It certainly felt that way to me, but it could be that he had reflected on the matter for some time and received some favorable indications of which I was unaware. It is also possible that the State Oracle indicated that it was a promising time to make a renewed effort to reach out to Beijing.[1]

From that time forward I assumed responsibility for this effort and sought to approach the PRC leadership through various channels. I left no stone unturned, never hesitating to reach out to any institution or individual I thought might be of some help. Initially Beijing was in no mood to deal with us directly; it adopted a very rigid and confrontational posture. With no opportunity to establish direct contact, I sought to intensify our efforts to gain international support for Tibet. In consultation with my colleagues in Dharamsala, some of the heads of the internationally based Offices of Tibet, and a few close friends, we developed a step-by-step strategy with the ultimate goal of directly reaching the Beijing authorities.

## TWO-PRONGED INITIATIVE: RALLY SUPPORT OF THE INTERNATIONAL COMMUNITY AND ARRANGE A MEETING BETWEEN HIS HOLINESS AND JIANG ZEMIN

After intense discussions, we agreed that rather than trying to engage Beijing on the complex political issue of Tibet, we should explore the possibility of His Holiness making a pilgrimage to a holy site in China that would enable him to renew a direct personal relationship with the current PRC President, who by this time was Jiang Zemin. His Holiness had not met with any major PRC leader since 1955 when he was in Beijing, except for some brief encounters with Premier Zhou Enlai in India in 1956.

His Holiness approved the idea and started publicly talking about such a possibility. As I continue to note, His Holiness has always believed meetings between him and the PRC's top leaders are key to resolving the parties' differences. We believed a one-on-one meeting between His Holiness and President Jiang was essential to jump-start this initiative. We thus reinvigorated our efforts to make it happen.

We also knew that we must simultaneously build global awareness and interest in the proposal to complement our direct efforts, even though Beijing might not appreciate such activity. This was when we accelerated our work both in the United States and in Europe.

Even though His Holiness had previously communicated his desire to visit Tibet to the PRC leadership, all our prior attempts to arrange it had failed. As a result, Dharamsala's position had hardened; it had completely given up on the idea. This feeling definitely contributed to the Kashag's decision not to approve His Holiness's proposed visit to Beijing in the context of Panchen Rinpoche's memorial service.[2] The Kalons thought that a visit should not happen before certain concrete steps were taken or a measure of success had been achieved. But I never believed in that approach. This is one area where Gyalo Thondup and I were in complete agreement: any opportunity for a meeting between the principals should be facilitated to the best of our abilities.

Many of us advising His Holiness have always felt that nothing will move forward until there is a personal relationship between His Holiness and senior Chinese leaders. Our belief is based on the nature and strength of His Holiness's personality, as I have noted. While it is difficult to describe, anyone who has been in

His Holiness's presence will agree. Simply being in the same room with him and feeling his gaze, much less meeting and talking with him, brings a sense of serenity, confidence, and trust that is unrivaled. Even the memory of a meeting with him, however brief, can trigger the same reaction years later.

I emphasize this truly exceptional quality of His Holiness because the biggest impediment to improved relations between the parties is lack of trust. While there are large areas of substantive disagreement, it is this ongoing mutual suspicion that is the root of the problem. While decades of broken promises have poisoned the Tibetans' attitude, it is the Chinese who suffer most from this affliction. They don't trust His Holiness. They cannot embrace his true nature despite all of His Holiness's sustained, sincere efforts to quell their anxiety and dispel their misgivings. Their impression of him remains based on decades of distorted information intentionally transmitted by unscrupulous parties, from both Lhasa and Beijing, to serve their own narrow interests.

So, for that reason, in my position as His Holiness's Special Envoy charged with establishing direct relations with the PRC leadership, one of the first things I made a serious effort to arrange was a meeting between the principals. I worked together with many others who held the same beliefs to get a consensus among Tibetan leaders and final approval from His Holiness to concentrate our efforts on realizing a meeting between him and Jiang Zemin.

Western leaders were also very comfortable with this proposal. Comfortable for two reasons. Many of them had personally met His Holiness and experienced the power of his presence. They also knew firsthand of his genuine sincerity, having felt it themselves and, shall we say, having been transformed as a result. A second, less subjective reason was the very pragmatic desire to forge a strong relationship with the PRC, an understandable objective. In the late 1980s, the PRC was not only an emerging power but also a perceived economic oasis, both as a source of inexpensive goods and labor and a destination for Western-produced luxury products and technological expertise.

Accordingly, Western leaders were hard pressed not to jeopardize their relationship with Beijing. They were not so much "pro-PRC" but rather self-centered, looking after the interests of their constituents. Economic prosperity is the driving force behind every military or political decision we see today. Given that reality, I'm not terribly critical of corporate leaders who justify their actions in the pursuit of profits. Trying to remain on the PRC's good side, and thus unwilling to support Tibet, they shouldn't be vilified for their greed, as they are fulfilling their responsibility to their shareholders. I say that with several exceptions, Rupert Murdoch being one of the most notable. His attempted denigration of His Holiness by repeating the statements of cynics, calling him a "very political old monk shuffling around in Gucci shoes," sadly, does nothing but reveal his ignorance.

*The Tibet Initiative at the Carter Center (1997–1999)*

I reached out to former President Carter as part of our effort to reengage Beijing. The President not only gave us his personal attention but also involved senior staff at the Carter Center, as well as other eminent experts. He wanted to establish a Tibet initiative at the Center, but it didn't have funds for the project. Joel McCleary once again came to the rescue, and his then wife Lavinia Currier graciously offered to finance the initiative. I would also like to recognize Lavinia's brother, Michael Currier, at this point for his generosity in furtherance of our cause.[3]

With the funds in place, in 1997 President Carter reached out to his top China expert, Michel Oksenberg, to head the Tibet Initiative. Mike had played a key role in assisting the President in normalizing relations with the PRC, along with

His Holiness's meeting with President Jimmy Carter at the Carter Center in Atlanta, Georgia, May 11, 1998. The author is to the left, Joel McCleary to the right.
International Campaign for Tibet

other Carter White House staff including Zbigniew Brzezinski, the President's National Security Advisor.

I first met Mike in the mid-1990s when he was heading the East-West Center in Honolulu. There is no doubt that he was one of the most well-informed China scholars in the United States at the time. It was also clear that he had very little knowledge of or interest in Tibet, and what he did know came from Beijing. Not surprisingly, however, as an American, he was sympathetic to our plight, particularly when fundamental human rights such as freedom of religion were involved.

When President Carter first shared with me his decision to tap Mike to head the initiative, I was pleased, although a bit worried because of his lack of knowledge about Tibet. President Carter and John Hardman, CEO of the Carter Center, both assured me that Mike was a professional with unquestionable integrity. They further promised to impress upon him the need to understand the situation from the Tibetan point of view. At my request, the President agreed to appoint Ambassador Harry G. Barnes as the cochair. He was already involved in some other Carter Center initiatives.

As advised by President Carter, I briefed Mike numerous times, accompanied on several occasions by Tenzin Namgyal. I think we did a solid job of educating him on the complex issue of Tibetan–Chinese relations, and he proved to be an excellent listener. Sadly, he passed away in 2001, before we were able to start a formal dialogue with Beijing. He would have been of invaluable assistance as the dialogue progressed.

I met with Ambassador Barnes many times as well, usually in Washington, D.C. While Mike acted very professionally, I was glad for Harry Barnes's participation. He helped give the initiative the proper balance. My extensive contact with the Carter Center also provided me with an excellent learning opportunity. You could find no better "tutor" than President Carter and no better "adversary" than Mike Oksenberg. I used the word "adversary" because Mike would challenge us on the proposals we were advocating, helping us hone our talking points and shape our strategy.

This collaborative work also gave us the opportunity to reinforce our bottom-line position with President Carter and those involved in the Center's Tibet Initiative. In one of my communications to President Carter, for example, I emphasized:

> There are certain issues that are fundamental to both the Tibetans and the Chinese which cannot be up for discussions. The Chinese side, for example,

> have made it clear that there cannot be any discussion about Tibetan independence or nationhood. We have reconciled ourselves to this Chinese position although the majority of Tibetan people would desire us to seek for nothing less than independence. Similarly, on our side one non-compromisable position is that any solution that is considered should include the entire Tibetan people. This is an issue that His Holiness has already discussed with you and which I have also talked [about] at length with your team.
>
> While a negotiated settlement can be reached and signed by a few people, any solution to be successful would have to be accepted both by the Tibetan and Chinese peoples. The Tibetans are a united people, and any solution that fails to recognize this will not be long lasting. I emphasize this issue at this time in order to highlight its importance in our efforts at starting a negotiation so that there is no misunderstanding whatsoever on this basic point.[4]

As part of the Carter Center Initiative, Mike traveled to several Tibetan areas and met with numerous Chinese officials and scholars. Because of the Carter Center's prestige, his team was warmly hosted by the Chinese People's Institute of Foreign Affairs. In addition, because of the key role that Mike had played in the normalization of Sino-American relations during Carter's presidency, he had access to the highest authorities in the PRC leadership. But he did not limit himself to meetings with Chinese officials and academicians. He also tried to meet with Tibetans both in Lhasa and in the Tibetan areas of Sichuan and Gansu. I insisted that his team not limit its visits to the TAR but include other Tibetan areas so that he and his colleagues could fully understand the unified identity of the Tibetan people. Unfortunately, I believe many of the Tibetans they met ostensibly "toed the official Chinese line," being afraid to candidly offer their views, a concern I shared with Mike both before and after his visits.

Mike took two American scholars well versed in the Tibet issue with him when he traveled to Tibet: Melvyn Goldstein, an anthropologist from Case Western University, and Tibetan Buddhist scholar Matthew Kapstein, of the University of Chicago. I had suggested some other experts but did not object to the Carter Center's choices, even though Dharamsala had some reservations about Melvyn Goldstein. I have to say that I respect him as a scholar and believe that he cares deeply about Tibet, despite the fact that some of his views on history differ from ours. We met periodically while working on the initiative and had very candid discussions. I have always found it beneficial to engage with people who hold different views, as it sharpens my understanding and strengthens my arguments.

In 1999, Mike Oksenberg and Harry Barnes submitted their report entitled "Reflections on Tibet, China, the Dalai Lama and the United States." On February 16, President Carter forwarded it to His Holiness, President Jiang, and President Clinton. While all three received the same report, President Carter's cover letters had different questions and recommendations for each recipient. I have no idea what was the thrust of President Carter's letter to President Jiang, but some concerned officials at the White House shared with me the gist of his letter to President Clinton.[5]

The report makes a sincere effort to present the conflicting views and positions of the parties and also the then prevailing conditions in Tibetan areas. Quoted here is a portion of the report's conclusion that reflects the essence of its findings:

> Finally, Tibet is an indicator of the Chinese future. China is poised to achieve greatness in the twenty-first century: to become, as President Jiang Zemin stated at the Fifteenth Congress of the Chinese Communist Party, a prosperous, socialist, democratic, and culturally advanced country by 2050. To achieve that lofty goal will require the drawing upon the diverse talents and traditions of all its peoples. Such a China will be a natural partner of the United States. But China also could become a militaristic and oppressive state. Such a China would likely be an adversary. Tibet, then, provides a significant litmus test; its future will reveal much about the direction in which China is headed.
>
> It is therefore quite appropriate for the United States and the American people to be concerned about Tibet, to observe carefully its evolution, to assist in the efforts to develop Tibet and improve its educational system, and to encourage a reconciliation between the government of China and the followers of the Dalai Lama.[6]

The litmus test that the report highlights is as relevant today as it was when it was first presented. While I felt that some of the report's recommendations would be difficult for us to accommodate, it did include a number of constructive ideas I thought we could pursue. I don't know how or even if the Chinese ever responded to President Carter. They may well not have, as it is generally not their practice to engage with outsiders on so-called "internal" matters. But the fact remains, this initiative and the resulting report are a direct result of our strategic decision to bring the issue of Tibet to the eyes of the international community and educate world leaders about the benefits to their respective states of its resolution. By involving eminent personalities and institutions such as President Carter and the Carter Center, we had unquestionably elevated the issue on the international agenda, again all in the interest of bringing the PRC government back to the negotiating table.

### *Senator Feinstein and Richard Blum's Continuing Support*

While President Carter's relationship with Beijing was through Deng Xiaoping and the people of that generation, Senator Feinstein's connection was directly with President Jiang Zemin. President Carter's interest in our issue was very much a part of his global commitment to conflict resolution, an admirable effort that has brought success on many occasions, affecting the lives of millions of people. By contrast, Senator Feinstein and Richard Blum's interest was very specific. They were doing it for their friend the Dalai Lama, whom they deeply love and respect, and for the Tibetan people, whose suffering they had come to embrace. Their persistent efforts, in fact, played a major role in President Jiang's decision to start informal discussions with us.[7]

His Holiness with (left to right) Richard Blum, Senator Dianne Feinstein, the author, and Tenzin Geyche

When I went through my files to refresh my memory of our various efforts in reaching out to the PRC leadership, I came across the notes of a meeting between Senator Feinstein, her husband, and President Jiang on September 28, 1997, that the Senator had shared with me soon after her return from Beijing. Reading through them, I could not help but feel a genuine sense of gratitude for this husband-and-wife team. The notes show how difficult the issue is, but at the same time make clear that a solution is achievable if both sides have the political will and make serious efforts. It was to this meeting that they carried the third and last hand-delivered communication from His Holiness to President Jiang.

The meeting lasted nearly three hours. It was, to my knowledge, one of the most candid and extensive discussions on Tibet by any foreign dignitary with a senior Chinese leader. The Senator and her husband tried very hard to counter every misgiving and piece of misinformation that President Jiang seemed to have about His Holiness. They were forceful and on occasion, undiplomatically blunt. The notes also show that this meeting was not the only heated discussion the parties had on the Tibet issue, President Jiang remarking at one point: "You are old friends, so we can discuss this openly and frankly. I remember once with Mr. Blum we discussed this in Diaoyutai[8] for three hours."

Whenever President Jiang brought up the need for the Dalai Lama to give up his "separatist tendencies," the Senator had her staff read portions of His Holiness's statements disavowing any such intention. Several times during their long conversation, the pair specifically asked President Jiang to give them the exact words he needed to hear from His Holiness to assure him of His Holiness's sincerity in rejecting independence or separation from the PRC and his commitment to finding a solution with Tibet remaining in the PRC. They also told President Jiang that President Clinton would appreciate President Jiang's agreeing to meet His Holiness. Their visit to Beijing took place just a few months before President Jiang's scheduled trip to Washington. They strongly argued that a favorable decision on Tibet would make the PRC President's US visit that much more beneficial. He would be warmly received by the American people if before he arrived, he publicly announced his willingness to meet the Dalai Lama.

The couple's efforts had immediate results. President Jiang sent Chen Yunlin, a senior staff member from his Secretariat, and K. S. Wu, a mutual friend of his and Richard's, to visit Lhasa in July 1997 to personally assess realities on the ground. Richard had shared with President Jiang and others close to him evidence of "State sponsored terror and discrimination against the Tibetans" and how "deeply the Tibetan people resented Chinese rule and how immense their devotion and loyalty remained to His Holiness." The team's findings, presented after their visit, exposed the false reports being sent to Beijing by TAR officials and the United Front. K. S. Wu told President Jiang and other Chinese leaders: "I believe Richard Blum. I don't believe the United Front." In his book, Richard comments: "His (President Jiang's) decision to fire that administrator in Lhasa may be my major accomplishment on the issue of Tibet with the Chinese government."[9]

Richard is referring to Chen Kuiyuan, who was transferred from the TAR Party Secretary post in 2000. Other sources also confirmed that President Jiang's unhappiness with Secretary Chen's handling of Tibet was a factor in his transfer. Chen Kuiyuan was an active member of the hard-liners' camp. This group single-mindedly sought to impose repressive policies in Tibet and further obstructed the effort by farsighted leaders in Beijing to work with His Holiness to find a mutually beneficial solution to the conflict. People such as Chen Kuiyuan played a major role in making the central government's policy more confrontational, as seen in this statement from the Third Tibet Work Forum held in 1994: "The focal point in our region in the struggle against splittism is to oppose Dalai clique. As the saying goes, to kill a serpent, we must first cut off its head. If we don't do that, we cannot succeed in the struggle against separatism."[10] This comment could be interpreted as going so far as to advocate physical harm to His Holiness.

The fruits of the Senator's meeting with President Jiang could also be seen during the PRC President's visit to France on October 23, 1999. He confided to President Chirac that he had "received several messages from the Dalai Lama, looking for a way to come back" using "different channels, including that of President Clinton."[11] In the same conversation President Jiang also described K. S. Wu as an emissary of the Dalai Lama, saying: "He has sent lots of emissaries, including Dr. Wu Gongtan,[12] the son of the president of the commission that presided over the reincarnation of the Dalai Lama."[13]

K. S. Wu was the son of Wu Zhongxin, a senior KMT official who was present in Lhasa representing the KMT government at the enthronement of His Holiness in 1940, as the president of the Mongolian Tibetan Affairs Commission. K. S. Wu had a distorted and exaggerated view of the role his father played at the ceremony. Despite that, he had genuine feeling for Tibet and was sincerely interested in trying to help us resolve the Tibet issue. He was spending quite a bit of time in Shanghai as a banker and had a close personal relationship with the Jiang family, whose base is also in Shanghai. I had personally worked with K. S. Wu and even arranged an audience for him with His Holiness during one of His Holiness's visits to the United States. It is unfortunate that he died so young. He would have been of much help as we began our formal dialogue with Beijing.

As I have previously noted, Senator Feinstein had strong reservations about our insistence that any solution to the Tibet question must include all areas inhabited by Tibetans.[14] A few weeks before one of His Holiness's visits to Washington, the Senator told me that she would like to share her concerns on this issue with him personally. She asked me if I was comfortable with this. I told her that as she is one of His Holiness's closest friends, he would give serious thought to her views, but reconsidering his commitment to seeking a solution for the entire Tibetan people was not something he would be able to do. When Senator Feinstein subsequently hosted His Holiness at her residence for lunch, she did share her general concerns but refrained from any detailed discussion, as she had come to appreciate His Holiness's position.

I further shared my personal views with Senator Feinstein, as I did with other seasoned diplomats and politicians, that a mutually acceptable and lasting solution could never be reached in the absence of consideration of the concerns of all Tibetans. If Beijing thinks rationally, it cannot disagree. Armed resistance against the Chinese began in the early 1950s in eastern Tibet and over the ensuing ten years spread throughout Tibet, culminating in the 1959 uprising and His Holiness's escape into exile. Resentment continues to this day, evidenced by the Plateauwide protest demonstrations in 2008 and the ongoing tragic self-immolations by Tibetans in all areas of Tibet. The anger, pain, and sorrow felt by the Tibetan people are not limited to one particular region and can never be rectified by the institution of artificial internal boundaries that exclude vast segments of the population. Attempts to compartmentalize the problem or address it in a piecemeal manner are destined for failure. Only a holistic approach, one that meets the physical and emotional needs of all Tibetans residing in the PRC can provide the framework for a lasting solution.

Taking my words to heart, as a true friend, the Senator started thinking creatively about finding a solution to this most delicate and vexing question. I remember a lot of brainstorming sessions with her, and sometimes with her husband and other friends, including Jeff Bader and Greg Craig. As an experienced politician, she continued to see our position as "unachievable." But as a true friend of His Holiness, and understanding the aspirations of the Tibetan people, she gave serious thought to finding a way of fulfilling His Holiness's commitment to the

Tibetan people without the issue becoming unnecessarily contentious and confrontational.

Of course, as the chief interlocutor representing the Tibetan people in the negotiations with the PRC, I have also given serious thought to this issue. In addition, I know that at least a few institutions in the PRC have also been examining the question, as they have shared some of their ideas with us. While it would be premature for me to discuss any of these proposals in detail, I sincerely believe that His Holiness and the Beijing leadership can find a mutually acceptable solution based on some of these creative ideas if the requisite political will can be generated.

As in the case of President Carter's efforts on our behalf, I made sure that the Clinton White House, and later the Bush White House, was aware of Senator Feinstein and Richard Blum's efforts. In many ways, their activities complemented each administration's work. Senior State Department and White House officials were regularly in touch with them, from time to time including me in their meetings.

### *Supportive Individuals Within the Chinese Community*

In addition to President Carter and Senator Feinstein, there are a number of individuals both inside and outside the PRC who have been very helpful. For a variety of reasons, quite a few of them must remain anonymous. These friends offered their heartfelt assistance, appreciating the wisdom of His Holiness's Middle Way Approach and recognizing that its implementation is for the long-term benefit of both the Tibetan and the Chinese people. In soliciting their views throughout my professional career, I hoped to further genuine understanding of the Tibet issue by the broader Chinese community in addition to the leadership in Beijing, knowing that the best outcome is one achieved by joint effort. For this reason, I have also always been a firm believer in the "Chinese outreach" program initiated by His Holiness. Just as we have approached governments, institutions, and individuals with the sole purpose of seeking their help in reaching out to the PRC government, our outreach to the Chinese community must be undertaken with the same purpose.

In addition to K. S. Wu and Youyi Li, I would like to acknowledge Chang-Lin Tien, who was the Chancellor of the University of California at Berkeley from

1990 to 1997. I benefited greatly from his wisdom. He was very well respected in the PRC and maintained personal friendships with a number of senior Chinese leaders, including Premier Zhu Rongji. He not only hosted a large faculty and student get-together with His Holiness but also helped me reach out to the Committee of 100, trying to encourage the group to take an active interest in Tibet. This association of prominent Chinese Americans was established in 1990 with the specific purpose to "pool their strengths and experience to address important issues concerning the Chinese American community, as well as issues affecting US–China relations."

Given its express mandate, the Committee could have played a positive role in our efforts, had it so chosen, as many of its members are well respected within their professions and enjoy special connections with influential Chinese individuals inside the PRC. Unfortunately, the majority of its members were unwilling to embrace our cause. Of course, there were exceptions. Yo-Yo Ma, the world-famous cellist, for example, didn't shy away from performing at several Tibet-related events. He is a wonderful person with deep respect for Tibetan culture. He and I had even dreamed of going to the Tibetan Plateau together to fulfill his desire to write a musical score based on the legends of the Ling Gesar.

Chang-Lin Tien passed away in October 2002 at the age of sixty-seven, prior to a meeting we had scheduled to discuss how to involve other prominent Chinese Americans in helping bridge the gap between His Holiness and the PRC leadership. In some of our earlier meetings, we had shortlisted a few individuals who he felt would be willing to help, provided their roles were not publicized. Many years later while giving a talk at the University of Denver, Colorado, I met a prominent Chinese businesswoman who mentioned his having approached her in that regard before he passed away.

Tu Weiming, who headed the Harvard-Yenching Institute promoting higher education in Asian studies, was another friend with whom I shared my thoughts and whose advice I sought. He is one of the most well-regarded Confucian scholars. I had met him many years before I moved to the United States, sharing a platform with him at several conferences. While highly respected in the PRC, he did not hesitate in publicly hosting His Holiness at Harvard.

Bette Bao Lord is another dear friend. She and her husband, the veteran American diplomat Winston Lord, had their door open for me at all times. Bette offered the use of the couple's spacious apartment in Manhattan for special gatherings and other Tibet-related events. Bette used to humorously tell me, however, that my association with her might not be of much benefit, as she was not popular in Beijing because of her frank and outspoken comments on controversial matters such as human rights.

Winston Lord was US Ambassador to the PRC from 1985 to 1989. He not only is one of the most well-informed individuals on the situation there but also holds the most balanced view. Starting from the day he accompanied Secretary of State Kissinger on his secret trips to Beijing, Ambassador Lord took part in every meeting that Presidents Nixon and Ford had with Mao Zedong and Zhou Enlai in the 1970s, and attended one meeting between President George H.W. Bush and Deng Xiaoping.

Individuals inside the PRC have also been very helpful. Some of them are academicians, but quite a few are serving or retired government officials. I will not jeopardize anyone's career or livelihood by revealing their names, even though some of them were in touch with me with the knowledge of their superiors. This group also included some Tibetans.

One person I can mention is Wang Yao. I first met him in 1982 at the Central Institute for Nationalities, Beijing, when I visited the PRC as a member of the first High-Level Exploratory Talks Delegation. We were given the opportunity to have informal roundtable discussions with some of the senior faculty members. Wang Yao was among the senior teachers who received us upon our arrival. Approaching me with a broad, welcoming smile, he unhesitatingly proclaimed: "You must be the elder brother of Pema Gyalpo la." With his perfect Tibetan and refined Lhasa dialect, I thought he must be a former Tibetan aristocrat working as a teacher at the institute. Sensing my surprise, he immediately said, again in flawless Tibetan: "I am Wang Yao." It turned out he had met my brother two years earlier when Pema Gyalpo visited Beijing as a member of the Second Fact-Finding Delegation sent by His Holiness.

I had the opportunity to meet Wang Yao again in 1984 in Beijing during our second High-Level Exploratory Talks mission and several times outside the PRC, including at international conferences. Because of his extensive knowledge of Tibet, senior CCP leaders and government officials often sought his advice. From time to time, he was also assigned specific tasks on their behalf, including preparing briefs and even accompanying them on trips to Tibetan areas. As I previously discussed, when Party Secretary Hu Yaobang traveled to Tibet in May 1980, Wang Yao accompanied him, and I am told Hu Yaobang relied heavily on his expertise. Wang Yao prepared the influential report chronicling the Party Secretary's visit that incorporates the main essence of Hu Yaobang's thinking and efforts to address the dismal conditions he witnessed in Tibet.[15]

Wang Yao went in and out of favor over the years depending on the mood of the hierarchy in Beijing. It has been my personal experience, over the years, however, that many Chinese officials and scholars who have a deep understanding of Tibetan culture have always been keen to make some effort for reconciliation and better understanding between the Tibetan and Chinese peoples, and of course between His Holiness and the PRC leadership. I also know that there are others with the opposite view. They advocate suppressing every aspect of Tibetan culture and identity, fearing that without its elimination, Tibetans will always have the desire to assert their separateness, a possibility they simply cannot countenance.

From time to time, Wang Yao sent messages of encouragement to me through mutual friends, as well as some valid criticism of our handling of the situation. To the extent possible, he would also share with me the efforts he was making on his end. During his career he was affiliated with several important institutions, including Tsinghua University and Beijing University. From 2004 until his passing away in December 2015, he was the Honorary Dean and Doctoral Supervisor at the Institute of Tibetan Studies, Central University for Nationalities in Beijing.

Another individual I must mention is Yan Mingfu, who at one time was viewed as an "up and coming" future leader. For years he headed the United Front. He was one who truly tried to make the organization perform the responsibility its name implies. He made sincere efforts to move forward on the Tibet issue, but both internal and external circumstances left little room for him to exert any meaningful influence. I stayed in touch with him quite regularly through Lily Sun, granddaughter of Sun Yat-sen, who lived in Honolulu. On her visits to the PRC, she regularly brought up the issue of Tibet. She had access to some high-level Chinese leaders and officials, as Beijing was at the time interested in giving recognition to Sun Yat-sen's descendants. A devout Buddhist, she was always available to me. While I was generally aware of Yan Mingfu's progressive views, being in touch with him through this intermediary also convinced me of his very genuine and sincere desire to find a way to resolve the Tibet issue. I truly valued his advice and suggestions.

Yan Mingfu was purged from all his positions in 1989, but a few years later he was partially rehabilitated, returning to public life as Vice Minister for Civil

Affairs in 1991. After his return, he tried to liberalize rules for international NGOs seeking to work in the PRC and also established the China Charity Federation, which he led until 2002. I met him when he visited Washington, D.C., greeting him with the traditional Tibetan *khata*. I told him that he was the first senior official of the PRC government to whom I had ever offered this ceremonial scarf in recognition of my genuine respect and admiration for him. At my request, his Federation embraced an international NGO trying to help Tibetans inside Tibet, providing it much-needed guidance and protection.

### *Other Outreach*

While direct involvement of third parties in any restarted discussions with Beijing was not feasible and actually might have been harmful, we knew that we must have as much international involvement as possible without unnecessarily creating suspicion and anger in the minds of the Chinese. We also felt the need for more input from Chinese scholars, preferably those residing in mainland China, but also from those teaching or working in various institutions or think tanks outside the PRC. Understanding the Chinese psyche was crucial; as I have repeatedly expressed, final resolution of the Tibet issue must come from the Tibetans and the Chinese working together.

The Washington-based Brookings Institution was home to some well-connected and well-informed Chinese scholars, including a few from the mainland. I had a close personal friendship with some of them, and they were eager to help. Richard Blum once again offered his assistance. He not only encouraged his friend Strobe Talbott, President of Brookings, to start a series of roundtable discussions on Tibet but also underwrote the program's costs. Starting in 2005, we were able to have ten separate meetings that were of immense value. The Brookings Institution has an excellent reputation in Beijing and was thus able to attract the participation of quite a few prominent mainland scholars.

The unique and most valuable aspect of the meetings was the opportunity for dialogue exclusively between the Chinese and Tibetan participants. After President Talbott and other senior Brookings officials welcomed the delegates, they voluntarily excused themselves from the ensuing meetings, leaving the substantive discussions solely for the Chinese and Tibetans to conduct. His Holiness personally participated in at least three of these meetings. We even arranged for the group to visit India twice to meet with His Holiness, the Kalon Tripa, and other CTA officials. One of these visits took the participants all the way to Leh, Ladakh, because His Holiness was there giving teachings.

Huang Jing, who was with Brookings at the time, was of great help in handling this initiative, particularly in arranging the participation of the mainland academicians. After he left Brookings to join the National University of Singapore, Cheng Li assumed his position. He was equally committed to the success of the program. In addition to their involvement with this initiative, both Huang Jing and Cheng Li were always available for consultation. A number of other eminent former diplomats and scholars in residence at Brookings were also of immense help. Jeff Bader, who joined Brookings after leaving the White House, and Richard Bush, a longtime friend and Sinologist, provided invaluable assistance. I was greatly honored when Brookings invited me to become a Nonresident Senior Fellow in Foreign Policy after I retired as Special Envoy of His Holiness, making an exception to their usual practice by allowing me to hold this position for three consecutive years.

## CHALLENGES OF THE PRC'S PROPAGANDA MACHINE: CEMENTING THE CONCEPT OF A UNIFIED TIBET IN THE EYES OF THE INTERNATIONAL COMMUNITY

As I discussed in depth in part II, the PRC responded to our efforts to engage the international community by intentionally misconstruing our activities in an effort to thwart our initiative. Although we had enjoyed unprecedented success in creating awareness for Tibet and solidifying our support base in the United States and Europe, we were beginning to feel the negative effects of Beijing's countermeasures, which were becoming more aggressive and more skillfully executed. Beijing employed professional lobbyists, both directly and indirectly, to reach out to American politicians and policy makers.

We were fortunate in one respect, however. Seemingly unaware of the vibrant democratic system that prevails in Western nations, Beijing initially paid scant attention to the US Congress, concentrating its efforts on building relations with the executive branch and influential individuals. Only later did it begin to understand that Congress is not a "rubber-stamp" organization like the PRC's National

People's Congress, but rather an independent and very powerful institution with tremendous influence over policy formation. In belated recognition of this reality, Beijing increased the number of diplomats at its US embassy to liaison better with Congress. It also hired some of the most expensive public relations firms. Despite this extensive undertaking, the Tibet movement, led by the professional and dedicated team at the ICT with the backing of thousands of grassroots supporters, rose to the challenge.

But, Beijing was still able to plant doubts in the minds of some lawmakers. In distorting our position on the geographic scope of Tibet and falsely accusing the Dalai Lama of calling for the expulsion of all non-Tibetan people from areas traditionally inhabited by Tibetans, Beijing sought to undermine our credibility. We were able to repudiate the latter allegation relatively easily, as none of His Holiness's written or oral statements made any such demand. To maintain the distinct Tibetan cultural, religious, and national character, a demographic balance in favor of Tibetans in these areas was clearly the preferred choice. For how could the Tibetan language and traditional way of life be maintained if the Tibetans became a small minority of the local population? However, there was never a demand or even a suggestion that non-Tibetan people be removed from predominately Tibetan areas. How could such an idea even be considered in the twenty-first century? Moreover, the notion that someone of His Holiness's unimpeachable moral character would ever propose such a blatantly discriminatory action is simply not credible.

On the question of the geographic extent of Tibet, our position is more complex. Under the United Nations' definition of a "people," we Tibetans have the right to strive for unity and to express the desire to be governed as one administrative unit, particularly given the fact that the entire territory inhabited by the Tibetan people is contiguous. His Holiness understood the complexity of the issue but expressed his vision very clearly in his unique style:

> I am not talking about politics, law and history. My responsibility and commitment is to preserve the great Tibetan civilization with its very distinctive characteristics in every aspect from language, culture, art, religious practices, and social norms that are common and identical among all the Tibetans living on the plateau of Tibet. For the Tibetan people to be genuinely able to preserve these identities, they need to be given the opportunity to be together and part of one administration with a single policy.[16]

A very genuine and profound expression.

Because of the importance of this issue, on numerous occasions, His Holiness gave high priority to explaining his definition of Tibet. I remember one instance in 1997 when he raised the issue with President Clinton at the White House. It was during the last "drop-by" meeting in Vice President Gore's office. While waiting for the President, His Holiness brought up the issue with the Vice President. I remember the Vice President telling His Holiness very clearly that he needed to discuss it directly with the President. Vice President Gore understood the Tibet issue quite well from his days in the Senate, where he was very supportive of our efforts.

When the President appeared, His Holiness explained his concept using the human body as an analogy. He said: "What I am talking about is the Tibetan people as a single entity in order for us to survive and maintain our distinctive individual culture, religion, and way of life. That must be kept intact. Right now you see the limbs are separated, the arms are separated." He further likened the "head" to Lhasa, home of the three great monastic universities, Sera, Drepung, and Ganden, to which large numbers of Tibetan scholars from Tibetan areas both inside and outside the present Tibet Autonomous Region (TAR) traveled to study.

As His Holiness's analogy was very persuasive, we decided to adopt his comparison to convince the public of the merits of his argument. We realized that in addition to Beijing's rejection of our position, some prominent members of the international community had serious reservations about our position. Somewhat surprisingly, we also needed to educate some of our own supporters and sympathizers, as well as some members of the Tibetan community, on the bona fides of our view.

It became clear that this would require a tremendous effort. The reality was that we had done a rather poor job prior to this time. Even in documents we authored in support of our position, we often cited purported justifications that actually pertained only to the part of Tibet that was historically governed from Lhasa, which is more or less the same region as the present- day TAR. Moreover, we had erroneously assumed that when international organizations or important supporters talked about Tibet, they were referring to the broader definition we embraced. It was only with His Holiness's clear and explicit definition of a unified Tibet, first publicly articulated in his Strasbourg Proposal, however, that the outside world, including most of our friends, became aware of Tibet as we recognize it.

His Holiness himself spearheaded this educational effort both in his public comments and directly in his discussions with global leaders. I also spent considerable time and effort trying to educate key players on this important issue. As previously noted, the congressional resolution S. Con. Res. 41, is one important result of this effort.[17] This was the first time that a prominent legislative body formally recognized the geographic scope of the unified Tibet that His Holiness was and is pursuing. A major step forward in our campaign.

While I realized that the executive branch would never accept our concept of a unified Tibet, my goal was to neutralize its position. My specific worry was that the State Department or the White House might make some remark challenging or contradicting the resolution. Not only would the Chinese take full advantage of the conflicting views, there was a far worse danger that other Western nations might seek to avoid a similar controversy by limiting the meaning of Tibet solely to the TAR in any policy or legislative actions they might subsequently undertake.

It was quite a daunting task, but we were ultimately successful. I convinced both the State Department and White House officials that if a question concerning the US administration's definition of Tibet was raised, they should reply that these are matters for Beijing and the Tibetans to work out and the United States didn't wish to take a stand. I knew that no government was willing to formally endorse our position, but if we could forestall anyone from taking the opposite view, it would be of great value to us. Another important approach that we adopted was to talk more about the "Tibetan people" than "Tibet." In many important resolutions, including the Tibetan Policy Act of 2002, we deliberately emphasized the impacts on the Tibetan people as a whole. Even the Chinese do not dispute that no matter where they live, in either the TAR or any of the neighboring PRC provinces, Tibetans are all of the same nationality.

Not surprisingly, the Chinese lashed out against this concept of a unified Tibet. Beijing unleashed the full fury of its massive propaganda machine, telling the whole world that the Dalai Lama not only wanted to separate Tibet from China but also, in claiming the Tibetan areas within Qinghai, Sichuan, Yunnan, and Gansu in addition to the TAR, he was asserting title to almost one-fourth of the PRC's total landmass.

Despite this public rhetoric, there were individuals in the PRC government who recognized the importance of this fundamental concern to the Tibetan people. They knew that if they were sincere in their avowed desire to find a lasting solution, they must take into consideration the interests and aspirations of all Tibetans, regardless of where they resided. Accordingly, some Chinese scholars and even senior officials started to discuss the matter, seeking input from knowledgeable outsiders. They sometimes posed very explicit questions, not only to solicit alternative views but seemingly with a sincere desire to find a mutually acceptable solution. Given the issue's importance, I am including the full text of a memorandum that I prepared in response to a request by Minister Wang Zhaoguo for clarification on some points that was forwarded to me through our Norwegian diplomatic contacts.

**What Encompasses Tibet**

First, Minister Wang expressed his concern about the geographic area to which His Holiness the Dalai Lama refers when discussing a negotiated settlement for Tibet.

His Holiness is not seeking to resolve the Tibet issue through a legalistic or political approach. Instead, he is seeking a pragmatic solution that will provide for all the Tibetan people to live together under one administrative unit where they will be subject to the same rules and enjoy the same rights, freedoms and protections.

When His Holiness formulated the Middle Way Approach he made a bold and courageous decision not to seek restoration of Tibetan independence. Instead, he chose to look to the future and seek a solution that would preserve the distinct national and cultural identity of the Tibetan people within the People's Republic of China. He made this decision because he believes that the survival of our culture is not only paramount to the Tibetan people, but would also benefit China and the rest of the world. And, our culture can only survive if all the Tibetan people are able to contribute to it.

Of the roughly six million Tibetan people who share the same national and cultural identity, only 2.4 million reside in the TAR. The majority of the Tibetan people live outside of the TAR in a contiguous area on the Tibetan plateau. And, all areas inhabited by Tibetans are equally important to the survival of our way of life. His Holiness has often used an analogy of the human body—just as a person cannot thrive without its limbs, torso and head, the Tibetan culture cannot survive if dismembered. For example, even today many of Tibet's greatest scholars come from outside of the TAR, and people from all over Tibet rely on the learning and cultural traditions fostered in Kham and Amdo.

Tibet consists of three regions, U-Tsang, Kham and Amdo. U-Tsang and parts of Kham constitute the present TAR, while the whole of Amdo and greater parts of Kham are outside of the TAR, though designated as Tibetan Autonomous prefectures, counties and districts.

Developing a solution for all the Tibetan people is also a moral issue for His Holiness. It is a fundamental fact that the vast majority of the Tibetan people, no matter where on the Tibetan plateau they reside, look to His Holiness as their leader and spokesperson, as well as the embodiment of their ethos. To abandon them by seeking a solution that would affect only a portion of the Tibetan people would run counter to His Holiness' moral responsibility.

On a pragmatic level, a negotiated solution would be quite precarious if it did not take into account all of the Tibetan people. In fact many believe that one of the reasons that the Tibetan people rose up against the Chinese in 1959 was because most parts of Kham and almost all of Amdo were not included in the 17-Point Agreement, leading to unrest there that spread throughout Tibet. In other words, despite its shortcomings, if the 17-Point Agreement had dealt with all the Tibetan people this revolt most probably could have been avoided.

Similarly, it would be virtually impossible to develop a solution today that would last if it did not address the needs of the entire Tibetan people in a unified manner. It is important to note that the Chinese authorities also recognize that Tibet consists of more than the TAR, as they have designated more than 90% of those areas inhabited by Tibetans outside of the TAR as Tibetan autonomous prefectures, counties and districts. Even Chou Enlai, China's former premier, recognized the legitimacy of the Tibetan concerns on this point. In 1951 he stated that the Tibetans had a real concern in calling for all of contiguous Tibet to be placed under one administrative jurisdiction. He said that Tibet had to be divided up because the Tibetan areas outside of the TAR had different socioeconomic needs and he gave his assurances that these concerns would later be addressed. Thus he convinced the Tibetan delegate that the 17-Point Agreement itself should only deal with those areas that were yet to be "liberated," meaning Central Tibet (present-day TAR), because

China's People's Liberation Army had already penetrated into most of Kham and Amdo by that time.

Seeking a solution that would include all of the Tibetan people within one defined administrative area is something that the Tibetans have been raising from day one. As noted above, the Tibetans made a strong plea for a unified entity when "negotiating" the 17-Point Agreement. Another example occurred in the early 1980s when exploratory talks took place between His Holiness' representatives and the Chinese government. In fact as a member of the delegation I raised this issue at His Holiness' direction. At the time the Chinese officials told us that they would not entertain this issue because I was considered to be a "splittist," representing a "splittist" organization. They told me very clearly that if we made a clear declaration of our commitment to a unified China then we would have the right to raise this issue. Of course this is precisely what happened when His Holiness put forward his Strasbourg Proposal, declaring his commitment to not seek independence. And, since then he has clearly and categorically repeated this stand on an almost daily basis. Furthermore, the desire to be unified is not just confined to the Tibetan leadership in exile. As the Chinese are aware, even important Tibetan leaders who live in China and hold senior government and party positions share these aspirations. As a matter of fact we know that several such Tibetans presented a written petition to Chinese authorities urging the creation of a common autonomous region for all Tibetans. If one reads the writings of Tibetan scholars and researchers inside Tibet, and in most cases working for the Chinese government, almost universally they will refer to and write of Tibet as a single entity. These writings reflect the reality of the situation and their aspirations.

Of course Minister Wang is correct in saying that the question of what encompasses Tibet is a complicated issue that involves a number of provinces. But just as the authorities were able to redefine Inner Mongolia when necessary, if the political will exists, Tibet, too, can be redefined.

I assure you that if the Chinese begin to seriously pursue negotiations, His Holiness will approach the whole issue in his most pragmatic manner. He will focus on the need to develop a solution which will allow for the survival of the Tibetan identity, even though the Tibetans, like all human beings, are very attached to every square inch of their land. Once an agreement is reached in principle that addresses the needs and aspirations of the six million Tibetans to be treated as a single entity, I am sure that we can creatively work out the geographic details and a method for its implementation in such a way as to ensure its mutual acceptability and success.[18]

## FIRST SUCCESSFUL RECONNECTION: DECEMBER 1997 MEETING IN HONG KONG

Jiang Zemin continued Deng Xiaoping's policy of reaching out to the Western world, particularly the United States. In spite of many ups and downs, both Washington and Beijing considered their relations as one of the most important bilateral relationships in the world. I have been told this by quite a few highly placed US officials. In a way, President Jiang gave more importance to US-PRC relations than did Deng Xiaoping, who was not being fully supported by some of his senior colleagues within the Standing Committee, including Li Ruihuan.

We were able to take full advantage of President Jiang's interest by making Tibet very much a part of the US-PRC relationship. The US Congress passed several bills and conducted high-profile hearings urging not only Beijing but also the US administration to be proactive on the Tibet issue.[19] In the beginning, when the Tibet issue was raised by US government officials, it was by the State Department, and sometimes by the White House, in the context of human rights concerns. We succeeded in broadening the parameters, making Tibet a "stand-alone" issue. Even senior US officials dealing with economic and financial matters were instructed to make it a topic of discussion with their PRC counterparts. I worked closely with some of President Clinton's economic team, including Bo Cutter and Bob Rubin at the White House, to educate them on the full scope of issues.

Through very reliable and discrete channels, I was also able to establish connections with a few leading members of the CCP, including Li Ruihuan, Qiao Shi, and Zhu Rongji. While I knew that in the rigid Chinese Communist system even these highly placed individuals were not likely to be able to be proactive, I recognized that it was critically important that they and other senior Party members be kept informed.

By 1997, our strategy began to pay off. We established direct connections with President Jiang Zemin, and he began to take a personal interest in Tibet. He sent his trusted advisors to Lhasa to get an unbiased picture of the situation and appointed Wang Jungfu, a senior official with Deputy Minister rank, to meet secretly with me and start a conversation. At the same time, Beijing made it clear that these talks were informal and must be kept highly confidential. It did not want the talks to be held in the United States, India, or any other Western country, preferring Hong Kong, Thailand, or Singapore. We agreed on Hong Kong, where I traveled in December 1997 for the first of what became several informal but very productive meetings with Wang Jungfu and his colleagues.

Although he hailed from a strict military background, Wang Jungfu was cordial and extremely polite. We started off with a good chemistry between us. Conversation with him was very easy, and he was open to discussing any issue, giving us candid answers as well as his personal views. While he was fully authorized to speak on behalf of President Jiang, he never exaggerated his own position or influence. I remember asking him the chain of command through which he operated. His answer was very clear. He told me that he was meeting with me with the full authority of the President, but he himself did not report directly to him but rather through certain senior officials within the President's Secretariat.

Throughout our meetings, he continued to emphasize the importance of keeping them highly confidential. He was concerned that any premature leak would severely damage the process. He emphasized the great political risk Jiang Zemin was taking in reaching out to the Dalai Lama. On issues including relations with the United States and the Taiwan and Hong Kong situations, President Jiang was simply continuing policies established by his predecessor, Deng Xiaoping. By contrast, his decision to engage the Dalai Lama was the one area where he was reversing Deng Xiaoping's policy. As previously discussed, although Deng Xiaoping had originally reached out to His Holiness, in later years he had come to greatly mistrust[20] the Dalai Lama, cutting off all communications with him, and to the extent he addressed the situation in Tibet, limiting his efforts to improving economic and social conditions on the Plateau.

Wang Jungfu strongly urged that I convey President Jiang's concerns to His Holiness, particularly about maintaining confidentiality, but most importantly, that we reassure the President of His Holiness's seriousness and sincerity. It was clear that President Jiang was taking this initiative personally and did not want it jeopardized through premature disclosure either domestically or in the international community. Wang Jungfu's emphasis on confidentiality bordered on paranoia. To avoid other PRC agencies becoming aware of our Hong Kong meeting, he insisted on holding our first session on the open seas to avoid any possibility of electronic surveillance. Most of our subsequent meetings were held on land, however, as I suffered from terrible seasickness during that boat ride to our initial meeting.

I came back from Hong Kong convinced that this channel was authentic and that this would be an ongoing process. I therefore felt the need to have an additional person working with me to take full advantage of the opportunity. While I am a great advocate for a recognized chain of command, with the appointed individuals given a clear mandate and defined responsibilities, this monumental task needed the efforts of more than one person. Moreover, limiting the involvement to just one individual shuttling back and forth between meetings wouldn't convey the sense of seriousness and formality that the process deserved and that Beijing wanted to see from our side. On the other hand, had I continued to act alone, it might have more powerfully conveyed the impression that I enjoyed the full confidence of His Holiness. While in our system the number of participants has no political relevance, in the Chinese world, because of the lack of trust, there are always multiple participants, each of whom is keeping tabs on the others. In keeping with this practice, beginning with our first meeting, my Chinese counterpart had several staff members assisting him.

I therefore requested His Holiness to appoint Kelsang Gyaltsen to work with me. I specifically asked for him because at the time he was working as one of His Holiness's Secretaries. His position ensured that His Holiness would be kept thoroughly briefed on our progress and that the briefings would remain confidential. In addition, Kelsang Gyaltsen would be in a position to pass on any information that came to His Holiness's attention that might be relevant to our efforts. As it was essential to proceed in a coordinated and highly confidential manner, this path of communication was critical. I also felt strongly that whoever became my partner must be personally committed to His Holiness's Middle Way Approach. I had observed Kelsang Gyaltsen and knew that he supported both the strategy and the tactics we had adopted to implement it. As he and I had worked together for many years, I also knew that he appreciated and had confidence in my approach. From unfortunate experiences in the past, I knew that in dealing with Beijing we had to present a consistent and unified position. At the same time, I also knew Kelsang Gyaltsen would be invaluable in brainstorming and assessing different options. He takes a logical and analytical approach to issues and most importantly, is unafraid to voice an alternative opinion and take a stand on matters he feels strongly about.

## APRIL 1998 MEETINGS IN CHIANG MAI

After His Holiness designated Kelsang Gyaltsen to work with me, we had a series of intense, substantive meetings with our PRC counterparts in April 1998 in Chiang Mai, Thailand. The primary focus of our discussions was the possibility of His Holiness making a pilgrimage to Mount Wutai that would afford the opportunity to meet with President Jiang. While the main purpose of such a visit was, of course, the proposed meeting, His Holiness's wish to make a pilgrimage to Mount Wutai is also very genuine. When he was in China in 1954–55, he tried to visit, but poor road conditions and inclement weather precluded the trip.

Mount Wutai is a holy site deeply revered by the Tibetans that has been one of the most important pilgrimage destinations for hundreds of years. Mahayana Buddhists view this mountain as the abode of Manjushri, the Bodhisattva of Wisdom. Moreover, it also has a special connection with the Dalai Lamas. It was there that the 13th Dalai Lama had his first contact with then US Ambassador to China William Woodville Rockhill, in June 1908. The Ambassador trekked for five days to meet with the Great Thirteenth, who was returning to Tibet via China from Mongolia. This was the beginning of a long friendship between the two that was maintained through correspondence over the years in the Tibetan language as, somewhat surprisingly for the times, the Ambassador was fluent in Tibetan.

During the April meetings in Chiang Mai, each side offered clarifications to our respective positions. My counterparts were insistent that not only the fact of our meetings but especially their substance be kept highly confidential. I had the persistent feeling that they were most worried about the reaction within the PRC leadership if our efforts were disclosed prematurely. Not surprisingly then, they became quite unhappy and very worried when they believed we had leaked the idea of His Holiness making a pilgrimage to Mount Wutai.

The immediate cause of their concern came after my meeting with Wang Jungfu in Hong Kong. His Holiness publicly mentioned his desire to make a pilgrimage. Our counterparts thought His Holiness had made the suggestion based on the discussions we had had in Hong Kong. Kelsang Gyaltsen and I explained that His Holiness's recent remarks were not in any way related to our discussions. He had expressed a desire to visit Mount Wutai a number of times in the past, most often when he was giving Buddhist teachings. From our counterparts' response, it was very clear that they had no idea His Holiness had been making this suggestion over the course of several years. Despite this background, they urged us to understand the sensitivity of the issue and refrain from publicly discussing the possibility of an imminent visit. I was happy to accede to their wishes and relieved that they understood it was not a deliberate leak from our side.

The major stumbling block for His Holiness visiting the PRC has always been Beijing's precondition that he publicly state that Tibet was always a part of China. One of the major successes of our informal discussions with Wang Jungfu was that Kelsang Gyaltsen and I were able to explain the reasons His Holiness is unable to make such a statement. We first assured our counterparts that it was not motivated by any ill intentions or a hidden agenda for the future. While the historic relations between the Tibetans and Chinese have been very close and at times special, there is no commonly accepted interpretation of the status of that relationship. Besides the conflicting views of the Chinese and Tibetan people, historians and international legal experts also cannot agree. As we see no possibility of a common understanding being reached, this requirement only serves to create more and deeper mistrust and misunderstandings. We also made it clear that we were not questioning the present reality: Tibet became part of the newly created PRC after signing the Seventeen-Point Agreement on May 23, 1951. We suggested to our counterparts that because this important document articulated the relations between the parties, both sides should take a fresh look at it. We also assured them that His Holiness was willing to make an unambiguous statement that he was not seeking independence for Tibet, but rather was committed to Tibet remaining part of the PRC.

We further asked our counterparts to be mindful of His Holiness's status as an ordained Buddhist monk. As previously discussed, His Holiness simply could not agree to Beijing's request, as it is factually untrue. As a Buddhist monk, having taken a vow to tell the truth, he could not intentionally tell a lie. In addition to the significant substantive differences between Beijing's and Dharamsala's positions and perceptions, this clash between the Marxist Communist worldview of the PRC leaders and the moral and ethical position of His Holiness has constituted and continues to pose one of the major impediments to the parties' ability to reach a mutually satisfactory solution.

During our two days of meetings with Wang Jungfu and his associates, we were also able to discuss other important issues, some of which were not on the formal agenda. Toward the end of our discussions on the second day, for example, Wang

Jungfu asked if he could raise just such an issue. I responded by welcoming his suggestion because by then we had established a friendly personal relationship. His question was how to handle the troublesome issue of identifying Panchen Rinpoche's reincarnation. I told him that while we had no official instruction or guidance on the matter, I would be more than happy to give him my personal opinion. I further told him, that, because I was Tibetan and a practicing Buddhist, my view would not be different from that of the Tibetan people.

I first reminded him that earlier in our meetings, we had had lengthy discussions about the role of the PRC central government versus that of the local Tibetan administration in the truly autonomous framework we were proposing. We had emphasized that on issues of national defense and foreign relations, Beijing would have the primary role, but on all other matters including culture, religion, and language, the Tibetans must have control, as spelled out by His Holiness in the Strasbourg Proposal. Therefore, I responded to his question about Panchen Rinpoche's reincarnation saying that as it fell within the realm of religion and culture, the Tibetans should be the decision-making authority. The issue of reincarnation is not only a fundamental tenet of Buddhism in general but also a distinctive feature and core aspect of the Tibetan Buddhist religious tradition in particular. Accordingly, the recognition of one of the most senior Tibetan Buddhist figures should be in the hands of the Tibetans, specifically His Holiness, and the PRC government should respect his decisions in that regard.

Wang Jungfu didn't leap off his chair in response to my remarks, as some other Chinese officials might have done. But he did come back with a second, important question. Given that Beijing had already recognized Gyaltsen Norbu as the 11th Panchen Lama, the dignity and prestige of the central government must be considered. I responded by saying that although I could not make any formal commitment, if His Holiness's decision were respected, we could find a creative way to accommodate Gyaltsen Norbu. I concluded with a laugh, saying: "Vice Minister, Tibetans have handled very delicate reincarnation issues in the past, and I think we can find a way to handle this one also without anyone losing face."[21]

I saw great benefit in these informal consultations because they gave both sides the opportunity to put ideas on the table that could not have been broached in a formal setting. By the conclusion of our talks in Thailand, in my view, we had made significant progress in understanding each other's positions on certain very important issues. The Chinese now had an understanding and appreciation of the reasons behind His Holiness's inability to make the requested sweeping statement about Tibet's relationship with historic China and the newly formed PRC, as it disregarded history. From our part, we now understood the need to look for a formula for our next discussions that would satisfy the Chinese side. We agreed to work closely together and continue to share ideas, including preparing a statement agreeable to both sides.

As we had managed to involve a number of international figures and institutions to help us with this process, there was also a strong push by these mutual friends, on both sides, to find a formula that would allow our relations to move to the next level. We also thoroughly discussed President Clinton's upcoming June 1998 trip to Beijing and worked out some rough "to do" lists for each party that included the possibility of His Holiness making an important statement during his planned visit to Washington, D.C., later in the year.

## OUR PREPARATIONS FOR THE CLINTON–JIANG MEETING IN BEIJING

On my return from the Chiang Mai consultations, I updated His Holiness and the Dharamsala leadership on our discussions and started working on a statement by His Holiness that could pave the way for more formal relations, including a visit by His Holiness. Once back in Washington, I briefed senior administration officials, including Jeff Bader, on the substance of our talks. Jeff was the key person at the White House dealing with the PRC for President Clinton. As instructed by His Holiness, I also began consulting with these officials about the content of His Holiness's statement. As circumstances ultimately prevented him from issuing it, I can't disclose the content we drafted.

A few weeks before President Clinton's visit, I received an urgent message from Wang Jungfu saying that our discussions in Chiang Mai were well received in Beijing and that President Jiang would be responding positively on Tibet to President Clinton during his forthcoming trip. He suggested that a personal communication from His Holiness to President Jiang before the US-PRC summit, however, would help him counter a negative impression among some senior PRC leaders that he was acting at the behest of the United States.

I soon left Washington for Dharamsala to report to His Holiness and for consultations with the Tibetan leadership. In mid-June, I traveled to Shenzhen through Hong Kong to hand deliver a letter from His Holiness addressed to

President Jiang. My Chinese counterparts made elaborate arrangements to receive me and take me across the border for the meeting. The Hong Kong media seemed to have gotten wind of my visit, as my Chinese escorts were very nervous. They were very happy with the results of our joint efforts, however, rushing back to Beijing with His Holiness's letter just after escorting me back to Hong Kong.

His Holiness's letter was delivered just ten days before the Clinton–Jiang Summit. This direct communication made it possible for President Jiang to publicly engage President Clinton on the Tibet issue, as he had evidence that there were open channels of communication with the Dalai Lama. In fact, I later learned that during their private discussions, President Jiang gestured at a document, indicating to President Clinton that it was from the Dalai Lama. He was signaling his openness to discuss the Tibet issue, not only as a result of being encouraged by President Clinton but also because the Dalai Lama himself was in touch with him.

Our efforts for further engagement were moving along quite smoothly, and we were enjoying some substantive progress. For the first time, we were able to bypass dealing with the United Front and work with individuals who reported directly to President Jiang. As previously mentioned, at the time, our main focus was creating an opportunity for His Holiness and President Jiang to meet. We thus settled on the idea of His Holiness making a private visit to the PRC in his capacity as a Buddhist leader and while there, meeting with the President.

## THE CLINTON–JIANG SUMMIT

The inclusion of Tibet as an important agenda item for the Clinton–Jiang Summit was the result of many months of effort by numerous people and required meticulous planning and coordination. As I previously noted, we were so intimately involved with the US administration in preparing for this meeting that we had full knowledge of the details of the President's statement and, to a large extent, President Jiang's anticipated response.[22] Weeks ahead of time I was able to inform His Holiness and the Kalon Tripa, Sonam Topgyal, of the essence of what both leaders would say in their joint press conference. At the time of the actual meeting, I was in a car on my way to meet with the late Prince Sadruddin Aga Khan, accompanied by my colleague Chungdak Koren, who was then His Holiness's Representative in Geneva. A senior aid accompanying President

Clinton personally called me, saying: “Lodi, it happened.” He was confirming that the remarks we had so diligently crafted had actually been stated by the Presidents. This high-visibility exchange between the Presidents of the United States and the PRC attracted extraordinary international attention. Prominent statesmen including President Carter personally wrote to His Holiness expressing their joy at the substance of the two Presidents’ remarks, viewing President Jiang’s comments as very promising.

## CHAPTER 18

# Fits and Starts

*Reengaging the United Front*

Unfortunately, things did not turn out as we hoped. The widely publicized positive Clinton–Jiang Tibet remarks had the opposite effect in the PRC and soon led to the Chinese authorities shutting us out completely. It took us nearly three years to reconnect with Beijing after the unintentional fallout resulting from this promising event.

As previously mentioned, at the time there was escalating friction within the top Chinese leadership on a number of issues, especially how President Jiang was handling the US–PRC relationship. Although it is very difficult to acquire precise details concerning the internal conflicts in this group, it is now an open secret that President Jiang was facing strong opposition from quite a few of his colleagues. The very public discussion of Tibet by President Jiang with President Clinton seems to have become a major source of contention.

I later learned that Standing Committee member Li Ruihuan was unhappy that the President had opened a channel of communication with us, completely bypassing the United Front.[1] That said, he seemed to be surprisingly more liberal and open-minded than Jiang Zemin on certain issues, including Tibet. Tibetans inside Tibet, with more intimate knowledge of Li Ruihuan, confirmed this view. I am not saying that he was a strong advocate for reaching out to His Holiness to settle the Tibet issue. He was, in fact, supportive of some very tough measures Beijing imposed in Tibet in the 1950s. However, he definitely did not take a negative view of His Holiness. The following quote gives insight into his feelings: "In dealing with the Dalai Lama we don't have to take a hostile attitude and use excessive measures. Just as long as he doesn't engage in Tibetan independence [activities], we can talk with him. We should be clear, under present conditions, that no plan can last for long that doesn't include the Dalai Lama."[2]

One example of Li Ruihuan's open views was his response to my suggestion concerning the Panchen Lama reincarnation issue. Through very reliable intermediaries, I had the opportunity to urge him not to do anything to undermine His Holiness's choice, arguing that a hands-off approach was in the long-term interests of both parties. I believe he gave some serious thought to my argument, as the PRC leadership took considerable time before going ahead with its decision. While His Holiness recognized Gedun Choekyi Nyima on May 14, 1995, Beijing only first announced its choice of Gyaltsen Norbu on November 29, 1995, after a gap of more than six months. Even on matters including the Cultural Revolution and the Great Leap Forward, of the most senior leaders, Li Ruihuan was among the few who did not hesitate to speak his mind: "We had the courage to conclude that the Cultural Revolution was a disaster, so we should have the same courage to face and learn from other mistakes and harm we have brought to the people in fifty years of rule."[3]

Together with Zeng Qinghong, Li Ruihuan was the leading advocate for liberalization, strongly backed by his former Standing Committee Politburo colleague Qiao Shi. The Tibetan world has a mistaken image of Qiao Shi as an ultrahard-liner because of his official responsibility for national security combined with his reported remarks citing the need to impose "merciless repression" in putting down the late 1980s demonstrations in Tibet. In reality, Qiao Shi was liberal and quite modest.

## BREAKDOWN OF EFFORTS

It is unfortunate that Tibet became one of the issues that Li Ruihuan and others invoked to challenge President Jiang. Their differences with the President stemmed from much deeper ideological concerns. They were fundamentally opposed to President Jiang's philosophy of the "Three Stresses," an educational drive focusing on "theoretical study, political awareness and good conduct within the Party."[4] Qiao Shi disparagingly referred to the President's theory as "Three Stresses in name but a personality cult in nature."[5] In his trademark, straightforward manner, Li Ruihuan further urged President Jiang to "talk less theory and do more real work."[6]

But let me share the details of a situation created by our side that may have contributed to earning the displeasure of the United Front, thereby alienating

Li Ruihuan and others like him. It involves Gyalo Thondup's participation in my meetings with Wang Jungfu in Hong Kong.

Over the years of our outreach to Beijing, we never had any reservations in dealing with the United Front or any other agency or individuals designated by Beijing. We have always recognized that it is Beijing's prerogative to designate whomever it wants to talk with us, just as it is His Holiness's right to choose his emissaries. Beginning with Deng Xiaoping's initial overtures in 1979, the United Front was the agency that handled our relations, even though the Nationalities Affairs Commission of the State Council (NAC) formally hosted our delegations until the early 2000s. The relationship between the United Front and the NAC was very close. In the early days, the United Front Minister concurrently held the position of NAC Minister. As a Party functionary, the United Front Minister outranks the NAC Ministers from the executive branch. During Premier Zhu Rongji's time, he sought to create some distance between the CCP and the executive branch by discontinuing many of these dual appointments.

From our many years of experience in dealing with the United Front, however, it became clear that the department had preconceived views and positions that impeded our efforts to reach a mutually beneficial solution. Quite simply, it wanted to maintain the status quo. Any criticism of existing government policy was seen as a direct attack on the department, and any suggestion for change was seen as challenging or undermining its authority. This was a deeply entrenched characteristic of that office. While we were not naïve enough to think that we could ignore the United Front, we sincerely felt that to make a breakthrough, we must have the opportunity to bring our proposals directly to the senior leadership.

Over the years, I have come to know many of the United Front Ministers and other senior officials personally, even developing close friendships with quite a few of them—that is, to the extent possible given the PRC's rigid political system. Many of these individuals are dedicated, hardworking officials who in their own way care about the well-being of the Tibetan people. Surprisingly, and being careful to avoid making any sweeping judgments, I often found senior officials of Han nationality much easier to deal with than those of minority ethnicity. The latter were less accommodating. Perhaps driven by some type of inferiority complex, they wanted to prove they were more loyal to the CCP and the political system than their Han compatriots.

The United Front's intransigence provides the background leading to the secret meetings I had with Wang Jungfu in December 1997 in Hong Kong and in

April 1998 in Chiang Mai. When I was in Hong Kong for our first meeting, I learned that Gyalo Thondup was also in town. As I hold him in high regard, I felt it would be improper for me not to meet with him. In addition, as I have noted, on important issues such as dealing with the PRC, one of the mistakes Dharamsala perpetually made was not coordinating its activities among involved individuals. Accordingly, I asked my Chinese counterparts if they would agree to meet with him as a courtesy and share a meal that I would host.

They flatly refused. They were unwilling to meet with him because they had clear instructions from Beijing not to meet with anyone other than me. As noted in the previous chapter, many of the concerned agencies in Beijing had not even been informed of our meetings because of anticipated backlash that could jeopardize our nascent relationship. This was the reason Wang Jungfu was so concerned about maintaining confidentiality. I was quite persistent, however, that we at least meet Gyalo Thondup briefly for a cup of tea.

Recognizing that it was important to me, Wang Jungfu and his associates agreed to meet him for lunch, provided they had my full assurances that he would not disclose this meeting to any of his Chinese friends, at least for the time being. They were extremely respectful, acknowledging his position as well as his many friends and well-wishers in Beijing, but they emphasized that premature disclosure of our meetings would seriously jeopardize our joint efforts.

I was very pleased with this turn of events and immediately got in touch with him. I met him in person soon thereafter and told him the reason for my visit to Hong Kong, adding that, at my suggestion, my counterparts had agreed to have lunch with us the following day before their return to Beijing. I further told Gyalo Thondup that this was the first step in renewed communications that must be kept highly confidential; he should not share this information with any of his contacts until there was some further movement. He was very happy and quite excited to meet Wang Jungfu. He assured me that everything would be kept confidential, going so far as to lecture me on the importance of dealing with such sensitive matters in a very discreet manner.

As planned, Gyalo Thondup accompanied me to the lunch, and I made the formal introductions. To my dismay, he immediately took over the conversation, which continued for about two hours. As he spoke in Mandarin, I had no idea what was being discussed. He did most of the talking, and I heard him name-dropping, referring to Deng Xiaoping, Hu Yaobang, and even Chiang Kai-shek and Zhou Enlai, as well as many others I didn't know. I could tell from Wang

Jungfu's body language that he was feeling quite uncomfortable, not knowing how best to handle the situation. I could only guess that Gyalo Thondup was asking him lots of questions. He further invited them all for dinner that evening as his guests, but they declined, saying they had already made their departure arrangements for later that evening, which I knew to be true.

After the luncheon, Gyalo Thondup told me he was not very happy with the conversation. He kept saying that they had been very secretive and reluctant to discuss any substantive matters. He asked me more than once: "Are you sure these are authorized people?" I then realized I had probably made a big mistake in arranging the meeting. I reiterated my admonition that he kindly keep the entire matter highly confidential. I assured him that Wang Jungfu and his companions were fully authorized representatives reporting directly to President Jiang.

Several months later, Gyalo Thondup telephoned me from Hong Kong, which he did quite often. He said to me: "Rinpoche, people in Beijing do not seem to know the people that you have been meeting." I literally fell off my chair in shock. I then knew he had breached his promise of confidentiality and had been talking to his United Front contacts about my meetings with Wang Jungfu. I became deeply worried and disappointed and said: "Oh, no! You have shared that information with others." Despite my anxiety, he was dismissive of my concerns, continuing to assert that Wang Jungfu and his associates were not authorized individuals because the "people who really matter" were not aware of their actions.

Later, we learned that the United Front not only was very unhappy about our meetings with Wang Jungfu but also had informed their superiors that contact was taking place without the knowledge of concerned agencies. After the Jiang-Clinton press conference, Li Ruihuan confronted President Jiang at a meeting of the Politburo Standing Committee, directly asking whether there had been any contacts with the Dalai Lama's representatives in recent days. While there is no way of knowing how Jiang Zemin responded, one thing became very clear: he squashed the initiative that he had personally set in motion, curtailing any further communications between the parties and once again effectively shutting us out.

While I am not saying that our failure to keep this contact confidential was the only reason for the breakdown of this important channel of communication, it certainly gave needed ammunition to those waiting for an opportunity to derail the effort. I must acknowledge, however, that at the same time, US-PRC relations were in one of their periodic downswings. One disadvantage of our having succeeded in making Tibet an integral part of that relationship was that whenever it was under stress, the Tibet issue suffered.

In retrospect, I knew I had erred in inviting Gyalo Thondup to meet the delegation, allowing my personal sentiments to override my professional responsibilities. I thus went to Dharamsala to brief His Holiness and then the Kalon Tripa, informing each of them of my decision and apologizing for my mistake in judgment. Later, when we were discussing how my premature involvement of Gyalo Thondup might have contributed to the breakdown of contacts, I remember Kalon Tripa Samdhong Rinpoche saying: "Now you have learned your lesson." This chastening was really directed to my long-standing position advocating inclusion of Gyalo Thondup in all our efforts at renewed contact with Beijing. And in this circumstance, he was correct.

In the preceding paragraphs, I have been talking a lot about being "shut out" by Beijing. When the Chinese shut you out, they do a thorough job. As I have discussed, over the years we managed to establish communications through a variety of channels, only to have them closed down. But when the United Front reasserted control, not only the door but also the windows and the entire ventilation system were slammed shut. Even individuals living outside the PRC who had been involved with the logistics for our meetings in Hong Kong and Thailand became unreachable. Previously we had had direct communications with Wang Jungfu, including the mobile number of his English-speaking assistant and his direct fax line. Communications via these avenues evaporated. We simply couldn't reach him.

Whatever may have compelled President Jiang to freeze our direct contact, he seems not to have completely turned his back on us. Sometime in November 1998, K. S. Wu visited the US and called me with a personal message from the President advising us of the need for a "cooling-off" period for the time being. Contact could be reestablished in the future, but in the meantime His Holiness and the Tibetans must help create a more congenial atmosphere. Any action by our side criticizing the PRC would only serve as an excuse for the hard-liners to block renewal of relations. I should not try to reach out to Wang Jungfu or his associates, as they were no longer authorized to deal with the Tibet issue, and any overtures in that regard would only cause the President serious inconvenience.

I was scheduled to meet K. S. Wu in New York before he returned to the PRC, but a pressing matter preempted my trip. Instead, we had another long telephone conversation, and I followed up with a personal note recapping our discussion. I also forwarded him a statement that His Holiness had issued at the end of his Washington visit to share with President Jiang. The original statement we intended to issue included a proposal for a pilgrimage by His Holiness to the PRC. Given the break in communications, we deleted that part of the text. In my November 20, 1998, letter to him, I suggested six points to share with President Jiang:

1. It is our mutual interest to resolve the Tibet issue.
2. [President Jiang] . . . needs to show leadership and boldness in learning to trust the Dalai Lama, and he should not be misled. President Jiang has shown a number of times that he has the courage and ability to exert real leadership on Tibet and other issues. As yet he can enter into the new millennium as one of the great statesmen of the world.
3. His Holiness the Dalai Lama is sincere and is willing to trust President Jiang.
4. Even though various circumstances, both internal and external, may make it necessary to slow the process of formal dialogue and negotiations, we must keep active a credible and reliable backchannel.
5. It would be beneficial for President Jiang to take us into confidence regarding what we can do to help create the right environment for him, both internally and externally.
6. We have no reservation as to which agency or individual to deal with—this is the prerogative of President Jiang and the Chinese government to determine. Whichever agency or individual is designated should be instructed to work with me as His Holiness's principal authorized person.[7]

I thought it was very important to stress our willingness to talk with any individual or institution Beijing wanted to designate. By then it was quite obvious that the United Front was making an issue of its exclusion from the confidential talks we had started, and I wanted to soothe their fears. I also acknowledged the need for a "cooling-off" period, but I argued that "we should not let the current situation cut off the communications we have established." K. S. Wu thought he would be back in the United States in December with more explicit information, but he didn't return. While I am not certain what prompted him to stop acting as our intermediary, I believe it was due to his poor health, which was apparently quite critical even before he returned to the PRC.

## EFFORTS FOR RENEWAL OF DIRECT CONTACTS

In spite of being officially shut out by Beijing, we didn't abandon all our efforts to reconnect. The messages that I had received from K. S. Wu and through some other channels indicated that Beijing was considering reestablishing relations with us, but the appropriate opportunity and the timing were problematic. We thus continued our efforts in the international community, and I began my outreach to Asian nations, seeking their advice in reengaging Beijing.[8]

At the same time, I continued trying to establish, or reestablish, direct connections with PRC officials but to no avail. They became intent on breaking off contact with me and resurrecting their relationship with Gyalo Thondup. Their efforts were perhaps unintentionally assisted by the inability of the Kashag to send a unified message about who was the designated interlocutor. Even though the Kashag has always been very supportive of me, for some reason it was unable to convey unequivocally that Kelsang Gyaltsen and I were the authorized representatives. At the same time, other interested parties were implying that they, too, had His Holiness's approval to proceed on his behalf and that there was no specific person designated as interlocutor.

I personally never gave Beijing any cause to believe that there was internal competition among individuals or that there were major differences within the Tibetan leadership as to who should lead the outreach effort, even when I was fully aware that Gyalo Thondup's continued relations with the United Front were sending the wrong signals. In fact, while his trips to the PRC were mostly met with strong opposition by our leadership, I always took the opposite view. I believe that individuals with his experience have much to teach us. We thus needed to try to actively include him in our efforts. Having said that, I was and remain fully aware of the difficulties in reining him in and including him as a formal team player. I have, however, continued to work closely with him as much as possible on a personal level. In some cases, I think the Chinese would have preferred it if I indicated some displeasure with the situation.

This lack of clarity, combined with the number of people going back and forth projecting themselves as authorized emissaries, did give Beijing an excellent excuse for refusing to acknowledge Kelsang Gyaltsen's and my roles. During a visit to London, Bi Hua, an official of the United Front dealing with Tibetan affairs, for example, bluntly informed the British Foreign Office that there was intense disagreement in Dharamsala over who should be the designated interlocutor. This uncoordinated approach was not only sending the wrong message to Beijing but also deeply hurting our efforts overall. I had never asked the Kashag to make any public announcement of my role or complained about the difficulties that its ambiguity was causing, even though many friends, including senior US administration officials, were also concerned about Dharamsala's seeming ambivalence. Several of them, including the President and the Secretary of State, knew firsthand from His Holiness that I was the principal interlocutor, so they couldn't understand Dharamsala's silence.

As previously noted, by mid-2000 the United Front had reconnected with Gyalo Thondup, either on its own initiative or at his instigation. It was somewhat confusing, because earlier Gyalo Thondup had several times told Dharamsala and me personally that he was consciously distancing himself from the United Front. Perhaps his inquiry about my meeting with Jiang Zemin's emissary in Hong Kong rekindled their relations. Khun Anand's private disclosure to me of this rejuvenated relationship was publicly revealed when Chinese Vice President Hu Jintao told him: "We are in touch with the Dalai Lama and in fact his elder brother visited Beijing just recently."[9]

I believe it was sometime in early August that I received a call from Sonam Topgyal, who was then the Kalon Tripa, asking me to visit Dharamsala at my earliest convenience. I could sense some urgency in his voice and left for Dharamsala immediately. After an exchange of pleasantries, he expressed his appreciation for my making the trip, saying the Kashag needed to discuss certain very important matters with me concerning our relations with the PRC. When I walked into the room to meet the Kashag members, I sensed some uneasiness among them. The Kalon Tripa then handed me a copy of the minutes recorded during a meeting between Wang Zhaoguo, then Minister of the United Front, and Gyalo Thondup during the latter's visit to the PRC in July.

The crucial point chronicled in the minutes was the statement: "We do not support the Dalai Lama's assigned person, who is controlled by the United States, who is radical Tibetan independence activist." After I read it, the Kalon Tripa said that Gyalo Thondup had recently brought the minutes to the attention of the Kashag, triggering a serious discussion. While the Kashag wanted me to continue as the key person dealing with the PRC, as designated by His Holiness, they also wanted to take advantage of the contacts Gyalo Thondup had to offer. They wanted to discuss the matter with me, come to a decision, and then seek His Holiness's approval.

For several years I had been spearheading our efforts to reengage the PRC leadership as instructed by His Holiness, but in an informal and highly confidential manner. During His Holiness's April–May 1998 visit to the United States, he instructed his Private Secretary Tethong Tenzin Geyche and me to prepare a letter in his name appointing me as the principal interlocutor. I think this occurred when we were in Atlanta, Georgia. Some days later, when His Holiness was at Deer Park in Wisconsin, he inquired if we had prepared the letter. Leaving His Holiness's room, I remember telling Tenzin Geyche that as I was the subject of the appointment, I was uncomfortable assisting in its drafting. As His Holiness had given clear guidance as to its contents, Tenzin Geyche should prepare the draft for his approval.

On May 16, 1998, His Holiness issued the authorization, instructing that it be conveyed to President Jiang, President Clinton, and others who were helping us. The statement read as follows:

> I hereby authorise Lodi Gyaltsen Gyari, my Special Envoy, as the principal person to act on my behalf in dealing with matters concerning resolution of the Tibetan problem with Chinese Government officials, as well as with other concerned people. Lodi Gyaltsen Gyari enjoys my full confidence and trust and will be reporting directly to me.

Because the Kashag was aware of this formal authorization, it felt obliged to include me in the discussion about the opportunity advanced through Gyalo Thondup, while at the same time urging me to continue in the lead role. Even though I was quite certain that the United Front's message rejecting my participation was not coming from the highest leadership, I told the Kashag that our relations with Beijing were far more important than the role of any particular individual, and that it must take whatever steps necessary to take advantage of the renewed contact through Gyalo Thondup. I knew that by this time President Jiang was fully aware of my role, as he had received His Holiness's letter designating me as principal interlocutor. Moreover, I had been receiving messages from Beijing indicating that contact would be reestablished after the "cooling-off" period. Nevertheless, I counseled that the Kashag should appoint someone else, as the United Front was only rejecting one specific individual, me. It appeared willing to reopen dialogue with anyone else, and there was no question we should avail ourselves of the opportunity.

My friends in the Kashag were genuinely relieved by my accommodating response. We then spent considerable time discussing suitable candidates to take my place. They had compiled a good list of possibilities, most of whom were senior civil servants, and I suggested only a few additional names. The Kashag settled on the composition of the delegation for which it would seek His Holiness's approval, with the further recommendation that I remain involved by providing support and guidance to the delegates.

Kalon Tripa Sonam Topgyal immediately requested an audience with His Holiness. If I remember correctly, His Holiness asked us to come that very afternoon. The Kalon Tripa reported the Kashag's decision, noting my express support for the proposal, and further asking for His Holiness's approval. After reflecting for a while, he commented: "Now the Chinese are saying that they also want to decide who should be my representatives." His Holiness was not at all happy. He then instructed the Kalon Tripa to have the Kashag ask Gyalo Thondup to take a message back to the United Front in the form of minutes of a meeting between it and Gyalo Thondup. The minutes should state that the Dalai Lama had appointed Lodi Gyari as principal interlocutor because he is someone who could clearly explain the Middle Way Approach. Sending Lodi Gyari should be seen as a demonstration of the Dalai Lama's sincerity in engaging Beijing to resolve the Tibet issue.

With this instruction, we apprised the Kashag and the following day returned with a draft memo for His Holiness's approval. He was very happy with the substance, choosing to add one further sentence in his own writing: "Lodi Gyari has already visited China twice in 1982 and 1984 as part of His Holiness the Dalai Lama's three-member High-Level Exploratory Talks Delegation."

Despite Beijing's pressure to designate someone else as his interlocutor, His Holiness remained firm. I sincerely thought that we should seize the opportunity of Wang Zhaoguo's offer to resume talks without making an issue of my participation. Looking back, however, His Holiness made the right decision by sending the strong message that it is his prerogative to choose his own emissaries. It took some time, but finally the Chinese "blinked." While His Holiness's uncompromising position may have initially taken the United Front by surprise, it finally acceded to his position and began contacting me directly.

Its first move was to issue an invitation for me to make a personal visit to my birthplace in Nyarong. I do not know whether they were trying to be nice to make up for their previous vigorous opposition to my involvement or had some other, more duplicitous agenda in mind, one that could have inured to their benefit by creating misperceptions in the minds of Tibetans. To be fair, it could have been a genuine gesture. It is very unfortunate that both we Tibetans and the Chinese always jump to the conclusion that there must be some sinister design behind any proposal or idea put forth by the other side. I confess to reacting that way myself all too frequently.

Sometime after K. S. Wu stopped acting as our intermediary, another mutual friend stepped in to assist us in our efforts to reconnect. To respect his wishes, his identity must remain confidential, but I can say he was a person with deep reverence for Buddhism and solid connections to the highest leadership levels in Beijing. His only condition, relayed to both sides, was that he would act solely as a reliable messenger, with no wish to be dragged into substantive matters. He also had no desire for any recognition, expressly prohibiting his name from being linked in any way with the process.

I have always thought that unlike Chinese Buddhists in Taiwan and other South Asian countries, those from the mainland or even Hong Kong would be much more reluctant to have any association with the Tibet issue, and especially with His Holiness. To my pleasant surprise, I found I was very wrong in my thinking. When I shared this perception with a group of Chinese Buddhist friends in Hong Kong, they corrected me. Until the Tibet issue is resolved and Beijing's attitude toward His Holiness becomes positive, they said, they face limitations on their ability to fully practice Tibetan Buddhism, the form of Buddhism that many of them follow. As it would benefit their practice, many of them wanted to make whatever contribution to resolving the issue that they could. Later, many Chinese Buddhists from the mainland whom I met expressed similar views. Unlike their peers under PRC control, Chinese Buddhists outside the PRC need not worry about Beijing's view of their relations with His Holiness. But ironically, quite a few seem to be more obedient to Beijing's directives than those from the mainland.

Sometime during this "cooling-off" period, a senior official of the Clinton White House introduced me to a prominent Washington-based Chinese journalist. He opened up yet another channel of communication for me with Beijing. The PRC government also sometimes used him to convey highly important communications to the White House, bypassing the usual State Department channel. Its 2002 decision to release some Tibetan political prisoners was in fact conveyed to the White House by this journalist, even before the US Ambassador to the PRC or the State Department was formally notified.

This individual became a regular, reliable contact for us, not even hesitating to visit me and some of my colleagues at my ICT office. With his fluent English, he became very much a part of our conversations with Beijing. In fact, he was the one who conveyed first to the White House and then to me that Beijing might renew direct contacts and that I would likely soon be hearing that from authorized channels. He further hinted that it would probably be the United Front that reopened the dialogue.

## INDICATIONS OF CHINESE WILLINGNESS TO RENEW CONTACT

By the end of 2000, I found many of the communication channels that had been closed for quite some time starting to reopen. I began receiving messages from not one, but several sources saying that the United Front was keen on establishing contact with me. Through my good friend Youyi Li, I was asked if I could encourage the Fairbank Center at Harvard to invite some United Front officials to the then upcoming PRC–Tibet Conference. For some time, I had been working with Ezra Vogel, one of the most eminent Chinese studies scholars, and his colleague and former student, Hu Xiaojiang,[10] to organize a conference at the Center exclusively dealing with PRC–Tibet matters. I had two meetings with Ezra Vogel on this matter. Knowing of the Center's prestige, combined with the professor's credibility, I was certain the conference would attract important individuals and provide an opportunity for a serious exchange of views.

Following his unanticipated retirement, Elizabeth Perry took over. She continued to take an interest in organizing the conference. After my conversation with Youyi Li, I immediately contacted the Center and forwarded the names of Zhu Xiaoming, Deputy Secretary of the United Front, and Bi Hua, his Deputy, to Professor Hu and the conference organizers. The United Front's idea was that the conference would afford an excellent opportunity for me to meet with their representatives to discuss the next steps in reestablishing communication.

To my surprise, sometime later the conference organizers called me to say that certain people had strongly warned that my participation might cause the United

Front officials to boycott the conference. I was truly puzzled, and the organizers were unsure what to do, as I had played a major role in initiating it. I told them I would not attend, and they should move forward because the conference had been in the works for a long time. As I was no longer participating, I decided to leave for Dharamsala for consultations that I had been postponing for quite some time.

Another surprise! I was reinvited. The day of my departure to India, the organizers called and followed up with a written invitation to speak at the conference. By then it was too late to change my plans. Moreover, as the United Front was supposed to have raised objections to my participation, I did not see any possibility of having an opportunity to meet with Zhu Xiaoming or his associates at the conference. Later, however, it became clear that the United Front had not made any objections. In fact, one of the main purposes of their attending the conference was to meet with me. At the same time, they needed to give the public impression that it was an unplanned encounter.

In the end, the situation worked to our advantage. With the failure of this "accidental meeting," the Chinese had to get in touch with me directly. While I was in Delhi, a mutual friend called on behalf of Zhu Xiaoming, asking to meet me in Washington on January 14, 2002, just a few days away. I welcomed the opportunity but responded that prior commitments in India wouldn't allow me to return to the States that soon. I would be very happy to meet him upon my return, however, anywhere in the United States he was planning on visiting, as I didn't want him to have to wait in D.C. until I returned.

The United Front was not pleased with my response, urging me to rearrange my schedule to accommodate Zhu Xiaoming's request, as the meeting was "very important." Well, of course, it was "important," but as I politely explained, it was very difficult for me to change my itinerary on such short notice. Within hours, I received a call asking if it would be convenient for me to come to Ottawa, Canada, on January 22 for a meeting at the Lord Elgin Hotel. Of course, I readily agreed.

On the 22nd, I flew to Ottawa for the day, going directly from the airport to meet Zhu Xiaoming. He was accompanied by several staff members including two translators, one for Tibetan and the other for English. I think he was quite surprised to see me arrive by myself. While our conversation began on a slightly sarcastic note referencing the "difficulty" in meeting me, Zhu Xiaoming immediately became very professional.

Our meeting began at 2:00 p.m. One of Zhu Xiaoming's translators, Huo Zhongquan, spoke excellent Tibetan. He had spent many years in Tibet, as well as two years at the PRC embassy in Kathmandu. Zhu Xiaoming's young assistant took notes. As the meeting was in Canada, I couldn't take Bhuchung Tsering with me because he would have needed a Canadian visa that frequently takes some time to obtain.[11] I didn't want to take anyone else because of the confidential nature of the discussions. While I initially had some misgivings about going alone, in retrospect, I am glad I was unaccompanied. It showed the PRC representatives that I had the authority to conduct this serious and sensitive discussion without "chaperoning," unlike in the Chinese system, as I have previously noted.

Below are my reflections on the meeting, prepared soon after my return to Washington and immediately forwarded to Kalon Tripa Samdhong Rinpoche and Tethong Tenzin Geyche, Principal Secretary to His Holiness. As this meeting ultimately led to Beijing's invitation for my team to begin formal dialogue, I am including the full text to give a clear picture of our position and efforts from the very beginning.

**ZHU:** It was quite a task to meet with you. I am very glad that we finally are meeting. How much time do you have? Are you staying overnight? (Introductions of his two assistants and himself.)

Because we have only a few hours, we should use it by being very frank and blunt.

**LGG:** I am very pleased to meet with you personally. I have heard much about you from quite a few mutual friends. We definitely must use the time that we have to exchange our views very frankly. You know that I am a Khampa and that we are well known for being quite blunt.

I would have liked to have met you in Boston at the Harvard conference. In fact, this conference was planned with the express purpose of creating an opportunity for people like us to meet. Prior to the conference it was suggested to me through our mutual friends, Professor Li and his daughter, that I support your participation as well as the participation of one of your deputies. So I passed on your names to the organizers of the conference. But after having done this I got all kinds of mixed signals from the organizers, to the extent that I came to the conclusion that you were opposed to my participation.

As you know, in the end I received an invitation to attend the conference as a guest, but it arrived on the day that I was departing for India. And, I did not receive your message expressing your desire to meet with me in Washington, DC, on the 14th of January until I was already in New Delhi, India. By that point it was not possible for me to cancel my other engagements and return to the US. However, I am happy that we are finally meeting.

Since our time is limited I would like to first talk a little about myself. This is something I do not usually do, but I think it is vitally important that those of us with the key responsibility of dealing with the issue of Tibet come to understand each other better as human beings. To start with, you can see that I do not have horns on my head, as some in Beijing sometimes seem to believe or at least give the impression that they believe. (He laughs at this.)

You may or may not be aware of the fact that I personally have no desire to be a key interlocutor with your government. You know that I visited China both in 1982 and 1984 as a part of the three-member, high-level delegation sent by His Holiness the Dalai Lama. During these visits I spent a fairly long period of time in China, meeting with a number of senior leaders and many of your former colleagues. These visits led me to conclude that I was not the best person to be involved with this task. Soon after my return to India in 1984, I had a private audience with His Holiness the Dalai Lama during which I clearly told him of my feelings in this regard and requested that I not be involved as his emissary to your government. Instead I suggested that he use my experience and services in other ways. Among other reasons, I cited my total lack of understanding of China, my inability to speak even one syllable of the Chinese language, and above all the fact that I was pretty convinced that your government was not serious about negotiations at the time.

Despite all this, in the latter part of the 1980s when His Holiness decided to make renewed efforts to reach out to your government by making important statements such as the Strasbourg Proposal, he suggested that I head the team that was being put together to start a dialogue. Normally, such nominations are considered to be a great honor and privilege, and almost no Tibetan would refuse such an appointment by the Dalai Lama. But I, with a great deal of difficulty, declined to head the team. Subsequently I agreed to the appointment, but with my own added request that I be named the number 2 and that my colleague, Tenzing Geyche Tethong, be designated as the team leader. His Holiness concurred with this plan. All of these efforts came to an end, however, when Tiananmen Square happened.

More recently, His Holiness has once again appointed me to spearhead his efforts to reach out to your government. As you know, he not only issued a formal letter of appointment to me, but he conveyed his decision to President Jiang more than once. Subsequently, in response to my request for a colleague to work on this most important task, His Holiness named his then-Secretary, Mr. Kelsang Gyaltsen, to work with me.

Having now explained my reluctance in taking on this responsibility, I must tell you that having accepted this post, I am devoting all my energy to the effort with complete sincerity and loyalty to His Holiness the Dalai Lama. First of all, I have come to the clear conclusion that the approach that His Holiness has adopted, namely to find a solution for Tibet within the framework of the PRC, is in the best interest of the Tibetan people. Furthermore, I strongly feel that the Tibetan people must take this great and historic opportunity of having such a great leader as His Holiness.

I have accepted this post with the clear understanding that it is very likely that in the end I will be labeled as someone who betrayed the interests of the six million Tibetan people. This is much more likely to happen than getting any credit, even if I am able to help His Holiness find a solution providing maximum benefit to the Tibetans. I won't blame the Tibetans if they come to such a conclusion, because almost every Tibetan strongly believes that the best outcome is to have a free and independent Tibet.

Let me tell you a personal story to illustrate this point. When I was working in preparation for His Holiness's Strasbourg Proposal, I would quite often sleep with my small briefcase under my pillow when staying with my parents in New Delhi en route from my travels to and fro. When I finally returned to New Delhi from Europe after His Holiness had delivered his proposal, my younger mother, who in my memory had never said a harsh word to me, said with such strong bitterness, "Had I known that the precious thing that you were holding on to so dearly was this document of betrayal, I would have torn it to pieces." I am sharing this very personal experience with you to illustrate to you the sentiments of the Tibetan people.

So, despite the potential negative repercussions of my work, I am engaged in this effort because of my deep, personal loyalty to my leader and love for my people.

I want to assure you that as long as I am responsible for this task I will not only work hard, but I will be totally sincere. You can count on this. To do otherwise would be disloyal to my leader and my teacher, His Holiness the Dalai Lama.

I know I have spent quite a bit of time talking about myself, but I thought that since this is our first meeting it would be very important that you understand who I am and what I believe in. Like I said earlier, developing a personal understanding between the two of us today is an important step forward toward our goal. (I gave this rather detailed personal explanation out of this sincere motivation; but I also did so because, as you will both [referring to His Holiness and Prof. Samdhong Rinpoche] recall, the Chinese government officials have been telling various people that there is an almost cutthroat race going on amongst the Tibetan leaders to be the one to talk to the Chinese.)

Because we don't have so much time today, I don't want to talk too much about the issues. Let me just say that I believe that if we are both sincere and have the political will to resolve the issue, then the gap between the views of the Chinese government and the vision of His Holiness is not so wide. In fact I think the differences are quite resolvable. On the other hand, if you deliberately look at the issue from the point of view of our greatest differences, then the gap can seem almost unbridgeable. From this perspective, the next few hours, days, and months will not bring us any closer. My hope is that you will look at this issue from the view of our commonalties, and seriously make an effort to resolve the situation.

ZHU: The Central Government is always ready to talk, but the Dalai Lama must be sincere. He must make a clear statement that Tibet is a part of China and because of his visits to Taiwan he needs to also make a statement that Taiwan is a province of China.

In our view, from the very beginning the Dalai Lama has been insincere. For example, when the Central Government, with an open mind, invited the Dalai Lama's delegation to visit Beijing but also to various parts of Tibet to see the actual situation, they used every visit to make propaganda against China and to further encourage and instigate a separatist movement. His delegations also distorted the facts and made false representations.

Furthermore, the Dalai Lama has internationalized the issue of Tibet and is trying to put international pressure on the Chinese Government to negotiate with him. The Chinese Government will never give in to such international pressure. The issue of Tibet is an internal matter for China and it has to be dealt with in that manner. You have also been a key person in internationalizing the issue of Tibet—you make many of the international visits with the Dalai Lama and are instrumental in arranging many of his meetings, including his meetings with the US Presidents.

**LGG:** You have mentioned, among other things, this issue of the "internationalization" of the Tibet issue. Yes, it is true that Tibet has become an international issue. It is also true that His Holiness and many of us working for him have been going around the world knocking at the doors of governments, parliaments, organizations, and individuals. But we do not do this for the purpose of embarrassing China or "splitting" China. We do it because we are compelled to do it. We do it because you have shut us out completely for a very long time.

If you will reflect, you will agree that starting from the late 1970s till the mid-1980s our efforts were going forward—we sent delegations and fact-finding missions, and we made every effort to keep in touch with various agencies of your government. During this period there was hardly any effort by us to "internationalize" the issue of Tibet, as you say. But when it became clear to us in the late 1980s that, for whatever reason, you had decided to shut us out, we were compelled to go in that direction.

What do we say to the world? Just one simple thing. "Please encourage the Chinese leadership to have a dialogue with us so that we can negotiate a solution to Tibet." We always make it very clear that we are not seeking independence but are trying to find a solution where the six million Tibetans can maintain their identity and preserve their culture.

If you want the so-called "internationalization" of Tibet to come to an end, it is very simple: start a formal dialogue with us to seriously negotiate a solution. Then we will have no reason whatsoever to plead with others to help.

I also want to make it very clear to you that we have never asked any government, institution, or individual to mediate. As a matter of fact, we always make it very clear that we have no desire to have anyone participate in the actual dialogue as a mediator. We are committed to proceed with the dialogue and negotiations directly with the Chinese government without any direct third-party participation.

It is true that personally I am very much involved in our efforts to meet with governments and individuals around the world. As a matter of fact, having had no direct access to your government, the only way that I have been able to pursue my responsibilities has been to approach governments, institutions, and individuals that have some relations with your government to help convey our message to your government. I am surprised that you see this act as hostile. As far as I am concerned, we have always gone to governments, institutions, and individuals that have friendly and sometimes close relations with your government. In fact, we have always made an effort to see that we did not approach or involve any government or individual that might bear ill will toward the PRC. You must advise me if we have gone to any governments or individuals that you consider to bear your government ill will, as we will immediately cease approaching you through them.

One of the key governments that we have approached is the United States. The United States and China are both great nations, and you have very close and complex relations. My understanding is that both Washington and Beijing have a keen desire to further improve your relations. Of course, because you are both big nations, it is natural that you will have some disagreements.

As I said at the very beginning, I do not want to spend our short time together listing the efforts that we have made and the lack of response from your side. Let me simply assure you that His Holiness has never ceased making efforts and has always been very sincere and transparent on his position. He has made it as clear as he can that he is not seeking independence. He has done this in his communications to your leaders, in his public statements, and in his conversations with world leaders.

ZHU: We know that you are designated by the Dalai Lama to talk with the Central Government, but you are also his Special Envoy to Washington, DC. This is a contradiction. Also, the talks cannot happen in Washington, DC.

It is wrong to say that we have shut out efforts for dialogue. We have always kept channels of communication open through our embassy in New Delhi and the Xinhua News Agency in Hong Kong. You know that even with Taiwan we do not deal with the government or the so-called "foreign office" of Taiwan. They have established a separate entity to deal with us since we do not accept the government. Similarly, we do not accept the so-called "exile government." Therefore, you being the Special Envoy to Washington, DC, and also the person to deal with us is a contradiction.

We know you are against violence like the Dalai Lama, which is good. Our head asked me to personally convey again his invitation for you to visit your hometown in your individual capacity. Since you last visited China there have been so many changes that you will be surprised to see how advanced China has become. It is very important for you to witness this transformation.

LGG: I know your position in not dealing with the exile government. It is precisely because of this sensitivity that I have stayed out of the government. You must be aware that I am His Holiness's Special Envoy and that I do not represent the exile government. My interactions with governments and institutions are mainly on the subject of our efforts to begin a dialogue with your government. If and when a real dialogue starts, my need to interact with others will naturally come to an end.

Nevertheless, I have taken note of your view that there are some contradictions in my role. I think it is mainly due to a misunderstanding of my position. However, you are candidly sharing your views with me and I will certainly convey them to His Holiness.

I must strongly disagree with your statement that you have always had doors open to us. This is simply not the case. For example, you talked about the Chinese Embassy in New Delhi as one of the channels open to us. I know from personal experience that it is not even useful as a letter box. At least a letter box will, without protest, accept letters to be posted in it. On more than one occasion your embassy has been incapable and unwilling to accept communications from us. If you are sincere, there needs to be a proper channel to communicate. With regard to the venue for negotiations, I do not think we have ever suggested that Washington be the venue for a dialogue. Therefore this is a nonissue.

ZHU: I want to share with you the great importance that the Central Leadership attaches to the well-being of the Tibetan people and the current major initiative that is under way as a part of the West China Development Program. (This was followed by a long narration, providing figures of billions of yuan designated for Tibet, the same figures that we have lately been reading about.)

We are also making much progress in bringing modernization to, for example, Ganze Autonomous Prefecture and to your hometown. (Again, here he gave a lot of statistics that he clearly loved about electricity, communication, etc.)

**LGG:** Thank you for sharing with me this detailed information about economic and other development efforts that your government is making in Tibet. I am aware of those figures, as I have read them. I believe that this is exactly what a government should provide for its citizenry. But you will agree that alone it will not help and satisfy the Tibetan people. To win the Tibetans' love, these efforts must be accompanied by a solution which will make it possible for the Tibetan people to be reunited with their leader. Economic and other incentives alone will not resolve the problem. How much of these efforts will really benefit the Tibetan people is also questionable. Again, however, I do not want to address the specifics of these programs because of a lack of time and because I believe we should address such details at a later date. Let me simply say that in principle, any effort made to advance the livelihood of the Tibetan people in any aspect is most welcome.

**ZHU:** You should understand that the United Front is the principal department responsible for dealing with this issue and that everything that is happening on this issue ultimately comes to us and we are aware of all the moves and efforts that you make. (This, of course, was his way of expressing disapproval and displeasure of our earlier dealings with people designated by President Jiang, as well as a kind of warning that in the future that we should only deal with them.)

**LGG:** I know that the United Front is the principal agency dealing with such issues. As far as I am concerned, I am prepared to deal with any individual or agency that is designated by the Chinese Government for this purpose. I am now happy that we have met, even though it is in a personal and informal manner and I look forward to working with you and your agency. The understanding that I have of your agency, which is also clearly indicated by its title, United Front, is that it is appropriate for it to lead the effort to bring closer relations between His Holiness and the Chinese leadership, and not to do the opposite. If working together we can bring His Holiness the Dalai Lama and some of your key leaders together in the same room like you and I sit here today, then I will say that the United Front has certainly done its job of creating a united front.

I believe with all sincerity that if we work hard and somehow make it possible for a personal meeting between His Holiness the Dalai Lama and President Jiang or any other Chinese leader, a solution to this problem can be found.

I would like to emphasize the importance of recognizing His Holiness not as the problem but as the solution. It is critical that a solution to Tibet be found during his lifetime, because he is the only person who can not only bring about a lasting solution but also give legitimacy to whatever conclusion is reached.

Kindly convey my personal appreciation to Minister Wang for his gesture in inviting me to visit my hometown. As I mentioned in my communication to him, even though it was inconvenient for me to make the visit at this time, if such a visit serves the purpose of starting the process and if that is precisely and explicitly the reason for such a visit, then I am obligated to give it the most serious consideration.

We must stay in touch, and I hope it will not be too much of a delay before some real meetings can take place.

In addition to the foregoing, several other topics came up. At one point Zhu Xiaoming talked about the need to create the right environment for dialogue. As a negative example, he cited the embarrassment to the PRC leadership when senior officials on international visits are besieged by public demonstrations and protests by Tibetans and friends of Tibet. He said that he had heard there might even be protests at the Winter Olympics in Salt Lake City. I responded:

I am aware that your leaders strongly resent demonstrations against them and they find it personally embarrassing to be confronted by protestors. In fact, when I was in Beijing in the early 1980s the Panchen Lama advised us to refrain from public demonstrations. He told us that such actions are not appreciated or understood by the Chinese leaders and they are taken very personally. I understand this sentiment in your leaders because in your kind of political system such expressions of protest are not tolerated. But in the free world, expressing one's views through public demonstrations is a common occurrence. Thus, Presidents, Prime Ministers and other important political leaders not only tolerate these activities but accept them as a part of the freedom of expression inherent in a democratic society.

You must also understand that demonstrations are not directed or organized exclusively by the Tibetan leadership in exile but are rather spontaneous expressions of support by Tibetans and friends of Tibetans. As I said earlier, we are fully aware that this does cause embarrassment and that it is

> taken personally by the Chinese leadership. We would therefore like to try, if possible, to encourage Tibetans and Tibetan friends to refrain from such activities. But this can only happen if and when there is some visible movement toward a sincere dialogue.
>
> I certainly agree with you that we all have to make an effort to create the proper environment for a dialogue. I therefore again encourage your leadership to resume a formal dialogue so that it will give His Holiness and other Tibetan leaders room to encourage our friends and supporters to stop engaging in public demonstrations. It is important to remember, however, that even under such circumstances there will still be some who will continue to demonstrate, given the fact that there is a segment of the population which opposes His Holiness the Dalai Lama's Middle Way Approach.

At another point, Zhu Xiaoming raised Arjia Rinpoche's name, asking if he had gone to India. I took the opportunity to explain that Arjia had gone on a pilgrimage and would visit Sera Monastery.

> Aja [*sic*] Rinpoche chose this time to visit India because he wanted to have the opportunity to receive teachings by His Holiness the Dalai Lama both in South India as well as at Bodh Gaya. As you are aware, Aja Rinpoche has made no political statements criticizing the Chinese government other than a candid statement about his opposition to the Chinese government's selection of the Panchen Lama and his concerns regarding the overall restrictions and limitations on religious freedom. We have also encouraged Aja Rinpoche to maintain contact with concerned people in your government. We have done this to give a clear indication that we do not intend to take advantage of situations such as his to our political benefit.

Ngawang Choephel's[12] release also came up. While Zhu Xiaoming did not try to portray it as a major step forward, he obviously wanted it to be recognized and appreciated. I told him that of course, we were pleased with his release. I had in fact sent representatives to receive him on his arrival in Detroit, and I personally met him when he arrived in D.C. I then jokingly said that while I was pleased that at least one Tibetan had been freed, I actually believed that it was a case of mistaken identity, that the man released was another who happened to share the "real" Ngawang Choephel's name.

Our discussion about Ngawang Choephel came toward the end of our conversation, after Zhu Xiaoming lectured me on why Beijing would not tolerate any interference from the outside world, clearly meaning the United States. I told him that while he had given me much advice about not seeking support from the "outside world," I felt that the release of Ngawang Choephel, as well as its timing, was orchestrated more to please the United States, in particular President George W. Bush, than to send a positive message to the Tibetans. However, I did express my hope that this would not be an isolated case but rather the beginning of a trend. Moreover, if it were followed by the release of other political prisoners, particularly those who have spent decades in prison, it would definitely be seen as a positive gesture that we, in turn, would publicly acknowledge. As I explicitly mentioned to the Kalon Tripa over the telephone when I was discussing the meeting, Zhu Xiaoming's response indicated that further releases were a possibility.

Another important matter that I mentioned toward the end of our meeting was that I was in the process of preparing a comprehensive memo on the Tibet issue that I would forward him when it was completed. I wanted to expressly mention this ongoing project to avoid being accused of being "insincere and manipulative" during our meeting for failure to inform them about my contemporaneous activities. As I discussed with the Kalon Tripa, one of my main concerns prior to the meeting was that unless our counterparts were aware of my ongoing work, they might try to preempt me in issuing their own statement first. I therefore said:

> I am very pleased that we have had the opportunity to meet face to face, although informally. I would like to emphasize that I feel no loss of pride in strongly urging, even pleading with the Chinese leaders to take advantage of working with His Holiness, who has such a consistent and forward-looking approach. We must meet and start a dialogue so that we can come to a negotiated conclusion. As His Holiness has said many times, a negotiated solution will make a strong contribution to the unity and prosperity of the PRC.
>
> Since I have this most important task of pursuing the dialogue, I have, in consultation with my colleague Kelsang Gyaltsen, been preparing a detailed memo where we try to share with the Chinese government some of our thoughts. Meeting with you today and having the opportunity to talk with you for a few hours has given me some encouragement. But it has also made me realize more than ever before how important it is for me to finish up this memo and without too much delay submit it to your government. I want to

> caution you that there will be some views contained in this memo which you may not like, but since we are here, meeting in person, I want to assure you that these views are being stated with the sincerest motivation. And, while we must be forward-looking, we must also acknowledge certain realities because to ignore them would be to perpetuate a deception.

Zhu responded that he understood and that he very much looked forward to receiving the memo. I am pleased that he said this, because when we do eventually send the communication, they will have been forewarned and will hopefully see it as a genuine effort to communicate.

I thought it interesting that Zhu Xiaoming did not mince words regarding the PRC's strong resentment of the United States. Even in his opening remarks, he cautioned me to avoid becoming a pawn in the effort of some countries to block the PRC's development into a global power. He talked in the usual Chinese way of how the PRC was progressing and becoming respected throughout the world, but said that its success in this regard had made some countries uncomfortable, driving them to try to do everything possible to create obstacles. In this discussion it was very clear that he was singling out the United States. I heard him say "Meiguo," which is the Chinese word for the United States, although the translator said "certain countries." At one point, he in fact turned toward his translator and explicitly told him to say "America."

In response to his accusation that His Holiness and the Tibetan leadership were collaborating with anti-PRC forces, I told him that this was simply not true. I used the example of Falun Gong, where we had made a conscious decision to keep a distance. I also pointed out that His Holiness and the Tibetan leadership did not oppose the PRC's receipt of "Most Favored Nation" status, that His Holiness had further issued a number of statements supporting the PRC's admittance to the WTO, and finally that he had recognized the PRC's legitimacy in hosting the Olympics.[13] I did point out, however, that it would be our moral responsibility to take a public position on any matters that were Tibet-related.

I also told him that contrary to becoming a "pawn" in anyone's effort to stop the PRC's advancement, His Holiness believes each nation has a right to aspire to greatness. He views the PRC as a nation with a beautiful, ancient civilization, home to almost a quarter of the world's population. It would therefore be immoral for anyone to try to block the country's global ascendance. I did qualify these remarks, however, noting that it takes more than size or wealth to make a country into a global power.

I continue to be amazed at how chauvinistic the Chinese can be. Somewhere toward the end of our meeting, in a very sincere manner, Zhu Xiaoming had the audacity to compare my work to that of Ngapo Ngawang Jigme, who, as previously noted, was the governor of eastern Tibet at the time of the Chinese invasion and subsequently represented the Lhasa government in the events leading to the Seventeen-Point Agreement. As if he were paying me a compliment, he said that if I were to make a serious and sincere effort to resolve the issue, the nation (meaning the PRC) would greatly honor me and respect my effort. He then said: "Look at how the Chinese people and the government respect and honor Ngapo Ngawang Jigme for his dedication to the interests of national unity."

I really couldn't help but be a little sarcastic in my response:

> I know Ngapo and I personally respect him. Nevertheless, to be very candid, I find our contributions to be totally incompatible. First of all, Ngapo did not have a choice about the role that he was compelled to play. He happened to be the Governor and commanding officer of the army in Chamdo when the PLA entered Tibet. This led him to take some unavoidable actions. I, on the other hand, have the complete choice as to whether or not I play any role in this effort. And, like I said at the beginning of our meeting, I am playing this role at the moment because of my devotion to my leader and love for my people.
>
> (I then said laughingly) I do hope that the end result of my efforts at the direction of His Holiness will differ and be more meaningful than the ones that Ngapo achieved in 1951. The fact of the matter is that the issues he dealt with remain unresolved after so many decades, and this clearly demonstrates that the solution reached at the time was not satisfactory to the Tibetan people. Please don't think I am responding arrogantly to your compliment. I know you meant well, and as I said earlier, I hold Ngapo in high regard and I think he cares about the well-being of his people.

This represents the bulk of our conversation. Even though Taiwan was mentioned as an important issue by him, I deliberately declined to address it. While my notes may not be in chronological order, they accurately relate the essence of our meeting. Nothing substantive has been omitted. I am also confident that I was able to convey all of the messages that I had wanted to relay.

I would also like to acknowledge Zhu Xiaoming's mostly positive demeanor during our meeting. His words, as well as his body language, were cordial, almost respectful. At one point he asked whether I would consent to have my photo taken with him. I agreed, and his staff then asked if they could be included. The only time he spoke with what initially seemed to me to be a degree of arrogance was when he discussed the Harvard conference that was originally slated to be the venue for our initial contact. He was "surprised" at the lack of understanding and performance of the scholars, clearly meaning the Tibetan participants. His reaction was so extreme that it was clear to me that he was not simply being arrogant. It seems that in the isolated political circles of Beijing, the policy makers addressing the Tibet issue have come to believe their own propaganda. When they are confronted with positions that differ from the official line, they immediately assume these views are incorrect.

The only moment that Zhu Xiaoming showed some real displeasure or discomfort was when I was responding to his comparison of me to Ngapo Ngawang Jigme. I don't know if he felt embarrassed for making an analogy that didn't sit well with me or viewed my response as arrogant or unappreciative. The only other "testiness" I noted was his strong insistence that our meeting be kept highly confidential and that it be characterized as nothing more than "personal and informal."

I was, in fact, pleased to see a marked change in both the style and the behavior of the United Front representatives from my last encounter with them in 1984. Zhu Xiaoming did not modify or disguise his views; his words were at times harsh and sometimes critical, but he was a good listener. We also had good chemistry, and our conversations, while quite frank and even blunt at times, were also very constructive. He did take pains, however, to warn us not to try to bypass the United Front in the future. Reiterating that the United Front was the principal department responsible for the Tibet issue, he sternly reminded me that any activity on this issue would ultimately come to the department's attention and that he was fully aware of all our past efforts that had not involved the United Front. This message I took to heart.

In September 2002, when we went to Beijing for the First Round of dialogue, Zhu Xiaoming was one of the senior officials assisting United Front Minister Wang Zhaoguo. Having become "old friends" with Zhu Xiaoming as a result of our January meeting in Ottawa, I was received very cordially. I have found that with the Chinese, if you have met someone before, you will receive this welcoming treatment during later encounters, provided they want to confer that honor upon you. I had the clear impression that during this First Round of dialogue, Zhu Xiaoming was being quite proactive, stepping in to clarify or explain certain points that, in the main, bolstered our position.

## SUCCESSFUL RENEWAL OF DIRECT CONTACTS

After the Ottawa meeting, United Front officials began communicating with me directly as well as sending messages via other channels, including through senior US officials. There were clear indications that Beijing was preparing to restart dialogue with us. The Tibetan leadership also began a series of internal discussions, with His Holiness actively participating and guiding the deliberations. With Samdhong Rinpoche becoming the first directly elected Kalon Tripa, or Chair of the Kashag, we at last had strong leadership in Dharamsala. Beginning when he was Chair of the Assembly of Tibetan People's Deputies (ATPD), Samdhong Rinpoche has been one of the key leaders involved with His Holiness's efforts to reengage Beijing. Before he assumed the Kalon Tripa role, I remember more than one occasion when I sought His Holiness's permission to brief the Kashag Chair and other concerned ministers on an issue, and His Holiness expressly said: "Yes, of course, but make sure you also brief and consult Samdhong Rinpoche."

Samdhong Rinpoche assumed full responsibility for communicating the results of our dialogue with Beijing to His Holiness. I decided to refrain from continuing to directly brief His Holiness as I had in the past, respecting his wish to empower the elected leadership, especially the Kalon Tripa. For his part, Samdhong Rinpoche always included me and Kelsang Gyaltsen in all the relevant discussions. In addition, the two of us also accompanied him to every important briefing and discussion on the matter with His Holiness.

Even though Beijing both publicly and privately strongly criticized any third-party involvement on the Tibet issue, we realized that a major factor in our success in reengaging the Chinese was the interest shown by the international community, especially the United States. With the possibility of direct talks resuming, we started briefing the US administration as well as other previously involved European governments. Of course, we also kept New Delhi fully informed. During my visits to India, I accompanied Samdhong Rinpoche in his briefings of important Indian officials such as the National Security Advisors and Foreign Secretaries. Even though Beijing chastised us for involving outsiders, senior PRC leaders and diplomats were also beginning to convey to other governments their willingness to engage in talks with us.

With the possibility of direct talks on the horizon, His Holiness and the Kalon Tripa felt that we must convey to President Jiang a clear picture of what we hoped to achieve by direct engagement. By then we knew that the President was once again taking a personal interest in the issue. However, while we were on the verge of restarting talks, we were worried that we might fall into a trap with the United Front taking full control of the agenda. Under Kalon Tripa Samdhong Rinpoche's direct supervision, we formulated a step-by-step approach through which a mutually beneficial solution could be reached between His Holiness and Beijing.

I discussed the possibility of the US administration helping convey this proposal to the PRC government ahead of our actual talks, but we came to the conclusion that direct US involvement at this juncture would do more harm than good. Senior White House officials were very helpful, however, in encouraging the Norwegians to act as the intermediary conveying our proposal to Beijing. I have no doubt that they must have quietly discussed their possible participation with PRC officials before deciding to help us. As previously discussed, on April 18, 2002, the Norwegian Ambassador in Beijing hand delivered a memorandum signed by Kelsang Gyaltsen and myself to Chinese officials for onward transmittal to President Jiang.[14] I also made sure that the United Front and other important people in Beijing were aware of this communication ahead of time to avoid any embarrassment or risk of precipitating yet another situation where the United Front might think we were trying to bypass it.

Once again, I am taking the liberty of sharing the full text of our proposal, as it lays out the framework of our vision for resolving the Tibet issue.

Your Excellency–

As Your Excellency is aware, His Holiness the Dalai Lama has designated us as his emissaries for contacts with your government. It is in this capacity that we write directly to Your Excellency. We write to call Your Excellency's attention to this matter and to the fact that time is running out for both the sides, time for finding a solution to the Tibetan issue that is mutually-beneficial as well as satisfactory to the Tibetan people. We write also to frankly state the problems that are being faced by the Tibetan people. Our aim is to enable Your Excellency to understand the ground reality and, thus, facilitate the creation of a viable basis for dialogue.

It is quite possible that, in the past, some of us working closely with His Holiness the Dalai Lama were unable to comprehend some of the Chinese central government's initiatives, such as the invitation to His Holiness to attend the memorial service for the late Panchen Lama, thus failing to respond positively to them. We believe the same may be true of the analysis done of our initiatives by your government. This may have led to the loss of opportunities for dispelling misperceptions and for understanding each other better.

We, on our part, wish to prevent such mistakes in the future. Should Your Excellency be able to resolve the problem of Tibet, it will undoubtedly win you great respect and admiration from the Tibetans, Chinese and the international community.

The problem of Tibet has remained unresolved for over 50 years. Right from the beginning of this conflict, His Holiness the Dalai Lama has sought a peaceful resolution through dialogue and negotiations. It is in this spirit that His Holiness, despite strong urgings from various groups, chose not to go into exile when the PLA marched into Tibet in 1949/1950. Instead, he returned from Dromo to Lhasa in 1951 with the aim of seeking peaceful co-existence. In 1954 he traveled to Beijing for face-to-face meetings with Chinese leaders. In 1956, when he was on a visit to India, he chose to return to Tibet despite strong requests against this from Tibetan officials and many other quarters. From 1950 to 1959, His Holiness made every possible effort to achieve peaceful co-existence with the Chinese central government.

However, in the course of the second half of the 1950s the policies of the Chinese government leadership swung toward ultra-leftism, bringing about turmoil and waves of purges throughout the People's Republic of China. In Tibet, too, the situation became increasingly critical, compelling Tibetans to rise up against the Chinese authorities. In 1959, when the situation became completely unmanageable, His Holiness went into exile in India. From 1979—when China emerged from the Cultural Revolution—to now, His Holiness has left no stone unturned to reach out to the Chinese leadership. When Mr. Deng Xiaoping signalled willingness for contacts, His Holiness responded immediately by sending his emissary to Beijing. His Holiness wrote personally to Mr. Deng, commending the policy of "opening" and "seeking truth from facts." Since then, His Holiness has undertaken a series of initiatives to establish dialogue with the Chinese leadership. He sent delegations for exploratory talks in Beijing and fact-finding delegations to tour Tibet. On a number of occasions, His Holiness addressed the Chinese leadership directly and personally in writing, outlining in detail his thinking on the issue of Tibet and urging for the resolution of the issue through dialogue. His Holiness used both formal and informal channels to reach out to the Chinese leadership. He used the offices of governments and private individuals to communicate with the Chinese government. His Holiness proposed meetings with Chinese leaders, either during his foreign visits or on a visit to Tibet when senior Chinese leaders could accompany him. He also expressed his desire to make a pilgrimage to some sacred Buddhist sites in China, which would provide him with an opportunity to meet senior Chinese leaders.

1. It is in the interest of the People's Republic of China's fraternal nationalities, particularly of the Tibetan and Chinese people, to resolve the Tibetan problem through negotiations.

The current situation in Tibet benefits neither the Tibetans, nor the government of the People's Republic of China. Tibetan religion, culture and way of life are under threat of extinction. The way to avoid this situation is for the central leadership and local officials in Tibet to change their policies and practices in line with the stated aims of the People's Republic of China's constitution and as per the stated desires of successive leaders, who visited Tibet, to respect and encourage the development of Tibet's precious national heritage. If this is not done, the resentment of the Tibetan people, which has remained unabated since the 1950's, and the mutual hostility that is growing between the Tibetan and Chinese peoples in Tibet hamper the realization of unity, stability and harmony between nationalities which are your government's fundamental principles.

The present policies have had devastating effects on the Tibetan people's distinct identity. Lhasa, the heart of the Tibetan civilization, has now been turned into just another ordinary Chinese city. Even fundamental attributes of our culture, such as the Tibetan language, are at great risk.

Although there have been some positive infrastructure and economic developments in Tibet in recent decades, appalling poverty continues to be the feature of rural and nomadic areas, where the vast majority of Tibetans live. His Holiness the Dalai Lama has made it very clear that Tibetans want and need development and that the Chinese government can certainly help in this respect. However, development will become meaningful and beneficial to the Tibetan people only if it is planned and implemented in such a way that it does not damage the culture and environment of Tibet, and if it does not serve to marginalize the Tibetan people further. If there were a true and genuine partnership between the Tibetans and Chinese in the development of Tibet, the Tibetan people would be able to realize their maximum potential, thus relieving the Chinese government of the current drain on its resources.

As you are aware, an increasing number of prominent Chinese, including party members, officials and intellectuals, have been voicing the need for a resolution of the Tibetan problem that too, through dialogue with His Holiness the Dalai Lama. Recently, a Chinese scholar has written a publicly distributed article to this effect. These Chinese people recognize His Holiness as the "key to the solution of the Tibetan problem;" they do not see him as a problem.

The resolution of the Tibetan problem would contribute greatly to the peace and stability in Asia, including improved relations between Asia's leading powers, China and India. There seems to be a suspicion that His Holiness the Dalai Lama and the government of India are in collusion to engage in activities to bring instability in Tibet. On the contrary, His Holiness' wish is to resolve the problem of Tibet, thus facilitating harmonious relationship between China and India, two leading powers.

On the global level, China is a huge country with enormous economic and military power. However, the Chinese government's policies in Tibet are damaging her image, thus undermining her efforts to assume a leadership role in the international community.

2. His Holiness' middle way approach envisages genuine autonomy, not independence, for the Tibetan people.

There is no insurmountable major difference between His Holiness' vision and that of the Chinese government concerning Tibet's future situation. His Holiness has formulated his proposal well within the framework set by Mr. Deng Xiaoping in 1979, when he stated that anything other than independence could be discussed and resolved. In acceptance of Mr. Deng Xiaoping's offer, His Holiness has stated both in public and in private communications to Your Excellency that he is not seeking separation of Tibet from the People's Republic of China, or Tibet's independence. He is calling for genuine autonomy for Tibet within the framework of the People's Republic of China.

As recent as in his annual statement on the anniversary of the Tibetan national uprising on March 10, 2002, His Holiness said, "My position on the issue of Tibet is straightforward. I am not seeking independence. As I have said many times before, what I am seeking is for the Tibetan people to be given the opportunity to have genuine self-rule in order to preserve their civilisation and for the unique Tibetan culture, religion, language and way of life to grow and thrive."

Under the constitution and laws of the People's Republic of China, Tibetans in the Tibet Autonomous Region and the Tibetan Autonomous Prefectures and Counties are entitled to enjoy autonomy. However, the reality is not like that. Tibetans do not have the opportunity to run their own affairs and are consequently not able to protect and develop their own culture and way of life. This is precisely the reason why His Holiness is calling for real, genuine autonomy. The Chinese government has accepted that Tibet's situation is unique and not comparable to any other autonomous region or province. This was evident from the 17-point Agreement signed in 1951. It is significant that Tibet is the only region with which such an agreement was concluded.

3. His Holiness' plan for Tibet's future includes all the Tibetan people.

When His Holiness the Dalai Lama formulated the Strasbourg Proposal, he made a bold and courageous decision of not seeking the restoration of Tibetan independence. In it, instead of seeking independence, His Holiness chose to look to the future and presented a solution that would help preserve Tibet's distinct national and cultural identity within the People's Republic of China. His Holiness reached on this decision as he believes that this arrangement is the most effective way to ensure the survival of Tibet's culture. This is not only of great benefit to the Tibetan people, but also to the Chinese people and the rest of the world. This solution, however, can become practical only if all the Tibetans are included in it and have the opportunity to participate in its implementation and contribute to it.

Of the roughly six million Tibetans, who share the same national and cultural identity, only 2.4 million reside in the Tibetan Autonomous Region (TAR). The majority live in Tibetan areas outside of the TAR. We believe all the Tibetan-inhabited areas are equally important to the survival of the Tibetan way of life. His Holiness has often used an analogy of the human body: just as a person cannot thrive without his/her limbs, torso and head, the Tibetan culture too cannot survive if the Tibetan areas remain separated.

On a pragmatic level, it would be useless to envision a solution that did not take into account all Tibetans as one entity. In fact, some political analysts believe that the Tibetan uprisings in 1956–1959 were on account of the exclusion of Amdo and the Kham area to the east of Drichu river from the terms of the 17-point

Agreement. If a solution is found which did not meet the aspirations of the entire Tibetan people, it will not be a lasting one.

In practice, the Chinese government recognizes that Tibet consists of more than just the TAR and that all Tibetans should be granted autonomy. This is evident from the fact that almost all Tibetan areas outside the TAR are designated as ten Tibetan Autonomous Prefectures and two Tibetan Autonomous Counties. Tibetans, who hold important positions in the party and government of the People's Republic of China, share the desire to see all Tibetan areas unified.

In 1951, when Tibetan representatives expressed the need for all Tibetan areas to be under one administrative jurisdiction at the time of the signing of the 17-point Agreement, Prime Minister Zhou Enlai recognized the legitimacy of the Tibetan wish. In 1952, when a delegation from Chamdo proposed a single autonomous region to include all the Tibetan people and areas, the Chinese leaders stated that this idea would be considered later when the conditions were right. Similarly, Vice-Premier Chen Yi, who headed the central government delegation to the inauguration of the TAR Preparatory Committee in April 1956, said that it would be logical to merge all Tibetan-inhabited areas as one entity. And, this has a precedent. The Chinese government has reunified all the Mongolian areas into the inner Mongolian autonomous region. A similar step was taken to unite all Hui people under the Ningxia-Hui autonomous region. These were wise and just decisions. The same wisdom and pragmatism should be applied in the case of Tibet.

His Holiness wants to approach the issue of administrative boundaries pragmatically and on the basis of democratic principles. He is not concerned about the historical or legalistic issues. What he is seeking is an administrative structure that will enable all Tibetans to live together under the same rules, enjoying the same protection. This situation needs to be created through a mutually agreed upon process.

4. His Holiness wants to empower the Tibetan people inside Tibet, not revive the old society there.

Some people have attempted to mislead others into believing that His Holiness wants to reinstall the old Tibetan government in Tibet. This is not at all true. His Holiness has made it very clear that he seeks no future political role for himself, nor for the government-in-exile once an agreement is negotiated and implemented. He has emphasized that Tibet belongs to Tibetans, and especially to those who are in Tibet. One need only look at the remarkable democratic system that has been set up in exile under His Holiness' direction to see if he is seeking to revive the old system.

As a matter of fact, some Chinese leaders, in light of His Holiness' decision not to assume a political role in future Tibet, are said to be asking the question as to how the Tibetan people would honor a negotiated settlement with the People's Republic of China government. We can see that this is a reasonable concern. Nevertheless, we must not forget that while His Holiness seeks no political role for himself, he has unambiguously stated that he will use his historical and moral authority "to persuade the Tibetans to accept and abide by the agreement that we will have reached." This is of critical importance since he is the only person who has the ability and moral stature to persuade all elements of Tibetan society to accept a solution that is short of independence. In addition, His Holiness' commitment to fostering cordial relations between the Tibetan and Chinese peoples will greatly facilitate the necessary healing between the two sides. And, it is His Holiness' belief that he will be better able to accomplish this goal if unfettered by the political office.

5. His Holiness is the key to ensuring the Tibetan people's acceptance of a negotiated settlement.

His Holiness is the key to the solution of the Tibetan issue. A small section of people object to dialogues with His Holiness by reasoning that the Tibetan issue will die naturally when the Dalai Lama is no longer around. This is a completely mistaken view. As well as obstructing negotiations, this self-deceptive view continues to create problems for the Tibetan people and the People's Republic of China government.

His Holiness is the only person who could persuade Tibetans to accept an agreement that recognizes Tibet as part of the People's Republic of China. In the absence of His Holiness, it would be extremely difficult for China to ever legitimize its presence in Tibet in the eyes of Tibetans and the international community. It is a fact that the international public perception considers Tibet as a country that has been invaded and occupied by China. Although many governments recognize Tibet as part of China, they append a special qualifier to this statement. There is no denying that the People's Republic of China government faces a serious problem of legitimacy concerning its presence in Tibet. Some ill-informed people have argued that your government should stall negotiations until His Holiness passes away. This advice to "raise the banner of negotiations high, while working to stop the Dalai Lama's return" reflects a lack of foresight, courage and political vision. To be candid, policies such as this are the result of leftist adventurism—which still seems to have considerable influence on issues such as that of Tibet—hijacking the national interests of China. In fact, ultra-leftist policies still hold sway in Tibet despite the changes carried out by the Chinese government and party elsewhere.

The Chinese government must understand the depth of Tibetan resentment against ultra-leftist policies. Based on the past experiences, the Tibetans view ultra-leftist policies as extremely damaging to the preservation and promotion of the Tibetan culture and way of life. Even the third and fourth generations of Tibetans—those born under Chinese communist rule—resent and resist the policies of ultra-leftists. So far, His Holiness has exerted restraining influence on the Tibetan people. The majority of Tibetans support the nonviolent path of His Holiness, but they do so largely because of their reverence for His Holiness. Without His Holiness, it would be very difficult to maintain this moderate and peaceful approach in the long run.

The passing away of His Holiness in exile would only radicalize the Tibetan struggle, making it infinitely more difficult to achieve and implement a negotiated settlement. At such a time, the Chinese government will lose any hope of legitimizing its presence in Tibet, since it will be forever recorded in history that His Holiness has never accepted Tibet as being part of the People's Republic of China. Therefore, time is neither on the side of Tibetans, nor of the People's Republic of China government. Time is running out for both of us to reach a mutually acceptable solution.

On the other hand, a Chinese leader who is able to conclude a mutually beneficial agreement with His Holiness, thus facilitating his return, will have brought about a new and genuine measure of unity to the People's Republic of China. Such a leader will gain enormously in the esteem of the Tibetan and Chinese peoples, and of the international community as well.

The issue of Tibet has, indeed, been internationalized. Millions of people throughout the world feel deeply committed to the Tibetan cause as a matter of moral principle. They have persuaded their governments to act to promote a just and peaceful solution to the problem. They will welcome a positive response from your government to His Holiness' initiatives.

Chinese leaders have repeatedly expressed concerns that foreign powers are using the Tibetan issue against China. As a matter of fact, it is the unquestioned leadership of His Holiness that has prevented just that from happening. But if His Holiness is no longer around, the situation may very well change.

It is evident that His Holiness is the key to a peaceful resolution of the Tibetan problem, a solution that serves the interests of both China and the Tibetan people.

6. The return of His Holiness the Dalai Lama will be of enormous benefit in creating unity among the peoples of the People's Republic of China.

The Chinese leaders must understand that the bond between His Holiness and the Tibetan people is profound and unique. It is a bad mistake and futile to attempt to separate His Holiness from the people or to emotionally divide them. The bond between His Holiness and the Tibetan people stems from hundreds of years of history and is deeply rooted in the Tibetan culture and psyche. Attempts to disseminate wrong information about His Holiness' health or inflate the significance of fringe group activities in the Tibetan community are ill advised and do disservice to the Chinese government, revealing as it does, the lack of proper information and understanding by the Chinese leaders of the Tibetan people. These efforts also ignore the many and profound links that exist between Tibetans in and outside Tibet. One of the clearest examples of this lack of understanding is the perpetuation of the policy, which has existed for several years. Those who understand Tibetans know that such policies to denigrate His Holiness the Dalai Lama can only serve to further alienate the Tibetan people from the People's Republic of China government.

In the 1980s Mr. Deng Xiaoping and other senior officials of the People's Republic of China recognized the importance of His Holiness' return to Tibet. In keeping with this view, a senior Chinese central party official remarked that the return of His Holiness—or even one word from him—would do more for the promotion of unity among the nationalities in the People's Republic of China than years of slogans the government might raise. Needless to say that it is the wish of all Tibetans that His Holiness return to Tibet. But in order to make it possible, we need to have dialogues with representatives of the Chinese government and bring about positive changes in Tibet.

Since social stability is an important principle of the People's Republic of China, advice from His Holiness the Dalai Lama for unity among the peoples, such as between the Tibetans and Chinese, will be immensely effective, both for social stability and national security. This is because His Holiness commands tremendous respect from the people.

7. Now is the time to act by beginning a dialogue.

The issue of Tibet can be resolved if it is tackled with sincerity and in an atmosphere of mutual respect and trust from both the sides. As interlocutors designated by His Holiness, we would like to take this initiative to urge you to appoint your representatives to begin constructive dialogue with us. We are ready to discuss the issues seriously and with complete sincerity. As we have mentioned earlier, on many fundamental issues the gap between our positions are [sic] not insurmountable through dialogues. Presently, one of the biggest problems we face, in our view, is the lack of mutual trust.

You will recall that we had the opportunity to engage in informal discussions with some of your officials in 1997–1998. We had hope at the time, and felt (as we believe your designated people did too) that such face-to-face encounters could lead to a breakthrough. In fact, soon after your joint press conference with the visiting United States President Bill Clinton in 1998, His Holiness acknowledged publicly that he felt there had been real progress over the previous 18 months. Unfortunately, however, the contact that could have produced results came to an abrupt end.

On account of its complexity, efforts for resolving the Tibetan issue will require a delicate process, involving both quiet diplomacy and some very public initiatives. We believe that a face-to-face meeting between Your Excellency and His Holiness would make a breakthrough possible. We would propose and urge you to consider the following steps toward initiating the process of dialogue and negotiations:

1. Your Excellency immediately designates representatives to engage in dialogue on the Tibetan issue. We, on our part, will sincerely accept the representatives appointed by you.

2. Your representatives and we meet at the earliest convenience and initiate a frank and sincere dialogue.

3. Representatives of the two sides meet and His Holiness issues a statement, addressing the major concerns that the Chinese government has raised on Tibet. Your Excellency, too, issues a statement on meeting His Holiness and thereafter beginning a dialogue leading to a negotiated settlement of the Tibetan problem.

4. His Holiness meets Your Excellency in the context of his publicly known visit to certain holy places in China to start the process of dialogue.

5. Following the meeting between His Holiness and Your Excellency, the two sides start earnest negotiations in order to find a dependable solution to the problem of Tibet.

We, on our part, have discussed this kind of scenario in the past, and we believe it provides a balance between confidence-building gestures and substantive action.

We consider it a great honour to be of service to His Holiness as well as to the cause of unity between the Tibetan and Chinese peoples. We are personally committed to serving His Holiness to realize his mutually beneficial approach. Prof. Samdhong Rinpoche, Chairman (Kalon Tripa) of the Kashag, has given us full support to undertake this responsibility laid on us by His Holiness. You are no doubt aware that His Holiness has transferred a major portion of his responsibility to the elected Chairman of the Kashag as part of the ongoing democratic reforms he has initiated. The Kalon Tripa expressed his full support to the approach of His Holiness and to our designated roles, when he invited us for consultations as one of his first actions after he assumed office.

We trust that you will respond positively to this sincere and direct communication from us.

We are convinced that a settlement can be reached, which greatly benefits both the Tibetans and Chinese. We cannot change the past, but we have a choice to change the future.

We remain, Your Excellency,
Lodi Gyaltsen Gyari
Special Envoy of H.H. the Dalai Lama
Kelsang Gyaltsen
Envoy of H.H. the Dalai Lama

## LAST-MINUTE GLITCHES

As a result of these efforts, in mid-June I received a clear message from the United Front saying they were ready to receive our delegation for the start of formal dialogue. Preparations for the visit were at times quite stressful, but both sides worked very closely together making the necessary adjustments to accommodate each other's positions and situations. I was handling the logistics and other details directly with United Front representatives. I was also regularly in touch with Kalon Tripa Samdhong Rinpoche, sometimes speaking with him several times a day, as well as with His Holiness's Private Office. The Kalon Tripa and I discussed even the most minor details so that everything was done in a professional way. Because of the urgency of the situation, our consultations were by telephone, but I always followed up with written memos so there was a detailed account of our work.

Initially, I faced a very delicate and quite serious obstacle: Beijing was rejecting the participation of my colleague Kelsang Gyaltsen as part of the delegation, just as two years back it had rejected my appointment. Minister Wang Zhaoguo's concerns were based on some remarks Kelsang Gyaltsen had made in Europe that the Minister believed were not supportive of the Dalai Lama's position. Thus, his participation would be "counterproductive." As in the past, the United Front agreed that I could bring anyone else and further, that I could increase the size of my delegation over the suggested number.

I went out on a limb and decided to handle the matter myself without consulting either the Kalon Tripa or His Holiness. My reservation in referring the matter to Dharamsala was that I might be advised not to object to the United Front's demand, as restarting the dialogue was the paramount consideration, not the identity of the participating individuals. There was merit to that view, as I have previously expressed with respect to my own participation.

I immediately wrote to Minister Wang, politely but firmly insisting that Kelsang Gyaltsen be part of the team if we were to come for dialogue. In this July 1, 2002, note, I praised Kelsang Gyaltsen as "someone who is fully committed to the vision of His Holiness the Dalai Lama in finding a solution through dialogue. Rather than being a critical voice, Kelsang Gyaltsen has always spoken for a rational and proactive approach."

I spent two very stressful weeks fearing that my unilateral decision might have jeopardized the opportunity of reengaging with Beijing. With the matter languishing in limbo, I decided to reach out to President Jiang through a back channel, knowing that he was once again supportive of our efforts. To my relief, I soon received assurances through this informal avenue that President Jiang himself had suggested to the United Front Minister to be "accommodating." Within days I received a message directly from the department saying that it had agreed to my request, but that I should come first with two senior staff members as originally planned, with Kelsang Gyaltsen joining the group a few days later in Beijing for the actual talks. Some other United Front officials sent a separate message saying that I should agree to that condition to reduce embarrassment for Minister Wang, as quite recently he had even told Gyalo Thondup that the United Front would not accept Kelsang Gyaltsen's participation.

Because having Kelsang Gyaltsen included in the substantive dialogue was the most important result, agreeing to this minor delay would have been the proper gesture to satisfy the Minister. But, knowing that our visit had been approved by

President Jiang himself, I responded with the sincere request that Kelsang Gyaltsen participate from the beginning. I argued that it was important for him to accompany us on the scheduled tour preceding the start of our discussions to see the situation on the ground. He would also be very disappointed to miss seeing some of the Tibetan areas that we were supposed to visit.

When I reported to the Kalon Tripa how I had already responded to the United Front's objection to Kelsang Gyaltsen's participation, I was relieved at his approval of my actions. I realized that even if I had referred the matter to him in advance, he would have sanctioned my approach. Everything worked out well in the end, even though the United Front never sent a formal reply accepting my request but simply asked us to forward our travel documents and arrival information. Again, through our back channel, I was advised not to worry about not receiving explicit agreement to Kelsang Gyaltsen's early participation. The department's request for our travel information was its indirect acceptance, specifically designed to avoid further embarrassment to the United Front, which was once again having to retreat from its initial position. And that was exactly how it happened. Our delegation was finally able to leave for Beijing for our First Round of dialogue on September 9, 2002.

One normally thinks of negotiations as two groups of people actually sitting down together to sort out the issues. In reality, negotiations start way ahead of the actual talks. All the predialogue arrangements, including composition of the team, date and venue, and of course, the text of any press releases announcing the event are very much a part of the premeeting negotiations. The initial rejection of Kelsang Gyaltsen's participation, as well as the offer for me to make a personal visit to my hometown, could all have been part of Beijing's tactics designed to throw us off guard. It must be said that it is not only the Chinese who play such mind games.

While it is very important to be sincere and honest when one negotiates, it is equally important to take a firm position when necessary. If I had succumbed to the United Front's demand to exclude Kelsang Gyaltsen, it could have not only weakened my position as team leader but also harmed the status and authority of our delegation. Being firm with the United Front only inured to our benefit. We remained stalwart, and there were no negative repercussions. In fact, when we actually met him, Minister Wang was very welcoming of our team, including Kelsang Gyaltsen.

Although the parties had agreed to issue a press release announcing the visit, it took several weeks of back-and-forth negotiations before we were able to agree on mutually acceptable language. In the beginning, the Chinese were quite adamant that there shouldn't be any publicity at all about the visit. They strongly advised us not to leak even the possibility of such a trip being planned for the future, as even that distant option could lead to postponement or even cancellation of the pending visit. The advice through our back channel was similar; the first visit should happen without any publicity to help stabilize the relationship that had been under strain for such a long time.

I responded that, unlike in the PRC, we lived in a world where it would be impossible to keep the visit secret. Moreover, it was important for Beijing to publicly announce the meeting because it would generate a positive reaction in the international community, benefiting the PRC government. It took a long time, however, even to reach an agreement in principle calling for some kind of announcement. Finally the United Front came back with suggestions as to the wording of the statement. In short, their suggestion was to announce that Kelsang Gyaltsen and I were returning to visit relatives in our native areas. Our counterproposal described the delegation as being officially sent by His Holiness to start a dialogue with Beijing. Our suggestion was flatly rejected. We ultimately agreed on the following:

> Mr. Lodi Gyaltsen accompanied by Mr. Kelsang Gyaltsen along with two assistants are arriving today in Beijing.
>
> During the visit Mr. Lodi Gyaltsen Gyari and the team will also visit Lhasa. His Holiness the Dalai Lama is very pleased that the team is able to make such a visit.
>
> Mr. Lodi Gyaltsen Gyari is the Special Envoy of His Holiness the Dalai Lama and Mr. Kelsang Gyaltsen is the Envoy of His Holiness the Dalai Lama.

After each of the Nine Rounds of formal dialogue, the accompanying announcements gradually became less ambiguous and more detailed. This initial release spoke only about our having arrived in Beijing. The United Front insisted our departure be kept confidential, worried that contemporaneous media coverage could include comments or remarks that in their minds could harm the process. I think their concerns were based on domestic considerations. Having denounced

His Holiness vehemently, even describing him as a "wolf in monk's robe," it was difficult for them to admit that they were now receiving his envoys as government guests.

The first sentence mentioning Kelsang Gyaltsen and me by name was our counterparts' suggestion. They agreed to our proposed second paragraph, wherein His Holiness expresses his pleasure about our trip, to accommodate our need to indicate that the trip was made at his direction. The final paragraph, stating that Kelsang Gyaltsen and I were envoys of the Dalai Lama, was also formulated at our insistence. Moreover, it was like pulling teeth to get them to agree to mention our Lhasa visit. They wanted to keep the language vague, characterizing it only as "visiting our home places."

During our back-and-forth, I somewhat humorously told them that neither Kelsang Gyaltsen nor I was born in Lhasa or anywhere near there. But I must acknowledge that the possibility of visiting Lhasa offered by Beijing really took us by surprise. During our pretrip negotiations, we hadn't insisted on visiting any Tibetan areas. We were worried that they would only take us to the areas where Kelsang Gyaltsen and I were born to reinforce their public position that we were there solely to visit relatives. There is no doubt that arranging for us to visit Lhasa at the very beginning of the resumption of formal relations was an unequivocal message from the Chinese side of their seriousness and commitment to the process. Their openness provided the opportunity for us to suggest visiting other Tibetan areas during our subsequent visits.

While our initial work together on this press release looked as if it were doomed to failure, it was our first lesson showing that if we were persistent and skillful, common ground could be found. Samdhong Rinpoche, Kelsang Gyaltsen, and I spent days working on the terminology of this statement. During later rounds, together with Task Force members and the Task Force Secretariat,[15] we carefully drafted all future press statements as well as other documents. Of course, in their own media, Beijing described our visit as "private" and arranged to "see relatives." Sadly, some Tibetans opposed to the dialogue process took pleasure in quoting from the Chinese media in an attempt to diminish the importance of the event. As the release was prepared jointly, however, no PRC government officials or spokespersons even attempted to challenge or disown our statement. As the talks progressed, not only were we able to add more detail to our press releases, but also Beijing gradually moved from describing the visits as "private,"[16] to calling us people "with close ties to the Dalai Lama,"[17] and finally describing us as the Dalai Lama's "representative"[18] in their own official publications.

Our success in reengaging the PRC government was a major breakthrough, coming to fruition principally because of the wise guidance and leadership provided by His Holiness himself. I was also fortunate at this critical time to have the support of Kalon Tripa Samdhong Rinpoche, who not only made the dialogue process his highest priority but also provided solid backing to my team's efforts. And finally, I could not have had anyone better than Kelsang Gyaltsen as my colleague. His eminent reliability, in conjunction with his outspoken nature, perceptive insights, and analytical abilities, were of inestimable value throughout the dialogue process.

CHAPTER 19

# Formal Dialogue Begins

It has been my great honor and privilege to represent His Holiness the 14th Dalai Lama for nine rounds of formal talks with the PRC government—the most long-lasting and stable relationship that both sides have acknowledged. As I discussed in the preceding pages, it took years of effort on our part, with the tireless assistance of many others, to achieve this milestone. While it may appear that the dialogue happened solely because of international attention and persistent efforts by His Holiness and the Tibetan leadership, that is not entirely correct. I must also acknowledge and give credit to the PRC leadership, because in the absence of its willingness to participate, the talks never would have happened. While for many years, some senior leaders, and other concerned officials were aware of the importance of resolving the Tibet issue for the PRC's own benefit and made efforts to move forward, ultimately they failed, falling victim to the opposition of hard-liners holding a very conservative approach. International and domestic events confronting Beijing, and even some of our own actions and inaction, also contributed to weakening the efforts of these proactive and pragmatic leaders.

The 1989 Tiananmen Square demonstrations are one example of events that hindered any rapprochement from Beijing's side. I have the greatest admiration for those courageous individuals who participated in the demonstrations. Many of them forfeited their lives for their beliefs. Sadly, I believe that Tiananmen set the clock back for decades for the PRC to move toward a more liberal society. Combined with the contemporaneous breakdown of the former Soviet Union, Tiananmen terrified Deng Xiaoping. He was convinced the PRC would be the next to disintegrate unless political liberalization was curtailed. From then on, he single-mindedly moved aggressively to promote economic liberalization while restricting political modernization equally forcefully.

I am not contending that absent these events Deng Xiaoping would have transformed the PRC into a fully democratic society or that we would have been able to resolve our differences overnight. What I am saying is that any political matter, including the Tibet issue, cannot be examined in isolation; the impact of contemporaneous events must be considered. In this case, without the events at Tiananmen Square, I believe Deng Xiaoping likely would have moved the PRC toward a political system similar to that then existing in South Korea, Singapore, and even Taiwan. The gradual transformation that was happening in Taiwan didn't go unnoticed in Beijing. Whether this would have been enough to further Tibet's interests, we'll never know for certain, but it is clear that these identified, challenging externalities definitely hampered our efforts.

Before addressing the specifics of the nine rounds of dialogue, I would like to share some information about the logistics of the talks, including the composition of the negotiating teams, the chosen venues, areas we visited and people we met, as well as the structure and format of the formal sessions (see table 19.1).

## THE TIBETAN NEGOTIATING TEAM: IMPLEMENTING THE "ONE CHANNEL, ONE AGENDA" POLICY

As the relationship with Beijing was of the highest priority, His Holiness himself provided overall leadership for the dialogue process. Every major decision was made either at his direction or with his approval. His Holiness's wisdom and farsightedness were the major factors inspiring this endeavor.

We were also very fortunate to have Kalon Tripa Samdhong Rinpoche as the team's leader in Dharamsala. His intellect, combined with his "no-nonsense" approach and calm personality, provided stability and much-needed confidence. With him in charge, the delegates could concentrate on the task at hand without worrying about internal Dharamsala politics. Samdhong Rinpoche stood solidly behind our efforts. He made it known to everyone that there was but "one channel and one agenda" in our dialogue with the PRC: "The approved channel is the one being pursued by Special Envoy Gyari Lodi Gyaltsen and Envoy Kelsang Gyaltsen and the approved agenda is seeking genuine autonomy for the Tibetan people." This clearly articulated and resolute position left no room for speculation or rumors within the Tibetan community, as had occurred too frequently in the past, nor any ability of Beijing to say it didn't know who

TABLE 19.1 Logistics of the Nine Rounds of Talks between the envoys of His Holiness the Dalai Lama and PRC representatives from 2002 to 2010

| Rounds of Talks | Date | Tibetan delegation | Chinese delegation | Other dignitaries met | Meeting venue/places visited |
|---|---|---|---|---|---|
| 1st Round | September 9–24, 2002 | 1. Special Envoy Kasur Lodi G. Gyari<br>2. Envoy Kelsang Gyaltsen<br>3. Sonam N. Dagpo, Additional Secretary, DIIR<br>4. Bhuchung K. Tsering, Task Force Member | 1. Wang Zhaoguo, Vice Chair of the CPPCC and Minister of the UFWD<br>2. Li De Zhu, Minister of Nationalities Affairs and Vice Minister of the UFWD<br>3. Zhu Xiaoming, Deputy Secretary-General of the UFWD<br>4. Chang Rongjun, Director of the 2nd Bureau<br>5. Mrs. Be Hua, Deputy Director of the 2nd Bureau<br>6. Wangdu, Deputy Director of the Bureau (interpreter)<br>7. Sithar, Deputy Director of the Bureau | 1. Ngapo Ngawang Jigme, Vice Chair of the CPPCC<br>2. Ragdi, Chair of the TAR People's Congress<br>3. Legchok, Governor of the TAR<br>4. Samdup, Head of the TAR United Front<br>5. Atrin, Vice Chair of the Sichuan People's Political and Consultative Conference | **Beijing**<br>**Places visited:** Chengdu, Shanghai, Lhasa (Jokhang, Potala Palace, Norbulingka, and Gaden Monastery), Kongpo, Shigatse (Tashi Lhunpo) |
| 2nd Round | May 25 to June 8, 2003 | 1. Special Envoy Kasur Lodi G. Gyari<br>2. Envoy Kelsang Gyaltsen<br>3. Sonam N. Dagpo, Additional Secretary, DIIR<br>4. Bhuchung K. Tsering, Task Force Member | 1. Liu Yandong, Vice Chair of the CPPCC and Minister of the UFWD<br>2. Zhu Weiqun, Vice Minister of the UFWD<br>3. Chang Rongjun, Deputy Secretary-General of the UFWD<br>4. Sithar, Director of the Bureau (interpreter) | 1. Master Yicheng, Head of the Chinese Buddhist Association (CBA)<br>2. Master Shi Jia Jie Ren, Deputy Head of the CBA<br>3. Jampa Gyaltsen, Vice Chair of the Yunnan People's Congress<br>4. Kelsang Dhondup, Director of the Yunnan Ethnic Affairs Commission<br>5. Nima Tsering, Deputy Director of the Yunnan Ethnic Affairs Commission<br>6. Latse Dala, Head of the Dechen Tibetan Autonomous Prefecture Government<br>7. Tashi Topgyal, Deputy Secretary of Dechen CCP (Chinese Communist Party)<br>8. Trongye Tsering, Head of the Dechen United Front | **Beijing**<br>**Places visited:** Shanghai, Jiangsu, Zhejiang, Dechen Tibetan Autonomous Prefecture in Yunnan |

| | | | | | |
|---|---|---|---|---|---|
| 3rd Round | September 12–19, 2004 | 1. Special Envoy Kasur Lodi G. Gyari<br>2. Envoy Kelsang Gyaltsen<br>3. Sonam N. Dagpo, Secretary, DIIR<br>4. Bhuchung K. Tsering, Task Force Member | 1. Liu Yandong, Vice Chair of the CPPCC and Minister of the UFWD<br>2. Zhu Weiqun, Vice Minister of the UFWD<br>3. Chang Rongjun, Secretary-General of the UFWD<br>4. Sithar, Director of the Bureau (interpreter)<br>5. Yao Mao Chen, Deputy Director of the Bureau<br>6. Xu Zhitao<br>7. Passang Tsering<br>8. Lin Jian | 1. Ogyen Phuntsok, Vice Governor of Kardze<br>2. Tsebo, Deputy Secretary of CPC Kardze<br>3. Jampa Thinley, Staff of Kardze Religious Department<br>4. Gawu Yeshi Tsultrim, Chairman of Kardze People's Congress<br>5. Lobsang Choephel, Chairman of Kardze People's Political Consultative Conference<br>6. Khangsar Kyabgon<br>7. Lingtsang Sey<br>8. Getak Trulku | **Beijing**<br>**Places visited:** Guangdong, Shanghai, Hebei, Chengdu, Kardze Tibetan Autonomous Prefecture in Sichuan |
| 4th Round | June 30 to July 1, 2005 | 1. Special Envoy Kasur Lodi G. Gyari<br>2. Envoy Kelsang Gyaltsen<br>3. Sonam N. Dagpo, Secretary, DIIR<br>4. Ngapa Tsegyam, Representative of His Holiness, Taipei<br>5. Bhuchung K. Tsering, Task Force Member | 1. Zhu Weiqun, Executive Vice Minister of the UFWD<br>2. Sithar, Director of the 2nd Bureau (interpreter)<br>3. Xu Zhitao Juzhang, Secretary to Executive Vice Minister<br>4. Hua, Secretary to Executive Vice Minister<br>5. Zhu Huang Gang, Staff of Switzerland Chinese Embassy<br>6. Lin Jian | None | **Bern, Switzerland** (Embassy of the People's Republic of China) |
| 5th Round | February 15–23, 2006 | 1. Special Envoy Kasur Lodi G. Gyari<br>2. Envoy Kelsang Gyaltsen<br>3. Sonam N. Dagpo, Secretary, DIIR<br>4. Bhuchung K. Tsering, Task Force Member | 1. Zhu Weiqun, Executive Vice Minister of the UFWD<br>2. Sithar, Director of the 2nd Bureau (interpreter)<br>3. Yao Mao Chen, Deputy Director of the 2nd Bureau<br>4. Xu Zhitao Juzhang, Secretary to Executive Vice Minister<br>5. Penpa Tashi<br>6. Lin Jian | 1. Jiang Xinhe, Head of Guangxi Zhuang Autonomous Region United Front<br>2. Huang, Deputy Head of Guangxi Zhuang Autonomous Region United Front | **Guilin City** (Guangxi Zhuang Autonomous Region), Guangdung |

(*continued*)

TABLE 19.1 (Continued)

| Rounds of Talks | Date | Tibetan delegation | Chinese delegation | Other dignitaries met | Meeting venue/places visited |
|---|---|---|---|---|---|
| 6th Round | June 29 to July 5, 2007 | 1. Special Envoy Kasur Lodi G. Gyari<br>2. Envoy Kelsang Gyaltsen<br>3. Sonam N. Dagpo, Secretary, DIIR<br>4. Bhuchung K. Tsering, Task Force Member | 1. Zhu Weiqun, Executive Vice Minister of the UFWD<br>2. Sithar, Vice Minister of the UFWD<br>3. Penpa Tashi, Head of the Seventh Bureau (interpreter)<br>4. Yao Mao Chen, Deputy Head of the Bureau<br>5. Lin Jian<br>6. Gao Xi (a Tibetan from Derge) | 1. Yang Buzhang, Deputy Head of Shanghai United Front<br>2. Ms. Zhou Min, Head of the Jiangsu United Front<br>3. Ms. Qian Ji Hong, Head of the Nanjing United Front | **Shanghai and Nanjing**<br>**Place visited:** Jiangsu Province (Suzhou) |
| Informal meeting | May 4–5, 2008 | 1. Special Envoy Kasur Lodi G. Gyari<br>2. Envoy Kelsang Gyaltsen | 1. Zhu Weiqun, Executive Vice Minister of the UFWD<br>2. Sithar, Vice Minister of the UFWD (helped in interpretation also) | This meeting was mutually restricted to four persons with no assistance from either side | **Shenzhen** |
| 7th Round | June 30 to July 3, 2008 | 1. Special Envoy Kasur Lodi G. Gyari<br>2. Envoy Kelsang Gyaltsen<br>3. Sonam N. Dagpo, Secretary, DIIR<br>4. Bhuchung K. Tsering, Task Force Member<br>5. Jigmey Passang, Task Force Secretariat | 1. Du Qinglin, Vice Chairman of the CPPCC and Minister of the UFWD<br>2. Zhu Weiqun, Executive Vice Minister of the UFWD<br>3. Sithar, Vice Minister of the UFWD<br>4. Chang Rongjun, Secretary-General of the UFWD<br>5. Yao Mao Chen, Deputy Director of the Bureau<br>6. Xu Zhitao Juzhang, Secretary to Executive Vice Minister<br>7. Damdul, a scholar from *the CTRC (interpreter)<br>8. Lin Jian | 1. Lhakpa Phuntsog, Director of the China Tibetology Research Center (CTRC)<br>2. Zhu Xiaoming, Deputy Director of the CTRC and other scholars at the CTRC | **Beijing**<br>UFWD Office, Olympic Stadium, and China Tibetology Research Center |

| | | | | | |
|---|---|---|---|---|---|
| 8th Round | October 30 to November 5, 2008 | 1. Special Envoy Kasur Lodi G. Gyari<br>2. Envoy Kelsang Gyaltsen<br>3. Sonam N. Dagpo, Secretary, DIIR<br>4. Bhuchung K. Tsering, Task Force Member<br>5. Kalsang Tsering, Task Force Secretariat | 1. Du Qinglin, Vice Chair of the CPPCC and Minister of the UFWD<br>2. Zhu Weiqun, Executive Vice Minister of the UFWD<br>3. Sithar, Vice Minister of the UFWD<br>4. Pema Trinley, Executive Vice Governor of the TAR<br>5. Chang Rongjun, Secretary-General of the UFWD<br>6. Yao Mao Chen, Deputy Director of the Bureau<br>7. Xu Zhitao Juzhang, Secretary to Executive Vice Minister<br>8. Damdul, a scholar from the CTRC (interpreter)<br>9. Lin Jian, Staff of the UFWD (note taker) | 1. Mr. Ma, Head of the Ningxia United Front<br>2. Mr. Yang Hong, Deputy Head of the Ningxia United Front<br>3. Mr. Lan De Ming, Head of the Religion and Ethnic Affairs Bureau of the Ningxia United Front<br>4. Lhakpa Phuntsog, Director, CTRC<br>5. Zhu Xiaoming, Deputy Director, CTRC, and other legal experts invited | **Beijing**<br>UFWD Office and China Tibetology Research Center<br>**Places visited:**<br>Yinchuan (Ningxia Hui Autonomous Region) |
| 9th Round | January 26–31, 2010 | 1. Special Envoy Kasur Lodi G. Gyari<br>2. Envoy Kelsang Gyaltsen<br>3. Tenzin Phuntsok Atisha, Secretary, DIIR<br>4. Bhuchung K. Tsering, Task Force Member<br>5. Jigmey Passang, Task Force Secretariat | 1. Du Qinglin, Vice Chairman of CPPCC and Minister of the UFWD<br>2. Zhu Weiqun, Executive Vice Minister of the UFWD<br>3. Sithar, Vice Minister of the UFWD<br>4. Nyima Tsering, Vice Chairman, the TAR People's Congress<br>5. Chang Rongjun, Secretary-General of the UFWD<br>6. An Qi Yi, Deputy Secretary-General and head of the Seventh Bureau of the UFWD<br>7. Yao Mao Chen, deputy head of the Seventh Bureau of the UFWD<br>8. Damdul, a scholar from the CTRC (interpreter)<br>9. Hua, Secretary to Executive Vice Minister<br>10. Lin Jian, Staff of the UFWD (note taker)<br>11. Taga (Tashi Choegyal from Kardze), Staff of the UFWD | 1. Mrs. Li Wei Wei, Head of Hunan UFWD<br>2. Tang Xin Hua, Deputy Head of Hunan UFWD<br>3. Guo Zheng Gui, Changsha City Vice Mayor<br>4. Mrs. Jiang, Deputy Head of Xiangxi Tujia and Miao Autonomous Prefecture | **Hunan**<br>Changsha City, Shoashan, Feng Huang County, Zhangjiajie City, Xiangxi Tujia, Miao Autonomous Prefecture<br>**Beijing**<br>UFWD Office, Beijing Capital Museum |

the authorized interlocutor was. International leaders and governments also appreciated the clear message being sent by Dharamsala, one they felt had been lacking in the past.

I want to emphasize once again that the dialogue with Beijing has always been between His Holiness's personal representatives and the PRC government. The CTA has never been an official party to the proceedings. From the very beginning of our relations, this has been the accepted fact on both sides. However, it has also always been equally clear that the reality is about resolving the broader Tibet issue and has nothing to do with the personal status of His Holiness the 14th Dalai Lama, regardless of any contradictory PRC propaganda. Many of the negotiating team members were in fact CTA officials.

While I had retired from CTA service long before, my negotiating colleague Kelsang Gyaltsen, Envoy to Europe, maintained full Secretary rank until July 2016. In addition, we deliberately included two senior CTA officials, Dagpo Sonam Norbu and Ngapa Tsegyam, in the negotiating team to emphasize the CTA's involvement. Dagpo Sonam Norbu first participated in his capacity as the Additional Secretary of the DIIR. In 2004 he was promoted to Secretary. Ngapa Tsegyam was initially His Holiness's representative in Taiwan, but in 2008 he was appointed Secretary of the Office of His Holiness the Dalai Lama. In October 2009, when Dagpo Sonam Norbu was appointed His Holiness's Representative in Australia, Atisha Tenzin Phuntsok succeeded him as DIIR Secretary. He simultaneously assumed Dagpo Sonam Norbu's position on the negotiating team, participating in the Ninth, which turned out to be the final, Round of talks. The other team member was Bhuchung Tsering, who had been assisting me at the ICT with most of our PRC-related work. He was included in the team in his capacity as a Task Force[1] member because of his knowledge and ability to help me with follow-up work.

It was a great pleasure to lead a team so rich in experience and professional skills. All of the members had previously served the Tibet cause in some capacity or another, and most importantly, they had all been associated with our PRC outreach effort for many years. While as leader of the delegation I did most of the talking during the negotiations, sometimes assisted by Kelsang Gyaltsen, in our internal strategy discussions each team member contributed as an equal. There was not one moment when I felt there was any difficulty or misunderstanding within the team. Given the stress of the situation and the critical importance of the matters we were addressing, there could have been any number of occasions creating friction among us. That never occurred. Our team's deportment was exemplary. As I reflect back upon our work, it makes me proud to be a Tibetan, and I can guarantee that our professionalism didn't go unnoticed by our counterparts. It is unfortunate that many of the investigative teams sent in the early years of engagement, including the Fact-Finding Delegations, had internal differences that detracted from their efficacy.

We did encounter one initial disappointment. Beijing refused to allow one of our team members, Ngapa Tsegyam, our Mandarin speaker, to participate in any meetings held in the PRC. Beijing initially tried to justify its objection by differentiating those team members who left Tibet early on from those who left only after Deng Xiaoping's policy of liberalization. Later, its objection was based on Ngapa Tsegyam's position as the head of His Holiness's office in Taipei. For my part, I refused to remove him from the delegation even though Beijing offered to accept any other Tibetan who spoke Mandarin in his place. Some of our advisors in Dharamsala felt it was essential to have someone with these language skills, so they supported finding a substitute. As we had chosen Ngapa Tsegyam not only for his language skills but also for his substantive knowledge of the issues, I kept his name as a member of our team, and each time we were about to begin a round of talks I resubmitted it for consideration. If the dialogue had continued beyond the Ninth Round, I am confident that ultimately, I would have succeeded in getting him accepted.

After a few rounds of talks, both Kelsang Gyaltsen and I were comfortable with the official translators arranged by our counterparts, but we still needed Ngapa Tsegyam's participation because of his familiarity with the subject matter and associated expertise. He had been a member of the Task Force from its inception in 1998. He was ultimately able to join us for the Fourth Round of dialogue that was held in Switzerland, even though the talks were conducted at the PRC embassy. During the meetings, he developed a good chemistry with the PRC delegates and made some excellent contributions to the discussions. As a result, I felt confident that he would be able to join us for the Fifth Round of talks in the PRC, but to my disappointment Beijing once again raised its objections.

As the dialogue process progressed, it became more established and increasingly serious. To handle the associated additional work, we decided to enlarge the team by including staff members of the Task Force Secretariat.[2] We also thought it important to start training members of the younger generation in this important and delicate work. Accordingly, from the Seventh Round forward, we included either Jigmey Passang or his colleague Kalsang Tsering on our negotiating team. Had the discussions continued, I was considering having both of them participate, as the volume of work was escalating and the team needed more help.

While the negotiating team carried out the formal dialogue, the role and contributions of the Task Force members was enormous. It was a highly efficient and professionally run group under the direct supervision of Samdhong Rinpoche. While it was not a policy-making entity, most of its recommendations were subsequently approved by the Kashag and His Holiness and were adopted as our negotiating positions. With the start of the formal dialogue process, the Task Force met several times a year, usually just before the talks, to brainstorm on the topics to be discussed, and after our return, for debriefing.

The Task Force members included senior CTA officials. Kasur Tashi Wangdi, with his long familiarity with our relations with the PRC and his excellent memory of past decisions and events, was of immense value. Similarly, Kasur Tempa Tsering was yet another member with rich experience and understanding of the issues. The Kalon of the DIIR and its Secretaries, as well as Senior Secretaries of His Holiness's Private Office, were ex officio members. The Kalon for the Security Department, Dongchung Ngodup, was a special permanent invitee because of his comprehensive understanding of the subject and his contemporary knowledge about conditions inside Tibet, gathered from his personal contact with Tibetans living there. Several other Task Force members were chosen because of their respective backgrounds and expertise.

In addition, we formed a group of consultants with either substantive knowledge or an ardent interest in the proceedings. They included Tsering Shakya of British Columbia University; Tseten Wangchuk, senior editor of the Voice of America Tibetan Service; Nawang Phuntsog from California State University; Lobsang Sangay, who was then at Harvard University; and Tashi Tsering, founder and director of Amnye Machen Institute.

During the dialogue process, Kelsang Gyaltsen and I benefited immensely from the research, discussions, and secretarial assistance the Task Force provided. The professionalism, knowledge, expertise, and especially dedication of this group was equal to that of the other participants in the process. I can also proudly say that there was no breach of trust or leaking of information by either the negotiating

Members of the Tibetan Task Force on Sino-Tibetan Negotiations, Snow Hermitage Resorts, Dharamsala, December 2007. (Seated, middle row, left to right) Kalon Tempa Tsering (Representative of His Holiness, New Delhi), DIIR Kalon Takla Kesang Yangkyi, Kalon Tripa Prof. Samdhong Rinpoche, the author, Security Kalon Dongchung Ngodup. (Standing, back, left to right) Tsewang Phuntso (Liaison Officer, Latin Americas), Ngapa Tsegyam (Representative of His Holiness, Taipei), Kasur Tashi Wangdi (Representative of His Holiness, Brussels), Kasur Tethong Tenzin Geyche (Private Secretary to His Holiness), Chhoekyapa Chhime Rigzing (Private Secretary to His Holiness), Envoy Kelsang Gyaltsen, Dawa Tsering (Head of China Desk, DIIR). (Seated, front, left to right) Kalsang Tsering (Task Force Secretariat Staff), Dr. Kunchok Tsondue (Chief Planning Officer), Dagpo Sonam Norbu (DIIR Secretary), Thubten Samphel (DIIR Secretary), Mevo Gonpo Tso (China Desk Staff), Jigmey Passang (Task Force Secretariat Staff)

team or Task Force members. This is actually quite an achievement given Dharamsala's rather poor reputation when it comes to keeping confidences.

We decided not to include any non-Tibetans in the dialogue process or on the Task Force, because we felt that all of the formal roles should be held by Tibetans. However, we did regularly consult with Indian and other friends experienced in negotiations and with knowledge of international law.

## OUR DIALOGUE COUNTERPARTS

Our formal counterpart for the dialogue was the United Front. Wang Zhaoguo was the United Front Minister with whom I dealt for over a year in preparing for the negotiations. Minister Wang was very close to President Jiang. We started to develop a relationship ahead of our first face-to-face meeting that turned out to be very useful. Minister Wang knew that the initiative had not only the President's blessing but also his personal interest. This benefited us greatly. My impression was that Minister Wang was also personally invested in the talks, hoping that they would progress toward a resolution of our differences. Having someone who enjoyed the confidence of Jiang Zemin, coupled with a personal interest in resolving the issue and a decisive personality, helped lay a good foundation for our renewed efforts at dialogue.

Other United Front Ministers involved at various times included Liu Yandong and Du Qinglin. Usually, United Front Ministers are also Vice Chairs of the Chinese People's Political Consultative Conference (CPPCC), placing them in the national leadership. They were formally introduced to us not as United Front Ministers but in their capacities as CPPCC Vice Chairs. In emphasizing their national leadership role, Beijing was conveying that we were being received at a high level of the leadership. In fact, Wang Zhaoguo was soon promoted to the Politburo.

Liu Yandong, one of the few women in a high position in the PRC system, succeeded Wang Zhaoguo and became our principal counterpart. She had a very warm personality and was quite sophisticated, but less decisive than her predecessor. I believe her more cautious stance reflected a less close relationship with President Jiang than Wang Zhaoguo enjoyed, combined with her own ambition. She came from the Communist Youth League faction and was considered to be much closer to Hu Jintao, but she was always careful not to cause any displeasure to Jiang Zemin. As a potential Politburo member, she was unwilling to take any initiatives on her own on Tibet or any other matter in the absence of clear directions or indications from her superiors. Her cautious behavior ultimately paid off. She was promoted to the powerful Politburo in 2007, serving for two terms until 2017.

Liu Yandong was not without a personal Tibet connection. Her father was a Red Army officer who had participated in the Long March in Tibetan areas and had developed personal relationships with quite a few Tibetans. When she was at the United Front, she went on a trip following in her father's footsteps. During our Third Round of talks, we had the opportunity to visit some places within the Kardze Tibetan Autonomous Prefecture and meet with a number of Tibetans, including Getak Rinpoche. On our return to Beijing, I shared with her some of my personal experiences of the trip, and when I mentioned Getak Rinpoche, she was sincerely delighted. She then spoke of her late father's relationship with his predecessor and referred to the present Getak Rinpoche with much affection. During that discussion she also expressed her personal interest in Tibet, all of which gave us good insight into her personality.

In 2007, Du Qinglin became Minister of the United Front, assuming the additional role of Vice Chair of the CPPCC in March 2008. From the Seventh Round of talks through the Ninth, he was the seniormost Chinese leader with whom we interacted. While our relations with Beijing had become well established, we started facing major obstacles, including the Plateauwide demonstrations in Tibet and Beijing's brutal suppression of them in 2008. Added to this was President Hu Jintao's hands-off attitude. Both before and after his inauguration as PRC

The author with Liu Yandong, United Front Minister, and Zhu Weiqun, Deputy UF Minister, during the Second Round of talks, Beijing, June 7, 2003

President, there was considerable optimism in some circles that because of his personal experiences and firsthand knowledge of Tibet, he would pay much more attention to resolving the issue, which in turn might lead to some form of breakthrough. In this hope, we even carried a personal communication from His Holiness to him in 2004 during the Third Round of talks.

Unfortunately, the opposite turned out to be true. I would not say that he was hostile or indifferent, but for whatever reason, he took no special interest in helping bring about any progress in our dialogue. At least during Hu Jintao's first term, Jiang Zemin's personal interest and influence were still evident. At times I could reach out to the former President or people close to him, such as Jia Qinglin, to help move the issue forward. Jia Qinglin was a Politburo Standing Committee member and Chair of the CPPCC, the CCP organ with jurisdiction over the United Front, as well as Chair of the Tibet Working Group. Starting with Hu Jintao's second term, however, it became quite clear that Jiang Zemin was either unwilling or unable to help. Although we may have had more meetings with Minister Du Qinglin than some of his predecessors, and his personal behavior was always pleasant and warm, without upper-level political support, there was little he or the United Front Minister could do to advance the issue.

Provided our talks moved steadily forward, Beijing indicated its willingness to upgrade our level of access within the national leadership. At one point, our counterparts recounted the history of His Holiness's relations with Beijing and said that if there were marked progress in our current discussions, the level of dialogue and access could be restored to that existing in early 1982. During that time period, senior leaders including Deng Xiaoping, Li Xiannian, Xi Zhongxun, and Ulanhu were personally receiving Tibetan delegations. This was very encouraging. The Chinese are very protocol-minded, and the way things are handled at every meeting is meant to convey a message. We became very adept at reading these signals.

Starting with the Second Round of talks, Vice Minister Zhu Weiqun became the principal interlocutor from the PRC side. In 2005 he was promoted to Executive Vice Minister. He was assisted by Sithar, a Tibetan who became a Vice Minister in 2006, a position he held until 2016. Sithar was a decent fellow and very loyal to his job. He was involved in all Nine Rounds of dialogue. I had the feeling, however, that had he had the option, he might have preferred a career in education over his responsibilities working for the United Front.

During the last two rounds of talks, the PRC delegation included a senior Tibetan leader from the TAR. In November 2008, during the Eighth Round, Pema Trinley, then Executive Vice Governor of the TAR, was present. In January 2010, during the Ninth, and final, Round, Vice Chair of the TAR People's Congress Nyima Tsering attended. The presence of these two Tibetan leaders was largely symbolic. Their participation was limited to reciting prepared written statements that primarily lauded the progress and changes taking place in the TAR. It was clearly designed to show that such officials more than ably represented the Tibetan people and the local Tibetan government. In fact, in a not-so-subtle remark, it was conveyed that these individuals were the true representatives of the Tibetan people.[3]

I directly challenged this assertion, saying that it was undeniable that the only person who truly represents the Tibetan people is His Holiness the 14th Dalai Lama. While we had taken a policy decision to avoid becoming confrontational with fellow Tibetans participating in any of the meetings, we recognized exceptions would need to be made either to set the record straight or to refute a baseless allegation. While these Tibetan officials made no real effort to participate in the discussions, their personal attitude toward us was very warm. Regardless of Beijing's intent, we were actually very happy they were present. It gave us the opportunity to explain to them the reason His Holiness was pursuing dialogue with the PRC leadership. In fact, after the Ninth Round of talks, we had an informal meeting during which Nyima Tsering expressly endorsed my remarks, calling for the need to find a mutually beneficial solution to our differences, stating: "What you said is convincing." We hoped that he would carry that message back to the Tibetan community at large.

Like our counterparts, we tended to look at and interpret actions taken by the other side negatively and with suspicion. Yet, my misgivings about Beijing's inclusion of these senior Tibetan officials proved incorrect. Some years later I learned from a well-informed Tibetan from inside Tibet that their involvement was for a good reason. Beijing wanted to show the Tibetan leadership inside that serious negotiations aimed at reaching some solution on the Tibet issue were, in fact, taking place with His Holiness's participation.

Vice Minister Zhu Weiqun became one of the most well-known senior Chinese officials responsible for handling the Tibet issue. He held this position for nearly two decades. His role as "flag bearer" of the old school of thought on Tibet became even more prominent upon his retirement from the United Front in 2013 and his appointment as Chair of the Ethnic and Religious Affairs Committee of the CPPCC.

Zhu Weiqun was a very tough negotiating opponent, but his conduct was always professional and courteous. He was very committed to the communist ideology, however, and I think he was not comfortable with the liberalization then taking place within the CCP. His ideology and analysis of issues, including Tibet, were very much based on a Marxist view of the world. I was pleased to see, however, that he didn't evince the chauvinistic attitude or sense of arrogance on a personal level that I had encountered in some other Chinese officials. I found him to be both a good interlocutor and a comparatively good listener. Both Kelsang Gyaltsen and I enjoyed working with him, as he was both challenging and provocative, spurring us to sharpen our own line of argument. But his worldview was unabashedly old Marxist school. If Beijing were seriously interested in making bold moves on Tibet, Zhu Weiqun was not the best choice of representative. In fairness to him, the position he advocated on Tibet, as well as on all other minority and religious issues, perfectly reflected Chinese government policy that had been in place for decades. Tibetans, and even some outside experts, who try to hold him responsible for the hard-line approach he took in our discussions need to understand that he was accurately espousing the long-held official Chinese position.

Accordingly, I was not surprised by Zhu Weiqun's conservative views. I did, however, become deeply concerned in later years with an idea floated by a small group of individuals, including him, to do away with the system of nationality identities. In 2012 he authored an article in *The Study Times*, the newspaper published by the Party School of the Central Committee of the CCP, advocating the revocation of PRC constitutional provisions and laws on autonomy applicable to nationality minorities within the PRC, including the Tibetans. This was far more serious than personally insulting His Holiness. If minorities were to lose their "autonomous" status under the PRC constitution, the very premise of His Holiness's Middle Way Approach would be eliminated. Many Chinese scholars both inside and outside the PRC were also deeply troubled by this proposition.

To highlight my concerns about this idea, on April 23, 2012, I made a presentation on this and several other issues at the Council on Foreign Relations, a Washington, D.C.-based think tank. My remarks were intended to bring the negative consequences of such a profound policy change to the attention of the international community. I include them in detail here, as they reflect my continuing strong reservations about such a proposal.

> Turning to Chinese policies on Tibet, I note with concern the recent article by a person of standing within the Chinese Communist Party advocating the scrapping of the Chinese constitutional provisions and laws on autonomy as they apply to the Tibetans and other nationality minorities within the PRC. This should not be read as an expression of an over-zealous individual's view. Since some years, a certain academician with strong ties to the Communist Party leadership dealing with the Tibetan issue has also been advocating this view in various forums. It is important to understand the consequences of the implementation of such ideas, for they are considerable.
>
> His Holiness the Dalai Lama's proposals and the position of the Tibetan exile administration, supported by many international experts and governments alike, is that the situation in Tibet should be resolved by transforming what is now merely a nominal autonomy for Tibetans under the Chinese constitution and laws into a genuine and effective autonomy. We are convinced that our primary goal of restoring the right of Tibetans to live as Tibetans according to our culture, values and religious traditions can best be achieved if Tibetans can govern themselves under a system of devolution of power from the central government to the Tibet Autonomous Region and its contiguous Tibetan autonomous prefectures and counties in the People's Republic of China (where half of all Tibetans live). The international community is increasingly aware of the benefits of decentralization of power and the contribution of autonomy arrangements in the resolution and prevention of conflicts, especially in multi-ethnic states. The autonomy Tibetans are asking for, as set out in detail in the Memorandum on Genuine Autonomy for the Tibetan People that my delegation presented to the Chinese government in our 8th round of dialogue in November 2008, respects the Chinese constitutional framework and is in line with the best practice of states in the area of autonomy.
>
> Instead of supporting the implementation of real autonomy in Tibetan areas within the People's Republic of China, the proposal I am referring to advocates the opposite position. In the name of promoting Chinese nationalism, it calls for eliminating ethnicity and minority status for Tibetans coupled with assimilationist policies, such as requiring that Tibetan children

study Chinese culture as the aspirational culture. The policy being advocated is one that negates the distinctiveness of Tibetans and other non-Chinese and would hasten the serious cultural destruction already underway in Tibet.

The recently concluded session of the Chinese National People's Congress did not take up these suggestions, but these ideas are dangerous all the same. If these ideas were to lead to changes in the autonomy laws, such a development would have serious ramifications internationally, in Tibet, and for prospects of achieving a negotiated solution to the Tibet question—because it is on the basis of a genuinely autonomous Tibet that His Holiness the Dalai Lama has been able to build a consensus among Tibetans for a future of coexistence with the Chinese.

The international ramifications should be carefully weighed by any Chinese leader contemplating this radical policy move. It is necessary to consider that the recognition by certain governments of China's claim to Tibet was conditioned through various diplomatic exchanges on the understanding that Tibet's distinctive identity would be respected as an autonomous area within the People's Republic of China. Perhaps most important in this regard was India's demand and China's explicit assurance, given by Prime Minister Chou Enlai to Prime Minister Pandit Jawaharlal Nehru in 1956. Given India's proximity to Tibet and its long relations with that country and with China, the Indian government's position and the assurances given to it by the People's Republic of China are particularly important because these factors clearly affected the actions and positions of other states whose governments have continued, as has the Government of India, to emphasize the autonomy of Tibet while recognizing it to be a part of the People's Republic of China. Joint communiqués between India and China make the important distinction when dealing with Tibet of referring to the autonomous status of the Tibetan region. A revocation of Tibet's autonomy by China or a further dilution of its meaning cannot be taken lightly by these governments and could have serious consequences for China and the region.

What China's leaders must also realize is that by [*sic*] reneging on the promises of autonomy in the constitution—even if they are unfulfilled—would severely impact the Tibetan position on the question. His Holiness the Dalai Lama's Middle Way Approach is premised on the supposition that a middle ground between independence and the current centralist dictatorship is possible within the framework of the People's Republic of China and its constitution. That middle ground is genuine autonomy. If the constitutional basis for autonomy were to be removed from the Chinese constitution and if, therefore, a Middle Way Approach could no longer be accommodated within the People's Republic of China and its constitution, then Tibetans would be compelled to look for a totally different approach.

When we look at the volatile situation in Tibet today, we could well be witnessing a preview of what is yet to come if Tibetans there do not soon experience a considerable, tangible and meaningful change in China's policies and practices or are at least given a realistic expectation for such change. The terrible and tragic wave of self-immolations in eastern and northeastern Tibet—the Tibetan areas of Kham and Amdo—are unquestionably the direct result of Tibetans living under daily circumstances of oppression. The Chinese government's failure to grasp the reality of this situation and to act responsibly is of serious concern to many governments.

Prospects for deepening religious repression in Tibet, continuing vituperative attacks against His Holiness the Dalai Lama, constraints on culture, including in the area of Tibetan language use, escalating tensions between Tibetans and Chinese as a result of economic disparities, the yet unknown impact of China's radical social experiment with nomad settlement—all of these developments forecast an intensification and broadening of the protest movement in Tibet.

His Holiness the Dalai Lama has always called on the people to refrain from using violence and has courageously reached out to China's leaders over the years. The willful disregard of Chinese leaders to his proposals—and to the plight of the Tibetan people—has placed at risk the peace and stability of Tibet. I do not expect Tibetans to turn to violence as long as His Holiness is present as the symbol of the Tibetan nation and its spirit. However, a continuation of the current level of repression in Tibet—or a worsening of it, which some observers expect—will increase Tibetan resistance, as people feel they have little left to lose.

In circumstances of intense government repression against its own citizens—or of open conflict—the international community has coalesced around the Responsibility to Protect or R2P principle. This principle has been invoked in UN debates on Darfur, Burma, Libya and elsewhere, and the UN has established a framework for its implementation, including the role of early warning. The exercise of sovereignty is a privilege and responsibility that is derived

> from the will of the people, and it prohibits their abuse. In the case of mass atrocities, the international community has a responsibility to intervene to assist the people and protect them from intolerable harm. Intervention need not be military in nature: that is clearly a measure of last resort.
>
> China, with Russia, has used its veto in the Security Council to block a UN Resolution on Syria that would have embraced R2P as a justification of intervention, claiming the Security Council had no role in the internal affairs of a state. But the People's Republic of China is not immune to the will of the people it governs or to the condemnation of the international community when it violates international norms of behavior. And Tibetans will inevitably continue to appeal to the international community, despite the major obstacles they may encounter in that endeavor. They have no choice but to do so in the face of the Chinese government's refusal to address their real and legitimate grievances. The risk factors are in place in Tibet. Unless China's leaders change their course, with a more responsible approach, I believe that the international community must be increasingly vigilant and prepared to act in a qualitatively different manner to help save Tibet.[4]

Following my speech, I received some words of encouragement from a well-connected individual in the PRC, saying that my remarks were very timely and had been noted by government individuals with responsibility for such matters. As of this writing, no important organ of the PRC political system seems to have given formal consideration to this idea, but we cannot and should not rule out the possibility of its being resurrected.

## VENUE OF TALKS AND PLACES VISITED

From the beginning of our outreach to Beijing, with his usual pragmatic approach, His Holiness advised us to focus our efforts on substance rather than form, not worrying about the rank of our counterparts or logistics. Nevertheless, in our numerous strategy sessions, the issue of venue was identified as an important element. At one stage in the late 1980s, we felt that we should try to meet our counterparts outside of the PRC, at least for the first few rounds of dialogue. The earlier Fact-Finding Delegations and the High-Level Exploratory Talks Delegations had been under serious limitations that hampered our abilities to conduct ourselves effectively while in the PRC. In addition, there was the tremendous stress resulting from simply being in the PRC. This changed over time, however; gradually we began to see the benefits of conducting our talks there, especially in Beijing.

Thus, by the time we started our formal talks in the early 2000s, we made a greater effort to conduct the talks in the PRC, with the option of periodically meeting outside. We did manage to persuade the PRC delegation to come to Switzerland for the Fourth Round. They were very nervous about meeting outside the PRC, especially in Western countries, fearing that we would orchestrate massive demonstrations or ambush them with unflattering media exposure. We took great care that none of this ever happened. By the conclusion of the Fourth Round, our negotiating counterparts had become very relaxed, even agreeing that future meetings could be held outside the PRC. Nevertheless, our further talks were held in the PRC, all but two of them in Beijing. The non-Beijing sites were not chosen to distance us from the capital; logistics and timing simply made these alternative venues more convenient.

Along with every meeting in the PRC, we were invited to visit various provinces, Tibetan autonomous areas, and major Chinese cities. While Beijing's primary goal in taking us on these excursions was certainly to show off its "progress" in these areas, it was equally important for us to get as much knowledge and understanding of conditions on the ground as possible. We needed not only to see the situation in Tibetan areas but also to understand life in the PRC if we ultimately hoped to live peacefully with the Chinese side by side. Accordingly, we took these tours seriously, while trying to visit as many Tibetan areas as possible. Even though we were not as successful as we would have liked, we were able to visit fourteen different Tibetan areas, in addition to several important religious sites and some major Chinese cities, as identified in the list below.

## PLACES VISITED DURING THE NINE ROUNDS OF NEGOTIATIONS

Fourteen Tibetan areas, including Lhasa, Shigatse, Kongpo and Gyaltse (Gyangtse) in Tibet Autonomous Region, Dartsedo, Nyarong, Drago, Gyalrong, Tawu, Rongdrag, Kardze and a few other counties of Kardze Tibetan Autonomous Prefecture, and Gyalthang in Dechen Tibetan

Autonomous Prefecture. These visits took place during the first three rounds of dialogue.

Forty-one Chinese cities, including Beijing, Shanghai, Nanjing, Guangdong, and Shenzhen, as well as several other provinces and autonomous regions, including Guangxi and Ningxia.

Fifteen religious sites and Buddhist temples, including Mount Putuo (Potala) in Zhejiang Province; Mount Jizu (Riwo Jakang) in Yunnan Province; Lingyin Temple, Liefang Pagoda, Jingci Temple, and Puji Temple in Hangzhou, Zhejiang Province; the Buddhist Association of China, Hongluo Temple, and the Temple of Heaven in Beijing; Xiangfu Temple in Mianzhu; Hengshan Hanging Temple in Datong; Guang Xiao Buddhist Temple in Guangzhou; and Bao Guang Temple in Chengdu.

Almost all of these sites were visited in connection with the Second Round of talks. Having the opportunity to visit Lhasa and other Tibetan areas is, of course, a once-in-a-lifetime opportunity for any Tibetan visiting the PRC. But what made it more important for us was the opportunity to meet some resident Tibetans. Although they were hand selected by our hosts, even that limited opportunity, in my mind, was very important. We often had to choose among competing itineraries. During our 2002 visit to Lhasa, for example, we had only a few days. We were given two possible options: a trip to Samye Monastery and some of the historical areas in the Yarlung Valley or a visit to Shigatse and the surrounding area. From a historical point of view, I definitely would have chosen to go to the Yarlung valley, the cradle of Tibetan civilization, and also visit Samye, the first Buddhist monastery ever built in Tibet. A visit there would have given me the further opportunity to visit Mindrolling Monastery, with which I have a special connection. However, we chose to go to Shigatse, giving more importance to contemporary matters.

Shigatse is the site of Tashi Lhunpo Monastery, the seat of the Panchen Lamas. I tried to bargain with our United Front guides to forego Kongpo so we could go to both Shigatse and Samye, but Kongpo was a must for them. I believe their intransigence had more to do with health concerns than any political motivations. The Shigatse area is at quite a high altitude. Our guides felt it necessary to acclimatize in Kongpo for a few days. And, as a Tibetan, I must make a very embarrassing confession: the first night in Shigatse I felt mild altitude sickness and needed some oxygen. Living in exile in India for so many years has taken a toll not only on my psyche but also on my physical body.

Of the Tibetan areas we were able to visit, the TAR was much more rigidly controlled, and the local officials more cautious, than in other Tibetan regions. While all Tibetan autonomous areas are regulated by the same central government policies, each one manifests its own version of these tenets, down to the manner in which guests are welcomed. For example, during our 2003 visit to Gyalthang, we were received at the airport with a very visible Tibetan traditional greeting ceremony. Local government and Party officials were dressed in traditional Tibetan attire; young people performed the traditional welcoming song and offered the *droso-chema*, the most formal way to welcome visitors. Similarly, during our 2004 visit to Kardze Tibetan Autonomous Prefecture (home to both Kelsang Gyaltsen and myself), our local hosts followed tradition in organizing receptions for us at three different points before we reached Dartsedo, the capital. The first reception committee was waiting for us just before we entered the tunnel leading into the Tibetan Prefecture. This attention to detail and protocol respected the well-established Tibetan tradition of providing three receptions for important visitors before they reach their final destination.

By contrast, the behavior was quite different in Lhasa and other areas of the TAR. In 2002, when we arrived at Gongkar Airport outside Lhasa, officials were waiting for us when we deplaned, but there was no ceremonial presentation, not even the offering of *khata*, traditional welcoming scarves. These relatively low-level officials then took us to an empty hall within the airport that was out of public sight. Only there did senior TAR officials greet us and offer the customary *khata*. Upon arrival in the TAR, even Sithar, the Tibetan United Front official accompanying us, started addressing me as "Mr. Gyari Lodi" rather than the more deferential "Rinpoche" he had been using.

For a Khampa, I have an uncharacteristically mild nature, but I really lost my temper during our Lhasa visit. One of the most irritating things was not knowing our itinerary until the last moment. When we arrived in Lhasa, we were told that early the next morning we would go to lower-altitude Kongpo to see some new projects, but primarily to acclimatize so we would not have any health problems because of Lhasa's high altitude. Sithar had further told us that, because of my keen desire to visit as many holy sites as possible, we would visit Ganden Monastery on the way. We were advised to dress casually and to wear comfortable walking shoes for the trip. I repeatedly conveyed to our hosts that we would appreciate it if we could pay our respects at the Jokhang at the start of our program. They were noncommittal. We got up very early the next morning and when we assembled in the hotel lobby, Sithar greeted us with a big, happy smile. He rushed over to me, saying that he had very good news: The local authorities had decided to take us to visit the Jokhang!

I was furious. I railed at Sithar: "You may be a nonbeliever, but you are a Tibetan and you know very well that visiting the Jokhang is not something that we do casually. Except for me, all my colleagues are visiting for the first time in their lives. How can you people be so casual about it? We are not even wearing proper Tibetan dress, and we have special offerings that we need to make." I not only showed my temper but also raised my voice, which made not just Sithar but the entire entourage very nervous. Our hosts began talking among themselves, while Sithar and others were busy on their phones. After some time they returned, urging us to make the visit as planned but giving us assurances that a second, more formal visit would be organized. At this point, I acquiesced. Recognizing that we could pay our proper respects later, I thought it was auspicious for us to begin our travels in Tibet by visiting the Jokhang and receiving the blessings of Jowo Rinpoche.[5]

Our official guides did make arrangements for my team to pay a second visit to the Jokhang in a more proper and respectful manner. Of course, they cleared out any unauthorized Tibetans not only from the temple but also from the whole Barkor plaza area in front so there could be no chance meetings. As our visit to Lhasa was confirmed before our departure from Dharamsala, at our last audience, His Holiness personally handed me a Dharmachakra, or "Wheel of Dharma," made of pure gold decorated with precious stones to be offered to Jowo Rinpoche on his behalf. The Dharmachakra is the most important, universal symbol of Buddhism and also the highest offering symbolizing sovereign power. I had the extraordinary honor to be the individual to bring this precious offering from His Holiness to Jowo Rinpoche. The monks who were taking care of the Jokhang recognized the offering's significance. They went out of their way to help so that I could make this special offering by placing it right in the lap of Jowo Rinpoche. I was so fortunate. I will never forget that moment. It was absolutely overwhelming.

This visit to the Jokhang was both the highlight and the most memorable moment of our trip, but at the same time extremely sad. During our Lhasa visit, we got a glimpse of the real situation under which our people live. Even with all the restrictions imposed, it was evident that some Tibetans were aware of our presence. We saw many people standing at a distance or peering around corners of buildings and from side streets, trying to steal a glance at our group.

We were also taken on a guided tour of the Potala Palace and the Norbulingka, the Dalai Lamas' winter and summer residences, respectively. In all these places the caretakers, whether monk or lay, old or young, made extraordinary efforts to take us to special shrines, explaining to us the significance and importance of some of the images and shrine rooms. At the Potala Palace, the caretakers literally formed a cordon, making it physically difficult for some of the accompanying officials to be near me. It was quite heartening to see this subtle, yet significant act of defiance by these proud Tibetans, allowing us the opportunity to say our prayers undisturbed.

These tightly controlled tours were organized by the Lhasa Municipality Administration. As the Mayor was away during our visit, Deputy Mayor Chakra Tulku showed us around and also hosted a lunch for us. I found him to be a bit self-absorbed, and even though he was supposed to be a reincarnate, he acted very indifferently toward His Holiness. Through their body language and other mannerisms, even lay Tibetans holding high positions convey some reverence or admiration toward His Holiness. I do not want to be too judgmental, however, as that was the only time I met him.

Strangely, we were not given the option to visit Mount Wutai. I was able to visit in 1982 when it was just being renovated, but I understand that now it is easily accessible and has become a major tourist attraction as well as pilgrimage site for overseas Chinese. I believe Beijing's indecision about the possibility of a visit by His Holiness was the reason we were not offered the opportunity. I can only think that our hosts were concerned we might interpret a visit by us as foreshadowing one by His Holiness in the near future, a message they were not prepared to communicate. We were, however, invited to visit Mount Putuo and Mount Emei, as well as Mount Jizu (Riwo Jakang) in Yunnan. A responsible Chinese official with us during our visit to Mount Putuo made an interesting comment that since it is dedicated to Avalokiteshvara, the Bodhisattva of Compassion, wouldn't it be a more appropriate site for the Dalai Lama to visit than Mount Wutai?[6] It certainly was a remark intended to convey a message.

We were also taken to Shaoshan in Hunan Province, the birthplace of Mao Zedong. There has been some criticism of our visiting Mao's ancestral home, and I understand the concern. I am certainly no admirer of Mao, his policies, and his practices. In 1982, when I arrived in Beijing as part of the three-member Exploratory Talks Delegation, our host shared with us an itinerary that included a visit to Mao's mausoleum. I firmly told him that I needed to be excused from the program. The deep wounds in my heart for the immense suffering that Mao caused millions of people, including members of my immediate family, who had become victims of the misguided Great Leap Forward and Cultural Revolution programs would not allow me to even consider such a visit. To my surprise, my hosts took my objection very well. They did say that earlier delegations, including the First Fact-Finding Delegation, of which my two colleagues had been a part, had visited the site. But without much protest, they revised the itinerary and never again sought to include it. I was told they even stopped taking other visiting Tibetans there.

As a student of history, I felt differently about Mao's birthplace. My deep dislike of Mao doesn't diminish the fact that although he created havoc and caused widespread pain and suffering, he fundamentally changed China, and for that matter became a historical figure of importance who could not be ignored. I went to learn more about him in the hope of understanding how the environment and circumstances under which he was born and raised might have influenced his outlook and policies.

## CONNECTIONS WITH THE CHINESE BUDDHIST COMMUNITY

In addition to our dialogue with PRC officials, we also gave high priority to establishing personal relationships with Chinese Buddhist leaders and scholars during our visits. Our efforts had one immediate and one long-term aim. In the short run, we thought the invitation for a pilgrimage visit by His Holiness would most probably come from the head of the Buddhist Association of China, as had the prior invitation for him to attend the 10th Panchen Rinpoche's memorial service. We thought this was a very acceptable arrangement, making it politically convenient for both His Holiness and the PRC government. From a long-term perspective, the most cohesive link between our two peoples is our shared Buddhist religion. While there are differences, and sometimes even critical comments about each other's practices, there is a common respect and unity between the Tibetan Buddhist and Chinese Mahayana traditions. Even under very strict Communist control, His Holiness's fame and reputation have not gone unnoticed in the PRC, especially among Chinese Buddhists.

We were therefore quite pleased when our hosts facilitated a visit with Master Yicheng during our 2003 trip. He was specially invited to come from his native province of Hunan to Beijing to receive us. He needed two translators: one to translate from his native dialect to Mandarin and one from Mandarin to Tibetan. Because of his senior status and advanced age Master Yicheng was assisted by Master Sheng Hui, Executive Vice-President of the Buddhist Association of China, the person who actually runs the organization. The latter was both well informed and well traveled.

It was immediately apparent that Master Yicheng was a genuine monk and Buddhist practitioner. Every time I mentioned His Holiness's name, he folded his hands in prayer as a sign of respect. We gave him a special *thangka* painting of the seventeen Nalanda masters[7] whom His Holiness has personally identified as the foremost masters of the Nalanda tradition. Master Yicheng received this gift with profound reverence, recognizing its true significance, as Chinese Buddhists also trace their lineage back to Nalanda.

Some of the connections that I made with senior Chinese monks in various parts of the PRC continued after our departure. A few of them even came to visit

Kelsang Gyaltsen and the author presenting the painting of the seventeen Nalanda masters to Master Yicheng, Head of the Chinese Buddhist Association, with CBA Executive Vice President Sheng Hui attending, Beijing, June 7, 2003

me in the United States. I firmly believe our common faith in the Buddha Dharma can be the cornerstone of future relations between our peoples. One of my sincerest disappointments is that most of the time, CCP leaders don't seem to understand or appreciate the possibility of this connection for revitalizing the ties between our peoples. I hope that they will one day realize the precious value of the Buddha Dharma and its value in helping foster closer understanding between us, leading to a mutually beneficial resolution of our differences. Encouragingly, some remarks by current President Xi Jinping seem to indicate that he has a better understanding of the value of Buddhism, respecting it as a part of the PRC's national heritage. In a speech delivered at UNESCO headquarters in Paris on March 27, 2014, President Xi said: "Buddhism originated in ancient India. After it was introduced into China, the religion went through an extended period of integrated development with the indigenous Confucianism and Taoism and finally became Buddhism with Chinese characteristics, thus making a deep impact on the religious belief, philosophy, literature, art, etiquette, and customs of the Chinese people."[8]

Chinese Buddhists who are actively helping restore and revitalize Tibetan Buddhism in Tibetan areas, in fact, have made the greatest contribution to date in bringing harmony between our peoples. This is the job institutions such as the United Front are tasked to perform. They should take a lesson from these devout Chinese Buddhists rather than continuing to take actions that undermine this special link between us. Indeed, our First Round of talks in 2002 took place a year after a major governmental crackdown on Larung Gar, the largest Buddhist academy on the Tibetan Plateau. Numerous huts and other structures were bulldozed and thousands of monks and nuns, including large numbers of Chinese practitioners, expelled. We raised the issue of religious freedom and specifically brought up the disturbing situation prevailing at Larung Gar during this meeting. I remember asking our counterparts why the government was so intent on trying to destroy this most precious common link between us. I specifically referred to the expulsion of Chinese monks and nuns because their participation at this important Buddhist institution conveyed a very strong image of a common bond.

It is truly sad that recently this famed institution is facing yet another round of destruction. I met with some of the teachers from Larung Gar when they came to the West to give teachings. Most of their entourage were Chinese students, and the bond between them was truly inspiring. The Chinese students were totally devoted to their teachers, while their Tibetan teachers treated them with the fondness showered on all students, regardless of their ethnicity or heritage. There is such promise in these relationships, if only they could be harnessed in resolving our political differences.

## TIBETAN LEADERS INSIDE

I would also like to share some observations of prominent Tibetan leaders inside Tibet whom I had the opportunity to get to know. I met a number of officials in Lhasa, other parts of the TAR, and the Kardze and Dechen Tibetan Autonomous Prefectures. We also had meetings with quite a few Tibetans in Beijing, especially those working at the China Tibetology Research Center.

My overall impression of Tibetan leaders inside has always been positive and favorable. Many of us in exile fail to take into consideration the circumstances and situations under which they live. It is true that the older generation of leaders, those who grew up during the chaotic period of the Cultural Revolution, tend to be more submissive than the younger generation in an attempt to appease their Chinese overlords. I noticed that even some very senior Tibetan leaders were very careful not to deviate from the party line as evinced by their Chinese compatriots. They would study the body language of even their young Chinese assistants and hardly depart from the prepared scripts they were handed to recite. They were not confrontational toward us; rather, they seemed a bit intimidated by our presence. Perhaps it was just the aura of us representing His Holiness the Dalai Lama.

Ragdi was one exception of this generation. When we visited Lhasa in 2002, he was Chair of the TAR People's Congress. He was spending most of his time in Beijing, however, as a member of the CCP's Central Committee, where he was being officially groomed to follow in the elder Ngapo Ngawang Jigme's[9] footsteps. In fact, the year after our visit he became one of the Vice Chairs of the National People's Congress, a position elevating him into the elite category of national leaders.

I know Lhasans tell all kind of jokes about Ragdi, treating him with the condescending attitude they visit on all non-Lhasan Tibetans. I found him to be assertive and well informed, as well as possessing a good sense of humor. He seemed to be taking full advantage of his rank and position and was certainly not one of

The Tibetan delegation visiting Lhasa during the First Round of talks, 2002. (Left to right) Sithar (translator for the Chinese delegation), Bhuchung Tsering, Lhakpa Phuntsog (head of the China Tibetology Research Center in Beijing), the author, Ragdi (Chairman of the TAR People's Congress), Envoy Kelsang Gyaltsen, Samdup (Head of the TAR United Front), Dagpo Sonam Norbu, Wangdu (UF official and translator)

those looking at his Chinese assistants for guidance. I learned that he was sent to Lhasa around the time of our visit specifically to receive us. After the formal dinner he hosted for us, he pulled me aside for a quick chat. He strongly urged that we try our best not to cause any personal embarrassment to President Jiang during his forthcoming visit to the United States. He also added that there "is some hope," clearly conveying that he was in favor of progress in our dialogue. After the dinner he invited us to join him and others for a cultural show that was attended by a few hundred specially invited guests. Throughout the performance, he kept on chatting with me, with the obvious intention of showing all those present that he was paying special attention to His Holiness's delegation. I later learned that his behavior didn't go unnoticed, becoming the hot topic around Lhasa.

Tibetan leaders and officials who had better educational opportunities and grew up after the Cultural Revolution behave with much more confidence than the older generation. They take full advantage of their ranks and positions. This generation is more conscious of their Tibetan identity. For some of our meetings, they came wearing traditional Tibetan dress, proudly exhibiting their cultural identity. During our visit to Gyalthang in Dechen Tibetan Autonomous Prefecture in Yunnan in 2003, for example, the local government presented each of us with Tibetan dress, no doubt a subtle message that they were not pleased by us not wearing traditional attire.

Our decision to wear Western dress for the dialogue meetings was not taken lightly, but only after considerable debate. Of course, we did bring traditional Tibetan attire with us to wear when visiting holy sites such as the Jokhang. I also wore Tibetan dress in 2004 when I had the opportunity to make a short visit to Nyarong, my birthplace, to visit two monasteries with which my family and I are associated. I declined to visit my parent's hometown as it was in ruins, even though the Chinese made some last-minute renovations before my visit, going so far as to build a bridge to make it more accessible. We did get out of our vehicles at our host's urging and take some photos to appease them, but I steadfastly declined to visit the village itself. It would not have given me any pleasant memories, and I didn't want to give Beijing the propaganda advantage of telling the world that I had visited my family home. I later learned that several of my relatives had gathered there specifically to meet me. My failure to meet them saddens me to this day, as many of them have since passed away.

We did have a few very important messages to convey to our fellow Tibetans, whether we met them individually or in groups. I started all our encounters greeting them on behalf of His Holiness and giving them a brief introduction to the purpose of our visit. I emphasized that His Holiness was looking for a solution for the benefit of all Tibetans, regardless of where they lived, without seeking independence or separation from the PRC. I assured them that whatever the outcome of our dialogue, it would have relevance to every Tibetan living within the PRC. We reinforced this message every time we met with any Tibetans, as we knew that there was a deliberate propaganda campaign in progress contending that His Holiness was making an effort to reintroduce the old system of governance and that there would be an overhaul of the present system if he were successful. We also knew that some Tibetan officials had sent memos to the PRC leadership expressing their concern in this regard.

I believe we were able to convey a very clear message that there was no such intention even in our wildest dreams. Indeed, the opposite was true. If His

Holiness's efforts succeeded, it would empower the Tibetans inside Tibet, including those currently holding office, making their positions more stable and authoritative. I could clearly see that our messages were being well-received, and in some instances our listeners' body language could be read to say: "Ah, now we understand the truth."

Even while the dialogue was ongoing, from May 2006 to June 2007, just prior to the Sixth Round of talks, certain agencies of the PRC government were intensifying their vicious personal attacks against His Holiness. I protested these activities at every opportunity, especially when meeting with Tibetans holding official positions. I told them that as members of the CCP they might not believe in religion, including Buddhism, and therefore might not revere His Holiness from a religious perspective. Nonetheless, I said that "as Tibetans, I know that you are all tremendously proud of the great son of Tibet named Tenzin Gyatso, who has become a global leader admired by millions for his compassion and unassailable moral character." I further added: "When you hear a malicious remark against His Holiness, it feels like a sharp knife piercing our collective hearts." I commiserated with them, saying I knew they felt that way, just as we all do. Beijing accuses His Holiness of being a "splittist," but in truth, it is this baseless allegation that is causing the real split.

Many times when watching the faces of these Tibetans as I shared with them the disparaging remarks made by some PRC officials, I could see a strong sense of sadness and even anger surfacing. All of our meetings were conducted in the presence of United Front officials. Our hosts were clearly uncomfortable with our remarks and a number of times cautioned us to be careful with our words. Nevertheless, we persisted. We felt it was essential to continue conveying this message at every meeting despite the risk of further opportunities for meetings being reduced or denied, which unfortunately turned out to be the case.

## STRUCTURE AND FORMAT OF THE NEGOTIATIONS

While the essence of any negotiations is obviously the substance of the talks, the style and format of the discussions also play a significant role and can contribute to success or failure. From the very beginning of the dialogue process, we were keen to bring about some structural changes in the way our meetings were conducted. During the First and Second Rounds we participated according to the plans that our hosts had arranged. By the Third Round, however, we suggested that we forego some of the ceremonial niceties and instead conduct our meetings in a more businesslike manner. Our counterparts agreed, as we had established some degree of confidence as a result of our first two meetings.

Beginning with the Third Round of dialogue, all of our talks took place with my team sitting directly across from our counterparts. Our discussions also became very structured, with an explicit but broad agenda. I think our PRC interlocutors also appreciated this style. In the beginning, it was always our counterparts who made the opening and closing remarks, but this also changed: if the PRC delegation made the opening remarks in the morning session, I would inaugurate the afternoon proceedings. This became so ingrained in our sessions that during one of our visits, Zhu Weiqun remembered that he had made the opening remarks at our meeting a year earlier and offered me the opportunity to speak first, as it was my turn.

Besides these formal discussions, we also had informal sessions and principals-only meetings. When the debate during our formal talks became heated, with

The Fourth Round of talks. Zhu Weiqun, Deputy UF Minister in the center with Sithar (translator) to his left and Xu Zhitao (another UF official) to his right, Chinese Embassy, Bern, Switzerland, June 30, 2005

both sides taking uncompromising positions, we would break for an hour or so. We would meet in a different room and continue the discussion, but in an informal manner, sometimes removing our neckties and even kicking off our shoes. This was very helpful in reducing tensions and getting our talks back on track. On quite a number of occasions, it was my negotiating counterpart who would suggest retiring to our informal setting when he could see us not getting anywhere. In our principals-only meetings, Kelsang Gyaltsen and myself would meet with Executive Vice Minister Zhu Weiqun alone, with Vice Minister Sithar acting as translator. In these meetings no notes were taken. Each side could speak freely, quite often departing from our respective official lines, in an attempt to find common ground.

## INSTITUTIONALIZATION OF THE DIALOGUE PROCESS BOTH IN DHARAMSALA AND IN THE INTERNATIONAL COMMUNITY

I am a strong proponent of institutionalization, accountability, and discipline, without which no major task can be accomplished with the desired result. I have already written about how the structure of the Tibetan leadership became more institutionalized under His Holiness's guidance. The same became true as we prepared to undertake the formal dialogue process.

As in every democracy, foreign relations are the responsibility of the administrative branch of government. However, from the very beginning when His Holiness conceived of the Middle Way Approach, he sought the advice and approval of the elected assembly, now known as the Tibetan Parliament-in-Exile. After tense and sometimes chaotic deliberations, the Parliament repeatedly endorsed His Holiness's policies. When His Holiness decided to send my team to engage in formal dialogue, it was done in full compliance with resolutions[10] unanimously passed by Parliament. Moreover, the strategy accorded with recommendations by the general public[11] requesting His Holiness to spearhead our efforts to reach out to the PRC leadership to resolve the Tibet issue. Indeed, every time we returned from a round of dialogue, my colleague Kelsang Gyaltsen and I personally briefed both the Speaker and the Deputy Speaker.

In addition to seeking the approval of the elected Parliament, Kalon Tripa Samdhong Rinpoche called a special meeting of all the former Kalons to seek their advice and support. Some of these occurred before the start of the formal dialogue process, when core issues were being discussed. Unlike consultations with the Parliament, there was no institutional obligation for the Kalon Tripa to reach out to former Kalons. Understanding the immense importance of the issue, however, he wanted to be inclusive, taking advantage of as much institutional knowledge as possible.

We didn't restrict our efforts at institutionalizing the dialogue process to the administration in Dharamsala but extended it to our international relations. While Beijing was adamant in opposing any third-party direct involvement, and, as I have already mentioned, we did not favor any formal role for third parties, we did seek to integrate international participation. We believed this was essential to ensure that the dialogue would be an ongoing process, not an isolated event. Accordingly, we used our contacts with heads of state, other government officials, and eminent international personalities to keep our issue at the highest leadership level in the PRC. At the start and conclusion of each round of talks, I personally briefed many of the interested governments and individuals. Kalon Tripa Samdhong Rinpoche participated in some of these briefings, including our meetings with the National Security Advisor and Foreign Secretary of the Indian government. Seeking help from these quarters solidified our actions, brought credibility to the process, and institutionalized our efforts on the broader world stage.

I have already discussed the importance of properly prepared press releases. This applied not only to statements issued by Dharamsala but also to those of other governments reporting on the dialogue process. After we had had a few rounds of dialogue and our relations with Beijing had stabilized, the US State Department began including remarks about our efforts in its press briefings. On occasion, it issued the standard statements welcoming the participants and encouraging the dialogue. The US Congress, the European Parliament, and other institutions released similar statements.[12] While these sometimes irritated Beijing, they enhanced the PRC's international image, as Beijing was seen as becoming more accommodating, a position appreciated by at least one section of the leadership.

As previously discussed, the Tibet issue, and particularly the dialogue process, is now so institutionalized in the United States that in 2002 Congress made it mandatory for the President and Secretary of State to submit a yearly report explaining the efforts the US administration took during the preceding year to encourage Beijing to engage in dialogue with us.[13] The elevation of the Tibet issue to this level of concern is one of the milestones of our international efforts. As an example of the US's ongoing desire that dialogue continue to take place, not only for the parties' benefit but also for that of the PRC's relations with the international community, I have provided relevant excerpts from the 2009 report that are representative of the US administration's annual filings.[14]

## REPORT ON TIBET NEGOTIATIONS AS REQUIRED BY SECTION 611, FOREIGN RELATIONS AUTHORIZATION ACT, 2003, "TIBETAN POLICY ACT OF 2002"

## MARCH 2008–FEBRUARY 2009

I. Executive Summary

The Dalai Lama's Special Envoys and Chinese officials from the United Front Work Department (United Front) met three times in 2008. . . .

The first round of dialogue took place in September 2002, followed by meetings in May 2003, September 2004, June 2005, February 2006, and late June/early July 2007. The United States has consistently urged Chinese officials to continue such contacts and, in public statements and through diplomatic channels, has pressed for direct and substantive dialogue, without preconditions, which will lead to a negotiated settlement of outstanding differences.

The United States believes that the Dalai Lama can be a constructive partner for China as it deals with the difficult challenges of continuing tensions in Tibetan areas. He represents the views of the vast majority of Tibetans and his consistent advocacy of non-violence is an important principle for making progress toward resolution of ongoing tensions. China's engagement with the Dalai Lama or his representatives to resolve problems facing Tibetans is in the interest of both the Chinese Government and the Tibetan people. Failure to resolve these problems will only lead to greater tensions inside China and will be a stumbling block to fuller engagement with the United States and other nations.

II. Tibet Policy

Encouraging substantive dialogue between Beijing and the Dalai Lama is an important foreign policy objective of the United States. We continue to encourage China and the Dalai Lama to hold direct and substantive discussions aimed at resolution of differences at an early date, without preconditions. The administration believes that dialogue between China and the Dalai Lama or his representatives will alleviate tensions in Tibetan areas and contribute to the overall stability of China. . . .

The United States continues to believe that meaningful dialogue represents the best way to resolve tension in Tibet. We are disappointed that, after seven years of talks, there have not been any concrete results. We are concerned that in 2008, the Chinese government increased its negative rhetoric about the Dalai Lama, increased repression in Tibetan areas, and further restricted religious freedom. We continue to urge both sides to engage in substantive dialogue and hope to see a ninth dialogue round in the near future that will lead to positive movement on questions related to Tibetans' lives and livelihoods.

III. Steps Taken by the President and the Secretary to Encourage the Government of the People's Republic of China to Enter into a Dialogue with the Dalai Lama or his Representatives Leading to a Negotiated Agreement on Tibet

A. Steps Taken by the President

Throughout his tenure, President George W. Bush consistently urged the Chinese government to engage in substantive discussions with the Dalai Lama or his representatives, and to respect the unique cultural, linguistic, and religious heritage of the Tibetan people. In 2008, he continued this appeal. He also encouraged Beijing to invite the Dalai Lama to visit China as a way of building trust between the two sides. . . .

In his 2006 meetings with President Hu at the White House and at APEC in Vietnam, President Bush encouraged the dialogue and reiterated the importance of a face-to-face meeting with the Dalai Lama at the earliest possible date. During President Bush's November 2005 visit to China, he urged Chinese Premier Wen Jiabao and Chinese President Hu Jintao to increase religious freedom and human rights in China and encouraged them to engage in a dialogue with the Dalai Lama.

B. Steps Taken by the Secretary. . . .

Over the previous four years, Secretary Condoleezza Rice consistently raised the issues of human rights and religious freedom at the highest levels, including in meetings with the Chinese President, Premier, State

Counselor, and Foreign Minister. In her meetings, she highlighted the need for progress on the dialogue with the Dalai Lama's representatives as well as the need for greater human rights and religious freedom in Tibet. During her trip to China in February 2008, the Secretary reiterated this message with Foreign Minister Yang Jiechi.

C. Steps Taken by Other Department of State Officials. . . .

Deputy Secretary John Negroponte raised Tibet when State Councilor Dai was in Washington in December 2008, for the final Senior Dialogue of the Bush Administration. He encouraged the Chinese to consider a discussion on the issues raised in the 2008 Memorandum on Genuine Autonomy for the Tibetan People, a document presented by the Tibetans to the Chinese during their November dialogue which specifies the Tibetans' position on autonomy. . . .

On May 17, 2001, Secretary of State Colin Powell designated Paula Dobriansky as Special Coordinator for Tibetan Issues. . . . As the Special Coordinator for Tibetan Issues, Under Secretary Dobriansky's responsibilities included promoting substantive dialogue between the Chinese government and the Dalai Lama or his representatives. . . .

Under Secretary Dobriansky accompanied President Bush to China in October 2001 and February 2002. She traveled to Beijing in August 2006 and in April 2002. On all these occasions, she discussed Tibetan human rights and religious freedom issues as well as the importance of dialogue between Chinese officials and the Dalai Lama or his representatives.

IV. Status of any Discussions between the People's Republic of China and the Dalai Lama or His Representatives

A. History of Discussions. . . .

Lodi Gyari and Kelsang Gyaltsen traveled to China for a third time in September 2004. They visited Beijing, Hebei, and Guangdong, and several counties of the Kardze Tibetan Autonomous Prefecture in western Sichuan province, including Lodi Gyari's hometown. The envoys were again hosted by the United Front, and met with United Front Head and Vice Chairperson of the Chinese People's Political Consultative Committee Minister Liu Yandong and other officials. Lodi Gyari issued a statement after the visit noting that they had "so far the most extensive and serious exchange of views on matters relating to Tibet," conducted in "a frank but cordial atmosphere." He noted that "both sides acknowledged the need for more substantive discussions in order to narrow down the gaps and reach a common ground."

From February 15–23, 2006, the Dalai Lama's envoys met in Guilin, China. In previous meetings, the envoys had requested to visit other autonomous regions of China, which is why Guangxi Autonomous Region was chosen. After the meetings concluded, Lodi Gyari reported that there was "a growing understanding between the two sides, though fundamental differences persisted." He made clear, however, that the Tibetans remained committed to the dialogue process and were hopeful that progress would be possible by continuing the engagement.

The Dalai Lama's envoys were hosted by the United Front in Shanghai and Nanjing from June 29 to July 5, 2007. Following this meeting, the envoys reported that "our dialogue process has reached a critical stage" and that "we . . . made some concrete proposals for implementation if our dialogue process is to go forward."

B. Current Status of Discussions

The Dalai Lama's representatives and officials of the UFWD held their seventh and eighth round of dialogue in 2008, as well as an informal round in the weeks immediately following the unrest in Tibetan areas in the spring. . . .

After months of continuing repression in Tibet, harsh rhetoric from Chinese officials, and the inconclusive dialogue round in July, the Dalai Lama publicly expressed his frustration on several occasions over the failure of his "Middle Way" approach aimed at greater autonomy for Tibet. As a result, Tibet's "government in exile" held a meeting in Dharamsala, India, with hundreds of Tibetan leaders to debate whether to continue to pursue a measured path of compromise with China or if another path should be taken. After five days of deliberation, the majority of Tibetans decided not to break with Dalai Lama's vision of finding a peaceful solution to Tibet within the framework of the People's Republic of China. There was also a strong endorsement of the Dalai Lama's continued leadership. . . .

In early November, the Dalai Lama expressed frustration with the dialogue while on a trip to Japan. Speaking at a press conference the Dalai Lama said, "My trust in the Chinese government has become thinner, thinner,

> thinner. Suppression [in Tibet] is increasing and I cannot pretend that everything is OK." Lodi Gyari said in Dharamsala, India, on November 16, the "we have told the Chinese very clearly this time that we have now reached the crossroads."
>
> While the United States remains supportive of the talks, after seven years we are disappointed and concerned that the dialogue, including the two rounds in 2008, has not produced concrete results. Dialogue is better than its absence; we expect, however, this dialogue to lead to negotiated solutions to the real problems that Tibet and its people face.

## HANDLING OF MEDIA REPORTING ON THE DIALOGUE PROCESS

The handling of the media was an important part of the dialogue process. This has historically been quite a challenging area for us. While we understood the need for comprehensive media coverage, we gave more importance to maintaining the dialogue process and not allowing impulsive or naïve remarks or responses to harm our efforts. The Chinese are extremely sensitive when it comes to media reporting. This wariness is very much a part of the culture prevailing in authoritarian governments, and the Chinese top the list in this regard. But is that the only reason? Certainly not. Some of their concerns with unrestrained media would have harmed our interests as well as theirs. Those PRC leaders in favor of maintaining dialogue with His Holiness faced serious challenges from within. An unflattering or biased story could potentially endanger their efforts. Even well-intentioned, complimentary remarks by certain world leaders, rather than pleasing the Chinese, could cause embarrassment and even make them less proactive on our issue. Even a "pat on the back" by His Holiness was not something that necessarily endeared them to their colleagues.

I have already shared the delicate negotiations that accompanied the announcement of our first visit. We were equally careful with the press release issued after each succeeding visit. Unlike for the statements preceding our visits, there were no explicit directives about the content of our postmeeting releases. These were factual, restrained, and forward-looking, but also communicated our deeply held concerns about the overall situation. Sometimes our statements reflected optimism, while in others, we deliberately conveyed a profound sense of discouragement, even questioning the benefit of the dialogue process. Each word was carefully discussed and phrased before any statement was released.[15] Whatever we said or did was to enhance our efforts to move the process forward.

Both Beijing and Dharamsala had several audiences to address. That has never been an easy task. For the Tibetan leadership, as long as we are interested in pursuing a negotiated solution, the most important audience is the leadership in Beijing. But we have always been mindful of how the Tibetans inside Tibet would react to what we said. After all, His Holiness's efforts are for their well-being. Our strength at the negotiation table is the determination and courage of the Tibetan people inside Tibet.

At the same time, we had to be mindful of how our statements would be viewed by the international community. We had to convey a message of hope to keep its support. No one would seriously want to continue helping us if they could not see even the slightest chance of success. But we also had to articulate the difficulties we were confronting and our concerns that the negotiations were not yielding substantive results. Without communicating that sentiment, we couldn't continue to lobby them to maintain their efforts to urge Beijing to be more accommodating.

I am not excluding the Tibetan community in exile as one of our relevant audiences. However, unlike their compatriots in Tibet, they have total freedom of expression and can exercise it either in support of or in opposition to, our efforts. While many of their concerns are legitimate and sincere, to be candid, there is a small but vocal group that has for whatever reason adopted an attitude opposing His Holiness's efforts. The very idea of engaging with the Chinese in dialogue is something they have vehemently opposed from the beginning. While I respect their views, I wish they would put forward some concrete alternatives for bringing some help and solace to our people inside Tibet, rather than opposing the dialogue merely to disagree for disagreement's sake.

## CHAPTER 20

# Nine Rounds of Dialogue

Our discussions during the Nine Rounds of formal dialogue and one additional, informal meeting were serious, extensive, and illuminating. The ten years over which they continued constitute the longest period of uninterrupted contact we have had with the PRC leadership. We engaged in 75 hours of talks. Notes from our sessions alone total over 600 pages. In addition, we provided our negotiating counterparts with two major memoranda and fourteen other documents, totaling over 200 pages. The latter included summaries of important issues raised by our side as well as detailed rebuttals of assertions and accusations propounded by the other side during either earlier meetings or the intervening periods, and further offered a number of proposals.

The two most important documents we gave our negotiating counterparts were the Memorandum on Genuine Autonomy for the Tibetan People,[1] presented in 2008 during the Eighth Round of talks, and the follow-up Note on the Memorandum on Genuine Autonomy for the Tibetan People,[2] provided in 2010 during the Ninth Round. I discuss them later in this chapter. Among the other significant documents was a handwritten letter from His Holiness to President Hu Jintao, along with a Chinese translation, that I personally presented to Liu Yandong, Vice Chair of the CPPCC and Minister for the United Front, in 2004 during the Third Round of talks for onward transmission to the President. In the letter, His Holiness expressed: (1) his happiness at being able to send his envoys for the Third Round; (2) his wish to make a pilgrimage to the PRC, including a visit to Mount Wutai; and (3) his view that President Hu Jintao's personal experience in Tibet could be a positive factor in resolving the Tibet issue. He concluded the letter stating his desire to meet with the PRC leadership in an effort to secure a mutually acceptable solution to the Tibet issue.

During our meetings, we also put forth a number of different proposals, both orally and in writing, with the aim of creating favorable circumstances for the dialogue to move forward. In the Fourth and Fifth Rounds, for example, we fervently pursued the long-standing suggestion for His Holiness to make a pilgrimage to some sacred sites, and in the Sixth and Eighth Rounds, we proposed setting up a Joint Study Group of Tibetan and Chinese members to ascertain conditions in Tibetan areas and to explain in depth the essence of His Holiness's Middle Way Approach.

The idea for the Joint Study Group arose in response to concerns routinely raised by our counterparts. During the Fifth Round of dialogue, they made a very detailed presentation of the major development activities undertaken in the TAR and other Tibetan autonomous areas. They highlighted projects in Lhasa and in some Tibetan areas in Sichuan and Yunnan Provinces. They were deeply disappointed over His Holiness's and the Tibetan leadership's failure to acknowledge any of this progress, construing our silence as a deliberate attempt to project an erroneous, dark picture of conditions in Tibetan areas to the international community.

We indeed expressed amazement at the virtually unimaginable progress Beijing had achieved in many areas of the PRC, but at the same time highlighted the fact that compared to the national standard, Tibetan areas remained very backward. Further acknowledging that definite improvements had been made in some areas, including infrastructure, that no doubt benefited resident Tibetans, we were concerned about the burdens and disadvantages that some of the other projects had occasioned. We wanted an opportunity to assess these "developments" firsthand and, via the efforts of a joint group, generate an unbiased report that might contribute to both sides having a more uniform view of the actual situation that would materially advance our talks. Our desire to have a better understanding of the actual conditions was genuine. But, had we suggested visiting these areas without the cloak of the Joint Study Group, we were concerned the authorities might not agree to our request, as they had not been pleased with the conclusions reached by our earlier Fact-Finding Delegations. We thought that the idea of a joint group might make our request more palatable.

We also thought that a Joint Study Group could set the stage for a healthy discussion of His Holiness's Middle Way Approach. We wanted to take the opportunity once again to dispel any doubts or suspicion that his proposal was a veiled attempt to seek independence or to restore the old aristocratic system of governance. PRC propaganda at the time was not limited to labeling His Holiness a "splittist" but further accused him of wanting to restore the old system, adopting the Tibetan expression for "resurrecting the dead" to bolster Beijing's contentions. In rebutting this strange accusation, I bluntly told my counterparts that in exile, His Holiness had introduced unprecedented changes in the system of governance, and that today it would be very difficult to find even one former feudal lord or aristocrat holding any official position. If there were any younger officials from former aristocratic families, they were chosen solely because of their personal qualifications and capabilities. By contrast, I told them how astounded I was by the number of former lords and lamas who had been inducted into the PRC system. To me, the situation looked more like the "dead had been resurrected" in the PRC than it had with us in exile. I also contrasted the genuine democratic system we had instituted in Dharamsala with the class-based system that was adopted in the early years of the PRC, when individuals of targeted classes were victimized.

One of Beijing's persistent accusations has been its unfounded labeling of His Holiness as a "splittist." This is and has been a constant refrain by Beijing that we take every opportunity to expose as baseless. Neither prior to nor during our formal discussions did Beijing ever provide any evidence even remotely supporting its allegations. The situation remains the same as of the writing of this book. Its propaganda campaign fomenting this accusation has actually backfired, deeply eroding Beijing's credibility in the international community. Responsible governments recognize the sincerity of His Holiness's explicit decision to forego seeking independence in favor of genuine autonomy for the Tibetan people within the PRC, where they can live with the Chinese as equals and with dignity. Since 1979, when His Holiness publicly announced his decision, he has never wavered in his commitment to it, unambiguously reaffirming it in all his writings and public statements.

> On the future of Tibet, let me take this opportunity to restate categorically that I am not seeking independence. I am seeking a meaningful autonomy for the Tibetan people within the People's Republic of China. If the real concern of the Chinese leadership is the unity and stability of PRC, I have fully addressed their concerns. I have chosen to adopt this position because I believe, given the obvious benefits especially in economic development, this would be in the best interest of the Tibetan people. Furthermore, I have no

> intention of using any agreement on autonomy as a stepping-stone for Tibet's independence.
>
> I have conveyed these thoughts to successive Chinese leaders. In particular, following the renewal of direct contact with the Chinese government in 2002, I have explained these in detail through my envoys. Despite all this, Beijing continues to allege that my "hidden agenda" is separation and restoration of Tibet's old socio-political system. Such a notion is unfounded and untrue.[3]

I have never understood why PRC officials won't accept His Holiness's forthright and unambiguous position. Seeking advice on how to convince Beijing of his sincerity and overcome its false perceptions, I have spoken to a number of scholars, including some Chinese friends. Most of them, with one notable exception, seem as puzzled and disappointed as I am. It was my late friend Youyi Li, who, in his typical unabashed manner, lectured me: "Lodi la, of course they understand His Holiness is not seeking separation. But they must continue to label him as a 'separatist.' Otherwise, how can they justify to the Chinese people continuing to deny him the opportunity to visit China? Only when they make up their mind to welcome him back will they stop calling him a splittist."

How true! I now understand that no matter what efforts we make, Beijing is not likely to change its tune. As with other contentious issues, the accusation of His Holiness being a "splittist" is a standard Chinese smokescreen for Beijing's refusal to deal with a complicated problem. That doesn't mean we stop publicly refuting it. We need to continue protesting such accusations at every turn while recognizing that the rhetoric will only subside when Beijing feels it opportune to do so.

In addition to the discussions during our formal meetings, I kept in close touch with our counterparts between our meetings on important matters, including a desire by His Holiness to make a personal visit to the region affected by the devastating 2008 earthquake to console the affected populace. Facilitating this personal visit not only would have been a major breakthrough in our relations but also would have generated praise from both the international community and local Tibetans, all of whom would have seen this as a very genuine and sincere expression of Beijing's desire to resolve the Tibet issue. Knowing how complicated a personal visit by His Holiness would be, I was disappointed but not surprised by Beijing's unwillingness to provide this opportunity.

As a Tibetan with a deep belief in my own Buddhist tradition, however, what personally saddened and actually surprised me was the government's refusal to allow a small group of monks to visit some holy sites in Tibet to perform religious rites for the long life of His Holiness. We made this request based on our deeply held religious traditions. While we recognize that the Chinese leaders do not subscribe to our beliefs, they were fully aware of the importance of the request at the time. His Holiness was turning seventy-two years old (according to Tibetan tradition) in 2006. In our culture, when one attains this age, it is considered the beginning of a critical period in one's life that can benefit from the performance of religious ceremonies and other prescribed rites. We made it very clear that the delegation would not include the heads of any Tibetan religious lineages, as we knew the participation of individuals of such stature would be difficult for Beijing to accept.

Recognizing that a kind gesture of this type would not go unnoticed inside Tibet and believing that Beijing would grant our request, we had already selected monks from each of the Tibetan religious traditions to make the trip. We had even submitted the list of names to our counterparts for their consideration during the Fourth Round of talks in Switzerland. The subsequent denial of this immensely personal request added yet another layer of deep resentment in the hearts of Tibetans everywhere, especially those inside Tibet. It was a callous and very blunt message of Beijing's disapproving attitude of His Holiness. Had Beijing acted wisely and agreed to the visit, not only would it have had quite a profound, positive impact on the Tibetans because of their love and respect for His Holiness, but it would also have burnished the PRC's image in the international community.

## SUMMARY OF THE FIRST SIX ROUNDS OF DIALOGUE

Rather than give a lengthy discussion of each of the Nine Rounds of dialogue, I will summarize the earlier meetings and focus on the Seventh through Ninth Rounds, as these held the most substance.

The First and Second Rounds in 2002 and 2003 were designed to reestablish formal contact between the parties and to cement our relationship so that serious discussions could begin. His Holiness and Kalon Tripa Samdhong Rinpoche were very clear that this should be our focus and we should be extremely careful not to say or do anything that could create obstacles in reestablishing this connection.

We embarked on our maiden visit to Beijing in the second week of September 2002, almost twenty years after our last formal, direct contact with the PRC leadership. The visit was kept low profile and, as previously discussed, a press release from the Office of His Holiness the Dalai Lama was issued in Dharamsala only after our arrival in Beijing. We hoped to accomplish two objectives: reestablish direct contact with the leadership in Beijing and create an atmosphere conducive to continuing face-to-face meetings on a regular basis in the future; and explain His Holiness's Middle Way Approach to resolving the issue of Tibet and the mutual benefits that could be gained if a solution were premised on that vision. For their part, our counterparts reiterated their long-standing position concerning His Holiness and the situation in Tibet, but also spent some time discussing the economic and infrastructure development that was occurring in the PRC, in particular those activities taking place in Tibet.

On our return from Beijing, we reported to His Holiness and the Kashag. To encourage a receptive attitude on Beijing's side, the Kalon Tripa inaugurated an affirmative policy to continue building trust between the parties. He urged all Tibetans and friends of Tibet to refrain from public rallies and demonstrations against the PRC, including during President Jiang Zemin's upcoming October visit to the United States and Mexico.

In May 2003, our delegation returned to the PRC for the Second Round of talks. In addition to the main objective of continuing the process begun in September 2002 to meet Beijing leaders responsible for Tibetan affairs, we had three specific aims for this visit: broadening our overall understanding of the situation in the PRC through visits to different areas and meetings with officials; meeting Chinese Buddhist leaders and visit Buddhist holy sites; and above all, visiting Tibetan areas and meeting Tibetan officials.

Changes in the leadership of the CCP as well as in the PRC government since our first meeting resulted in a change in our counterparts' delegation. In Beijing we met with Liu Yandong, Minister of the United Front; Zhu Weiqun, Vice Minister; and Chang Rongjun, the Deputy Secretary-General, among others. We were impressed by the attention and candor displayed by these representatives during our meeting. Both sides agreed that our past relationship had had many twists and turns and that many areas of disagreement still existed. We further recognized the need for enhanced efforts to overcome the existing problems and bring about a climate of mutual understanding and trust.

We left the 2003 meetings greatly encouraged by this first encounter with our new negotiating counterparts. They explicitly acknowledged the positive efforts the Tibetan leadership had taken to create a favorable environment for continuing the dialogue. Both sides agreed to take further steps toward that end. In his 2004 annual statement commemorating the 1959 Tibetan National Uprising, His Holiness expressed a willingness to meet with the new PRC leaders to secure a mutually acceptable solution to the Tibet issue. In welcoming the dialogue between his envoys and their PRC counterparts, His Holiness said: "I consider it of highest importance to maintain the momentum and to intensify and deepen this process through regular face-to-face meetings and substantive discussions."

These two initial meetings, however, were very much "form over function." We were initially received at the Great Hall of the People and then "treated" to overly elaborate banquets. Discussions with the United Front Minister were then conducted in a reception room where we were positioned side by side on overstuffed, doily-laden sofas, a setting more conducive to formal social gatherings than hardball political negotiations. This protocol was in line with the way all prior Tibetan delegations had been received in the past.

Beginning in 2004 with the Third Round of talks (September 12–29), we were able to move from this largely ceremonial structure to one reflecting the seriousness of the discussions. From then on, we would first meet with the United Front Minister at a formal reception. This was followed by substantive discussions with the Vice Minister that were conducted in a very professional manner. The initial meeting with the Minister was not solely ceremonial; it reflected the importance senior leaders attached to our visit. In addition to the United Front Minister, many other senior officials attended this reception, including the Vice Minister and the United Front Secretary General or his deputy, as well as directors of various other bureaus. These encounters were not just social events; we were given the opportunity to make formal presentations of our views as well as to offer responses to any questions, or rebut inaccuracies or misperceptions, raised at the time.

During this round of dialogue, held in Beijing, we again met with Minister Liu Yandong, Vice Minister Zhu Weiqun, and Secretary General Chang Rongjun. To this third meeting we brought two additional objectives: creating a stable dialogue process and bringing the status of the dialogue to a higher level. And indeed, this was the first meeting in which we had significant substantive discussions. We identified our major differences and acknowledged the need for further meetings to try to narrow the gaps between our respective positions. Both sides stressed the need for flexibility, farsightedness, and vision to bridge our differences.

The Fourth Round of talks took place on June 30 and July 1, 2005, at the PRC embassy in Bern, Switzerland. Once again, we had very frank and serious discussions. While major differences remained, the parties exchanged views on many core issues. From our side, we offered several concrete proposals to help build trust and confidence between us, with the goal of moving the dialogue to a new level of engagement. We once again raised the idea of a pilgrimage by His Holiness to some holy sites in the PRC. We also reiterated our view that a meeting between His Holiness and the PRC leadership would be a major step forward in resolving the parties' differences. To reaffirm His Holiness's sincerity in seeking a resolution that was premised on Tibet remaining part of the PRC, we explained the crux of the Middle Way Approach and provided a thirty-three-page document addressing concerns raised in prior meetings.

During this round of talks we reaffirmed our commitment to creating an environment of trust and respect conducive to the continuation of the dialogue. We urged our counterparts to join us in this effort, highlighting the absence of any such gestures from their side. We noted that the Kashag would be issuing a second appeal to all Tibetans and Tibet support groups to refrain from any negative actions, including the staging of protest demonstrations or any other activities that would be embarrassing to President Hu Jintao during his forthcoming trip to the Americas.

Both sides left the meeting with a positive assessment of the ongoing dialogue process. Now Executive Vice Minister Zhu noted that the central leadership of the CCP attached great importance to this contact with His Holiness. He was further pleased that direct contact between the parties had now become stable and an "established practice." Moreover, he counseled us not to be pessimistic about the existing differences between us, that it would be possible to narrow the gaps in subsequent meetings. His Holiness was also very pleased with the Bern round, noting that it had provided a further opportunity to deepen the relationship through a candid exchange of views.

The Fifth Round of talks took place from February 15 to 23, 2006. As had become standard practice, for the first few days we toured different areas, including the Guangxi Zhuang Autonomous Region. On February 22, the day before our departure, we had a day-long meeting with Zhu Weiqun in Guilin City during which we dealt with substantive issues. We presented a nineteen-page document responding to questions and concerns raised by our counterparts during the Fourth Round. However, during this meeting it was apparent that major differences between the parties, even regarding the approach to take in addressing the issue, still existed. Nevertheless, both sides remained committed to the dialogue process. Our counterparts stated their firm belief that the obstacles could be overcome through further discussion.

We met for the Sixth Round of talks from June 29 to July 5, 2007, amid a further hardening of attitude on behalf of Beijing and an unexpected propaganda campaign vilifying His Holiness and objecting to the Middle Way Approach. The atmosphere both inside Tibet and in the exile community was tense as supporters of our cause prepared to stage demonstrations against the upcoming 2008 Olympic Games in Beijing. Discussions were held in three sessions over a day and a half in Shanghai and Nanjing. Once again, Executive Vice Minister Zhu Weiqun, and now Vice Minister Sithar, led the discussions from the PRC side. In strong terms, both sides articulated our respective positions. This was the first meeting in which we proposed sending a Joint Study Group to assess the situation on the ground. Our proposal was flatly rejected.

The dialogue had reached a critical stage. Upon our return to Dharamsala, His Holiness instructed us to submit a comprehensive analysis of the process to date. Because of the hardening in Beijing's attitude, we felt the prospect of moving forward with the dialogue was diminishing. Kalon Tripa Samdhong Rinpoche convened a meeting of the Task Force to consider our options. In an earlier Task Force meeting in 2004, we had formulated an "exit strategy" to curtail discussions with our counterparts, should the hard-liners in Beijing prevail in playing the "waiting game." As I have said on many occasions, that policy is a fundamentally misguided and dangerous approach.

> Some detractors in the Chinese Government seem to believe that the aspirations of the Tibetan people will fizzle out once the Dalai Lama passes away. This is a most dangerous and myopic approach. Certainly, the absence of the Dalai Lama would be devastating for the Tibetan people. But more importantly his absence would mean that China would be left to handle the problem without the presence of a leader who enjoys the loyalty of the entire community and who remains firmly committed to non-violence. It is certain

> that the Tibetan position would become more intractable in his absence, and that having had their beloved leader pass away in exile would create deep and irreparable wounds in the hearts of the Tibetan people. In the absence of His Holiness the Dalai Lama, there is no way that the entire population would be able to contain their resentment and anger. And it only takes a few desperate individuals or groups to create major instability. This is not a threat, but a statement of fact. . . . The Dalai Lama's world view, his special bond with the Tibetan people and the respect he enjoys in the international community all make the person of the Dalai Lama key both to achieving a negotiated solution to the Tibetan issue and to peacefully implementing any agreement that is reached. This is why we have consistently conveyed to our Chinese counterparts that far from being the problem, His Holiness the Dalai Lama is the solution.[4]

## INFORMAL MAY 2008 MEETING IN SHENZHEN

In early 2008, not only were there widespread protests all over the Tibetan Plateau arising from the terrible conditions suffered by the Tibetan people, there were also international demonstrations against the Beijing Olympics. While in the past, the PRC leadership had claimed that His Holiness had little influence over the Tibetans inside Tibet, by March 2008, the unprecedented protests on the Plateau were so beyond Beijing's control that, during his state visit to Laos, Premier Wen Jiabao asked His Holiness to use his "influence" to calm down the situation in Tibet.[5] Deeply concerned about the deteriorating situation, His Holiness offered to negotiate directly with President Hu Jintao. He further appealed to the Chinese people to help dispel the misunderstandings between the two communities and create an environment conducive to negotiating a peaceful, lasting solution to the problem of Tibet in the spirit of understanding and accommodation. His Holiness further expressed his appreciation and gratitude to the many world leaders, Parliamentarians, NGOs, and members of the public who expressed their deep concern over the tragic events in Tibet.

Indeed, there was unprecedented support and sympathy for the Tibetan cause worldwide, including within the Chinese community. Chinese intellectuals both inside and outside the PRC, including Liu Xiaobo, the future Nobel Peace Prize laureate, authored more than a thousand articles supporting the Tibetan cause,

Meeting in Shanghai during the Sixth Round of talks, June 30, 2007. Participating United Front officials include Sithar (Vice Minister, Central United Front), Penpa Tashi, Lian Jian, Yao Mao Chen, Gao Xi

urging the PRC leadership to engage in substantive dialogue with His Holiness and criticizing Beijing's policies toward the Tibetan people. Particularly remarkable and encouraging for our side was a signed petition delivered to the PRC leadership by a group of Chinese intellectuals residing in the PRC, urging it to rethink its Tibet policy.

Many human rights groups and world leaders, including US President George W. Bush, French President Nicolas Sarkozy, Japanese Prime Minister Yasuo Fukuda, British Prime Minister Gordon Brown, and European Parliament President Hans-Gert Pottering, urged the PRC leadership to have substantive talks with His Holiness's representatives. President Bush spoke by phone with his PRC counterpart Hu Jintao, reiterating the need for substantive dialogue with the Dalai Lama. Many heads of state threatened to boycott the Olympic Games' opening and closing ceremonies, while prominent athletes announced their intentions to boycott the games.

The protests over participation in the Olympic Games seriously annoyed Beijing, and while I am confident that they knew these events were spontaneous and certainly not instigated by us,[6] they nevertheless blamed us for the global embarrassment they faced. This, combined with the Plateauwide demonstrations Tibetans undertook against Chinese misrule, deeply disturbed and worried them. But rather than taking any active steps to correct wrongdoing and reduce tensions, Beijing began a vicious campaign maligning His Holiness and the Tibetan people.

For the first time, Beijing's propaganda tactics were successful in creating a big divide between the Chinese and the Tibetans. His Holiness was deeply saddened by the events. In all my decades of service to him, I have never seen him as agitated as he was during this time. He felt helpless to do anything to bring any comfort to his people. This tragic and seemingly intractable situation made His Holiness, who is always full of optimism and hope, doubt the benefits of continued dialogue. But despite our despair, we did not retreat from our engagement. In fact, we urgently redoubled our efforts to see if we could find some way of defusing the situation. We asked for an informal, emergency meeting of the principals only. Beijing agreed, and Kelsang Gyaltsen and I traveled to Shenzhen to meet with Zhu Weiqun and Sithar on May 4, 2008.

When our counterparts agreed to this meeting, we were hopeful, thinking that Beijing finally realized we needed to put our heads together first and foremost to calm conditions on the ground. Our discussions were difficult but honest. We left believing that some positive steps would be taken. But, once again to our grave disappointment, after this meeting there was no concrete follow-up by the PRC authorities. Instead, they did just the opposite, totally inflaming the situation. Beijing's massive negative propaganda campaign painted every Tibetan as ungrateful and untrustworthy. As 2008 unfolded, countless Tibetans holding high government and Party positions in the PRC were subject to discrimination, intimidation, and other abuses. They were denied accommodations in hotels where they held confirmed reservations, and many were prevented from traveling to international conferences despite having formal invitations and the requisite official permission to attend. In the short period of a few months, the PRC government managed to make every Tibetan feel as if he were a second-class citizen.

During our informal May 4 meeting, as well as in subsequent formal meetings, I proffered my harshest criticism of the PRC government for its conduct. I am on record explicitly telling them that future generations, and the history books, would never forgive them for this egregious error that created such a deep rift between the Tibetans and the Chinese. Their actions constituted the most provocative and devastating acts of "splittism" that could be imagined. Their propaganda was so intense, extensive, and unrelenting that it had dramatic negative effects even among people in generally sympathetic places like Hong Kong. What Chinese person wouldn't feel disturbed and threatened by the distorted images circulated by Beijing's propaganda machine showing Tibetans armed with knives chasing and kicking Chinese individuals identified as innocent bystanders? The most publicized image of His Holiness Beijing circulated in those days showed him with a raised fist and strained look on his face, implying that this evinced his deep anger with the Chinese. In fact, the image was taken completely out of context and had absolutely nothing to do with that particular event or period.

## THE SEVENTH ROUND OF TALKS

At the Shenzhen informal meeting in early May 2008, we proposed having the Seventh Round of talks in early June, but due to the devastating Sichuan earthquake, they were postponed. We ended up visiting Beijing from June 30 to July 3, 2008. We first met with Du Qinglin, Vice Chairman of the CPPCC and the newly appointed Minister of the United Front, on July 1. He gave us a brief overview of the PRC's domestic and international situation as well as its policy on Tibet. We took the opportunity to explain His Holiness's basic approach in resolving the Tibet issue. On July 2, we had a day-long meeting with Zhu Weiqun and Sithar.

This was one of the most difficult sessions held so far. Even though the recent events in Tibet clearly demonstrated the Tibetan people's genuine and deep-rooted discontent over Beijing's policies, our counterparts could focus on nothing but the security of the upcoming Olympic Games. We highlighted the urgent need for serious and sincere efforts to address conditions on the Plateau with courage and vision in the interests of stability, unity, and harmony of all the peoples within the PRC. To our dismay, our pleas fell on deaf ears. In the course of our discussions, we felt compelled to candidly convey to our counterparts that in the absence of any serious steps on their part, continuation of the dialogue process would serve no purpose.

At the time, there was a widespread belief, not only in the Tibetan world but also in the broader international community, that the PRC representatives were only meeting with us to dispel international criticism prior to the Olympics. As all the efforts to create an atmosphere of respect and restraint had come from our side, I was beginning to find myself among this group of doubters as well. The Tibetan leadership was equally disappointed with the status of the talks. In his statement on the occasion of His Holiness's seventy-third birthday, Kalon

Negotiations during the Seventh Round of talks led by the author and Envoy Kelsang Gyaltsen on behalf of the Tibetans and Executive Vice Minister Zhu Weiqun and Vice Minister Sithar on behalf of the Chinese, Beijing, July 2, 2008

Tripa Samdhong Rinpoche said: "Unfortunately, the seventh round of talks—as we have suspected from the very beginning—did not at all go in accordance with our hopes and expectations. Moreover, the Chinese government has indulged in a selfish act of spewing one-sided propaganda on Tibet. Greatly disturbed by these negative developments, we are doubtful, more than ever before, whether the leaders of the People's Republic of China have the determination and sincerity to work toward achieving a reconciliation on the issue of Tibet."[7]

At the conclusion of the Seventh Round, our counterparts tried to allay our fears. They countered our pessimism by stating that the discussions had been productive so far and that we needed to keep in mind that a half-century-old issue of great complexity could not be resolved in just a few years. Our displeasure did generate one positive effect. Responding to our concerns, Minister Du explicitly invited us to present suggestions from His Holiness to promote stability and development in Tibet, while Zhu Weiqun further solicited our views on the degree or form of autonomy His Holiness envisioned. Despite our misgivings, but guided by the Tibetan leadership's policy of engagement, we agreed to hold another round of discussions at the end of October. Our negotiating counterparts' overtures, in fact, led to preparation of the landmark Memorandum on Genuine Autonomy for the Tibetan People (Memorandum) that we subsequently presented during the Eighth Round of talks and which laid out in detail His Holiness's Middle Way Approach.

## INTERNAL POLITICS GENERATE DIALOGUE UNCERTAINTY

The dialogue process that I led was conducted as part of a unified effort under the direct guidance of His Holiness with Kalon Tripa Samdhong Rinpoche's assistance. From the beginning, however, a small group within the Tibetan community started questioning, and in some cases opposing, the dialogue. It is understandable for those affected by policy decisions to raise concerns. In fact, I was deeply disappointed that many Tibetans lacked any interest at all in the dialogue process. Such apathy is at a minimum disrespectful, given that His Holiness is working on behalf of all the Tibetan people to improve our collective future. But even worse, some of the opposition put forward by these critics seemed to be motivated more by their own selfish concerns than by the greater good of the Tibetan people. Sadly, the most outspoken of these individuals held, and in some cases continue to hold, responsible positions within the Tibetan leadership, exercising considerable influence over some sectors of the exile community.

During the course of the dialogue, written statements by some Tibetan activists criticizing both the process and His Holiness for adopting the Middle Way Approach became more frequent. This deteriorating situation, combined with the lack of any signs of progress in the dialogue and the worsening state of affairs inside Tibet, prompted His Holiness and the Tibetan leadership to convene a Special General Meeting. Authorized under Article 59 of the Tibetan Charter, it was set for November 17–22, 2008, and given the unusually broad mandate of addressing the advisability of continuing the dialogue. The widespread perception within the exile community was that discontinuation of the talks would be recommended. I myself became quite alarmed about that possibility.

Unfortunately, the Eighth Round of talks had already been scheduled for October 30 to November 5, preceding the Special Meeting by several weeks. As the sole purpose of the Eighth Round was to present the Memorandum, our most important proposal, I was reluctant to make the trip before the outcome of the meeting was known. Even with my limited diplomatic experience, I was concerned that a document of such historic importance should not be put forward in a situation of uncertainty where the delegation's authority and the continuation of the dialogue process were in question. But His Holiness, with his customary farsighted wisdom, instructed that the delegation must visit as planned. As in so many cases, it proved to be a very wise decision, even though at the time it generated some ill will among our counterparts. Had we not gone ahead with the trip, however, we never would have had the opportunity to put forth and discuss this momentous proposal with the PRC leadership.

## THE EIGHTH ROUND OF DIALOGUE AND PRESENTATION OF THE MEMORANDUM ON GENUINE AUTONOMY FOR THE TIBETAN PEOPLE

In many ways the Eighth Round was the most important because of our presentation of the Memorandum. It was the most thoughtful and comprehensive proposal we provided to Beijing during the dialogue process and remains His Holiness's fundamental position on the subject. It outlines the specific needs of the Tibetan people for autonomy and self-government and how they can be met through application of the principles on autonomy set forth in the PRC Constitution. One of the main goals of this book is to provide a better understanding of the issues involved and the efforts we have made to resolve them in our direct negotiations with Beijing. The Memorandum is an essential document from this perspective that must be carefully reviewed.

### *The Memorandum Was Prepared in Response to Chinese Overtures*

The decision to prepare the Memorandum was not ours alone; not only was it drafted with the full knowledge of our negotiating counterparts, it was initiated in response to the suggestion of Du Qinglin, Vice Chair of the CPPCC, and Executive Vice Minister Zhu Weiqun of the United Front. When the genesis of the document became controversial, Zhu Weiquan did try to distance himself from it, contending that he had only asked for the proposal "to test the sincerity of the

Dalai Lama." He stopped short of denying his involvement, however, and in the introductory section of the Memorandum, we highlighted our counterparts' invitation requesting its preparation:

> During the seventh round of talks in Beijing on July 1 and 2, 2008, the Vice Chairman of the Chinese People's Political Consultative Conference and the Minister of the Central United Front Work Department, Mr. Du Qinglin, explicitly invited suggestions from His Holiness the Dalai Lama for the stability and development of Tibet. The Executive Vice Minister of the Central United Front Work Department, Mr. Zhu Weiqun, further said they would like to hear our views on the degree or form of autonomy we are seeking as well as on all aspects of regional autonomy within the scope of the Constitution of the PRC.

Our cover letter transmitting the Memorandum, addressed to Du Qinglin, further referenced our counterparts' invitation:

> During the seventh round of talks you explicitly invited His Holiness the Dalai Lama to provide suggestions for the stability and development of Tibet. Similarly, the Executive Vice-Minister of the Central United Front Work Department, Mr. Zhu Weiqun, said your side is willing to hear our views on the degree or form of autonomy we are seeking as well as on all aspects of regional autonomy within the scope of the Constitution of the People's Republic of China. We are hereby providing this Memorandum on Genuine Autonomy for the Tibetan People outlining their basic needs. In the past, too, we have had the opportunity to present to you the basic points contained in this memorandum.
>
> Since our aim is to find a mutually acceptable approach within the scope of the Constitution of the People's Republic of China, we are fully confident that, given goodwill, the issues raised in our memorandum can be implemented within its framework.
>
> We are presenting these suggestions with the sole purpose of making a sincere effort at addressing the real problems in Tibet, and in ensuring the full implementation of the regional national autonomy status, in accordance with the spirit of the Constitution. We strongly believe that this will contribute to the stability and development of Tibet, promote peace, harmony, and unity

of all nationalities, and serve the interest of the Tibetan and Chinese peoples. It is not our intention to continue the arguments of both sides on the current exercise of autonomy status for the Tibetan people.

The resumption of our contact in 2002 has resulted in establishing a stable contact enabling both sides to explain and understand each other's position. However, on the fundamental issue there has not been any meaningful outcome. On the contrary, the situation in Tibet has deteriorated during this period, rather than there being any positive changes. Thus, our contact has reached a most critical stage. Therefore, we strongly urge that we discuss and agree on a mutually acceptable mechanism to address the issues raised in this memorandum, and to set up a timetable to do so effectively.

So far, despite growing difficulties, we have been able to maintain the contact and thus demonstrate our sincerity. However, in the absence of any concrete outcome resulting in a forward movement in our contact, the signs of frustration and disappointment among Tibetans, both inside and out of Tibet, have been growing. We are, therefore, afraid that the obvious reality then would be that if the eighth round of talks fails to bring about concrete results, the present process cannot continue.

In conclusion, it is our hope that the Central Government, considering the unity of the country, friendship of nationalities, the establishment of a harmonious society, and the long-term common interest of the Tibetan and Chinese peoples, will act on this memorandum with farsightedness and vision.

I would also like to make one other thing perfectly clear. Despite contrary rumblings in some sectors of the Tibetan exile community, the Memorandum was never "rejected" by Beijing. This mistaken perception may be the result of a failure by some to understand the difference between the terms "rejection" and "objection" when they are used in the diplomatic context. In the diplomatic world, when one of the involved parties is unwilling to entertain a proposal, quite often it will refuse even to accept a document—a clear message of rejection. At other times, documents may initially be accepted but subsequently be returned to the author, sometimes without any formal notes attached—again a clear sign of rejection, sending the message that the recipient doesn't even want to hint at the possibility that it has seen the material.

This was simply not the situation in our case. Not only was our Memorandum presented in response to Beijing's explicit suggestion, it was neither rejected nor returned to us but actually became the main discussion item on the agenda during the remainder of the Eighth Round of talks and into the Ninth.

### *Circumstances Affecting Presentation of the Memorandum*

When we arrived in Beijing on October 30 for the Eighth Round of talks, we were initially told that we would first visit Ningxia Hui Autonomous Region and only meet with senior leaders upon our return to Beijing on November 5, the last day of the dialogue. With this restricted timetable in mind, I decided to give the Memorandum to Vice Minister Sithar immediately, requesting that he share it with senior leaders so that they would have some time to review it and we could have informed discussions on our return to Beijing.

Had I had complete control over the situation, I would have handled this most important task differently. The short time before our formal meeting and the need to discuss the Memorandum's substance at that time, however, required me to submit the document in this rather haphazard manner. In the absence of any time constraints, and had there not been the existing political uncertainty back home in Dharamsala, we would have presented this instrumental document in a formal meeting with the United Front Minister and Executive Vice Minister. We would have concurrently discussed the context in which the Memorandum should be considered, highlighted its major provisions, and sought to ease any concerns arising from the most challenging proposals. Unfortunately, this was not to be the case. The complex and tense situation prevailing within the exile leadership at the time and the uncertainty over the outcome of the Special General Meeting scheduled for mid-November gave us envoys very little room to maneuver. Circumstances compelled me to act informally, hurriedly handing the document to the Vice Minister with no ability to set the tone or explain the substance of the Memorandum in its most promising and compelling light.

When we returned to Beijing, we found our counterparts highly agitated. Despite this, none of our previously established activities was disturbed, including our meeting with the Vice Chair of the CPPCC and United Front Minister Du, during which we formally made our presentation. Our day-long working discussions addressing the Memorandum were held with Zhu Weiqun, assisted by Sithar, and for the first time, as I previously mentioned, a senior leader from the TAR, Pema Trinley.

### *The Essence of the Memorandum*

In the Memorandum, we initially cite the rights of the Tibetan people for unity and autonomy as guaranteed in the PRC Constitution and related laws.

> The Tibetan nationality lives in one contiguous area on the Tibetan plateau, which they have inhabited for millennia and to which they are therefore indigenous. For purposes of the constitutional principles of national regional autonomy Tibetans in the PRC in fact live as a single nationality all over the Tibetan plateau. . . .
>
> The uniqueness of the Tibetan situation has consistently been recognised within the PRC and has been reflected in the terms of the '17-Point Agreement' and in statements and policies of successive leaders of the PRC since then, and should remain the basis for defining the scope and structure of the specific autonomy to be exercised by the Tibetan nationality within the PRC.

The Memorandum then identifies the major considerations required to *implement* these existing guarantees. Two of the most important are:

> **1. Respect for the Integrity of the Tibetan Nationality**
>
> As a part of the multi-national state of the PRC, Tibetans can benefit greatly from the rapid economic and scientific development the country is experiencing. While wanting to actively participate and contribute to this development, we want to ensure that this happens without the people losing their Tibetan identity, culture and core values and without putting the distinct and fragile environment of Tibetan plateau, to which Tibetans are indigenous, at risk. . . .
>
> For this to happen, it is imperative that the right of Tibetans to govern themselves be recognised and implemented throughout the region where they live in compact communities in the PRC, in accordance with the Tibetan nationality's own needs, priorities and characteristics.
>
> The specific matters that the Memorandum identifies as the "basic needs of Tibetans" over which they should have control to realize the goal of

self-government are: language, culture, religion, education, environmental protection, utilization of natural resources, economic development and trade, public health, regulation of population migration, and cultural, educational and religious exchanges with other countries.

### 2. Application of a Single Administration for the Tibetan Nationality in the PRC

In order for the Tibetan nationality to develop and flourish with its distinct identity, culture and spiritual tradition through the exercise of self-government on the above mentioned basic Tibetan needs, the entire community, comprising all the areas currently designated by the PRC as Tibetan autonomous areas, should be under one single administrative entity.

Bringing all the Tibetans currently living in designated Tibetan autonomous areas within a single autonomous administrative unit is entirely in accordance with the constitutional principle contained in Article 4, also reflected in the LRNA [Law on Regional National Autonomy] (Article 2), that "regional autonomy is practiced in areas where people of minority nationalities live in concentrated communities."

*Reaction to the Memorandum*

Not surprisingly, our counterparts' substantive reaction to the Memorandum was negative. Executive Vice Minister Zhu was critical of the proposal, beginning with the title itself. In extremely harsh words, he voiced his strong objections to the term "genuine autonomy." With his anger barely restrained, he called our use of these words "a serious criticism" that could not be tolerated because the Tibetans were already enjoying "genuine autonomy" in the existing autonomous areas. He further labeled our proposal as an act abridging both the Constitution and the national regional autonomy system of the PRC.

### Tibet's Geographical Boundaries: Beijing's Primary Objection to Our Proposal

Our counterparts' main objection to the proposals included in the Memorandum was, once again, the geographic scope of the region that comprises a unified

Tibet. They continued to make the timeworn allegation that we were demanding establishment of an exaggerated and unwarranted area they denigrated as "greater Tibet," further characterizing our position as nothing more than a thinly masked attempt to "split" the PRC that would remove one-fourth of the PRC's total landmass from its control. Such a proposal, in their view, was against "history," "ground reality," and the "constitution and laws" of the land.

The tension between the genuine desire of the Tibetan people to be unified under one autonomous governing body and Beijing's vehement opposition to that concept was, in fact, the most difficult issue we addressed during the dialogue process.

### The Tibetan People's Claim for a Unified Tibet Is Consistent and Long-Standing

As previously discussed, this argument is not something that arose for the first time when we presented the Memorandum. The proposal for a unified Tibet to fulfill the aspirations of the Tibetan people was initially given to the Chinese leadership as early as 1951 during the negotiations over the Seventeen-Point Agreement, as well as on other occasions thereafter, as cited in the Memorandum. A unified Tibet has been a topic of discussion throughout our engagement with PRC officials, including during the secret talks I had with President Jiang's emissaries before the start of the formal dialogue process in 2002. From the very beginning, we have made it clear that His Holiness was committed to an outcome that would benefit all Tibetans, but one that was based on Tibet remaining within the PRC.

Moreover, when Deng Xiaoping took the initiative in reaching out to His Holiness in 1979 through Gyalo Thondup, he explicitly stated that other than independence, *everything else* could be discussed. At times, our negotiating counterparts have contended that Gyalo Thondup distorted Deng Xiaoping's words. But it was not only Deng Xiaoping who conveyed this message. In 1980, for example, Li Xiannian delivered a similar message to the First Fact-Finding Delegation. And when our three-member High-Level Exploratory Talks Delegations went to the PRC in 1982 and 1984, we often referred to Deng Xiaoping's statement. I remember no one seeking to refute it. In fact, PRC leaders and official publications have acknowledged this fact on numerous occasions.[8] Because Beijing aired its accusations against Gyalo Thondup in the international media,[9] however, Kalon Tripa Samdhong Rinpoche invited Gyalo Thondup and Juchen Thubten Namgyal to

Dharamsala in November 2008 to take part in a press conference[10] to share their personal recollections of the official statements.

When I was in Beijing in 1982 with the Exploratory Talks Delegation, I also raised the issue of a unified Tibet at the highest level. In one of our meetings, Yang Jingren, then Minister for Nationality Affairs, responded quite harshly, saying: "You have no right to even raise such issues." He absolutely refused to discuss the desire of the Tibetan people to be reunified despite my repeated demands for an answer. A few days later, when we were in Shanghai, Ren Rong, the United Front official accompanying us, asked for an informal meeting with the three members of our delegation. He told us he had been instructed by the Central Authority to "unofficially" answer my question. The leadership didn't wish to give the impression that it was being personally rude to me. He further added that my youthful frankness was actually very much appreciated.

Ren Rong explained that Yang Jingren's refusal to discuss the matter was because of my association with an organization that was not committed to the unity of the motherland and was still advocating Tibet independence. It was not clear to me whether he was referring to the exile leadership, of which I was still a part, or the Tibetan Youth Congress, with which I maintained a close association. In any case, he made it very clear that only those Tibetans committed to national unity and accepting Tibet as part of the PRC had such rights. After I returned to Beijing, I remember telling Phuntsok Wangyal and, I believe, Ngapo Ngawang Jigme, of the United Front's position, counseling them that in light of that view, Tibetan leaders such as themselves who are part of the system should raise the matter more vigorously.

Ren Rong bolstered his contentions by giving us a rather detailed account of a July 1957 meeting in Qingdao[11] during which Premier Zhou Enlai discussed the future administrative structure of the PRC's minority areas. Mindful of his commitment to consider the Tibetans' views regarding unification in one autonomous area versus maintaining the status quo of discrete regions, Premier Zhou consulted with a number of Tibetan leaders. Ren Rong then recounted a long list of names of Tibetan aristocrats, important religious leaders, and chieftains who participated in the meeting. The outcome, he contended, was that a majority of Tibetans favored maintenance of the present situation rather than integration into one autonomous region.

At the end of his remarks, Ren Rong turned to me and rather sarcastically said: "When you return to India you should ask your father, Gyari Nyima, who is very knowledgeable about these matters, about this conversation." He was implying that my father's generation not only had agreed to the retention of independent autonomous regions but actually preferred it. I responded that I did not need to consult with my father about the Qingdao conference. While Ren Rong was correct that Zhou Enlai did consult a number of Tibetans, by the time of the meeting, many of them had already been "encouraged" or otherwise influenced to take a position opposing a unified Tibet. In any case, I reminded him that he was now dealing with my generation, which had the further responsibility of safeguarding the interests and aspirations of future generations.

Ren Rong is one of those elder Chinese cadres who have worked in Tibet and have a good knowledge of Tibetan matters. Although his views are rooted in old-school thinking, he is among those who genuinely wish for the Tibet issue to be resolved and His Holiness to be invited to come back. I kept up relations with him after his retirement and even went to visit him once in Vienna, Austria, when he was vacationing there with his wife. From time to time, he has provided me with both verbal and written messages of encouragement. He has also urged the officials who succeeded him at the United Front to try to keep the dialogue alive so that some solution can be found.

I am sharing this rather lengthy narrative on the "greater Tibet" issue to emphasize that it has been in discussion for decades. Those Tibetans mistrustful of Gyalo Thondup doubted whether he faithfully conveyed Deng Xiaoping's message to His Holiness. Questions of his veracity aside, other Tibetan leaders received similar commitments from other senior Chinese leaders, as I have already mentioned. Moreover, I have personally seen PRC documents that confirm Gyalo Thondup's having raised the matter with Hu Yaobang. While the latter's immediate reaction showed that he had not been thoroughly briefed about Deng Xiaoping's discussions with Gyalo Thondup, his response was something to the effect of: "Although I am hearing this for the first time, we can discuss it."

When Beijing accuses His Holiness of demanding an unjustified "greater Tibet," it is trying to create the impression that we are distorting history. In fact, the opposite is true. It is the Chinese who assert an incorrect historical view of their relations with Tibet, thereby imposing a major obstacle to our moving forward. We have repeatedly told our negotiating counterparts that we are neither trying to restore the rule of the Dalai Lama nor bring the aristocrats back to power. Our request to be united under a single administrative unit is based on the deeply held aspirations of the Tibetan people. The existing situation poses insurmountable barriers for Tibetans trying to maintain their identity as a distinct people, despite provisions of the PRC Constitution guaranteeing this right.

### *The PRC Constitution Explicitly Guarantees Autonomy for Minority Nationalities, Including the Tibetan People*

The question is sometimes asked why, in addition to seeking a solution to the Tibet issue that envisions Tibet remaining a part of the PRC, His Holiness further states his commitment to finding one that also comports with the PRC Constitution: "I have only one demand: self-rule and genuine autonomy for all Tibetans, i.e., the Tibetan nationality in its entirety. This demand is in keeping with the provisions of the PRC Constitution, which means it can be met."[12] Critics of His Holiness's approach cite his position as a further example of concessions made by our side in the absence of any reciprocal accommodation by Beijing. What they fail to realize is that, if the PRC's existing constitution is faithfully implemented, there is ample room to implement our proposal as explicitly outlined in the Memorandum. Moreover, Beijing's failure to respect our aspirations could be interpreted as violating the constitutionally established rights and privileges for minority nationalities, including the Tibetans, as well as those enumerated in other PRC laws. Article 4 of the PRC Constitution explicitly states:

> All nationalities in the People's Republic of China are equal. The State protects the lawful rights and interests of the minority nationalities and upholds and develops a relationship of equality, unity and mutual assistance among all of China's nationalities. Discrimination against and oppression of any nationalities are prohibited; any act which undermines the unity of the nationalities or instigates division is prohibited.
>
> The State assists areas inhabited by minority nationalities in accelerating their economic and cultural development according to the characteristics and needs of the various minority nationalities.
>
> Regional autonomy is practiced in areas where people of minority nationalities live in concentrated (contiguous) communities; in these areas organs of self-government are established to exercise the power of autonomy.
>
> All national autonomous areas are integral parts of the People's Republic of China. All nationalities have the freedom to use and develop their own

> spoken and written language and to preserve or reform their own folkways and customs.

The Preamble of the Law on National Regional Autonomy further provides:

> Regional national autonomy means that the minority nationalities, under the unified state leadership, practise regional autonomy in areas where they live in concentrated (contiguous) communities and set up organs of self-government for the exercise of power of autonomy. Regional national autonomy embodies the state's full respect for and guarantee of the right of the minority nationalities to administer their internal affairs and its adherence to the principle of equality, unity and common prosperity for all its nationalities.[13]

During one of our rounds of talks, our counterparts regaled us with a so-called comprehensive "history lesson" of our relations as seen by Beijing. They accused us of mischaracterizing Beijing's treatment of the Tibetans as "divide and rule" tactics designed to create regional discord. They said our contention was baseless because the present regional division of Tibet happened long before the PRC was established.

I don't disagree with this specific argument. As previously noted, I am one of those people who has been uncomfortable with some of our writings in which we have used terms, and even included some "facts," without proper verification. There is a widely held belief among Tibetans, as well as many of our friends in the international community, that before Mao's Liberation Army marched into Tibetan areas, the whole of Tibet was a unified sovereign nation. This is simply not true. False proclamations to this effect actually weaken our position.

With his characteristic insight, His Holiness the Dalai Lama initiated his effort to fight for the fundamental rights of the Tibetan people without resorting to legalistic or purportedly history-based arguments that are too easily subject to debate. Rather, he chose to focus on the Tibetan people's distinct identity covering every aspect of our lives, from culture to religion, language, and way of life. His position is that because of this common bond, we as a people have every right to be unified. Moreover, this right is expressly guaranteed in the PRC Constitution. Beijing's refusal to acknowledge it abridges the express guarantees of both that document and other laws of the PRC governing the treatment of nationalities. His Holiness's argument and our proposed resolution strictly comply with the Marxist-Leninist principles that the CCP claims it upholds. While we ourselves do not subscribe to this ideology, we fully recognize that it is the foundation of the PRC's political system and the one under which we must live. Accordingly, we consciously designed a proposal that fully complies with these realities.

With the exception of His Holiness, Samdhong Rinpoche is perhaps our most eloquent spokesperson on this issue. In numerous formal presentations and interviews he has lucidly and unambiguously articulated our proposal for genuine autonomy while rebutting Beijing's intentional mischaracterization of it as an unjustified demand for creation of a region disparagingly referred to as "greater Tibet." For example, in his keynote address to the Round Table Discussion on "Greater Tibet" held in New Delhi on August 27, 2009, he stated:

> In reality, Tibet is Tibet. There is no greater or smaller Tibet. All Tibetans belong to one minority nationality among the 55 minority nationalities of the PRC. Beijing tries to mislead the international community by saying that His Holiness the Dalai Lama is demanding "Greater Tibet" which is one fourth of the PRC's territory. This propaganda is done to make people believe that His Holiness the Dalai Lama's aspiration is unreasonable and that he is asking for separation of one fourth of the PRC or that His Holiness is asking for inclusion of certain areas into an autonomous region that are not already declared as Tibetan autonomous areas.
>
> In reality, His Holiness the Dalai Lama has never used the word "Greater Tibet" at any time verbally or in written documents. If someone surveys the entire correspondences, statements, documents and any other written dossiers of the Tibetans since 1979, one will not find a single instance of the word "Greater Tibet" being used. This is the PRC's word which they are trying to project as if it is His Holiness the Dalai Lama's position.[14]

Many international institutions and scholars have gradually come to appreciate our proposal as a legitimate aspiration. No serious, unbiased expert has subscribed to Beijing's propaganda characterizing it as a hidden agenda for separation. The US Congressional-Executive Commission on China, for example, correctly interpreted it, explicitly recognizing its potential for resolving a principal area of dispute between us:

> With respect to the meaning of "Tibet," there have been two principal areas of disagreement between the Chinese government and the Dalai Lama and his envoys. One issue is the territory to be recognized as "Tibet"; the other issue is whether or not all of such territory should be unified into a single administrative area.
>
> The Memorandum's description of territory to be included in a single Tibetan administrative area appears to resolve the first of the two principal areas of divergence between the Chinese government and the Dalai Lama. The Memorandum states explicitly that a single Tibetan administrative area should comprise "all the areas currently designated by the PRC as Tibetan autonomous areas."[15]

While our proposal for a unified Tibet is sincere, legitimate, and in full compliance with the PRC Constitution and other relevant laws, I appreciate that realizing it will not be an easy task. But, rather than continuing to mischaracterize our proposal, make baseless criticisms, and launch a war of words, if Beijing's representatives were willing to sit down with us and genuinely seek a way out that meets the needs of both parties, I am among those who firmly believe we can find a mutually agreeable solution. I shouldered the important task of negotiating on behalf of my fellow Tibetans at the behest of not only my political leader but especially my revered spiritual teacher, Tenzin Gyatso, the 14th Dalai Lama of Tibet. It would have been disingenuous and against my personal ethics to have undertaken this responsibility without believing in the possibility of achieving some positive result.

But to realize what should be our common goal, the first step Beijing must be willing to take is acknowledging the legitimate right of the Tibetans to be administratively unified no matter in which autonomous area or region, or in which PRC province, they currently reside. As I told United Front officials as early as 1982, the aspiration of the Tibetan people to be unified will never go away. It will only strengthen as the Tibetans become more aware of their rights and privileges guaranteed under PRC law, and as they rediscover their great national heritage. Beijing endeavors to paint our proposal as sinister and complex. It is not. It is very simple. What His Holiness the Dalai Lama requests, and has always sought, is preservation of the rich and vibrant Tibetan civilization. It is nothing more than that.

The proposal for a single administration and common policy governing Tibetans is one viable tool for achieving this end. I have presented this option numerous times, in US Congressional hearings, before other parliamentary bodies, and at gatherings sponsored by research institutions and think tanks including: the Brookings Institution and the Center for Strategic & International Studies (CSIS) in Washington, D.C.; the Asia Center in Paris; the Asia Society in New York; and the Institute of South Asian Studies of the National University of Singapore, to mention just a few. For example, in November 2006, soon after the Fifth Round of talks, I made the following remarks at a Brookings Institution forum.

### Single Administration for the Tibetan People

Since His Holiness the Dalai Lama has addressed the fundamental concern of the Chinese government about the status of Tibet, it is our expectation that they should reciprocate by acknowledging the legitimate needs of the Tibetan people.

Today, less than half of the Tibetan people reside in the Tibet Autonomous Region. The rest reside in Tibetan autonomous counties and prefectures in Qinghai, Gansu, Sichuan and Yunnan provinces. All Tibetans residing in these Tibetan areas share the same language, ethnicity, culture, and tradition.[16] Furthermore, just as the Chinese nation has sought to unify many different regions into one nation, the Tibetan people, too, yearn to be under one administrative entity so that their way of life, tradition, and religion can be more effectively and peacefully maintained.

Historically the division of a nationality area into many administrative units contributed to the weakening and erosion of that nationality's unique characteristics, as well as its ability to grow and develop. This can also hinder or even undermine the nation's peace, stability and development. Such a situation is in contradiction to the founding goals of the People's Republic of China, namely the recognition of the equality of all nationalities. Thus in order to thrive, the Tibetan people cannot remain divided, but must be accorded the equality and respect befitting a distinct people.

The Chinese side makes the argument that the present-day Tibet Autonomous Region parallels the area under the former Tibetan government. Thus, their argument continues, our position that the entire Tibetan people need to live under a single administrative entity is unreasonable. This question will lead us inevitably to the examination of Tibet's historical legal status under the Tibetan government and will not help in reaching a common ground on which to build a common future. The Chinese Government has redrawn internal boundaries when it has suited its needs and could do so again in the case of Tibet to foster stability and to help ensure Tibet's characteristics remain intact. The point here is not about territorial division, but how to best promote Tibet's culture and way of life.

The Chinese side is also characterizing our position as a demand for the separation of one-fourth the territory of China. First of all, since the Tibetans are not asking for the separation of Tibet from China, there should be no concern on this front. More importantly, it is a reality that the landmass inhabited by Tibetans constitutes roughly one-fourth the territory of the People's Republic of China. Actually, the Chinese government has already designated almost all Tibetan areas as Tibet autonomous entities: the Tibet Autonomous Region, Tibet Autonomous Prefectures or Tibet Autonomous Counties.[17] Thus, our positions on what constitutes Tibet are really not so divergent.

Having the Tibetan people under a single administrative entity should not be seen as an effort to create a "greater" Tibet, nor is it a cover for a separatist plot. It is a question of recognizing, restoring and respecting the integrity of the Tibetans as a people and distinct nationality within the People's Republic of China. Furthermore, this is not a new or revolutionary idea. From the beginning, the Tibetans have raised this issue and representatives of the Chinese government have recognized it as one that must be addressed. In fact during the signing of the 17 Point Agreement in 1951, Premier Zhou Enlai acknowledged that the idea of unification of the Tibetan nationalities was appropriate.[18] Similarly, in 1956 Vice-Premier Chen Yi was in Lhasa and said that it would be good for Tibet's development as well as for the friendship of Tibetans and Chinese if in the future the Tibet Autonomous Region included all ethnic Tibetan areas, including those now in other provinces.[19]

The Tibetan people are striving for the right of a distinct people to be able to preserve that very distinctiveness through a single administrative entity. This would give the Tibetans a genuine sense of having benefited by being part of the People's Republic of China and would embody the respect for the integrity of the Tibetans as a distinct people.

The Chinese leadership is clearly aware that this aspiration of the Tibetan people is voiced not just by His Holiness the Dalai Lama and the Tibetans in

> exile, but by Tibetans inside Tibet, including prominent members of the Communist Party. Knowing this, certain elements of the Chinese leadership have lately been trying to alter the public perception by orchestrating and arranging written opposition to the aspiration by some of the Tibetans inside Tibet.[20]

Throughout this section I have emphasized our long-standing position on the geographic scope of our proposal, incorporating quotes from documents, speeches, and other presentations showing our transparent and consistent viewpoint. As previously acknowledged, however, I know that implementing our proposal will require serious work. Recognizing the attendant complexity, concerned individuals have suggested we look for creative ways of realizing our objective, employing methods as palatable to Beijing as possible. China experts, including some from the mainland, have raised the issue at different times, including at Brookings Institution Round Table discussions on Tibet. Below is an excerpt from an interview Kalon Tripa Samdhong Rinpoche gave to Chinese scholar Bi Yantao in February 2010. As noted by the Kalon Tripa, we are open to any suggestions from our PRC counterparts on alternative methods for realizing our objective.

**PROFESSOR BI:** I think "Greater Tibet" is the biggest obstacle for people inside China to understand the issue of Tibet. Apart from that, other concerns of the TGiE (Tibetan Government in Exile) such as religious freedom, economic development, promotion of education, protection of the Tibetan culture, etc. are understandable and I believe people inside China will also extend their support.

However, it appears that the "unification of all Tibetan areas" is the biggest difference between Beijing and the TGiE at present. If the dialogue process does not move forward, will the TGiE change its position on "One administration for all Tibetan areas" in the future? Will the Dalai Lama's side change its strategy of the dialogue process?

**KALON TRIPA:** This question cannot be entertained at this moment because there are no alternative suggestions that are forthcoming.

From our side, we consider the request for one administration for all the Tibetan nationality as reasonable and constitutional, apart from being the legitimate right of the Tibetan people. There will be no problem in implementing it if there is political will in the PRC leadership. As we have mentioned before the objective of our request is for the preservation of Tibetan language, culture and spiritual heritage.

If there is [*sic*] more logical and convincing alternative suggestions coming forth, His Holiness the Dalai Lama is always very open to any idea which is based on truth and reason.[21]

I have had serious and in-depth discussions with a number of concerned officials and experts, including some China scholars, of creative ways for realizing His Holiness's vision in a manner that Beijing can accommodate. While it would be premature to discuss these ideas in this book, I am aware that a number of people within the PRC leadership are also considering possible alternatives.

## IMPACT ON THE NEGOTIATIONS OF THE SPECIAL GENERAL MEETING

I did feel a profound sense of helplessness when I had to decline Executive Vice Minister Zhu's suggestion for us to go into a principals-only meeting at the concluding session of the Eighth Round of talks. His gesture was no doubt to show the seriousness with which they were treating the negotiations, wanting an opportunity to discuss the issues in a more intimate and informal manner.

As the future of the dialogue process was uncertain given the upcoming Special General Meeting, scheduled for less than two weeks after our return from Beijing, my colleague Kelsang Gyaltsen and I felt a sense of disempowerment precluding us from entering into any serious discussion of the Memorandum. I also thought it very important that we at least preserve the integrity and sincerity of our efforts, even if the whole dialogue process were subsequently discontinued. We did not want our counterparts to think that we had engaged in discussions leading to commitments that we had no authority to make.

Throughout the formal discussions of the Eighth Round, we had been very candid in telling our counterparts that we might not be back for any future talks, depending on the outcome of the Special General Meeting. While PRC officials generally dismiss comments about potential negative impacts of such internal meetings as political grandstanding, I had the feeling they were also very concerned. They actually tried to give us moral encouragement that the meeting would go well and that we would be able to return to continue our discussions.

Even though Zhu Weiqun criticized the proposals offered in the Memorandum in his November 10 press release following the Eighth Round of talks, he explicitly acknowledged the serious nature of our ongoing dialogue:

> As Dalai Lama's private representatives, Mr. Lodi, Mr. Kelsang Gyaltsen and three other persons came back to China and stayed from October 31 to November 5. This is the ninth contact and talk since 2002, and the third of this year. Mr. Du Qinglin, Vice-Chairman of the Chinese People's Political Consultative Conference and minister of the United Front Work Department of CPC Central Committee, had an interview with them. Mr. Sita, Vice-Minister of the United Front Work Department of the CPC Central Committee, Mr. Pelma Trilek, Executive Vice-Chairman of Tibet Autonomous Region and I, held a whole day's talk with them. In addition, we also invited relevant domestic experts and scholars to brief them on the laws, policies and practices concerning China's regional autonomy system for ethnic minorities and arranged them to tour in Ningxia Hui Autonomous Region. Though there existed serious divergences of views in this contact and talk, the atmosphere generally remained frank and sincere.

His statement also shows that, despite the cover story of our discussions being limited to the position and role of the Dalai Lama, the talks actually concerned the legitimate rights of the Tibetan people. I want to further dispel the contention by some critics of the dialogue process that Beijing's reference to the negotiating team as "personal representatives of the Dalai Lama" somehow diminishes our discussions or renders them irrelevant. At the time, His Holiness was the Head of State of the exile government. Anyone representing him in any capacity was representing the Tibetan people. As previously mentioned, referring to us as His Holiness's personal representatives gave the more reform-minded senior PRC officials a convenient "fig leaf" to counter the objections of their hard-line peers that they were dealing with the "illegitimate" exile government. Now, with the change of political system in the exile administration, as discussed in part II, this reference becomes problematic.

In light of the distorted criticisms contained in Zhu Weiqun's press release, however, we decided to publicly release the Memorandum. The Tibetan leadership felt that it was important for the Special General Meeting participants to see the full text of the Memorandum as presented to Beijing, rather than solely its interpretation by the Chinese. Thus, on November 16, 2008, in Dharamsala, on the eve of the Special General Meeting, we held a press conference releasing the Memorandum.

In response, Beijing published a rather lengthy article outlining eight major areas in which the Memorandum purportedly contradicted the PRC Constitution and other laws addressing the rights of nationalities.[22] Review of these criticisms not only provides insight into the vision and scope of the proposals outlined in the Memorandum but also refutes any contention that our counterparts "rejected" our submission.

Frankly, we were not surprised by the vast majority of our counterparts' objections. Beijing had voiced many of them in the past. Others were based on distorted facts or misrepresentations of our proposals. Some of their accusations were, in fact, totally unrelated to the proposals put forth in the Memorandum. They were simply regurgitations of the same contrived criticisms presented in opposition to His Holiness's Five-Point Peace Plan of 1987 and the Strasbourg Proposal of 1988.

Knowing how the Chinese in particular operate, and also how parties in any negotiations stake out the playing field, we were for the most part actually pleased with their response. Quite a few "China watchers," as well as officials from observing governments, were also encouraged that Beijing had limited its reaction to this anticipated rhetoric and hadn't rejected the Memorandum outright. We were better off, in a way, as Beijing's concerns were now stated in a precise and orderly manner. This enabled us to specifically address them in our subsequent Note on the Memorandum on Genuine Autonomy for the Tibetan People (Note on the Memorandum) that we presented during the Ninth Round of talks in 2010.

One other major grievance our negotiating counterparts raised during the Eighth Round was our lack of acknowledgment of the role of the CCP. They had continuously leveled this criticism over the course of the dialogue. Beijing interpreted our silence as somehow opposing the Party's authority. It is true that neither in His Holiness's speeches nor in any of our communications during the dialogue, including the Memorandum, is there any mention of the CCP. While our omission is intentional, we have never challenged the Party's role. All of our proposals for the future were specifically crafted to fit within the existing situation in the PRC, which we acknowledge is totally under CCP control. As we explicitly stated in the follow-up Note on the Memorandum:

> The position of His Holiness the Dalai Lama, as presented in the Memorandum, in no way challenges or brings into question the leadership of the Chinese Communist Party in the PRC. . . . The Memorandum also does not

> challenge the socialist system of the PRC. Nothing in it suggests a demand for a change to this system or for its exclusion from Tibetan areas. As for His Holiness the Dalai Lama's views on socialism, it is well known that he has always favored a socialist economy and ideology that promotes equality and benefits to uplift the poorer sections of society.[23]

Indeed, one of the issues that we raised during our formal talks was the need for Tibetan cadres to be given meaningful positions within the CCP hierarchy, including Party Secretary in the TAR, a position, at least as of this writing, never held by a Tibetan. If we were opposing any role for the Party in our future relations, why would we continue arguing in favor of Tibetan participation therein? Moreover, as early as 1982, when we mentioned the idea of "one country, two systems" as a solution to our problem, based on Beijing's offer to Taiwan and Hong Kong, PRC leaders strongly objected to its applicability. They explained that in Tibet, unlike these other two regions, the rule of the Communist Party had been firmly established. How ironic! As previously discussed, the "one country, two systems" approach was first enshrined in the Seventeen-Point Agreement that the then Tibetan government signed under duress.

The Special General Meeting convened as scheduled on November 17 and lasted for six days. All the participants had the opportunity to express their views, in plenary sessions and in smaller groups, not only on the ongoing dialogue with the PRC but also on other important issues confronting the Tibet movement. While the vast majority of delegates expressed strong mistrust of the sincerity of the PRC government in undertaking the negotiations, they nevertheless formally endorsed His Holiness's Middle Way Approach and supported continuing the dialogue for at least a few more years to give Beijing the benefit of the doubt. Of course, there were several naysayers who strongly voiced their support for total independence and opposition to any dialogue with the PRC leadership.

## THE NINTH ROUND OF TALKS

After a gap of about fifteen months, my delegation was able to return to the PRC in January 2010 for the Ninth, and what turned out to be the final, Round of talks. In the interim, we had kept in close touch not only with our negotiating counterparts but also with many world leaders, including the US President, to encourage Beijing to continue the dialogue. As previously noted, many individuals with excellent connections in the PRC as well as our Chinese friends also stepped in to help. Gradually we could sense Beijing becoming more inclined toward resumption of the dialogue and more willing to listen to our clarifications of the essential points of the Memorandum.

To remove any ambiguity in our position, Kalon Tripa Samdhong Rinpoche took the lead in working with Kelsang Gyaltsen, myself, and the Task Force in preparing the Note on the Memorandum that offered further explanation of the key points in the Memorandum that Beijing was either deliberately distorting or simply misunderstood.

Our visit to the PRC for the Ninth Round of talks began on January 26th and lasted until the 31st. During this visit, we were once again received by Du Qinglin, Vice Chair of the CPPCC, and held our formal talks with Zhu Weiqun and Sithar. This time, Nyima Tsering, who was then a Vice Chair of the TAR People's Congress, also participated. As in the past, our discussions were very frank and businesslike, with the usual heated arguments on certain issues. Nevertheless, we were able to formally share with them the Note on the Memorandum and further elaborate on its contents item by item. The substance of our presentation and Beijing's response is accurately summarized in the following press statement I issued on February 2, 2010.

> Before beginning our programmes there, we formally presented to the Central United Front Work Department, a Note relating to the Memorandum on Genuine Autonomy for All Tibetans that we had given during the previous eighth round of dialogue in November 2008. The Note contained seven points that addressed the fundamental issues raised by the Chinese leadership during the eighth round and some constructive suggestions for a way forward in the dialogue process. The seven points include respecting sovereignty and territorial integrity of the PRC, respecting the Constitution of the PRC, respecting the "Three Adherences," respecting the hierarchy and authority of the Chinese Central Government, Concerns raised by the Central Government on specific competencies referred to in the Memorandum, recognising the core issue, and offering His Holiness the Dalai Lama's cooperation for a mutually beneficial solution. The Note made clear that His Holiness the Dalai Lama and other members of the exiled leadership have no personal demands to make. His Holiness' concern is with the rights and welfare of the Tibetan people.

Therefore, the fundamental issue that needs to be resolved is the faithful implementation of genuine autonomy that will enable the Tibetan people to govern themselves in accordance with their own genius and needs.

His Holiness the Dalai Lama speaks on behalf of the Tibetan people, with whom he has a deep and historical relationship and one based on full trust. It cannot be disputed that His Holiness legitimately represents the Tibetan people, and he is certainly viewed as their true representative and spokesperson by them. It is indeed only by means of dialogue with His Holiness the Dalai Lama that the Tibetan issue can be resolved.

The recognition of this reality is important. We emphasised the point that His Holiness' engagement for the cause of Tibet is not for the purpose of claiming certain personal rights or political position for himself, nor attempting to stake claims for the Tibetan Administration in Exile. We called upon the Chinese side to stop the baseless accusations against His Holiness and labelling him a separatist. Instead, we urge the Chinese leadership to work with him to find a mutually acceptable solution to the Tibetan problem based on the Memorandum. This will ensure stability, unity and the development of a harmonious society.

The Chinese side laid out "Four Not to Indulge In" points to outline their position. They also provided us with a detailed briefing on recent developments relating to Tibet, particularly on the important Fifth Tibet Work Forum. They said the Forum decided to further improve the livelihood of Tibetans in the Tibet Autonomous Region and all Tibetan areas, specifically in public services, such as education, medical services, and environmental protection. Based on the initial reports that we had of the Forum, we welcomed the issues it has taken up to improve the lives of the Tibetan people especially in rural areas. We welcome the fact that the Fifth Tibet Work Forum has looked into the issues of development in all Tibetan areas—The Tibet Autonomous Region as well as other Tibetan areas. It is our strong belief that all the Tibetan areas must be under a uniform policy and a single administration. If we take away the political slogans, many of the issues that have been prioritised by the Forum are similar to the basic needs of the Tibetan people outlined in our Memorandum.

A major difference between the two sides is the conflicting perspectives on the current situation inside Tibet. So, in order to have a common understanding of the real situation, we suggested a common effort to study the actual reality on the ground, in the spirit of seeking truth from facts. This will help both the sides to move beyond each other's contentions.[24]

The apparent gap between the parties' positions continued to look significant at this juncture, particularly if one assigns any credence to the contemporaneous PRC propaganda. Despite adopting a very rigid and uncompromising public position, in our view, Beijing was taking some steps in the right direction. For example, our negotiating counterparts conveyed to us the serious measures to improve the lot of the Tibetans that Beijing planned to undertake in both the TAR and the other Tibetan autonomous areas. One decision of great importance was Beijing's recognition of the need to include both Tibetans and Chinese officials from *all* the Tibetan regions as participants in the Fifth Tibet Work Forum. In the past, these meetings had been solely TAR-focused. This inclusiveness, in our minds, signaled a major step forward.

In spite of continuing disagreements and conflicting positions, we left Beijing with full confidence that the dialogue process had taken firm root and that both sides had managed to handle the recent challenges relatively well and were now set to move forward. While I knew that with the leadership changes in Dharamsala, I would not be spearheading the dialogue process for much longer, I did feel a great deal of satisfaction believing that this critically important dialogue would continue. I further hoped that I might at least be in a position to introduce the next Special Envoy to Beijing's representatives.

Prior to this round of dialogue, I had publicly announced my decision to step down from my position as Special Envoy. I appreciated the fact that the front-runner for the Kalon Tripa position, Lobsang Sangay, would prefer appointing his own team for this crucial task. The success of this endeavor depends a great deal on the personal trust and understanding among the team members as well as with the Dharamsala leadership. One of the reasons my team had achieved a measure of success was the complete trust among Kalon Tripa Samdhong Rinpoche, the two of us in our roles as the envoys, and the Task Force members.

## CONTINUING INTERNAL CHALLENGES

Even though the November 2008 Special General Meeting had endorsed the continuation of dialogue with the PRC leadership, from time to time, we continued to encounter opposition from some members of our own community. Of most concern were the misleading and irresponsible remarks about the Memorandum and the Note on the Memorandum which some influential individuals were peddling. They alleged that neither document had been approved by the Tibetan Parliament or authorized by His Holiness, in an attempt to create the impression that Kalon Tripa Samdhong Rinpoche and we envoys were acting without the proper authorization. This misinformation campaign led His Holiness to send a communication on March 8, 2010, to the Tibetan Parliament during its budget session, requesting action to clarify the facts.

In his statement, His Holiness said that he had been trying his best to work with Beijing based on the successive resolutions passed by the Tibetan Parliament-in-Exile. To dispel any confusion and prevent misleading the general public, he requested the Parliament to engage in thorough deliberations on these fundamental and important issues during its current session. At His Holiness's urging, a day-long, special hearing attended by all members of the Parliament and the Kashag, as well as many former Kalons, His Holiness's envoys, and the members of the Task Force on Negotiations was convened.

The disingenuous campaign instituted by disgruntled members of the Tibetan exile community actually gave the Kashag an excellent opportunity to articulate its position. As a result, the Parliament once again unanimously passed a resolution reaffirming its faith in His Holiness and respecting his wisdom in determining how to resolve the issue of Tibet. This resolution supported the prior unanimous resolution passed by the Parliament on September 18, 1997. The new resolution further stated that the Parliament was fully convinced that the Memorandum and the Note on the Memorandum were in accordance with the wishes of His Holiness and therefore needed no further discussion.

I want to conclude this chapter by highlighting the fundamental point we consistently reiterated during the dialogue process, and which remains true: His Holiness the 14th Dalai Lama is the true representative of all the Tibetan people, regardless of where they reside. As such, he represents their collective interests that are at the core of any negotiations with the PRC leadership. In this regard, his personal status is irrelevant. Moreover, only through negotiations with his Holiness through his representatives can an acceptable resolution of the Tibetan people's differences with Beijing be reached and implemented. As stated in the Note on the Memorandum:

His Holiness the Dalai Lama's concern is with the rights and welfare of the Tibetan people. Therefore, the fundamental issue that needs to be resolved is the faithful implementation of genuine autonomy that will enable the Tibetan people to govern themselves in accordance with their own genius and needs.

His Holiness the Dalai Lama speaks on behalf of the Tibetan people, with whom he has a deep and historical relationship and one based on full trust. In fact, on no issue are Tibetans as completely in agreement as on their demand for the return of His Holiness the Dalai Lama to Tibet. It cannot be disputed that His Holiness the Dalai Lama legitimately represents the Tibetan people, and he is certainly viewed as their true representative and spokesperson by them. It is indeed only by means of dialogue with His Holiness the Dalai Lama that the Tibetan issue can be resolved. The recognition of this reality is important.

This emphasises the point, often made by His Holiness the Dalai Lama that his engagement for the cause of Tibet is not for the purpose of claiming certain personal rights or political position for him, nor attempting to stake claims for the Tibetan administration in exile. . . . His Holiness the Dalai Lama made it clear on numerous occasions that he will not hold any political position in Tibet. . . .

His Holiness the Dalai Lama has offered, and remains prepared, to formally issue a statement that would serve to allay the Chinese Central Government's doubts and concerns as to his position and intentions on matters that have been identified above.[25]

CHAPTER 21

# Status of Relationship, Obstacles to Reconnection, and Recommendations

It is most unfortunate that our dialogue with the PRC leadership, which had been firmly established, has come to an end. My disappointment is deep, because more than anyone else, I am aware of the extraordinary effort His Holiness put into this process. In addition, many foreign governments, heads of state, organizations, and individuals not only lent their support to this effort but also actively contributed to it in the hope of achieving a breakthrough. Finally, and most disturbing, is the negative impact of the lapse in negotiations on the Tibetan people, particularly those inside Tibet, who placed their faith in the process, believing it would bring some relief from their long-standing suffering.

## EVENTS FOLLOWING THE NINTH ROUND OF DIALOGUE

To state the obvious, our relations with Beijing are of paramount importance. From this perspective, the formal dialogue process became the key factor. With Samdhong Rinpoche's imminent departure from his position as Kalon Tripa in 2011, we were heading into unknown territory. I have learned from many years of experience that our relations with Beijing are difficult to sustain without a strong and unified team handling it from our side. I thought that whoever was the next Kalon Tripa must have a team in which he or she had full confidence. Thus, as I previously noted, in early 2010, I decided to step down from my position as Special Envoy leading the dialogue process. Both His Holiness and Samdhong Rinpoche were well aware of my decision at the time.

By the end of 2010, after the preliminary election, Lobsang Sangay emerged as the front-runner for the Kalon Tripa position. There were two other prominent candidates, Kalon Trisur Tethong Tenzin Namgyal and Kasur Tashi Wangdi. Kelsang Gyaltsen and I felt that at the earliest opportunity, we should brief all three of them on the status of the dialogue. It is natural for an outgoing administration to brief the incoming one, and we wanted each of the candidates to be careful that their campaign-related remarks did not inadvertently harm the ongoing negotiations. We conveyed our thinking to Samdhong Rinpoche and also sought His Holiness's approval. Both of them not only agreed but also encouraged us to contact the candidates immediately, recognizing the importance of such a briefing.

The Task Force Secretariat approached the three candidates to find a convenient time for them to be together in Dharamsala. This took some time to arrange, as all of them were in the middle of their respective campaigns. The Secretariat finally received confirmation that February 2, 2011, would work for them all. Unfortunately, because of prior commitments, I was unable to attend. Kelsang Gyaltsen and the Task Force Secretariat staff, however, gave an extensive, confidential briefing to the three candidates. Because of the sensitive nature of the dialogue, no documents were released to them; however, they were given a PowerPoint presentation and thoroughly briefed on the status of the negotiations. All of their questions were answered.

Lobsang Sangay ultimately won the election. While he had identified the dialogue process as important during his campaign, he indicated he had major changes in mind, including reshuffling the Task Force and appointing new envoys should he be elected. I had my first one-on-one meeting with him as the Kalon Tripa-elect in July 2011 when he came to Washington, D.C., during His Holiness's visit to give the Kalachakra initiation. I briefed him on the status of the dialogue and further assured him that I would try to make one more trip to Beijing after he assumed his post so that the dialogue could continue. He knew that I had already decided to leave my position as Special Envoy, as by this time it was public knowledge.

At the meeting, I suggested that it would be useful if he could appoint the next envoy soon after he assumed office so that I could personally brief our dialogue counterparts ahead of time. Providing them with this important information in advance, based on my experience, would give us the best chance of their accepting the new team without protest. I also told him that as the outgoing Special Envoy, I thought it was my responsibility to recommend a strong candidate to take my place. My choice was my colleague Kelsang Gyaltsen, who had a lot of experience and a thorough understanding of the issue. At the time, there were rumors of a former Kalon being considered for my position. If that were the case, I strongly urged Lobsang Sangay to retain Kelsang Gyaltsen in the number two position.

With the full devolution of political authority by His Holiness to the elected leadership, things became much more complicated. Nevertheless, I was still prepared to make one last trip to Beijing to maintain the fragile relationship that we had so carefully nourished. I started receiving messages from my PRC counterparts, however, posing two questions: First, were we still committed to or interested in dialogue? And second, who was it that we now represented? The first question was not difficult for me to answer because the Kalon Tripa-elect not only was publicly committed to the dialogue process but also had very strongly reaffirmed his position in a personal discussion with me.

The second question was much more difficult to answer. Given the history of our discussions, I knew that Beijing would not accept anyone other than the personal representatives of His Holiness as their counterparts in negotiations. But with his official devolution of political authority to the elected leaders, I knew any attempt to discuss this political matter with His Holiness would not be appreciated. Aware of the difficulties resulting from these major changes in Dharamsala but wishing to keep the existing relationship alive, our PRC counterparts not only agreed to another round of dialogue but further offered to have informal, off-the-record meetings with me and Kelsang Gyaltsen. I think it is important to acknowledge their efforts, because even though they recognized that the individuals participating from our side might change, they were committed to the credibility and long-term interests of the process.

In October 2011, Kelsang Gyaltsen and I went to Dharamsala to consult with the Kalon Tripa. A Task Force meeting was also scheduled to take place. We were finally able to discuss the predicament we faced in the absence of clear guidance from the CTA on whether or not we should remain in touch with United Front officials. As a result of our meeting, Lobsang Sangay issued a press release acknowledging that because we envoys were not part of the CTA, the changes in Dharamsala had not affected our representation of His Holiness. He further noted: "I have consistently stated that one of my foremost priorities as the Kalon Tripa is to make every possible effort to find a peaceful and negotiated resolution to the issue of Tibet. . . . I have therefore asked the two envoys of His Holiness the Dalai Lama to make efforts to resume the dialogue at the earliest convenience."[1] With this acknowledgment, it became much easier for me to renew contact with Beijing. After several months, I was able to reconnect with my Chinese contacts.

In early March 2012, however, when Kelsang Gyaltsen and I were in Dharamsala for another meeting with Lobsang Sangay, it became clear that for some unexplained reason, Dharamsala was rethinking its decision to pursue further dialogue with Beijing. Because I was no longer in direct communication with His Holiness's office, I had no understanding of the factors motivating this change in thinking. In the wake of this apparent policy reversal, on March 29, 2012, Kelsang Gyaltsen and I sent a joint communication to the Kalon Tripa, stating our belief that it was "important that the Tibetan people see that the decision to end the dialogue was taken by the Kashag with thorough deliberations and executed with due institutional process." We further urged that Dharamsala's public statement explaining its action be unequivocal and "not leave any room for misinterpretation of the Tibetan leadership's continued commitment to the Middle Way Approach and dialogue with the PRC."

The main purpose of our submission, however, was to offer our resignations, ostensibly due to our inability "to continue our efforts successfully mainly on account of the intransigent Chinese position as well as other factors. . . . [We thus] request our leadership to relieve us from our present responsibilities." We thought it far better to make us envoys the scapegoats responsible for walking away from the dialogue process than to expose the monumental policy shift undertaken by the new leadership in Dharamsala.

But Dharamsala once again shifted its position. I was not privy to the discussions in this apparently ongoing debate and have no idea what precipitated the policy reversal. We were simply informed that a meeting with Beijing's representatives would be acceptable as long as it was held outside the PRC. Hong Kong was identified as a suitable venue. With this new information, I contacted our counterparts, who readily agreed to meet with us in Hong Kong on June 4. When apprised of the potential meeting, the Kalon Tripa called Kelsang Gyaltsen, expressly telling him that the CTA had no objection to our meeting.

When the two of us traveled to Dharamsala in late May for another Task Force meeting and expressly to prepare for the June 4 meeting, we were once again blindsided by a Dharmasala policy reversal. Lobsang Sangay informed us that the Hong Kong meeting should actually be "unofficial" because Kelsang Gyaltsen was still active in the CTA's service. As I was retired, however, I was free to go in my personal capacity.

I can honestly say that for the first time in my life, I was outraged. Not only did I feel totally unappreciated for all the decades of service I had devoted to the cause of Tibet, I felt used and exploited. The dialogue for which we had worked so hard for so many years, and the relationship we had so carefully nurtured with our counterparts, was being precipitously terminated. And, to this day, I have no understanding of the underlying reasons . In language totally out of character, and which I will not repeat here, I exploded. While I am not saying it was anyone's intention to cause me this anguish, I am only being truthful in relaying the profound disappointment I experienced over the demise of a process and a relationship to which I had devoted virtually my entire professional life. The cause that was, and remains, so dear to my heart, and to which I had given my all, was being unceremoniously dismissed.

I further recall being reminded at the time of what, in retrospect, was an all-too-prescient quote. Inscribed on a plaque given to me by a senior Norwegian diplomat at the start of our formal negotiations with Beijing are the following words:

> Six Phases of a Project:
>
> 1. Enthusiasm 2. Disillusionment 3. Panic 4. Search for the Guilty 5. Punishment of the Innocent 6. Praise & Honors for the Non-Participants

The plaque was further addressed: "To Lodi, Prophetic words? Hope not. Your friend and partner." How disturbingly accurate this sentiment proved to be.

After this meeting with the Kalon Tripa, on May 29, Kelsang Gyaltsen and I formally submitted our resignations. The press release ultimately issued by the Kashag accepting our resignations explicitly adopted the rationale we submitted in our original offers to resign back in March, without even hinting at the real reason for terminating the dialogue process.

> Despite Mr. Gyari's desire to step down in April 2011, the two envoys were asked to continue their efforts to reach out to their Chinese counterparts by Kalon Tripa-elect Dr. Lobsang Sangay. The envoys met and briefed the Kalon Tripa on twelve separate occasions since May 2011. At the Task Force meeting on May 30–31, 2012 in Dharamsala, the envoys expressed their utter frustration over the lack of positive response from the Chinese side and submitted their resignations to the Kalon Tripa.[2]

Kelsang Gyaltsen and I did stay on as members of the Task Force, primarily to avoid any negative speculation by the public about a rift in the Tibetan leadership. As of this writing, we both continue as members.

I do regret not being able to make the scheduled trip to Hong Kong to meet with Zhu Weiqun of the United Front. In my view, this meeting could have helped maintain our delicate relationship. I wrote to Lobsang Sangay on October 20, 2013: "It was unfortunate that I was unable to make one last trip after you assumed Office. There would not have been any significant breakthrough, but at least the fragile relation could have been continued." I also candidly told him:

> The Chinese Leadership obviously will not enter into direct formal relation with you and the Kashag, and the relations must be accepted and projected as being between His Holiness and the Chinese government. In fact this has always been the case. The Chinese even had problems and reservations about Professor Samdhong Rinpoche's role in the dialogue process, but gradually they came to acknowledge the pivotal role of the Kalon Tripa. As both Kelsang Gyaltsen and I have suggested, the crucial factor is His Holiness's personal involvement and also the two of you having clear understanding of the specific steps that need to be taken.

I am in no way trying to hold Lobsang Sangay responsible for the breakdown of the dialogue process. By the time of the CTA decision not to engage in further dialogue, I was no longer privy to the deliberations in Dharamsala. I have no doubt there must have been a number of factors leading to it. I also sincerely respect the prerogative of any elected Kalon Tripa and the Kashag to make whatever policy decisions they deem appropriate.

## OBSTACLES TO CONTINUED DIALOGUE

### *Philosophical Differences Between Beijing and Dharamsala*

In addition to the obvious differences in Beijing's and Dharamsala's positions and perceptions, there are several other factors that impede our relations. The most important is the philosophical divide between the parties, specifically His Holiness's Buddhist ethics versus the Marxist-communist worldview of the PRC's leaders.

In the past, whenever PRC government officials or important leaders met with global leaders and discussed the Tibet issue, they always acknowledged that "the Dalai Lama is not just a religious leader, but he is also a political leader." Until the 2011 political changes in Dharamsala, Beijing was making a correct statement. Tibetans both inside and outside Tibet considered His Holiness their undisputed spiritual and temporal leader. But it is important to remember that for both the Dalai Lama and the Tibetan people, his role as a religious leader is far more important than any political position he might occupy. Simply put, no political interests will cause him to compromise his ethics. PRC leaders, on the other hand, see everything through a political lens that necessarily entails compromise. These two contradictory perspectives are a fundamental problem in resolving our differences.

As a religious leader, His Holiness feels passionately about issues such as human rights, democracy, freedom of religion, freedom of speech, and protection of the environment. He considers them of great importance from his perspective as a Buddhist monk. Imagine the Tibet movement without the Dalai Lama, without his unwavering moral code and ethical principles. Sadly, the PRC government is unable to understand or appreciate the sincere motives underlying his comments on these global matters. Instead, Beijing deeply resents his outspokenness, misconstruing it as intentional criticism of the PRC.

This disparity in viewpoints has caused major schisms between the parties over the course of our relations. Deng Xiaoping, for example, never forgave His Holiness for his response to the government's brutal crackdown on the prodemocracy movement in Tiananmen Square in June 1989. His Holiness's deep expression of anguish was both spontaneous and heartfelt. It was never meant to embarrass the PRC or Deng Xiaoping. It was simply the natural expression of His Holiness's boundless compassion, one of the two major tenets of Tibetan Buddhism and the trait for which His Holiness is revered by Buddhists and non-Buddhists around the world. This, in combination with his uncompromising commitment to the truth, renders His Holiness constitutionally incapable of remaining silent in the face of the PRC government's brutality aimed at its own citizens, no matter what the cost. And in this case, it was a very high price. My personal experience of His Holiness's reaction to this tragedy, as captured in the following question-and-answer passages of Victor Chan's book *The Wisdom of Forgiveness*, coauthored with His Holiness, reveals His Holiness's truly unparalleled commitment to morality and ethics.

Lodi Gyari arrived fifteen minutes late and slightly harried. He had just come from a meeting between the Dalai Lama and Richard Holbrooke in the Tibetan monk's hotel suite [in Washington, D.C.]. Holbrooke, the American diplomat who had brokered the Balkan peace treaty in 1995, was in town for the celebrations. . . .

Lodi Gyari, together with Tenzin Geyche Tethong, is one of the Dalai Lama's closest advisers. After his boss, Lodi Gyari is arguably the most effective advocate for Tibet in the West. I wanted to glean some insights about the Tibetan leader from the one man who has been his confidant for four decades.

"What's it like to work for the Dalai Lama?" I asked him.

"Everyone knows that His Holiness is very compassionate," Gyari replied. "But he's also a very strong-willed person. This is something people working close to him know. This draws people like me to him."

"His strength," I said.

"Yes, there is no doubt his compassion is all-encompassing. But to be frank, he is not an easy boss. And the yardstick with which he measures you is phenomenal. I'm very conscious that I work for someone who has high ideals. This is useful because it restrains me. I won't cross certain lines in my personal conduct.

"Let me tell you something that happened during the Tiananmen Square incident,"[3] Lodi Gyari said. "I was his foreign minister when the tragedy occurred. At that time, despite several ups and downs, we were on the verge of starting a dialogue with the Chinese. Yang Minfu was the head of the United Front Works department, and somehow we had managed to reestablish contacts. There was agreement in principle for a preliminary meeting in Hong Kong, which would set the actual venue and the date of negotiations."

I knew that there is nothing more crucial for the Dalai Lama and the other exiled Tibetans than to coax the Chinese to the negotiating table. Everything they have worked for in the past four decades is geared toward this objective. The consensus among many thoughtful Tibetans is that a genuine rapprochement with the Chinese is the only way to save the Tibetan way of life and stop Tibet from being swamped by a tidal wave of Chinese migrants. But despite the prodigious moral authority of the Dalai Lama, the Chinese have rarely shown signs that they're willing to talk.

Gyari continued, "I was busy preparing for that, and then Tiananmen Square happened. I remember it well. I was at home in Dharamsala. One of

His Holiness' drivers came with a vehicle to fetch me. I was wanted immediately in the palace. I quickly put on my Tibetan dress. The driver had instructions to bring me to His Holiness' residence instead of the office. When I arrived, Tenzin Geyche was already waiting for me. The two of us went straight to the Dalai Lama's room.

"For the first time ever, I saw that His Holiness was very, very agitated. He was like Napoleon. He didn't turn around to face us when we walked in; he had his hands clasped behind his back. He was deep in thought. He dispensed with the usual greetings and immediately asked us. Did you see? Did you see?

"Of course we had seen. There was nothing else on TV. We knew what he was referring to. So we said yes. He said, 'You two get to work on a statement I want to issue; the strongest condemnation of the Chinese government and their policy of brutalizing their own people, my unconditional support for the youngsters on the Square.'

"My selfish Tibetan mind immediately said: 'Oh, my God, this is going to ruin any opportunities for negotiations, something we have worked hard on for decades.' His Holiness turned, read my body language right away, and said curtly, 'What is it?' I said, 'Your Holiness, of course you realize this will derail our efforts at negotiations maybe for a very long time.' I felt that he had registered my views, and for one brief moment I thought he would modify his position. But then he turned around. I felt intense energy, like that of a tiger. He said, 'Yes, it's true, you have a point. But if I do not speak out now, I have no moral right to ever speak out for freedom and democracy. Those young people are asking for nothing more, nothing less than what I have been asking for. And if I can't speak for them'"—Lodi hesitated, searching his memory for the right words—"'I'll be ashamed to ever talk about freedom and democracy.'"

Lodi grew silent. Out of habit, I tried to keep my face impassive. But it was difficult. I was deeply moved by the Dalai Lama's response. He had squarely placed the welfare of the Chinese students ahead of the hopes of his countrymen. I looked away. The hum of conversation in the crowded lounge continued, unabated.

"I felt a tremendous respect for His Holiness," Gyari went on. "I also felt very small, very selfish. Of course, in retrospect, I was right in my assessment that His Holiness' stance would kill the negotiations. Deng Xiaoping never forgave him. He took it very personally, as we learned later on. But it is things like this that make me feel honored to serve His Holiness, because he is genuine. He believes in what he preaches, and he acts according to that."[4]

In that same interview, I recounted another instance when His Holiness's compassion for the problems of others prevailed over the narrower interests of Tibet:

> As we sat back in our chairs, Gyari picked up his story again. "His Holiness' first ever visit to Europe was in 1973," he said. "I was very young, very radical in those days. Halfway into our six-week tour, we were in Switzerland. His Holiness was staying at a private home near Zurich. I was beginning to feel frustrated because so far he had said very little about Tibet in public."
>
> "He was talking about religion instead?" I asked.
>
> "He was talking about the things he talks about all the time—universal responsibility, compassion, the good heart. But lots of people also wanted to know about Tibet. I felt he was not doing enough for the Tibetan people. I remember well the house he was staying in, a huge chalet, full of beautiful stained-glass windows. One early morning, I walked into his room. He knew immediately that I was agitated, that I had something on my mind."
>
> "He could read you very well." I said.
>
> "Yes. He said to me. 'What is it?' I said, 'Your Holiness, I think you should speak more about Tibet. This is a tremendous opportunity, we need to tell the world more about the suffering of our people.' He said: 'It's true, yes, I understand. In fact, I have also thought I should talk more about Tibet. But you know, many of these people have so many problems on their minds. They come to me with some kind of false hope that I'll be able to lift their burden, which I can't. I feel that I have no right to send them out with an extra burden, a burden of my own.' Tears came into my eyes when I heard that."
>
> Lodi Gyari paused and looked away. I could tell he was moved by that memory. Finally it was time for him to leave. As we stood up, his eyes held mine. "Victor, I'm sure of one thing. His Holiness is the most altruistic person I have ever known."[5]

Senior PRC leaders such as Deng Xiaoping, deeply imbued in their own ideology, have never understood or appreciated what His Holiness the 14th Dalai Lama embodies. For Buddhists around the world, the Dalai Lama is compassion incarnate. As such, it would be anathema for him not to speak out on issues of human rights, religious freedom, protection of the environment, democracy, etc. I have to admit that at times, as a selfish Tibetan, I myself have felt some reservations when His Holiness publicly addressed those issues, seemingly at the expense of Tibet's interests. But I always conclude that the Tibetan people are truly blessed to be represented by a person with his unrivaled level of concern and compassion for all beings. The benefits to Tibet and the Tibetan people gained precisely because of His Holiness's compassionate nature and unwavering commitment to the good of all beings, or in his own words, "a free spokesperson on their behalf," simply defy measurement.

### *Lack of Trust*

Some of the differences between the Chinese and the Tibetans are fundamental in nature, making it hard for either party to compromise. The biggest problem, however, is lack of trust. No one can fault the Tibetans for deeply mistrusting the PRC government and its motives. Beginning with Beijing's failure to implement the provisions of the Seventeen-Point Agreement signed on May 23, 1951, the Tibetan people have been the victims of continued deception by the Chinese on issues both big and small. This experience is not limited to Tibetan officials or the Dalai Lama. Many lamas, chieftains, and even ordinary Tibetans have encountered this duplicitous behavior since the Chinese Communists entered Tibetan areas.

At the same time, PRC leaders from their side formed an opinion that the Tibetans, and especially His Holiness the 14th Dalai Lama, are not trustworthy. Individuals and institutions with vested interests in both Lhasa and Beijing succeeded in planting this mistrust from the beginning. As early as 1955, when His Holiness was concluding a rather meaningful visit to Beijing and felt that Mao was someone he could count on for support, this group of troublemakers was already at work undermining the burgeoning relationship. In addition, as I have previously noted, our lack of response to some of Beijing's initiatives, combined with miscommunications within Dharamsala, no doubt also contributed to its suspicions. It is also truly unfortunate that His Holiness was unable to cultivate relations with any of the "second-generation" leaders he met during his mid-1950s visit to Beijing. Those potential relationships would have been of inestimable value today in resolving the parties' differences.

During our High-Level Exploratory Talks in 1982 and 1984, we gave the highest priority to trying to restore some form of mutual trust but were not successful.

Even today, it is my belief that this remains the most important issue to be addressed. As long as the parties regard each other through this mutual lens of deep mistrust, no serious breakthrough in our relations can happen. We must be transparent, candid, and sincere in our dealings with each other.

Even in 2002, after being entrusted by His Holiness to lead his team for formal dialogue with Beijing, I continued to be truthful in discussing its policies in private meetings with government officials as well as in public forums. PRC officials warned me that, as the designated interlocutor for His Holiness with Beijing, I must cease all my so-called "splittist" activities and stop "internationalizing" the Tibet issue. Even some Tibet supporters and experienced negotiators suggested that I curtail these activities. I, however, felt that it gave us greater leverage if I pursued these opportunities as before, provided I continued to act responsibly. Thus, in my capacity as His Holiness's Washington-based Special Envoy, for example, I continued to meet with senior US administration officials and members of Congress and also took part in public discussions, including testifying before congressional committees. I had similar meetings outside of the United States with government leaders and parliamentarians and spoke at a number of public events.

On all these occasions, while I was blunt in my criticism of PRC government policies and lobbied tirelessly to hold the PRC accountable for its unjust treatment of the Tibetan people, I never said anything or even used a critical term against either the PRC or any Chinese official that I had not already stated in a face-to-face meeting. Even in interviews with radio organizations including Voice of America, Radio Free Asia, and Voice of Tibet, I always concluded my remarks by expressly stating that all of my criticisms had previously been conveyed to my negotiating counterparts during our in-person discussions.

As much as Beijing dislikes criticism, what it really resents is duplicity. While early on, differing versions of conversations reported to different parties at different places might have been tolerated, this is no longer the case. Today, you cannot play this game. Yet, some of our people persist in the practice, to both their personal and Tibet's detriment.

I can say with a high degree of confidence that my team was able not only to formalize our dialogue process with the PRC government but also to gain considerable trust and respect, at least regarding our conduct. Because of my role as Special Envoy of His Holiness and the lead negotiator with Beijing, I had the opportunity to establish relationships with a number of Chinese government officials, mainland-based Chinese scholars and individuals, as well as Tibetans from various walks of life, when they were either traveling in the West or visiting India or Nepal. In all my dealings with these individuals, I have been consistent in my positions and approach. While highly critical of Beijing's wrong policies, I have remained firmly committed to the dialogue process as guided by His Holiness. Not once have I tried to solicit information from someone who was not authorized to provide it or uncomfortable in sharing it. Above all, I have never asked anyone—private individual, organization, or government representative—to undertake any activity that might cause personal harm or create a misunderstanding with Beijing.

This includes my contacts with Western NGOs and individuals working on the Tibetan Plateau who have sought my guidance and, on occasion, brought publications or other information to me describing conditions there. Expressing my gratitude for their desire to help, I have always explicitly told them never to get involved in activities that may be seen as sensitive or provocative by PRC authorities. I emphasized that such actions could not only harm their projects but most importantly, jeopardize the dialogue process. I further explained that my personal status is irrelevant, but in my official capacity I bear a huge responsibility that cannot be compromised. If I succeeded in the work entrusted to me by His Holiness, there could be immense benefit not only to the Tibetans but also to the Chinese. To certain individuals and organizations, I even conveyed these sentiments in writing.

Chinese government officials are not by nature inclined to compliment Tibetans. Therefore, I am pleased to say that after many years of working closely with a number of them, they formally acknowledged the benefits of our dialogue, going so far as to expressly compliment the contributions of our negotiating team during conversations with diplomats from other nations. Not surprisingly, Tibetans are suspicious of Chinese praises, even leading some to hint that these "compliments" could only have been the result of improper concessions on our part. But there is absolutely no justification for such contentions in this case. These compliments addressed the efforts of the Tibetan negotiating team and were solely related to our professional conduct, as can be seen, for example, from Zhu Weiqun's comment: "Despite our conflicting viewpoints, I respect Mr. Lodi Gyari."[6]

That said, the parties' deeply rooted mistrust of each other has historically hindered our relations and unfortunately continues to this day. Until we can learn to trust each other, believe in the sincerity of each other's proposals, and respect each other's views in those areas where compromise cannot be reached, a resolution of our differences will remain elusive.

I recognize that much of my narrative recounts the efforts made by delegations I led at the behest of His Holiness on behalf of the Tibetan people. I am not trying to inflate my role or glorify my activities, but rather to put the record straight, and most importantly, to encourage both the Tibetans and the Chinese to move forward in finding a mutually acceptable resolution.

In that regard, I have words of advice for both parties. First, to the PRC leadership: Let me be very clear, the Tibet issue will not go away unless and until the grievances and wounds of the Tibetan people are addressed and healed. Building highways, airports, and glitzy townships is not the remedy. The only cure is for the PRC government to be responsive to the genuine aspirations of the Tibetan people. Beijing must allow us to maintain our distinct identity by providing the conditions under which we can live and thrive with pride and dignity. Giving the Tibetan people this opportunity will not encourage any of us to become "splittists" but on the contrary, will make us more committed to remaining a part of the big family of peoples residing within the PRC.

To my fellow Tibetans, with equal seriousness and conviction: We must take advantage of the compassion and vision of our leader, His Holiness the 14th Dalai Lama, and under his guidance try to find a place for the Tibetan people within the PRC. We must stop fooling ourselves with empty slogans. We must wake up from our make-believe world. We always love to cite the famous Tibetan proverb: "Tibetans are ruined by hope and Chinese by suspicion." There is definitely some truth there, but as veteran Tibetan politician Ngapo Ngawang Jigme told the Second Fact-Finding Delegation in the 1980s, the reverse is sometimes true: "Tibetans are ruined by suspicion and Chinese by hope."

It is true that historically we have been let down and deceived by a succession of Chinese leaders. It is thus natural that we give little credence to the words of those who now rule from Beijing, especially in the face of our current experiences under the Chinese Communist regime. However, I am a firm believer that not everything Beijing does and says is motivated by the intention to deceive. During my days of service and interaction with PRC officials, I encountered a number of senior leaders in Beijing who saw the need to resolve the Tibet issue and, realizing their policies in Tibet were misguided, reached out to His Holiness. I can also say with certainty that there are still many such people at various governmental levels who desire to do the right thing. I also have more faith in the future, in spite of our history of taking one step forward and two steps back, as today the PRC is vastly different from even a few decades ago.

I say again to my fellow Tibetans, the future of six million of your compatriots, or whatever may be the exact number, is in the balance. We owe it to them to take the matter seriously. We must continue to make informed and conscientious efforts to reach a solution. A strategy that focuses on scoring points over the PRC leaders on an international chessboard or, even more tragically, reduces this critically important matter to a playing piece in some kind of internal political game is not only useless but a repudiation of our commitment to bettering the lives of the larger Tibetan community.

Sadly, a small section of the Tibetan exile community, including a few people who held official or other responsible positions, created serious obstacles for the success of this precious effort. I call this work "precious" because it is a vision of His Holiness formulated with uncompromising courage and farsightedness. I call it precious because it directly affects each and every Tibetan inside Tibet. The Tibetan community as a whole must recognize this opportunity and work together, doing everything in our collective power to engage the PRC leadership and reach a comprehensive solution to the crisis that brings so much misery to our compatriots suffering on the Tibetan Plateau.

## RECOMMENDATIONS

Despite these obstacles, I remain optimistic that a solution to the Tibet issue can be reached. We have learned so much, dedicated so much energy, and made so many strides forward that it would be heartbreaking to abandon the process. That said, I fully recognize the remaining difficulties as well as the changed circumstances under which any restart to the discussions must take place. While at first glance my major suggestion might sound like a revised approach, it is really more a restatement of the situation as it actually exists.

### *The CTA Focuses on Its Role as an Active Member of Civil Society*

When His Holiness came into exile, he traveled not just as an individual but also, and more importantly, as the leader of the Tibetan government, bringing the legitimacy of the Gaden Phodrang, as well as its institutions and representatives, along with him. That historical reality and the associated moral authority are accepted by the vast majority of Tibetans both inside and outside Tibet. The Tibetan people look to the physical location of His Holiness as the locus of the Tibetan government. From a historical, legal, and moral perspective, as well as in developing a current strategy for negotiating with Beijing, this is crucial to understand.

Upon their arrival in India, however, His Holiness and his accompanying senior Tibetan government officials recognized that they could no longer function in all capacities as a "government." They could not establish many of the institutions formerly used to fulfill the needs and aspirations of the Tibetan people through that vehicle. Equally importantly, they realized that neither any state within the international community of nations nor any international organization was prepared to deal directly with a "Tibetan Government-in-Exile." So from the very beginning, with the advice of friends, including Indian officials, they made the wise decision to set up every Tibetan ministry, department, and related entity in their exile home in accordance with India's laws regarding nongovernmental organizations. It is precisely because of its formal status as an NGO that the CTA is able to receive financial and other assistance not only from India but also from governments and other NGOs around the world.

This dual or hybrid system of administration gradually took root and for many years has been able to function very smoothly. More recently, some members of the younger generation have sought to emphasize the "governmental" nature of the CTA. Perhaps motivated by a desire to demonstrate their "coming of age" and differentiate themselves from their elders, they are eager to don the trappings of a full-fledged government, including adoption of positions and titles befitting high-ranking officials. This has generated something of a split personality within the CTA, with the older generation concentrating more on its activities as a participant in civil society while younger members embrace a more aggressive posture emphasizing its governmental status.

With His Holiness devolving his political power, totally separating the Gaden Phodrang from the CTA, a huge change has occurred. We cannot ignore that fact. But then the question arises: What now is the true status of the CTA? When His Holiness held a political position as the Head of State, he undertook all the major political decisions. He appointed government officials, and major official publications were issued in his name. At that time, the CTA could legitimately claim that it represented all Tibetans, those residing in Tibet as well as those in exile, because its leader, His Holiness the 14th Dalai Lama, had the unprecedented mandate from and support of all the Tibetan people. I can't help but ask myself now: To whom or what did my father and the others of his generation, who played such crucial roles in launching the historic move galvanizing the allegiance of *all* Tibetans to one common leader, His Holiness the 14th Dalai Lama, and to a common platform and common institution, make their pledge? History is unambiguous and conclusive in this regard: it is, without a doubt, to His Holiness.

Given this history, in the aftermath of His Holiness's devolution of political authority, can the CTA continue to claim that it represents the interests of all Tibetans? It can certainly assert with confidence that it represents the Tibetan community in exile. The officials heading executive and other branches of the CTA are now democratically elected by the Tibetan diaspora as representatives of the three regions of Tibet and its various religious sects. But is a broader assertion of representation still justified?

As someone who remains deeply concerned about the future of Tibet and wants to take all positive measures to reestablish connections with Beijing, while avoiding any actions that might hinder that reengagement, I suggest that the more prudent course is for the CTA to emphasize its status as an active member of civil society, representing the interests and aspirations of the Tibetan people, rather than its governmental role. I am not saying that the CTA should abandon its governmental status, but only that in certain circumstances, before certain audiences, it should highlight its position as a member of civil society to most effectively further the Tibetan people's interests. The vast majority of its current activities, in fact, address the economic, social, and cultural needs of the Tibetan exile community, traditional areas of emphasis for civil society participants. Legally constituted as a nongovernmental actor, it is accepted as such by governments the world over, including those of both India and the United States, two of its most important supporters.

In embracing this role, the CTA might look to the activities of other organizations championing the interests of peoples who have taken advantage of the opportunities nongovernmental status can provide. Two organizations immediately come to mind: the Palestine Liberation Organization (PLO) and the African National Congress (ANC). As the "voice of the people," each of these organizations has been widely accepted by the international community, giving them direct access not only to many international organizations but also to a number of governments.

For example, in 1974, as leader of the PLO, Yassar Arafat became the first representative of an NGO to address a plenary session of the United Nations. His impassioned remarks elevated the Palestinian cause on the international community's agenda, dramatically increasing support for the Palestinian people's plight. Had Arafat presented himself as the purported "president" of the Palestinian "government," he never would have been accorded this unprecedented opportunity. The PLO went on to become the ruling party within his lifetime.

The forerunner of the ANC was the South African Native National Congress (SANNC), formed in 1912 with the objective of endowing black and mixed-race Africans with the right to vote. From the 1940s, the ANC's mission included ending apartheid. Although the ANC was banned in 1960 and forced to leave South Africa, it maintained a strong international presence with offices in many capitals around the world, including New Delhi, where I often met with the office head. From its position outside South Africa, the ANC remained the main opposition to the government's apartheid policies and, in participating in peacebuilding activities, played a major role in resolving the conflict. Largely as a result of its efforts, in 1990, South African President F. W. de Klerk lifted the ban on the ANC and released Nelson Mandela from prison. On March 17, 1992, voters approved a referendum removing apartheid and paving the way for full participation by the ANC as a political party in South Africa.

What these examples demonstrate is that participation in civil society does not relegate an organization to undertaking purely social or cultural activities, such as running schools or opening medical clinics on behalf of its beneficiaries, but allows for much, much more activity and participation in the international community.

Recognizing the advantages inherent in civil society participation, I would like to share an idea that, if one is willing to carefully consider it, may be of some benefit. During the 2011 election of the Kalon Tripa, now Sikyong, my sister Gyari Dolma was initially a candidate. Early in the campaign, I met with her for about an hour in Dharamsala, where I expressed my support for her candidacy. I told her: "Whether you win or lose, you have taken the courageous and admirable step of offering yourself as a candidate. You have all the necessary credentials, and I know if elected you will be a great Kalon Tripa. Most importantly, I am happy that you, as a woman, are running for office, whether or not Tibetans, even Tibetan women, are ready for or enthusiastic about having a woman as Kalon Tripa."

My sister then asked if I had any advice for her. I laughed and said I did, but I didn't think she would find it acceptable because I knew the current thinking and environment in Dharamsala and my proposal wouldn't align with those interests. "But since you asked," I told her, "I'll tell you, but I won't blame you at all for not listening to me." I said: "Dolma, if you really want to run, I wish you would come out with a totally new approach to resolving the Tibet issue." I could see she was excited, anticipating that she would get some grand idea from me to make her an appealing candidate. I continued:

> If I were you, I would announce the following policy: If elected, it is my intention that anything to do with the political aspect of Tibet, including the delicate and important issue of our relations with the PRC, will be off limits to my Cabinet. I am going to formally request His Holiness, regardless of any political office he may or may not keep,[7] to continue in his position as the only person who can legitimately speak for, and act on behalf of, all Tibetans, especially those inside Tibet. Similarly, in the international arena, all important political matters, including those relating to any dialogue with Beijing, will be handled directly by His Holiness and his staff.
>
> Second, I have no illusions that the Chinese government wants to talk to me, as head of the Tibetan Parliament-in-Exile, or to my Kashag, neither of which it recognizes as a "government" or as representatives of the Tibetan people's interests. That said, I give you my word that I and my Kashag will faithfully carry out any specific instructions that His Holiness gives, including how and in what manner I, my cabinet, or the CTA can play a role in the dialogue process. I will be ready at any moment to implement His Holiness's vision and follow through on his commitments on behalf of the Tibetan people.
>
> Instead of focusing on our relations with the PRC, I will dedicate all my energy, time, and experience to maintaining the distinct identity of the Tibetan people inside Tibet, where, in spite of some positive changes and opportunities, Tibetans are still being marginalized. At the end of the day, if I and my Kashag can become the instruments for realizing that goal, it will be a historic achievement.

I summarized my proposal advising that the CTA should openly embrace its position as a member of civil society. I went on to say:

> I have been in the Kashag. We suffer from split personalities. Yes, we are a government in some respects, but we want to believe, and we further pretend, that we are a government for all purposes. And that is our mistake, even though some of our friends do us the honor of treating us with that respect. What we have actually been doing on a day-to-day basis, at least during my tenure as a Kalon, is focusing on the needs of the Tibetan exile community. Maybe things have changed in your time as Deputy Speaker in Dharamsala, but most of the things we dealt with or confronted were matters concerning the approximately 150,000 Tibetans in exile who mostly live in India. From time to time, we would address matters with a larger impact, for example, events including the March 10th Anniversary, when we needed to make statements. But in reality, the work that the CTA does is that of a civil society organization, but we simply don't want to admit it.
>
> I continued:
>
> If you are bold enough to say that your administration will function in its civil society capacity with the lofty goal of preserving the distinct Tibetan identity that is being threatened and marginalized, you will advance the Tibetan people's interests exponentially. The CTA already has this mandate; it is just sometimes obscured or lost in the political intrigue that accompanies the Tibet question. If you adopt this approach, I guarantee that if you are elected and position yourself not as the prime minister or head of state but rather as leader of this uniquely positioned and empowered nongovernmental entity, you will have greatly expanded access to governments and organizations in the international community. For example, I am quite sure that with some effort you will be able to walk right into the U.S. State Department and plead our case about the importance of maintaining the living Tibetan culture, its language, and every other core aspect of what we are struggling for.

My sister and I did not have time to discuss my proposal or for me to learn her ideas on the subject. I had a flight to catch, and even without the time constraints,

I'm not sure how candid her response would have been. While she is strong-minded with her own ideas, she is also very respectful of me as her elder brother.

I share this family encounter because the idea of the CTA emphasizing its role as a civil society participant is not something that I am proposing or advocating for the first time now. I have seriously thought about it for quite some time. But let me be perfectly clear, I am in no way challenging the validity or credibility of the CTA. I am only advocating that it put less emphasis on its quasi-governmental activities, in favor of highlighting its civil society persona.

In a way, I think the present CTA leadership already sees the benefits of projecting itself as a civil society participant. The elected leader is now called the President, in line with the organizational structure of many other international NGOs. As the CTA's adoption of this moniker can in no way be viewed as implying the existence of a presidentially based system of governance, its use is a possible indicator of organizational intent to emphasize its civil society leanings.

### *His Holiness the 14th Dalai Lama Becomes the Formal Representative of the Tibetan People in Re-engaging Beijing*

The main reason I have devoted my time and energy to writing this book and in particular, to extensively discussing our relationship with Beijing, is not simply to recite history or explain the parties' respective actions. It is my fervent hope that this chronicle will motivate the Tibetan leadership and His Holiness to consider restoring relations with Beijing. Building on the foundation we have established, I sincerely believe that there is still an opportunity to resolve our differences.

Initially, I want to emphasize that in considering my proposal for His Holiness to resume representation of the Tibetan people in their dealings with Beijing, one must accept the underlying premise and inalterable fact that Beijing will never negotiate directly with the CTA. No one should labor under any delusions to the contrary. When His Holiness was the Head of State, we devised a creative way of getting around this obstacle. We accepted from the very beginning Beijing's uncompromising position that it would only talk with His Holiness or his personal representatives, and certainly not with the CTA. We very carefully deliberated how to address this challenging restraint. Recognizing that His Holiness was the *only* individual who undisputedly represented the interests of the Tibetan people, both inside and out of Tibet, and at the same time was the Head of the

CTA, we capitalized on his dual role. Even though throughout the process, many of us involved in the discussions with Beijing were at times CTA Ministers, Secretaries, or other senior leaders, we interacted with Beijing as His Holiness's Representatives, not in our capacity as CTA officials. While Beijing was well aware of our governmental positions, it was able to work with us as the personal emissaries of His Holiness, which also reflected reality. With the political changes in Dharamsala, however, this camouflaged representation is no longer available.

As I have already noted, I was not in favor of His Holiness's decision to relinquish his political position and distance himself from the dialogue process. But, at least with respect to the relationship with the PRC, there may be one real advantage. With no formal connection to the CTA, His Holiness is now in a position to represent the Tibetan people without any of the political baggage that his prior position occasioned in the minds of the PRC leadership. In other words, there is no longer any need to maintain the "fig leaf" of "personal representation of His Holiness" under which we previously operated. He can now forthrightly proclaim that he represents the interests of all Tibetans, both inside and outside the PRC. With the unwavering support of all the Tibetan people and his sincere belief in the Middle Way Approach, he is, in fact, the only person who can undertake this responsibility on our behalf.

Tibetan leaders, and the exile community at large, must recognize this reality and act accordingly. The Kashag should explicitly request His Holiness, the current Dalai Lama, to assume a formal role to reach out to Beijing to reestablish communication and negotiate a solution that will enable the Tibetans inside Tibet to enjoy the rights and privileges to which they are entitled and that they so richly deserve.

While forcefully advocating a solution to the Tibet issue based on His Holiness's Middle Way Approach, I am not in any way saying that the Tibetan people have great enthusiasm for this result. Their heartfelt aspiration, as exemplified by my own mothers' deeply held views,[8] is for freedom. I have always been open and truthful about this pervasive and strongly held sentiment among the Tibetan people, never hiding or attempting to minimize this fact in all my dealings with my dialogue counterparts, as official transcripts of our meetings and my public comments plainly show. My remarks in a 2006 interview are illustrative:

> It has been extremely difficult for His Holiness. When he chose "the Middle Way" path, there were tremendous protests from his own people. This strong

> opposition came from people who were ready to give their lives for the cause. And as someone who served His Holiness very closely and has been intimately involved in the process, I can tell you, it was very painful. It was certainly a difficult thing for those of us who had the honour to be associated with him. But it was even more difficult for His Holiness to take such a decision.
>
> He showed that he was a real leader, because a real leader has sometimes to take unpopular decisions. He showed that he had the courage to take difficult decisions. I always share this with my Chinese colleagues to give them an idea of the extent His Holiness has gone to work for a mutually satisfactory solution.
>
> I would like to mention a personal experience. My mother was one of the first women to take on the fight against the Chinese. She was quite well known. Though she was a very gentle woman, she never hesitated to fight the Chinese.
>
> When I accompanied His Holiness to Strasbourg to present the Proposal, she was deeply upset with me. Until His Holiness' presentation of his proposal to the European Parliament, I would keep this document under my pillow because it was extremely confidential.
>
> When I returned from Strasbourg, the first thing my mother told me: "If I had known that the documents that you were so preciously guarding were this Proposal, I would have ripped it apart."
>
> This is just to give you an idea about the mindset of the Tibetan people when they first heard of the Proposal. This shows how difficult the process has been.[9]

At the same time, the majority of Tibetans understand that their leader and spiritual teacher, His Holiness the 14th Dalai Lama, knows what is most beneficial for their interests and, most importantly, what is achievable.

His Holiness's position based on the Middle Way Approach represents his sincerely held beliefs. He has no hidden agenda. He genuinely believes that if the Tibetan people are allowed to live as equals with respect and dignity, they can lead peaceful and productive lives contributing to the welfare and benefit of the family of peoples residing together in the PRC. He has publicly stated that it would actually be of benefit to the approximately six million Tibetan people to be part of a nation of over one billion. While His Holiness definitely believes this, I must admit that I see the possibilities for some discomfort in this association, at least in the early stages.

His Holiness took the historic decision to devolve his political authority with his, what should by now be anticipated, brilliant insight and long-term perspective. For us to now disavow his intentions by arguing a different rationale for his actions would be a great disservice to His Holiness's vision and efforts. But should the CTA play any role in the resolution of the conflict? Absolutely. I know from my own personal experience that His Holiness will fully involve the CTA in the process. He has no personal agenda or differences to work out with the CTA. His only goal is to negotiate a settlement with Beijing that gives the Tibetan people a place within the PRC where they can live with dignity and respect, and most importantly, the ability to retain and foster their distinct identity.

As I said earlier, even if the CTA does not technically represent the Tibetans inside Tibet, as it was not elected by them, no one would question its right to represent those in exile. And even though it no longer has any connection with the Gaden Phodrang, for over sixty years it has represented the aspirations of the Tibetan people and thus has the legitimacy and credibility to continue in that role. Moreover, it is the only institution in which all three regions of Tibet are represented. For this reason alone, it should continue to play a major role in reflecting the hopes of the Tibetan people. As His Holiness has formally devolved his political power to the CTA, it is also only proper that the CTA exercise its newly acquired authority to request this service of him. Should the CTA take the step of formally requesting His Holiness to represent the Tibetan people's interests in seeking to resolve their differences with Beijing, it will gain instant credibility in the international community, demonstrating that it fully understands the reality of the situation and is ready to participate in solving the problem in a constructive and meaningful way.

On several occasions in the past, I have both orally and in writing suggested how the CTA can continue to play a crucial role in helping resolve the Tibet issue while formally ceding full responsibility to His Holiness for reengaging Beijing in dialogue. But in a way, His Holiness does not need to be empowered by the CTA. Even though he devolved power to this elected body, there are certain things inherently invested in him that even he cannot transfer, his status as the one true representative of all the Tibetan people being paramount.

In earlier drafts of this chapter, I referred to some memoranda I had prepared in this regard that are much more explicit, providing details about the logistics of an arrangement authorizing His Holiness to represent the Tibetan people in its dealings with the PRC. Since then, I have participated in two Task Force meetings in Dharamsala, leading me to believe that it might not be proper to publicly share any further information at this time. In offering my thoughts on the subject during these meetings, I went into considerable detail fleshing out the associated mechanics. The Task Force has an internal rule that nothing that has been shared or discussed at its meetings should be circulated outside the group. So, concerned about finding myself in that prohibited position, I feel constrained in offering any further details of my proposal.

I have also revised these last few paragraphs, hoping to avoid excessive focus on my proposal. I do not want it to become the focal point of discussion of my book, knowing that it is a suggestion that some people in the Dharamsala leadership may find a bit challenging. I remain concerned, however, that the public, in the absence of a full and proper explanation of my proposal, may think I am questioning the legitimacy of the CTA. Absolutely not. The motivation underlying my reticence to elaborate also stems from personal considerations that may limit my ability to respond to any concerns raised by my suggestions. I simply don't want to raise any issues that I may not have the opportunity to fully explain. Therefore, in this narrative, I am consciously trying to make things as clear, nonconfrontational, and straightforward as possible.

The Tibetan people, who have so much love, faith in, and respect for His Holiness, and who rely on him so much—as His Holiness sometimes says, "more than he can deliver"—would certainly welcome his resumption of what would now be clearly articulated representation. But Beijing should be just as pleased. It would no longer have any concerns that it was dealing with a purported "government" that it doesn't recognize. Given His Holiness's moral authority and unquestionable support from Tibetans everywhere, the PRC leadership can have full confidence that any settlement reached will be honored on the Tibetan side. Beijing could not have a more open-minded and principled counterpart in negotiations than His Holiness. He has demonstrated his love and concern not only for the people of Tibet but also for the welfare of all mankind, including the Chinese. As I have previously recounted, he has shown his steadfast commitment to this overriding ethical principle, despite the negative consequences sometimes inuring to the narrower Tibetan cause. If Beijing can take His Holiness at his word, specifically that he is committed to finding a solution by which the Tibetan people remain part of the larger PRC family, it should applaud his return to the negotiating table in this newly defined capacity.

One thing I can say for certain is that I know, more than anyone else, the positions and proposals for which we can expect international support. I believe this is one of them. I also know there are a number of matters dear to our hearts for which there will never be international, much less Chinese, support. We must recognize this reality and move forward with the options and resources available to us.

### *The International Community Plays a Supporting Role*

His Holiness the 14th Dalai Lama has personally led our efforts in seeking a resolution of our differences with Beijing. He is the one who devised the Middle Way Approach and brought it to the attention of the international community to galvanize support for its substantive proposals. I was fortunate to be included in almost all of his meetings with world leaders and hear him explain our rationale for reaching out to them for their support. To this day, our goal has never changed—to use whatever means available to reach out to Beijing, restart direct communications, and find a mutually acceptable solution to our differences. In pursuit of this objective, we must continue to make use of any and all international support we have developed over the decades to encourage the PRC to reengage with us.

I vividly remember, not once but several times during my official talks with PRC representatives, being accused of positioning the Tibet issue on the global stage with the intention of creating a bad image for the PRC. I always replied that this was absolutely not the case. I gave them the names of the international leaders with whom we were talking, and I asked: "Aren't they your friends?" We were also always careful not to approach either individuals or organizations that could be perceived as anti-PRC or even anticommunist, recognizing that this would be counterproductive. Even during the Cold War, when some Tibetans did get involved with anticommunist efforts, His Holiness remained steadfastly opposed to any such collaboration.

Under His Holiness's guidance, we Tibetans have always made our own decisions. Some may have been shortsighted, and I am sure we have made mistakes. But it is my belief that we shouldn't have any regrets. Instead, we should move forward and continue to be our own masters. While we are blessed to have so many well-intentioned supporters who care deeply about Tibet, their emotional attachment and exuberance have sometimes overcome their judgment and intruded upon our need to take the lead in decision making.

Burma is a good case study in this regard. I know many Westerners who were staunch supporters of Aung San Suu Kyi while she was under house arrest but became disaffected once she became part of the government and her policies appeared to have changed. I have told them that she is a Burmese, and as such she has to think about the future of her country just as Nelson Mandela did about his. Even in South Africa's case, when he started reaching out to the white minority government to find a solution, many antiapartheid groups in the West were unhappy, thinking that he had "sold out." To the contrary, his actions were very wise.

There was a time when he was involved in armed resistance, but he later chose to work closely with white South Africans for the benefit of his country and all its people, both black and white. He stepped down at the peak of his popularity, even though he could have hung on to power for decades without any difficulty. Nelson Mandela is one leader I regret never having met despite several opportunities to do so. He was deeply loved by his people and equally respected by the international community. But most importantly, as the appointed leader, he decided what policies and strategies to pursue. Our kind supporters in the international community need to accord us the same respect.

His Holiness has said that as Buddhists, we take refuge in the Buddha, the Dharma, and the Sangha, but as Tibetans we have a fourth refuge: Tibet supporters. But this is our movement, and being a supporter means standing behind us, pushing and helping us, but not getting out in front. This position has made me unpopular with some, and I have even been labeled "a control freak." But I am a Tibetan and I believe that Tibetans must control their own destiny.

I have conveyed this same message to the Tibetan people, yet some of them persist in holding on to the ancient practice of *jindak* or seeking patrons for all their needs. I believe that Tibetans should stop looking for surrogates to fight on our behalf. Under the farsighted policies of His Holiness, we are seeking a solution through the Middle Way Approach, and we must be the leaders in that pursuit.

While I am sure the foregoing proposals, and perhaps I personally, will be criticized, I feel I owe it to the Tibetan people to candidly share my thoughts. My suggestions are motivated solely by my unflagging desire to bring some relief to

The author bidding farewell to His Holiness upon his departure from the United States after a visit, Washington, D.C., May 2001
International Campaign for Tibet

my fellow Tibetans inside the PRC and are based on several decades of experience trying to realize this goal.

## CONCLUSION

From the very beginning of our struggle, His Holiness has been clear that we must reach out to the PRC government to find a solution that is mutually beneficial and acceptable. While we have used different methods at different times, His Holiness has remained steadfast in this pursuit. Even though I have now been retired for a few years, I am certain this remains His Holiness's firm commitment, one that I wholeheartedly share.

Given the advances we have made over the past three decades, it is clear that our strategy has been a tremendous success. Negotiations are complex, time-consuming, and challenging. I think it is quite remarkable that we sustained the dialogue for so many years, seriously discussing issues of tremendous importance with far-reaching implications, without deviating from our fundamental positions and long-term goals. But we are currently at a standstill and must figure out a way to move forward.

His Holiness has now severed his formal connection with the CTA. He is the ideal, and in fact only, person who can legitimately represent the interests of the Tibetan people in their relations with Beijing. As His Holiness expressly admonished following abdication of his political position, exercise of his power and authority must be reserved for those "critical situations only the Dalai Lama can handle, at which time, I will put all my strength." This is one of those situations. The Tibetan people must earnestly request His Holiness to assume the mantle of representation he has identified and implement his promise "to serve the Tibetan people until my death."

The PRC government has never acknowledged the legitimacy of the CTA, even when it was led by His Holiness. Any notion that the CTA can directly engage Beijing in negotiations is pure fantasy; it will not happen. While it is beneficial for Chinese members of the intelligence community, businesspersons, academicians, and followers of the Buddha Dharma to have confidential meetings with members of the Kashag, these activities can never take the place of formal dialogue.

This is an unprecedented moment in time that the Tibetan people must not squander. To maintain our distinct cultural identity and for the sake of future generations, we should formally request His Holiness to lead us in reestablishing relations with Beijing. In support of His Holiness's resumed efforts on our behalf, the Tibetan community at large must at the same time be scrupulously honest and forthright in our conduct, following his example. We must not do anything to cast doubt on His Holiness's veracity and sincerity in advocating the Middle Way Approach as the solution to our differences with Beijing. Of most importance, we must avoid any actions that might be viewed as calling into question his commitment to that proposal or as indicating that it is nothing more than "a stepping-stone to independence."

If we fail to adopt these measures, we will do nothing but perpetuate the climate of distrust, doubt, and suspicion that has plagued our relationship with Beijing for so long. Strong statements vilifying the Chinese or casting doubt on their motives cause more harm to our cause than any personal satisfaction we may derive from publicly expressing them. Moreover, each time such an unfortunate word is uttered, it casts suspicion on our brothers and sisters inside Tibet, further worsening their plight. It became crystal clear during the 2008 nationwide protests that sheer mistrust of our motives triggered Beijing's adoption of its extremely unfortunate policy putting every Tibetan, including very senior leaders in Tibet, on a "suspect" list.

The PRC leaders did not take those steps with the intention of causing anguish. They acted out of deep-seated mistrust. Accordingly, we in exile must make every effort to allay their misgivings, both to alleviate some of the suffering of Tibetans inside Tibet and to diminish this climate of suspicion and fear. Otherwise, Beijing will keep up the pressure in every area of Tibetan daily life, contributing to the misery of our compatriots and maintaining obstacles to the resumption of contact between the parties. When rhetoric in the exile community is more restrained, Tibetans inside tell me that conditions improve. Accordingly, Tibetan leaders of this and future generations must take every step possible to demonstrate our sincerity in looking for a mutually acceptable solution, based on the Middle Way Approach, to our differences with Beijing.

At the same time, the CTA must continue to devote its efforts to preserving and bolstering the unique Tibetan identity. During its multiple decades in existence, the CTA has enjoyed tremendous success in this regard. It should be very proud of its achievements and continue its good work, particularly in fostering the unity of Tibet's three regions. Even though I have sometimes been appalled at the conduct of individual Parliamentarians and their regional perspectives, I recognize the importance of the institution, at least symbolically, in maintaining our unity. And to continue receiving the support of the international community, it needs to enthusiastically embrace its position as an active member of civil society and deemphasize its governmental status to avoid placing any unnecessary obstacles in the path of reengagement with Beijing.

I conclude part III of my book in the hope not only that the narration of my experiences will lead to a better understanding of the Tibet issue but also, most importantly, that it will convince Dharamsala and Beijing that direct communication is the only viable way to bring closure to this unfortunate and tragic situation. To be very candid, because of the changes in Dharamsala and Beijing, formal dialogue in the manner we established in the past cannot be restored. But the PRC leadership must not fool itself into thinking that time is on its side and that the issue will disappear once His Holiness the 14th Dalai Lama is no longer with us. His Holiness's approval of any agreement is the only way to defuse the situation inside Tibet and for Beijing to achieve the legitimacy it desires. From their side, Tibetans must also recognize that the only person who can help resolve this issue is the current Dalai Lama. We must not waste our limited time, and our precious resource in the person of His Holiness, Tenzin Gyatso, the 14th Dalai Lama, by continuing to forego this unique opportunity in the deluded view that there are any other possible options. Time is not the friend of either the Chinese or the Tibetans. The clock is ticking.

# APPENDIX A

## *Na-gan Thumoche: The Great Oath of Unity*

### གནས་མཆོག་རྡོ་རྗེ་གདན་དུ་ཆོལ་གསུམ་སེར་སྐྱ་ཡོངས་ནས་ ཕུལ་བའི་མནའ་གན་མཐུ་མོ་ཆེའི་ཞལ་བཤུས།

༄ རྒྱ་གར་འཕགས་པའི་ཡུལ་དུ་བདག་ཅག་གི་སྟོན་པ་ཐུགས་རྗེ་ཅན་མངོན་པར་རྫོགས་པ་སངས་རྒྱས་པའི་གནས་མཆོག་རྡོ་རྗེ་གདན་དུ་༧གོང་ས་སྐྱབས་མགོན་༧རྒྱལ་དབང་སྐུ་ཕྲེང་ ༡༤ པ་ཐམས་ཅད་མཁྱེན་ཅིང་གཟིགས་པ་ཆེན་པོ་མཆོག་ཆིབས་བསྒྱུར་སྐབས་རྒྱ་གར་ཁུལ་དུ་སྤྱི་རྗེས་འབྱོར་བའི་བོད་མི་སྟོང་སྐོར་སོ་སོའི་སྤྱི་འཐུས་རྣམས་འདུ་འཛོམས་སེར་སྐྱ་མི་མང་སྤྱི་མཐུན་ནས་བརྟན་བཞུགས་༧ཞབས་བརྟན་བསྐུར་འབུལ་དང་ཆབས་ཅིག་འབྱུང་འགྱུར་བོད་རིགས་རྣམས་མཐུན་ལམ་རྡོག་རྩ་གཅིག་བསྒྲིལ་ཞུ་རྒྱུའི་གན་རྒྱ་འབུལ་ལམ་ཞུས་པ་གཤམ་གསལ།

༄༅།། རབ་བྱུང་ ༡༦ པའི་བོད་ས་ཕག་ཟླ་ ༡༣ ཚེས་ ༢ ལ། དཔལ་མྱུར་མཛད་ཡེ་ཤེས་ཀྱི་མགོན་པོ་ཕྱག་དྲུག་པ་དང་། དཔལ་ལྡན་དམག་ཟོར་གྱི་རྒྱལ་མོ་རེ་མ་ཏི། བསྟན་སྲུང་དམ་ཅན་རྒྱ་མཚོ་དཔང་དུ་བཙུགས། ཕན་བདེའི་འབྱུང་གནས་ལུགས་གཉིས་༧གོང་མ་ཁྲིམས་བདག་རིན་པོ་ཆེའི་༧ཞབས་དྲུང་དུ།

བདག་མིང་རྟགས་ཁུངས་གཤམ་གསལ་རྣམས་བློ་ཡིད་གཅིག་ཏུ་མཐུན་པའི་རང་མོས་བློས་བླངས་ནས་ཡང་འགྱུར་མེད་ཀྱི་གན་རྒྱ་མཐུ་མོ་ཆེ་གཙང་མར་འཛུགས་སྙིང་། དོན་རྩ། འཇིག་རྟེན་ཡོངས་ལ་ཕན་བདེ་གང་ལས་བྱུང་བའི་རྩ་ལག་དམ་པ་སངས་རྒྱས་ཀྱི་བསྟན་པ་རིན་པོ་ཆེ་དར་རྒྱས་ཡུན་རིང་དུ་གནས་ཐུབ་པ་དང་། རང་ཅག་སྟོད་མངའ་རིས་སྐོར་གསུམ། བར་དབུས་གཙང་རུ་བཞི། སྨད་མདོ་ཁམས་ཆུ་བཞི་སྒང་དྲུག་ཨ་མདོ། འབྲུ་ལོག་བཅས་བོད་ཆོལ་ཁ་གསུམ་གྱི་མི་མང་ཡོངས་ལ་བདེ་སྐྱིད་ཀྱི་དཔལ་ཡོན་རྟག་ཏུ་བཞད་པའི་ཐབས་ཚུལ་ལ་གངས་ལྗོངས་རྒྱལ་བསྟན་ཆབ་སྲིད་ཡོངས་ཀྱི་བདག་པོ་སྤྱི་ནོར་༧གོང་ས་༧སྐྱབས་མགོན་ཆེན་པོས་ཉིན་མཚན་དུས་དྲུག་ཏུ་ཐུགས་ཁུར་ཟབ་བཞེས་བཀའ་དྲིན་སྤུ་མཐའ་མེད་པ་བསྐྱངས་རུང་། རང་ཅག་བོད་རིགས་མི་མང་ཡོངས་ནས་ད་བར་མཐུན་ལམ་རྡོག་རྩ་གཅིག་ཏུ་བསྒྲིལ་བའི་ཁུར་བབས་སྲི་ཞུ་ལྷག་བསམ་རྣམ་དག་ཅིག་སྒྲུབ་མ་ཐུབ་པའི་ཉེར་ལེན་དང་། བསྟན་པ་སྤྱི་བགེགས་གཉིས་ཀའི་ངན་འབྲས་བཟློག་ཏུ་མེད་པ་རང་ས་དགྲ་ཡིས་ཧམ་བཟུང་གིས་བོད་ཆོལ་ཁ་གསུམ་གྱི་ཁོངས་སུ་གཏོགས་ཚད་ཀྱི་མི་རྒྱུ་ཟོག་གསུམ་གང་ལའང་ལྷ་བཟོ་སྤུ་ཙམ་མེད་པར་ད་ཆ་བོད་མི་ཀུན་གྱི་ཡིད་ལ་བཟོད་པར་དཀའ་བའི་སྡུག་བསྔལ་གྱི་ཚོར་བ་དྲག་པོ་མྱོང་སྲུས་ཀྱང་། ད་དུང་གནས་སྐབས་རང་གི་བདེ་དོན་ཐ་མོར་ཞེན་པའི་འཁྲི་བ་མ་བཅད་པར། མཁྲིགས་ཆོས་སུ་བཟུང་སྟེ་བསྟན་པ་སྤྱི་དོན་

ལ་རང་ཅག་བོད་རིགས་ཚང་མས་སྔར་ཐུས་ལྟར་སྤྱི་ཐོམ་ཡལ་ཡོལ་འབབ་ཞིག་གི་དབང་དུ་མ་སོང་བར་སྤྱི་ནོར་༧གོང་ས་༧སྐྱབས་མགོན་ཆེན་པོ་མཆོག་སྐུ་ངལ་ཁྱད་བསད་ཀྱིས་རྒྱ་གར་འཕགས་པའི་ཡུལ་དུ་ཆིབས་བསྒྱུར་བཀའ་དྲིན་ཆེ་སྟེ་བོད་ལྗོངས་ཆོལ་ཁ་གསུམ་གྱི་ཁྲོད་ལ་ཆོས་སྲིད་རང་དབང་བདེ་སྐྱིད་རྫོགས་ལྡན་གསར་པའི་དགེ་མཚན་གསར་དུ་བཞེད་ཐབས་ལ་༧སྐུའི་གསང་བ་གསུམ་གྱི་ཡོན་ཏན་མ་ལུས་པ་གཅིག་ཏུ་སྤུངས་ཏེ་མཐུ་སྟོབས་ནུས་པའི་རྣམ་འཕྲུལ་ནི་རང་ཅག་སོ་སྐྱེ་རྣམས་ཀྱི་བསམ་བརྗོད་ཀྱི་ཡུལ་ལས་འདས་པའི་མཐའ་ཡས་རྒྱ་ཆེའི་མཛད་འཕྲིན་གྱི་འོད་སྟོང་འཛམ་གླིང་ཡངས་པའི་གོ་ལར་མངོན་པར་དུ་འཕགས་པ་འདི་ནི་འཛམ་གླིང་ནང་གི་སངས་རྒྱས་པའི་རིང་ལུགས་ལ་ཞུགས་པ་རྣམས་དང་། སྤྲོས་སུ་རང་ཅག་ཁ་བ་རི་པའི་སྐྱེ་འགྲོ་ཡོངས་ལ་བསམ་བཞིན་དད་པའི་སྣ་ལོང་དབང་མེད་དུ་གཡོ་བའི་བཀའ་དྲིན་གྱི་ཚད་མཐའ་གཞལ་དུ་མེད་པ་དེ་ལྟ་བུའི་དུས་སྐབས་འདིར་རང་ཅག་བོད་རིགས་ཚང་མས་སྔར་བྱུས་ལ་འགྱོད་སྡོམ་དྲག་པོ་དང་། ཕྱིས་ཀྱི་ཁུར་བབས་ཞུ་བྱའི་ཐད་༧གོང་ས་༧སྐྱབས་མགོན་ཐམས་ཅད་མཁྱེན་གཟིགས་ཆེན་པོའི་དགོངས་གཞི་ཟབ་མོ་དང་མཐུན་པའི་བོད་རིགས་ནང་ཁུལ་རང་རང་མིང་གི་རྗེས་སུ་བསྙེགས་པའི་ཕྱོགས་འཛིན་ཕྲག་དོག་རྣམས་ཞེ་ནས་སྤྲངས་ཏེ་མཐུན་བསྒྲིལ་རྡོག་རྩ་གཅིག་བསྒྲིལ་ལྷུགས་ཀྱི་གོང་བུ་བཞིན་བྱེད་རྒྱུ་དང་། ༧གོང་ས་༧སྐྱབས་མགོན་ཆེན་པོའི་ཡང་དག་པའི་དབུ་ཁྲིད་འོག་ང་ཚོས་བཀའ་དགོངས་ཟབ་མོ་དང་མཐུན་པའི་ཁུར་བབས་ཞུ་བྱ་ཅི་མཆིས་ན་ནུས་འཆི་ཐུབ་ཞུས་ཆེ་བོད་སྤྱིའི་འཕྲལ་ཕུགས་བདེ་དོན་སྒྲུབ་པར་འདི་ལས་དགེ་མཚན་ཆེ་བ་མ་མངོན་པར་ཚང་མའི་མཐོང་སྣང་གཅིག་ཏུ་མཐུན་ཏེ་མ་བསྐུལ་དང་བླངས་དགའ་སྤྲོའི་སེམས་པས་ཁེངས་པའི་ངང་ནས་གྲོས་ཐག་གཅང་མར་བཅད་ཟིན་པ་འདི་ལས་ནམ་ཡང་མི་འགལ་ཞིང་། གལ་སྲིད་འགལ་ཚར་འགྲོ་རིགས་དྲག་ཞན་སེར་སྐྱ་སུ་ཐད་ནས་བྲ་མོ་ཙམ་ཤར་རུང་ཡུལ་ཁྲིམས་དང་མཐུན་པའི་ལུགས་གཉིས་ཁྲིམས་ཀྱི་བདའ་འདེད་ཡན་ཐོན་མ་སོང་བ་བྱེད་པོ་སུ་ཡིན་རྣག་ཐོག་གཙག་འཕེལ་གྱི་བཀའ་དབྱད་ཞུ་རྒྱུ་སྨོས་ཅི། དེས་ན་ཕྱིན་ཆད་མི་དམངས་ཀྱི་དཀྲར་ཟིན་པ་མ་ཟད། ནང་པ་སངས་རྒྱས་པར་ཁས་འཆེ་བའི་མི་རིགས་ནས་རང་གི་ཁས་ལེན་དམ་བཞག་ལས་བཟློག་པའི་བགྱི་བ་ངན་པ་བྱེད་སྲིད་ན་བསྟན་སྲུང་དམ་ཅན་རྒྱ་མཚོའི་ཚོགས་ཀྱི་ལས་འབྲས་དུས་སུ་བཏོད་པའི་དྲག་པོའི་ཆད་པ་གཅོད་པར་མཛོད་ཅིག་ཅེས་ཇི་སྲིད་བར་དེ་སྲིད་རྩ་འཛིན་སྤྱི་མཐུན་གན་རྒྱར་མིང་རྟགས་རིམ་འབུལ་ཞུས་གྲས།

༡ གདན་ས་ཆེན་པོ་དཔལ་ལྡན་འབྲས་དཀར་སྤུངས་པའི་སྤྱི་འཐུས་བློ་གླིང་སློབ་དཔོན་པདྨ་རྒྱལ་མཚན་གྱི་རྟགས།
༢ སེ་ར་ཐེག་ཆེན་གླིང་གི་སྤྱི་འཐུས་བྱེས་སློབ་དཔོན་བློ་བཟང་དོན་ཡོད་ཀྱི་རྟགས།
༣ དགའ་ལྡན་རྣམ་པར་རྒྱལ་བའི་སྤྱི་འཐུས་ཤར་རྩེ་སློབ་དཔོན་བློ་བཟང་ཆོས་འཕེལ་གྱི་རྟགས།
༤ རྒྱུད་གྲྭ་སྟོད་སྨད་ཀྱི་སྤྱི་འཐུས་རྒྱུད་སྨད་སློབ་ཟུར་དགེ་དབང་ལེགས་ལྡན་གྱི་རྟགས།
༥ བཀའ་རྙིང་ས་གསུམ་གྱི་སྤྱི་འཐུས་དཔལ་སྤུངས་དབོན་སྤྲུལ་ཀརྨ་བདེ་ཆེན་ངེས་དོན་གྱི་རྟགས།
༦ ཀ་སྨྱུག་ཐར་ཆོས་དགོན་གྱི་སྤྱི་འཐུས་མཁན་པོ་ངག་དབང་སྦྱིན་པའི་རྟགས།
༧ རྫོར་གདན་བོད་གཞུང་དགོན་འཕེལ་རྒྱས་གླིང་གི་སྤྱི་འཐུས་དགེ་བསྐོས་སྦྱིན་པ་རྒྱ་མཚོའི་རྟགས།
༨ གཞུང་ཞབས་རྩེ་སྒོར་སྤྱི་འཐུས་མཁན་དྲུང་ངག་དབང་དོན་གྲུབ་གྱི་རྟགས། (ཨ་གུག་ལགས།)
༩ ཤོད་སྐོར་སྤྱི་འཐུས་རྩིས་དཔོན་རྣམ་གླིང་དཔལ་འབྱོར་འཇིགས་མེད་ཀྱི་རྟགས།
༡༠ བོད་གཞུང་དམག་སྒར་ཁག་གི་སྤྱི་འཐུས་ཀ་དང་སྐུ་སྲུང་རུ་དཔོན་བསོད་ནམས་བཀྲ་ཤིས་དང་། ངག་དབང་དོན་གྲུབ་གཉིས་ཀྱི་རྟགས།
༡༡ ཚ་སྒང་ཨ་མདོ་འགུ་ལོག་བཅས་དང་བླངས་འགོ་མང་གི་སྤྱི་འཐུས་བྲ་གོད་རྣམ་རྒྱལ་རྡོ་རྗེ་དང་ཨ་མདོ་ཆོས་གྲགས་གཉིས་ཀྱི་རྟགས།

༡༢ མི་མང་སྤྱི་འཐུས་སྟོན་འཁོར་སེར་སྐྱ་ཕྱག་དགེ་བློ་བཟང་རྡོ་རྗེའི་རྟགས། (ཤེལ་ཕྱག)
༡༣ མི་མང་སྤྱི་འཐུས་སྟོན་འཁོར་ཨ་མདོ་རྒྱལ་སྟོང་(ཚེ་རིང་)གི་རྟགས།
༡༤ སྟོད་གཙང་སྤྱི་འཐུས་གཞིས་རྩེ་ལམ་གཙོ་སྨི་ཟུར་རྡོ་རྗེ་ནོར་བུའི་རྟགས།
༡༥ མི་མང་སྤྱི་འཐུས་ཆུ་ཤུར་སྐྱན་གྲོང་ཚེ་རིང་སྟོབས་རྒྱལ་གྱི་རྟགས།
༡༦ མི་མང་སྤྱི་འཐུས་སྡེ་གདོང་གཙོ་དྲུག་དབང་འདུད་རྡོ་རྗེའི་རྟགས།
༡༧ མི་མང་སྤྱི་འཐུས་བསོད་ནམས་བསྟན་འཛིན་གྱི་རྟགས།
༡༨ མི་མང་སྤྱི་འཐུས་འཕྱོངས་རྒྱས་གཙོ་དྲུག་ཤེས་རབ་ཀྱི་རྟགས།
༡༩ མི་མང་སྤྱི་འཐུས་རྨར་ལམ་མཛོད་པ་ཚེ་བརྟན་རྣམ་རྒྱལ་གྱི་རྟགས།
༢༠ མི་མང་སྤྱི་འཐུས་མར་ནང་པདྨ་ཚེ་དབང་གི་རྟགས།
༢༡ ཀོང་པོ་སྤྱི་འཐུས་རྩེ་སྨན་ལྷ་དབང་ཚེ་རིང་གི་རྟགས།
༢༢ ཀ་སྨུག་པང་ཚའི་སྤྱི་འཐུས་རྨར་ཁམས་ཐོས་བསམ་ཅན་ནས་སྤྱི་ཐམ།
༢༣ ཀ་སྨུག་ཡིད་མཐུན་སྤྱི་འཐུས་བསོད་ནམས་ཚེ་དབང་གི་རྟགས།
༢༤ མི་མང་སྤྱི་འཐུས་གྲོ་མོ་གོང་འཐུས་ཨ་ཕྱུར་གྱི་རྟགས།
༢༥ མི་མང་སྤྱི་འཐུས་འཇིགས་མེད་རྣམ་རྒྱལ་གྱི་རྟགས།
༢༦ ཌལ་ཧ་བོད་དགོན་བཤད་སྒྲུབ་འདོད་རྒུ་འཁྱིལ་གྱི་གནས་འཛིན་དགེ་སློང་ཐུབ་བསྟན་འབྱུང་གནས་ཀྱི་རྟགས།
༢༧ རྡོར་གླིང་མི་མང་སྤྱི་འཐུས་བཟོད་པ་དང་། སྐྱན་གྲགས། ཨ་ཟླ། ཕུར་བུ། ཨ་ཁྲུ། ཡེ་ཤེས་ཚེ་རིང་བཅས་སྤྱི་
ལག་སྐོར་བའི་རྟགས།
(ཞེས་བཀའ་ཐམ་འབྱར་མའི་ཞལ་བཤུས་ཤིག་ནས་ཞུས་དག་སོང་།། །།)

ORAL HISTORY SERIES 24 (pages 217–222)


## THE GREAT OATH TAKEN BY ALL THE MONASTIC AND LAY COMMUNITY OF THE THREE PROVINCES AT THE HOLY PLACE OF BODHGAYA

During the visit of His Holiness the Fourteenth Dalai Lama to the most sacred place of Bodhgaya in India, the land of Arya, where Buddha attained complete and perfect enlightenment, representatives of Tibetans, who have arrived in India at various times, gathered together. The representatives of secular and lay communities in unanimity made a long-life prayer offering, and at the same time took the following oath stating that henceforth all Tibetans will maintain harmony and unity:

On the seventh day of the twelfth month of the Tibetan Earth-Pig year in the Sixteenth Rabjung (sixty-year cycle) with the six-armed wisdom protector Gonpo who is endowed with the power for swift action, Palden Lhamo and oath-bound protectors of doctrine—who are the source of happiness and providers of justice for temporal and religious spheres—as witnesses, we, the following signatories, united by our mind and hearts voluntarily and clearly take this unshakable great oath.

Purpose:

His Holiness the Dalai Lama, the supreme temporal and spiritual leader of the Land of Snow, has been striving in all six stages of day and night with his deepest concern and kindness for the flourishing of the precious Buddha Dharma—the source of happiness for the entire world—and for the blossoming of happiness and well-being of all the people of the Three Provinces of Tibet from the Three Rings of Ngari in the upper region, the Four Mountain Ranges of U-Tsang in the middle, and the Four Rivers and Six Ranges of Do-Kham in the lower region as well as Amdo and Golog;

Yet, until now, because of our inability to take up our responsibility in unity with sincerity and the general obstacles to the Dharma, the irreversible negative outcome has led to the forceful takeover of our land by the enemy who spared not a hair's worth of our people, property, and livestock in all Three Provinces of Tibet. This has plunged every Tibetan into an unbearable and continued suffering;

Nevertheless, for the larger cause of the Tibetan people's welfare and Buddha Dharma, we must abandon the careless attitude of still stubbornly clinging to short-term and self-centered meager benefits. Particularly, by acknowledging the tireless effort that His Holiness the Dalai Lama has made to come to India and making every endeavor to restore religious and political freedom for all the Three Provinces of Tibet, thus to usher in a new virtuous era of happiness through combination of his all three secrets wisdom, the manifestation of his ability, which is beyond the comprehension of the ordinary people like us. His limitless activity is as evident as the thousands of dazzling rays across the globe, and his immeasurable kindness causes hair-raising faith in followers of Buddhism around the world in general and the people of the Land of Snow in particular.

At such a time, all Tibetans will strongly atone for their past misdeeds, and in future shoulder our responsibility in accordance with the visions of His Holiness the Dalai Lama. Furthermore, we will eschew pursuance of personal name and fame driven by mutual jealousies and narrowmindedness, and remain united like an iron ball.

There is no better way to achieve the short- and long-term collective happiness for all Tibetans other than for each of us to carry out his responsibilities per each person's ability, in accordance with His Holiness the Dalai Lama's deep vision and guidance;

This being the unanimous observation of all of us, we have voluntarily and with our minds filled with happiness resolutely passed this resolution, and pledge never to violate it.

If even a minor transgression takes place, whether by the powerful or weak, or by the religious or lay community, they will be subject to the dual system of decree in accordance with the laws of the land, and prosecuted accordingly like a medicinal lancet is inserted to take the pus out. Afterward, not only will they be considered the enemies of the public but also, for breaking their pledge and committing evil deeds in a community upholding Buddhism, may the oath-bound protector deities of the Dharma take forceful actions bringing timely fruition of the karmic deed.

The following signatories on this oath commit to uphold it for as long as it is needed:

1. Signature of Loling Abbot Pema Gyaltsen as the representative of the great seat of Glorious Drekar Pungpa [Drepung]
2. Signature of Serjey Abbot Lobsang Dhonyo as the representative of Sera Thekchen-ling
3. Signature of Shartse Abbot Lobsang Choephel as the representative of Gaden Nampar Gyalwa
4. Signature of former Abbot Ngawang Legden as the representative of Gyuto and Gyumed
5. Signature of Palpung Ontrul Karma Dechen Ngedhon as the representative of Kagyu, Nyingma, and Sakya
6. Signature of Khenpo Ngawang Jinpa as the representative of Tharpa Choeling Monastery in Kalimpong
7. Signature of Disciplinarian Jinpa Gyatso as the representative of Phelgyeling, Tibetan Government monastery in Bodhgaya
8. Signature of Khendrung Ngawang Dhondup (Agug lak) as the representative of government officials from the clergy
9. Signature of Tsee-pon Namling Paljor Jigme as the representative of government officials from the lay community
10. Signatures of Rupon Sonam Tashi and Ngawang Dhondup as the representatives of all military regiments of the Tibetan Government, Ka- Regiment and Bodyguard Regiments

11. Signatures of Jagoe Namgyal Dorjee and Amdo Choedrak as the representatives of the officers and members of the Voluntary Resistance Force (Chushi Gangdrug), including Amdo Golog
12. Signature of Sermey Chagzoe Gan Lobsang Dorje (Shelchag) as the representative of the public who arrived in India earlier
13. Signature of Amdo Gyetong (Tsering) as the representative of the public who arrived in India earlier
14. Signature of Shitse Leytso Pesur Dorjee Norbu as the representative of Toe and Tsang regions
15. Signature of Chushur Kandrong Tsering Topgye as the representative of the general public
16. Signature of Nedong chief Wangdu Dorje as the representative of the general public
17. Signature of Sonam Tenzin as the representative of the general public
18. Signature of Chong-gye chief Sherab as the representative of the general public
19. Signature of Marlam Zodpa Tseten Namgyal as the representative of the general public
20. Signature of Marnang Pema Tsewang as the representative of the general public
21. Signature of Tsegang Lhawang Tsering as the representative of Kongpo
22. Stamp of Markham Thoesam as the representative of Panchayat, Kalimpong
23. Signature of Sonam Tsewang as the representative of Yithun, Kalimpong
24. Signature of Dromo Gongthue Aphur as the representative of the general public
25. Signature of Jigme Namgyal as the representative of the general public
26. Signature of Gelong Thupten Jungney as the Manager of Shedrup Doegu-khyil Tibetan monastery, Varanasi
27. Signatures of Soepa, Nyendrak, Atra, Phurbu, Akhu, and Yeshe Tsering as representatives of the Darjeeling public

(Copied and proofread from a sealed copy of the original document)

## APPENDIX B

*Tibetan Policy Act*

TIBET POLICY ACT (excerpt)

H.R. 1646

Foreign Relations Authorization Act, Fiscal Year 2003

P.L. 107–228

Subtitle B—Tibet Policy

### SEC. 611. SHORT TITLE.

This subtitle may be cited as 'Tibetan Policy Act of 2002.'

### SEC. 612. STATEMENT OF PURPOSE.

The purpose of this subtitle is to support the aspirations of the Tibetan people to safeguard their distinct identity.

### SEC. 613. TIBET NEGOTIATIONS.

(a) POLICY

(1) IN GENERAL—The President and the Secretary should encourage the Government of the People's Republic of China to enter into a dialogue with the Dalai Lama or his representatives leading to a negotiated agreement on Tibet.

(2) COMPLIANCE—After such an agreement is reached, the President and the Secretary should work to ensure compliance with the agreement.

(b) PERIODIC REPORTS—Not later than 180 days after the date of the enactment of this Act, and every 12 months thereafter, the President shall transmit to the appropriate congressional committees a report on:

(1) the steps taken by the President and the Secretary in accordance with subsection (a)(1); and

(2) the status of any discussions between the People's Republic of China and the Dalai Lama or his representatives.

## SEC. 614. REPORTING ON TIBET.

Whenever a report is transmitted to Congress under section 116 or 502B of the Foreign Assistance Act of 1961 (22 U.S.C. 2151m, 2304) or under section 102(b) of the International Religious Freedom Act of 1998 (22 U.S.C. 6412(b)), Tibet shall be included in such report as a separate section.

## SEC. 615. CONGRESSIONAL-EXECUTIVE COMMISSION ON THE PEOPLE'S REPUBLIC OF CHINA.

Section 302(h) of the US-China Relations Act of 2000 (Public Law 106-286), relating to the Congressional-Executive Commission on the People's Republic of China, is amended:

(1) by striking 'shall include specific information' and inserting the following: 'shall include:

(a) specific information;'

(b) by striking the period at the end and inserting ;' and;' and

(c) by adding at the end the following:

(2) 'a description of the status of negotiations between the Government of the People's Republic of China and the Dalai Lama or his representatives, and measures taken to safeguard Tibet's distinct historical, religious, cultural, and linguistic identity and the protection of human rights.'

## SEC. 616. ECONOMIC DEVELOPMENT IN TIBET.

(a) DECLARATIONS OF POLICY—It is the policy of the United States to support economic development, cultural preservation, health care, and education and environmental sustainability for Tibetans inside Tibet. In support of this policy, the United States shall use its voice and vote to support projects designed in accordance with the principles contained in subsection (d) that are designed to raise the standard of living for the Tibetan people and assist Tibetans to become self-sufficient.

(b) INTERNATIONAL FINANCIAL INSTITUTIONS—The Secretary of the Treasury shall instruct the United States executive director of each international financial institution to use the voice and vote of the United States to support projects in Tibet, if the projects are designed in accordance with the principles contained in subsection (d).

(c) EXPORT-IMPORT BANK AND TDA—The Export-Import Bank of the United States and the Trade and Development Agency should support projects proposed to be funded or otherwise supported by such entities in Tibet, if the projects are designed in accordance with the principles contained in subsection (d).

(d) TIBET PROJECT PRINCIPLES—Projects in Tibet supported by international financial institutions, other international organizations, nongovernmental organizations, and the United States entities referred to in subsection (c), should:

   (1) be implemented only after conducting a thorough assessment of the needs of the Tibetan people through field visits and interviews;
   (2) be preceded by cultural and environmental impact assessments;
   (3) foster self-sufficiency and self-reliance of Tibetans;
   (4) promote accountability of the development agencies to the Tibetan people and active participation of Tibetans in all project stages;
   (5) respect Tibetan culture, traditions, and the Tibetan knowledge and wisdom about their landscape and survival techniques;
   (6) be subject to on-site monitoring by the development agencies to ensure that the intended target group benefits;
   (7) be implemented by development agencies prepared to use Tibetan as the working language of the projects;

(8) neither provide incentive for, nor facilitate the migration and settlement of, non-Tibetans into Tibet; and
(9) neither provide incentive for, nor facilitate the transfer of ownership of, Tibetan land or natural resources to non-Tibetans.

## SEC. 617. RELEASE OF PRISONERS AND ACCESS TO PRISONS.

The President and the Secretary, in meetings with representatives of the Government of the People's Republic of China, should:

(1) request the immediate and unconditional release of all those held prisoner for expressing their political or religious views in Tibet;
(2) seek access for international humanitarian organizations to prisoners in Tibet to ensure that prisoners are not being mistreated and are receiving necessary medical care; and
(3) seek the immediate medical parole of Tibetan prisoners known to be in serious ill health.

## SEC. 618. ESTABLISHMENT OF A UNITED STATES BRANCH OFFICE IN LHASA, TIBET.

The Secretary should make best efforts to establish an office in Lhasa, Tibet, to monitor political, economic, and cultural developments in Tibet.

## SEC. 619. REQUIREMENT FOR TIBETAN LANGUAGE TRAINING.

The Secretary shall ensure that Tibetan language training is available to Foreign Service officers, and that every effort is made to ensure that a Tibetan-speaking Foreign Service officer is assigned to a United States post in the People's Republic of China responsible for monitoring developments in Tibet.

## SEC. 620. RELIGIOUS PERSECUTION IN TIBET.

(a) HIGH-LEVEL CONTACTS—Pursuant to section 105 of the International Religious Freedom Act of 1998 (22 U.S.C. 6414), the United States Ambassador to the People's Republic of China should:

(1) meet with the 11th Panchen Lama, who was taken from his home on May 17, 1995, and otherwise ascertain information concerning his whereabouts and well-being; and

(2) request that the Government of the People's Republic of China release the 11th Panchen Lama and allow him to pursue his religious studies without interference and according to tradition.

(b) PROMOTION OF INCREASED ADVOCACY—Pursuant to section 108(a) of the International Religious Freedom Act of 1998 (22 U.S.C. 6417(a)), it is the sense of Congress that representatives of the United States Government in exchanges with officials of the Government of the People's Republic of China should call for and otherwise promote the cessation of all interference by the Government of the People's Republic of China or the Communist Party in the religious affairs of the Tibetan people.

## SEC. 621. UNITED STATES SPECIAL COORDINATOR FOR TIBETAN ISSUES.

(a) UNITED STATES SPECIAL COORDINATOR FOR TIBETAN ISSUES—There shall be within the Department a United States Special Coordinator for Tibetan Issues (in this section referred to as the 'Special Coordinator').

(b) CONSULTATION—The Secretary shall consult with the chairmen and ranking minority members of the appropriate congressional committees prior to the designation of the Special Coordinator.

(c) CENTRAL OBJECTIVE—The central objective of the Special Coordinator is to promote substantive dialogue between the Government of the People's Republic of China and the Dalai Lama or his representatives.

(d) DUTIES AND RESPONSIBILITIES—The Special Coordinator shall:

(1) coordinate United States Government policies, programs, and projects concerning Tibet;

(2) vigorously promote the policy of seeking to protect the distinct religious, cultural, linguistic, and national identity of Tibet, and pressing for improved respect for human rights;

(3) maintain close contact with religious, cultural, and political leaders of the Tibetan people, including regular travel to Tibetan areas of the People's Republic of China, and to Tibetan refugee settlements in India and Nepal;

(4) consult with Congress on policies relevant to Tibet and the future and welfare of the Tibetan people;

(5) make efforts to establish contacts in the foreign ministries of other countries to pursue a negotiated solution for Tibet; and

(6) take all appropriate steps to ensure adequate resources, staff, and bureaucratic support to fulfill the duties and responsibilities of the Special Coordinator.[1]

## APPENDIX C

# *Selected Press Releases*

## FOURTH ROUND STATEMENT, 2005

*Statement of the Special Envoy of His Holiness the Dalai Lama Kasur Lodi Gyari, Head of the Tibetan Delegation, for the Fourth Round of Meetings with the Chinese Leadership*

Envoy Kelsang Gyaltsen and I, accompanied by three senior assistants, Sonam N. Dagpo, Ngapa Tsegyam, and Bhuchung K. Tsering, met with Vice-Minister Zhu Weiqun and his six-member delegation on June 30 and July 1, 2005 at the Embassy of the People's Republic of China in Berne, Switzerland. This is the fourth round of meetings since the resumption of direct contact in 2002.

Vice Minister Zhu Weiqun is the deputy head of the United Front Work Department of the Chinese Communist Party and also a member of the Central Commission for Discipline Inspection of the Communist Party.

The discussions were concrete and substantive, and held in a cordial, frank, and business-like atmosphere. Obviously, major differences on a number of issues, including on some fundamental ones, continue to remain. But the Berne round gave both sides yet another opportunity to extensively share with each other their views and perspectives on core issues.

We put forward some concrete proposals that will help build trust and confidence and move the ongoing process to a new level of engagement aimed at bringing about substantive negotiations to achieve a mutually acceptable solution to the Tibetan issue.

We reiterated our commitment to continue making every effort to create a better environment. At the same time we urged the Chinese side to join in this effort, and highlighted the absence of such obvious gestures from their side.

It was apparent that both sides had a positive assessment of the ongoing process. Despite the existing areas of disagreement, Vice-Minister Zhu was pleased that our direct contact had now become stable and an "established practice." He also conveyed to us that the Central leadership of the Chinese Communist Party attached great importance to the contact with His Holiness the Dalai Lama. He stated that we need not be pessimistic about the existing differences and that it was possible to narrow down the gaps through more meetings and exchange of views. This shows the degree of trust and confidence that the present process has been able to build.

At the third round of meetings in Beijing last year we had discussed the increase in the number of meetings and to consider periodic meetings at any convenient place, including outside of China, and the inclusion of Mr. Ngapa Tsegyam as a member of our team.

We have reported to His Holiness the Dalai Lama today on our discussions. His Holiness is very pleased with the Berne round, which has provided another opportunity to further deepen the ongoing process. He was also pleased that we had the opportunity to address extensively the issues raised by the Chinese government and to clarify in detail our positions on fundamental issues. His Holiness instructed the Kalon Tripa and us to continue to push this process forward and pursue the issues discussed at the Berne round.

On our arrival in Dharamsala on July 5, 2005 we reported to Kalon Tripa Samdhong Rinpoche on the Berne round. We will also be briefing the Chair and the Vice-Chair of the Assembly of Tibetan People's Deputies and members of the Kashag.

Dharamsala, July 7, 2005

https://tibet.net/important-issues/sino-tibetan-dialogue/statement-on-sino-tibetan-dialogue-by-envoys-of-his-holiness-the-dalai-lama/ statement-of-special-envoy-of-his-holiness-the-dalai-lama-kasur-lodigyari-head-of-the-tibetan-delegation-for-the-fourth-round-of-meetings-withthe-chinese-leadership-dharamshala-7-july-2005/

## SHENZHEN INFORMAL MEETING STATEMENT, MAY 2008

*Statement by Special Envoy of His Holiness the Dalai Lama, Kasur Lodi Gyaltsen Gyari*

The two envoys of His Holiness the Dalai Lama held informal talks on Tibet with their Chinese counterparts in the Chinese city of Shenzhen on Sunday, 4 May.

Envoy Kelsang Gyaltsen and I had the honour of briefing His Holiness the Dalai Lama immediately after our arrival yesterday from China. Kalon Tripa, Prof. Samdhong Rinpoche, joined us in the briefing. We also briefed the Deputy Speaker, Mrs. Dolma Gyari, this morning. The Speaker, Mr. Karma Choephel, is currently on an official visit.

On 4 May 2008 in Shenzhen, China, we met with Executive Vice-Minister Zhu Weiqun and Vice-Minister Sithar of the United Front Work Department of the Chinese Communist Party. We would like to express our appreciation to the hosts for accepting our suggestion to hold this informal meeting in Shenzhen as well as agreeing to a meeting of principals without aides. Executive Vice-Minister Zhu Weiqun and Vice-Minister Sithar were our counterparts for the last several years. This long relationship made it possible to have open and frank discussions in a friendly and respectful atmosphere, despite the prevailing tense and grave situation in Tibet.

Our main purpose of seeking this urgent informal meeting was to discuss the critical situation in Tibet. There were strong and divergent views on the nature as well as the causes of the recent tragic events in Tibet. These views were expressed in a frank and candid manner. On our part we rejected categorically the accusation made against His Holiness the Dalai Lama of instigating the demonstrations and unrest in Tibet. Instead we made it clear that the events in Tibet are the inescapable consequences of wrong policies of the authorities towards the Tibetans, which goes back several decades. The recent crisis in Tibet is a clear symptom of deeply felt grievances and resentment of the Tibetans with these policies. The task at hand is to address the legitimate concerns of the Tibetan people in a realistic and constructive way.

We have stressed the importance of ending the current repression throughout Tibet. We have called for the release of prisoners, to allow those injured to be given proper medical treatment and give unfettered access to visitors, including the media. We have also called for an end to the "patriotic re-education" campaign which is deeply resented by the Tibetan people.

We also rejected the accusation that His Holiness the Dalai Lama is sabotaging the Olympic Games 2008. On the contrary, we made it clear that His Holiness the Dalai Lama has consistently and unambiguously supported the Beijing Olympic Games right from the beginning.

Despite major differences on important issues both sides demonstrated a willingness to seek common approaches in addressing the issues at hand. In this regard, each side made some concrete proposals, which can be part of the future agenda. As a result an understanding was reached to continue the formal round of discussions. A date for the seventh round will be finalised soon after mutual consultations.

We welcome the recent statement of President Hu Jintao that his government is "serious" about the dialogue and his acknowledging that His Holiness the Dalai Lama is being "conscientious and serious." This statement is encouraging at a time when there is growing scepticism about China's sincerity in resolving the Tibet issue through dialogue.

May 8, 2008

Dharamsala

https://tibet.net/2008/05/statement-by-special-envoy-of-his-holiness-thedalai-lama-kasur-lodi-gyaltsen-gyari-2/

## SEVENTH ROUND STATEMENT, JULY 2008

*Statement by Special Envoy of His Holiness the Dalai Lama, Kasur Lodi Gyaltsen Gyari*

Envoy Kelsang Gyaltsen and I accompanied by senior aides Sonam N. Dagpo, Bhuchung K. Tsering, both members of the Task Force on Sino-Tibetan Negotiations, and Jigmey Passang from the Secretariat of the Tibetan Task Force, visited Beijing from June 30 to July 3, 2008.

We met with Du Qinglin, Vice-Chairman of the Chinese People's Political Consultative Conference and Minister of the Central United Front Work Department, on July 1, 2008. This was our first meeting with Minister Du who had taken over the present post after the 17th Party Congress. He gave us a brief overview of China's domestic and international situation as well as on China's policy on Tibet. We took the opportunity to explain His Holiness the Dalai Lama's basic approach in resolving the issue of Tibet and also expressed our heartfelt condolences to the victims of the earthquake in Sichuan.

We visited the China Centre for Tibetan Studies and were received by Director Lhakpa Phuntsok and Deputy Director Zhu Xiaoming.

We had a good discussion with the scholars who briefed us about their research projects. We appreciated the work of the scholars in various fields and had the opportunity to emphasize the importance of scholars engaging in unbiased and independent research on issues such as the history of Tibet, which will contribute to a better understanding of the different perceptions. We had a day-long discussion with Executive Vice-Minister Zhu Weiqun and Vice-Minister Sithar on July 2, 2008.

This meeting took place at a crucial time in our relationship. The recent events in Tibet clearly demonstrated the Tibetan people's genuine and deep-rooted discontentment with the People's Republic of China's policies. The urgent need for serious and sincere efforts to address this issue with courage and vision in the interest of stability, unity and harmony of all nationalities of the PRC is obvious. In addition even though His Holiness the Dalai Lama is seeking a solution to the issue of Tibet within the PRC, it is a fact that it has become an issue of great international concern. In this context, we had hoped that the Chinese leadership would reciprocate our efforts by taking tangible steps during this round. On the contrary, due to their excessive concern about legitimacy the Chinese side even failed to agree to our proposal of issuing a joint statement with the aim of committing both parties to the dialogue process.

While the Chinese side finally seems to have realized that their allegations against His Holiness for instigating the recent events in Tibet and sabotaging the Olympics Games have become untenable, they are now urging His Holiness not to support violence, terrorism, and sabotaging the Olympics. We stated in the strongest possible terms that no one needs to urge us on this as His Holiness and the Tibetan struggle are universally acknowledged and appreciated for consistently rejecting and opposing such acts. While the Tibetan Youth Congress does not support the Middle Way Approach of His Holiness the Dalai Lama and stands for independence of Tibet, we categorically rejected the Chinese attempt to label it as a violent and terrorist organization. His Holiness has repeatedly and clearly stated publicly he is not seeking separation and independence of Tibet.

Throughout our talks we have reiterated to our counterparts that the issue at hand is the welfare of the Tibetan people and is not about the personal status and affairs of His Holiness the Dalai Lama or that of the Tibetans in exile. In the course of our discussions we were compelled to candidly convey to our counterparts that in the absence of serious and sincere commitment on their part the continuation of the present dialogue process would serve no purpose. The Chinese side expressed the view that the dialogue process has been productive and that we need to keep in mind that a half-a-century-old issue of great complexity, cannot be resolved in a matter of years.

Guided by the Tibetan leadership's policy of engagement, we agreed with our counterparts to have the next round of discussions in October and discussed some points that could serve as the basis of the agenda.

We briefed His Holiness the Dalai Lama today. We also briefed Speaker Karma Chophel and the Deputy Speaker Dolma Gyari this morning. On our arrival in Dharamsala on July 4 we briefed Kalon Tripa Samdhong Rinpoche.

We thank our host the Central United Front Work Department of the Chinese Communist Party for its hospitality and assistance.

July 5, 2008

Dharamsala

https://tibet.net/2008/07/statement-by-special-envoy-of-his-holiness-thedalai-lama-kasur-lodi-gyaltsen-gyari/

## APPENDIX D

# *Memorandum on Genuine Autonomy for the Tibetan People*

(Translated from the original Tibetan)

## I. INTRODUCTION

Since the renewal of direct contact with the Central Government of the People's Republic of China (PRC) in 2002, extensive discussions have been held between the envoys of His Holiness the 14th Dalai Lama and representatives of the Central Government. In these discussions we have put forth clearly the aspirations of Tibetans. The essence of the Middle Way Approach is to secure genuine autonomy for the Tibetan people within the scope of the Constitution of the PRC. This is of mutual benefit and based on the long-term interest of both the Tibetan and Chinese peoples. We remain firmly committed not to seek separation or independence. We are seeking a solution to the Tibetan problem through genuine autonomy, which is compatible with the principles on autonomy in the Constitution of the People's Republic of China (PRC). The protection and development of the unique Tibetan identity in all its aspects serves the larger interest of humanity in general and those of the Tibetan and Chinese people in particular.

During the seventh round of talks in Beijing on 1 and 2 July 2008, the Vice-Chairman of the Chinese People's Political Consultative Conference and the Minister of the Central United Front Work Department, Mr. Du Qinglin, explicitly invited suggestions from His Holiness the Dalai Lama for the stability and development of Tibet. The Executive Vice-Minister of the Central United Front Work Department, Mr. Zhu Weiqun, further said they would like to hear our views on the degree or form of autonomy we are seeking as well as on all aspects of regional autonomy within the scope of the Constitution of the PRC.

Accordingly, this memorandum puts forth our position on genuine autonomy and how the specific needs of the Tibetan nationality for autonomy and self-government can be met through application of the principles on autonomy of the Constitution of the People's Republic of China, as we understand them. On this basis, His Holiness the Dalai Lama is confident that the basic needs of the Tibetan nationality can be met through genuine autonomy within the PRC.

The PRC is a multi-national state, and as in many other parts of the world, it seeks to resolve the nationality question through autonomy and the self-government of the minority nationalities. The Constitution of the PRC contains fundamental principles on autonomy and self-government whose objectives are compatible with the needs and aspirations of the Tibetans. Regional national autonomy is aimed at opposing both the oppression and the separation of nationalities by rejecting both Han Chauvinism and local nationalism. It is intended to ensure the protection of the culture and the identity of minority nationalities by powering [*sic*] them to become masters of their own affairs.

To a very considerable extent Tibetan needs can be met within the constitutional principles on autonomy, as we understand them. On several points, the Constitution gives significant discretionary powers to state organs in the decision-making and on the operation of the system of autonomy. These discretionary powers can be exercised to facilitate genuine autonomy for Tibetans in ways that would respond to the uniqueness of the Tibetan situation. In implementing these principles, legislation relevant to autonomy may consequently need to be reviewed or amended to respond to the specific characteristics and needs of the Tibetan nationality. Given good will on both sides, outstanding problems can be resolved within the constitutional principles on autonomy. In this way national unity and stability and harmonious relations between the Tibetan and other nationalities will be established.

## II. RESPECT FOR THE INTEGRITY OF THE TIBETAN NATIONALITY

Tibetans belong to one minority nationality regardless of the current administrative division. The integrity of the Tibetan nationality must be respected. That is the spirit, the intent and the principle underlying the constitutional concept of national regional autonomy as well as the principle of equality of nationalities.

There is no dispute about the fact that Tibetans share the same language, culture, spiritual tradition, core values and customs, that they belong to the same ethnic group and that they have a strong sense of common identity. Tibetans share a common history and despite periods of political or administrative divisions, Tibetans continuously remained united by their religion, culture, education, language, way of life and by their unique high plateau environment.

The Tibetan nationality lives in one contiguous area on the Tibetan plateau, which they have inhabited for millennia and to which they are therefore indigenous. For purposes of the constitutional principles of national regional autonomy Tibetans in the PRC in fact live as a single nationality all over the Tibetan plateau.

On account of the above reasons, the PRC has recognised the Tibetan nationality as one of the 55 minority nationalities.

## III. TIBETAN ASPIRATIONS

Tibetans have a rich and distinct history, culture and spiritual tradition all of which form valuable parts of the heritage of humanity. Not only do Tibetans wish to preserve their own heritage, which they cherish, but equally they wish to further develop their culture and spiritual life and knowledge in ways that are particularly suited to the needs and conditions of humanity in the 21st century.

As a part of the multi-national state of the PRC, Tibetans can benefit greatly from the rapid economic and scientific development the country is experiencing. While wanting to actively participate and contribute to this development, we want to ensure that this happens without the people losing their Tibetan identity, culture and core values and without putting the distinct and fragile environment of the Tibetan plateau, to which Tibetans are indigenous, at risk.

The uniqueness of the Tibetan situation has consistently been recognised within the PRC and has been reflected in the terms of the '17 Point Agreement' and in statements and policies of successive leaders of the PRC since then, and should remain the basis for defining the scope and structure of the specific autonomy to be exercised by the Tibetan nationality within the PRC. The Constitution reflects a fundamental principle of flexibility to accommodate special situations, including the special characteristics and needs of minority nationalities.

His Holiness the Dalai Lama's commitment to seek a solution for the Tibetan people within the PRC is clear and unambiguous. This position is in full compliance and agreement with paramount leader Deng Xiaoping's statement in which he emphasised that except for independence all other issues could be resolved through dialogue. Whereas, we are committed, therefore, to fully respect the territorial integrity of the PRC, we expect the Central Government to recognise and fully respect the integrity of the Tibetan nationality and its right to exercise genuine autonomy within the PRC. We believe that this is the basis for resolving the differences between us and promoting unity, stability and harmony among nationalities.

For Tibetans to advance as a distinct nationality within the PRC, they need to continue to progress and develop economically, socially and politically in ways that correspond to the development of the PRC and the world as a whole while respecting and nurturing the Tibetan characteristics of such development. For this to happen, it is imperative that the right of Tibetans to govern themselves be recognised and implemented throughout the region where they live in compact communities in the PRC, in accordance with the Tibetan nationality's own needs, priorities and characteristics.

The Tibetan people's culture and identity can only be preserved and promoted by the Tibetans themselves and not by any others. Therefore, Tibetans should be capable of self-help, self-development and self-government, and an optimal balance needs to be found between this and the necessary and welcome guidance and assistance for Tibet from the Central Government and other provinces and regions of the PRC.

## IV. BASIC NEEDS OF TIBETANS

## SUBJECT MATTERS OF SELF-GOVERNMENT

### *1) Language*

Language is the most important attribute of the Tibetan people's identity. Tibetan is the primary means of communication, the language in which their literature, their spiritual texts and historical as well as scientific works are written. The Tibetan language is not only at the same high level as that of Sanskrit in terms of grammar, but is also the only one that has the capability of translating from Sanskrit without an iota of error. Therefore, Tibetan language has not only the richest and best-translated literatures, many scholars even contend that it has also the richest and largest number of literary compositions. The Constitution of the PRC, in Article 4, guarantees the freedom of all nationalities "to use and develop their own spoken and written languages . . ."

In order for Tibetans to use and develop their own language, Tibetan must be respected as the main spoken and written language. Similarly, the principal language of the Tibetan autonomous areas needs to be Tibetan.

This principle is broadly recognised in the Constitution in Article 121, which states, "the organs of self-government of the national autonomous areas employ the spoken and written language or language in common use in the locality." Article 10 of the Law on Regional National Autonomy (LRNA) provides that these organs "shall guarantee the freedom of the nationalities in these areas to use and develop their own spoken and written languages . . ."

Consistent with the principle of recognition of Tibetan as the main language in Tibetan areas, the LRNA (Article 36) also allows the autonomous government authorities to decide on "the language used in instruction and enrolment procedures" with regard to education. This implies recognition of the principle that the principal medium of education be Tibetan.

### *2) Culture*

The concept of national regional autonomy is primarily for the purpose of preservation of the culture of minority nationalities. Consequently, the Constitution of PRC contains references to cultural preservation in Articles 22, 47 and 119 as also in Article 38 of the LRNA. To Tibetans, Tibetan culture is closely connected to our religion, tradition, language and identity, which are facing threats at various levels. Since Tibetans live within the multinational state of the PRC, this distinct Tibetan cultural heritage needs protection through appropriate constitutional provisions.

### *3) Religion*

Religion is fundamental to Tibetans and Buddhism is closely linked to their identity. We recognise the importance of separation of church and state, but this should not affect the freedom and practice of believers. It is impossible for Tibetans to imagine personal or community freedom without the freedom of belief, conscience and religion. The Constitution recognises the importance of religion and protects the right to profess it. Article 36 guarantees all citizens the right to the freedom of religious belief. No one can compel another to believe in or not to believe in any religion. Discrimination on the basis of religion is forbidden.

An interpretation of the constitutional principle in light of international standard would also cover the freedom of the manner of belief or worship. The freedom covers the right of monasteries to be organised and run according to Buddhist monastic tradition, to engage in teachings and studies, and to enroll any number of monks and nuns or age group in accordance with these rules. The normal practice to hold public teachings and the empowerment of large gatherings is covered by this freedom and the state should not interfere in religious practices and traditions, such as the relationship between a teacher and his disciple, management of monastic institutions, and the recognition of reincarnations.

*4) Education*

The desire of Tibetans to develop and administer their own education system in cooperation and in coordination with the central government's ministry of education is supported by the principles contained in the Constitution with regard to education. So is the aspiration to engage in and contribute to the development of science and technology. We note the increasing recognition in international scientific development of the contribution which Buddhist psychology, metaphysics, cosmology and the understanding of the mind is making to modern science.

Whereas, under Article 19 of the Constitution the state takes on the overall responsibility to provide education for its citizens, Article 119 recognises the principle that "[T]he organs of self-government of the national autonomous areas independently administer educational . . . affairs in their respective areas . . ." This principle is also reflected in Article 36 of the LRNA.

Since the degree of autonomy in decision-making is unclear, the point to be emphasised is that the Tibetan need to exercise genuine autonomy with regard to its own nationality's education and this is supported by the principles of the constitution on autonomy.

As for the aspiration to engage in and contribute to the development of scientific knowledge and technology, the Constitution (Article 119) and the LRNA (Article 39) clearly recognise the right of autonomous areas to develop scientific knowledge and technology.

*5) Environment Protection*

Tibet is the prime source of Asia's great rivers. It also has the earth's loftiest mountains as well as the world's most extensive and highest plateau, rich in mineral resources, ancient forests, and many deep valleys untouched by human disturbances.

This environmental protection practice was enhanced by the Tibetan people's traditional respect for all forms of life, which prohibits the harming of all sentient beings, whether human or animal. Tibet used to be an unspoiled wilderness sanctuary in a unique natural environment.

Today, Tibet's traditional environment is suffering irreparable damage. The effects of this are especially notable on the grasslands, the croplands, the forests, the water resources and the wildlife.

In view of this, according to Articles 45 and 66 of the LNRA, the Tibetan people should be given the right over the environment and them allow [*sic*] to follow their traditional conservation practices.

*6) Utilisation of Natural Resources*

With respect to the protection and management of the natural environment and the utilisation of natural resources the Constitution and the LRNA only acknowledge a limited role for the organs of self-government of the autonomous areas (see LRNA Articles 27, 28, 45, 66, and Article 118 of the Constitution, which pledges that the state "shall give due consideration to the interests of [the national autonomous areas])." The LRNA recognises the importance for the autonomous areas to protect and develop forests and grasslands (Article 27) and to "give priority to the rational exploitation and utilization of the natural resources that the local authorities are entitled to develop," but only within the limits of state plans and legal stipulations. In fact, the central role of the State in these matters is reflected in the Constitution (Article 9).

The principles of autonomy enunciated in the Constitution cannot, in our view, truly lead to Tibetans becoming masters of their own destiny if they are not sufficiently involved in decision-making on utilisation of natural resources such as mineral resources, waters, forests, mountains, grasslands, etc.

The ownership of land is the foundation on which the development of natural resources, taxes and revenues of an economy are based. Therefore, it is essential that only the nationality of the autonomous region shall have the legal authority to transfer or lease land, except land owned by the state. In the same manner, the autonomous region must have the independent authority to formulate and implement developmental plans concurrent to the state plans.

*7) Economic Development and Trade*

Economic Development in Tibet is welcome and much needed. The Tibetan people remain one of the most economically backward regions within the PRC.

The Constitution recognises the principle that the autonomous authorities have an important role to play in the economic development of their areas in view of local characteristics and needs (Article 118 of the Constitution, also reflected in LRNA Article 25). The Constitution also recognises the principle of autonomy in the administration and management of finances (Article 117, and LRNA Article 32). At the same time, the Constitution also recognises the importance of providing State funding and assistance to the autonomous areas to accelerate development (Article 122, LRNA Article 22).

Similarly, Article 31 of the LRNA recognises the competence of autonomous areas, especially those such as Tibet, adjoining foreign countries, to conduct border trade as well as trade with foreign countries. The recognition of these principles is important to the Tibetan nationality given the region's proximity to foreign countries with which the people have cultural, religious, ethnic and economic affinities.

The assistance rendered by the Central Government and the provinces has temporary benefits, but in the long run if the Tibetan people are not self-reliant and become dependent on others it has greater harm. Therefore, an important objective of autonomy is to make the Tibetan people economically self-reliant.

*8) Public health*

The Constitution enunciates the responsibility of the State to provide health and medical services (Article 21). Article 119 recognises that this is an area of responsibility of the autonomous areas. The LRNA (Article 40) also recognises the right of organs of self-government of the autonomous areas to "make independent decisions on plans for developing local medical and health services and for advancing both modern and the traditional medicine of the nationalities."

The existing health system fails to adequately cover the needs of the rural Tibetan population. According to the principles of the above-mentioned laws, the regional autonomous organs need to have the competencies and resources to cover the health need of the entire Tibetan population. They also need the competencies to promote the traditional Tibetan medical and astro system strictly according to traditional practice.

*9) Public Security*

In matters of public security it is important that the majority of security personnel consists of members of the local nationality who understand and respect local customs and traditions.

What is lacking in Tibetan areas is absence of decision-making authority in the hands of local Tibetan officials.

An important aspect of autonomy and self-government is the responsibility for the internal public order and security of the autonomous areas. The Constitution (Article 120) and LRNA (Article 24) recognise the importance of local involvement and authorise autonomous areas to organise their security within "the military system of the State and practical needs and with the approval of the State Council."

*10) Regulation on population migration*

The fundamental objective of national regional autonomy and self-government is the preservation of the identity, culture, language and so forth of the minority nationality and to ensure that it is the master of its own affairs. When applied to a particular territory in which the minority nationality lives in a concentrated community or communities, the very principle and purpose of national regional autonomy is disregarded if large scale migration and settlement of the majority Han nationality and other nationalities is encouraged and allowed. Major demographic changes that result from such migration will have the effect of assimilating rather than integrating the Tibetan nationality into the Han nationality and gradually extinguishing the distinct culture and identity of the Tibetan nationality. Also, the influx of large numbers of Han and other nationalities into Tibetan areas will fundamentally change the conditions necessary for the exercise of regional autonomy since the constitutional criteria for the exercise of autonomy, namely that the minority nationality "live in compact communities" in a particular territory is changed and undermined by the population movements and transfers. If such migrations and settlements continue uncontrolled, Tibetans will no longer live in a compact community or communities and will consequently no longer be entitled, under the Constitution, to national regional autonomy. This would effectively violate the very principles of the Constitution in its approach to the nationalities issue.

There is precedent in the PRC for restriction on the movement or residence of citizens. There is only a very limited recognition of the right of autonomous areas to work out measures to control "the transient population" in those areas. To us it would be vital that the autonomous organs of self-government have the authority to regulate the residence, settlement and employment or economic activities of persons who wish to move to Tibetan areas from other parts of the PRC in order to ensure respect for and the realisation of the objectives of the principle of autonomy.

It is not our intention to expel the non-Tibetans who have permanently settled in Tibet and have lived there and grown up there for a considerable time. Our concern is the induced massive movement of primarily Han but also some other nationalities into many areas of Tibet, upsetting existing communities, marginalising the Tibetan population there and threatening the fragile natural environment.

### *11) Cultural, educational and religious exchanges with other countries*

Besides the importance of exchanges and cooperation between the Tibetan nationality and other nationalities, provinces, and regions of the PRC in the subject matters of autonomy, such as culture, art, education, science, public health, sports, religion, environment, economy and so forth, the power of autonomous areas to conduct such exchanges with foreign countries in these areas is also recognised in the LRNA (Article 42).

## V. APPLICATION OF A SINGLE ADMINISTRATION FOR THE TIBETAN NATIONALITY IN THE PRC

In order for the Tibetan nationality to develop and flourish with its distinct identity, culture and spiritual tradition through the exercise of self-government on the above mentioned basic Tibetan needs, the entire community, comprising all the areas currently designated by the PRC as Tibetan autonomous areas, should be under one single administrative entity. The current administrative divisions, by which Tibetan communities are ruled and administered under different provinces and regions of the PRC, foments fragmentation, promotes unequal development, and weakens the ability of the Tibetan nationality to protect and promote its common cultural, spiritual and ethnic identity. Rather than respecting the integrity of the nationality, this policy promotes its fragmentation and disregards the spirit of autonomy. Whereas the other major minority nationalities such as the Uighurs and Mongols govern themselves almost entirely within their respective single autonomous regions, Tibetans remain as if they were several minority nationalities instead of one.

Bringing all the Tibetans currently living in designated Tibetan autonomous areas within a single autonomous administrative unit is entirely in accordance with the constitutional principle contained in Article 4, also reflected in the LRNA (Article 2), that "regional autonomy is practiced in areas where people of minority nationalities live in concentrated communities." The LRNA describes regional national autonomy as the "basic policy adopted by the Communist Party of China for the solution of the national question in China" and explains its meaning and intent in its Preface:

> the minority nationalities, under unified state leadership, practice regional autonomy in areas where they live in concentrated communities and set up organs of self-government for the exercise of the power of autonomy. Regional national autonomy embodies the state's full respect for and guarantee of the right of the minority nationalities to administer their internal affairs and its adherence to the principle of equality, unity and common prosperity of all nationalities.

It is clear that the Tibetan nationality within the PRC will be able to exercise its right to govern itself and administer its internal affairs effectively only once it can do so through an organ of self-government that has jurisdiction over the Tibetan nationality as a whole.

The LRNA recognises the principle that boundaries of national autonomous areas may need to be modified. The need for the application of the fundamental principles of the Constitution on regional autonomy through respect of the integrity of the Tibetan nationality is not only totally legitimate, but the administrative changes that may be required to achieve this in no way violate constitutional principles. There are several precedents where this has been actually done.

## VI. THE NATURE AND STRUCTURE OF THE AUTONOMY

The extent to which the right to self-government and self-administration can be exercised on the preceding subject matters largely determines the genuine character of Tibetan autonomy. The task at hand is therefore to look into the manner in which autonomy can be regulated and exercised for it to effectively respond to the unique situation and basic needs of the Tibetan nationality.

The exercise of genuine autonomy would include the right of Tibetans to create their own regional government and government institutions and processes that are best suited to their needs and characteristics. It would require that the People's Congress of the autonomous region have the power to legislate on all matters within the competencies of the region (that is the subject matters referred to above) and that other organs of the autonomous government have the power to execute and administer decisions autonomously. Autonomy also entails representation and meaningful participation in national decision-making in the Central Government. Processes for effective consultation and close cooperation or joint decision-making between the Central Government and the regional government on areas of common interest also need to be in place for the autonomy to be effective.

A crucial element of genuine autonomy is the guarantee the Constitution or other laws provide that powers and responsibilities allocated to the autonomous region cannot be unilaterally abrogated or changed. This means that neither the Central Government nor the autonomous region's government should be able, without the consent of the other, to change the basic features of the autonomy.

The parameters and specifics of such genuine autonomy for Tibet that respond to the unique needs and conditions of the Tibetan people and region should be set out in some detail in regulations on the exercise of autonomy, as provided for in Article 116 of the Constitution (enacted in LRNA Article 19) or, if it is found to be more appropriate, in a separate set of laws or regulations adopted for that purpose. The Constitution, including Article 31, provides the flexibility to adopt special laws to respond to unique situations such as the Tibetan one, while respecting the established social, economic and political system of the country.

The Constitution in Section VI provides for organs of self-government of national autonomous regions and acknowledges their power to legislate. Thus Article 116 (enacted in Article 19 of the LRNA) refers to their power to enact "separate regulations in light of the political, economic and cultural characteristics of the nationality or nationalities in the areas concerned." Similarly, the Constitution recognises the power of autonomous administration in a number of areas (Article 117–120) as well as the power of autonomous governments to apply flexibility in implementing the laws and policies of the Central Government and higher state organs to suit the conditions of the autonomous area concerned (Article 115).

The above-mentioned legal provisions do contain significant limitations to the decision-making authority of the autonomous organs of government. But the Constitution nevertheless recognises the principle that organs of self-government make laws and policy decisions that address local needs and that these may be different from those adopted elsewhere, including by the Central Government.

Although the needs of the Tibetans are broadly consistent with the principles on autonomy contained in the Constitution, as we have shown, their realisation is impeded because of the existence of a number of problems, which makes the implementation of those principles today difficult or ineffective.

Implementation of genuine autonomy, for example, requires clear divisions of powers and responsibilities between the Central Government and the government of the autonomous region with respect to subject matter competency. Currently there is no such clarity and the scope of legislative powers of autonomous regions is both uncertain and severely restricted. Thus, whereas the Constitution intends to recognise the special need for autonomous regions to legislate on many matters that affect them, the requirements of Article 116 for prior approval at the highest level of the Central Government—by the Standing Committee of National People's Congress (NPC)—inhibit the implementation of this principle of autonomy. In reality, it is only autonomous regional congresses that expressly require such approval, while the congresses of ordinary (not autonomous) provinces of the PRC do not need prior permission and merely report the passage of regulations to the Standing Committee of the NPC "for the record" (Article 100).

The exercise of autonomy is further subject to a considerable number of laws and regulations, according to Article 115 of the Constitution. Certain laws effectively restrict the autonomy of the autonomous region, while others are not always consistent with one another. The result is that the exact scope of the autonomy is unclear and is not fixed, since it is unilaterally changed with the enactment of laws and regulations are [sic] higher levels of the state, and even by changes in policy. There is also no adequate process for consultation or for settling differences that arise between the organs of the Central Government and of the regional government with respect to the scope and exercise of autonomy. In practice, the resulting uncertainty limits the initiative of regional authorities and impedes the exercise of genuine autonomy by Tibetans today.

We do not at this stage wish to enter into details regarding these and other impediments to the exercise of genuine autonomy today by Tibetans, but mention them by way of example so that these may be addressed in the appropriate manner in our dialogue in the future. We will continue to study the Constitution and other relevant legal provisions and, when appropriate, will be pleased to provide further analysis of these issues, as we understand them.

## VII. THE WAY FORWARD

As stated at the beginning of this memorandum, our intention is to explore how the needs of the Tibetan nationality can be met within the framework of PRC since we believe these needs are consistent with the principles of the Constitution on autonomy. As His Holiness the Dalai Lama stated on a number of occasions, we have no hidden agenda. We have no intention at all of using any agreement on genuine autonomy as stepping stone for separation from the PRC.

The objective of the Tibetan Government in Exile is to represent the interests of the Tibetan people and to speak on their behalf. Therefore, it will no longer be needed and will be dissolved once an agreement is reached between us. In fact, His Holiness has reiterated his decision not to accept any political office in Tibet at any time in the future. His Holiness the Dalai Lama, nevertheless, plans to use all his personal influence to ensure such an agreement would have the legitimacy necessary to obtain the support of the Tibetan people.

Given these strong commitments, we propose that the next step in this process be the agreement to start serious discussions on the points raised in this memorandum. For this purpose we propose that we discuss and agree on a mutually agreeable mechanism or mechanisms and a timetable to do so effectively.

## APPENDIX E

# *Note on the Memorandum on Genuine Autonomy for the Tibetan People*

(Translated from the Tibetan original)

### INTRODUCTION

This Note addresses the principal concerns and objections raised by the Chinese Central Government regarding the substance of the Memorandum on Genuine Autonomy for the Tibetan People (hereinafter "the Memorandum") which was presented to the Government of the People's Republic of China (PRC) on October 31, 2008 at the eighth round of talks in Beijing.

Having carefully studied the responses and reactions of Minister Du Qinglin and Executive Vice-Minister Zhu Weiqun conveyed during the talks, including the written Note, and in statements made by the Chinese Central Government following the talks, it seems that some issues raised in the Memorandum may have been misunderstood, while others appear to have not been understood by the Chinese Central Government.

The Chinese Central Government maintains that the Memorandum contravenes the Constitution of the PRC as well as the "three adherences."[1] The Tibetan side believes that the Tibetan people's needs, as set out in the Memorandum, can be met within the framework and spirit of the Constitution and its principles on autonomy and that these proposals do not contravene or conflict with the "three adherences." We believe that the present Note will help to clarify this.

His Holiness the Dalai Lama started internal discussions, as early as in 1974, to find ways to resolve the future status of Tibet through an autonomy arrangement instead of seeking independence. In 1979 Chinese leader Deng Xiaoping expressed willingness to discuss and resolve all issues except the independence of Tibet. Since then His Holiness the Dalai Lama has taken numerous initiatives to bring about a mutually acceptable negotiated solution to the question of Tibet. In doing so His Holiness the Dalai Lama has steadfastly followed the Middle-Way approach, which means the pursuit of a mutually acceptable and mutually beneficial solution through negotiations, in the spirit of reconciliation and compromise. The Five-Point Peace Plan and the Strasbourg Proposal were presented in this spirit. With the failure to elicit any positive response from the Chinese Central Government to these initiatives, along with the imposition of martial law in March 1989 and the deterioration of the situation in Tibet, His Holiness the Dalai Lama felt compelled to state in 1991 that his Strasbourg Proposal had become ineffectual. His Holiness the Dalai Lama nevertheless maintained his commitment to the Middle-Way approach.

The re-establishment of a dialogue process between the Chinese Central Government and representatives of His Holiness the Dalai Lama in 2002 provided the opportunity for each side to explain their positions and to gain a better understanding of the concerns, needs and interests of the other side. Moreover, taking into consideration the Chinese Central Government's real concerns, needs and interests, His Holiness the Dalai Lama has given much thought with due consideration to the reality of the situation. This reflects His Holiness the Dalai Lama's flexibility, openness and pragmatism and, above all, sincerity and determination to seek a mutually beneficial solution.

The Memorandum on Genuine Autonomy for the Tibetan People was prepared in response to the suggestion from the Chinese Central Government made at the seventh round of talks in July 2008. However, the Chinese Central Government's reactions and main criticisms of the Memorandum appear to be based not on the merits of that proposal which was officially presented to it, but on earlier proposals that were made public as well as other statements made at different times and contexts.

The Memorandum and the present Note strongly reemphasise that His Holiness the Dalai Lama is not seeking independence or separation but a solution within the framework of the Constitution and its principles on autonomy as reiterated many times in the past.

The Special General Meeting of the Tibetans in Diaspora held in November 2008 in Dharamsala reconfirmed for the time being the mandate for the continuation of the dialogue process with the PRC on the basis of the Middle-Way approach. On their part, members of the international community urged both sides to return to the talks. A number of them expressed the opinion that the Memorandum can form a good basis for discussion.

## 1. RESPECTING THE SOVEREIGNTY AND TERRITORIAL INTEGRITY OF THE PRC

His Holiness the Dalai Lama has repeatedly stated that he is not seeking separation of Tibet from the People's Republic of China, and that he is not seeking independence for Tibet. He seeks a sustainable solution within the PRC. This position is stated unambiguously in the Memorandum.

The Memorandum calls for the exercise of genuine autonomy, not for independence, "semi-independence" or "independence in disguised form." The substance of the Memorandum, which explains what is meant by genuine autonomy, makes this unambiguously clear. The form and degree of autonomy proposed in the Memorandum is consistent with the principles on autonomy in the Constitution of the PRC. Autonomous regions in different parts of the world exercise the kind of self-governance that is proposed in the Memorandum, without thereby challenging or threatening the sovereignty and unity of the state of which they are a part. This is true of autonomous regions within unitary states as well as those with federal characteristics. Observers of the situation, including unbiased political leaders and scholars in the international community, have also acknowledged that the Memorandum is a call for autonomy *within* the PRC and not for independence or separation *from* the PRC.

The Chinese government's viewpoint on the history of Tibet is different from that held by Tibetans and His Holiness the Dalai Lama is fully aware that Tibetans cannot agree to it. History is a past event and it cannot be altered. However, His Holiness the Dalai Lama's position is forward-looking, not backward grasping. He does not wish to make this difference on history to be an obstacle in seeking a mutually beneficial common future within the PRC.

The Chinese Central Government's responses to the Memorandum reveal a persistent suspicion on its part that His Holiness' proposals are tactical initiatives to advance the hidden agenda of independence. His Holiness the Dalai Lama is aware of the PRC's concerns and sensitivities with regard to the legitimacy of the present situation in Tibet. For this reason His Holiness the Dalai Lama has conveyed through his Envoys and publicly stated that he stands ready to lend his moral authority to endow an autonomy agreement, once reached, with the legitimacy it will need to gain the support of the people and to be properly implemented.

## 2. RESPECTING THE CONSTITUTION OF THE PRC

The Memorandum explicitly states that the genuine autonomy sought by His Holiness the Dalai Lama for the Tibetan people is to be accommodated within the framework of the Constitution and its principles on autonomy, not outside of it.

The fundamental principle underlying the concept of national regional autonomy is to preserve and protect a minority nationality's identity, language, custom, tradition and culture in a multi-national state based on equality and cooperation. The Constitution provides for the establishment of organs of self-government where the national minorities live in concentrated communities in order for them to exercise the power of autonomy. In conformity with this principle, the White Paper on *Regional Ethnic Autonomy in Tibet* (May 2004), states that minority nationalities are "arbiters of their own destiny and masters of their own affairs."

Within the parameters of its underlying principles, a Constitution needs to be responsive to the needs of the times and adapt to new or changed circumstances. The leaders of the PRC have demonstrated the flexibility of the Constitution of the PRC in their interpretation and implementation of it, and have also enacted modifications and amendments in response to changing circumstances. If applied to the Tibetan situation, such flexibility would, as is stated in the Memorandum, indeed permit the accommodation of the Tibetan needs within the framework of the Constitution and its principles on autonomy.

## 3. RESPECTING THE "THREE ADHERENCES"

The position of His Holiness the Dalai Lama, as presented in the Memorandum, in no way challenges or brings into question the leadership of the Chinese Communist Party in the PRC. At the same time, it is reasonable to expect that, in order to promote unity, stability and a harmonious society, the Party would change its attitude of treating Tibetan culture, religion and identity as a threat.

The Memorandum also does not challenge the socialist system of the PRC. Nothing in it suggests a demand for a change to this system or for its exclusion from Tibetan areas. As for His Holiness the Dalai Lama's views on socialism, it is well known that he has always favoured a socialist economy and ideology that promotes equality and benefits to uplift the poorer sections of society.

His Holiness the Dalai Lama's call for genuine autonomy within the PRC recognises the principles on autonomy for minority nationalities contained in the Constitution of the PRC and is in line with the declared intent of those principles. As pointed out in the Memorandum, the current implementation of the provisions on autonomy, however, effectively results in the denial of genuine autonomy to the Tibetans and fails to provide for the exercise of the right of Tibetans to govern themselves and to be "masters of their own affairs." Today, important decisions pertaining to the welfare of Tibetans are not being made by Tibetans. Implementing the proposed genuine autonomy explained in the Memorandum would ensure for the Tibetans the ability to exercise the right to true autonomy and therefore to become masters of their own affairs, in line with the Constitutional principles on autonomy.

Thus, the Memorandum for genuine autonomy does not oppose the "three adherences."

## 4. RESPECTING THE HIERARCHY AND AUTHORITY OF THE CHINESE CENTRAL GOVERNMENT

The proposals contained in the Memorandum in no way imply a denial of the authority of the National People's Congress (NPC) and other organs of the Chinese Central Government. As stated in the Memorandum, the proposal fully respects the hierarchical differences between the Central Government and its organs, including the NPC, and the autonomous government of Tibet.

Any form of genuine autonomy entails a division and allocation of powers and responsibilities, including that of making laws and regulations, between the central and the autonomous local government. Of course, the power to adopt laws and regulations is limited to the areas of competency of the autonomous region. This is true in unitary states as well as in federal systems.

This principle is also recognised in the Constitution. The spirit of the Constitutional provisions on autonomy is to give autonomous regions *broader* decision-making authority over and above that enjoyed by ordinary provinces. But today, the requirement for prior approval by the Standing Committee of the NPC for all laws and regulations of the autonomous regions (Art. 116 of the Constitution) is exercised in a way that in fact leaves the autonomous regions with much less authority to make decisions that suit local conditions than that of the ordinary (not autonomous) provinces of China.

Whenever there is a division and allocation of decision-making power between different levels of government (between the Central Government and the autonomous government), it is important to have processes in place for consultation and cooperation. This helps to improve mutual understanding and to ensure that contradictions and possible inconsistencies in policies, laws and regulations are minimised. It also reduces the chances of disputes arising regarding the exercise of the powers allocated to these different organs of government. Such processes and mechanisms do not put the Central and autonomous governments on equal footing, nor do they imply the rejection of the leadership of the Central Government.

The important feature of entrenchment of autonomy arrangements in the Constitution or in other appropriate ways also does not imply equality of status between the central and local government nor does it restrict or weaken the authority of the former. The measure is intended to provide (legal) security to both the autonomous and the central authorities that neither can unilaterally change the basic features of the autonomy they have set up, and that a process of consultation must take place at least for fundamental changes to be enacted.

## 5. CONCERNS RAISED BY THE CHINESE CENTRAL GOVERNMENT ON SPECIFIC COMPETENCIES REFERRED TO IN THE MEMORANDUM

### *a) Public security*

Concern was raised over the inclusion of public security aspects in the package of competencies allocated to the autonomous region in the Memorandum because the government apparently interpreted this to mean defence matters. National defence and public security are two different matters. His Holiness the Dalai Lama is clear on the point that the responsibility for national defence of the PRC is and should remain with the Central Government. This is not a competency to be exercised by the autonomous region. This is indeed the case in most autonomy arrangements. The Memorandum in fact refers specifically to "internal public order and security," and makes the important point that the majority of the security personnel should be Tibetans, because they understand the local customs and traditions. It also helps to curb local incidents leading to disharmony among the nationalities. The Memorandum in this respect is consistent with the principle enunciated in Article 120 of the Constitution (reflected also in Article 24 of the LRNA), which states: "The organs of self-government of the national autonomous areas may, in accordance with the military system of the state and practical local needs and with approval of the State Council, organise local public security forces for the maintenance of public order."

It should also be emphasised in this context that the Memorandum at no point proposes the withdrawal of People's Liberation Army (PLA) from Tibetan areas.

### *b) Language*

The protection, use, and development of the Tibetan language are one of the crucial issues for the exercise of genuine autonomy by Tibetans. The emphasis on the need to respect Tibetan as the main or principal language in the Tibetan areas is not controversial, since a similar position is expressed in the Chinese Central Government's White Paper on *Regional Ethnic Autonomy in Tibet*, where it is stated that regulations adopted by the Tibet regional government prescribe that "equal attention be given to Tibetan and Han-Chinese languages in the Tibetan Autonomous region, *with the Tibetan language as the major one* . . ." (emphasis added). Moreover, the very usage of "main language" in the Memorandum clearly implies the use of other languages, too.

The absence of a demand in the Memorandum that Chinese should also be used and taught should not be interpreted as an "exclusion" of this language, which is the principal and common language in the PRC as a whole. It should also be noted in this context that the leadership in exile has taken steps to encourage Tibetans in exile to learn Chinese. The Tibetan proposal which emphasises the study of the Tibetan people's own language should therefore not be interpreted as being a "separatist view."

### *c) Regulation of population migration*

The Memorandum proposes that the local government of the autonomous region should have the competency to regulate the residence, settlement and employment or economic activities of persons who wish to move to Tibetan areas from elsewhere. This is a common feature of autonomy and is certainly not without precedent in the PRC.

A number of countries have instituted systems or adopted laws to protect vulnerable regions or indigenous and minority peoples from excessive immigration from other parts of the country. The Memorandum explicitly states that it is *not* suggesting the expulsion of non-Tibetans who have lived in Tibetan areas for years. His Holiness the Dalai Lama and the Kashag also made this clear in earlier statements, as did the Envoys in their discussions with their Chinese counterparts. In an address to the European Parliament on December 4, 2008, His Holiness the Dalai Lama reiterated that "our intention is not to expel non-Tibetans. Our concern is the induced mass movement of primarily Han, but also some other nationalities, into many Tibetan areas, which in turn marginalises the native Tibetan population and threatens Tibet's fragile environment." From this it is clear that His Holiness is not at all suggesting that Tibet be inhabited by only Tibetans, with other nationalities not being able to do so. The issue concerns the appropriate division of powers regarding the regulation of transient, seasonal workers and new settlers so as to protect the vulnerable population indigenous to Tibetan areas.

In responding to the Memorandum the Chinese Central Government rejected the proposition that the autonomous authorities would regulate the entrance and economic activities of persons from other parts of the PRC in part because "in the Constitution and the Law on Regional National Autonomy there are no provisions to restrict transient population." In fact, the Law on Regional National Autonomy, in its Article 43, explicitly mandates such a regulation: "In accordance with legal stipulations, the organs of self-government of national autonomous areas shall work out measures for control of the transient population."

Thus, the Tibetan proposal contained in the Memorandum in this regard is not incompatible with the Constitution.

### *d) Religion*

The point made in the Memorandum, that Tibetans be free to practice their religion according to their own beliefs, is entirely consistent with the principles of religious freedom contained in the Constitution of the PRC. It is also consistent with the principle of separation of religion and polity adopted in many countries of the world.

Article 36 of the Constitution guarantees that no one can "compel citizens to believe in, or not to believe in any religion." We endorse this principle but observe that today the government authorities do interfere in important ways in the ability of Tibetans to practice their religion.

The spiritual relationship between master and student and the giving of religious teachings, etc. are essential components of the Dharma practice. Restricting these is a violation of religious freedom. Similarly, the interference and direct involvement by the state and its institutions in matters of recognition of reincarnated lamas, as provided in the regulation on the management of reincarnated lamas adopted by the State on July 18, 2007 is a grave violation of the freedom of religious belief enshrined in the Constitution.

The practice of religion is widespread and fundamental to the Tibetan people. Rather than seeing Buddhist practice as a threat, concerned authorities should respect it. Traditionally or historically Buddhism has always been a major unifying and positive factor between the Tibetan and Chinese peoples.

*e) Single administration*

The desire of Tibetans to be governed within one autonomous region is fully in keeping with the principles on autonomy of the Constitution. The rationale for the need to respect the integrity of the Tibetan nationality is clearly stated in the Memorandum and does not mean "Greater or Smaller Tibet." In fact, as pointed out in the Memorandum, the Law on Regional National Autonomy itself allows for this kind of modification of administrative boundaries if proper procedures are followed. Thus the proposal in no way violates the Constitution.

As the Envoys pointed out in earlier rounds of talks, many Chinese leaders, including Premier Zhou Enlai, Vice-Premier Chen Yi and Party Secretary Hu Yaobang, supported the consideration of bringing all Tibetan areas under a single administration. Some of the most senior Tibetan leaders in the PRC, including the 10th Panchen Lama, Ngapo Ngawang Jigme and Bapa Phuntsok Wangyal have also called for this and affirming that doing so would be in accordance with the PRC's Constitution and its laws. In 1956 a special committee, which included senior Communist Party member Sangye Yeshi (Tian Bao), was appointed by the Chinese Central Government to make a detailed plan for the integration of the Tibetan areas into a single autonomous region, but the work was later stopped on account of ultra-leftist elements.

The fundamental reason for the need to integrate the Tibetan areas under one administrative region is to address the deeply felt desire of Tibetans to exercise their autonomy as a people and to protect and develop their culture and spiritual values in this context. This is also the fundamental premise and purpose of the Constitutional principles on regional national autonomy as reflected in Article 4 of the Constitution. Tibetans are concerned about the integrity of the Tibetan nationality, which the proposal respects and which the continuation of the present system does not. Their common historical heritage, spiritual and cultural identity, language and even their particular affinity to the unique Tibetan plateau environment is what binds Tibetans as one nationality. Within the PRC, Tibetans are recognized as one nationality and not several nationalities. Those Tibetans presently living in Tibet autonomous prefectures and counties incorporated into other provinces also belong to the same Tibetan nationality. Tibetans, including His Holiness the Dalai Lama, are primarily concerned about the protection and development of Tibetan culture, spiritual values, national identity and the environment. Tibetans are not asking for the expansion of Tibetan autonomous areas. They are only demanding that those areas already recognised as Tibetan autonomous areas come under a single administration, as is the case in the other autonomous regions of the PRC. So long as Tibetans do not have the opportunity to govern themselves under a single administration, preservation of Tibetan culture and way of life cannot be done effectively. Today more than half of the Tibetan population is subjected to the priorities and interests first and foremost of different provincial governments in which they have no significant role.

As explained in the Memorandum, the Tibetan people can only genuinely exercise regional national autonomy if they can have their own autonomous government, people's congress and other organs of self-government with jurisdiction over the Tibetan nationality as a whole. This principle is reflected in the Constitution, which recognises the right of minority nationalities to practice regional autonomy "in areas where they live in concentrated communities" and to "set up organs of self-government for the exercise of the power of autonomy," (Article 4). If the "state's full respect for and guarantee of the right of the minority nationalities to administer their internal affairs" solemnly declared in the preamble of the Law on Regional National Autonomy is interpreted not to include the right to choose to form an autonomous region that encompasses the whole people in the contiguous areas where its members live in concentrated communities, the Constitutional principles on autonomy are themselves undermined.

Keeping Tibetans divided and subject to different laws and regulations denies the people the exercise of genuine autonomy and makes it difficult for them to maintain their distinct cultural identity. It is not impossible for the Central Government to make the necessary administrative adjustment when elsewhere in the PRC, notably in the case of Inner Mongolia, Ningxia and Guangxi Autonomous Regions, it has done just that.

### *f) Political, social and economic system*

His Holiness the Dalai Lama has repeatedly and consistently stated that no one, least of all he, has any intention to restore the old political, social and economic system that existed in Tibet prior to 1959. It would be the intention of a future autonomous Tibet to further improve the social, economic and political situation of Tibetans, not to return to the past. It is disturbing and puzzling that the Chinese government persists, despite all evidence to the contrary, to accuse His Holiness the Dalai Lama and his Administration of the intention to restore the old system.

All countries and societies in the world, including China, have had political systems in the past that would be entirely unacceptable today. The old Tibetan system is no exception. The world has evolved socially and politically and has made enormous strides in terms of the recognition of human rights and standards of living. Tibetans in exile have developed their own modern democratic system as well as education and health systems and institutions. In this way, Tibetans have become citizens of the world at par with those of other countries. It is obvious that Tibetans in the PRC have also advanced under Chinese rule and improved their social, education, health and economic situation. However, the standard of living of the Tibetan people remains the most backward in the PRC and Tibetan human rights are not being respected.

## 6. RECOGNISING THE CORE ISSUE

His Holiness the Dalai Lama and other members of the exiled leadership have no personal demands to make. His Holiness the Dalai Lama's concern is with the rights and welfare of the Tibetan people. Therefore, the fundamental issue that needs to be resolved is the faithful implementation of genuine autonomy that will enable the Tibetan people to govern themselves in accordance with their own genius and needs.

His Holiness the Dalai Lama speaks on behalf of the Tibetan people, with whom he has a deep and historical relationship and one based on full trust. In fact, on no issue are Tibetans as completely in agreement as on their demand for the return of His Holiness the Dalai Lama to Tibet. It cannot be disputed that His Holiness the Dalai Lama legitimately represents the Tibetan people, and he is certainly viewed as their true representative and spokesperson by them. It is indeed only by means of dialogue with His Holiness the Dalai Lama that the Tibetan issue can be resolved. The recognition of this reality is important.

This emphasises the point, often made by His Holiness the Dalai Lama that his engagement for the cause of Tibet is not for the purpose of claiming certain personal rights or political position for him, nor attempting to stake claims for the Tibetan administration in exile. Once an agreement is reached, the Tibetan Government-in-Exile will be dissolved and the Tibetans working in Tibet should carry on the main responsibility of administering Tibet. His Holiness the Dalai Lama made it clear on numerous occasions that he will not hold any political position in Tibet.

## 7. HIS HOLINESS THE DALAI LAMA'S CO-OPERATION

His Holiness the Dalai Lama has offered, and remains prepared, to formally issue a statement that would serve to allay the Chinese Central Government's doubts and concerns as to his position and intentions on matters that have been identified above.

The formulation of the statement should be done after ample consultations between representatives of His Holiness the Dalai Lama and the Chinese Central Government, respectively, to ensure that such a statement would satisfy the fundamental needs of the Chinese Central Government as well as those of the Tibetan people.

It is important that both parties address any concern directly with their counterparts, and not use those issues as ways to block the dialogue process as has occurred in the past.

His Holiness the Dalai Lama is taking this initiative in the belief that it is possible to find common ground with the People's Republic of China consistent with the principles on autonomy contained in PRC's Constitution and with the interests of the Tibetan people. In that spirit, it is the expectation and hope of His Holiness the Dalai Lama that the representatives of the PRC will use the opportunity presented by the Memorandum and this Note to deepen discussion and make substantive progress in order to develop mutual understanding.

# *Notes*

## HOMAGE

1. Atisha was an eleventh-century Indian Buddhist scholar and saint whose arrival in Tibet initiated the period of the "second transmission" of Buddhism to Tibet, formative for the Sakya, Kagyu, and Gelug schools.

## PART I. LAND OF MY ANCESTORS

1. Mike and Greg were each of great help to me during their professional careers under several US administrations. Mike was the Senior Director for Asian Affairs for President George W. Bush at the White House, while Greg served in several senior-level positions at the State Department and at the White House during the Clinton presidency. He was the very first Special Coordinator for Tibet, appointed by Secretary of State Madeleine Albright. They have both become very close personal friends, and I have immensely benefited from their guidance and friendship.
2. Dr. Pemba, an English-trained surgeon at the Planters Hospital, Darjeeling, was highly respected and deeply admired by the Tibetan people because he was the first Tibetan to become a surgeon and doctor in Western medicine.

## 1. HISTORY OF NYARONG, KHAM, MY BIRTHPLACE

1. The time periods of the Tibetan emperors are taken from Thupten Phuntsok, *Bod kyi lo rgyus spyi don padma ra g'i lde mig* (*General Theme of the Tibetan History Padma ragai de mig*) (Beijing: Tibet Nationality Publishing House, 2006).
2. *Gyalpos* include such influential figures as Derge Gyalpo, Lingtsang Gyalpo, and Nangchen Gyalpo. The rulers of principalities in the Gyalrong area were also referred to as *gyalpo*. While the term *gyalpo* would seem to designate a more powerful individual than a chieftain or *ponpo*, the reverse is actually more accurate. Chieftains were generally more influential, exerting control over larger areas in terms of both territory and population.
3. Yudru Tsomu, *The Rise of Gönpo Namgyel in Kham: The Blind Warrior of Nyarong* (Lanham, Md.: Lexington Books, 2014), 223.

4. Tsewang Yishey Pemba, *White Crane, Lend Me Your Wings: A Tibetan Tale of Love and War* (New Delhi: Niyogi Books, 2017), 63.
5. Adding *tsang* to a surname means "house of." Thus, *Gyaritsang* means "House of Gyari."
6. *Gothak—go* means "head" and *thak* is "to bind or attach." *Gothak* thus literally means "submitting to the head" or "coming under the protection of."
7. Pemba, *White Crane*, 83.
8. Pemba, *White Crane*, 176.
9. The honorific title of "Rinpoche" is bestowed on both reincarnated lamas and learned Buddhist scholars. *Khenchen* means "Great Abbot." *Kyabjé*, meaning "Lord of Refuge," is a mark of respect reserved for the most senior lamas whose realization and powers are extraordinary. See https://www.rigpawiki.org/index.php?title=Kyabjé.
10. Pemba, *White Crane*, 255.
11. Kyabjé Jigmé Phuntsok Rinpoche was instrumental in helping revive Buddhism in Tibet after the Cultural Revolution. In his later years he gathered more than 10,000 students around him at Larung Gar in Sertar in eastern Tibet. https://www.rigpawiki.org/index.php?title=Khenpo_Jikme_Phuntsok.
12. A few years later, my son was recognized by His Holiness Minling Trichen Rinpoche as an incarnated lama and given the name Gyurmé Kunzang Namgyal. He was subsequently enthroned at Mindrolling Monastery in Dehradun by His Holiness Minling Trichen Rinpoche as the reincarnation of Minling Trichen Rinpoche's uncle, Minling Penam Rinpoche.

## 2. THE GYARI FAMILY

1. Yudru Tsomu, "Constructing Images of Gönpo Namgyel: A Hero or a Villain?" *Revue d'Etudes Tibetaines* 26 (April 2013): 61. See also Yudru Tsomu, *The Rise of Gönpo Namgyel in Kham, The Blind Warrior of Nyarong* (Lanham, Md.: Lexington Books, 2014).
2. Meaning the Central Government based in Lhasa that at varying times exerted control not only over U-Tsang, but also Kham and Amdo.
3. Feathers of different colors with jewels, such as turquoise and jade, at the tips of Manchu hats denoted different ranks within Manchu society.
4. The Gaden Throne is the highest position in the Gelug tradition, one of the four main branches of Tibetan Buddhism that also includes the Nyingma, Sakya, and Kagyu schools. The Gelug hierarchy is similar in some respects to the Vatican system. Succession to this position is not hereditary but based on merit and scholarship. Most of the holders of the Gaden Throne came from humble backgrounds and from very remote areas of Tibet. What Gönpo Namgyal is implying is that, just as for the holders of the Gaden Throne, if one is capable, one can aspire to reach the highest position.
5. Sherab Özer Rinpoche, *Nyag rkyed bu long ma'i lo rgyus mdo tsam brjod pa* (*Brief History of Nyakyedtsang's Blind Son*), 50. The last line of this quote refers to Liu Ma who brought the gifts and communication from the Manchus.
6. W.D. Shakabpa, *Tibet, A Political History* (New York: Potala Publications, 1984), 187. A Kalon is a minister in the Tibetan cabinet, the Kashag.
7. See, e.g., Tsomu, "Constructing Images," 86.

8. Aten Doyaltshang, *A Historical Oration from Kham: The Ancient Recitation of Nyagrong* (*Nyag rong gtam rgan ma*) (Dharamsala: Amnye Machen Institute, 1993), 82.
9. Eric Teichmann, *Travels of a Consular Officer in Eastern Tibet: together with a History of the Relations Between China, Tibet and India* (Cambridge: At the University Press, 1922), 33.
10. Nyarong is also considered to be one of the four great valleys of Tibet along with Powo-rong, Tsawa-rong, and Gyalmo-rong. It is further mentioned in some treasure texts as one of the important hidden valleys including Dremojong (Sikkim) and Pema-kod.
11. Sherab Özer Rinpoche, *Brief History of Nyakyedtsang's Blind Son.*
12. See Thupten Phuntsok, *Bod kyi lo rgyus spyi don padma ra g'i lde mig*, (*General TTtheme of the Tibetan History Padma ragai de mig*) (Beijing: Tibet Nationality Publishing House, 2006).
13. Phuntsok, *General Theme of the Tibetan History, Padma ragai de mig*, 464.
14. I interchange "Gyaritsang" and "Gyari family" in referring to my family. Most Khampas add the word *tsang*, meaning "household," after their family names. My family simplified the nomenclature, preferring to use Gyari standing alone.
15. Shakabpa, *Tibet*, 187.
16. "Pledge my loyalty to Gaden Phodrang" means pledging loyalty to the Lhasa government, while prostrating to the Dalai Lama means giving allegiance to him.
17. The title of Drung-ney was conferred on the Gyari family and three other important chieftains. *Drung* is an abbreviated form of *Drung-khor*, which is the fifth ranking official of the Central Tibetan Government. *Ney* translates to "rank," in this case meaning "equivalent." Unlike a true Drung-khor, people who were given the equivalent rank were not allowed to wear their hair in a knot.
18. Gyari Samdrub and his older brother, Gyari Sonam Norbu, had a common wife at home in Nyarong. Because he was posted in Derge for a long period of time, Gyari Samdrub also married a local woman and had several children. Polygamy was a common custom in those times. It was a way of maintaining both economic and political strength as well as family influence. Gyari Samdrub's children maintained very close ties with their paternal family in Nyarong.
19. As discussed in part II, this is no longer the case. After the democratization of the system by His Holiness the 14th Dalai Lama in 1991, members of the Kashag are now elected rather than appointed.
20. Phuntsok Gelek Rabten was the sixty-fourth direct descendent of Denma of Ling, who was the foremost general among the heroes of Ling.
21. In those days one of the US aid organizations, most probably USAID, provided some food packages for Tibetan refugees including canned pork, oil, powdered milk, and corn flour.
22. A *sangha* is a community of Buddhist practitioners including both monastic and lay individuals.
23. In Kham, "a family without sons was like one without yaks or guns or horses, an edifice with no core." Tsewang Yishey Pemba, *White Crane, Lend Me Your Wings: A Tibetan Tale of Love and War* (New Delhi: Niyogi Books, 2017), 190.
24. A daughter in a family with no sons was often "brought up as a mixture of tomboy and nun: strict, chaste and, once she had entered her teens, always with a chaperone. . . . She

was thus religious and knew all her prayers; but she could saddle a horse, ride and shoot as well as any . . . [boy]." Pemba, *White Crane,* 190.

25. The Taksen-Drukchu, which literally means the "Sixty Tigerlike Retainers," were people of proven loyalty and bravery.
26. It is called the "speaking Tara" because it is said to have actually spoken and to sometimes turn its head in different directions. It is also known to have shown various emotions through changing facial expressions, including the shedding of tears.
27. Melvyn C. Goldstein, Dawei Sherap, and William R. Siebenschuh, *A Tibetan Revolutionary: —The Political Life and Times of Bapa Phüntso Wangye* (Berkeley: University of California Press, 2004), 251–52.
28. A *labrang* is the monastic household or residence of the lama. Here it refers to the private Bureau of Panchen Rinpoche.
29. After the Communist takeover, he continued to be involved with Tibetan affairs, and even Marshal He Long consulted him. However, he was later classified and purged as a "Rightist" during the Cultural Revolution.
30. Communicated in a conversation between the author and Bapa Phuntsok Wangyal.
31. Maura Moynihan, private correspondence with the author (February 2, 1995).
32. Moynihan, private correspondence.
33. Moynihan, private correspondence.

### 3. MY SPIRITUAL LINEAGE

1. The term *tertön* refers to enlightened Buddhist masters who reveal hidden teachings concealed by Guru Rinpoche. This term is used widely in the Nyingma tradition, where it refers to an individual who, in a previous life, was a student of the master Padmasambhava. A *tertön* is one who was later reincarnated to spread the teachings he had once received, but that had been hidden until the appropriate time for their dissemination to occur. https://rywiki.tsadra.org/index.php/Terton.
2. Minling is the abbreviated form of Mindrolling. I use these terms interchangeably.
3. Attaining the "rainbow body" is the process by which an accomplished practitioner's body gradually becomes smaller and smaller, ultimately dissolving into the elements while emanating rainbow light. Sometimes the whole body dissolves, leaving only the hair and nails.
4. Dudjom Rinpoche, *The Nyingma School of Tibetan Buddhism: Its Fundamentals and History* (Somerville, Mass.: Wisdom, 1991), 919.
5. Matteo Pistono, *In the Shadow of the Buddha: One Man's Journey of Discovery in Tibet* (New York: Dutton, 2011).
6. In earlier days there were many Tibetan oracles, but only a few remain today, the main one being the Nechung Oracle. Through him manifests Dorje Drak-Den/Nechung, the principal protector divinity of the Tibetan Government in Exile and the Dalai Lama. See The Nechung Foundation, http://nechungfoundation.org/oracle.html.
7. The Mindrolling and the Sakya throne holders are hereditary, but the monastic community members of these traditions are celibate.
8. *Tri* means "throne." *Tsab* means "acting" or "regent." Pema Wangchen ascended to the throne of Mindrolling but, as he was not a male descendant of the family, he was not

considered a throne holder but a regent. His son, Gyurmé Döndrub Wangyal, became the Tenth Mindrolling throne holder with the full title of *Trichen*.

9. Many people, including Kyabjé Dudjom Rinpoche (1904–1987), also called him Jurme Phendei Özer.
10. A "heart disciple" is the main or principal student of a Buddhist master.
11. Yamantaka is the wrathful expression of Manjushri, a Bodhisattva associated with wisdom. Bodhisattvas are deities who have postponed their own enlightenment to help others achieve liberation. They are traditionally depicted in a variety of both peaceful and wrathful forms.
12. *Wangpo* is not a name, but a title given to those who manage the administrative work of a monastery. This practice is more common in Kham than in other areas of Tibet. *Wangpo* literally means the "mighty one, ruler or lord." Lumorab had three to four people with the title. They held the second-most important positions and responsibilities after the Rinpoches.
13. Sera Monastery is one of the three famous Gelug monastic universities in Lhasa. With over five thousand monks, it was the second largest monastery after Drepung, which had over seven thousand monks in its heyday.
14. As is the case for many other monasteries, their destruction in Tibet by the Chinese and the subsequent flight of many Tibetans into exile resulted in the reestablishment of these institutions in India, where many Tibetans took up residence.
15. In Vajrayana Buddhism *tsok* has a central role. This important practice of offering and purification is practiced on the tenth and twenty-fifth day of each Tibetan month of the lunar calendar. Through the practice of *tsok*, one accumulates immense relative and absolute merit and in the process purifies oneself. Relative merit is related to worldly merit and absolute merit helps toward enlightenment.
16. My great grandfather was an avid practitioner of Vajra Yogini, a semiwrathful meditation/tutelary deity. She is red in color with one face and two arms, wearing ornaments of human bones. She represents the transformation of ignorance and passion into emptiness and compassion. Just before he passed away, Gyari Dorjé Namgyal asked his attendants to help him stand up. Using the wall as a back support, he adopted one of Vajra Yogini's traditional postures by standing on his left leg. He then passed away in this position. For the final last rites, his body was brought all the way to Lumorab, which was a two-day horse ride. More than fifty days after his passing, his body still showed no signs of decomposition or rigor mortis. His body remained supple and childlike. I remember elders telling me that these were the signs of his accomplishing the highest state of the Vajra Yogini practice.
17. Dartsedo is the administrative headquarters for the Kardze Tibetan Autonomous Prefecture. An important Sino-Tibetan trade route for centuries, it is also called Kangding and Dajianlu.

### 4. THE GYARITSANG'S INVOLVEMENT IN THE TIBETAN RESISTANCE

1. During the final editing of this book, my mothers allowed me to read this section to them. I have added their comments as a postscript to this chapter.

2. Gyari Samdrub's grandson Dzonor Kunzang spent long periods of time in Nyarong helping my parents rebuild the Gyari manor.
3. Jamyang Norbu, *Horseman in the Snow: The Story of Aten, an Old Khampa Warrior* (Dharamsala: Information Office, Central Tibetan Secretariat, 1979), 70–72.
4. Tashi Namgyal, the younger brother of Dromo Wangchen, made it into exile as the senior attendant of Jamyang Khyentse Chökyi Lodrö, one of the greatest Buddhist masters of our time. Both my father and Tashi Namgyal felt bound by the oath that my father had previously taken with Tashi's elder brother, Dromo Wangchen.
5. For more details on the schism among Khampa families once they were in exile, see chapter 9.
6. Shiwa Monastery is the ancestral monastery of the Gyari family, and the resident monks have always been loyal to the Gyari clan. Gyase Monastery is another monastery that has been historically close and loyal to the Gyari family.
7. Sometimes people get a little confused between the Group of Eighteen and the Bhutsa Chogyed, a group of eighteen families that had the responsibility to provide domestic services to our family. While most of these families took care of our needs at the Gyari manor, four or five of them looked after the family's livestock that was pastured in nomadic areas. These eighteen families were exempt from taxation and other responsibilities.
8. This elderly warrior was able to make it into exile, and I was able to arrange a personal audience for him and his family with His Holiness the 14th Dalai Lama in 1974 at Bodhgaya. He presented to His Holiness a very precious family heirloom, a unique statue that even His Holiness could not identify. His eldest son, Drapa Anor, was among the few important Nyarongwa leaders who survived imprisonment. When I went to Nyarong in 2004, he was among the few relatives I was able to meet.
9. Aten refers to the originally scheduled date of the revolt. I assume he forgot that my mother preempted the Chinese attack by two days.
10. Jamyang Norbu, *Warriors of Tibet: The Story of Aten and the Khampas' Fight for the Freedom of Their Country* (London: Wisdom Publications London, 1986), 106–7.
11. My mothers tell me that this young officer's name was Yi Mang Tra. He shared with them his memory of his father, who was also a devout Buddhist and landed gentry. While sharing this, he at one time broke down and pleaded with my parents not to disclose the details of their conversation, as it would create serious problems for him.
12. At a much later age, when I came into exile, I discovered that the Chinese way of pronouncing Buddha Amitabha was "Omitobho," and that's exactly how I remember the young officer pronouncing it.
13. Edgar Snow, *Red Star Over China* (New York: Pelican Press, 1973), 235.
14. Norbu, *Warriors*, 110.

### 5. OUR FLIGHT FROM NYARONG

1. I believe that when Gyato Wangdu briefed the CIA that there were over 50,000 Tibetan resistance fighters in the region, desperately in need of arms and ammunition, the CIA dismissed his report as a gross exaggeration. Whatever the reason, no help came, and

Gyato Wangdu himself soon headed back to Central Tibet. More information on the role of Gyato Wangdu can be found in chapter 10.

2. See discussion in chapter 10.
3. Yachen Gar is also known as Yachen Orgyen Samten Chöling, a Buddhist community founded by Akhyuk Rinpoche in 1980. More than 10,000 monks and nuns reside there, second in size only to the famous Larung Gar Buddhist Academy.
4. See discussion in chapter 12.

## 6. THE JOURNEY TO LHASA

1. The Tibetan divination system called *mo* has been relied upon for centuries to give insight into future turns of events, undertakings, and relationships. https://www.shambhala.com/mo-2303.html.
2. My mothers cannot recall the name of this person, but he was from the Dhargye area and known to the Tasotsang, a family related to us.
3. While Tulku Angak was my mothers' actual uncle, Minling Penam was their cousin. Due to the large age difference between them, however, they referred to him as their uncle. Similarly, because of the substantial age difference between my mothers and Jetsün Kunzang Chödrön, they called her their great aunt when she was, in fact, their aunt. Finally, because of their close ages, my mothers referred to Minling Shabdrung as their cousin even though he was their nephew.
4. In Buddhist and Hindu mythology, a garuda is a creature combining the features of humans and birds, having a wingspan of many miles, and often depicted holding a snake in its beak and arms. It represents the various elements of the Buddhist path.
5. Gyalo Thondup and Anne F. Thurston, *The Noodle Maker of Kalimpong: The Untold Story of My Struggle for Tibet* (New York: Public Affairs, 2015), 66–67, 86.
6. As previously mentioned, the Kagyu school, founded by Marpa the Great Translator (1012–1097), is one of the four major sects of Tibetan Buddhism.
7. A *stupa* is a structure in the shape of a semi-hemispherical dome housing Buddhist relics. It represents the enlightened mind of the Buddha. The Tibetan *chorten* and the pagodas of some Asian countries are examples of stupas.
8. Khenpo Aten was considered a great yogi in the tradition of the Yamantaka practice, the initiation for which he received from the great Mipham Rinpoche.
9. Dharmapala are protectors of the Dharma, who vow to protect and guard the teachings of the Buddha and its followers. They appear as either virtuous samsaric beings or emanations of Buddhas or Bodhisattvas. https://www.dhammawiki.com/index.php/Dharmapala.
10. Andruk Gonpo Tashi was a successful and prominent businessman from Lithang. He became the leading figure establishing the Chushi Gangdrug resistance movement. He was a very close collaborator of Gyalo Thondup. This resistance movement was also supported by the US CIA. *Chushi* means "Four Rivers" and *Gangdrug* means "Six Ranges," referring to the areas where the resistance forces came from. This group also had prominent leaders from the Amdo region but after coming into exile, the Amdo people gradually withdrew. Today, Chushi Gangdrug is an exclusively Khampa organization that functions as an NGO. See also chapter 9.

11. Trehor is a region in Kham. Each monastery is made up of several "*Khamstens*," or hostels, each of which houses monks coming from the same region, who thus share the same local customs and dialect.
12. See discussion in chapter 19.

### 7. FROM MINDROLLING TO EXILE IN INDIA

1. *Dungse* means "noble son." This is a title given to sons of important religious families such as the Sakyas and the Mindrollings. The Eleventh Mindrolling throne holder, Trichen Gyurmé Kunzang Wangyal, was at the time not yet enthroned, hence the title.
2. *Khen* is the short form for *khenpo*, meaning "abbot." The title "Rinpoche," meaning "Precious One," is automatically attached to a khenpo who is a realized practitioner as well as to the seniormost khenpo in a monastery.
3. See the Homage for further discussion of the texts I studied.
4. In those days it was common to see pilgrims coming from Kham carrying a *khur-shing*.
5. Ngari Panchen Pema Wangyal, *Perfect Conduct: Ascertaining the Three Vows* (Boston: Wisdom, 1996).
6. The Ri-me movement is an ecumenical, nonsectarian group started in the nineteenth century in Kham by Jamyang Khyentse Wangpo, Jamgön Kongtrul, and their disciples.
7. The full text of this prayer is included in the introductory materials following the Homage.
8. My sister Yulzin Dolma, and later my brother Kunzang Tsewang, both had their names altered at the time of their admission to Tibetan schools. Even for Tibetans their names may have sounded rather unusual. The school authorities arbitrarily decided to call my sister Rinzing and my brother Kalsang.
9. Some people refer to him as "Yonru king," no doubt showing respect and also acknowledging the importance of the Yonru clan, but the Yonru family is always called *pon*, meaning "chieftain," not "king." In fact, chieftains such as Yonru are far more powerful and wealthy than some kings. And in Kham, a *pon* is not considered less than a king.
10. See chapter 9.
11. It is a sad thing that even with the tremendous hardships faced by Tibetans in escaping from Tibet and adjusting to life in exile, many Tibetans persist in wasting their precious time addicted to this and other habit-forming games.
12. Padmasambhava was invited to Tibet by Trisong Detsen, the thirty-eighth Tibetan emperor. He brought the Vajrayana form of Buddhism to the country and is affectionately known as the "Second Buddha" to his followers. His appearance was prophesied by the Buddha himself. He altered the entire landscape of Tibet and her people in reintroducing and firmly establishing Buddhism. His kindness for Tibet can thus never be repaid.
13. A *gar-thue* is a group representative.
14. *Tulku* is the Tibetan word for a reincarnate.
15. The Joint Center was set up by the Indian Intelligence, the CIA, and the Tibetans to supervise or coordinate their joint activities.
16. Tibet's landmass is huge. The vast western and northern plateaus are dry with some grasslands, their beauty being equated by some with that of the lunar surface. By contrast,

the eastern and northeastern parts of Tibet have deep gorges and support much more vegetation, including thick forests. When people describe Ladakh to me as reminding them of Tibet, it doesn't sound right because Nyarong, my ancestral home, is more similar to Bhutan. Yet, Tibetans from Lhasa and western Tibet find Ladakh very much like Tibet.

17. In Buddhism, the Three Jewels refers to the Buddha, the Dharma (the scriptures), and the Sangha (the community of practitioners).
18. I remember sometime in 1955 or early 1956, Uncle Tsultrim and I dug holes underneath the horse stable of Lumorab Labrang, the residence of the monastery's Rinpoches, to hide several items including the Nationalist government flag as well as medals and badges conferred on the Gyari family by the KMT.
19. See chapter 8.
20. Direct translation from the taped message given to the author and his younger mother, Gyari Dorjé Yudrön, at the Ashoka Hotel in New Delhi.
21. *Kundun* is one of the several respectful names for the Dalai Lama in the Tibetan language.
22. See discussion in chapter 3.

## PART II. TIBET RESTORED

1. Contemporary popular song translated by High Peaks Pure Earth. https://highpeakspureearth.com/2013/music-video-from-tibet-letsgo-together-by-dekyi-tso/.
2. See appendix A for the full text of the Great Oath of Unity and its signatories.

## 8. A UNIFIED TIBET

1. The author's personal files.
2. *Chakravartin* is the Sanskrit word for a universal monarch who rules ethically and benevolently.
3. Namkhai Norbu, *The Necklace of gZi: A Cultural History of Tibet* (Dharamsala: Narthang Publications, 1989).
4. In 1642, the Fifth Dalai Lama was conferred the title of Supreme Head of Tibet at Shigatse. Later that year, he made a proclamation declaring that Lhasa would be the capital of Tibet and that the government would be known as Nam-koi Gaden Phodrang Chok-le Namgyal, named after the Labrang of the Dalai Lamas. The government would exercise political as well as religious control over the whole of Tibet from Lhasa. Desi Phagmo Drupa's residence at Drepung Monastery called Do-khang Ngon-po (Blue-Stone House) was offered to the 2nd Dalai Lama in 1518 by Ne-dong Miwang Tashi Drakpa and became the Gaden Phodrang Labrang or palace of the subsequent Dalai Lamas until the Great Fifth moved to the Potala Palace after its renovation and expansion that began in 1645.
5. See chapter 9 for more details about the SFF and my near appointment to it in the role of Political Officer.
6. See chapter 10 for further details regarding the Mustang guerilla base.
7. See appendix A.

8. In Tibet when a person dies, his body is kept in a corner of the house with a white cotton curtain to cover it from view, but a butter lamp is lit on the floor to make it visible.
9. Today, the Hotel Mahayana occupies this historic site.
10. To avoid confusion, I use the term "Parliament" in the text when I am referring to either the Tibetan Parliament-in-Exile, as the body was renamed in 2006, or its prior designations, the Commission of Tibetan People's Deputies and the Assembly of Tibetan People's Deputies.
11. Prior to the adoption of the 1991 Charter, the CTA functioned roughly along the lines of the Constitution for the Future Tibet that had been promulgated by His Holiness on March 10, 1963. See chapter 14 for more discussion of the dissolution of the Kashag and election of the interim Kashag members.
12. Samdhong Rinpoche is popularly known as Professor Samdhong Rinpoche.
13. See discussion of the Seventeen-Point Agreement in chapter 12.
14. Chiang Kai-shek, "Documents: The Question of Tibet," *Taiwan Review*, December 1, 1959, https://taiwantoday.tw/news.php?unit=12,29,33,45&post=23544.
15. The prominent role of Gyalo Thondup in the Tibetan freedom struggle is discussed in chapter 9.
16. See discussion in chapter 1.

## 9. TIBETAN EXILE ORGANIZATIONS

1. Tsepon W. D. Shakabpa was, in fact, one of the key individuals of the anti-Reting faction. In his memoirs, Gyalo Thondup, who is much more knowledgeable about that era than I, makes serious allegations about Shakabpa's role in the demise of Reting Rinpoche. See Gyalo Thondup and Anne F. Thurston, *The Noodle Maker of Kalimpong: The Untold Story of My Struggle for Tibet* (New York: Public Affairs, 2015), chapter 9, 86.
2. *Dzasa* is a Mongolian title previously used to address high-ranking Tibetan officials.
3. *Jindak* translates as "master" and was the title used by many Tibetans to address Andruk Gonpo Tashi.
4. *Jhatsak* is the Tibetan word for "tea strainer."
5. Jagoe Namgyal Dorjee was the most prominent leader in exile from the Derge region and the nephew of Jagoe Topden, referred to earlier in the book. Sadu LoNyendak was from a well-known and influential business family in the Trehor region. Drawu Pon Rinchen Tsering is from one of the most influential chieftain families under the nominal rule of the King of Nangchen. His family's domain is in Kyegudo in present-day Yushu Tibetan Autonomous Prefecture, Qinghai Province. Jagoe Namgyal Dorjee and Drawu Pon Rinchen Tsering were two of the most prominent Khampa leaders in the Group of Thirteen.
6. David Lague, Paul Mooney, and Benjamin Kang Lim, "China Co-opts a Buddhist Sect in Global Effort to Smear Dalai Lama," *Reuters*, December 21, 2015, https://www.reuters.com/investigates/special-report/china-dalailama.
7. Khenpo Tsewang Dongyal, *Light of Fearless Indestructible Wisdom: The Life and Legacy of H.H. Dudjom Rinpoche*, (Ithaca, N.Y.: Snow Lion, 2008), 129.

8. Dongyal, *Light*, 129–30.
9. The Sakya Trizin, the Sakya Throne Holder, is the traditional title of the head of the Sakya school of Tibetan Buddhism. Until recently, it was a lifetime title. On December 11, 2014, however, a resolution was passed during the 23rd Great Annual Sakya Monlam announcing a new succession system under which the role of Sakya Trizin is limited to a single three-year term based on seniority and qualifications. At the time of this writing, Ratna Vajra Rinpoche is the 42nd Sakya Trizin. He was enthroned in 2017 and is the elder son of His Holiness the 41st Sakya Trizin, Ngawang Kunga.
10. The author's personal files.
11. I had this audience with Bokar Rinpoche, heart disciple of Kalu Rinpoche, because he knew of the previous (16th) Karmapa's close relationship with my family.
12. This shrine, which still exists, is a tribute to Dzongnang Rinpoche and his legacy. I only wish the Sikkimese royal family could have provided a better location for it and more support. Many of my Sikkimese friends feel that if the shrine had been built in a more prominent place and enjoyed strong royal patronage, it would have benefited both Sikkim and the royal family.
13. The SFF was very involved in the liberation of Bangladesh. Major General S. S. Uban, the founding Inspector General, includes a vivid description of the critical role the SFF played and the sacrifices its forces made in his book *The Phantoms of Chittagong: The Fifth Army in Bangladesh* (New Delhi: Allied Publishers, 1985).
14. King Gesar of Ling is a historical personage highly revered by the Tibetan people as an inspired warrior-king. The epic tale of his life and exploits is in the tradition of the King Arthur legends and Homer's *Iliad.*
15. Lodi Gyari, "Status and Position of the Tibetan Youth Congress When It Was Initially Established, and Some Issues Pertaining to the Just Cause of Tibetan Struggle," 2014, http://tibet.net/2014/10/kasur-lodi-gyari-on-genesis-of-tyc-and-tibetan-struggle/.
16. See discussion in chapter 10.
17. See discussion in chapter 11.
18. Virendra Kumar, *Chin Up, Chest Out* (India, 1976). The work is a self-published lawyer's analysis of the socioeconomic and political situation in India during the pre- and post-Emergency days.
19. CTA Department of Information and Publicity, *Tibetan Bulletin* (March/April 1977): 35.
20. *Tibetan Review* (April 1977): 8.
21. George Fernandes, interview by Claude Arpi, 2006, http://www.sify.com/news/we-will-neither-forget-nor-forgive-for-a-100-years-news-national-kcuuJrjhajcsi.html.
22. *Lhacham Kusho* is a highly honorific term used to refer to the wife of a Kalon or spouse of one of the Dalai Lama's siblings. It could also be translated as "Princess" or "Divine Consort."
23. *Chogyal* means "Dharma King" or "Righteous Ruler," the title conferred upon Sikkim's Buddhist kings of the Namgyal monarchy. Founded by the fifth-generation descendants of Guru Tashi, a prince of the Minyak House who came to Sikkim from Kham in eastern Tibet, this monarchy ruled the kingdom of Sikkim from 1642 to 1975, when the monarchy was abolished and the Sikkimese voted by referendum to make Sikkim India's twenty-second state.

## 10. REPERCUSSIONS FROM DIVISIONS WITHIN THE TIBETAN COMMUNITY IN EXILE

1. The author's personal files.
2. Dudjom Rinpoche, *Counsels from My Heart*, trans. Padmakara Translation Group (Boston: Shambhala, 2003), 45.
3. Dudjom Rinpoche, *Counsels from My Heart*, 44.
4. See discussion in chapter 7.
5. Another son of Gyatotsang, Gyato Dhondup, became a casualty of the Bangladesh Liberation War. He was a very popular young political leader at the SFF. This family thus sacrificed two of its sons to the Tibetan cause.
6. Lodi Gyari, "My Personal Words of Gratitude," December 31, 1974, https://www.savetibet.org/my-personal-words-of-gratitude/.
7. Gyalo Thondup and Anne F. Thurston, *The Noodle Maker of Kalimpong: The Untold Story of My Struggle for Tibet* (New York: Public Affairs, 2015), chapter 19.
8. Ringo Tulku Rinpoche may possibly have a copy of this letter, because he played a very important role in the reconciliation process.
9. See chapter 16.
10. Not surprisingly, her revealing answer to the final question was not translated by the interpreter, as this was a program sanctioned by Beijing, yet it is included in the archives.

## 11. TIBETANS INSIDE TIBET

1. I discuss these events in detail in chapter 12.
2. The author's personal files.
3. Central Tibet Administration, Research and Analysis of Department of Security, *Ngapo Ngawang Jigme kyi Ched Pel Tam-tsok* (Collected speeches) (Dharamsala, 1999).
4. A live recording of the song is available at https://www.youtube.com/watch?v=oaBtni3UFkM.
5. According to the Tibetan method of calculating age, a person is considered to be one year old at birth. Using the Western method, he would have been fifteen at the time.
6. "Kasur Lodi Gyari on Genesis of TYC and Tibetan Struggle," October 6, 2014, https://tibet.net/kasur-lodi-gyari-on-genesis-of-tyc-and-tibetan-struggle/.
7. Appeal by His Holiness the Dalai Lama of Tibet to the United Nations (1950), UN Document A11549-11, Kalimpong, November 1950, http://www.tibetjustice.org/materials/un/un2.html.
8. See discussion in chapter 20.

## PART III: THIRTY YEARS OF ENGAGEMENT WITH THE PRC

## 12. THE EARLY YEARS

1. I refer to the government established in Dharamsala alternatively as the Central Tibetan Administration (CTA) or as the Tibetan Government-in-Exile (TGiE), the latter reflecting its roots in Lhasa prior to 1959.

2. The trip never took place, as Beijing refused to accept the teachers' travel documents issued by the Indian government. This failure did not cause a major setback in Dharamsala-Beijing relations, however. Toward the end of that year, the first Fact-Finding Delegation appointed by His Holiness was able to leave for Tibet.
3. The focus of my narrative in this part is contemporary Dharamsala-Beijing relations. I begin with Deng Xiaoping's initiative reaching out to His Holiness in 1979 through Gyalo Thondup. As Gyalo Thondup explicitly chronicles his activities in his memoir, I don't go into too much detail about his efforts, only focusing on those areas in which I disagree with his depiction.
4. See discussion in chapter 8.
5. Gyalo Thondup and Anne F. Thurston, *The Noodle Maker of Kalimpong: The Untold Story of My Struggle for Tibet* (New York: Public Affairs, 2015), chapters 28–29.
6. See chapter 8.
7. The Tsuglagkhang complex houses the Phodrang (the Dalai Lama's residence), the Tibet Museum, the Institute of Buddhist Dialectics, the Tsuglagkhang Temple, and Namgyal Monastery in Dharamsala.
8. Central Tibet Administration, Research and Analysis of Department of Security, *Ngapo Ngawang Jigme kyi Ched Pel Tam-tsok (Collected Speeches)* (Dharamsala, 1999).
9. The United Front maintains a firm grip on Tibet-related matters even though at some points other senior leaders, as well as some Chinese specialists on Tibet, tried to broaden the involvement of other stakeholders.
10. Hu Yaobang's "Speech to the Meeting of Cadres in the TAR, 29th May 1980" (extracts), https://tibet.net/important-issues/sino-tibetan-dialogue/an-overview-of-sino-tibetan-dialogue/sino-tibetan-dialogue-hopes-and-suspicions-1978-1987/; John Garnaut, "Decades After Call for Reform, Tibet Remains in Crisis," *Sydney Morning Herald*, September 4, 2010.
11. Melvyn Goldstein, Dawei Sherap, and William R. Siebenschuh, *A Tibetan Revolutionary: The Political Life and Times of Bapa Phüntso Wangye* (University of California Press, 2004), 286–87. Whenever I refer to this work, I call it Phuntsok Wangyal's book because it is about his political life and times, as the authors state.
12. Goldstein, Sherap, and Siebenschuh, *A Tibetan Revolutionary*, 288.
13. Wang Yao, "Hu Yaobang's Visit to Tibet, May 22–31, 1980, An Important Development in the Chinese Government's Tibet Policy," http://www.archieve.claudearpi.net/maintenance/uploaded_pics/1980HuavisittoTibet.pdf.
14. Hu Yaobang's "Speech to the Meeting of Cadres in the TAR, 29th May 1980" (extracts), https://tibet.net/important-issues/sino-tibetan-dialogue/an-overview-of-sino-tibetan-dialogue/sino-tibetan-dialogue-hopes-and-suspicions-1978-1987/.
15. Goldstein, Sherap, and Siebenschuh, *A Tibetan Revolutionary*, 288.
16. See discussion in chapter 11.
17. Quoted in Goldstein, Sherap, and Siebenschuh, *A Tibetan Revolutionary*, 71.
18. The book is available in both English and Tibetan. When I was at the ICT, we funded the first publication of the Tibetan translation and distributed it free of charge to Tibetan educational institutions.
19. DIIR publication entitled "From the Heart of the Panchen Lama (Major Speeches and a petition: 1962–1989)," https://tibet.net/1998/04/.

20. See discussion in Thondup and Thurston, *The Noodle Maker of Kalimpong*, chapter 11.
21. See discussion in chapter 11.
22. Central Tibet Administration, Research and Analysis of Department of Security, *Ngapo Ngawang Jigme kyi Ched Pel Tam-tsok* (*Collected Speeches*) (Dharamsala, 1999).
23. *Indian Parliament on the issue of Tibet—Lok Sabah debates 1952–2005* (New Delhi, Tibetan Parliamentary and Policy Research Centre, 2006), 102; http://www.archieve.claudearpi.net/maintenance/uploaded_pics/lok_sabha_debates_on_tibet-2006.pdf.
24. CTA DIIR, *Tibet Under Communist China: 50 Years* (Dharamsala, 2001), 11.
25. Derong Tsering Dhondup, born in Derong, Kardze, in 1954, was a historian and the author of petitions to the PRC leadership that heavily criticized the central government's policies concerning Tibetan areas. These petitions were later translated into Tibetan and incorporated in a book, along with the original Chinese text, entitled *Wode xinyuan* (Tibetan: *bDag Gi Re sMon*) (Ganzi Newspaper Office Printing Press, 1995), which served as an internal reference document for the CTA. In 1997, the Tibet Information Network translated the book into English under the title *My Aspirations*.
26. Goldstein, Sherap, and Siebenschuh, *A Tibetan Revolutionary*, 303.
27. 1) In May 1977, Ngapo Ngawang Jigme announced that His Holiness could return to Tibet "as long as he stands on the side of the people."

    2) On March 13, 1979, Deng Xiaoping told Gyalo Thondup, "the Dalai Lama and Tibetans in exile can either return permanently to Tibet or come for a visit. The Dalai Lama should not worry about the arrangement upon his return. He can live in Beijing and visit Tibet occasionally. Living in China would be more convenient for him."

    3) During the visit of the First Fact-Finding Delegation, Li Xiannian reiterated what Deng had previously said to Gyalo Thondup.

    4) On May 1, 1979, Ulanhu told Gyalo Thondup that the Dalai Lama and the Tibetans in exile were welcome to return to their homeland and contribute toward the development of the nation, with "suitable" arrangements being made for everyone upon their return.

    5) On June 11, 1980, the Chinese Ambassador in New Delhi appealed for the early return of His Holiness during a meeting with Takla Phuntsok Tashi. He further said: "If the Dalai Lama does not prefer to stay long there, he can return. The central government will respect his decision."

    6) On July 21, 1981, Ulanhu suggested to Gyalo Thondup that "it would be better for His Holiness and his followers to return at the earliest."

    Excerpts of meeting minutes from the author's personal files.

## 13. TIBET'S RISE TO PROMINENCE ON THE INTERNATIONAL STAGE

1. The full text can be found online at https://www.dalailama.com/messages/tibet/five-point-peace-plan.
2. See His Holiness the Fourteenth Dalai Lama, "The Global Community and the Need for Universal Responsibility," in *Imagine All the People: The Dalai Lama on Money, Politics and Life as It Could Be* (Boston: Wisdom, 1999).
3. CTA, DIIR, "Memorandum from Yan Mingfu, Head of the United Front Work Department of the CCP Central Committee to the Exiled Tibetan Administration,"

October 17, 1987, translated from the Chinese and included in *DHARAMSALA AND BEIJING Initiatives and Correspondences 1981–1993*, March 1996, https://tibet.net/wp-content/uploads/2014/10/Dharamsla-and-Beijing.pdf.

4. The full text can be found online at https://www.dalailama.com/messages/tibet/strasbourg-proposal-1988.
5. ICT, "Where is China Heading on Tibet? Remarks by Lodi Gyaltsen Gyari to the Council on Foreign Relations Washington, DC," April 23, 2012, https://www.savetibet.org/where-is-china-heading-on-tibet/.
6. See discussion in chapter 16.
7. See appendix B and chapter 20.
8. These include Kanlho (Ch: Gannan) Tibetan Autonomous Prefecture (Gansu), Tsojang (Ch: Haibei) Tibetan Autonomous Prefecture (Qinghai), Tsolho (Ch: Hainan) Tibetan Autonomous Prefecture (Qinghai), Malho (Ch: Huangnan) Tibetan Autonomous Prefecture (Qinghai), Golog Tibetan Autonomous Prefecture (Qinghai), Yulshul (Ch: Yushu) Tibetan Autonomous Prefecture (Qinghai), Tsonub (Ch: Haixi) Tibetan Autonomous Prefecture (Qinghai), Ngawa Tibetan Autonomous Prefecture (Sichuan), Kardze Tibetan Autonomous Prefecture (Sichuan), Dechen (Ch: Deqen) Tibetan Autonomous Prefecture (Yunnan), Pari (Ch: Tainzhu) Tibetan Autonomous County (Gansu), and Mili (Ch: Muli) Tibetan Autonomous County (Sichuan).
9. My colleague Rinchen Dharlo may have been the first Tibetan official to meet with the Carters. They had visited Nepal with Richard Blum when Rinchen Dharlo was the Representative of His Holiness the Dalai Lama in Nepal.
10. Richard C. Blum and Thomas C. Hayes, *An Accident of Geography* (Austin, Texas: Greenleaf Book Group Press, 2016), 215.
11. CTA, *Sino-Tibetan Dialogue: A Chronological Account since 1978*, subsection "A row over the internationalization of Tibet issue (1987–1990)," https://tibet.net/important-issues/sino-tibetan-dialogue/an-overview-of-sino-tibetan-dialogue/sino-tibetan-dialogue-a-row-over-the-internationalisation-of-the-tibet-issue-1987-1990/.
12. Gyalo Thondup and Anne F. Thurston, *The Noodle Maker of Kalimpong: The Untold Story of My Struggle for Tibet* (New York: Public Affairs, 2015), chapter 30.
13. Tethong Tenzin Geyche, His Holiness's other Secretary, was already participating in his capacity as a Kalon.
14. See Thondup and Thurston, *The Noodle Maker of Kalimpong*, chapter 31.
15. See discussion in chapter 21.

### 14. DEVELOPING UNITED STATES SUPPORT FOR TIBET

1. The author's personal files.
2. See discussion in chapter 21.
3. Editor's note: Congresswoman Pelosi resumed her role as Speaker of the House after the November 2018 US elections.
4. Their son Michael is about the same age as my two youngest children. My daughter Tenzing Tsering has many fond memories of the Senator, how lovingly he cared for her and her brother, Penam Rinpoche, when they were at his home.
5. See appendix C.

6. During this time period, there was only one Deputy Secretary of State, occupying the second position, with multiple Under Secretaries next in the hierarchy. Now there is more than one Deputy Secretary.
7. After explaining the symbolism of Losar to the Tibetan people, I commented on how I saw the reception as the US government implementing its policy "to assist in preserving the distinct religious, cultural, and linguistic heritage of the Tibetan people." ICT, "US Government Celebrates for the First Time Losar, the Tibetan New Year, in Recognition of Tibetan Culture and Identity," February 23, 2015, https://savetibet.org/us-government-celebrates-for-the-first-time-losar-the-tibetan-new-year-in-recognition-of-tibetan-culture-and-identity/.
8. He visited a nomadic area once by himself and later, in June 1993, he traveled to the Phala area, where Melvyn Goldstein was doing field studies. Phala is directly north of Sangsang, located on the east-west road to Mount Kailash. It is in the area of two lakes joined together and known as *tsho punnyi*. "My most recent trip to Tibet was by all measures the most extraordinary. I took my two sons and accompanied Professor Goldstein and Professor Bealle to the area in the Changtang where they have conducted their research among the Nomads. We spent five days in a tent above 16,000 feet with the Nomads, and, as you can imagine, it was one of the most extraordinary experiences of our lives." Richard Holbrooke, letter to Lodi Gyari, Special Envoy of the Dalai Lama, August 3, 1993.
9. Many even referred to him as the Kissinger of the next generation.
10. See discussion in chapter 18.
11. I wrote to Ambassador Paul Bremer to inform him that I was planning to write this book and that I might reference this meeting. He did not object.
12. See full transcripts of speeches at ICT, "Congressional Gold Medal Ceremony: transcripts of speeches," October 31, 2007, https://savetibet.org/congressional-gold-medal-ceremony-transcripts-of-speeches/.
13. Sichan Siv was the principal staff member at the White House with whom I worked to arrange this meeting. He was also the note taker when the President and His Holiness met. As a Cambodian Buddhist, he has deep reverence for His Holiness, and he was personally very helpful to me. I kept in touch with him when President Bush appointed him US Ambassador to the UN Economic and Social Council, a position in which he served from 2001 to 2006.
14. A video of the joint press conference can be viewed online at https://www.youtube.com/watch?v=2LpzElEiNoM (courtesy William J. Clinton Presidential Library).
15. See chapter 18.
16. This was also the case with Ambassador Jeff Bader when he was at the White House in the Clinton administration. Not once but several times he encouraged and also helped me to meet with James Steinberg, then Deputy National Security Advisor.
17. Richard Blum and Thomas C. Hayes, *An Accident of Geography* (Austin, Texas: Greenleaf Book Group Press, 2016), 227.
18. See Jeff A. Bader, *Obama and China's Rise: An Insider's Account of America's Asia Strategy* (Washington, D.C.: Brookings Institution Press, 2013), 73.
19. Daniel Russel was one of Evan Medeiros's senior colleagues at the White House. He subsequently went to the State Department as Assistant Secretary of State for East Asian and Pacific Affairs.

20. The author's personal files.
21. Kori Schulman, "The President's Meeting with His Holiness the XIV Dalai Lama," July 17, 2011, https://obamawhitehouse.archives.gov/blog/2011/07/17/president-s-meeting-his-holiness-xiv-dalai-lama.
22. Bader, *Obama*, 75.

## 15. INDIA, OUR HOME AWAY FROM HOME

1. Lodi Gyari, "My Personal Words of Gratitude." December 31, 2014, https://www.savetibet.org/my-personal-words-of-gratitude/.
2. *Indian Parliament on the issue of Tibet—Lok Sabha Debates 1952 to 2005*, translated from Hindi (New Delhi: Tibetan Parliamentary and Policy Research Centre, 2006), 267, http://www.archieve. claudearpi.net/maintenance/uploaded_pics/lok_sabha_debates_on_tibet-2006.pdf.
3. Much later, for political reasons, the Tibet issue was moved to the East Asia Division.
4. I think I was close to nineteen years old, because sometime around that period I was featured as an "Editor under 19" in the *Junior Statesman* magazine, which had a column in every edition profiling a person of that age in various professions.
5. See discussion in chapter 14.
6. One contemporary example is the impact of climate change on the Tibetan Plateau that is causing negative downstream effects on the Indian subcontinent. While Beijing participates in multilateral discussions addressing environmental concerns on the Mekong River, to date it has not held any international meetings addressing the situation on the Tibetan Plateau because of the potentially attendant political considerations. For India's welfare, as well as that of the global community, meaningful discussion of the effects of climate change and measures that can be taken to alleviate them must be undertaken.
7. Gyalo Thondup and Anne F. Thurston, *The Noodle Maker of Kalimpong: The Untold Story of My Struggle for Tibet* (New York: Public Affairs, 2015), 91.
8. Thondup and Thurston, *The Noodle Maker of Kalimpong*, 93.
9. B. N. Mullik, *My Years with Nehru: The Chinese Betrayal* (Bombay: Allied Publishers, 1971).
10. R. K. Sinha, "Why Is the Dalai Lama Silent?," *Statesman*, July 24, 2017, https://www.thestatesman.com/opinion/why-is-the-dalai-lama-silent-1500930385.html.

## 16. ASSISTANCE FROM OTHER ASIAN NATIONS, EUROPE, NONGOVERNMENTAL ORGANIZATIONS, AND DHARMA CENTERS

1. *Ajahn*, meaning "teacher," is the respectful form of address used by many Thais for beloved spiritual masters.
2. George Yeo, "Tibet in the 21st Century," in *Bonsai, Banyan and the Tao* (Singapore: World Scientific Publishing, 2015).
3. Yeo, *Bonsai, Banyan and the Tao*, 557.
4. See discussion in chapter 14.
5. This relationship reflects the high regard Senator Kerry and many other prominent politicians have for His Holiness and their concern over the plight of the Tibetan people.

6. Jacques Chirac, *My Life in Politics*, trans. Catherine Spencer (New York: St. Martin's Press, 2012), 224–30.
7. Hugh Richardson was the last British diplomat posted in Tibet. He stayed on to represent India after the transfer of power from Britain to India.
8. I am referring to U.S. Representative Tom Lantos and his wife, Annette, and Senator Dianne Feinstein and her husband, Richard Blum.
9. In addition to his substantive contributions, Christian Schwarz-Schilling funded these discussions largely through his own foundation. He was recognized for his efforts on our behalf in receiving the ICT's Light of Truth award in 2013.
10. See discussion in chapter 11.
11. See discussion in chapter 8.
12. UK Parliament, Written Ministerial Statements, FOREIGN AND COMMONWEALTH OFFICE: Tibet, Wednesday, October 29, 2008, https://hansard.parliament.uk/lords/2008-10-29/debates/08102936000006/Tibet.
13. Lodi Gyari, "Tibet, China, and the Twenty-First Century: The Role of the Dalai Lama," remarks delivered at the Third Annual Lord Ennals Memorial Lecture hosted by the Tibet Society of the United Kingdom (London, October 1, 1998). The author's private files.
14. I would love to acknowledge my friend's name, but knowing his nature, I will refrain from doing so. He has been of major help in many other regards, including reaching out to important Chinese leaders and senior administration officials in Washington, D.C.
15. The author's personal files.
16. His Holiness the 14th Dalai Lama, "Nobel Peace Prize Acceptance Speech," December 10, 1989, https://www.dalailama.com/messages/acceptance-speeches/nobel-peace-prize/nobel-peace-prize.
17. His Holiness the 14th Dalai Lama, "The 14th Dalai Lama's Nobel Lecture," December 11, 1989, https://www.dalailama.com/messages/acceptance-speeches/nobel-peace-prize/nobel-peace-prize-nobel-lecture.
18. See discussion of the Task Force in chapter 19.
19. See discussion in chapter 13.

## 17. THE 1990S

1. In his autobiography, His Holiness discusses his consultations with the State Oracle and how he considers its advice in addition to that of the Kashag in making decisions, while expressly acknowledging, "This may sound far-fetched to twentieth-century western readers. Even some Tibetans, mostly those who consider themselves 'progressive,' have misgivings about my continued use of this ancient method of intelligence gathering. But I do so for the simple reason that as I look back over the many occasions when I have asked questions of the oracle, on each one of them time has proved that his answer was correct." *Freedom in Exile: The Autobiography of the Dalai Lama* (London: Hodder and Stoughton, 1990), 233–34.
2. See discussion in chapter 13.
3. Michael Currier was the first individual to contribute one million U.S. dollars to the CTA. It was an enormous gift in those days. Michael and I were very close friends.

Seeing that I had six children to support and was hoping to send to US colleges, he offered to fund a Tibetan restaurant in Washington, D.C., for my wife, Dawa, to run, even hiring a real estate agent to look for an appropriate site. In the end we did not feel that we should take advantage of Michael's generous offer, as Dawa had her hands full caring for me and the children, and if the business didn't succeed, we would have felt terrible. Tragically, Michael died in 1998 at the young age of thirty-seven. He was a truly generous and thoughtful friend, and I miss him to this day.

4. Lodi G. Gyari, letter to President Carter, January 6, 1999, the author's personal files.
5. The Clinton White House was appreciative of former President Carter's efforts, believing they would complement its own work. I always kept senior officials at the White House informed about my meetings with President Carter and his team. While the two didn't see eye to eye on some issues, their disagreements did not take away from the cooperation between them.
6. The author's personal files.
7. See discussion later in this chapter, "First Successful Reconnection: December 1997 Meeting in Hong Kong" and "April 1998 Meeting in Chiang Mai."
8. Diaoyutai is a historic state guesthouse located in Beijing.
9. R. C. Blum and Thomas C. Hayes, *An Accident of Geography* (Austin, Texas: Greenleaf Book Group Press, 2016), chapter 11, "Small Successes Matter."
10. Tibet Information Network and Human Rights Watch/Asia, *Cutting off the Serpent's Head: Tightening Control in Tibet, 1994–1995* (March 26, 1976), vi, quoting Ragdi, Deputy Executive Secretary of the Communist Party of the Tibetan Autonomous Region, on September 5, 1994, at the Seventh Plenum of the Sixth Standing Committee Session of the TAR Communist Party, https://www.hrw.org/reports/pdfs/t/tibet/bktibet.pdf.
11. Jacques Chirac, *My Life in Politics*, trans. Catherine Spencer (New York: St. Martins' Press, 2012), 227.
12. Wu Gongtan's English name is K. S. Wu.
13. See discussion in chapter 12. This claim of having "presided" over the ceremony is false. Likewise, the event that he attended was the enthronement ceremony, not a "reincarnation" as quoted in President Chirac's book.
14. See discussion in chapter 13.
15. See discussion in chapter 11.
16. The author's personal files.
17. See discussion in chapter 14.
18. The author's personal files.
19. Beginning in 1988, the U.S. Congress passed more than fifty resolutions relating to Tibet. See, e.g., 1988 resolution (S. Con. Res. 129) expressing the support of Congress for the Dalai Lama and his proposal; 1989 resolution (S. Res. 82) expressing the concern of the Senate about the ongoing human rights abuses in Tibet; 1990 resolution (S.J. Res. 275) designating May 13, 1990, as the "National Day in Support of Freedom and Human Rights in China and Tibet"; 1991 resolution (S. Con. Res. 41) expressing the sense of Congress that "Tibet" refers to all Tibetan-inhabited areas; 1992 resolution (S. Res. 271) that the US government should raise human rights abuses in Tibet with senior officials of the PRC; 1993 resolution (H. Con. Res. 106) urging the President to raise, at the highest

levels of the government of the PRC, the issue of Chinese population transfer into Tibet; 1995 resolution (S. Res. 169) expressing the sense of the Senate welcoming His Holiness the Dalai Lama on his visit to the United States.

20. We had become aware of Deng Xiaoping's change of attitude through several other sources. When Yan Mingfu was Minister of the United Front, he had expressed experiencing similar difficulties.

21. I have intentionally decided not to address the Panchen Lama controversy in this book, as others with more thorough knowledge, including Isabel Hilton (*The Search for the Panchen Lama* [New York: Norton, 1999]) and Arjia Rinpoche (*Surviving the Dragon: A Tibetan Lama's Account of 40 Years under Chinese Rule* [New York: Rodale, 2010]), have written extensively about it.

22. See discussion in chapter 14.

### 18. FITS AND STARTS

1. Li Ruihuan ran the United Front in his capacity as Chair of the CPPCC. While the United Front Minister reported to him, the United Front Minister is also a Vice Chair of the CPPCC.
2. Andrew J. Nathan and Bruce Gilley, *China's New Rulers: The Secret Files* (New York: New York Review Books, 2003), 218.
3. Nathan and Gilley, *China's New Rulers*, 81.
4. President Jiang's Speech at the Symposium Commemorating the 78th Anniversary of the Founding of the Communist Party of China (June 28, 1999), https://www.cpim.org/marxist/199904_marxist_china_jiang.htm.
5. Nathan and Gilley, *China's New Rulers*, 166.
6. Nathan and Gilley, *China's New Rulers*, 191.
7. The author's personal files.
8. See discussion in chapter 16.
9. See discussion in chapter 16, "Support in Southeast Asia."
10. Hu Xiaojiang went on to become a professor at Beijing Normal University's School of Social Development and Public Policy.
11. At that time Bhuchung Tsering was traveling on an Identity Certificate, a travel document in lieu of a passport issued by the Indian government for which a Canadian visa is required.
12. Ngawang Choephel is a documentary filmmaker, director, and producer born in Tibet in 1966 but whose family fled the region in 1968. He returned to Tibet in 1995 to record Tibetan folk songs for a documentary film. He was arrested by the Chinese authorities under a charge of espionage and counter-revolutionary activities, for which the Chinese produced no evidence but sentenced him to eighteen years in prison without a trial. He was released in 2002 on "medical parole" after six years' imprisonment.
13. See, e.g., "Dalai Lama Backs Olympics Bid if Boosts Rights," CNN.com, May 11, 2001, https://edition.cnn.com/2001/WORLD/asiapcf/east/05/10/tibet.olympics/.
14. See discussion chapter 14.
15. See discussion of the Task Force Secretariat in chapter 19.

16. Chinese Ministry of Foreign Affairs spokesperson Kong Quan, September 10, 2002, https://2001-2009.state.gov/p/eap/rls/rpt/45015.htm.
17. Chinese Ministry of Foreign Affairs Spokesperson Kong Quan, June 12, 2003, https://2001-2009.state.gov/p/eap/rls/rpt/45015.htm.
18. Xinhua, "Beijing Holds Talks with Dalai's Representatives," reprinted in *China Daily* (online), July 3, 2008, and State Council Information Office News Briefing, November 10, 2008.

## 19. FORMAL DIALOGUE BEGINS

1. The Task Force on Sino-Tibetan Negotiations was created in 1998 to act as an internal think tank, helping recommend policies and strategies designed to find a peaceful and mutually acceptable solution to the Tibet issue.
2. When Samdhong Rinpoche became Kalon Tripa, to institutionalize the dialogue process, he organized a permanent Task Force Secretariat under his direct supervision within the Kashag Secretariat.
3. As of this writing, Pema Trinley is one of the Vice Chairs of the National People's Congress Standing Committee, and as such is the highest-ranking Tibetan in the Chinese leadership, while Nyima Tsering is a Vice Chair of the TAR People's Congress.
4. ICT, "Where Is China Heading on Tibet?," remarks by Lodi Gyaltsen Gyari to the Council on Foreign Relations, Washington, DC, April 23, 2012, https://savetibet.org/where-is-china-heading-on-tibet/.
5. Jowo Rinpoche, also known as the Jowo Shakyamuni, is the central Buddha figure in the Jokhang Temple in Lhasa. It is the most revered image of the Buddha, believed to have been carved during Buddha Shakyamuni's life (sixth–fifth centuries BCE).
6. In the Tibetan Buddhist tradition, the Dalai Lama is considered to be the incarnation of Avalokiteshvara, the Bodhisattva of Compassion, who is further regarded as Tibet's "patron saint."
7. These masters include: Nagarjuna, Aryadeva, Buddhapalita, Bhavaviveka, Chandrakirti, Shantideva, Shantarakshita, Kamalashila, Asanga, Vasubandhu, Dignaga, Dharmakirti, Arya Vimuktisena, Haribhadra, Gunaprabha, Shakyaprabha, and Atisha.
8. See speech by H.E. Xi Jinping President of the People's Republic of China at UNESCO Headquarters, March 28, 2014, https://www.fmprc.gov.cn/mfa_eng/wjdt_665385/zyjh_665391/t1142560.shtml.
9. See discussion in chapter 12.
10. On September 18, 1997, based on a preliminary opinion survey reflecting the Tibetan people's profound trust in His Holiness, the Tibetan Parliament adopted a unanimous resolution stating that His Holiness should decide on the issue of Tibet, from time to time, in accordance with the changing political situation in the PRC and in the world. It was further resolved that whatever decisions His Holiness took would be regarded by all the Tibetan people as no different from a decision made through the referendum process.

    On March 20, 2010, the Parliament unanimously passed a resolution reaffirming its faith in His Holiness the 14th Dalai Lama in using his wisdom to resolve the issue of Tibet in accordance with the September 1997 resolution. It further stated that the

Parliament was fully convinced that the Memorandum on Genuine Autonomy for the Tibetan People and the Note on Memorandum were in accordance with the wishes of His Holiness and that these documents needed no discussion by the Parliament, as they implemented the dictates of the prior resolution.

11. *Middle Way Policy and All Recent Related Documents* "The Middle-Way Policy was Adopted through a Democratic Process," 5, https//tibet.net/wp-content/uploads/2012/06/MID WAY-ENGLISH.pdf.
12. For example, on July 6, 2005, just a few days after the Fourth Round of talks began, the European Union Presidency issued the following statement: "The European Union welcomes the fourth round of talks between the envoys of the Dalai Lama and members of the Chinese Government that took place at the Embassy of the People's Republic of China in Bern, Switzerland, on June 30 and July 1, 2005. The EU strongly supports the continuation of dialogue which it hopes will bring about serious negotiations leading to a peaceful and sustainable solution for Tibet that both sides agree upon. The Acceding Countries Bulgaria and Romania, the Candidate Countries Turkey and Croatia, the Countries of the Stabilization and Association Process and potential candidates Albania, Bosnia and Herzegovina, the former Yugoslav Republic of Macedonia, Serbia and Montenegro, EFTA countries Iceland, Liechtenstein and Norway, members of the European Economic Area, as well as Ukraine and the Republic of Moldova align themselves with this declaration." https://ec.europa.eu/commission/presscorner/detail/en/PESC_05_68.
13. See Section 611, Foreign Relations Authorization Act, 2003, Tibetan Policy Act of 2002, discussed in detail in chapter 14. https//www.savetibet.org/policy-center/us-government -and-legislativeadvocacy/state-department-annual-reports-on-tibet/.
14. The full report can be accessed at https://2001-2009.state.gov/p/eap/rls/rpt/2007/88157 .htm.
15. See examples of press releases in appendix C. Full texts of all the related press releases can be found at https://tibet.net/important-issues/sino-tibetan-dialogue/.

## 20. NINE ROUNDS OF DIALOGUE

1. See appendix D.
2. See appendix E.
3. Excerpt from His Holiness's speech accepting the U.S. Congressional Gold Medal on October 17, 2007, https://www.dalailama.com/messages/acceptance-speeches/u-s -congressional-gold-medal/congressional-gold-medal.
4. Lodi Gyaltsen Gyari, Special Envoy of H.H. the Dalai Lama, remarks prepared for delivery at the Brookings Institution, "Seeking Unity Through Equality:The Current Status of Discussions Between His Holiness the Dalai Lama and the Government of the People's Republic of China," Washington, D.C., November 14, 2006, https://www.brookings .edu/wp-content/uploads/2012/04/20061114-1.pdf.
5. "China says it's open to talks with Dalai Lama," *Indian Express*, April 1, 2008, http://archive .indianexpress.com/news/china-say-it-s-open-to-talks-with-dalai-lama/290656/.
6. In his Congressional Gold Medal Acceptance Speech, His Holiness expressly stated: "The Chinese authorities assert that I harbor hostility towards China and that I actively seek

to undermine China's welfare. This is totally untrue. I have always encouraged world leaders to engage with China; I have supported China's entry into WTO and the awarding of summer Olympics to Beijing. I chose to do so with the hope that China would become a more open, tolerant and responsible country." https://www.dalailama.com/messages/acceptance-speeches/u-s-congressional-gold-medal/congressional-gold-medal.

7. "The Kashag's statement on His Holiness' 73rd Birthday," *Tibetan Bulletin* 12, no. 4 (July-August 2008), https://tibet.net/wp-content/uploads/2014/02/july-aug-08.pdf.

8. See, e.g., (a) On March 1, 1979, Ulanhu, Chairman of the United Front Work Department and Minister for the Nationality Affairs Commission, met Gyalo Thondup and said: "The Dalai Lama and the Tibetans in exile are welcome to return to their home and contribute towards the development and progress of the nation. Suitable arrangements can be made for everyone upon their return. The Dalai Lama has not made contacts with the Soviet Union. Therefore, 'apart from independence, we can solve any problem.'" The author's personal files.

(b) On May 19, 1991, Premier Li Peng in an interview with Xinhua News Agency said, "All matters except 'Tibetan independence' can be discussed."

(c) On September 23, 1991, the newsletter released by the Embassy of the People's Republic of China, Washington, D.C., regarding the "Questions concerning negotiations between the Central Government of China and the Dalai Lama," reiterated what Premier Li said in the interview with Xinhua News Agency and emphasized, "Except for the independence for Tibet, all other issues may be negotiated."

(d) Premier Li stated to the visiting Indian President R. Venkataraman to China in May (18–23) 1992, "We . . . are willing to talk to him about anything except the issue of the so-called independence of Tibet." Ramaswamy Venkataraman, *My Presidential Years* (New Delhi: HarperCollins, 1994), 529.

(e) Premier Li's interview with Xinhua News Agency again emphasized: "All matters except 'Tibetan independence' can be discussed." White Paper 1992: "Tibet—Its Ownership and Human Rights Situation," Beijing, Information Office of the State Council of the PRC, September 1992. http://ie.china-embassy.org/eng/zt/ChinasTibet/t1145462.htm.

(f) *100 Questions About Tibet* (Beijing: Beijing Review Press, 1989):

"Q 38: How does the Chinese Government view the Dalai Lama's 'New Proposal' on Tibet he put forward in Strasbourg, France?"

A: The Dalai Lama said that he was ready to send his representatives to hold discussions. He or his representatives are welcome: "The channel is always open for dialogue," in China or at any Chinese embassy abroad, or at any other place. "But no foreigners can be allowed to attend. Any issue is open for discussion except the question of 'Tibetan independence.'"

9. "This is the question that Mr. Lodi Gyari repeatedly raised to me. Actually, Mr. Deng Xiaoping never said this, and this is a distortion of Mr. Deng Xiaoping's remark." Zhu Weiqun, State Press Conference, State Council Information Office, November 10, 2008, in DIIR publication, "A Compilation of the Memorandum on Genuine Autonomy for the Tibetan People, His Holiness the Dalai Lama's Brussels Statement of 4 December 2008, and the Chinese State Council's Press Briefing of 10 November 2008,"

December 2008, https://tibet.net/wp-content/uploads/2014/10/memorandum-on-Gen-autonmy..1.pdf, 35.

10. See Phurbu Thinley, "Gyalo Thondup reconfirms Deng Xiaoping's offer on Tibet talks," November 19, 2008, https://www.phayul.com/2008/11/19/23254/. Juchen Thubten Namgyal was the head of the First Fact-finding Delegation and a member of the 1982 and 1984 Exploratory Talks teams.
11. Some discussion of this meeting is offered in Melvyn Goldstein, Dawei Sherap, and William R. Siebenschuh, *A Tibetan Revolutionary: The Political Life and Times of Bapa Phuntso Wangye* (Berkeley: University of California Press, 2004), chapter 18.
12. His Holiness the Dalai Lama, "Statement of His Holiness the Dalai Lama on the Forty-Seventh Anniversary of the Tibetan National Uprising Day," https://www.dalailama.com/messages/tibet/10th-march-archive/2006.
13. Preamble of the Law on National Regional Autonomy. https://www.china.org.cn/english/government/207138.htm.
14. "Kalon Tripa Samdhong Rinpoche's Keynote Address on Round Table Discussion on 'Greater Tibet,'" New Delhi, August 27, 2009, in DIIR publication, *Middle Way Policy and All Recent Related Documents*, October 2012, 81, https://tibet.net/wp-content/uploads/2012/06/MIDWAY-ENGLISH.pdf.
15. Congressional Executive Commission on China, *Special Topic Paper: Tibet 2008–2009*, October 22, 2009, https://www.cecc.gov/sites/chinacommission.house.gov/files/CECC%20Special%20Topic%20Paper%20-%20Tibet%202008%20-%202009%20-%2010.22.09.pdf.
16. *White Paper on Tibetan Culture,* Information Office of the State Council of the People's Republic of China, June 22, 2000, http://www.chinamission.be/eng/zywj/bps/200403/t20040309_8301617.htm, "China Issues White Paper on Tibetan Culture (Jun 22 2000)," March 9, 2004, http://www.chinamission.be/eng/zywj/bps/t72378.htm.
17. "Administrative Division of Tibetan Areas," website of the Ministry of Foreign Affairs of the People's Republic of China, www.fmprc.gov.cn.
18. Ngapo Ngawang Jigme, conversation with Zhou Enlai, May 1951. This was confirmed by senior PRC leader Ulanhu to Tibetan official Takla Phuntsok Tashi during their meeting in Beijing on May 29, 1982.
19. Goldstein, Sherap, and Siebenschuh, *A Tibetan Revolutionary*, 206. Chen Yi was leading the central government's delegation to launch the Preparatory Committee for the establishment of the Tibet Autonomous Region.
20. https://www.brookings.edu/wp-content/uploads/2012/04/20061114-1.pdf.
21. Bi Yantao, "Written Interview with Kalon Tripa Prof. S. Rinpoche," *Boxun News*, February 25, 2010, https://samdhongrinpoche.com/en/written-interview-with-kalon-tripa-prof-s-rinpoche/.
22. Xinhua News Agency, "On The 'Memorandum' Of The Dalai Clique," November 21, 2008, https://china.usc.edu/xinhua-news-agency-memorandum-dalai-clique-november-21-2008.
23. See appendix E.
24. "Statement By Special Envoy Kasur Lodi Gyari On 9th Round of Talks With China," February 2, 2010, https://tibet.net/statement-by-special-envoy-kasur-lodi-gyari-on-9th-round-of-talks-with-china/
25. See appendix E.

## 21. STATUS OF RELATIONSHIP, OBSTACLES TO RECONNECTION, AND RECOMMENDATIONS

1. CTA press release, "Task Force Meeting Held in Dharamshala," October 12, 2011, https://tibet.net/task-force-meeting-held-in-dharamshala/.
2. CTA press release, "Kalon Tripa Accepts Resignations of Special Envoy Lodi G. Gyari and Envoy Kelsang Gyaltsen," June 3, 2012, https://tibet.net/kalon-tripa-accepts-resignations-of-special-envoy-lodi-g-gyari-and-envoy-kelsang-gyaltsen/.
3. When the Tiananmen tragedy took place, we were actually hoping to renew some contact with Beijing. There was even the possibility of a meeting between our respective representatives in Hong Kong that could have led to His Holiness meeting with some top PRC leaders. The possibility of this high-level meeting was confirmed in President Carter's 1997 China trip report: "We spent a lot of time on the Tibet issue, with my reminding that Deng Xiaoping had let me arrange for talks with the Dalai Lama in July 1989, that were prevented by the Tiananmen Square tragedy."
4. Victor Chan, *The Wisdom of Forgiveness: Intimate Conversations and Journeys* (New York: Riverhead Books, 2005), excerpt from chapter 4, "A Most Altruistic Person," 78–81.
5. Chan, *The Wisdom of Forgiveness*, 82.
6. Memoir of Zhu Weiqun's talks with Beat U. Wieser, a reporter for the Swiss newspaper *Neue Zuercher Zeitung,* on October 18, 2013 (*China Tibet Online*, November 21, 2013). Reprinted in *News from China* XXVI, no. 1 (New Delhi: Embassy of the People's Republic of China, January 2014), 60.
7. By this time, it was becoming quite clear that His Holiness would disassociate himself from the political leadership.
8. See discussion in chapter 18.
9. Interview with Claude Arpi, "Why China Will Change: The Tibet Factor," *Rediff News*, April 3, 2006, http://www.rediff.com/news/2006/apr/03inter1.htm.

## APPENDIX B. TIBETAN POLICY ACT

1. https://www.savetibet.org/policy-center/tibetan-policy-act/. See https://www.savetibet.org/wp-content/uploads/2013/01/hres1646.pdf for the full text of the legislation.

## APPENDIX E. NOTE ON THE MEMORANDUM ON GENUINE AUTONOMY FOR THE TIBETAN PEOPLE

1. The "three adherences" as stipulated by the Central Government are: (1) the leadership of the Chinese Communist Party; (2) the socialism with Chinese characteristics; and (3) the Regional National Autonomy system.

# *Selected Bibliography*

## BOOKS AND ARTICLES


Bader, Jeff A. *Obama and China's Rise: An Insider's Account of America's Asia Strategy*. Washington, D.C.: Brookings Institution Press, 2013.

Blum, Richard C. *An Accident of Geography*. Austin, Texas: Greenleaf Book Group Press, 2016.

Chirac, Jacques. *My Life in Politics*. Trans. Catherine Spencer. New York: St. Martin's Press, 2012.

Dongyal, Khenpo Tsewang. *Light of Fearless Indestructible Wisdom: The Life and Legacy of H.H. Dudjom Rinpoche*. Ithaca, N.Y.: Snow Lion, 2008.

Doyaltshang, Aten. *A Historical Oration from Kham: The Ancient Recitation of Nyagrong (Nyag rong gtam rgan ma)*. Dharamsala: Amnye Machen Institute, 1993.

Dudjom Rinpoche. *Counsels from My Heart*. Trans. Padmakara Translation Group. Boston: Shambhala, 2003.

Dudjom Rinpoche. *The Nyingma School of Tibetan Buddhism: Its Fundamentals and History*. Somerville, Mass.: Wisdom, 1991.

Goldstein, Melvyn C., Dawei Sherap, and William R. Siebenschuh. *A Tibetan Revolutionary: The Political Life and Times of Bapa Phüntso Wangye*. Berkeley: University of California Press, 2004.

His Holiness the Dalai Lama. *Freedom in Exile: The Autobiography of the Dalai Lama*. London: Hodder and Stoughton, 1990.

His Holiness the Dalai Lama and Victor Chan. *The Wisdom of Forgiveness: Intimate Conversations and Journeys*. New York: Riverhead Books, 2005.

His Holiness the Dalai Lama with Fabien Quaki. *Imagine All the People: The Dalai Lama on Money, Politics, and Life As It Could Be*. Boston: Wisdom, 1999.

Kumar, Virendra. *Chin Up, Chest Out*. India: Virendra Kumar, 1976.

Mullik, B. N. *My Years with Nehru: The Chinese Betrayal*. Bombay: Allied Publishers, 1971.

Nathan, Andrew J., and Bruce Gilley. *China's New Rulers: The Secret Files*. New York: New York Review Books, 2003.

Norbu, Jamyang. *Horseman in the Snow: The Story of Aten, an Old Khampa Warrior*. Dharamsala: Information Office, Central Tibetan Secretariat, 1979.

—. *Warriors of Tibet: The Story of Aten and the Khampas' Fight for the Freedom of Their Country*. London: Wisdom, 1986.

Norbu, Namkhai. *The Necklace of gZi: A Cultural History of Tibet.* Dharamsala: Narthang Publications, 1989.

Pemba, Tsewang Yishey. *White Crane, Lend Me Your Wings: A Tibetan Tale of Love and War.* New Delhi: Niyogi Books, 2017.

Phuntsok, Thupten. *Bod kyi lo rgyus spyi don padma ra g'i lde mig* (General theme of the Tibetan history *Padma ragai de mig*). Beijing: Tibet Nationality Publishing House, 2006.

Pistono, Matteo. *In the Shadow of the Buddha: One Man's Journey of Discovery in Tibet.* New York: Dutton, 2011.

Shakabpa, W. D. *Tibet: A Political History.* New York: Potala Publications, 1984.

Snow, Edgar. *Red Star Over China.* New York: Pelican Press, 1973.

Teichmann, Eric. *Travels of a Consular Officer in Eastern Tibet: together with a History of the Relations Between China, Tibet and India.* Cambridge: At the University Press, 1922.

Thondup, Gyalo, and Anne F. Thurston. *The Noodle Maker of Kalimpong: The Untold Story of My Struggle for Tibet.* New York: Public Affairs, 2015.

Tsomu, Yudro. "Constructing Images of Gönpo Namgyel: A Hero or a Villain?" *Revue d'Etudes Tibetaines* 26 (April 2013): 57–91.

—. *The Rise of Gönpo Namgyel in Kham: The Blind Warrior of Nyarong.* Lanham, Md.: Lexington Books, 2014.

Uban, S. S. *The Phantoms of Chittagong: The Fifth Army in Bangladesh.* New Delhi: Allied Publishers, 1985.

Venkataraman, Ramaswamy. *My Presidential Years.* New Delhi: HarperCollins, 1994.

Wangyal, Ngari Panchen Pema. *Perfect Conduct: Ascertaining the Three Vows.* Boston: Wisdom, 1996.

Yeo, George. "Tibet in the 21st Century." In *Bonsai, Banyan and the Tao.* Singapore: World Scientific Publishing, 2015.

## MISCELLANEOUS SOURCES

Central Tibetan Administration, Department of Information and International Relations (DIIR). *From the Heart of the Panchen Lama (Major Speeches and a petition: 1962–1989).* https://tibet.net/1998/04/.

—. "Memorandum from Yan Mingfu, Head of the United Front Work Department of the CCP Central Committee to the Exiled Tibetan Administration," October 17, 1987. Translated from the Chinese and included in *DHARAMSALA AND BEIJING Initiatives and Correspondences 1981–1993* (March 1996). https://tibet.net/wp-content/uploads/2014/10/Dharamsla-and-Beijing.pdf.

—. *Middle Way Policy and All Recent Related Documents* (May 2011), 5. https//tibet.net/wp-content/uploads/2012/06/MIDWAY-ENGLISH.pdf.

Central Tibet Administration, Research and Analysis of Department of Security. *Ngapo Ngawang Jigme kyi Ched Pel Tam-tsok (Collected Speeches).* Dharamsala, 1999.

Central Tibetan Administration, Sino-Tibetan Dialogue. https://tibet.net/important-issues/sino-tibetan-dialogue/.

Chiang Kai-shek. "Documents: The Question of Tibet, March 26, 1959." *Taiwan Review*, December 1, 1959. https://taiwantoday.tw/news.php?unit=12,29,33,45&post=23544.

Congressional Executive Commission on China. *Special Topic Paper: Tibet 2008–2009* (October 22, 2009). https://www.cecc.gov/sites/chinacommission.house.gov/files/CECC%20Special%20Topic%20Paper%20-%20Tibet%202008%20-%202009%20-%2010.22.09.pdf.

Embassy of the People's Republic of China. *Tibet—Its Ownership and Human Rights Situations* (Beijing: Information Office of the State Council of the PRC, September 1992). http://ie.china-embassy.org/eng/zt/ChinasTibet/t1145462.htm.

Gyari, Lodi. "My Personal Words of Gratitude." December 31, 1974. https://www.savetibet.org/my-personal-words-of-gratitude/.

Gyari, Lodi G., Special Envoy of H.H. the Dalai Lama. Remarks as prepared for delivery at the Brookings Institution, "Seeking Unity Through Equality: The Current Status of Discussions Between His Holiness the Dalai Lama and the Government of the People's Republic of China," Washington, D.C, November 14, 2006. https://www.brookings.edu/wp-content/uploads/2012/04/20061114-1.pdf.

International Campaign for Tibet. "Where is China Heading on Tibet?" Remarks by Lodi Gyaltsen Gyari to the Council on Foreign Relations, Washington, D.C., April 23, 2012. https://www.savetibet.org/where-is-china-heading-on-tibet.

Xinhua News Agency. "On The 'Memorandum' Of The Dalai Clique." November 21, 2008. https://china.usc.edu/xinhua-news-agency-memorandum-dalai-clique-november-21-2008.

Yao, Wang. "Hu Yaobang's Visit to Tibet, May 22–31, 1980: An Important Development in the Chinese Government's Tibet Policy." http://www.archieve.claudearpi.net/maintenance/uploaded_pics/1980HuavisittoTibet.pdf

# Index

CPSIA information can be obtained
at www.ICGtesting.com
Printed in the USA
BVHW041651051222
653486BV00018B/275/J